QUANTITATIVE METHODS
IN MANAGEMENT

Text and cases

QUANTITATIVE METHODS
IN MANAGEMENT

Text and cases

PAUL A. VATTER
STEPHEN P. BRADLEY
SHERWOOD C. FREY, JR.
BARBARA B. JACKSON

all of the
Graduate School
of Business Administration
Harvard University

1978
RICHARD D. IRWIN, INC.
Homewood, Illinois 60430

ISBN 0-256-02006-X
Library of Congress Catalog Card No. 77–089790

Printed in the United States of America

12 13 14 15 MP 9 8 7 6 5 4

Dedicated to the former course heads of Managerial Economics

Robert O. Schlaifer
Arthur Schleifer, Jr.
John E. Bishop
John W. Pratt

Preface

Perspective

The objective of this book is to supply prospective managers with the skills necessary to make effective use of formal quantitative analyses, whether the details of those analyses are performed by themselves or by a technical specialist. The book has grown out of a required course in Managerial Economics at the Harvard Graduate School of Business Administration. The course is presented to students with diffuse interests and diverse backgrounds who nevertheless have the common objective of enhancing their abilities to confront complex management decisions in a practical fashion. An origin such as this has a profound influence on the objectives, the content, and the form of a text treating quantitative methods.

This book is written for the manager or student whose needs are not the complete mastery of the technical details of mathematical techniques, but rather the development of formal analytical processes that contribute to an individual's decision-making skills. It is not a survey of operations research/management science techniques, but instead it develops those fundamental concepts that we believe are most important for the practical analysis of management decisions. As a result, we focus on developing alternative strategies; considering uncertainty explicitly; identifying the relevant criteria; using historical data and limited information effectively; anticipating competitive reactions; and allocating scarce resources.

In each of these areas, the relevant techniques are developed and applied in the context of real business situations. While we develop those mechanical skills necessary to manipulate the quantitative techniques appropriately, we also use case studies to emphasize the crucial skills of describing and defining the problem before the conduct of any analysis, and interpreting and implementing the results of whatever analysis is performed. Because the focus of our attention is the development of analytical processes, we have presented the technical material without the use or development of calculus or linear algebra. Despite this choice, we believe that we have preserved the mathematical integrity of the techniques. In summary, this book is directed primarily to readers who do not intend to be specialists in the development of quantitative techniques, but who seek a managerial perspective in the use of quantitative methods of analysis.

Organization and contents

The book is organized into six parts: Part I, A framework for analyzing decisions under uncertainty; Part II, Judgmental assessment and limited information; Part III, Using historical data to develop probabilities; Part IV, Simulation in the analysis of complex decisions; Part V, Accounting for competitive reaction; and Part VI, Allocating scarce resources. The first three parts are subdivided into chapters treating specific aspects of the more general rubric. The last three parts are each supported by single chapters presenting particular techniques. Each chapter is composed of expository material, exercises to develop skill in the manipulation of the methodologies, and a number of cases of increasing complexity to place those methodologies in a management setting.

Part I has four chapters, the first of which presents an overview of decision analysis. Chapter 1 develops the basic framework for analyzing decisions in which uncertainty is an important component. This framework consists of articulating the alternatives and the risks, evaluating the consequences, assessing the uncertain future, developing a consistent strategy, and determining its sensitivity to the inputs of the analysis. This chapter forms the foundation for a more detailed development in later chapters. A major goal of the chapter is to demonstrate that quantitative analysis is a tool whose most important ingredient is the decision maker's own judgments. The analysis aims at improving the decision-making process by requiring decision makers to consider all the relevant aspects of problems and to focus on each of these components individually. As a result the methodology provides managers with a broader and more systematic basis for acting in accordance with their personal judgments.

The remaining three chapters of Part I address specific aspects of the framework by treating in detail the structuring of alternatives and the evaluation of consequences. In Chapter 2, we focus on the appropriate identification and measurement of returns and on the significance and evaluation of the timing of those returns. We develop the concept of cash flow as a measurement of economic value, and the techniques of discounted cash flow as a method to evaluate systematically situations in which the cash returns are spread over a long period of time. Chapter 3 considers the elements important in effectively using decision diagrams as a means for structuring decisions. The goal of the chapter is to assist the student in answering the difficult questions: What actions and uncertainties do I include in the diagram? In what sequence do I place them? How do I select the horizon for my evaluation? In Chapter 4 we present a method for systematically evaluating alternatives whose consequences span a range large enough to require the careful consideration of the manager's attitude toward risk. In the earlier chapters, risk attitudes were either ignored because the spread of potential consequences was relatively small, or they were included in the decision-making process through an implicit and internalized evaluation. In this chapter we show that, by making a few subjective judgments concerning simple alternatives, a procedure can be followed for systematically and consistently comparing complex risky alternatives.

Part II is directed at enlarging the student's ability to describe and forecast the uncertain future. Chapter 5 introduces the concept of the continuous probability distribution as a description of uncertainties for which there are a large number of possible outcomes. In Part I we had restricted our attention to situations in which the relevant uncertainty could be adequately described by a limited number of outcomes. There are a vast number of decision problems for which this condition is simply not met. The goals of Chapter 5 include expanding our terminology so that we will be able to describe the more complicated uncertainties involving many outcomes, addressing the difficult task of meaningfully assessing probability distributions for these uncertainties, incorporating the more complex probability descriptions into the decision diagram framework of Part I, and suggesting methods for making assessments by breaking the uncertainty into natural and more easily assessible parts. Chapter 6 continues the discussion of probability assessment by developing procedures for evaluating the worth of refining probability assessments through the collection of additional information. Since a manager can often choose to postpone judgment until more information has been collected and a more definitive specification of the problem has been obtained, a careful and explicit treatment of the uses and value of additional information is particularly relevant to the development of a decision-making process. In this chapter we develop techniques for updating probability assessments based on new information and use those techniques in evaluating the potential worth of collecting such information.

Part III continues the discussion of forecasting the uncertain future by considering the effective use of historical data as a guide in the forecasting process. There is comfort in basing decisions on hard data rather than on judgmental assessments, but there are pitfalls. An essential consideration when using the past as a guide for the future is the relevancy of the data. If environmental conditions change substantially, we must be careful in converting inferences drawn from the past into implications for the future. In Chapter 7 we present two simple methods for making use of historical data that are usually available. The first applies to the situation in which the past and the future are sufficiently similar to allow the data to be used directly without any interpretation or adjustment. The second method deals with the more common situation in which the environment has been changing. Within this setting, if there has been and will continue to be a forecaster providing predictions, we present a procedure by which the use of past predictions makes the past data useful. Chapters 8 and 9 continue the discussion of forecasting in a changing environment by developing more formal techniques for the interpretation of historical data. In some circumstances the available data may consist of observations made at regular intervals of time on the quantity to be forecasted. Chapter 8 discusses the use of time series data in the assessment of a probability forecast. In Chapter 9 we develop the use of regression analysis, which allows us to make adjustments in the data to remove the effects of identifiable causes that underlie the changing environment. Forecasting with regression analysis is essentially a process of identifying factors which influence the quantity to be forecasted, evaluating the magnitude of those influences, and allowing for these influential factors in the development of a forecast.

The last three parts of the book each contain a single chapter dealing with a specific technique: simulation, competitive analysis, and linear programming. Chapter 10 presents the technique of simulation as a tool for analyzing complex decisions under uncertainty. There are many situations for which the decision analysis techniques of Part I become too cumbersome to apply. Such complexity may be due to a large number of relevant uncertainties, each with many possible outcomes. Problems of this form have far too many consequences to permit the explicit evaluation of each outcome as required by decision analysis. The analysis we propose involves the selection of a sample of the possible consequences; and simulation is a technique for appropriately making that selection. The chapter also explores the interpretation of the output from simulation studies and the application of those results to decision problems.

Many of the decisions faced by managers must include explicit consideration of competitive reactions. To perform a purely internal analysis would be myopic. In Chapter 11, therefore, we discuss the concepts and techniques of competitive analysis, drawing on the framework of game theory. We develop a structure for assisting the manager in compactly displaying and analyzing the complex reflexive interactions of a competitive environment, including as part of that structure a terminology useful in describing these interactions. In addition, the chapter emphasizes the need in competitive situations not only for setting clear objectives but also for carefully and thoughtfully conceiving a plan for communicating those objectives.

Chapter 12 deals with the problems of allocating scarce resources to competing activities in a fashion that satisfies financial, technological, marketing, and organizational constraints. Linear programming is introduced as a technique in this problem area, with the focus on the conceptualization of problems in the format of linear programming, the underlying logic of linear programming, and the interpretation of linear programming results. The discussion emphasizes the need to include the managerial considerations of the value of changing constraints, the design of new alternatives that make more efficient use of the scarce resources, and the establishment of appropriate controls to monitor changes in the sensitive inputs to the allocation decision.

Potential audiences

The material of this book originates from an MBA course whose students come from diverse educational backgrounds, including many who have taken no business or mathematics courses in college. As a result, the most obvious audiences for this book lie in the MBA curricula with similarly diverse student interests and backgrounds. However, the mathematical level and the pragmatic approach that we have adopted make this book appropriate for use in a variety of other settings.

First, there is the introductory undergraduate course for students in business and economics that is likely to be the only course in quantitative methods for those students. Generally, this course faces the difficulty of teaching within a single framework a group of students with a broad range of mathematical aptitudes and inclinations. By limiting the mathematical prerequisites to a level essentially equivalent to basic algebra, and by emphasizing the recognition and conceptualization of problems, the interpretation of analytical results, and the translation of these results into specific courses of action, we believe that this book makes available to this student group the important perspective of quantitative analysis in a relevant and understandable form.

Another group of students for whom this book is appropriate are the mid-career general managers who are interested in strengthening their knowledge of the modern tools for the analysis of decisions and their ability to interpret analyses that use these tools. Their needs are not the mathematics of the techniques, but rather a conceptual approach to applying quantitative methods to their business decisions. This book presents those quantitative methods essential to the general manager in the context in which they are most likely to be applied. In this way the book provides insights to the general manager for making effective use of quantitative methods and for understanding and directing technical specialists.

A final non-MBA use of this book is as an undergraduate course for students in business and engineering, for whom this course would be an introduction to operations research/management science. A course based on this book would provide a pragmatic decision-making context to which more technique-oriented courses could relate. It would offer the student the managerial point of view currently lacking in many undergraduate curricula.

Acknowledgments

This book presents the expository material and cases of a course that has evolved over the last 15 years. As a result, the book not only reflects the work and ideas of the authors who are involved in the current course, but is greatly influenced by the work of individuals and groups who developed the earlier versions of the course. Those earlier versions provided the foundation upon which the current course has been built. We are thus tremendously indebted to these previous teaching groups and to the men who headed them: Professors Robert O. Schlaifer, Arthur Schleifer, Jr., John E. Bishop, and John W. Pratt. Our gratitude toward these four men is great, and thus to them we respectfully dedicate this book.

In addition to the former course heads, we specifically would like to thank a number of our colleagues, present and past, who have written or supervised the writing of cases included in the book. They are: Robert N. Anthony, Stanley H. Buchin, Charles J. Christenson, Victor Fung, Regina E. Herzlinger, Jay O. Light, Paul W. Marshall, Richard F. Meyer, Howard Pifer, Roy D. Shapiro, Steven C. Wheelwright, and William B. Whiston. We are particularly indebted to John S. Hammond, III, who not only was involved in a number of cases used in the book, but was instrumental in the development of notes which form the basis for the text material in Chapter 11.

The preparation of a casebook is possible only through the help of an effective staff. Although we cannot cite all those who have contributed, we would especially like to thank Nancy Hayes for coordinating the manuscript preparation and Martha Laisne for copy editing.

December 1977   *Paul A. Vatter*
                                                     Stephen P. Bradley
                                                     Sherwood C. Frey, Jr.
                                                     Barbara B. Jackson

Contents

Acts and events to be included in a decision diagram. The order of acts and events in a decision diagram. Where to stop a decision diagram.

Certainty equivalents for reference profiles. Certainty equivalents for actual risk profiles. Assessing preference values. Assessing certainty equivalents. Choice of reference consequences. Decreasing risk aversion. Stability of preference curves over time and the selection of a criterion. Operating decisions. Expected monetary value and linear preference. Preference analysis and the evaluation of a decision diagram.

PART II
JUDGMENTAL ASSESSMENT AND LIMITED INFORMATION

Describing probability distributions. The probability mass function. The cumulative distribution function. Continuous and many-valued uncertain quantities. Describing a distribution using measures of central tendency. Assessing probability distributions for uncertain quantities. Using bracket medians to approximate probability distributions. Obtaining probability distributions from other probability distributions.

6. UPDATING PROBABILITY ASSESSMENTS WITH
ADDITIONAL INFORMATION 209

Conditional probabilities and Bayes Theorem. Joint outcomes and joint
probabilities. Conditional probabilities. Probability calculations without
counting. The tabular method. The tree method. Expected value of perfect
information. Expected net gain from sampling.

PART III
USING HISTORICAL DATA TO DEVELOP PROBABILITIES

7. ELEMENTARY FORECASTING 261

Historical data from indistinguishable situations. Developing probability
distributions from point forecasts. Absolute-error model. Relative-error
model. Adjusting data for one distinguishing factor.

8. DEVELOPING FORECASTS WITH THE AID OF TIME
SERIES DECOMPOSITION 303

Measuring the combined effect of trend and cycle. Separating the effects of trend and cycle. Determination of trend. Describing cyclical variations. Measuring the combined effects of seasonal and unexplained movements. Separating the effects of seasonal and unexplained variations. Measuring the seasonal pattern. Measuring the unexplained variations. Developing a probablistic forecast. Other uses of seasonal indices.

9. DEVELOPING FORECASTS WITH THE AID OF
REGRESSION ANALYSIS 347

Inputs to a regression analysis. Outputs from a regression analysis. Regression coefficients. Measures of goodness of fit. Estimates or forecasts. Developing the model. Selection of the dependent variable. Selection of explanatory variables. Lagged variables. Dummy variables. Determining the nature of relationships. Two warnings in developing models.

PART IV
SIMULATION IN THE ANALYSIS OF COMPLEX DECISIONS

10. SIMULATION AS A DECISION AID 425

An overview of the simulation approach. Deterministic simulation models. Probabilistic simulation models. Sampling the possible consequences. Example of a probabilistic model: The Weatherburn Aircraft Company. Decision diagram for the problem. Simulation of the problem. Interpreting the results of the simulation. Including continuous uncertain quantities in simulations. Including more complexity in the model.

PART V
ACCOUNTING FOR COMPETITIVE REACTION

11. GAMES AND COMPETITIVE SITUATIONS 483

An example: The battle for transcontinental air passengers. Elements shared by all competitive situations. Significant differences among competitive situations. Two-person zero-sum games. Analysis by iterated dominance. Mixed strategies. Nonzero-sum games: Games with no conflict. Threat and forcing potentials. The Prisoner's Dilemma. The Battle of the Sexes.

PART VI
ALLOCATING SCARCE RESOURCES

12. AN INTRODUCTION TO LINEAR PROGRAMMING 553

Formulating linear programming problems. A geometrical overview. Graphical representation of the decision space. Finding the optimal solution. Integer solutions. Shadow prices on the constraints. Ranges on objective coefficients. Ranges on the right-hand-side values. Computational considerations. Reduced costs and pricing out. 100 percent rules. Computer solution of a linear program. Solution stages of a linear programming problem.

APPENDIXES

_____ PART I

A framework for analyzing
decisions under uncertainty

Chapter 1

An introduction to
decision analysis

To introduce the basic ideas of decision analysis, we will consider a simple decision facing a hypothetical real estate agency. Let us see if we can apply a formal analysis to help the owner, Thadeus Warren, make his choice.

Warren is faced with the opportunity of offering for sale three residential properties, one located in Arlington, one in Belmont, and one in Cambridge, all suburbs of Boston. Several conditions are placed on the proposal. The first stipulates a definite sales price for each property: $25,000 for the house in Arlington, $50,000 for the one in Belmont, and $100,000 for the one in Cambridge. The second condition indicates that the properties must be sold one at a time, starting with the house in Arlington. If the Arlington property is sold, then Warren, if he wishes to continue, can choose to offer next either the Belmont or the Cambridge property. If he continues and succeeds in selling his second choice, then he will have the option to place the third property on the market. A third condition calls for a commission of 4 percent of the selling price for any successful sale. The final condition states that once a particular property is offered for sale, it will have to be sold within 30 days, or the entire arrangement will be terminated.

Assuming that these are the best terms Warren can obtain, should he accept or reject this proposal? To help Warren make this choice, a decision analysis would suggest that he break the problem down into a number of simpler questions, exercise his judgment on each of these issues, and then recombine his judgments to develop a consistent course of action. Thus, decision makers should first concentrate on understanding their alternatives and the risks these alternatives involve. Then they should

3

evaluate the potential consequences they perceive in the situation. Finally, they should assess the uncertainties involved in the decision. After these judgments have been made, the final step in the analysis will involve recombining the judgments to develop a consistent strategy.

THE ALTERNATIVES AND RISKS

During the first stage of the analysis, Warren is asked to consider all of the choices open to him, the uncertainties he will be required to face, and the time sequence in which these acts and events will occur. He will be asked to consider them in such detail that he can draw a diagram representing his view of his problem.

This process begins with Warren identifying the choices that are open to him at the present time. In this situation Warren may see only two choices: to reject the deal, or to offer the Arlington home for sale. Notice that the choice of whether or not to offer the Arlington property is Warren's; it is a decision he must make. This can be depicted graphically by an *act fork,* in which each branch of the fork represents a potential choice open to Warren. By convention, the node from which an act fork emanates is drawn as a square. Warren's decision diagram would begin with the two branches shown in Figure 1–1. Warren will be asked to push himself into the conceptual future down each branch of this diagram, asking at each point the critical question of decision diagramming: Then what?

Figure 1–1

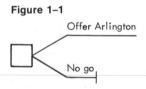

Offer Arlington

No go

In the example we are considering, Warren might indicate that if he turned the deal down this would end the situation, but if he tried to sell the Arlington house he would face the uncertainty of whether he would succeed or fail. Warren at this time cannot be sure which of these possibilities will occur. He can certainly affect what will happen. How well he has selected, trained, and motivated his sales staff; how effective his advertising and promotion are, and how well organized his agency is all will influence whether he will sell the Arlington property or fail to do so. The important point to note, however, is that although he can affect the result, he cannot completely control it; there is still *uncertainty.*

In this type of situation the uncertainty can be depicted graphically by an *event fork,* in which a branch of the fork represents each possible event or occurrence. The node from which an event fork emanates is, by con-

Figure 1–2

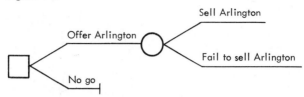

vention, depicted by a circle. The diagram for Warren's decision would be developed as shown in Figure 1–2.

To continue, Warren will now consider what would be involved if he fails or if he succeeds in his attempt to sell the Arlington property. Suppose he concludes that were he to fail, the deal would terminate, but were he to succeed then he would have to select one of three options: (1) stop, (2) offer Belmont, or (3) offer Cambridge. The diagram would be developed along the lines shown in Figure 1–3. The square node indicates

Figure 1–3

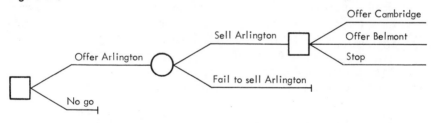

that at this point Warren will have control; he will have a decision to make. The three branches of the act fork indicate that he is willing to consider the three possible courses of action indicated by the labels on the branches.

A continuation of this process would result in the structure depicted in Figure 1–4.[1] In this first step in the problem-solving process Warren has been asked to concentrate on identifying his alternatives and the uncertainties facing him. It has been up to Warren to use his ingenuity and creativity to make sure that he has become aware of all of the options that are available to him.

The problem of generating all of the relevant alternatives for an act fork depends for its solution on the judgment and imagination of the decision maker. A creative manager sees more options for action than does one who is more pedestrian in outlook. The process of generating a rich

---

[1] We have not yet considered the numbers that appear in Figure 1–4; they will be discussed in the next section of this chapter.

Figure 1–4

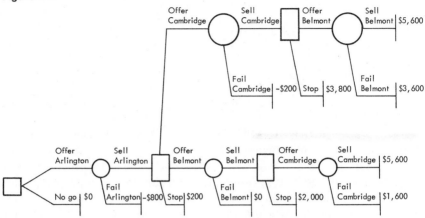

set of alternatives is not a mechanical one but rather rests heavily on the imagination and creativity of the decision maker. The discipline of systematically describing alternative strategies through a decision diagram should be a reminder of the desirability of looking for some less obvious but potentially valuable strategies which may otherwise have been overlooked. An exploration of possible answers to the "Then what?" question whenever there is a choice (including the choice to stop) may help to uncover some of the less obvious options.[2]

THE MONETARY CONSEQUENCES

At the second stage in the analysis, Warren will be asked to direct his attention exclusively to the evaluation of the potential monetary consequences: the relevant costs and the pertinent revenues. At each of the terminal points shown in Figure 1–4 he will be asked to answer the question: "If you were to conclude the deal at this particular end point, what in your judgment would be the net monetary flow that would result?" To answer this question Warren will have to identify *all* of the relevant costs incurred in the various activities involved and *all* the pertinent revenues that would result from the sales.

In this situation the revenues are found simply by applying the commission rate (4 percent) to the fixed selling prices. Unfortunately, the costs cannot be developed so easily. *All* of the relevant costs must be identified and evaluated. Thus, if in order to take on this business the Warren Agency had to cut out some other profitable endeavor, then this opportunity cost would be a relevant one. If funds had to be tied up over a period of time,

---

[2] A more detailed treatment of the issues involved in developing a decision diagram is given in Chapter 3.

their interest cost at an appropriate rate would be just as relevant as the more obvious sales, legal, advertising, and promotional costs. In this illustration we will assume that Warren has exercised his judgment on the costs and concluded that the cost for attempting to sell the Arlington property (which, since it is first, must also bear the setup costs for the entire deal) would be about $800. The corresponding figure for the Belmont property is $200, and for the Cambridge property, $400.

Once Warren has made these judgments, their consequences can be considered by summing all the partial monetary flows leading to each end point in Figure 1–4. If Warren accepted the deal and failed to sell the Arlington property, in his view he would have a net monetary *outflow* of $800. Were he to take the deal, succeed in selling the property in Arlington, and then decide to stop, the $800 cost and the $1,000 commission for Arlington would leave him with a net monetary *inflow* of $200. In a similar way, the remaining end points on the diagram have been evaluated to show the net monetary consequences as judged now by Warren.

CONSEQUENCES NOT CONTAINED IN THE MONETARY FLOWS

In most decisions, consequences other than purely monetary ones also exist, in the view of the decision maker. These nonmonetary consequences should be evaluated and taken into account. As a third step in the analysis Warren is asked to address himself to this dimension of his decision.

To illustrate the type of factor involved and the process of evaluation, imagine that Warren indicates that the prospective client who has made this proposal to him is one of the major landowners in the greater Boston area. Imagine also that Warren believes that if only he can impress this person favorably by the sale of all three properties, his success will provide an "open sesame" to a great deal of profitable future business. In that case (as we hope you would agree), to take the deal and succeed in all three sales would be worth more than the net monetary flow of $5,600 to Warren; it would also be worth a good deal of profitable future business.

In general, if decision makers believe that various end points on their decision diagrams leave them with different prospects for the future, they should assess the value for these future differences and add them to the monetary flow consequences. Thus, a decision maker who found different customer relations, employee morale, equipment, or inventories at various end points would take these differences into account at this stage.

In this illustration we will assume that upon considering this issue, Warren decided that there were no differences in future prospects among the end points other than those contained in the monetary flow evaluations. Having dealt with the third dimension of his problem, and in this situation finding it not relevant, Warren is ready to move on to the next step in his attempt to deal with his actual decision by concentrating on the separate aspects of the situation, one at a time.

THE UNCERTAIN FUTURE

In almost every decision made by a manager, its consequences are unfolded in the uncertain future. In every decision there is therefore contained, either implicitly or explicitly, a forecast of future events. At this stage in the analysis, Warren is asked to provide a forecast by exercising his judgments about the future and indicating his assessment of the probability that he would succeed were he to attempt to sell each of the properties involved.

Warren would, of course, wish to become as knowledgeable as he could about each of these properties and about the real estate market in the Boston area, so he has a basis for making these assessments. Imagine that he has gone out and appraised each of the properties, looked at his past records to see how successful he has been in moving similar properties within a month, talked to his sales staff about prospects who might potentially be interested in such homes, become aware of other competitive properties on the market, and thought about the state of the mortgage market. With this work as a background, suppose that (using a type of procedure described below) Warren indicates that were he to try to sell the Arlington house, he thinks the chance of success would be about 70 percent. This judgment also implies, of course, that he assesses the probability of failure at 30 percent. When he considers the house in Belmont he is less optimistic and assesses the probability of success at 60 percent. With the expensive Cambridge house he evaluates the chances at 50/50. Warren also states that the three houses are in such different price segments of the market that he would not change his assessments for any of the properties if he were informed of success or failure in the attempt to sell any of the other properties involved.

Now we can take one of Warren's assessments, the .60 for Belmont, and explore two questions related to it:

1. What does a probability mean in a one-time decision such as this?
2. How can an individual go about assessing a probability?

In order to understand the basic meaning of a probability as used in a one-time decision-making situation, you may have to change an attitude that many people form quite early in their schooling: A number is used to measure some objectively "true" value, and thus it is either right or wrong; or, if methods of approximation are employed, it is within or outside of a range of allowable error. If we ask, in the example, of Warren's 60 percent probability of sale, what the objectively "true" value he is attempting to measure is, we run into a stone wall. The only "true" value in this one-time decision would be a very hollow one. If Warren tried to sell the Belmont property and succeeded it could perhaps be said that the "true" probability was 100/0. On the other hand, if he failed, it could similarly be argued that the "true" probabilities were 0 and 100.

Unfortunately, this information does not make it easier to understand the 60/40 probabilities at all. In order to put these probabilities in proper perspective, they must be considered not as a measure of some objectively "true" value but rather as a language—a device to communicate the decision maker's judgment about the uncertain future. We might note that this "language" of probability is not much different from a language that decision makers have been using for centuries, in statements such as "I think there is a *pretty good chance* that this year our sales will be at an all time high," or "It's *not very likely* that our competitor will change prices in the near future," or even "I'm *quite uncertain* about how the government will act on this issue." These weasel phrases are attempting to perform the same function that the probabilities perform: to communicate a judgment about the uncertain future. The probabilistic language merely asks for a higher informational content in the message and for more explicit descriptions of judgments. Instead of merely saying there is a *pretty good chance,* the decision maker is asked to indicate (in her or his opinion) how good a chance. It suggests that instead of being satisfied with saying they are *quite uncertain,* people evaluate the degree of their uncertainty.

Probabilities in essence constitute a language, which leads directly to the question of how one learns to speak this language. How can Warren describe in this "language" his informed view of the uncertainty he would face in attempting to sell the house in Belmont?

To illustrate this assessment process, Warren would first be asked to think of some desired outcome. It does not matter what the outcome is as long as Warren would rather have it occur than not. For example, assume Warren would find a one-month, all-expense-paid vacation attractive. In the light of Warren's knowledge about the Belmont property and the real estate market in the Boston area, he then is asked to choose between two alternative ways by which he could have a chance of obtaining the vacation. He might be asked, for instance, to select one of the two following ways as a basis for attempting to win the trip:

1. You win if you sell the Belmont property under the terms of this proposal and by using your normal sales effort.
2. You win if your number is drawn in a fair lottery in which you hold 50 percent of the tickets.

If after careful thought Warren chooses the first alternative, to obtain the trip conditional on the successful sale of the Belmont property, what would this indicate about his assessment of the probability of success? Clearly it can now be inferred that he is assessing a probability of sale greater than 50 percent, because he will certainly have chosen the alternative in which he feels he has the larger chance of winning. In the beginning situation, his assessment could have been anywhere between 0 and 100 percent. In answering this question, he has indicated that his probability of selling the Belmont property lies between 50 and 100 percent. Had he answered by choosing the second alternative, it would have indicated that his assessment of success was between 0 and 50 percent.

Warren is now asked to make a second choice. Again thinking of a desired outcome, he is asked to choose between two alternative chances to obtain it:

1.   You win if you sell the house in Belmont under these terms and with normal activity.
2.   You win if your number is drawn from a fair lottery in which you hold 75 percent of the tickets.

Assume that this time, again after careful thought, Warren says, "If I have three quarters of all the tickets and if I want that vacation, I would take my chances on winning in the lottery." Now we would be able to conclude that Warren's probability of success falls between 50 and 75 percent. With one more question (with a lottery in which Warren held between 50 and 75 percent of the tickets) or perhaps two, Warren would very likely get to the point where he would be indifferent between the two alternatives. This point of indifference would identify his assessed probability of sale. In this example the probability of 60 percent indicates that in facing these choices Warren prefers the lottery when he has more than 60 percent of the tickets, and he prefers to take his chances on obtaining the trip as a sales bonus for selling the Belmont property when less than 60 percent of the lottery tickets are in his possession.

A probability thus describes a decision maker's view of the uncertain future by indicating how he or she chooses in a number of relatively simple one-time choices in which this uncertainty is the critical element. We might note that the choices Warren was asked to make in this case were much simpler than the actual decision with which he is attempting to deal. In these choices there were only two alternatives open, rather than the many strategies available in the real problem, and the consequences were the same for each alternative (the trip or nothing), whereas various consequences are shown at the many end points of the actual decision. The only factor influencing his choices in these questions was his view of the uncertainty he would face were he to attempt to sell the Belmont property.

DEVELOPING A CONSISTENT STRATEGY

Warren has now exercised his judgments separately on four different aspects of his decision. He started by considering the opportunities and uncertainties present in the situation, and from these he could draw his decision diagram. Then he concerned himself exclusively with the question of relevant costs and revenues; that is, he evaluated the monetary consequences. At the third stage he dealt with consequences not already reflected in the monetary flows, and at the fourth stage he expressed his judgment about the uncertain future, encoding it in the language of probability. The final step in his analysis will be to recombine these separate judgments in such a way that he can choose the course of action most consistent with the judgments he has made.

Certain rules of thumb for making a decision might quickly occur to you. One might be: Take the most likely outcome of each of the uncertainties and select as the choice of strategy the one that leads to the best consequence if that set of most likely outcomes were to occur. A moment's reflection indicates that this is not a satisfactory decision rule, since almost anyone, given a choice between the two proposals in Figure 1–5, would favor proposal B, and yet the one that does best under the most likely result is proposal A.

Figure 1–5

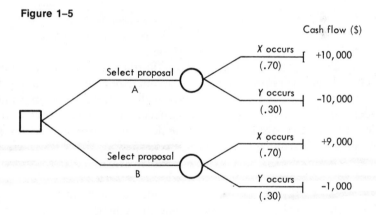

A second rule of thumb you might think about is: Never select a strategy where the probability of failure is greater than the probability of success. The fact that almost everyone would take the proposal in Figure 1–6 indicates the weakness of that rule.

Figure 1–6

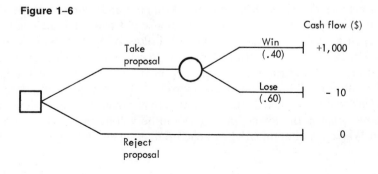

Another rule might suggest: Never take a strategy where the amount that could be lost is greater than the amount that might be gained. Slightly different but similar in nature would be a decision rule that prescribes: Select that strategy where the worst possible consequence under the strategy is better than the worst possible consequence of all the alternative strategies. The observation that almost everyone with adequate resources would prefer the go to the no-go alternative in Figure 1–7 again points to the flaw in these decision rules.

Figure 1–7

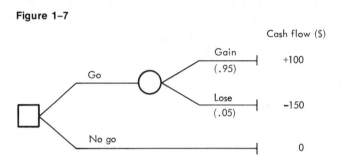

The difficulty with these various decision rules is that each eliminates from consideration at least one major relevant aspect of the decision. The first two rules consider the probabilities of the various events but fail to consider the relative magnitude of the consequences. The latter two rules consider the relative size of the consequences but ignore the likelihood of the possible events. What is needed is a criterion for combining both types of judgments, probabilities and consequences, so they will be reflected in the decision. The method described in the following section, using a decision criterion of *expected value,* provides such a combination.

Perhaps the simplest way to recombine these judgments mechanically is to start at the end points of the decision diagram—to analyze backward from the future to the present. In this way the judgments about what could happen later on will be brought to bear in determining what Warren should do in the present. An illustration of this type of analysis is given in Figure 1–8. Start by considering the values at *C* and *D*. The value at point *C* indicates that if Warren sold all three properties, he would value the consequences at $5,600. If he sold the Arlington and Belmont properties, and then failed in his attempt to sell the house in Cambridge, he evaluates the result at point *D* as a net monetary inflow of $1,600. Now Warren moves back one step toward the present, to point *G* on the diagram, and asks himself the question: "If I were at point *G*, what value would I place on the entire deal?" He might ask himself: "If I were guaranteed that I could get to point *G*, and someone wanted to purchase the entire deal from me now, what is the lowest price I would be willing to accept?" Notice that if Warren is at point *G* he can end up making either $5,600 or $1,600,

Figure 1–8

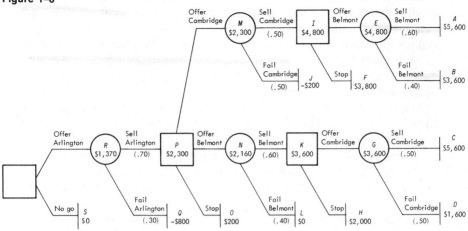

depending on whether or not he sells the Cambridge property. The lowest price he would be willing to accept for the entire deal would of necessity not be less than $1,600. The highest he would set for the minimum price he would accept would be $5,600. The more likely it is, in his view, that he will succeed, the closer he will set his price to $5,600. The more probable it is, in his opinion that he will fail, the closer it will be to the $1,600 value. We will call such a subjective valuation of a risky situation his *certainty equivalent* (CE) for that position; it is the minimum amount he would accept in exchange for the position.

If Warren is willing to make one more statement about his situation, it will be possible to establish a value he *should* put on the situation, conditional on a guarantee that he could reach point *G*. If Warren indicates that for the Warren Agency the amounts involved as potential consequences in this decision are not very large and, that essentially the decision entails financial consequences of a size to which the Agency is quite regularly exposed, then the value he should place at position *G*, or his certainty equivalent for that position, can be calculated. We have argued that this value will be between $5,600 and $1,600, and that the higher the probability of success the closer it will be to $5,600. At stage 4 of the analysis Warren indicated that the likelihood of success and failure in Cambridge was 50/50. It can thus be concluded that in this type of operating decision Warren should evaluate position *G* at a point midway (50 percent) between $1,600 and $5,600, or at $3,600. The same argument applied to point *E* in the upper branch would determine the value at 60 percent of the way from $3,600 *(B)* to $5,600 *(A)*, or at $4,800.

Remember the interpretation of the $3,600 value placed at point *G* in the diagram. It indicates that if Warren had a guarantee that he could get to point *G* and somebody now wanted to buy the rights to the entire deal from him, he would sell only if the best offer were better than $3,600. The results of this type of calculation are referred to as *expected monetary values* (EMV). This does *not* mean that if Warren is at point G he *expects* to make $3,600 from the entire situation, at least in the usual meaning of the word "expect." Rather it is a technical term that refers to a weighted average. In this illustration the $3,600 is an average of the $5,600 and $1,600 weighted by their respective probabilities, in this case .50 and .50.

The use of EMV criteria for routine decisions with small potential consequences (operating decisions) rests on the proposal that in a large number of such decisions the decision maker will "on the average" do best by selecting the strategy with the highest expected monetary value (or EMV). Thus for decisions in which he or she would be willing to "play the averages," the certainty equivalent would be the expected monetary value.

Warren can now be asked to move back one step toward the present to point K and again place a value on the entire contract, conditional on being at that point. Notice that at point K Warren must decide whether to stop, and thus move to an end point he has evaluated as worth $2,000 to him, or to offer the Cambridge property for sale and then move to point G, which would be evaluated at $3,600. This is not a very difficult choice. Warren can use what we might jokingly call a "criterion of greed." He will select the alternative which he believes is worth more to him and his organization, with all relevant consequences having been considered. Thus, if he is at point K he would not stop but rather would place the Cambridge property on the market—move to point G in the diagram. If Warren is guaranteed that he can get to point K, and if when he is there he knows he will move to point G, then to be guaranteed he will get to point K has the same value as to be guaranteed he will get to point G, namely $3,600.

Faced with a choice, the decision maker will look at the certainty equivalent for the node at the end of each branch of the act fork, pick the best one, prune off the other branches, and fold back the certainty equivalent of the best branch to the node of the act fork.

In general there are two ways of evaluating positions as one works back through a decision diagram. If the position is one at which the branching is uncertain, as indicated by a circle in the diagram, then it is evaluated by assessing probabilities over the uncertainty and using them as weights in averaging the consequences. If the position is one at which the decision maker must choose, as indicated by a square in the diagram, he or she chooses the best, prunes off the other branches, and folds back the best value to the position of choice. By this process of *averaging out and folding back,* Warren can analyze back through the diagram, as shown by the remaining values in Figure 1–5. You should work back through the rest of the figure and verify the consistency of Warren's choice to accept the proposal. You might also verify that if none of Warren's judgments change over the course of the decision, he would choose to exercise the option on the Cambridge property immediately upon the successful sale of the Arlington property.

SOME DOUBTS—A SENSITIVITY ANALYSIS

To develop a further concept useful in a decision analysis, assume that after making this analysis and deciding that he would accept the offer, Warren is told that he does not have to make the final, binding decision for another week or so. Also assume that Warren feels that he has a considerable amount of experience and knowledge relevant to the Belmont and Cambridge properties and has used his judgment well in assessing the 60/40 and 50/50 probabilities. However, he thinks that although the 70/30 for Arlington expresses the way he would act now if he had to, it is based on relatively little knowledge or fact. Warren believes that if he spent more time thinking about that property and investigating the price segment of the market in which it is located, his judgments on the uncertainty of its sale might change considerably. Should Warren be willing to act now, or should he at least consider further the possibility of refining his judgment on the Arlington property?

Warren might begin thinking about this question by asking himself, "What role does the 70/30, which is under consideration, play in the analysis?" Note in Figure 1–8 that, conditional on being at point P in the diagram, Warren places a value of $2,300 on the deal, while if he were at point Q he thinks the entire deal would result in an $800 loss. A value for point R was found by applying the 70/30 probabilities as weights in averaging these values, to obtain the $1,370 valuation shown at that position. If Warren considers the value assigned at R, he would soon recognize that the only thing that concerns him as a decision maker is the size of the value relative to its alternative: the value of position S, in this case $0.

Once Warren recognizes that his interest is not in the precise valuation of position R but merely whether the value is greater or less than the valuation of its alternative, position S, he can determine how low his assessment of the probability of success in Arlington would have to fall in order for him to change his preliminary decision. For example, if the assessed probability of success in Arlington fell to .50, the value node R would become

$$.5(2,300) + .5(-800) = 750,$$

and Warren would still accept the deal. At a .40 probability of a sale in Arlington, node R would be labeled

$$.4(2,300) + .6(-800) = 440,$$

and the decision would remain unchanged.

How low would the probability have to go before Warren would be entirely indifferent between accepting the deal and refusing it? Suppose p is that value. With p equal to the probability of success, $(1 - p)$ is the probability of failure, and node R will be labeled with $p(2,300) + (1 - p)(-800)$. For Warren to be indifferent, the value on node R must just equal the value on node S, or \$0.

Thus, the break-even (or indifference) probability can be found by solving the following equation:

$$p(2,300) + (1 - p)(-800) = 0.$$

The break-even probability is $8/31 = .258$. Thus Warren's probability of success in selling the Arlington house could drop to almost 25 percent before he would change his tentative decision and turn down the proposal. If Warren felt that no matter what he would learn, his probability would not drop down to that level, then he would recognize that he ought not to spend any of his time or energy attempting to refine his assessment. Only if he believed his new assessment might drop below that level would he have to consider the question further.

This example suggests that a decision analysis often involves a two-stage process. In the first stage, when a difficult judgment is encountered, rather than face it head on the decision maker may approximate it, remembering to come back to the point before a final decision is reached. Based on the approximations, a first preliminary analysis can be made leading to a first tentative conclusion. Then the judgment or set of judgments which have been approximated can be revisited and the question asked, "If this judgment or set of judgments were to vary over the entire range where I believe they could finally fall, would it change my decision?" If, as in this case, the answer is no, then the decision maker can recognize that the approximations are adequate for the decision, and no further time and effort should be expended. On the other hand, if the decision maker learns that the decision could change, depending on where in a conceivable range the judgment fell, then a critical judgment for the decision has been identified.

The ability to use a so-called *sensitivity analysis* to discriminate between judgments which may have to be refined further and those for which an approximation is adequate can apply to any of the judgments involved in the decision. In this example, Warren questioned a probability assessment. He could have used the same type of reasoning to decide whether he ought to spend time placing a value on some nonmonetary factor, such as improved reputation, or on making a more careful allocation of costs in determining his evaluation of the monetary flow at an end point.

RISK AVERSION AND DECISION MAKING

Throughout our discussion we have assumed that the range of potential consequences in this decision was small for the Warren Agency. We have assumed that the Agency will, over time, be faced with a large number of such small-consequence decisions and thus is willing in every one of them to play the averages, to be guided by the choice with the highest expected monetary value. Under these conditions, we have argued that a decision maker's valuation of a particular position (the certainty equivalent for that position) can be determined by calculating the expected monetary value.

Suppose you were the decision maker. How will the analysis change if you are not willing to make this assumption? How will you proceed if the range of potential consequences in a decision is, to you, very large? What can you do if you are not willing to say that your certainty equivalent for a position is even close to the expected monetary value?

In such a situation the first steps in the analysis remain unchanged. You can still identify the potential strategies and describe them through a decision diagram. You can evaluate the consequences at each end point with the relevant cash flows and adjust them for nonmonetary consequences. Your forecasts of the uncertain future can still be described through your assessment of the appropriate probabilities. The difference occurs when you try to combine these separate judgments. When you could obtain your certainty equivalent for a position by calculating an expected monetary value, you proceeded by averaging out and folding back through the diagram. In larger consequence decisions, since your certainty equivalents are not obtainable through the calculation of the expected monetary value, that procedure would have no justification. In such a case, you might obtain information useful in your decision by developing what is called a *risk profile* for each strategy.[3]

The purpose of a risk profile is to show the decision maker the possible final results of following a particular strategy and the likelihood or probability of each of these results occurring. Each strategy exposes the decision maker to different levels of risk and thus, of course, there are as many risk profiles involved in an analysis as there are strategies, one profile for each strategy. In the decision facing the Warren Agency, there are six strategies, starting at the one end with the no-go strategy and ending at the other with a strategy that states "Take the deal; if you sell the Arlington property exercise at that time your option on the Cambridge house, if you sell that property do not stop, but try to sell the Belmont house." (We will call this the A–C–B strategy. You may want to think about descriptions for the other four strategies.)

For a given strategy you can now list, from worst to best, the possible final results and then calculate for each the probability of that result being the one actually obtained. For the A–C–B strategy you would obtain the risk profile shown in Table 1–1.

---

[3] A strategy consists of a choice from the original act fork of the diagram, followed by contingent choices from each further act fork until there are no further levels of act forks possible. For example, "no go" is a simple strategy for Warren. Another strategy is: "Go, if you fail to sell the Arlington property you are through, if you succeed try next to sell the Belmont house, if you fail here you are through, if you succeed—stop."

Table 1–1
A–C–B strategy

Possible final results ($)	Probability
−800	0.30
−200	0.35
+3,600	0.14
+5,600	0.21
	1.00

The probability of not selling the Arlington house and thus losing $800 was assessed directly by Warren at .30. In order to end with a net cash flow of −$200, Warren would have to sell the Arlington house and then fail in his attempt to sell the Cambridge property. The probability of this joint occurrence, since the probabilities were assessed as independent by Warren, is the product of the two probabilities: .70 × .50 = .35. In a similar way, the probability of the successful sale of both Arlington and Cambridge followed by failure in the attempt to sell the Belmont house would be .70 × .50 × .40 = .14. You can verify that the probability of the successful sale of all these properties is .21.

If the potential consequences involved in a decision are so large that the decision maker is not willing to base the decision on expected monetary value, the risk profiles associated with each of the contending strategies can be developed. The decision maker can then make a judgmental tradeoff between return and risk and select as the decision the one with the preferred risk profile. Different individuals, or even the same individual in different contexts, might prefer different risk profiles. The analysis does not indicate a specific decision; it provides information useful in the decision-making process.[4]

By tracing through an analysis of Warren's decision, you should have developed an improved understanding of the reasoning involved in decision analysis. You should realize that what we have been dealing with is a tool to help Warren come to a decision. The basic ingredient, the important determinant of what he chose to do, was of course his own judgment. Decision analysis aims at improving the decision-making process by concentrating on one aspect of a problem at a time, thus providing managers with a more solid basis for acting in accordance with their best judgments.

Warren's problem is a relatively uncomplicated one which has allowed us to demonstrate in simple terms the basic ideas of decision analysis. Much of the remainder of this book will consider methods of analysis that can make you more adept at implementing the various steps in decision analyses of increased complexity. In Chapter 2 we consider more fully the

---

[4] Chapter 4 will deal more extensively with the problem of selecting among the risk profiles of different strategies.

evaluation of monetary consequences. Chapter 3 covers in more detail issues involved in developing decision diagrams. In Chapter 4 we look at ways of coping with decisions where the large magnitude of the potential consequences makes the decision maker adverse to risk and unwilling to use expected monetary value as a criterion. Chapters 5 through 9 deal with methods for assessing and using probability distribution, including the use of historical data in the development of assessments.

The decision analysis involving Warren's real estate problem has allowed us to consider decision diagraming, evaluation of cash flows and other consequences, probabilities, and attitudes toward risk. We will develop these methods of analysis in considerable detail in the chapters and cases that follow.

EXERCISES

1.1. Describe in words each of the six strategies perceived by Mr. Warren in his problem.

1.2. For each of the strategies described in Exercise 1, construct a risk profile. Be sure you understand the reasoning by which the probabilities of each possible final result are obtained.

1.3. Calculate the expected monetary value of each strategy in Exercise 1. If you were willing to decide on the basis of EMV, which strategy would you choose? What is the relationship between this analysis and the one described in the chapter?

Case 1–1

The Pillsbury Company*

In late January 1967 the Pillsbury Company of Minneapolis, which produced a wide range of convenience home foods, was trying to decide what quantity of pecans to order for the coming year. Orders for pecans were normally placed only once a year just before the crop was harvested— although for a slight premium additional purchases could often be made at other times.

During the 1967 season, however, the pecan growers had suffered extensive crop damage, and a considerably smaller crop than usual was coming onto the market at a much higher price. The purchasing department at Pillsbury realized that if it did not place a large enough order now it would not be able to buy any more pecans until the next crop was harvested in March 1968. In addition, because of the shortage, the 1967 price for pecans was considerably higher than normal. Thus the purchasing department knew that by placing too large an order it would unnecessarily increase the cost of future production—especially as the department was certain that the 1968 price for pecans would return to normal levels. (Excess stocks of pecans purchased now would be used for 1968 production.)

The uncertainty as to what quantity to order was further increased by the sales department's decision to introduce a new pecan product to the market during the coming year. The sales department was not sure how the new product would be received, and, consequently, it could only give the purchasing department a very vague idea of how many pecans would be needed.

Faced with having to place a firm order within seven days and with the uncertainty of demand for the new pecan products, the purchasing department believed that its normal procedure of estimating the average sales of the products and adding a little extra for inventory might not be the best course of action for the 1967 pecan purchase.

Consequently, it requested one of the company's staff department members to help lay out a decision tree. In this way the purchasing department felt that a more rational decision could be reached.

---

* The problem presented in this case has been slightly simplified over what actually occurred.

The staff member, in conjunction with the purchasing department, asked sales for an estimate of the demand for both the old and the new pecan products. The sales department replied that demand for 1967 could only be one of three values because of the manner in which the products were sold in bulk lots to wholesalers. The most likely demand was for 180,000 cases of the product. There were, however, two other possible demands; one was for 220,000 cases, and the other for 140,000 cases. When asked to estimate the probability of these levels occurring, the sales department replied that its best estimates of probabilities were .7, .2, and .1, respectively.

If the demand was for 180,000 cases, then the purchasing department calculated it would need to purchase 400 hundredweight of pecans in excess of the stock it already had on hand. If, however, the demand was for only 140,000 cases, then 120 hundredweight of pecans in excess of existing stock would be sufficient. Should the demand reach the high figure of 220,000 cases, however, purchasing decided it would then need to buy an additional 680 hundredweight over existing stock.

The staff member then asked the purchasing department the extent to which present prices were above normal (i.e., including 1968 prices). This figure was set at $40/hundredweight. He then asked sales for the net margin that accrued to the company from the sale of the pecan products. After some quick calculation the sales department decided that the figure was $2/case.

Armed with this information, the staff member returned to his office to prepare his recommendation to the purchasing department.

Case 1–2

Ventron Engineering (A)*

The Ventron Engineering Company has just been awarded a development contract by the U.S. Army Aviation Systems Command to design, develop, and demonstrate critical components of a new rotor system. The system will be part of the Heavy Lift Helicopter program which is currently receiving much attention in the industry.

An integral part of the rotor system is the blade spar. The blade spar is a metal tube which runs the length of and provides strength to the helicop-

---

* Copyright © 1972 by Applied Decision Systems, a division of Temple, Barker, & Sloane, Inc.

ter blade. Due to the unusual length and size of the Heavy Lift Helicopter blade, Ventron is unable to produce a single-piece blade spar of the required dimensions, using existing extrusion equipment and material.

The engineering department has prepared two alternatives for developing the blade spar: sectioning, and improvement of the extrusion process. Ventron is faced with a decision as to which process it should select.

Sectioning

This process involves joining several shorter lengths of extruded metal into a blade spar of sufficient length. This work will require extensive testing and rework over a 12-month period at a cost of $150,000 per month. While this process will definitely produce an adequate blade spar, it merely represents an extension of existing technology.

Extrusion

In order to extrude the blade spar as a single piece, it will be necessary to modify the extrusion press at a monthly cost of $160,000 and to improve the material used at a monthly cost of $50,000. Each of these steps would require six months of steady work.

If successful, this process would produce a blade spar of superior quality at a lower overall cost. Unfortunately, as opposed to sectioning, there is some risk that Ventron will be unable to perfect the process.

After studying the technical problems, the engineering department feels there is a nine in ten chance of perfecting the material. However, the other possibility (a one in ten chance) is that at the end of the six-month development effort it will know that a satisfactory material cannot be developed within any reasonable time and cost framework, and it will have to rely on sectioning.

The engineers believe there is a three in four chance of successfully modifying the press, but a one in four chance that at the end of a six-month press development project the extrusion process will have to be abandoned, because a press with the necessary capabilities will be shown to be infeasible.

Development of the blade spar must be completed within 18 months in order to avoid holding up the rest of the contract. It has also been determined that if necessary, the sectioning work could be done on an accelerated basis in a six-month period at a monthly cost of $400,000.

The Director of Engineering, Dr. Smith, is most interested in the opportunity provided by this contract to explore new technology in the extrusion process. He feels that if Ventron is successful in producing the blade spar as a single piece Ventron's reputation in the field will be greatly enhanced. In addition, it would be able to complete development of the blade spar well under budget.

After a preliminary review of the problem, Ventron's President, Bill Walters, has not yet reached a final decision. Like Dr. Smith, he is intrigued by the possibility of successfully developing the extrusion process. He feels that this would give Ventron an excellent chance at some additional contracts. He is concerned, however, about the possibility of wasting money on unsuccessful development or of being forced to do sectioning on an accelerated basis.

Ventron's contract with the Army is for a fixed total amount spread over several years. Walters wants to minimize the expenditures on the blade spar portion to free up money for technical developments on other components of the rotor system, which would improve Ventron's position for future business, both defense and commercial.

Exhibit 1
Risk report: Blade spar development

	Cost/month ($000)	Probability of success	Time required for effort (months)	Total cost ($000)
Extrusion development				
Material development	50	0.9	6	300
Press modification	160	0.75	6	960
Sectioning				
Normal basis	150	1.0	12	1,800
Accelerated	400	1.0	6	2,400

Case 1–3

Harvard Business School: Division of
Computer Services

In August 1972 the Division of Computer Services at Harvard Business School was involved in the final phases of installing a new DEC (Digital Equipment Corporation) system 1070 computer. Years before that time the School had kept an IBM 1401 computer in the Robinson Room in Baker Library, where the new computer would also be housed. In 1968 the 1401 had been removed, and since that time the Robinson Room had been used to store a variety of items, including used computer tapes. In August 1972 the room was being cleaned out to make room for the new installation. Professor Arthur Schleifer, who was then Director of the

Division of Computer Services at HBS, asked Mr. William Madison, who had recently been hired as Manager of Software Development, to collect the information needed to decide whether to try to salvage the tapes or simply to discard them.

The tapes had been in dead storage since the mid-1960s; they had been used on the 1401 and had been stored when that machine left the School. In 1972 there were still over 400 of these tapes in storage. Because they had been written in formats which were not easily read by the computers available to researchers in the university in 1972, they had been abandoned by the researchers who had used them. A quick look at a few of the name labels on the tapes indicated that most of them had belonged to faculty members, many of whom had long since left HBS (or, at least, had completed the projects for which the tapes had been used). Even for ongoing projects, researchers had copied their data onto newer tapes in formats acceptable to available machines. Mr. Madison could find out very little about what the tapes actually contained, what condition they were in, or precisely how old they were. He was particularly interested in these tapes since the Division would need a large number of tapes to support the operation of the new system; at the start, it would need about 400 tapes. Thus, if he could salvage some of the old tapes, he could save the cost of buying new ones.

Trying to salvage tapes of this sort would involve sending them out to be cleaned, recertified, and tested, a service which would cost $2,800 for the 400-plus tapes. When the tapes came back from being recertified, Mr. Madison would then have to decide how many of them were worth keeping.

The Appendix gives some background information about computer tapes. A key factor concerning the old tapes at HBS was that no one knew their exact age and, therefore, whether they were made under "old" or "new" technology. This factor would definitely influence whether the tapes would be worth trying to salvage. From the people he spoke with, Mr. Madison got the impression that all the tapes were likely to be within a narrow age range. Thus, it seemed highly likely that they were all (or almost all) "new" technology or all "old" technology. On the basis of the information which he collected, Madison assessed a 70 percent probability that the tapes were old technology and a 30 percent chance that they were new.

The decision facing Mr. Madison had other complexities. Among these was the need for a value judgment of the quality standard by which a tape was considered "good" or "bad." The analysis was also complicated by the fact that he could end up with any of a large number of possible mixes of good tapes, bad tapes, mediocre tapes, long tapes, and short tapes.

After some debate it was decided that the tapes would have to be in fairly good condition to be worth keeping. Madison considered whether or not to try to use tapes which had been salvaged but which were shorter than 2,400 feet in length; because the first portion of a tape receives most of the use, it is sometimes possible to restore a tape to usefulness by removing that heavily used part. Madison decided that while it was theoretically possible to use tapes of different lengths and different qualities for different purposes, doing so would create administrative complexities which would place an unacceptable additional workload on the operations staff at the new facility. Consequently, he decided that any tapes which were short or which did not meet a fairly strict quality standard would be classified as "bad"/discard; only tapes which were of high quality and standard length would be classified "good"/keep.

With these assumptions in mind, Professor Schleifer (a member of the Managerial Economics area as well as Director of Computer Services) and Mr. Madison proceeded to assess the probabilities of salvaging the tapes. First they looked at the probabilities of salvaging various numbers of the tapes if they had been fabricated with the "new" technology. They assessed about a 25 percent chance of being really lucky and salvaging 400 tapes. At the other extreme, even with the new technology, there was still a 25% chance of being able to reclaim only 200 tapes. Schleifer and Madison also estimated a 25 percent chance of 325 good tapes and a 25 percent chance of 275.[1]

If the tapes had been fabricated with the "old" technology, Madison and Schleifer knew they wouldn't be so lucky. They assessed a 25% probability that only 125 of the tapes would be any good. At the other extreme, there was a 25 percent probability that 325 tapes would be good. And, in the middle, they assessed a 25 percent chance of 250 being good and a 25 percent chance of 200 good.

Depending on how many tapes were salvaged, the computer center would need to buy different numbers of new tapes. Currently it could expect to pay $12 apiece for the first 100 tapes in an order and $11 for each tape above that number (thus, an order for 150 tapes would cost $12 × 100 + $11 × 50 = $1,750.)

If the Division decided not to try to salvage the tapes, it would give them all to the Braille Press, where they would be cut to one-fourth-inch width and used for talking books. Any tapes declared bad after recertification could similarly be given to Braille, although the money spent on recertification would be of no advantage as far as Braille Press was concerned. For HBS there would be no tax break or other financial benefit from the tape donation; however, there would at least be the nonmonetary satisfaction of knowing that the tapes would be put to good use.

The basic question facing Mr. Madison, then, was whether he should spend the $2,800 to recertify the tapes (buying new tapes to replace any judged to be too low in quality) or whether simply to abandon the project,

---

[1] In reality, of course, many intermediate numbers of good tapes were possible but the four numbers here were selected as representative of various ranges of possible values.

giving the óld tapes to Braille and buying 400 new ones. Madison also considered trying to find out more information about the tapes. By going through old invoices and lists of faculty projects, someone might be able to date the tapes more precisely and, thus, to determine whether the group was of old or new technology. Before trying to obtain this information, though, Madison wanted to determine how much it would be worth, since a temporary worker would have to be hired to go through the tapes and invoices and, thus, the search for information would have some tangible cost.

Appendix: Background information on computer tapes

A general-purpose computer is usually thought of as consisting of the following parts:

1. The central processing unit, or CPU—this part is the central "logic" of the computer. It performs the various arithmetic operations (such as addition or division) and logical operations (such as comparisons of two numbers) which are the basic part of the computer's work.

2. *Storage*—this portion of the machine holds the numbers on which the CPU can perform its operations. The storage unit of a machine contains space for a large number of individual pieces of information. When the CPU is instructed to perform one of its operations, the instruction must also include directions as to which of the items in storage to use. The CPU logic then requests that the appropriate numbers be fetched from storage, it performs the required operation, and it then may request that the result be stored in some location in the storage. The storage consists of a large number of individual slots or bins for information; each such slot is called a *location*.

3. The *I/O* (for input/output) equipment—these parts of the computer provide the interface with human users or mechanical users of the machine. Typical I/O equipment includes line printers (which provide the familiar printed computer forms), card readers (which read computer cards with holes punched in them, such as the cards which come with your telephone bill), card punches (which punch such cards), and terminals (which are used with time-shared computers such as the HBS machine).

The typical general-purpose computer would contain anywhere from about 10,000 to several hundred thousand storage locations, or *words,* as they are called. Such storage units are reasonably expensive; their prices depend on both their sizes and on the speeds with which individual numbers can be retrieved from or stored in them. For example, a 16,000-word storage with a fetch time of 0.75 millionths of a second might (in 1974) cost about $5,000. Surprising as it might seem at first, even relatively large storage units, with several hundred thousand words, do not provide enough storage for most computer facilities. Rather than buy more of the expensive fast storage (called core memory because it is usually constructed from magnetic cores), most users elect instead to buy what is called secondary storage. The various forms of secondary storage provide much less expensive (although much slower) storage space for very large amounts of information.

One very commonly used medium for bulk storage of computer information is magnetic tape. (Tapes are so common on computers that they have become the symbol for a computer; in movies or on TV, the whirring of a tape unit, called a tape drive, shows that there is a computer at work.) The information on magnetic tapes is stored in what are called bits; each individual bit is either a one or a zero (i.e., it is either magnetized or not magnetized). The bits are the basic building blocks of computer language. (Thus, in technical terms, although normal numbers used by humans are base 10, the computer numbers are base 2.) All information on the tapes (or inside the computer) is formed from codes of these bits; one typical code uses eight bits to make one ordinary character or number. (For example, the letter a might be encoded as 11000001.) As an example of the storage capacity of a magnetic tape, consider a 2,400-foot tape. A typical tape might contain 800 characters per inch of tape length. Thus, the 2,400-foot tape would be able to hold $2,400 \times 12 \times 800$, or 23,040,000, characters. As a comparison, the punched cards which are often used on computers hold 80 characters each. One magnetic tape is equivalent in capacity to about 300,000 cards (or 150 boxes of computer cards)!

Thus, magnetic tapes can hold extremely large amounts of information at very little cost. Their disadvantage is in speed. If the CPU needs a block of information which has been recorded somewhere in the middle of a tape's length, first the tape must be mounted on a special reading unit called a tape drive. Then the tape drive must read through the tape, sequentially, until it reaches the particular information required by the CPU.

In summary: To balance speed and expense the typical computer facility has a mix of available forms of storage—some high-speed but expensive core memory and various types of other slower and less expensive secondary storage.

Like other sorts of magnetic tape, computer tape, if properly cared for and cleaned, can be used over and over. With current tape technology, a clean used tape can give just as good performance as a clean new tape. However, tapes have not always had this property. The adhesive backing and oxides of tapes made under older technology tended to deteriorate more with time and usage.

Imperfections in a tape can cause a bit to be misread. Even with brand-new, cleaned tape, about one in every 10 million bits may "drop" out (or misread). Tape in less good condition might have a drop rate of one bit in every 100,000 to 1,000,000. Obviously, then, it is a value judgment at what point the tape is considered "bad" or "good."

Within the computer code there are schemes (such as making sure the numbers of 1's and 0's add up to what they should) to ensure that it is known if a bit is dropped. In most circumstances, therefore, the loss of a bit will be indicated to the user as an error in the code; the machine will not simply proceed along with an error in the data. Depending on the particular use of the data, a lost bit may or may not be a problem. In some cases the program would stop. In others, such as a large consumer survey where losing one piece of data doesn't matter so much, the program may be designed simply to proceed.

In the recertification process, after the tape is cleaned, number 1's are coded across the whole width and length of the tape. These bits are read back, and a map is made of all errors noted. These may simply be "soft errors" caused by dust or other foreign matter on the tape. Or, there may be "hard errors" caused by such physical damage to the tape as the oxide's being worn down, creases in the tape, nodules of oxide lifting the tape off the reading head, etc. These hard errors are not easily fixed.

Given their maps of errors, tapes could, theoretically, be rated in terms of their riskiness to the user. Some users might perhaps be willing to take riskier tapes for a cut in price. However, new 2,400-foot tapes only cost about $12, and given that this is more than enough tape for all but the most data-heavy of individual research projects, it seems unlikely that there would in most circumstances be much of a market for cut-rate tape.

Another consideration in the salvaging of computer tape is that the first 400 feet or so of a tape is inevitably used more and is damaged more than is the rest of the tape. By stripping off this portion, it may be possible to obtain an acceptable, even if somewhat shorter, tape. Tapes 2,400 feet long are typical, but shorter tapes, such as 1,200-foot or 600-foot ones, are often used for special purposes.

Chapter 2

The evaluation of monetary consequences

A promising new product is nationally introduced on the basis of its future sales and subsequent profits. A piece of real estate is developed for the rental income that can be derived from it, as well as its potential resale value. A corporate bond is purchased for its coupons and the ultimate repayment of its par value. These decisions are similar in that each involves the current investment of money with the anticipation and hope of future benefits.

The value of such an investment depends on several factors—the magnitude of the benefits, the timing of these benefits, and the uncertainty of actually receiving them. Each of these factors contributes to the difficulty of the investment decision. The prediction of future benefits is perhaps the most significant problem, but even if they are known with certainty, difficulties still persist in making the go–no go decision or in selecting among alternative investments. For example, a manager may be faced with an investment for which the total dollar return far exceeds the initial investment, but the return is delayed into the distant future. Does the magnitude of the return justify the wait? Or one investment may yield substantially greater returns than another, but the returns of the first are received over a longer period of time than the second. How do you know which is better, or even if either is desirable?

A systematic approach to this question is the topic of this chapter. We shall focus our attention on the appropriate identification and measurement of the returns (cash flow) and on the significance and evaluation of the timing of those returns (discounting). It will be assumed that the returns are known with certainty. The concepts and techniques for dealing with uncertainty explicitly are discussed in other chapters of the book.

CASH FLOW AS A CRITERION

Why are new products introduced, real estate developed, or bonds purchased? In each decision there are probably a host of reasons, ranging from the strategic goals of the corporation to the personal desires of the manager. But common to almost all investment decisions is the objective of financial returns from the invested money. In this section, we concentrate on the identification and measurement of these financial returns and ignore the other, more subjective considerations that surround most capital investment decisions.

Rather simply stated, the returns from a corporate investment can either be reinvested in the firm or distributed to the owners. Better investments will generate more money for reinvestment or distribution. So in evaluating an investment, the decision maker should be looking at its financial return in terms of money that can be "used." Likewise the outlays for the investment should be viewed as money withdrawn from the pool of "usable money." This means that investments should be evaluated in terms of *cash flow*—the inflow and outflow of real cash—and not in terms of earnings or profits as reported by the firm's accounting system.

Suppose, for example, that in a three-year insurance program a manager were offered the choice between prepaying the entire premium of $3,000 or paying the premium in three annual installments of $1,000 each. The manager would almost certainly select the deferred payment plan. But why? Under either plan, the firm's income statement would show the same annual insurance cost of $1,000 (since accrual methods would allow the prepayment to be spread evenly over the three-year life of the policy), and hence the same profits would be reported. The difference between the two options lies in their differing schedules of demand for cash, that is, in their differing cash flows. The deferred plan is preferred since it actually spreads the cash expenditure over the next three years; this is seen only by considering the cash flow and is obscured in the reported profits or earnings.

The facts that the cash flow is the relevant measurement of the returns from an investment and that profits or earnings are irrelevant for this purpose do not mean that the accountant's reports are for naught. They are designed with a different purpose in mind—the measurement of profitability over periods shorter than the life of the investments. If fiscal years were 100 calendar years long, the cash flow from projects would be the same as their profits after tax.

Differential cash flows

The usual technique for calculating the cash flows for an investment is to calculate the *differential cash flows*—the difference between the cash flows from the investment and the cash flows of a "do-nothing" alternative. If there are several alternatives to be evaluated, you do several cash flow calculations, comparing each alternative to the "do-nothing" option. In addition to treating the cash flows in a differential fashion, you must distinguish carefully between those flows that are really cash flows and those that are noncash flows that result from accounting conventions. A simple rule of thumb is: "If you write a check for it, it's a cash outflow, and if you can deposit it at the bank, it's a cash inflow." In the prepayment alternative of the insurance policy example above, the check is written now so the cash outflow is $3,000 now, and, regardless of how the cost might be expensed over the next three years for accounting purposes, there is no cash outflow in subsequent years from the insurance policy with the prepayment option.

The construction of an exhaustive list of the sources of cash flows would be an impossible task, but it is possible to be fairly comprehensive with the limited number of categories that are frequently encountered in practice. With regard to the initial outlays for an investment, look first for the obvious initial purchase or construction cost, and then note any *changes* in working capital (the holding of cash, inventories, and the net of accounts receivable and accounts payable) required to support the project, the salvage value of any equipment that is being replaced or discarded, and any investment incentives offered by the government. For cash flows subsequent to the initial outlay, look for revenues (sales, dividends, or interest payments if it is a purely financial investment) resulting from the investment, for cost of goods sold (materials, manufacturing costs), for changes in selling and administrative expenses, for possible subsequent investment costs, and for taxes.

Note that neither depreciation nor financing expense is included as cash flows. Depreciation is simply an accounting provision whose effects will be reflected in the calculation of taxes but is not itself a cash flow. The exclusion of the costs associated with financing the investment is the result of the widely accepted practice of separating the evaluation of the investment itself from the decision concerning the means of financing that investment. There are several reasons for keeping these two evaluations separate. The pool of investments is generally funded from capital that is raised through a combination of debt, equity, and retained earnings. In the evaluation of an investment it would be inappropriate to assume the cost of any one of these sources, but a composite cost would require the perspective of the total financial demands on the firm. Even if a project were clearly to be financed out of either debt or equity (but not both), the cost of either means would not reflect the real cost, since the funding of the investment would affect the firm's ability to acquire future capital by either means. Thus the financing decision is a global decision and should not be implicitly made (or assumed) at the individual investment decision level. Finally, if the means of financing an investment were included in the evaluation of the investment, the initial outlay would be reduced and subsequent interest charges would be incurred. This change in the cash flows would generally favor those investments with the greatest amount of debt. The result is a distortion of the true value of the investment. Of course, if an investment has been accepted and alternative financing arrangements for it are now being evaluated, then the financing cash flows are the only relevant ones.

Example of cash flow calculations

To illustrate these concepts, we will evaluate the cash flows for a proposed investment of $32,000 which will expand production operations for three years and allow a firm to satisfy sales that are currently being lost. It is anticipated that the new sales will generate $27,000 per year in revenue, at a cost of goods of $12,000 and with no increase in selling or general administrative expenses. To support the increased sales volume, $8,000 must be set aside at the time of the investment to cover increases in inventories and accounts receivable, all of which will be recoverable at the conclusion of the project. Also at the end of the project, there will be usable equipment with a salvage value of $2,000. The initial investment will be depreciated by a simple straight-line method in such a way that it has a book value of $2,000 at the end of the project. The marginal tax rate is assumed to be 48 percent.

The cash flows for this investment are shown in Figure 2–1. Note that the flows during each year have been aggregated to give an annual total, even though most of them will actually take place continuously during the year. The format of Figure 2–1 highlights the actual cash flows because it never includes *directly* in the calculations any noncash items such as de-

Figure 2–1
Cash flows

			Year		
Cash flows		*0*	*1*	*2*	*3*
Cost of project....................		$−32,000			
Sales			$ 27,000	$ 27,000	$ 27,000
Cost of goods....................			− 12,000	− 12,000	− 12,000
Taxes*			− 2,400	− 2,400	− 2,400
Changes in working capital..........		− 8,000			8,000
Salvage of equipment					2,000
Taxes on salvage†					0
Total cash flow		$−40,000	$ 12,600	$ 12,600	$ 22,600

* Tax computation: Revenues	$ 27,000	
Cost of goods	− 12,000	
Depreciation	− 10,000	
Profits before taxes	$ 5,000	
Taxes (48% of profit)	$ 2,400	

† Taxes are zero since equipment is sold at book value, that is, there is no capital gain or loss on the sale.

preciation. An alternative format which many find useful follows the layout of the standard income statement. This procedure will yield the same result as long as you are careful to account for the fact that noncash charges have been included in the calculation of profits after tax and must be "added back" to convert after-tax profits into cash flows. Figure 2–2 presents the calculation of the cash flows for the above example, using this alternative format.

Figure 2–2
Cash flows: Income statement format

		Year		
	0	*1*	*2*	*3*
Cash flow of initial investment	$−32,000			
Sales		$27,000	$27,000	$27,000
Cost of goods		12,000	12,000	12,000
Depreciation		10,000	10,000	10,000
Total costs		$22,000	$22,000	$22,000
Before-tax profits from sales		$ 5,000	$ 5,000	$ 5,000
Taxes (48% of profits)		2,400	2,400	2,400
After-tax profits from sales		2,600	2,600	2,600
Plus: Noncash charges to sales*		10,000	10,000	10,000
Cash flow from sales		$12,600	$12,600	$12,600
Salvage of equipment				$ 2,000
Book value of equipment				2,000
Profits from equipment salvage				0
Capital gains tax				0
After-tax profits from equipment salvage				0
Plus: Noncash charges to equipment salvage*				$ 2,000
Cash flow from equipment salvage				$ 2,000
Cash flow from working capital changes	$ −8,000			$ 8,000
Total cash flow	$−40,000	$12,600	$12,600	$22,600

* Since noncash items (depreciation and book value of equipment) have been subtracted in arriving at the after-tax profits, these must be added back to convert after-tax profits into cash flow.

TIME VALUE OF MONEY

Once the cash flows for a proposed investment alternative have been determined, the question remains as to whether or not the proposal is a sound investment. In addition, if there are several attractive alternatives but limited available cash, the alternatives must be evaluated to determine which ones make the most effective use of those limited funds. A systematic way to make evaluations when the cash returns are spread over a long period of time is the topic of this section.

To help in the development and understanding of the techniques to be discussed, we will work together in determining the better choice in the following numerical example. Suppose a manager is faced with two investment opportunities, A and B, each of which requires an initial investment of $37,000. The first alternative returns lump-sum cash flows of $15,000 at yearly intervals for each of the three years following the initial outlay. The cash flows for the second alternative, also annual, are $5,000 for each of the first two payments and $37,000 for the last one. The alternatives are graphically illustrated in Figure 2–3. Which one do you prefer?

Figure 2–3
Display of cash flows for investments A and B

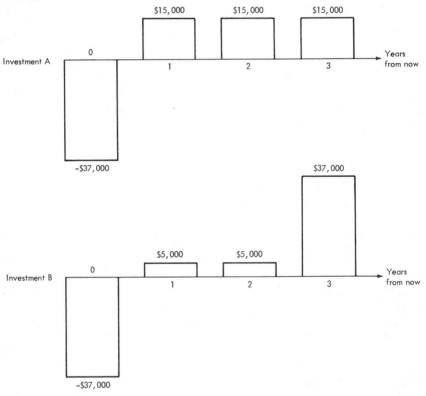

Accumulated value

We see in Figure 2–3 that over their lifetimes each of these investments will return more than the initial outlay of $37,000. Investment A results in a total cash return of $45,000, while investment B yields a total of $47,000. Since for the same initial outlay investment B returns more than investment A, it may seem that investment B is the clear choice.

The decision is clear until we notice that investment A yields its returns steadily, while investment B delays the bulk of its total return until the final year. If we were to select investment A, we would have more cash in hand at the end of years 1 and 2 than with investment B. This should make us question the impulsive choice of investment B. Surely, we would not leave the cash returns from either of these investments lying idle; rather we would reinvest them as soon as possible in other profitable opportunities. Since investment A offers more cash for reinvestment at the end of years 1 and 2, there might be enough additional return from these *re*investments to offset the greater total return of investment B. Whether it does so or not will depend on just how attractive the reinvestment opportunities are. Let us assume for now that our plans would be to aggressively manage any cash returns so that they would yield 10 percent after taxes. In this context, what would be the total returns (including reinvestment) from the two alternatives?

We can answer this question by using an approach that is identical to the one used to calculate interest on a savings account. The interest rate for each time period is applied to the balance in the account, and the resulting interest is added to the balance. Thus the balance of the account changes by the interest that is earned and by the deposits (or withdrawals) that are made. In the cash flow example above, the returns are analogous to the "deposits" to the savings balance, and the earnings from reinvesting the returns are the "interest payments." Applying this analogy to investment A, there are, as Figure 2–4 shows, zero dollars on deposit during year 1 but, at the end of year 1, a deposit of $15,000 is made. Thus during year 2 a balance of the $15,000 will be carried. That balance will earn $1,500 in interest at a 10 percent rate, giving an end-of-year balance of $16,500. But also at the end of the year the second deposit of $15,000 is

Figure 2–4
Comparing investment A and investment B (reinvestment at 10 percent)

	Year 1	Year 2	Year 3
Investment A			
Cash balance at beginning of year	0	$15,000	$31,500
Earnings from reinvestment of balance at 10%	0	1,500	3,150
Cash at end of year from investment A	$15,000	15,000	15,000
Total cash available at end of year for reinvestment next year	$15,000	$31,500	$49,650
Investment B			
Cash balance at beginning of year	0	$ 5,000	$10,500
Earnings from reinvestment of balance at 10%	0	500	1,050
Cash at end of year from investment B	$ 5,000	5,000	37,000
Total cash available at end of year for reinvestment next year	$ 5,000	$10,500	$48,550

made, so the total balance that will be on deposit during year 3 is $31,500 ($16,500 + $15,000). This balance will earn $3,150 during the year, so that along with another "deposit" of $15,000, the balance at end of year 3 will be $49,650. Similar reasoning can be applied to investment B (Figure 2–4).

Now, when we compare the two alternatives, investment A is by far the better choice, since it results in an accumulated value of $49,650, compared to $48,550 for investment B, at the end of three years. Remember that this is provided we can earn 10 percent on the cash that becomes available from the investments. Our choice now is different from the impulsive decision we made earlier. A careful look at the numbers in Figure 2–4 suggests the reason for the change. Investment A yields substantially greater earnings from reinvestment, since its cash flows in years 1 and 2 are greater than those for investment B. These added earnings are sufficient to offset the $2,000 difference in total return.

Investment A may not be better if we decide or are forced to follow a less aggressive policy with regard to reinvestment. Suppose we decide to put all of the cash spinoffs into U.S. government bonds that yield 4 percent after taxes. We can compare the two alternatives using the 4 percent rate just as we did with the 10 percent reinvestment rate. Which of the alternatives leaves us in the better position at the end of year 3? These calculations are shown in Figure 2–5. When the reinvestment rate is 4 percent, investment B will produce the greater accumulated value at the end of the third year. Why is this different from the ranking when the reinvestment rate was 10 percent? Again we should look at the earnings from the reinvestment of the cash spinoff. At 4 percent, the additional earnings from the accelerated payment scheme are not sufficient to offset the $2,000 difference in total return.

Figure 2–5
Comparing investment A and investment B (reinvestment at 4 percent)

	Year 1	Year 2	Year 3
Investment A			
Cash balance at beginning of year	0	$15,000	$30,600
Earnings from reinvestment of balance at 4%	0	600	1,224
Cash at end of year from investment A	$15,000	15,000	15,000
Total cash available at end of year for reinvestment next year	$15,000	$30,600	$46,824
Investment B			
Cash balance at beginning of year	0	$ 5,000	$10,200
Earnings from reinvestment of balance at 4%	0	200	408
Cash at end of year from investment B	$ 5,000	5,000	37,000
Total cash available at end of year for reinvestment next year	$ 5,000	$10,200	$47,608

The important conclusion that should be drawn from the above examples is that *in evaluating investments whose payoffs extend into the future, it is not only the magnitude of the cash flows that is important but also the timing of the flows and the subsequent use to which those flows can be put.* To appropriately evaluate alternative cash flow streams, the analysis must include all three aspects—magnitude, timing, and reinvestment rate. The method used above, which again is analogous to the compounding growth of interest-bearing accounts, does just this. Other techniques based on the same reasoning will be developed later.

Thus far in our analysis of the two alternative investments, we have concluded that investment A is better than investment B when the reinvestment rate is 10 percent. The question remains whether either one of them is an attractive use of the initial outlay of $37,000. Would it be better to put the $37,000 into our 10 percent investment opportunities rather than either of these alternatives? One way to answer this question is to compare the accumulated value of the initial investment to the accumulated values of investments A and B. At a 10 percent rate, with the earnings from one year reinvested for the next, the $37,000 would compound to $40,700 by the end of the first year, to $44,770 by the end of the second year, and to $49,247 by the end of the third year. You might find it helpful to check these numbers using the format of Figures 2–4 and 2–5. Now when we compare the accumulated values, we find that investment A ($49,650) is a slightly better use of the initial outlay than simply investing it in the 10 percent opportunities ($49,247). On the other hand, investment B ($48,550) is a poorer use of funds than the 10 percent opportunities. Even though the total return from investment B substantially exceeds the initial investment, it is still not a sound investment when 10 percent opportunities exist. What would you expect to happen if the investment opportunity rate were 4 percent? Check your intuition with the numerical calculation.

Present value

In the discussion above we focused attention on a future date and calculated the accumulated value of a stream of cash flows out to that point in time. This is a very natural way to think about evaluating the worth of cash flows, since it so closely parallels everyday savings account computations, but it does have drawbacks in business applications. One of these is that in the comparison of alternatives we are dealing in "future dollars," and with long-lived investments that "future" could be very distant. In this example, with its three-year future, this was not a problem, but consider an investment in a new plant with a 40-year useful life. To many decision makers it would seem rather unnatural to think in terms of dollars 40 years from now, particularly when the decision is being made now with "now dollars." A second difficulty arises out of the focus on future dollars—the need to compute the accumulated value of the initial investment in order to decide if the investment yields sufficient returns to make it attractive. If we change our perspective from "future dollars" to "now dollars," both of these problems are eliminated.

From the "future dollars" perspective, we saw that with a 10 percent rate, $37,000 would accumulate to $49,247 in three years. If we shift our perspective to "now," we could say that $37,000 is the *present value* of $49,247 received three years from now, when 10 percent opportunities exist. The $37,000 is a present value in the sense that if it were invested now at 10 percent it would grow to $49,247 three years in the future. In other words, the present value of a future payment is that amount which makes us indifferent between receiving the present value now or waiting for the future payment. *Present value is simply the inverse of accumulated value.*

Let us apply this concept to the cash flows from investment A, which is made up of three annual payments of $15,000 each. The present value of these flows at the assumed rate of 10 percent would be the sum of money we would require now in order to generate the future cash flows of investment A. The stream of cash flows is made up of three individual payments, so to calculate the present value of the returns we could calculate the present value of each component (i.e., the amount of money we need now to generate each of the components) and then sum the resulting present values. The accumulation over time of a reinvested dollar is the underlying concept of present value, so to assist us in finding the present value of investment A, let us determine the accumulation over time of a single dollar invested at 10 percent:

	Year 1	Year 2	Year 3
Beginning amount	1.00	1.10	1.21
Interest at 10%	0.10	0.11	0.121
Ending amount	1.10	1.21	1.331

The first component of the investment A stream is $15,000 one year from now. Each dollar that is invested at 10 percent will accrue to $1.10 one year from now. Thus $15,000 equals 110 percent of the amount we would need to invest now to have $15,000 at year's end. The present value of $15,000 is therefore $13,636 (or $15,000/1.10). Similarly, to create the investment A cash flows for years 2 and 3, we must now invest $12,396 (or $15,000/1.21) and $11,270 (or $15,000/1.331), respectively. Finally, to generate all of the future cash flows of investment A, we must now invest $37,302 ($13,636 + $12,396 + $11,270), and this is the present value of investment A at 10 percent.

To repeat an old question, is investment A an attractive prospect? Given our 10 percent opportunities, we would need $37,302 (the present value of investment A) to generate the same cash flows as investment A;

however, using investment A, we can "buy" those flows for $37,000. So, as we concluded when we considered accumulated value, it is an attractive alternative when 10 percent opportunities exist for investing the cash spin-off. This comparison of the present value of a stream of cash flows to its initial investment is often summarized by a single number, the *net present value* (NPV), which is simply the present value of the future cash flows minus the initial investment. As such, it is a measurement of the attractiveness of the investment. When the net present value is a positive number (as it is for investment A), the investment is attractive, since it would require more money than the initial investment to generate the same future flows through our 10 percent opportunities. When the net present value is negative, the prospect is unattractive. We would be indifferent between undertaking the investment and employing the funds in 10 percent opportunities when the net present value is zero. Among those investments with positive net present value, the larger the NPV the more attractive the investment, since its value to us (the present value) exceeds by a larger amount its cost to us (the initial outlay). In a sense, *the higher the net present value, the better the deal*.

In the above examples, notice that the present values of future cash flows are less than the flows themselves. The future flows have been "discounted" to account for the time value of money. At a 10 percent rate, $15,000 received one year from now has a present value of $13,636, or .9091 of its future value. To account for the time value of money, the flow one year from now has been multiplied by the factor .9091, to bring the flow to its present value. This factor is the *"one-year discount factor at 10 percent."* Similarly, the discount factors at 10 percent are .8264 for two years and .7513 for three years. Each of these can be easily calculated as the reciprocal of the accumulated values of a dollar—.9091 = 1/1.10, .8264 = 1/1.21, and .7513 = 1/1.331. Thus, the discount factors may be interpreted as the present values of future $1 payments. These discount factors can be used to calculate the present value of investment A:

$$($15,000 \times 0.9091) + ($15,000 \times 0.8264) + ($15,000 \times 0.7513)$$
$$= \quad $13,636 \quad + \quad $12,396 \quad + \quad $11,270$$
$$= \quad $37,302$$

In fact, the discount factors are what are most commonly used to calculate present values and are available in tables such as those in Appendix A, Table A–1.

Formulas for accumulated value and present value

Underlying the concepts of accumulated value and present value are several rather straightforward equations. You may have already noticed them in the above numerical examples. In calculating accumulated values, we went through the following mechanics:

	Beginning amount	*Interest at 10%*	*Ending amount*
Year 1	1.00	0.10	$1.10 = 1.00 \times 1.10$
Year 2	1.10	0.11	$1.21 = 1.10 \times 1.10$
Year 3	1.21	0.121	$1.331 = 1.21 \times 1.10$

If we take the ending amount for year 2 and go back to what happened in year 1, we can rewrite the equation as follows:

$$\begin{aligned} 1.21 &= 1.10 \times 1.10 \\ &= (1.00 \times 1.10) \times 1.10 \\ &= 1.00 \times (1.10)^2 \end{aligned}$$

Similarly, the ending amount for year 3 can be rewritten as

$$1.331 = 1.00 \times (1.10)^3 ,$$

and the pattern begins to become apparent. The general formula for the accumulated value n years hence of a single payment now is

$$A = P \times (1 + i)^n ,$$

where

  P = Initial amount
  i = Periodic earnings rate for reinvestments (expressed as a decimal, 0.10 in our examples)
  n = Number of periods of accumulation
  A = Accumulated value of P after n periods at rate i

To find the present value at rate i of an amount A which is available n years into the future, we need to solve the above equation for P, obtaining

$$P = \frac{A}{(1 + i)^n} .$$

Within-year payments

In these examples, we have assumed that all investment returns are received at the end of each year. In many of the business applications of present value, this is not the case. Taxes are paid quarterly; operating expenses are incurred weekly. Although the general formulas have been developed in terms of full years, they also hold for partial years. If a cash inflow of $32,000 will occur two years and four months from now, the present value at 10 percent of that flow is $\$32{,}000/(1.10)^{2.33}$, which is the above formula with n equal to 2.33. If we have a sufficiently powerful calculating device, we can calculate the exact present value using this formula. If not, we can easily compute a close approximation by *interpolating* between the discount factors for year 2 and year 3. Since two and one-third years is one third the way between two years and three years, the appropriate discount factor is approximately[1] one third of the way between the discount factors for two years and three years:

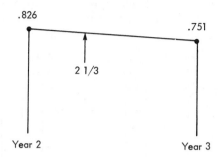

Specifically, .751 is .075 less than .826, so the discount factor which is one third of the way between .826 and .751 is .025 (⅓ of .075) less than .826; that is, .801. Thus the present value at 10 percent of $32,000 received two years and four months from now is *approximately* $25,632 ($32,000 × .801). The exact value is $25,620.

If a stream of cash flows were comprised of five years of quarterly payments, the treatment of each flow as an individually dated payment would entail very tedious computations by hand. Fortunately, when the payments within a year are periodic and of equal magnitude (a common occurrence in many applications), tables of factors which convert the installments into their year-end accumulated value are available. One of these is Table A–2 in Appendix A. An excerpt from that table is the following:

Interest rate	Period			
	1 year	*½ year*	*¼ year*	*1 day*
0.10	1.000	1.024	1.037	1.049

In this table, it is assumed that each installment is made at the end of its installment period; for example, if the payments are made quarterly, they are assumed to occur at the *end* of each quarter during the year. The factor 1.037 is the year-end accumulation at 10 percent of $1 paid in four quarterly installments of 25 cents. If a $6,000 annual payment were to be paid in quarterly installments of $1,500, the year-end accumulated value at 10 percent would be $6,222 (or $6,000 × 1.037). Note that it is the *total* annual payment (not the installments) which is multiplied by the factor in the table!

---

[1] It is "approximately" this figure because the discount factors do not decrease with time in a linear fashion. The approximation will slightly overestimate the true value of the discount factor.

To illustrate the fashion in which the year-end accumulation factors can be introduced into present value calculations, let us assume that the cash inflows of investment A occur quarterly. Since investment A has an annual cash flow of $15,000, the quarterly payments will be $3,750 each, and the returns from the investment can be visualized as follows:

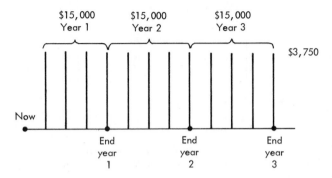

The present value of these cash flows, discounted at 10 percent, is evaluated by converting the quarterly installments into an equivalent end-of-year payment (the accumulated value of those installments) and then finding the present value of the year-end equivalents. During any one of the years, the quarterly installments will accumulate to $15,555 (or $15,000 × 1.037), and the present value of these year-end equivalent flows, discounted at 10 percent, is:

$$($15,555 \times 0.9091) + ($15,555 \times 0.8264) + ($15,555 \times 0.7513)$$
$$= \qquad $14,141 \qquad + \qquad $12,855 \qquad + \qquad $11,686$$
$$= \qquad $38,682$$

This is substantially larger than the present value when the cash flows were assumed to have occurred in a lump sum at the end of each year. The quarterly payment scheme has accelerated foward the cash flows and thus increased the present value of the stream.

The discount rate

Whether we are accumulating cash flows to a future date or discounting them back to the present, there is a need to do so at some interest rate. Throughout the previous sections we have simply assumed that this interest rate was known. We have suggested, however, the fundamental principle on which such a rate should be based. Cash that becomes available does not lie idle but rather is recommitted to other activities throughout the firm, and these activities give rise to future profits. Strictly speaking, the interest rate we seek is the amount that must be earned on a dollar so that the investor or manager is indifferent between receiving the dollar now and receiving the dollar plus its earnings a year from now. How to estimate this interest rate is a difficult question which has generated much controversy and very few answers. The details surrounding this debate go well beyond the scope of this book.

The flavor of the problem can be sensed by briefly examining two approaches to the issue. The first states that the appropriate rate is the *opportunity rate,* that is, the marginal rate of return of the pool of investment opportunities that the firm might undertake with its available cash spin-offs. It was in this context that we selected a 10 percent discount rate for the evaluation of investments A and B (4 percent if we were not aggressive). In practice, where the profile of potential investment opportunities is complex, this can be a difficult number to estimate.

An alternative approach is to seek the discount rate from the perspective of the company's *cost of capital.* The prices that investors are willing to pay for a firm's securities and the yields that they demand from these securities determine a market cost for capital raised through debt and equity. The cost of debt is easy to see, since it is simply the interest that must be paid. There is a corresponding cost for shareholder's equity, since investors in the company want to earn a satisfactory rate of return on their investment. This cost applies both to new investments made in the company through purchases of stock and to earnings that are retained in the company rather than paid out through dividends. These costs, combined with the capital structure of the firm, result in a weighted average cost of capital. Since this is the average rate demanded by the capital markets for the investment funds, the firm should consider only those investments whose cash flows will yield at least that rate. Thus the value of the investment, from the perspective of the capital markets, is the present value of the cash flows discounted at this average cost of capital. In a perfect environment, where both the firm and the investors have complete information, the cost of capital and the opportunity rate will be identical, since a firm will invest in projects until the present value at the cost of capital will be equal to the initial investments. But we never have the perfect marketplace, so the cost of capital cannot serve as a substitute for the opportunity rate. In addition, as you have probably sensed, it is exceedingly difficult to estimate exactly either the cost of capital or the opportunity rate.

In most cases, based on rough approximations of these two rates, firms will establish by policy the interest rate to be used in their investment decisions. This rate is called a *hurdle rate.* If, at the specified hurdle rate, an investment has a positive net present value, it is judged to be a financially attractive alternative. If the NPV is negative, the proposal can be rejected for financial reasons.

Internal rate of return

Frequently the accept/reject or good/bad decision is not particularly sensitive to the exact value of the hurdle rate. There may be a comfortable leeway for error in the determination of the hurdle rate. To find out how much leeway there may be, we could seek that specific interest rate which results in a zero net present value for the investment (the threshold for the accept/reject decision) and compare it to the hurdle rate. *The "break-even" hurdle rate is called the internal rate of return.*[2] There is no formula for computing the internal rate of return; we must in general find it by trial and error.

As an example, consider investment A. At a 10 percent rate, the net present value of the investment is $302. If the hurdle rate were 4 percent, investment A would be even more attractive and would have a net present value of $4,625. On the other hand, if the hurdle rate were increased to 16 percent, investment A would be viewed as undesirable, since its net present value would be −$3,310. As the hurdle rate is moved from 4 to 16 percent, the net present value changes from being very positive to being very negative.

This relationship between net present value and the hurdle rate is graphed in Figure 2–6, where it can be seen that the net present value of

Figure 2–6

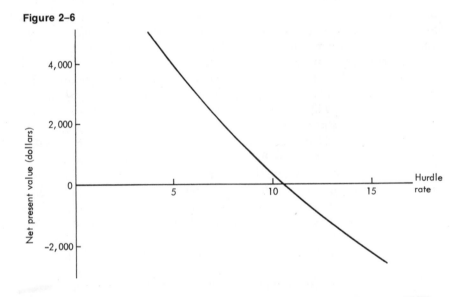

investment A is zero for a rate somewhere between 10 and 11 percent. Thus the internal rate of return, the break-even rate, is somewhere between 10 and 11 percent. By continuing the trial-and-error process, we can try values and in this range until a hurdle rate results in a net present value of zero or, more simply, we could approximate the break-even hurdle rate

[2] In certain circumstances there may be more than one interest rate which results in a zero net present value for an investment. For these cases, the internal rate of return is difficult to interpret. When an investment consists of an initial outlay followed by a stream of cash inflows, only one internal rate of return exists.

from the graph in Figure 2-6. For this example, the internal rate of return is 10.5 percent. If the specified hurdle rate is below 10.5 percent, the net present value will be positive, and the investment will be judged to be attractive. If the hurdle rate is greater than the internal rate of return of 10.5 percent, the net present value will be negative and the investment will be viewed as undesirable. With a hurdle rate of 10 percent, the project is acceptable but it is very close to the break-even rate.

In this analysis we used the internal rate of return as a means of assessing the sensitivity of our evaluations to a previously specified hurdle rate. The internal rate of return also is frequently used to determine if it is even necessary to establish a specific value for the hurdle rate. If the internal rate of return for an investment is so low that it is below the smallest reasonable value for the hurdle rate, the investment can be rejected without explicitly specifying the hurdle rate. Similarly, if the internal rate of return is very high, the investment can be accepted without a specific value for the hurdle rate.

The internal rate of return is also used in the role of ranking alternative projects by their relative attractiveness—the ones with the highest internal rate of return are judged to be the most attractive. In following this procedure, we are divorcing the evaluation of the project from the *actual* uses to which we might put its cash spin-offs. By definition, the internal rate of return is the interest rate that results in a zero net present value for the particular investment under consideration. The resulting rate is purely "internal" to the investment and bears no relationship to the external reinvestment rate facing the firm. In fact, for very profitable projects, the internal rate of return far exceeds the reinvestment rate. Thus the internal

Figure 2–7

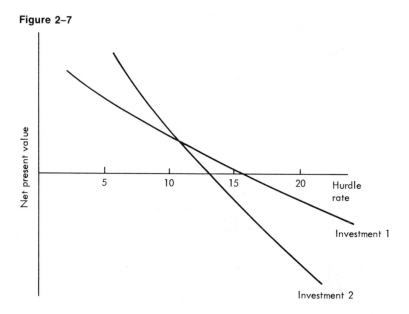

Figure 2–8
Discounted cash flow analysis (10 percent hurdle rate)

	Now	Year 1 Annual amount	Year 1 Accumulation factor	Year 1 Year-end equivalent	Year 2 Annual amount	Year 2 Accumulation factor	Year 2 Year-end equivalent	Year 3 Annual amount	Year 3 Accumulation factor	Year 3 Year-end equivalent
Cost of project (lump-sum payment)..........	$–32,000									
Sales (weekly flows)		$ 27,000	1.048	$ 28,296	$ 27,000	1.048	$ 28,296	$ 27,000	1.048	$ 28,296
Cost of goods (weekly flow)		–12,000	1.048	–12,576	–12,000	1.048	–12,576	–12,000	1.048	–12,576
Taxes (quarterly flow)		–2,400	1.037	–2,489	–2,400	1.037	–2,489	–2,400	1.037	–2,489
Changes in working capital (lump-sum payments)	–8,000							8,000		8,000
Salvage of equipment (lump-sum payment)								2,000		2,000
Total	$–40,000			$ 13,231			$ 13,231			$ 23,231
Present value	$ 12,027									
	10,929									
	17,446									
Net present value........	$ 402									

Discount factor 0.909

Discount factor 0.826

Discount factor 0.751

rate of return *incorrectly* assumes the reinvestment of the cash spin-offs at the internal rate rather than the assumed 10 percent opportunity rate. This incorrect reinvestment assumption may mean that a single investment, chosen from among a set of mutually exclusive alternatives because it has the highest internal rate of return, will turn out to be less attractive then some of the others if all alternatives are evaluated by their net present value with a realistic reinvestment rate.

To illustrate this point, consider the two investments whose net present values are shown in Figure 2–7. If we base our choice of one of these two alternatives on internal rate of return, we would select alternative 1—it has the higher internal rate of return. However, with a hurdle rate of 8 percent, the actual reinvestment rate for the firm, alternative 2 is better, since it has the higher net present value.

SUMMARY

In order to tie together the two major concepts of this chapter, cash flow and present value, we will return to the example we began to analyze in the cash flow section. The cash flows for the project were shown in Figure 2–1. Since we have seen that the timing of the flows is particularly important to the analysis, we should be a bit more careful in specifying the exact pattern in which these flows occur. Assume that sales and cost of goods occur in weekly installments and that the taxes are paid quarterly. In addition, we will do the evaluation of the project at a hurdle rate of 10 percent.

The analysis is shown in Figure 2–8. Note that the first step in the discounting process is to convert the installment flows into their end-of-year accumulated values. This gets all the flows dated on a common end-of-year basis. The second step is to find the present value of this equivalent stream of payments, all of which are dated at the end of the year. The resultant net present value is $402, which makes this project an attractive one at a 10 percent hurdle rate. The internal rate of return is only slightly less than 11 percent, since at 11 percent the net present value is −$353, and thus there is not a wide margin for error in establishing the hurdle rate.

EXERCISES

2.1. *a*. If you put $100 in the bank at 6 percent per year (computed annually), how much will you have in the account at the end of ten years?

b. How much must you deposit in a bank account today, at 10 percent interest computed annually, in order to have $2,000 ten years from now?

2.2. In each of the following situations, which alternative is the better, assuming that you would put whatever money you receive in a secure investment that returns 8 percent annually?

    a. $100 now, *or* $120 three years from now
    b. $150 now, *or* $250 five years from now
    c. $300 two years from now, *or* $450 five years from now

2.3. The Hi-Cap Company is considering the purchase of a piece of labor-saving machinery. The machine has a useful life of five years. It would result in a net cash outflow (after consideration of tax effects) of $25,000, immediately followed by net cash inflows (after tax) of $7,000 in each of the next five years. Is the equipment attractive if the company has adopted a hurdle rate of 10 percent? 12 percent? 14 percent? What is the internal rate of return?

2.4. The Leverage Company is considering two different options for repayment of a loan. The first option requires payments of $20,000 at the end of each of the next four years. The second option requires $10,000 at the end of the first year, $15,000 at the end of the second, $25,000 at the end of the third, and $35,000 at the end of the fourth. Thus the second option requires the payment of an extra $5,000 in all, but it allows Leverage to make smaller payments in the first two years. Which option should the company choose if its hurdle rate is 10 percent? 20 percent?

2.5. A company has an opportunity to invest funds in the projects shown in Table A.

Table A

	Net cash proceeds per year			
Year	Project A	Project B	Project C	Project D
1...........................	$ 5,000	$ 6,000	$ 3,000	$10,000
2...........................	5,000	6,000	3,000	−4,000
3...........................	5,000	5,000	3,000	10,000
4...........................	5,000	4,000	8,000	−4,000
5...........................	5,000	4,000	8,000	10,000
Required investment	$12,500	$12,500	$12,500	$12,500

    The investment outlays are made at the beginning of the first year, while net cash receipts occur in a lump sum at the end of the year. All the cash flows are known with certainty. Tax effects have already been taken into account in the computation of these cash flows.

    a. Compute the net present value of each of the projects, assuming a hurdle rate of 15 percent.

    b. Verify that for any interest rate, the NPV of Project B is higher than the NPV of Project A. What intuitive property of the time value of money does this reflect?

    c. What is the NPV of Project A if the total amount received during each year is received in two equal installments, one at midyear, the other at year end?

    d. Same as *c* except that the total amount is received in equal daily installments.

2.6. The Modern Company is considering the purchase of a new piece of equipment to perform operations currently being done on less efficient equipment. The purchase price is $15,000 delivered and installed. It has been estimated that the new equipment will produce annual savings of $4,000 in labor and other direct costs, as compared with the present equipment. The new equipment will have an economic life of ten years, at which time it will have zero salvage value over the costs of removal. The present equipment, which is fully depreciated, is in good working order and will last, physically, for at least 15 more years, but its present salvage value is zero, net of all costs of removal. The company has adopted a hurdle rate of 14 percent. For ease in calculation, assume that the marginal tax rate is 50 percent, that the new equipment will be straight-line depreciated over no less than 10 years (IRS regulations), and that the cash flows occur in a lump sum at year's end.

a. Show that the company cannot justify the equipment on purely economic grounds. What happens if the flows are assumed to occur quarterly?

b. What would the salvage value of the present equipment have to be to make the new equipment attractive? Assume that the salvage income is subjected to the 50 percent tax rate. Why does the old equipment's salvage value influence the new equipment's attractiveness?

c. Suppose again that the present equipment has zero salvage value. What would the salvage value of the new equipment at the end of its ten-year life have to be to make the new equipment attractive?

d. In either of the following two situations, should the company purchase the equipment? Note that in both situations, as well as in a, the new equipment yields a total savings of $40,000. If your recommendations are different for the different conditions, why?

   i. 20-year economic life with $2,000 per year savings.

   ii. 10-year economic life with $5,000 savings in each of the first five years and $3,000 savings in each of the remaining five years.

e. Modern decided to purchase the equipment described above and hereafter called Model A. Two years later, even better equipment (called Model B) comes on the market and makes Model A obsolete, with no resale value in excess of its cost of removal. Model B costs $28,000 delivered and installed and is expected to result in annual savings of $7,000 over the cost of operating Model A. The economic life of Model B is estimated to be 8 years and it may be fully depreciated over this period.

   i. What action should the company take?

   ii. If the company decides to purchase Model B, it seems that a mistake has been made somewhere because good equipment, bought only two years ago, is being scrapped. How did this mistake come about?

Case 2–1

Carob Company

In March 1972, the Carob Company was considering a proposal to replace four handloaded transmission case milling machines with an automatic machine. The company operated a large machine shop that did machine work on a subcontract basis for local industries in the Detroit area. One of the contracts was to machine transmission cases for truck engines for the Avida Automobile Company. The Carob Company had negotiated such a contract with the Avida Automobile Company for each of the previous ten years. For the last few years, the contract had been 60,000 transmission cases annually.

The unfinished cases were supplied by Avida. With a handloaded machine, all of the faces could not be machined at the same time. Each machine required the constant attention of one skilled machine operator.

The machines used by Carob were only three years old. Each machine had an annual output of approximately 15,000 cases on a two-shift, five-day week basis; therefore, four machines had been purchased at a total cost of $295,000.

The useful life of a handloaded machine on a two-shift, five-day week basis was estimated to be 15 years. Its salvage value at the end of its useful life was estimated to be $2,500. Depreciation of $57,000 had been built up for the four machines, representing three years' accumulation. The purchase of the machines had been financed by an 8 percent bank loan, and $90,000 of this loan had not yet been repaid. It was estimated that the four machines could be sold in their present condition for a total of $120,000 net, after dismantling and removal costs. The book loss resulting from the sale would be a deductible expense for income tax purposes and would therefore result in a tax saving of 52 percent of the loss.

The machine being considered in 1972 was a fully automatic transfer-type milling machine, equipped with four machining stations. Automatic transfer equipment on this machine moved the part progressively from one station to the next and indexed at each station, finishing a complete case with each cycle of the machine. One skilled machine operator was required to observe the functioning of the machine and make any necessary adjustments.

An automatic transfer-type machine with an annual output of 60,000 transmission cases on a two-shift basis would be specially built by a machine tool manufacturer, and it was estimated that such a machine would cost $340,000, delivered and installed. The useful life of this machine was estimated to be 15 years. No reliable estimate of scrap value could be made; a rough estimate was that scrap value would approximate the removal costs.

Automatic transfer-type machines similar to the one being considered had first been offered for sale in 1971 at a price of approximately $390,000. It was expected that the price would continue to drop somewhat over the next several years.

The Carob Company's engineering department was asked to prepare a study for use by the executives of the company in deciding what action to take. The direct labor rate for milling machine operators was $5 an hour, including provisions for social security taxes and fringe benefits, which varied with the payroll. There would also be a saving in floor space. This saving would amount to $800 annually on the basis of the charge made in 1972 for each square foot of floor space used, although the factory layout was such that it would be difficult to use this freed space for some other purpose, and no other use was planned. Out-of-pocket savings of $10,000 per year for other costs items were estimated if the automatic machine were purchased.

The Carob Company planned to finance any new equipment purchase with a bank loan at a rate of 8 percent. Some selected financial data for the company are shown in Exhibit 1. The company considered the picture given by these statistics to be normal and expected the same general pattern to prevail in the foreseeable future.

Exhibit 1
Selected financial information

Condensed Income Statement, 1971

Net sales	$10,728,426
Less: All costs and expenses	8,277,294
Profit before taxes..................	$ 2,451,132
Provision for income taxes	1,245,430
Net income.......................	$ 1,205,702

Condensed Balance Sheet, December 31, 1971

Current assets	$ 6,102,698	Current liabilities	$ 1,860,654
Fixed assets (net)	8,478,420	Six percent mortgage bonds...	1,000,000
Other assets	302,982	Capital stock...............	2,000,000
		Surplus....................	10,023,446
	$14,884,100		$14,884,100

Case 2–2

Leicester Polytechnic Institute

Leicester Polytechnic Institute was a small, private four-year college located in Atlanta, Georgia. The school was founded by Robert Leicester, a successful industrialist and a "Georgia Booster," who thought it important that the Atlanta area have a school to ensure a steady supply of top-notch engineers and other technical personnel. Over the years, Leicester Poly had fulfilled, and indeed exceeded, his expectations. It had an excellent reputation, and many of its graduates held responsible positions in the major firms located in Atlanta. Their loyalty to the school was legendary, and it evinced itself not only in their gifts to the school but also in their rate of hiring and promoting Leicester Poly's more recent graduates.

Paralleling the growth of the school was the rate of growth of the economy of the city of Atlanta; by 1976, both city and school were bursting at the seams. Leicester Poly's graduates had an average of three job offers, and a number of the large industrial concerns in the area were urging the Institute to expand its capacity. Given the rate and stability of Atlanta's economic development, it seemed that the demand for the Institute's graduates had nowhere to go but up. Further, the Institute was concerned over the fact that it was rejecting very attractive candidates for admission merely because of the limited capacity of the school.

The administrators of the school thought that over the next 12 years, at least 1,500 high-quality additional students could enter if there were sufficient space for them. A number of responsible people were consulted about the academic and financial viability of expanding the school's capacity. All agreed that it was desirable to do so. The issues were not those of whether to expand but of how to do it.

School requirements

The current enrollment in the college was distributed among 70 classrooms in four physically separate locations. Projections called for a requirement for 12 more classrooms after two years, and an additional 12 classrooms ten years thereafter. This expansion was required to meet the additional 1,500 students expected to be added to Leicester's enrollment over the next 12 years.

Alternative proposals

The following choices were facing the school:

1. Build one building with 12 classrooms now, and another 12 classroom building ten years from now, or
2. Build one 24-room building now.

The economies of scale of construction are such that the total cost of the two smaller separate buildings is 1½ times as large as the total cost of the one large building. In addition, the costs were expected to grow at an annual rate of 8 percent. As shown in Exhibit 1, the total cost of the first option was $9,489,000 (including the impact of inflation) and the total cost of the second was $4,023,500.

Exhibit 1
Preliminary analysis

		Conventional	Systems
1. Build one building now and another ten years thereafter			
a. First building			
Construction cost (@ 75 percent of Option 2)*		$2,730,000	$ 3,844,317
Design and supervision		273,000	384,432
		$3,003,000	$ 4,228,749
b. Second building			
Construction cost†		$5,896,500	$ 8,303,725
Design and supervision		589,650	830,373
		$6,486,150	$ 9,134,098
Total Cost		$9,489,150	$13,362,847
2. Build one building combining both sets of 12 classrooms			
Construction cost.............................		$3,639,450	$ 5,125,909
Design and supervision		384,050	512,591
Total Cost		$4,023,500	$ 5,638,500

* Does not include the cost of land which is already owned by the school.
† Second building construction cost inflated by 8 percent per annum, compounded.

During the interim ten-year period, when the extra classrooms in the 24-room building would not be fully utilized, it was anticipated that the various administrative agencies currently occupying space in the over-crowded administration building could usefully occupy the space. Plans called for the construction of a separate facility for this group at the end of the first ten years anyway, so little extra cost would be involved. In fact, the school would save approximately $26,000 annually in rent, which would have to be paid for the space needed by the administrative unit.

An additional issue was that of evaluating two competing proposals, both submitted by the same architectural consulting firm. Proposal A called for a conventional construction format. Proposal B called for a "systems building" format, a substantial departure from traditional school construction techniques, stressing modular flexibility.

The initial cost of the systems building exceeds the initial cost of a traditional building. (Exhibit 2 summarizes the projected costs of the competing proposals.) According to the architects' report, either building

Exhibit 2
Construction proposals

	Conventional	Systems
Initial cost	$4,023,500	$5,638,500
Annual maintenance—years 1 through 9 (per year)*	225,000	135,000
Remodeling and maintenance in year 10	3,975,000	1,635,000
Annual maintenance—years 11 through 20 (per year)*	225,000	135,000

* Maintenance services are purchased from a cleaning service and are directly proportional to the size of the building.

would meet the requirements of Leicester Poly for the period of 20 years from the completion of the construction. The additional cost in the tenth year for both proposals was the cost of remodeling the extra space vacated by the administrative agencies. Because of the different types of construction used, this remodeling would be much less expensive with the systems building. Since inside walls were partitions, relatively little cost and time would be involved in removing and replacing them. In the traditional building, the remodeling would represent a major undertaking since the superstructure of the building would have to be altered. Both construction proposals would achieve the same effect in terms of educational quality and aesthetic appeal.

Financing alternatives

In addition to choosing a construction format, there was the problem of recommending a financing alternative. The alternatives considered were limited to three options—10- and 20-year bonds and use of the college endowment. The bonds would probably carry a 5 percent interest rate. In addition, the school had a $2 million unexpended fund balance in the plant fund, donated by former graduates and built up from past transfers of funds resulting from current operations. The endowment was currently earning an 8 percent return, and it could be used to help finance the construction. The income was being transferred to finance current operations at the present time.

Case 2–3

Eric Goodling

It was August 1974, and Eric Goodling had just completed the largest financial transaction in his life. He had sold his town house in Boston in preparation for his move to Houston, Texas. He had been transferred by his employer, an engineering consulting firm. The house had sold for $50,000, which, after deduction of the 6 percent real estate commission, netted him $47,000. He had originally purchased the house in December 1969 for $32,600.

Eric was curious as to how "good" an investment this house had been for him. He had determined that the house had increased in market value at an annual rate of 9.2 percent during the 56 months of his ownership.[1] He was convinced, however, that this was not a true reflection of the economic growth on his initial investment because it ignored: (1) the costs of ownership; (2) the value of rent saved because of ownership; (3) the financial leverage that resulted from being able to mortgage the property; and (4) the income tax savings resulting from his home ownership. He had collected data on each of these categories and was interested in determining the return on his investment.

Costs of ownership

Eric had separated his costs of ownership into two categories. The first category was capital improvements and included all the expenditures that he felt had increased the value of the house. He had refinished the basement with paneling and new carpet in 1970. He had added a new hot-water heater in 1971 and made major modifications to the furnace in 1972. He had installed a dishwasher in 1973. The total of these expenses by year are summarized in Exhibit 1.

Exhibit 1
Costs of ownership (dollars)

	1970	1971	1972	1973	1974
Capital improvements	686	1,691	767	576	120
Real estate taxes	1,344	1,292	1,228	1,362	658
Insurance	262	131	156	188	58

---

[1] The component growth formula can be written as $P_0 e^{it} = P_t$. Where P_0 = starting value, P_t = value at time t, i = the annual growth rate, t = time in years, and e is the base of the natural logarithm. In this case, $P_0 = 32.6$, $P_t = 50$, $t = 4.67$.

The other category of costs he called expenses. There were two main items in this category: real estate taxes and insurance. The amount of these expenses is shown in Exhibit 1. He did not include utility costs like electricity or heating oil since he felt that these costs would have been incurred even if he had rented a comparable house.

Rent savings

It was not possible to determine exactly what rent would have been paid for a comparable house during the five-year period. Similar town houses were currently renting for $450 per month, and in 1970 they were renting for $350 per month. Therefore, Eric felt that $400 per month was a reasonable estimate. This would result in savings of $4,800 during the first four years and $3,200 during 1974.

Financial leverage

Eric had finished his doctorate degree at MIT in June 1968, and when he purchased his house in December 1969 he had very little capital, in fact next to none. He did have a good job and was able to convince creditors that his cash flow was sufficient to repay rather substantial loans. He had assumed the existing mortgage of the previous owner, and he also had been able to take advantage of a second-mortgage program sponsored by his new employer. Funds from these two mortgages had not been sufficient, and thus he had also taken a personal loan from a local commercial bank. These loans are summarized below.

The first mortgage, a 25-year loan, had originally been granted in March 1966 for $20,800 at 5¼ percent interest. This resulted in a monthly payment of $124.64. Eric had assumed this mortgage in the 46th month with a principal balance of $19,090. When this loan was repaid in August 1974, the principal balance was $16,538. The second mortgage from his employer was for $4,800 at 4 percent for 20 years. The monthly payment for this loan was $29.09. The final balance on this loan in August 1974 was $3,980.

The personal note secured by Eric was for $6,400 but had an additional charge for life insurance of $59. This total amount was borrowed for five years at 6.5 percent interest. The interest for all five years was added on at the beginning of the loan. The net result was a monthly payment of $142.58 per month. By early 1973 Eric had accumulated enough savings to pay off this note, and in February 1973 he repaid the principal balance of about $3,000.

Eric had made a down payment of $2,262 to complete the purchase of $32,552.

Exhibit 2 summarizes the interest and principal repayments on each of these loans during the five-year period.

Exhibit 2
Financial charges of repayments (dollars)

	1969	1970	1971	1972	1973	1974
Principal repayments						
First mortgage	—	505	533	562	592	16,898*
Second mortgage	—	173	167	173	181	4,106†
Personal note...............	—	960	1,126	1,291	3,082	0
Down payment	2,262	—	—	—	—	—
Interest payments						
First mortgage	—	990	963	934	904	590
Second mortgage	—	205	182	175	168	108
Personal note...............	—	750	584	419	70	0

* $16,538 as final payoff and $360 during the first eight months.
† $3,980 as final payoff and $126 during the first eight months.

Income tax savings

Eric realized that the IRS allowed some of these expenses to be deducted from his personal taxable income before taxes were computed. Specifically the interest payments and real estate taxes were deductible expenses. He had gone back over his income tax returns for the previous five years and had calculated both his average and marginal income tax rates. These are summarized in Exhibit 3.

Exhibit 3
Tax rates (in percent)

	1970	1971	1972	1973	1974*
Average tax rate	19.1	19.8	22.8	27.3	27.3
Marginal tax rate	28	28	36	42	42

* Estimated to be the same as 1973.

Case 2–4

Manufacturers Hanover Leasing Corporation

Over the past three months, Manufacturers Hanover Leasing Corporation, the leasing affiliate of Manufacturers Hanover Trust Company, and the Alamo Off-Shore Drilling Company[1] had been negotiating a 15-year lease of a $20 million semisubmersible oil drilling rig. The negotiations had been narrowed to two proposals, one a level series of equal payments and the other a step schedule involving different levels of payments in different years. Because of the close working relationship between Alamo and Manufacturers Hanover, Alamo had negotiated with this company only, feeling confident that Manufacturers Hanover would come up with as good a lease arrangement as possible. Alamo also relied on the company for extensive financial advice and so had requested Ms. Barbara Silber, leasing representative with Manufacturers Hanover Leasing, to prepare an analysis of the two proposed deals.

Alamo Off-Shore Drilling Company

Alamo Off-Shore Drilling Company was one of the medium- to large-sized oil drilling companies. In obtaining oil from offshore sites, the oil companies first used seismic and other testing procedures to explore potential sites. In the United States, they next engaged in competitive bidding to obtain leases from the federal government to explore for and produce oil (and gas) on specific parcels of the continental shelf. Next, they entered the drilling phase, in which wells were drilled in the ocean floor from large rigs on the surface of the water. The drilling operation was the most dangerous part of the oil business, for it involved drilling into layers below the surface whose contents were not known exactly. Drillers used a substance called drilling mud to provide a downward pressure in the drilling holes which was supposed to balance the pressures of gases and liquids in the layers below the surface (which would try to force their way upward through the drilled column). On occasion, however, even very experienced drilling crews could not maintain sufficient pressure in the wells they were constructing; the results were "blowouts," or uncontrolled eruptions from the well shafts. In some cases, blowouts led to very hazardous fires on the platforms.

After the completion of the drilling phase, if the initial results were favorable, a production platform was set up for the more routine process of extracting oil and gas from the new wells.

In large part because the drilling operation was so specialized, many of the major oil companies did not do their own drilling. Instead, they contracted out the work to specialist companies in the drilling business. The drilling companies usually worked on fairly short contracts, typically for about two years, and were paid on a daily rate. (Thus, for example, the oil company took the risks of poor weather interrupting operations.)

When a drilling crew finished a contract with one oil company, they moved on to another job.

---

[1] Alamo is not a real company. It is, however, a simplified example of a typical lessee of Manufacturers Hanover Leasing.

There were various types of drilling rigs or platforms used in offshore operations. In relatively shallow, calm water, a platform raised above the floor of the ocean on three legs could be used. For deeper water and in areas where there were storms and particularly large waves (such as in the North Sea), semisubmersible rigs were used extensively. These rigs were basically two ship hulls with six huge columns supporting the platform. When the rig reached the drilling site, the hulls were partly flooded and, as a result, were lowered below the surface. The platform stood on top of the columns, above the water surface. These rigs made for more stable operations than did the shallow-water varieties, for on the semisubmersible rigs only the six columns were exposed to wave action. Such rigs usually cost on the order of $20 million. Exhibit 1 shows a typical semisubmersible rig.

Exhibit 1

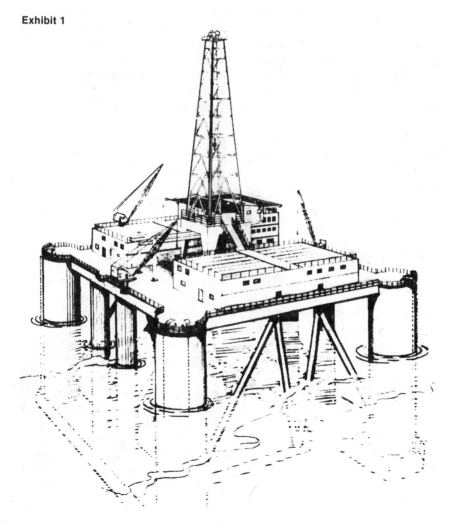

Manufacturers Hanover Leasing Corporation

Manufacturers Hanover Corporation, the fourth largest bank holding company in the United States, with assets of over $25 billion, was the parent of several companies, including the bank Manufacturers Hanover Trust and also Manufacturers Hanover Leasing Corporation. The leasing corporation was established as a separate company in early 1972, at which time it had had a staff of three people. Growth since that time had been substantial, so that in the middle of 1974 the staff numbered 170. The leasing corporation dealt in all types of big-ticket items—those costing at least several million dollars—and had investments in leverage leases running to approximately $1 billion worth of equipment.

Barbara Silber had been with Manufacturers Hanover Leasing Corporation for about six months. After finishing college with a B.S. degree in mathematics, she had worked in the operations research department of International Nickel, particularly in the areas of econometric model building, risk analysis, and market analysis of the marine industries. After that, she had worked in marketing software for time-sharing and computer companies. In mid-1974 she was just finishing the part-time MBA program at New York University with a major in quantitative analysis and a minor in finance. At Manufacturers Hanover Leasing, she was involved in marketing leases, in pricing leases, and in conducting market studies of industries which might provide the company with new lease customers. In a typical lease situation, Ms. Silber would be involved in the initial marketing phase, would deal with all aspects of the pricing (arranging the specific details of payments, structure of the lease, etc.), and would follow through on the final documentation of the lease.

Leverage leasing

The leasing offered by Manufacturers Hanover Leasing Corporation was a method of financing and complemented other methods, such as bank loans. The leases were typically written for even longer terms than were long-term bank loans. The user of the equipment made all of the arrangements involved in the purchase, took care of all maintenance and insurance, and contracted for a lease term of approximately the useful life of the equipment. In large transactions, such as those involving drilling rigs, it was common for MHLC to advance approximately 25 percent to 35 percent of the total cost of the equipment and to arrange to borrow the remaining 65 percent to 75 percent from institutional investors, such as life insurance companies or employee pension funds: hence the term *leveraged lease*. In a lease of this type MHLC was the owner of the equipment and was able to recover its investment in part through the tax benefits of ownership, such as depreciation and investment tax credit, as well as through the cash rentals. The lessee in effect was exchanging tax benefits in return for a substantially lower financing rate. This type of arrangement was particularly advantageous when the lessee was unable to utilize all of the tax benefits of ownership, as was often the case for drilling companies, airlines, and others in capital-intensive industries. Thus, an airline or drilling company could have the use of the equipment at a much lower financing rate than it would have to pay if it borrowed the money and bought the equipment outright.

Arranging a leverage lease was an extremely complex process and depended on the particular equipment, the availability of outside funds, and a number of other factors all specific to the individual deal. The entire procedure could take as long as a year of negotiations and could generate a two-inch-thick document at the end. Lease structures involving stepped or multilevel rentals often were used for economic reasons: that is, to obtain the lowest possible financing rate for the lessee. In some cases it was possible for Manufacturers Hanover to defer for some time the principal payments on the portions borrowed from the institutional investors. In such cases, in the early periods of the lease Manufacturers Hanover could require only low rents from the company leasing the equipment—when repayment of the principal by Manufacturers Hanover began, the company would require correspondingly higher lease payments. Such rental patterns were desirable from the lessee's standpoint, particularly in situations in which the peak revenue-generating years of a project were in the later years of the lease. Patterns of payments were also influenced by the creditworthiness of the company leasing the equipment. Before entering into lease negotiations, the leasing company obtained from Manufacturers Hanover Trust, the bank, a favorable credit rating for the company which would lease the equipment. The rating was based on the same criteria used by the bank in rating its loan customers.

The lease of the semisubmersible drilling rig

The negotiations between Alamo Off-Shore Drilling and Manufacturers Hanover Leasing Corporation had finally come down to two proposals. These were:

1. Proposal A
    15 equal annual payments of $1,897,784
2. Proposal B
    Years   1–5   ......$1,104,900
    Years   6–10 ......$2,761,504
    Years 11–15 ......$2,199,826

These were the proposals which Ms. Silber was asked to evaluate. For her calculations she was using $20 million as the cost of the rig.

Methods of evaluating lease proposals

Companies used several different indicators in evaluating leases. One commonly used measure was the *lease cost,* the financing charge on the lease; lease cost was entirely analogous to *internal rate of return*. In other words, it was the break-even interest rate at which rent payments just equaled the capital value of the equipment. The lease cost was calculated for all lease proposals by Manufacturers Hanover.

A second indicator used by most companies for evaluation was *net present value*. Alamo had been using a 6 percent discount rate but was considering using a higher rate for the future.

Normally the calculations to evaluate a lease were performed by the lessee's own financial office rather than by the leasing company, and such calculations were usually based on the company's cost of capital. In advising a company about specific leases, though, Manufacturers Hanover might also perform the calculations to evaluate the proposals.

Chapter 3

The development of decision diagrams

Chapter 1 introduced a decision diagram as a device which can help decision makers understand the structure of a decision: the alternatives they are willing to consider, and the risks or uncertainties that are important to them. The discipline of forcing one's self, at the start of the problem-solving process, to identify explicitly the possible strategies that are open, as well as the uncertainties that make the decision difficult, has great potential payoffs. By asking the "Then what?" question at every point where a choice is faced, including the "stop" options, decision makers are reminded of the desirability of using their imagination and creativity to develop strategies, some of which may not be obvious and might otherwise be overlooked.

The identification in the decision diagram of the uncertainties involved in the decision suggests the probability assessments that will be required before a decision can be made. The explicit recognition of the presence of these uncertainties and the point in time when they will be resolved might also suggest the possibility of obtaining information to eliminate, reduce, or modify the effects of major risks. This process in turn may help in the development of a richer set of strategies among which the decision maker can choose.

ACTS AND EVENTS TO BE INCLUDED IN A DECISION DIAGRAM

If you were asked to construct a decision diagram for a decision of your own, your first task would be to decide which acts and events to include. There must be *act forks* which describe all the choices you must make now and those you may be faced with while the results of the decision are being determined. Even though the decision maker is usually concerned only with the choice that must be made at the beginning of the diagram, in an analysis future choices which may affect the consequences of the present decision must also be considered.

The diagram must also include *event forks* representing the uncertainties about events which directly affect the consequence of the present choices. In addition, uncertain events which may provide information for the selection of future acts should be included, since by affecting future choices they may indirectly affect the consequences of the present choice.

The set of specific acts described by the branches at an act fork and the set of possible events described by the branches at each event fork must be *mutually exclusive* and *collectively exhaustive*. That is, no more than one of the branches from a given fork can be chosen or can occur at the same time, and one of them *must* occur or be chosen. It should be noted, however, that this requirement is a subjective one. You are free to exclude from your diagram acts you do not wish to consider or events you believe to be practically certain not to occur.

In many decisions there are choices or strategies which are possible, but where logic indicates these strategies could never be winners, never be the best acts to choose. Such *dominated strategies* obviously may be excluded from your diagram. For example, if you were trying to decide whether to buy a particular piece of information, you could conceive of a strategy whereby you bought the information but ignored it in your subsequent choices. Such a strategy could never be a winner; certainly, *either* buying the information and conditioning your action on it *or* not buying the information at all would be superior.

As you think through a decision you might also identify uncertainties which will affect the results of your choices, but where their magnitude is such that they could not affect your evaluation of the current choices. Such uncertainties could also be left out of the diagram. Remember, however, that a series of small uncertainties, none of which alone could affect your choice, might do so jointly. In that event, eliminating them one at a time could be dangerous.

THE ORDER OF ACTS AND EVENTS IN A DECISION DIAGRAM

The general principle for developing the time sequence in a decision diagram is one of *subjective chronology*. Under this principle, if you visualize a calendar running above your diagram from the present to the future, potential acts will be placed at the time when you must *commit* irrevocably to your choice, not necessarily at the time the actual choice is made. The uncertainties will occur at the time when you, the decision maker, *learn* what event occurred. This may be long after the event itself actually occurred.

For example, if on January you must either pass up the opportunity to buy a property or sign the contract to buy it, with the actual settlement to take place on June 1, the fork showing the acts "buy" and "don't buy" would be located at January 1. Similarly, if the as-yet uncertain amount a competitor will charge for a product is relevant to a decision of yours, the event fork representing the uncertain price will be located on your diagram at the time when you will learn about the price and thus be able to condition your future choices on that information, not necessarily at the time when your competitor actually makes the choice. If the competitor decided on the price at a meeting on September 17 but you only would learn about the decision when a catalog was released on November 15, the event node would be located at the November date. If you do not know when an uncertainty will be resolved before you must make a particular choice, you should include the uncertainty about the timing explicitly in your diagram.

Although an appropriate diagram can always be constructed following the subjective chronological order, there are circumstances in which a departure from strict chronological order is permissible and may facilitate the diagramming or the analysis. If you must make a sequence of choices and there is no uncertainty that will be resolved for you during the period of the choices, you can diagram the several act forks in whatever order you wish, or you can combine them into a single, complex act fork. For example, suppose you had to decide whether to accept a particular order and, before anything else was learned, you also had to decide which of two production processes (A or B) to employ if you accept the order. The two diagrams in Figure 3–1 ,are equivalent, provided that you will not learn of the resolution of some relevant uncertainty between the two acts.

Figure 3–1

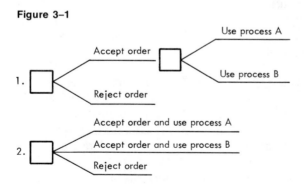

Two or more uncertainties can be diagrammed in other than a chronological order if the decision maker will not be faced with a choice of acts during the period between the resolution of the two uncertainties. Recognition of this principle can be useful, since it means that in such situations you need not worry about the order in which the string of uncertainties is resolved. It also means that you can place these uncertainties on your decision diagram in an order that makes it easiest to exercise your judgments on the uncertainties.[1]

WHERE TO STOP A DECISION DIAGRAM

Most decisions are made in the context of an organization that will operate continuously over a long period of time. In a sense, therefore, it is possible to argue that if you were to take into account *all* future acts and uncertain events that could *conceivably* affect the ultimate consequences of your present choices, you would have to develop your decision diagram indefinitely far into the future.

In order to analyze a problem in a practical way, you must select some *cutoff date* for the diagram and consider explicitly only those choices and uncertainties that pertain up to that point. In a number of situations a natural cutoff date suggests itself. In Thadeus Warren's problem presented in Chapter 1, the time when all three properties could be disposed of suggested the place to cut off the decision diagram. A decision maker faced with deciding on the number of items to produce for an upcoming selling season would consider the end of that season as a natural diagram cutoff date.

In other decisions no natural cutoff date is apparent. For a manager trying to decide whether to meet increased demand through the purchase and use of new equipment or through working the current equipment and labor force overtime, the choice of how many periods into the future to place the diagram cutoff point is not obvious or natural. You must, on a subjective and judgmental basis, decide on how far out you believe you can meaningfully identify potential choices and uncertainties and draw your diagram to that point, with the understanding that beyond that point you do not think it is worthwhile to take account of specific acts and events.

It is, of course, critical that the somewhat arbitrary choice of a diagram cutoff date does not affect the results of the decision analysis. Even though diagramming ends at a specific cutoff date, the stream of future consequences which result from the acts and events of the diagram must be considered until they have run their complete course, or at least until they could not affect the present evaluation of the alternative choices faced in the present. The fact that such streams of consequences may also continue indefinitely into the future gives rise to the need for still another choice in the analysis: the period of time for which you attempt to evaluate the future cash flows that will result from a given combination of acts and events. The future point beyond which you will no longer project the

---

[1] This idea will be developed more fully in Chapter 5.

cash flows explicitly is called the *cash-flow horizon* for the analysis. Such a point, of course, may be much further in the future than the cutoff date for your diagram. For example, for an innovator attempting to decide whether to introduce a proposed new product, the cutoff date for the diagram might be two or three years from now after choices have been made on the possible purchase of marketing research, production technology, and launching strategies, and after the uncertainties of the marketplace have been taken into account. At the end points on the diagram at the cutoff date you might evaluate not only the relevant cash flows to that date but the pro forma projections of cash flows for a period of time, say ten years into the future.

The selection of a cash flow horizon date is based largely on judgment. However, the analysis should be such that differences in the somewhat arbitrary selection of a horizon date should not bring about different decisions. This can be accomplished by recognizing that if there are differences among different end points in the future cash flows *beyond* the cash flow horizon date, they can be taken into account by assigning different *residual values,* based on your assessment of the value of the different flows beyond the horizon. The relevant cash flows at any end point can thus be thought of as composed of three components:

1. The relevant cash flows during the period from the present to the diagram cutoff point.
2. The projected cash flows from the cutoff date to the cash flow horizon.
3. The projected cash flows beyond the horizon as evaluated by a residual value at the horizon.

In the example of the new product introduction the cutoff date for the diagram might have been set at three years from now because the innovator felt the choices and uncertainties could be evaluated to that point. The horizon might have been set out to ten years and the projected cash flows evaluated year by year to that point. Beyond the ten years, the innovator might have assessed a residual value for each end point by considering what the innovator would be just willing to sell the equipment and the market position for at that point.

The art of developing a useful decision diagram hinges in part on the location of the horizon. The closer to the present you place the horizon, the clearer and stronger are your judgments about the appropriate cash flows, but the greater is the importance of making a sound evaluation of the residual value beyond the horizon. The further out in time you are willing to specify the cash flows that will result, the less is the burden placed on the establishment of a residual value. This is true because the magnitude of the residual is undoubtedly less and also because, under normal hurdle rates, its impact on any present value diminishes as the horizon date is placed further out.

EXERCISES

3.1. Evaluate the decision tree in Figure A and identify the optimal strategy. Be sure to show the EMV at each action and event point. (The numbers in parentheses on the branches of the tree are the partial cash flows associated with taking those paths.)

Figure A

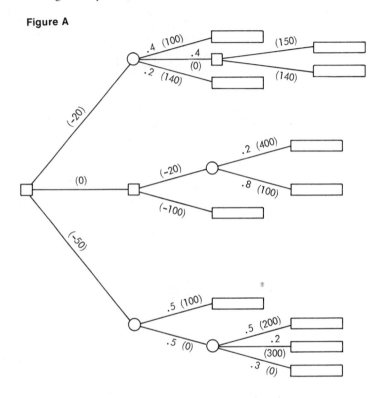

3.2. In September of 1971, Joe Doakes, a student, was trying to decide what he should do with his 1968 Buick. The Buick service department had telephoned that morning while performing routine service on the car and said that the engine was in bad shape, and in order to avoid permanent damage it needed some immediate work that would most likely cost $120. They wanted permission to go ahead with the work immediately. Joe wasn't sure, for several reasons. Uppermost in his mind was his critical cash position between now and when he would take a job in June 1972. Because of this fact and his already staggering student loans, he had resolved that he should decide what to do about his car on the basis of trying to minimize his cash expenses on it over the next 12 months.

To help him in making the best decision, Joe spent the morning investigating possible alternatives. By noon he had decided that the choice was really between trading his Buick in on a new Volkswagen and keeping the Buick. If he decided to trade it in, he could do so without having it repaired. The net cash outlay for the new VW would be $300, which he would have to pay immediately.

If he decided to keep the Buick, he still wasn't sure he should have the $120 repair made. Even if he had it made he would still have annual repairs of about $100 on the car. If he did not have it repaired, he figured that there was only a 40 percent chance it would have a breakdown and a 60 percent chance it wouldn't. If a major breakdown occurred, it appeared equally likely that the repair would cost $200 or $300. (Whether it had a breakdown or not, Joe estimated other service charges would run about $100.)

Since both cars would have roughly equal retail values in a year, Joe did not think this factor needed to be considered. However, he did feel oil and gas costs were relevant. He estimated them at $340 for the Buick and $210 for the VW over the next 12 months.

Analyze Joe Doakes' decision problem and recommend a strategy for him to follow.

3.3. An oil wildcatter must decide either to drill (act a_1) or not to drill (act a_2). He is uncertain whether the hole will be dry or wet. His payoffs, which are determined by the nature of the hole (the state) and his actions, are given in Figure B. Assume that the cost of drilling is $70,000. The net return of the consequence associated with action a_1 and wet is $100,000, which is interpreted as a return of $170,000 less the $70,000 cost of drilling.

Figure B
Monetary payoffs

State	Act	
	a_1	a_2
Dry	$-70,000	0
Wet	100,000	0

At a cost of $10,000, the wildcatter could take a series of seismic soundings which would determine the underlying geological structure at the site. The soundings will disclose whether the terrain below has (1) no structure—that's bad, or (2) open structure—that's so-so, or (3) closed structure—that's really hopeful. The experts have provided the wildcatter with Figure C, which shows the probabilities of various test results and hole states.

Figure C
A. No seismic
   Probability of dry = .5
B. Seismic
   i. Probability of no structure = .40
      Probability of open structure = .35
   ii. Probability of dry, given the seismic revealed no structure = .8
       Probability of dry, given the seismic revealed open structure = .5
       Probability of dry, given the seismic revealed closed structure = .1

What is the optimal action without running the seismic test? What is the optimal action if one considers the possibility of taking a seismic test before deciding to drill? Should the wildcatter take a seismic test?

Case 3–1

Edgartown Fisheries (A)

On a rainy day in March 1969, Lars Dyson, MBA '48, businessman and adventurer, president of Edgartown Fisheries, faces a difficult and perplexing decision problem.

Edgartown Fisheries is in the shark-fishing business and operates one fishing boat especially equipped for sharking in the North and Middle Atlantic. The company was formed in order to exploit a technique which had previously been little used for shark fishing, a technique called "long-line" fishing, in which arrays of long, baited lines are suspended from buoys. Dyson has now had a few years' experience using this technique, and he and his crew feel that they have acquired a substantial skill in catching shark this way. Nevertheless, he feels anxious about Edgartown Fisheries' future, largely because of uncertainties about the size of the catch and the price which the fish will command.

On this particular rainy day, Dyson has just received a letter from an Italian shark importer who offers to make a one-season contract with Edgartown Fisheries for 300,000 pounds of shark at 55 cents a pound, delivered in Italy. The shark is to be delivered by October 10, 1969, but Edgartown Fisheries may, under the terms of the proposed contract, divide the 300,000 pounds into partial shipments in any way it desires. Dyson has to decide whether or not to accept the contract within the next few days, and he has assembled the following information to help him with his decision.

Shark production and market

The Atlantic sharking season runs from April 1 through October 31. However, Edgartown Fisheries ordinarily obtains only about 120 days of active fishing, the other 90 days being spent either in port or traveling to and from the fishing grounds. (The travel and port time is somewhat affected by various factors, particularly the weather.) There are two distinct types of season. In a good season, Edgartown Fisheries can catch about 600,000 pounds of shark; in a bad season, about 480,000 pounds. The variation in the size of the catch from day to day is small enough to be ignored, so that Dyson is willing to think of his catch as being a constant 5,000 pounds per fishing day if the season is good or 4,000 pounds per fishing day if the season is bad. Thus it is possible to determine, after the first few weeks of the season have passed, whether the season will be good or bad. Unfortunately, it is impossible to tell ahead of the start of the season what kind of a season it will be.

Shark is caught not only in the Atlantic but also in the Pacific, primarily by the Japanese. The price for Atlantic shark, therefore, depends not only on whether the Atlantic catch is large or small, but also on the size of the catch in the Pacific. Table 1 shows the price per pound which Dyson expects for shark landed in New Bedford (his home port) under each of the four conditions that may occur. For example, if Dyson encounters a large catch (5,000 pounds per day) and the Pacific catch turns out small, Dyson expects to receive 40 cents per pound landed in New Bedford.

Table 1
Anticipated price per pound of shark landed in New Bedford (in cents)

Pacific catch	Atlantic catch	
	Large	Small
Large	30	35
Small	40	45

As with the Atlantic catch, it is impossible to tell before the start of the season whether the Pacific catch will be large or small. However, after the first few weeks of the season have passed, the size of the Pacific catch to date provides a reliable indication of the rest of the season. Dyson's wife can obtain this information and radio it to him.

As he looks forward to the season, the four possible conditions that may occur all seem equally likely to Dyson, so he assigns them the probabilities given in Table 2.

Table 2
Probabilities of various catch sizes

Pacific catch	Atlantic catch	
	Large	Small
Large	¼	¼
Small	¼	¼

Shipping to Italy

Dyson can store shark already caught in a cold-storage warehouse for as long as one season at essentially no cost. He is therefore not constrained to ship the fish to Italy as soon as they are caught. He can ship fish from New Bedford to Italy at a cost of 19 cents per pound by a standard freighter service offering weekly departures. Any one freighter will take all or any part of the 300,000-pound order.

Alternatively, Dyson could ship the 300,000 pounds by sending his own vessel to Italy. His boat can carry only 150,000 pounds of shark packed in ice, so that two trips of his own boat would be required to deliver the entire shipment of 300,000 pounds. In each round trip to Italy, his boat would lose the equivalent of about 20 fishing days. (Note that the 300,000 pounds must be delivered before the end of the season.) In comparing the cost of operating his boat for fishing with the cost of operating his boat for transporting fish to Italy, Dyson finds that the additional fuel required to transport the fish just about balances the cost of the bait that would have been used in the corresponding time spent fishing. Use of the boat to transport the fish will actually reduce the cost of tackle, since no tackle will be used in a transport operation, whereas tackle is regularly lost while fishing.

Costs and assets

On April 1, 1969, at the start of the season, Dyson will have assets which, besides his fully depreciated boat and some office equipment, include $20,000 cash and 40 miles of ready-to-use tackle. Excluding tackle, his total costs for the entire fishing season (interest payment on boat mortgage, crew's wages, office rent, etc., and fuel and bait) will be about $160,000. Regarding tackle, in his normal fishing operations Dyson carries 20 miles of tackle on board his boat; the other 20 miles he has are stock he carries for replacement purposes. Loss of tackle turns out to depend directly not on the number of days of fishing, but rather on the number of pounds of shark caught. Based on past experience, Dyson knows that he will have to replace about one mile of tackle for every 50,000 pounds of shark caught. The cost of ready-to-use tackle (including hooks, buoys, radar reflectors, etc.) from Dyson's regular supplier is $1,000 per mile. However, 30 miles of Dyson's present tackle were purchased used from the estate of another shark fisherman in New Bedford at a cost of $22,500. This is the only instance that Dyson has ever encountered of used tackle being for sale, and he considers the future availability of used tackle to be a virtual impossibility.

Case 3–2

Weston Manufacturing Company

At their quarterly meeting held on November 5, 1965, the directors of the Weston Manufacturing Company were informed that the company would probably finish the fiscal year ending December 31 with an operating loss of nearly $50,000 on sales of approximately $1.8 million. This would be the second year in succession of unprofitable operation, the only two such years in the company's 57-year history. The loss of $49,971.48 in 1964 followed a profit of more than $150,000 in 1963.

The financial statement for the period ending October 31, 1965, showed a loss of $48,915.56. This compared with the loss of $73,059.68 for the same period in 1964. Scott Howell, the Chairman of the Board, expressed disappointment in October's profit of $15,261.58 on net shipments of $217,245.97. Unfortunately, one big order did not come out as expected due to final design changes.

Shipments for November were projected to be $85,000, resulting in a loss of approximately $14,000. If shipments in December reached $240,000 as estimated, a profit of $13,000 was expected.

After dispensing with the financial projections for the remainder of the year, Scott Howell began to inform the directors of the background of negotiations with the Sheridan Electric Products Corporation. Sheridan was a national manufacturer of heavy-duty industrial electrical appliances, and the company's headquarters were in Dayton, Ohio, less than 100 miles from Weston.

"In 1958 Sheridan asked us to determine whether a flatbed car with 330-ton capacity and a bed height of 26 inches could be built. The car was needed to move one of a series of new transformers from the construction area to the testing shop, a distance of 2½ miles on the company's track. The low bed height was required because of vertical clearance constraints in the area of the construction shop. John Sanders did some figuring and wrote them that such a car could be built for about $20,000.

"It seemed to us that Sheridan was on the verge of placing the order but then decided instead to rent a car from the Baltimore and Ohio Railroad each time one of the large transformers needed to be moved. No reason was given for this decision, but I do know that we were the only people Sheridan had contacted with a view to having a car built for them. Over the next five years, Don Archer occasionally stopped by the Sheridan plant and found their interest in the purchase of the flatbed car to vary from time to time.

"Last year Sheridan indicated interest in resuming serious talks. Bert Stokes drew up some plans according to the gauge, capacity, height, and other specifications received from Fred Shillkof, Sheridan's Chief Engineer. Shillkof approved the plans, and, as usual, we took this as an assurance that the track was a normal, level, industrial installation, permitting the proposed simple nonoscillating design for the car. In spite of a general increase in costs in the interim, John was able to submit the original bid of $20,000. The production costs were actually $15,000. The order was placed, and the car was shipped March 23, on schedule.

"Unfortunately, Sheridan's track foundation was not adequate, and the car derailed on a banked portion of the track. Sheridan would not accept the car and returned it, at a cost of $550 to us. Bert then undertook an engineering restudy and concluded that the cost of rebuilding the car with oscillating trucks would be about $16,000. A further review of costs developed no useful shortcuts. On July 18, a revised total price of $36,000 was offered to Sheridan. If we decided to rebuild the car, the modifications could be completed in less than a week.

"As you know, I was more or less out of action for most of the fall due to a prolonged serious illness in the immediate family. Shortly after I returned, early in October, having received no reply to our July proposal, I sent a wire requesting that Bert and I meet with Sheridan's Chief Engineer, the Purchasing Agent, and the General Manager.

"I have asked Bert to report to the Board on that meeting. He will be along in a few minutes. In the meantime, has anybody any questions?"

"Yes, Scott, there is one point I'd like to clear up," said O'Brien. "Did anyone from Weston see the Sheridan track?"

"Bert and I inspected the track when we visited in October," replied Howell. "It was totally unsuited for a nonoscillating car. It turned out that Sheridan's people thought the car would flex, but any engineer could see that that would be impossible for a car with 330-ton capacity."

There was a knock at the door, and Albert Stokes entered. No introductions were necessary, so Howell asked Stokes to proceed immediately with the report of their joint visit to Dayton.

"On October 22, Scott Howell and I met at Dayton, Ohio, with Sheridan's Purchasing Agent, Mr. Robert Casey, and Mr. James Woodruff, their General Manager. Mr. Woodruff informed us that, according to a report from his Traffic Department dated October 8, there had been four instances since March when the Weston car could have been used if it had been operating satisfactorily. In each case it was necessary to pay the B&O Railroad $300 demurrage charges. However, they foresee that a car of 330 tons capacity could be used about 12 times a year—equivalent to $3,600 demurrage charges.

"Woodruff expressed the feeling that on the basis of a car life of 20 years, $36,000 was a greater investment than the company would consider. They felt that a suitable car should cost about $25,000. This figure was based on savings that would accrue to them if they did not have to pay the demurrage charges.

"We left the meeting with the understanding that we would review the design to see if costs could be reduced below the quotation of July 18. Scott had also suggested that they consider whether this car would not serve additional uses for Sheridan in moving and storing the new large transformers. We said we would keep in touch, although Woodruff and Casey indicated that there was 'no great rush.' "

"Bert, why wasn't Fred Shillkof at this meeting?" asked Hall.

"I don't know, Max," Stokes replied. "Neither Woodruff nor Casey gave any reason for his absence. He hasn't been fired, and he wasn't off sick. I know because we walked past his office on our way from the meeting; the door was open, and he was working at his desk."

"One more question, Bert," said O'Brien. "If we rebuild the car with oscillating trucks according to the revised design, what are the chances that it will again derail?"

"Very small, even though that track of theirs is not so hot. I'd say not more than one chance in a hundred."

There being no further questions forthcoming, Stokes collected his papers and left the room.

"Well, gentlemen," said Howell, "where do we go from here?"

The ensuing silence was broken by Sanders. "We quote them a figure of $36,000 based on the present estimate of the costs of modification and the production cost of the original car. Now, though, with an indication that a suitable car at $25,000 might be acceptable to them, we could reconsider. But I would like to remind you that it would have been impossible to have built an oscillating car originally for $25,000. Maybe we should split the difference and make a bid of $30,000. However, I would say that we would have less than an even chance of getting the order at $30,000, say, around two in five, whereas at $25,000 the odds would be about nine to one in our favor. By the same token, at $36,000 we'd be lucky to have one chance in ten."

"What about trying to sell the car to someone else if Sheridan turns us down?" asked Hall.

Don Archer shook his head. "Not very good—as is, we might have a one in twenty chance of selling the car. If we can find a customer, we might get between $10,000 and $18,000, and my best estimate is about $15,000. The market is pretty small, so I don't think our selling costs would run over $200. We should be able to survey this market in less than two weeks.

"If we rebuild the car with an oscillating truck, there are more firms that might be interested, and the chances are about one in five of finding a customer. We should get between $17,000 and $25,000, with an average of about $20,000, but in this market the selling costs would be around $500, with all prospective customers contacted in less than four weeks.

"Those are very reasonable prices, but that would be about the most we could expect in either case."

All agreed that the possibilities of bargaining further with Sheridan were nil. Sanders summarized the situation: "As I see it, we have two choices: make them a firm bid for the rebuilt car on a take-it-or-leave-it basis or absorb the loss ourselves. As scrap, the car might be worth about $3,000 to us. If we rebuild the car with oscillating trucks and it still doesn't work, its scrap value might go up to around $4,000."

"I think that just about says it, John," said Howell. "I certainly don't want to absorb any loss in view of our recent poor profit picture, but I would do so in preference to a legal battle. Our lawyers have assured me that we could force Sheridan to pay a substantial cancellation charge on the grounds that the track was substandard. Another, and perhaps stronger reason for demanding a cancellation charge would be the claim that Shillkof could have warned us when he saw and approved the plans. Legally, we are on sure ground, but this is our first contract with Sheridan, and possible future business from such a large company could substantially help us to halt, even reverse, our present sales decline. Besides, getting your name involved with a wrangle in court never does you any good in this business, no matter how right you are in the eyes of the law. For the same reason we have to give Sheridan the right of first refusal on a modified car. Only if they turn down our bid can we consider selling it elsewhere. Anyway, the next move seems to be ours, and it should be made soon. The sale of this car could significantly alter the profit projections discussed earlier. Given Bert and Don's estimates, I see no reason why we cannot resolve this transaction before the end of the fiscal year. I would like you to give some intensive thought to this matter, and for us to reach a decision before the end of the week. Now, John, let's have that general report of yours."

Sanders opened his briefcase and took from it four copies of his general report. He passed one copy to each of the other three directors so that they could refer easily to the quantitative data contained in the report. Having cleaned his spectacles and taken a drink of water, John Sanders, reading from his own copy, went to the next report on the agenda.

Case 3–3

Brunswick Corporation (A): School Equipment Division

In late April 1966, Mr. Baker,[1] the division president for the School Equipment Division of Brunswick Corporation, was trying to decide the bid price he should set for an Erehwon[2] State contract for lecture hall seating.

The contract was of a rather unusual nature, in that a successful bid now increased the possibility of a sizable additional business under several contract proposals that were known to be pending release in the near future. Consequently, Mr. Baker felt that it was extremely important to carefully evaluate the effects of this initial bid price upon future contract awards and to make his decision with these effects in mind.

The School Equipment Division

Brunswick's School Equipment Division (see Exhibit 1 for a partial organization chart) was located in Kalamazoo, Michigan, and although actual sales figures were not released, it was felt to be among the top two

Exhibit 1
Partial organization chart

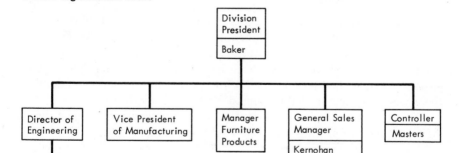

Source: Company records.

---

[1] All names used in this case are fictitious.
[2] Fictitious—pronounced "era-wun."

or three suppliers of school equipment in the United States. The major competition came from American Seating Company and Virco—a supplier on the West Coast—although there were many smaller suppliers, such as Heywood-Wakefield, Clarin, and Herman Miller. The product lines of these companies were not strictly comparable, however, as some favored manufacturing office furniture, and thus only entered the school equipment market in terms of seating and tables, while others concentrated on supplying a wide range of classroom equipment for only one or two segments of the total educational market.

Brunswick's product line included both classroom equipment and furniture. Their range comprised chairs, tables, cabinets, blackboards, desks, folding partitions, gymnasium seating, and folding stages. Although all of these items came in a wide variety of shapes, sizes, and colors, nearly 70 percent of the division's sales could be supplied from inventory. It was estimated that the total U.S. market for equipment of the type that Brunswick manufactured was approximately $150 million and that of this total Erehwon State accounted for around 9 percent, or $13.5 million.

Demand for Brunswick's products was highly seasonal, with a peak that occurred during July, August, and September. This peak was up to six times the level of demand during the remainder of the year. In order to avoid carrying excessive inventory during the off-season months, the level of production was changed in sympathy with the forecast demand. Thus, during the fall, winter, and early spring, the factory in Kalamazoo operated considerably below its rated capacity.

The Erehwon State contract

Mr. Kernohan, the General Sales Manager, first heard of the State University of Erehwon's requirement for lecture hall seating on October 25, 1965, from Brunswick's agent in Hamilton, Erehwon.

The agent stated that there were three lecture halls then under construction that had to be equipped with seating during 1966. In addition there were four lecture halls planned for completion during 1967.

The specifications compiled by the State University called for three different styles of seating—these were designated as the "A," "B," and "C" styles.

The "A" style was an entirely new seating arrangement that was not a standard product for either Brunswick or any other school equipment supplier. The design called for a combination tabletop and cantilevered hinged seat arrangement. It was envisaged that the tabletops would be continuous and that from each supporting post a pair of seats would be fixed so that, when not in use, the seats would fold under the table. To use the seat a student would swing the seat out against its closing spring to a position where the student could comfortably sit at the desk. The seat bucket was also required to be capable of swiveling and tilting at the end of its cantilevered supporting arm. Exhibit 2 shows the university's sketch of a typical unit.

Exhibit 2
State University of Erehwon, Office of Architecture and Facilities: Lecture hall seating—continuous tabletop (type A)

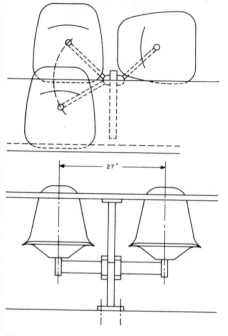

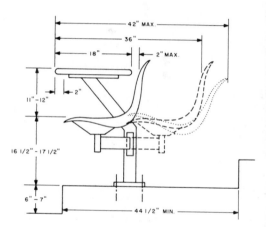

STATE UNIVERSITY OF EREHWON
OFFICE OF
ARCHITECTURE AND FACILITIES

LECTURE HALL SEATING
CONTINUOUS TABLE TOP-TYPE A

The State University's reason for requiring such a unit was an attempt to decrease the space between adjacent tabletops so that any given lecture hall could accommodate more students. To achieve this increased density the new seat design did not provide any aisle space between the back of the seat and the table behind when it was being used in the "swung out" or "operating" position. When the student left the seat, it would swing closed, thus providing the necessary aisle space through which other students could pass.

The "B"-style seat required only a minor modification to an existing Brunswick design. The specifications called for single seats that were equipped with folding tables and that were mounted in a fixed position by a central pedestal. Exhibit 3 shows an illustration of the standard Brunswick product.

The third seat arrangement, the "C" style, was simply a four-legged moveable chair with a hinged writing table. Exhibit 3 illustrates Brunswick's standard product that would meet this requirement.

Exhibit 3
Standard type B and type C seating

Type B: Brunswick Model - Riser Mount.

RISER MOUNTED SEATING

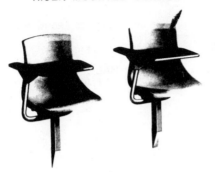

Perfect for lecture halls, demonstration rooms, any area which calls for tiered seating. Riser mounted units are available with CHANCELLOR, CONTEMPORARY or DYTRON shells; deskchair, tablet or fold-away Tab-Lette arms (see page 11); under-seat book racks (see page 13).

Brunswick riser mounted seating requires a minimum 5½" riser. Rise should not exceed 10½" if Tab-Lette units are planned. Riser pedestal is 1½" x 3", 14-gauge rectangular steel tubing; in-depth metallic grey finish.

Type C: Brunswick Model - UDC.

Model UDC–CHANCELLOR DESK CHAIR
Mocha black understructure. New, C/U fixed desk arm; walnut woodgrain plastic surface.

DIMENSIONS:
Seat Height—18"   Overall Height—31"
Seat Width—18¾"   Overall Width—22½"
Work Surface Height—28¼"   Overall Depth—30¾"
Work Surface—16" x 25½"

ALSO AVAILABLE AS:
Model UDC-C—Chrome understructure.

Source: Company records.

Having noted the requirements for the three styles of seats, Mr. Kernohan's interest was awakened by the agent's comments that (1) Erehwon State's *total* requirement for the type A unit, over the years, would be around 12,000 units and that (2) a manufacturer bidding on the contract would be required to supply all three seat styles for that portion of the contract for which it received an award. Thus, for Brunswick to be considered as suppliers of the B and C styles, which could be filled from the standard product line, it would have to develop a type A unit.

Mr. Kernohan immediately contacted the division's chief engineer, and he agreed to assign Mr. Carlaw, the liaison engineer, to investigate the contract's potential for Brunswick.

October 1965–April 1966

As the formal bid proposal had not been issued, Mr. Carlaw's first task was to collect the information that was available and then to make a decision concerning the feasibility of producing the type A unit.

After carefully reading the Hamilton agent's letter, he decided to call the agent in order to ascertain what steps would have to be taken if Brunswick was to file a successful bid. The agent, who had just returned from a discussion with the state authorities, outlined the following requirements. The actual bid proposal would not be distributed by the state until a satisfactory sample of the type A seat had been demonstrated. This delay was in order to prove the feasibility of the state's tentative specifications. The agent had received a copy of these specifications and was forwarding them to Brunswick for evaluation. In addition, Carlaw learned, the agent had scheduled an appointment with the state's division of standards on Thursday, February 10, 1966. The purpose of this meeting was for Brunswick, should it be interested, to present a working sample of its type A design so that the division of standards could evaluate the design's acceptability. The agent also told Carlaw that the state had decided on the amount and timing of its actual seating requirements and that a copy of this schedule would be enclosed with the promised seat specifications.

Several days later Mr. Carlaw received the specifications and schedule from the agent in Hamilton. The schedule is shown in Exhibit 4. Armed

Exhibit 4
Tentative schedule of lecture hall seating
requirements, State University of Erehwon*

Proposal No. ⟨⟨⟨ (to be distributed April 1966)

	Type A—continuous
Agency†	tabletop‡
Easton	1,000
Southfield	1,000
Middletown	1,000

Proposal No. ⟨⟨⟨ (to be distributed early 1967)

	Type A—continuous
Agency†	tabletop‡
Centerville	1,200
Westport....................	1,200
North Plains	1,200
Upton	1,200

Note: Contracts for each agency will be awarded separately.
* Figures disguised.
† Refers to campus where seating is to be installed.
‡ Each unit refers to a single seat.
Source: Company records.

with this information, Mr. Carlaw and Mr. Kernohan, made the decision to proceed with the construction of a prototype for submission to the state's division of standards in February 1966. Although they did not as yet know the extent of the total market, they did know that Erehwon State would be requiring 9,400 type A units within the next year and a half and possibly up to 12,000 units within the foreseeable future. They realized that it was very unlikely that they would be awarded 100 percent of the contract. However, the possibility of selling standard type B and C chairs from stock, coupled with the need to maintain a close contact with the state that accounted for 9 percent of total industry sales, suggested that Brunswick proceed with the construction of a sample.

On February 10, 1966, Brunswick presented the prototype type A seating together with sample type B and C seats to the authorities in Hamilton. The units, with some modifications, were accepted as fulfilling the basic specifications. Toward the end of March 1966 Brunswick submitted the further prototypes that incorporated the required modification. These prototypes were accepted as meeting the specifications in principle. If Brunswick decided to go ahead and bid on the contract, the prototype units would be subjected to the normal range of mechanical strength tests to ensure that they met the more detailed durability and safety standards expected of any school furniture.

In mid-April 1966, Brunswick received Erehwon State's formal bid proposal for the requirements of type A, B, and C lecture hall seating.

The bid proposal

The bid proposal received by Brunswick called for type A lecture hall seating to be delivered to the three campuses of Easton, Southfield, and Middletown during July, August, and September, respectively. The number of type A units required was as shown in Exhibit 4.

In addition to the type A units, each campus required type B and C units that totaled 50 percent and 25 percent, respectively, of the type A requirements. Thus, Easton, which required 1,000 type A units, would also need 500 type B units and 250 type C units. The same ratios applied to all of the campuses shown in Exhibit 4. These standard ratios were applicable because all of the campus lecture halls had been designed on a modular basis, so that the size and number of rooms using the three styles of chair remained in the same proportion.

The bid proposal also stated that in order to ensure uniformity in seating design and style, the contract for each campus would be awarded to the same contractor. This meant that if Brunswick received the contract for Easton, then it would supply all three styles of chair to that campus. However, it was quite possible that each campus contract would be awarded to a different contractor. Consequently, Brunswick, if it obtained any contract at all, might receive contracts for one, two, or perhaps all three campuses.

The bid opening was set for May 18, 1966 at 11:00 A.M., and contract awards were to be made, subject to sample seating passing the required durability and safety standards.

The decision to bid

On April 20, 1966, Mr. Baker called a preliminary meeting to discuss the Erehwon State contract.

After a few initial remarks that were followed by a general discussion, Mr. Baker decided to go ahead and put in a bid for the contract. He agreed with Mr. Kernohan that it was in the company's best interest to maintain or even improve its position as a supplier of school equipment to Erehwon State. Because of the goodwill or future benefit that a successful bid might produce, he believed that this factor should be specifically included in the decision on what price to submit. The meeting then assigned the different members the responsibility of bringing all the relevant data and information to a final bid price meeting to be held on the following Wednesday.

The price-setting meeting

Mr. Baker commenced the meeting at 10:00 A.M. Present were Mr. Masters, the controller; Mr. Kernohan, the general sales manager; and Mr. Carlaw, the liaison engineer.

After some general remarks, Mr. Baker called upon Mr. Masters to give some details of the costing of the different types of seating. Mr. Masters began by handing out a sheet (Exhibit 5) to the people present. After

Exhibit 5
School Equipment Division cost figures for type A, B, and C seating*

	Type A	Type B	Type C
Direct cost (including direct overhead) ...	$38.75	$18.45	$18.43
Freight	2.00	1.00	1.00
Installation	1.48	3.42	0.53
Service (percent of direct cost)	3.88 (10%)	0.92 (5%)	0.92(5%)
Total cost†	$46.11†	$23.79†	$20.88†

* Cost data have been disguised.
† To this figure must be added the agent's commission. The commission was 10 percent of the "equipment selling price," where the "equipment selling price" was equivalent to the actual selling price (bid price) less freight, installation, and service.
Source: Company records.

explaining that this cost information represented the most accurate data he could determine from the facts available, he drew the group's attention to three items of particular interest. First, because the type A unit was both unproved and technically complex, he anticipated that it might require more than the usual amount of service. He had therefore included a

10 percent service allowance for this product in lieu of the normal 5 percent. Second, he emphasized that until the bid prices were determined he could not include the agent's 10 percent commission, which had to be based on the equivalent selling price. However, the method of computing this commission was included in the paper (see Exhibit 5). Finally, he added that because the business with Erehwon State was important and because the seasonal demand for Brunswick's products meant that the factory would have excess capacity during the year, he had decided to marginally cost any items relating to the sale of type A units. He further justified this approach by stating that the annual budget had been developed without including any business resulting from these Erehwon State contracts and that consequently he had treated this revenue as extra and was willing to accept the contract on a marginal cost basis. Mr. Masters noted, however, that all fixed costs directly related to the project would need to be fully amortized over the course of the Erehwon State contracts. He then called upon Mr. Carlaw to present and describe the fixed costs involved.

Mr. Carlaw began by stating that up until the present, the engineering department had spent $5,500 on building and designing the prototypes and that if Brunswick went ahead with the decision to bid, a further $20,300 would be required for tooling and design. He emphasized that once the final decision to bid was made, these costs would be committed. This would be necessary because the tooling had to be subcontracted immediately if Brunswick was to have any chance of meeting and delivery dates called for on the bid proposal. In addition to tooling and design costs, Mr. Carlaw estimated that a further $4,700 opportunity cost would be incurred because of the delaying effect the type A unit was having on other design work in the engineering department.

Mr. Baker asked if anybody wanted to comment on the cost figures. After receiving no reply, he said that the figures looked fine to him and recommended that they be accepted. This was formally agreed to.

The next order of business, Mr. Baker stated, was to obtain some feel for the likely demand for type A units, and he asked Mr. Kernohan to present his estimates.

Mr. Kernohan began by saying, "Well, before I can give you any estimate of demand, we will have to settle on possible bid prices, because the demand very much depends on the price we set. I have discussed the matter at some length with Mr. Masters and Mr. Carlaw, and they have agreed that we consider only two prices for the first Erehwon contract. These would be $58.75 or $54.75 for the type A unit. We feel that both of these prices have a good chance of securing at least some of the campus contracts, although the $54.75 price would have a better chance of getting more schools than the higher price. Now the prices for the B and C units are fixed because we have sold these very successfully to Erehwon State before. These prices are $35.84 and $29.15, respectively."

"All right," Mr. Baker replied, "seeing that you three have discussed this already, I'm willing to accept those two bid prices as being the best two to consider. Now say we bid $58.75 for the type A unit, what are our chances of getting all or part of the first three school contracts?"

"There's no question in my mind," replied Mr. Kernohan, "that we have no chance at all of getting all three campuses. We know that one of the competition is a preferred bidder—in fact, we even suspect that he designed the original type A unit and submitted it to the state. So I'm certain we will not get all three schools. I would say we have a 20 percent chance of not getting anything and probably a 50 percent chance of getting one school. However, if we bid $54.75, then our chances improve. In this case I would say the probability of getting no schools is only 10 percent while the chance of getting two schools is now 60 percent. Again I'm convinced that no matter what happens we will not get all three schools."

"That's fine," said Mr. Carlaw. "Let me get my slide rule out, and I'll work out which price we should be bidding—that's if we should bid at all."

"Hold on a minute," said Baker. "Surely we have to consider the effect of the second contract for four schools. In fact, we should also think about the possible future market apart from the second contract. Well, that's how I see it anyway."

"I don't know," said Masters, "perhaps we should work out whether our estimates for the first contract say 'go' before we look at anything further."

"You may be right," concurred Baker, "but rather than break this meeting up now, we may as well get all the figures that seem appropriate so that we don't have to start all over again. Now, let's see, as far as I'm concerned, if we don't get any schools in the first contract, then we should take any losses we've incurred and forget the whole thing. It would seem that the prices you fellows have come up with are more than competitive, and if they don't land us at least one school, we might as well retire gracefully. Also, to be on the safe side, I suggest that we amortize all our fixed expenses over the first contract."

The meeting nodded its assent, and Mr. Kernohan began. "We know that in the second contract for four schools [see Exhibit 4 for details] the bidding is going to get tougher—especially as most of our competitors will probably have written off their tooling by then. So I feel that if we decide to submit a $58.75 bid for the first contract, then we *must lower* our bid for the second contract. I would suggest that in this case we only bid $54.75 for the second leg. It would be strategically unnecessary to jump from $58.75 to our low limit of $51.75 with the competition being what it is. If, however, we decide to bid the extremely competitive $54.75 for the first three schools, then we should consider bidding again at that price or else lowering the bid to a rock bottom $51.75."

"Can we go as low as $51.75?" queried Mr. Baker.

"Yes! Mr. Masters and I had a somewhat heated discussion on this," replied Mr. Kernohan, "but we feel this price is realistic if the volume is there. This second contract calls for four schools at 1,200 units each compared to the three schools at 1,000 units each for the first bid proposal."

"Well, what do you see the demand becoming?" asked Mr. Baker.

"This starts to get very complicated," replied Mr. Kernohan. "First, you've got to realize that a lot depends on events that we have no control over. In fact, we may not even be aware of them right now. There is an election for state school committee in November, and that may change the ground rules on everything in Erehwon's educational plan next spring. I've tried to be precise in my predictions. Let me explain how I got them."

Mr. Kernohan continued, "Just as for the first contract, I'm certain that there is no chance of our gaining all four schools whatever price we bid. I also have enough faith in our product that if we get some business on our first bid we won't get shut out on the second round. The real question is, Will we get one, two, or three schools? This depends on our initial bid, the success of that initial bid, and our second bid. If we get two schools on the first round and do not raise our price, I am certain that we will get at least as many on the second round. However, if we only get one school on the first round, I think it is impossible to get three on the next round. As an example, if we bid $54.75 on the first round, obtain two schools, and then lower our bid to $51.75, I am estimating that we have a 40 percent chance of getting two schools and a 60 percent chance of getting three schools on the second round."

Mr. Kernohan's assessments are summarized in Table 1.

Table 1
Assessment of probabilities

1st contract bid	*No. of schools obtained on 1st bid*	*2d contract bid*	*Probability of obtaining no. of schools shown on 2d bid*		
			1	*2*	*3*
$58.75	1	$54.75	0.5	0.5	0
58.75	2	54.75	0	0.4	0.6
54.75	1	54.75	0.8	0.2	0
54.75	1	51.75	0.5	0.5	0
54.75	2	54.75	0	0.8	0.2
54.75	2	51.75	0	0.4	0.6

Mr. Baker called for comments on these assessments. The discussion was vigorous, but after about an hour the group decided that the figures were as realistic as could be obtained with the knowledge available.

"Now, what about the future market potential apart from the Erehwon State contracts?" asked Mr. Willis.

"Well, it seems to me," began Mr. Kernohan, "that this market is dependent on the success we have in the first bid. If we obtain some part of the first contract, then I think we will sell 2,000 type A units for certain on the open market. These would provide us a contribution of $10,000. If we don't have any success in the first contract, I think the alternative markets are effectively zero. There's too much prestige attached to gaining a contract from Erehwon State for us to compete effectively on the open market under this circumstance. Of course, the open market sales would not include our standard B- and C-type units as it is unlikely that anybody else would want precisely these three units in a package like Erehwon did."

"I think we now have all the information," said Mr. Baker, "so Mr. Carlaw can, along with the rest of us, bring out his paper and pencil and calculate what we should do. I would like to meet again tomorrow at 10:00 A.M., so please bring along your firm recommendations then."

Case 3–4

Novon Cement Company

The Novon Cement Company was founded in 1922 in Falstaff, a small town in southern California. In early 1961, Novon was engaged in the manufacture and distribution of cement, as well as the mining of raw materials required in cement manufacture.

Novon's Falstaff operations included a large cement-producing plant which had an annual capacity of 3,500,000 barrels of cement. Initial construction of this plant had begun in 1922. Since that time, the plant had been expanded on several occasions. This plant was located on a 2,000-acre tract which contained valuable raw material resources. Novon also operated a second and larger plant at Plata, California, 125 miles southeast of Falstaff. The 5,000 acres of land on which this plant was located were acquired in 1927 for the raw material deposits which the property contained. The plant itself, with an annual capacity of 5,500,000 barrels of cement, was constructed in 1954–55. This plant was one of the most up-to-date facilities in the cement industry.

Each of Novon's plants was an independent, completely integrated operating unit. Each had, in addition to its own raw material deposits, complete crushing, grinding, clinker-burning, cement-grinding, and shipping facilities, as well as storage facilities and complete maintenance

Exhibit 1

NOVON CEMENT COMPANY
Balance Sheets

	April 30, 1960	*December 31, 1960 (unaudited)*
Current Assets:		
Cash	$ 3,900,095	$ 4,381,086
U.S. government and other securities (at cost)	1,210,000	2,725,959
Accounts receivable (net of allowance for doubtful accounts)	1,799,647	2,564,593
Inventories:		
Cement and process stock (at cost below market)	2,119,031	2,329,311
Packages and fuel (at cost)	440,646	632,870
General supplies (at cost)	1,544,328	1,676,674
Total Current Assets	$11,013,747	$14,310,493
Sundry Assets	138,986	143,496

Long-Term Assets:				
Land and quarries	$ 2,893,440		$ 3,079,000	
Building, machinery, and equipment	26,817,119		30,125,418	
	$29,710,559		$33,204,418	
Less depreciation:				
Amortization, depletion	12,060,570		13,618,177	
		$17,649,989		$19,586,241
Deferred charges		194,916		248,140
Total Assets		$28,997,638		$34,288,370

	April 30, 1960	*December 31, 1960 (unaudited)*
Current Liabilities:		
Accounts payable	$1,150,655	$ 888,786
Accrued expenses	398,723	941,114
Dividends payable	528,000	148,500
Federal income tax (estimated)		759,220
Total Current Liabilities	$ 2,077,378	$ 2,737,620
Stockholders' Equity:		
Preferred stock........................	$ 6,600,000	$ 6,600,000
Common stock........................	379,500	11,385,000*
Retained earnings	19,940,760	13,565,750
Total Liabilities	$28,997,638	$34,288,370

* In August 1960 the company increased the par value of the common stock and declared a stock split in the form of a stock dividend.

shops. Novon also operated modern powerhouse facilities at each plant which were sufficient to provide most of the plant's power requirements.

The primary raw materials used by Novon came from the limestone deposits adjacent to its plants. The company estimated that its raw material resources at each plant would be sufficient to sustain operations for more than 100 years. Besides the plants and property at Falstaff and Plata, Novon owned other raw material deposits in California, Utah, Wyoming, Arizona, and Texas.

Novon marketed various types of cement under the "Novon" and "White Dot" brand names. These products were sold exclusively in southern California. The company's customers included ready-mix concrete dealers, building material dealers, concrete products manufacturers, heavy engineering construction contractors who worked under government contracts, and the federal, state, and local governments. Within its southern California trading area, Novon experienced competition from five other cement plants that were operated by four companies.

Novon's balance sheets as of April 31, 1960, and December 31, 1960, and its statement of earnings for the fiscal years 1958, 1959, 1960, and for the first eight months of fiscal 1961, are shown as Exhibits 1 and 2, respectively. The company had recently adopted a 17 percent after-tax hurdle rate for use in evaluating proposed expenditures.

Exhibit 2
Operating statements

	Year ended April 30			Eight months ended December 31, 1960
	1958	1959	1960	(unaudited)
Sales	$26,317,229	$26,413,146	$30,959,062	$18,165,551
Cost of goods sold:				
Direct costs	15,531,755	14,305,431	17,377,504	10,598,456
Depreciation and depletion	1,425,703	2,129,969	2,464,134	1,605,541
Selling and administrative expenses	2,169,412	2,059,528	2,554,287	1,644,933
	$19,126,870	$18,494,928	$22,395,925	$13,848,931
Operating profit	7,190,359	7,918,218	8,563,137	4,316,620
Other income (expense)	(141,108)	84,633	(75,787)	(71,130)
Earnings before income taxes	7,049,251	8,002,851	8,487,350	4,245,490
Income taxes	3,084,178	3,584,841	3,528,602	1,771,000
Net profit	3,965,073	4,418,010	4,958,748	2,474,490

Investigation of new markets

In early 1960, Novon's top executives had begun to think about what plans the company ought to adopt so that it could continue to achieve sales increases. At that time, there was extra capacity at both the Falstaff and Plata plants, but the southern California market was steadily growing, and Novon's management believed that in the next several years Novon would be operating at capacity. The Executive Committee (composed of the President, Tom Denner; the Vice President–Production, George Ivers;

the Vice President–Sales, Joe Merlis; and the Treasurer, Ralph Coleman) believed that in addition to considering further expansion in southern California, Novon should seriously consider entering new markets. Because of the desire to have a source of raw materials at a plant site, primary attention was focused on locations where Novon already owned raw material deposits.

Upper Feather River Project

In June 1960, the state of California approved a bond program in the amount of $1,750 million to be expended for water resource development. A major phase of the state-supported water development program was the Upper Feather River Project in northeastern California. This project had been advocated for many years, but up until June 1960 conservation groups, principally the Sierra Club, had successfully argued against it. The primary component of the Upper Feather River Project was the construction of the Glenn Butte Dam, which would help control the frequent flooding by the Feather River. In addition to flood control, the reservoir would also provide water for irrigation, municipal and industrial needs, and power resource development. When full, the reservoir formed by this dam would have a volume of 3.5 million acre-feet. Five smaller earthen reservoirs, upstream from the Glenn Butte Dam, were included in the project. They would provide flood control and recreational facilities for northern California.

After approval of the bond, the state of California moved quickly to begin construction. The water requirement projections for the southern portions of the state were pressing, particularly in light of the pending *Arizona-California* lawsuit over Colorado River water rights.

In August 1960, Novon was asked by the state of California whether it "intended to bid on the Glenn Butte Dam and whether it was planning to build any new plants within economic shipping distances of the proposed structure." Novon replied that it was "interested in an opportunity to furnish the cement." In September 1960, Novon was informed by the state of California that invitations to bid on the 3-million-barrel cement contract would not be issued before November 1960 due to several minor changes required in the specifications for the cement. In late November, the state set 5:00 P.M., January 20, 1961, as the deadline for bids for the cement for the dam. The bids would be opened on February 6, 1961, and the contract would be awarded within a week of that date. The successful bidder would probably have to start supplying cement to the damsite in the summer of 1962. The company which was awarded the contract would be notified 15 days prior to the date on which the initial delivery would be required. In no case would cement be required after June 30, 1967. The anticipated delivery schedule was as follows:

Year	Barrels of cement
1962	400,000
1963	900,000
1964	800,000
1965	700,000
1966	200,000

Novon special projects

As soon as the 1960 water resource bond was approved, Novon began an intensive study of the feasibility of construction of a new plant on its property in Lowe, 80 miles from the damsite. Its investigation was conducted on two fronts—the costs of a new plant and the basic market demand of northern California.

The estimated cost for a plant with an annual capacity of 1,500,000 barrels of cement was $4 million, $3.5 million of this for bricks and mortar and $500,000 for anticipated increases in working capital. Construction time for the plant would be slightly less than a year. The bulk of the construction expense would be incurred in the last phases of construction, that is, in late 1961–early 1962. Mr. Ivers had estimated that the variable manufacturing cost would be approximately $1.50 per barrel. The variable manufacturing cost did not include an allowance for administrative expenses (salaries for accounting, purchasing, sales, and executive personnel and other related costs), depreciation, or depletion. The selling and administrative expenses were estimated to be $400,000 per year. For depreciation purposes, Mr. Ivers knew that Novon would use a straight-line method with a ten-year life. Mr. Ivers also estimated a percentage depletion deduction for federal income tax purposes that would result in a reduction in taxable income of approximately 20 cents per barrel of cement sold. With respect to delivery of the cement, the dam contract was unusual. Industry practice usually required that all transportation costs be borne by the purchaser; however, when large contracts were "let" by the state, delivery to the construction site was to be included in the bid. Since the damsite was so close to the Lowe property, Novon felt that it would be able to use its own trucks instead of contract trucks to transport the cement, and in so doing incur a cost of approximately $0.10 per barrel rather than $0.16 per barrel.

The analysis of the basic market demand for northern California was conducted by a well-known market research firm. The results are given in Exhibit 3. These numbers confirmed the Executive Committee's suspicions that a plant capacity of 1,500,000 barrels of cement would be adequate for at least the first eight years of the plant's life. Also it was clear to the Executive Committee that, if Novon were to lose the Glenn Butte contract, plans for the Lowe facility would have to be abandoned.

The basic market demand simply was not adequate to support a large plant in its early years, and a smaller plant would be far too inefficient. In addition, Novon would have to compete directly with the winner of the dam contract for that demand. Consequently, it would be foolish for Novon, or probably any firm, to build a plant in the area without having won the dam contract.

Exhibit 3
Estimates of basic cement demand,
proposed Lowe plant*

Calendar year	Basic demand (000 barrels)†
1962	800
1963	800
1964	900
1965	1,050
1966	1,200
1967	1,250
1968	1,350
1969	1,400
1970	1,600
1971	1,700
1972	1,900

* Estimates assume: (*a*) a price of $2.70, or 180 percent of variable manufacturing costs; (*b*) that Novon is the only cement manufacturer in the region; (*c*) the completion of the Lowe facility in the first quarter of 1962.

† Basic demand does *not* include the cement required for the dam.

While the final conclusions of the report supported its intuition, the Executive Committee was very excited about some of the supporting information. As part of the analysis of Novon's entrance in the northern California market, a careful study of the competition was conducted. This included estimates of the production costs of the three primary competitors. Presently none had plants in the vicinity of the damsite but each had resource holdings within an economic distance of the dam; and consequently the estimates were based on each firm's raw material sources, transportation costs, and production technology. The estimates of the competitors' costs initiated a debate over the chances that Novon had of winning the dam contract at various bid prices. Ivers and Merlis maintained that Novon's bid had to be low enough to guarantee winning the contract and thereby ensuring the success of a plant at Lowe. Denner and Coleman believed that Novon's bid price should be based on a fair estimate of costs plus a reasonable profit; they did not advocate setting "an unbeatable price." However, Ivers and Merlis thought that the contract was an opportune way of "getting the new plant rolling" and thereby ensuring production close to capacity while Novon was building a commercial market in the area. Denner and Coleman argued that if Novon submitted a very low bid and were awarded the contract, the amount of its winning bid would be published in many newspapers and trade journals. Because the low bid would be publicized, they thought that Novon would be receiving demands from its commercial customers for prices lower than what they were being charged, prices more in line with Novon's "unbeatable" price to the state.

At this point, Denner took control and insisted on estimating, based on the competitors' cost structure, Novon's chances of winning the Glenn Butte contract at various bid prices. Novon usually set its prices at 180 percent of variable manufacturing costs. Since the cement was to be delivered to the damsite, transportation costs would be added to the variable manufacturing costs. This implied a price of approximately $2.90 per barrel. The state contract was of such a magnitude that the full 180 percent pricing was probably inappropriate; but even so, a $2.90 bid would be discussed "just to see what it implied." Ivers and Merlis agreed that a factor of 130 percent was the lowest that Novon could economically go and thus wanted a bid of $2.10 per barrel included. Denner thought that a bid of $2.50 per barrel (160 percent) represented a reasonable profit and that there was probably a 50–50 chance of winning at that price. Others felt differently, but no more than 10 percent one way or the other. Ivers contended that the low bid was so low that the competition could not economically beat it since Novon's production technology and plant site were at least as good as any of the competitors'. Of course, there might be some factors, although he couldn't imagine what, that would motivate the competition to bid very low. So he argued that there was at least a 90 percent chance of winning. The high bid was much more difficult. Eventually, they agreed that if they made the high bid of $2.90 per barrel, there would be only a one in ten chance of winning.

Case 3–5

C. K. Coughlin, Inc. (A)

On a Sunday afternoon in mid-September 1973, Mr. Christopher Schilling was in the office of Mr. Ralph Purcell, President of C. K. Coughlin, Inc. Mr. Schilling, who was Mr. Purcell's assistant, was presenting the details of an analysis he had prepared on Saturday.

Mr. Purcell was hopeful that by the end of the afternoon he would be able to establish a course of action that might hasten the final settlement of a patent suit brought against Coughlin three years earlier by the Tolemite Corporation and its licensee, Barton Research and Development.

The contenders

C. K. Coughlin, Inc., had been founded in Milwaukee, Wisconsin, in 1926 as a commercial outlet for the inventive genius of Dr. Charles K. Coughlin, an astute organic chemist. In its early years the company had achieved sufficient strength to weather the depression and then to participate in the· prosperity that was associated with World War II and its aftermath. By 1950, annual sales were in the neighborhood of $1 million.

Dr. Coughlin had continued in his ownership and management role until 1962. At that time, nearing retirement age, he had sold the company and all of its patents and products to Arrow Industries, a small Chicago-based conglomerate. The company continued to prosper as an Arrow subsidiary and by 1973 had reached an annual sales volume of $3.5 million[1]—14 percent of the Arrow total. About 10 percent of Coughlin's 1973 sales were derived from a chemical component called Varacil. It was the manufacturing process for Varacil which was the subject of the patent suit. The remainder of Coughlin's sales comprised specialty organic chemical products sold, in relatively small volume, primarily to the pharmaceutical industry.

The Tolemite Corporation, also headquartered in Chicago, was a large chemical and pharmaceutical manufacturer with estimated 1973 sales in excess of $100 million. In 1964 Tolemite had been awarded a patent covering various aspects of a new, low-cost method for the synthetic production of the chemical compound Varacil. The techniques covered by the patent had been discovered at Tolemite's research facility in 1959 as an offshoot of another research project. Since Tolemite was neither a user nor a producer of Varacil, it had been decided to offer the use of the patent, under license, to Barton Research and Development, the principal Varacil producer in the United States.

Barton Research and Development (BARD) had begun as a small chemical research company located in Evanston, Illinois. By 1964, however, the company had dropped all research activities and was solely involved in the production of Varacil. To maintain its position as industry leader, BARD had accepted Tolemite's licensing offer and had at once begun conversion of all Varacil production to the new process. In return for the use of the patent, BARD had agreed to pay Tolemite a 4 percent royalty on all sales of synthetic Varacil. In addition, BARD had received permission to sublicense any other Varacil producers that became interested in the process. BARD was further authorized to work out indi-

---

[1] Based on actual sales for January–August and an estimate for September–December.

vidual royalty agreements with producing firms. Under these sublicensing agreements, royalties in excess of 4 percent would accrue to BARD, with 4 percent going to Tolemite.

In 1969, five years after Tolemite had received its patent, a research chemist at C. K. Coughlin had, quite independently, discovered a very similar process for the production of synthetic Varacil. The Coughlin researchers, however, had not felt that the new processing techniques could be patented. Thus, no patent search had been initiated and production facilities had simply been converted to the new process. At that time, no one at Coughlin had suspected the degree to which its new process was similar to the process originated by Tolemite and covered by Tolemite's patent. It was with some surprise then that Coughlin management had received notification that Coughlin was being sued by Tolemite and BARD for patent infringement.

Varacil

Varacil was a chemical substance sold almost exclusively to pharmaceutical manufacturers. Although it appeared as a component in a wide variety of drug preparations, Varacil itself contributed only a minor fraction to the composition of any one drug. The economics of its manufacture, however, suggested that it be made in relatively long runs involving substantial volume. Thus the major drug companies themselves were not involved in its preparation.

Before 1964, Varacil had been processed from naturally occurring organic chemicals found in animal tissue. As a result of the high cost of these natural chemicals, the cost of Varacil itself had been relatively high. With the advent, in the early 60s, of synthetic Varacil, this situation was dramatically changed. Variable costs in the manufacture of synthetic Varacil represented only about 15 percent of sales. For an investment of under $100,000 and annual fixed costs of about $65,000, anyone with the requisite skills in chemical technology could acquire the facilities to provide capacity for an annual volume of 5,000 pounds of a three-shift basis. Understandably, under these circumstances, synthetic Varacil soon drove the natural product virtually out of the market.[2]

In 1973 the national market for synthetic Varacil amounted to some $3 million in sales. On a unit basis this market had been relatively stable for the past several years. As drugs requiring Varacil had been phased out, new drugs—requiring similar amounts of the compound—had always seemed to appear. There was, furthermore, no reason to believe that this stability would be lost over the next several years. Industry unit sales projections thus tended to be quite flat as far out as five and ten years.

---

[2] A few Varacil users still specified the natural product in the belief that it had certain superior properties over the synthetic product.

On the dollar value side, however, the story was quite different. Prices for Varacil, and industry dollar sales as well, had been in decline for the past several years. When converting to the synthetic process, each competitor in the industry had tooled up to supply an optimistic share of the market. Then, when market share objectives were not met, prices were slashed in an attempt to keep manufacturing facilities operating at efficient levels and to bring in as much contribution as possible toward fixed costs. This situation was expected to continue for at least the next five years. Exhibit 1 indicates industry unit and dollar sales of synthetic Varacil for the period 1964 through 1973 as well as projections for the years 1974 through 1984.

Exhibit 1
Unit and dollar sales of synthetic* Varacil by company (actual: 1964–1973; projected: 1974–1984)

	BARD		*Coughlin*		*All others*	
Year	*(lbs)*	*($)*	*(lbs)*	*($)*	*(lbs)*	*($)*
1964	1,000	51,000	0	0	0	0
1965	5,000	246,000	0	0	0	0
1966	20,000	892,000	0	0	0	0
1967	60,000	2,523,000	0	0	0	0
1968	68,000	2,674,000	0	0	0	0
1969	76,000	3,015,000	0	0	0	0
1970	83,000	3,208,000	1,000	37,000	0	0
1971†	89,000	3,182,000	6,000	192,000	2,000	71,000
1972	94,000	2,633,000	11,000	312,000	19,000	536,000
1973*	100,000	2,000,000	17,000	350,000	35,000	700,000
1974	100,000	2,000,000	17,000	340,000	35,000	700,000
1975	100,000	1,900,000	17,000	323,000	35,000	665,000
1976	100,000	1,800,000	17,000	306,000	35,000	630,000
1977	100,000	1,600,000	17,000	272,000	35,000	560,000
1978	100,000	1,500,000	17,000	255,000	35,000	525,000
1979	100,000	1,500,000	17,000	255,000	35,000	525,000
1980	100,000	1,500,000	17,000	255,000	35,000	525,000
1981	100,000	1,500,000	17,000	255,000	35,000	525,000
1982	100,000	1,500,000	17,000	255,000	35,000	525,000
1983	100,000	1,500,000	17,000	255,000	35,000	525,000
1984	100,000	1,500,000	17,000	255,000	35,000	525,000

* Total annual sales of Varacil (including the natural product) were roughly 150,000 pounds for the period 1964–73.
† Estimated.
Source: C. K. Coughlin, Inc.

In 1973 there were seven principal competitors in the synthetic Varacil market. BARD, with $2 million in sales, took 65 percent of the market. Coughlin, with $350,000 in sales, was the second largest operator and held 11 percent of the market. The remaining five entrants, none of whose Varacil sales exceeded $190,000, then comprised that remaining 24 percent of the market. By 1970 all seven of the principal competitors were manufacturing synthetic Varacil by nearly identical processes. Only BARD, however, was paying royalties to Tolemite.

Background on the litigation

On June 12, 1970, Tolemite and BARD had jointly filed suit in the Superior Court of the Fifth District of Wisconsin charging C. K. Coughlin, Inc., with infringement of Tolemite's patent on the manufacturing process for synthetic Varacil. To remedy the infringement, Tolemite and BARD were seeking a royalty payment of 10 percent of all of Coughlin's future sales of synthetic Varacil over what remained on the 17-year life of the patent, as well as a lump sum indemnity to cover past sales.

When confronted with the suit, Mr. Purcell had immediately discussed the matter with Mr. Aaron Mantiris, General Counsel for Arrow Industries. Both men had felt that there was considerable evidence indicating that Tolemite's process might not be patentable. At Mr. Mantiris' suggestion, Coughlin had obtained the services of Evans and Blaylock, a well-known and highly reputable firm of patent attorneys in New York City. These attorneys had been in agreement with Mr. Mantiris on the potential weakness of the Tolemite suit. Thus, in 1970 Evans and Blaylock had begun preparation of a case for Coughlin's defense.

Tolemite's patent contained 12 claims of originality. To obtain it, Tolemite had had to demonstrate to the patent examiners that there was no "prior art" and that there was invention. This was the case with all patents. Prior art could consist of previous patents covering the applied-for patents, or processes in the public domain—unpatentable but generally known—that were similar. To show invention, it was necessary to demonstrate that the applied-for process was not obvious to a person reasonably knowledgeable about related chemical processes.

Any patent was always subject to later challenge in the courts. All or part of a patent could later be overturned on the basis of prior art or absence of invention. As a practical matter, it was sometimes possible, years later, to argue the absence of invention. Ideas that had seemed novel at the time of the invention often seemed far more obvious at a later date. The patent holder, in defense, attempted to reemphasize the novelty of the ideas at the time of the invention. Nevertheless, there were many instances of patents later being successfully challenged.

In the case of synthetic Varacil, Mr. Mantiris argued that Tolemite had not, in fact, introduced any novelty. It had merely observed and harnessed a naturally occurring process which, of itself, was not patentable.

From 1970 to 1973 a partner in Evans and Blaylock had worked intermittently in liaison with Mr. Mantiris researching and preparing the case. Coughlin had considered the suit to be little more than a nuisance and had been content to drag its feet in the hope that Tolemite's case might simply collapse from inertia. Late in 1972, however, a tentative trial date was set for January 1973. Before a firm date could be set, Mr. Purcell and Mr. Mantiris decided, with the concurrence of the patent attorneys, to make at least a token effort at pretrial settlement. Their offer amounted to the payment of all future liabilities at a royalty rate of 2.5 percent of sales. This offer was rejected out of hand by Tolemite and BARD. Following the failure of this effort at pretrial agreement, the case finally reached the court docket and a trial date was set in October 1973.

By September 1973 Mr. Purcell was becoming uneasy over the high—and increasing—level of attorneys' fees. These fees had already reached a total of $100,000, and if the trial were to take place as scheduled, they would surely loom large in comparison with the total value of any successful defense.

In response to this uneasiness about both the progress of the suit and the alarming accumulation, of the attorneys' fees, Mr. Purcell decided on two immediate actions. First, he arranged, through Mr. Mantiris, for a meeting in New York City to thoroughly review the case with the patent attorneys. Second, he asked his new assistant, Mr. Schilling, to review the case and, hopefully, to bring a fresh viewpoint to bear.

Mr. Schilling's analysis and the meeting with the patent attorneys

Chris Schilling was a recent graduate of the Harvard Business School. While pursuing his studies, he had become interested in the application of formal, quantitative frameworks to decision problems. Thus, his approach to this particular problem took the form of the decision tree. This analysis recognized two options open to C. K. Coughlin: (1) go to court and contest the patent, which would cost an additional $50,000 in legal fees and lead to winning the suit with probability X or losing it with probability $1 - X$; or (2) settle out of court for an amount Y percent of past and future sales. These options he summarized in the accompanying decision diagram.

The purpose of his analysis was to determine, for any given out-of-

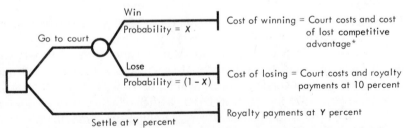

* If CKC *won* the suit, BARD would no longer have to pay 4 percent royalty to Tolemite. Because of the highly competitive nature of the industry, Mr. Schilling believed that BARD would pass this saving along to customers, forcing CKC to retaliate. Thus CKC's revenues would be *reduced* from the status quo by 4 percent if it won the suit.

court settlement offer Y, how large the probability X of winning the suit would have to be to justify rejecting the offer. To do this "break-even" analysis, he solved the following equation for X, given various values of Y:

$$(\text{Cost of winning})(X) + (\text{Cost of losing})(1 - X)$$
$$= \text{Cost of settlement at } Y \text{ percent.}$$

This resulted in the accompanying break-even curve. For all offers above the curve, it was preferable to go to court. Offers below the line were worthy of consideration. For example, if C. K. Coughlin personnel felt that the probability of winning was .6, then settling up to a 7.5 percent royalty rate (shown by the dotted line on the curve) could be justified.

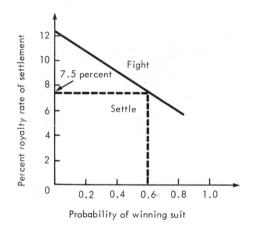

Schilling's principal conclusion from this analysis was that unless the odds on winning the suit were extremely good, any reasonable pretrial settlement was preferable to paying the additional costs and taking a chance on going to court. Mr. Purcell, a chemical engineer, was himself well attuned to quantitative analysis and, in fact, liked to support his own arguments with numerical data wherever possible. Thus, he was intrigued by Mr. Schilling's presentation. As a result, he invited Mr. Schilling to join Mr. Mantiris and himself on the trip to New York City to meet with the patent attorneys. At that meeting Mr. Purcell intended to confront the patent attorneys with Mr. Schilling's analysis and then to obtain their opinion on the benefits of pursuing the case to trial.

In New York the patent attorneys began the meeting by presenting an outline of their case. Everyone attending agreed that the case was indeed a strong one with a high probability of success in the trial phase. The attorneys demurred, however, when asked to give a precise figure for their probability of success in court. At that point, Mr. Purcell sketched out Mr. Schilling's analysis. He then asked the patent attorneys if they still felt that their probability of success was high enough to merit entering the trial phase. The attorneys were visibly uncomfortable with Mr. Schilling's approach. Although they remained convinced of the merits of their case, they agreed that some rethinking was probably necessary before proceeding to trial.

On the flight back to Milwaukee, Mr. Purcell discussed with his General Counsel and his assistant what had happened at the meeting. As a result of that conversation he decided that Mr. Schilling should pursue his analysis further to take into account such things as potential appeals, and to appraise the sensitivity of the analysis to changes in the underlying assumptions. All three men agreed that settlements well in excess of 2½ percent would, in all probability, be preferable to a court fight.

Further analysis

On Saturday, the day after returning to Milwaukee, Mr. Schilling broadened his analysis as requested by Mr. Purcell. This expanded analysis took into account the possibility of appeals by Tolemite or CKC

Exhibit 2
Results of Mr. Schilling's expanded analysis: Break-even
probability for going to court at various royalties

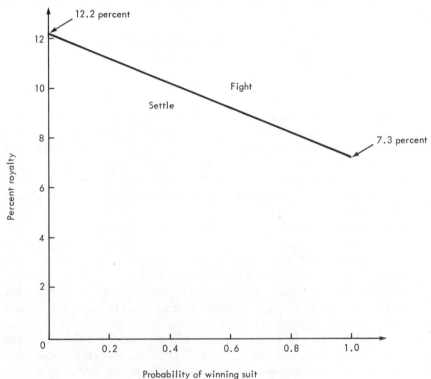

and the additional legal expenses in the event of appeals. The result of this analysis was the revised break-even curve shown in Exhibit 2, which strengthened the conclusion that any reasonable settlement would be preferred to going to court. (The interested reader will find the complete analysis in the Appendix.) On the Sunday afternoon following his return to Milwaukee, Mr. Schilling presented his findings to Mr. Purcell in an informal meeting, and the two men began to map a strategy for resolving the suit.

Appendix: Mr. Schilling's Expanded Analysis of *Arrow* vs. *Tolemite* Pretrial Settlement

September 23, 1973

Objective: To determine the range of payment Arrow Industries can afford to pay in pretrial settlement relative to future costs and the probability of success in court.

Conclusion: If the likelihood of winning the trial is between 75 percent and 100 percent, Arrow can pay a pretrial settlement royalty rate of up to 8.5 percent and save money. In fact, Arrow can afford to pay a royalty rate of 7 percent even if the probability of winning the trial is 100 percent, due to the magnitude of future attorneys' fees and subsequent appeals. (See Exhibit 2 for the break-even probability curve.)

Assumptions: 1. Expected proceedings:
      a. If Arrow wins the trial, there is a 90 percent chance that Tolemite will appeal.
      b. If Tolemite wins the trial, there is only a 10 percent chance that Arrow will appeal.
      c. If Arrow wins the trial, there is a 75 percent chance that Arrow will win the appeal.
      d. If Tolemite wins the trial, there is a 75 percent chance that Tolemite will win the appeal.
  2. Future attorneys' fees and court costs will be:
      a. For the trial—$50,000.
      b. For the appeal:
          (1) If Arrow wins the trial—$25,000.
          (2) If Tolemite wins the trial—$50,000.
  3. Exposure to liability:
      a. Past liabilities.
          (1) If Tolemite wins the trial, it will seek 10 percent of sales 1970–73—total liabilities of $89,100.
          (2) Tolemite will settle past liabilities prior to the trial at the same royalty rate applied in future sales. (See 3*b*(2) below.)
      b. Future royalties.
          (1) If Tolemite wins the trial, it will seek 10 percent of future sales.

(2) The Tolemite pretrial settlement royalty requirement is unknown but will be approached in this
analysis as that rate at which Arrow industries
would "break even" in the alternative of facing the
costs and risks of trial. (See Exhibit 2.)

4. Actual royalty costs involved:

   a. C. K. Coughlin will continue to produce 17,000 pounds
       of Varacil per year for the next seven years (the remain-
       ing life of the patent).

   b. The price/pound for Varacil will erode as expected and
       produce the total sales shown in Table A–1.

   c. In this industry of fixed costs and volume and severe
       pressure upon price, BARD will possess a competitive
       advantage directly proportional to the royalty differential
       between itself and C. K. Coughlin. The assumption is
       that it will lower price rather than simply absorb extra
       profit. The extent of BARD's use of this advantage and
       its significance to C. K. Coughlin profitability will be
       illustrated in the analysis.

   d. The "value of money" to the corporation is approxi-
       mately 10 percent.

Analysis: The object of this analysis is to define, in general terms, the
relationship between the future expenses and risks faced in the
Tolemite suit and the cost of an immediate settlement. An attempt has been made to break the overall problem into a number
of smaller events and action alternatives and to assess reasonable ranges of event probability and consequence; these elements are then related mathematically to obtain a solution.

There can be a substantial advantage in this approach in illu-
minating the basic issues which generally remain submerged in a
single assessment of the entire solution. There is also a potential danger in quantification and simplification of complex problems—the result is apparently so precise and straightforward
that it can be very easily overlooked that this result is no better
than the assumptions upon which it is based.

Based on the above assumptions and the decision diagram
shown in Exhibit A–1 the following costs were calculated:

1. Costs associated with Endpoint ① (Arrow wins trial,
    Tolemite appeals, Arrow wins appeal).

    Present value of 4 percent lost competitive advantage
    (see Table A–1) . . . . $ 56,900
    Appeal costs   25,000
    Trial costs   50,000

    Total $131,900

2. Costs associated with Endpoint ② (Arrow wins trial,
    Tolemite appeals, Arrow loses appeal).

Table A–1
Present value of royalties and lost competitive advantage (dollar amounts in thousands)

Year	Discount* factor	Sales	Cost of 10 percent royalty payments and past liabilities claims		Cost of 4 percent lost competitive advantage		Cost of settlement at 8 percent royalty	
			Royalty (10 percent)	Net present value	Lost competitive advantage (4 percent)	Net present value	Royalty (8 percent)	Net present value
0	1.000	$891†	$89.1	$ 89.1	—	—	$71.3	$ 71.3
1	0.909	340	34.0	30.9	$13.6	$12.4	27.2	24.7
2	0.826	323	32.3	26.7	12.9	10.6	25.8	21.3
3	0.751	306	30.6	23.0	12.2	9.2	24.5	18.4
4	0.683	272	27.2	18.6	10.9	7.4	21.8	14.8
5	0.621	255	25.5	15.8	10.2	6.3	20.4	12.7
6	0.564	255	25.5	14.4	10.2	5.8	20.4	11.5
7	0.513	255	25.5	13.1	10.2	5.2	20.4	10.4
				$231.6		$56.9		$185.1

* Rate = 10 percent.
† Past sales (1970–73).

Present value of royalty payments and past liabilities
    claims at 10 percent (see Table A–1) $231,600
Appeal costs   25,000
Trial costs   50,000
        Total $306,600

3. Costs associated with Endpoint ③ (Arrow wins trial, no appeal).

Present value of 4 percent lost competitive
    advantage .... $ 56,900
Trial costs   50,000
        Total $106,900

4. Costs associated with Endpoint ④ (Arrow loses trial, Arrow appeals, Arrow wins appeal).

Present value of 4 percent lost competitive
    advantage .... $ 56,900
Appeal costs   50,000
Trial costs   50,000
        Total $156,900

Exhibit A–1
Decision diagram

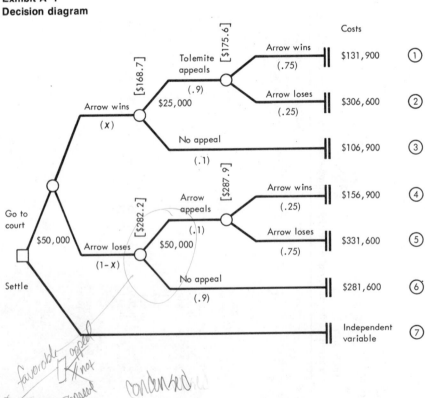

5. Costs associated with Endpoint ⑤ (Arrow loses trial, Arrow appeals, Arrow loses appeal).

Present value of royalty payments and past liabilities
  claims at 10 percent $231,600
Appeal costs   50,000
Trial costs   50,000
                                                   ──────────
     Total $331,600

6. Costs associated with Endpoint ⑥ (Arrow loses trial, Arrow does not appeal).

Present value of royalty payments and past liabilities
  claims at 10 percent $231,600
Trial costs   50,000
                                                   ──────────
     Total $281,600

The next step is to find, for a given settlement rate of Y percent royalty, the probability of winning the trial which will make the expected cost of going to court equal to the cost of the settlement. For example, assuming a settlement rate of 8 percent royalty payments, the present value of the cost of settlement is $185,100 as shown in Table A–1. The break-even probability of winning, X, could be calculated from the following equation:

Expected cost of going to court = Cost of settlement
$168,700 X + $282,200 (1 − X) = $185,100
To get: $X = 0.85$

Solving this equation for different settlement rates resulted in the break-even probability curve shown in Exhibit 2.

Chapter 4

Assessing certainty equivalents by assessing preference for consequences

In the analysis of a decision in which the spread of potential consequences is relatively small (an operating decision), we have said that expected monetary value (EMV) can be used to develop a decision maker's certainty equivalent (CE) for a strategy, and thus provide a guide for action. In cases where the range of consequences is substantial, however, we have noted that EMV would no longer necessarily reflect the decision maker's valuation of the strategy, and thus it would not provide a reasonable guide to action. In such cases we have developed risk profiles of the contending strategies, considering the risk profile as a form of information useful to the decision maker in choosing among strategies. If the strategy with the highest EMV is also the most conservative, the choice is usually clear. But when one strategy has the highest EMV but is more risky than another with a lower EMV, we have indicated only that a judgemental tradeoff has to be made. Can we develop a procedure for determining in such cases what strategy *should* be preferred, given the decision maker's desired degree of conservatism?

If each of the contending strategies had only two possible final results, and they were the same for every strategy, the choice of the preferred strategy would be obvious. If the risk profiles were those shown in Table 4–1, any decision maker, regardless of aversion to risk, would prefer strategy A to strategy B.

The difficulty in deciding among risk profiles arises when the various strategies result in different consequences, as well as different prob-

106

Table 4–1
Risk profiles of strategies A and B

Strategy A		Strategy B	
Possible final results ($)	*Probability*	*Possible final results ($)*	*Probability*
−10,000,000	0.30	−10,000,000	0.40
+50,000,000	0.70	+50,000,000	0.60

abilities of results. It is not clear which of the two strategies shown in Table 4–2 *should* be preferred.

If these consequences were over a range where the decision maker is willing to consider expected monetary value as his or her valuation (or certainty equivalent) of the strategy, the procedure would be straightforward. You can verify that the EMV of strategy X is higher ($10¼ million) than that for strategy Y ($6½ million). This would lead to a choice of strategy X. However, a decision maker in a relatively weak financial position who was not willing to operate on the basis of EMV in this range might well favor the more conservative strategy Y, where the poorest result is not so bad and where there is a smaller probability of loss.

Table 4–2
Risk profiles of strategies X and Y

Strategy X		Strategy Y	
Possible final results ($)	*Probability*	*Possible final results ($)*	*Probability*
−8,000,000	0.30	−5,000,000	0.20
−2,000,000	0.35	0	0.40
+25,000,000	0.15	+15,000,000	0.25
+48,000,000	0.20	+25,000,000	0.15

In the more general case in which there are many strategies and in which the various risk profiles have different possible outcomes and varying probabilities, is there some way, other than by an overall feeling, by which we can help the decision maker decide which risk profile should be preferred, given a particular degree of conservatism or risk aversion: In this chapter we adopt the role of the decision maker to show that there exists a procedure for comparing risk profiles which reduces our problem to one of deciding on our certainty equivalent for a very small number of risk profiles, each of which has only two possible payoffs. Once having done this, we will be able to *calculate* our certainty equivalent for each of the risk profiles in an actual decision and select the strategy we evaluate most highly.

CERTAINTY EQUIVALENTS FOR REFERENCE PROFILES

If we were faced with a number of strategies, each of which had, for example, a worst possible consequence that was no worse than −$10 million and a best consequence no better than +$50 million, we might begin by trying to assess our certainty equivalent for each of a set of simple risk profiles which have these two values as the only possible consequences but which differ in the probability assigned to each consequence. Three such risk profiles are shown in Table 4–3.

Table 4–3
Three reference profiles

Possible final results ($)	Probability	Possible final results ($)	Probability	Possible final results ($)	Probability
−10,000,000	0.75	−10,000,000	0.50	−10,000,000	0.25
+50,000,000	0.25	+50,000,000	0.50	+50,000,000	0.75

Our plan is to obtain *our* certainty equivalents for a large number of such profiles. Having done that, we hope to use the results to infer *our* certainty equivalents for the actual risk profiles involved in a given real-world decision. These certainty equivalents provide us with our evaluation of each potential strategy which gives rise to the corresponding risk profile. At that stage we have only to select as our decision the strategy we evaluate most favorably.

In principle, the procedure we are about to consider would require us to assess our certainty equivalent for a large set of such profiles, each of which has the same two possible results, but where the profiles differ in the probability of the better result (+$50 million), with the complementary probability of the poorer result (−$10 million).[1] In practice, however, we can generally get our needed results with much less effort. To see this, suppose that when faced with the three risk profiles shown in Table 4–3 we had made the following evaluations:

1. We assessed our certainty equivalent for a 25 percent chance at +$50 million and a 75 percent chance at −$10 million as −$5 million. That is, we would be just willing to pay $5 million for certain rather than be committed to a strategy with that risk profile. Notice that the expected monetary value of that profile is +$5 million. In choosing −$5 million instead, we have shown our unwillingness to use EMV as a criterion; we are *risk averse*. Notice also that the CE is based on a subjective assessment. A more

---

[1] Profiles with the same two possible results but differing probabilities, which we will use in assessing certainty equivalents, will be called *reference profiles*.

conservative individual would pick a lower CE; a less risk-averse individual would choose a higher one.

2. Our CE for a 50/50 chance at +$50 million and -$10 million was assessed at +$5 million. (Note that the EMV is +$20 million.)

3. Our CE for a 75 percent chance at +$50 million with a 25 percent chance at -$10 million was assessed at +$25 million (EMV = $35 million).

4. From the very concept of a certainty equivalent, we realize that the CE for a 100 percent chance at +$50 million (with zero percent chance at a loss of $10 million) is +$50 million. In a similar sense, a zero percent chance at a gain of $50 million and hence a 100 percent chance at a loss of $10 million is the same thing as a loss of $10 million for certain.

Table 4-4 summarizes these assessments.

Table 4-4
Certainty equivalents for selected
reference profiles

Probability of better result	Certainty equivalent ($)
0.00	-10,000,000
0.25	-5,000,000
0.50	+5,000,000
0.75	+25,000,000
1.00	+50,000,000

Before we proceed to try to assess our certainty equivalents for a number of other reference profiles with other probabilities of the better result, we might plot the results from the assessments we have already made. Such a graph is usually drawn with the CEs plotted along the horizontal axis and the probability of the better result along the vertical axis. A plot of the data from Table 4-4 results in Figure 4-1.

If we believe that our certainty equivalents for the reference profiles should increase smoothly as the probability of the better result increases, we might conclude that the five points shown in Figure 4-1 allow us to determine, as accurately as we need, our CEs for the other possible reference profiles by simply fairing a smooth curve through the five plotted points. Given any probability of the better result, we could then read the corresponding CE from the smooth graph.

If, on the contrary, we did not feel the five points were enough to tie down our other CEs as well as we would like, we could proceed to assess our valuations for other probabilities of the better result and continue plotting until we felt that for all practical purposes only one smooth curve could be drawn through the points.

Figure 4–1

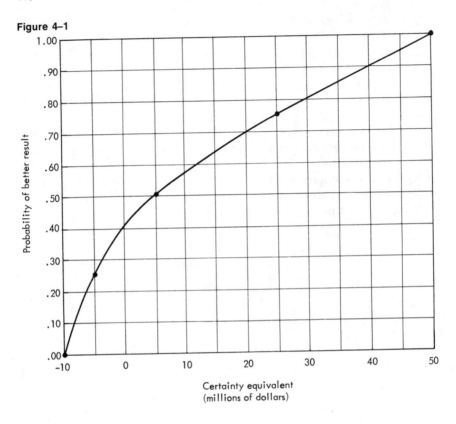

Certainty equivalent
(millions of dollars)

CERTAINTY EQUIVALENTS FOR ACTUAL RISK PROFILES

Once we are willing to accept the curve in Figure 4–1 as approximating closely enough our certainty equivalents for various reference profiles, we can use the results to help evaluate our CEs for the actual risk profiles in our real decision problems. If we were faced with a decision that has been reduced to a choice between the two actual risk profiles given in Table 4–5, the results from Figure 4–1 can aid us in making the choice.

Table 4–5

Risk profile of·strategy X		Risk profile of strategy Y	
Possible final results ($)	*Probability*	*Possible final results ($)*	*Probability*
−8,000,000	0.30	−5,000,000	0.20
−2,000,000	0.35	0	0.40
+25,000,000	0.15	+15,000,000	0.25
+48,000,000	0.20	+25,000,000	0.15
EMV = $10,250,000		EMV = $6,500,000	

Our difficulty in choosing between the two risk profiles, and thus the two strategies, arises because there are a number of different possible results and different probabilities in the two profiles. If we could convert each actual risk profile to its equivalent reference profile (i.e., a reference profile with the same certainty equivalent as the actual profile), the choice would be easy. We would simply choose the reference profile with the greater chance of winning.

Let us look, one at a time, at each of the possible results from the risk profile of strategy X.

1. The worst result is a loss of $8 million. Referring back to Figure 4–1, we can see that, based on our assessments, −$8 million is the CE for us of a reference profile with a 10 percent probability of +$50 million and thus a 90 percent probability of −$10 million. We obtain this data by going across to −$8 million on the horizontal axis, going up to the curve, and reading across on the vertical axis to determine the probability of the better outcome (+$50 million). This implies that we could substitute for −$8 million a situation in which we had a 10 percent chance at +$50 million and a 90 percent chance at −$10 million, and this would not make the strategy more or less attractive to us. Noting this equivalency, we could conclude that a 30 percent chance of −$8 million from the actual risk profile is the equivalent to us of a (.3) (.1) = .03 chance at +$50 million and a (.3) (.9) = .27 chance at −$10 million.

This can be shown in the following set of diagrams:

a. The .30 probability of a loss of $8 million can be diagrammed as:

$$\bigcirc \!\!\!\!\!\!\!\!\underset{}{\overset{(.30)}{\rule{3cm}{0.4pt}}}\!\!\!\dashv -\$8,000,000$$

b. From Figure 4–1, where we found that −$8 million was the CE for a .10 probability of +$50 million and a .90 probability of −$10 million we can obtain the following equivalent diagram:

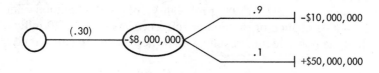

c. By combining the probabilities, we find that this in turn is equivalent to:

2. Similarly, we can read from Figure 4–1 that −$2 million for certain has the same value to us as a 35 percent chance at +$50 million, with a 65 percent chance at −$10 million. We can thus calculate that in the actual risk profile of strategy X, we could substitute, for a .35 probability of −$2 million, a .1225 probability of +$50 million, that is, (.35 × .35), and a .2275 chance of −$10 million, that is, (.35 × .65).

In diagram form, this is:

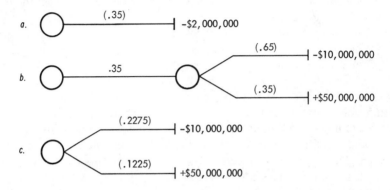

3. The third consequence in our actual risk profile for strategy X was +$25 million. Again going across to $25 million on the horizontal axis of Figure 4–1, going up to the curve, and reading across on the vertical axis, we see that we would be indifferent between $25 million for certain and a .75 chance at $50 million, with a .25 chance at −$10 million. Substituting this equivalence, we see that, for us, a .15 probability of a gain of $25 million has the same value as a .1125 chance at +$50 million (.15 × .75), and a .0375 chance at −$10 million (.15 × .25).

Can you develop the equivalent to this argument using appropriate diagrams?

4. Finally, you can verify that the .20 probability of a result of +$48 million in the actual risk profile of strategy X has the same attractiveness to us as a .2 × .99 = .198 probability of +$50 million and a .2 × .01 = .002 chance of the poorer reference result of −$10 million.

Each of the possible final results with its accompanying probability has

Table 4–6

Actual risk profile			
Possible final results ($)	*Probability*	*Equivalent probability on +$50,000,000*	*Equivalent probability on −$10,000,000*
−8,000,000	0.30	0.0300	0.2700
−2,000,000	0.35	0.1225	0.2275
+25,000,000	0.15	0.1125	0.0375
+48,000,000	0.20	0.1980	0.0020
	1.00	0.4630	0.5370

now been converted into an equivalent pair of probabilities on the better and poorer results in the reference profile. We can now find the reference profile which is equivalent for us to the actual profile of strategy X. The process of this conversion becomes apparent when we summarize the information from point 1 above in Table 4–6.

We can therefore conclude that, for us, given the risk aversion shown in our assessments leading to Figure 4–1, the actual risk profile of strategy X is the equivalent of the reference profile in Table 4–7.

Table 4–7

Possible final results ($)	Probability
−10,000,000	0.537
+50,000,000	0.463

Going back to Figure 4–1, we can now find that a reference profile with a probability of the better result of .463 has a CE to us of about +$3 million.

The calculation leading to the particular reference profile that is the equivalent of an actual risk profile can be made routine. The probability of the better result in the reference profile that corresponds to a given certainty equivalent can be defined as our *preference* value for that CE, relative to the two results in the reference profile. Thus in this example we would say that .75 was our preference value for $25 million relative to +$50 million and −$10 million. With that definition we could observe that the probability of the better result in the two resultant reference profiles can be found by converting each result in the actual risk profile to its corresponding preference value and then averaging (calculating the expected value), using the probabilities from the actual risk profile as weights. For strategy Y (see Table 4–5 above) we could lay out the calculation of the equivalent reference profile as shown in Table 4–8.

Table 4–8

Possible final results ($)	Probability	Preference (see Figure 4–1)	Preference × probability
−5,000,000	0.20	0.25	0.05
0	0.40	0.40	0.16
+15,000,000	0.25	0.64	0.16
+25,000,000	0.15	0.75	0.1125
			0.4825

You can verify that we could have found the .4825 value obtained in the table with the more laborious type of procedure we used for strategy X, instead.

Since there are only two possible results in our reference profile, if the probability of the better result is .4825, the probability of the poorer result must be its complement, or .5175. Thus, the actual risk profile for strategy Y is, for us, equivalent to the reference profile shown in Table 4–9.

Table 4–9

Possible final results ($)	Probability
– 10,000,000	0.5175
+ 50,000,000	0.4825

Finally, if we compare the reference profiles for strategies X and Y in Table 4–10, we find that our choice has been made easy. Since there are only two possible results and they are the same for both strategies, anyone should prefer the strategy with the higher probability of the better result. In this case they should prefer the reference profile corresponding to the actual risk profile of strategy Y to that of strategy X.

Table 4–10
Reference profiles for strategies X and Y

Strategy X		Strategy Y	
Possible final results ($)	Probability	Possible final results ($)	Probability
– 10,000,000	0.5370	– 10,000,000	0.5175
+ 50,000,000	0.4630	+ 50,000,000	0.4825

The certainty equivalent for this reference profile, which is equivalent to the actual profile of Y, can be obtained by reading from the probability scale at .4825 to the curve and down to a CE of about $4 million. To state we prefer strategy Y to strategy X is thus saying only that we prefer a strategy whose CE to us is worth $4 million to one we evaluate as worth $3 million.

You may recall that if the decision involving the choice of strategy X or Y had been an operating decision for us, we would have evaluated each strategy with its expected monetary value and chosen Strategy X ($10¼ million v. $6½ million). We have now seen that if we wish to be consistent with the degree of risk aversion indicated by our assessments of Figure 4–1, we should in fact prefer the risk profile of strategy Y.

This procedure for taking into account our desired degree of risk aversion in selecting among alternative strategies consists of four steps:

1. Determine the risk profile for each of the competing strategies based on the evaluation of consequences and the assessment of probabilities involved in the particular decision.
2. Assess a preference curve for reference consequences at least wide enough to encompass all of the consequences in all of the actual risk profiles.
3. For each strategy, convert the actual risk profile to an equivalent reference profile and determine the certainty equivalent of each strategy by reading from the preference value to the certainty equivalent scale on the preference curve.
4. Select as your decision the strategy with the highest certainty equivalent. Note that the certainty equivalent for each strategy is *your* certainty equivalent based on *your* preference curve and desired degree of conservatism.

ASSESSING PREFERENCE VALUES

A critical element in our procedure for choosing among actual risk pofiles is our ability to assess responsibly our certainty equivalents for various reference profiles. In the preceding section we arbitrarily selected the two consequences in the reference profiles. We assumed that we could indicate our CEs for a few selected profiles and that we would be willing to accept the curve faired through the assessed points as indicating the CEs for all of the other reference profiles in the set. In this section we will explore procedures which experience and research have shown to facilitate the responsible assessment of preference values.

Assessing certainty equivalents

In the preceding section we assessed our certainty equivalent for three reference profiles: one with a .25 probability of the better reference consequence, one with a .50 chance at the better consequence, and one with a .75 probability of the more favorable result. Experience has shown that most people find it easier to decide on their CEs when the chances of each of the two consequences are equal (.50 and .50). They find it much harder to assess their CEs when the probabilities on the two reference consequences are not equal (e.g., a probability of .25 on the better result and thus .75 on the poorer result).

For this reason, rather than assess our CEs for several profiles with the same reference consequences and different probabilities, we find it easier to assess them for several profiles with carefully selected different pairs of reference consequences, where equal probabilities (.50 and .50) are placed on the two reference results for each profile. This procedure, called *chained assessment*, would work in the following manner in the example where we wished, ultimately, to obtain our CEs for the set of reference profiles with consequences of −$10 million and +$50 million.

1. We would first assess our CE for a reference profile with a .50 probability at −$10 million and a .50 probability at +$50 million. As previously, we will assume that our answer to this question is a CE of +$5 million.

2. We might then proceed to ask for our CE for a reference profile with a .50 probability of the same poorer consequence of −$10 million and with a .50 probability of a different better consequence of +$5 million. (The selection of the +$5 million was not arbitrary. It was selected because it was our CE from the first assessment.) If we were to assess our CE for this second reference profile at, for example, −$5 million, we would be saying that we would be indifferent between a certain loss of $5 million and a risk profile with a .50 chance of a loss of $10 million and a .50 chance of a gain of $5 million.

3. Based on the two assessments made above, we can now *infer* our evaluation of a reference profile with a .75 probability of a loss of $10 million and a .25 chance at a gain of $50 million. The reasoning can be shown in the following sequence of diagrams:

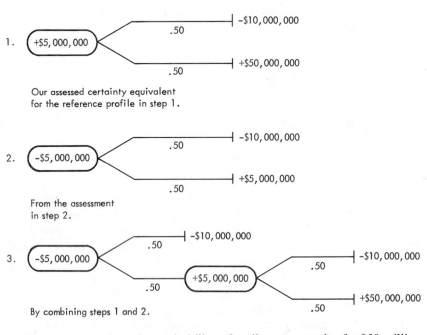

1.   Our assessed certainty equivalent
    for the reference profile in step 1.

2.   From the assessment
    in step 2.

3.   By combining steps 1 and 2.

If we now calculate the probability of ending at a result of +$50 million we find it is .5 × .5 = .25. Thus the preceding diagram is, for us, equivalent to:

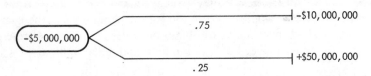

An extension of this reasoning allows us to assess a certainty equivalent for a set of three reference profiles, each of which has the same reference results but a probability of the better result of .25, .50, and .75, respectively. This can be done by directly assessing three reference profiles, each of which has a 50/50 chance on its two results and is thus easier to assess then if the reference result were fixed and the probability varied. If we denote the worse reference consequence in the profile as V_0 and the better reference consequence as V_1, the chaining procedure follows the following three steps:

1. We directly assess our CE for a reference profile that has a .50 probability of V_0 and a .50 probability of V_1. Let us symbolize this value as $V_{.5}$. (In our example V_0 is $-\$10$ million, V_1 is $+\$50$ million, and $V_{.5}$ is $+\$5$ million.)

2. Next we directly assess our CE for a 50/50 profile on V_0 and $V_{.5}$. This certainty equivalent is our valuation of a profile with a .25 chance at V_1 and a .75 chance at V_0. Let us denote this as $V_{.25}$. (In our example $V_{.25}$ is $-\$5$ million.)

3. Finally, we assess our CE for a 50/50 chance at $V_{.5}$ and V_1. This CE is then also our CE for a profile with a .75 chance at V_1 and a .25 chance at V_0—call it the $V_{.75}$ certainty equivalent ($+\$25$ million in our example).

To the extent that we feel more comfortable in making our valuation of 50/50 reference profiles rather than evaluating reference profiles with unequal probabilities, this method of chained assessment should be more reliable than the direct assessment described previously.

Choice of reference consequences

Before we can assess a curve showing our certainty equivalents for the complete range of reference profiles for use in analyzing a particular decision problem, we must decide what two consequences to use in our reference profiles. In the earlier example a choice had been made to select $+\$50$ million as the better of the two consequences and $-\$10$ million as the worse consequence. We shall call these extreme consequences our *reference consequences*.

Concerning the choice of these two values, only two facts are immediately apparent. First, the better reference results must be at least as good as the best result in any of the actual risk profiles being compared, otherwise we could not substitute for that result the equivalent reference profile and develop our comparison. And second, for a similar reason, the worse reference result must be at least as bad as the worse result in any of the actual risk profiles being compared.

Although these are the only theoretical requirements for the selection of the reference consequences, it would not be safe to say that any pair of consequences that meets these requirements would be as good as any other pair that meets them. If we are to assess our certainty equivalents for reference profiles with the consequences of $-\$10$ million and $+\$50$

million, we might then employ the results to evaluate a series of actual risk profiles in which the worst consequence was −$980,000 and the best +$1½ million. We could also have evaluated the same actual risk profiles after having assessed a certainty equivalent for reference lotteries involving a worse consequence of −$1 million and a better consequence of +$2 million. Would our two analyses have led to the same conclusion? If not, which should we believe?

There is no theoretical proof, but a lot of empirical evidence, to demonstrate that the two procedures would almost certainly lead to internally inconsistent results and could well lead to different decisions. At this point we may be tempted to conclude that the results of a preference analysis of a decision problem are meaningless because they could depend heavily on an apparently arbitrary choice of the reference consequence. Let us see if this is really so. More specifically, let us see whether there is some way of distinguishing between "bad" reference consequences that may yield meaningless results and "good" reference consequences that yield results in which the decision maker can place real confidence.

To look at this question, we will define as a risk premium for a particular risk profile *the difference between the expected monetary value of the profile and the decisionmaker's assessed certainty equivalent.* Thus if we had a risk profile with a .50 probability of −$10 million and a .50 probability of +$50 million and had assessed our CE as +$5 million recognizing that the EMV was +$20 million, the risk premium would be $20 million − $5 million = $15 million. Risk premiums for any profile are thus defined by:

$$\text{Risk premium (RP)} = \text{Expected monetary value (EMV)}$$
$$- \text{Certainty equivalent (CE)}$$

For conservative behavior, risk premiums are positive. If some decision maker assessed for a given profile a CE greater than the EMV, the risk premium would be negative and the decision maker would be described as risk seeking.

When we assess our certainty equivalents for various reference profiles with reference consequences of −$10 million and +$50 million, our assessments rest in a sense on our desired risk premiums for that "broad" risk. If we assessed our CEs for another set of reference profiles, with reference consequences of −$1 million and +$2 million, our results would rest ultimately on our risk premiums for the relatively "narrow" risks of either a loss of $1 million or a gain of $2 million. It has been consistently observed that *virtually every decision maker's judgmentally assessed risk premiums for narrow (but nontrivial) risks are far too large to be logically consistent with that same decision maker's judgmentally assessed risk premiums for broad risks.* By "too large to be logically consistent," we mean that any result that agrees with the assessed RPs for broad risks will imply RPs for narrow risks that are much smaller than those directly assessed by the decision maker.

Suppose now that we do in fact discover that our judgmentally assessed RPs for narrow risks are substantially too large to be logically consistent with our judgmentally assessed RPs for broad risks. *Whether or not* we propose to analyze our decision problem by use of a preference analysis, we will presumably want our general behavior under uncertainty to be internally consistent (or "coherent"). Therefore, we will feel that we ought either to reduce our RPs for narrow risks, increase our RPs for broad risks, or compromise and do some of both.

There is no mathematical or logical argument to tell us just which of our various RP assessments should be revised, and by how much, in order to make the whole set of assessments coherent. It is, however, an observable fact that virtually all responsible decision makers who face problems of this sort and think seriously about them finally decide that they are much more confident about the "rightness" of their RPs for broad risks than they are about the rightness of their RPs for narrow risks. Accordingly, they leave their RPs for broad risks essentially unchanged and adjust their RPs for narrow risks downward.

The reason for this greater confidence in the rightness of RPs for broad risks is probably the following. When decision makers assess a CE for a very broad risk, they can really *feel* ("internalize") the meaning to them of the various consequences involved. If the uncertainty is an even chance at fixed income of $10,000 or $100,000 for life, we can actually *visualize* the life-style we will have with either of these incomes, *visualize* the life-style we would be just willing to accept in exchange for the risk, and then assess our certainty-equivalent income by estimating the income required to support our certainty-equivalent life-style.

When, on the contrary, we are asked to assess our CE for a narrow risk—for example, one giving even chances at incomes of $30,000 and $31,000—we ordinarily cannot really feel anything at all because there is nothing real to feel. A person currently enjoying an income of $31,000 can live on $30,000 by making a few minor adjustments. A person currently getting by on $30,000 will be only imperceptibly better off with $31,000. What almost certainly happens, therefore, when we are asked to assess our CE for even chances at $30,000 and $31,000 is that we first compute EMV and then reach into the air and pull down some seemingly "reasonable" RP to use in computing $CE = EMV - RP$.

Whenever a spread is so narrow that the decision maker assesses the CE for a profile by first computing the EMV and then subtracting a "judgmentally" assessed RP, the resulting CE is almost certainly meaningless. The only CEs that are meaningful—the only ones that express the way a decision maker really wants to behave under uncertainty—are CEs for profiles so broad that the decision maker assesses the CE directly, without even thinking about EMV.

From the conclusion just reached, it is immediately apparent that when we wish to construct a preference curve for use in analyzing some deci-

sion problem we should not in general start by choosing reference consequences that are respectively equal or nearly equal to the worst and best
consequences in our decision problem. Rather, we should choose reference consequences that are respectively bad enough and good enough for
us to be able really to feel what it would mean to end up, not only with one
or the other of the reference consequences themselves, but also with any
one of the CE consequences that we will have to assess in order to establish the numerical basis for our preference curve.

On the other hand, if we picked reference consequences so large or so
small that we could again not feel what it would be like to end with those
results (e.g., annual income of $5 billion a year for life), we might
expect unreliable results as well. Hence, choosing reference consequences involves striking a balance between values that are too close and
values that are too different.

Decreasing risk aversion

The task of assessing our certainty equivalent for every one of a set of
reference profiles would be prohibitive if every one had to be assessed
individually. What makes the job possible is our willingness to believe
that our certainty equivalents would increase smoothly between the few
we did assess directly as the probability of the better consequence increased. The assessment process is further simplified if we are willing to
impose another nonnumerical requirement on our preference curve. It
may well be that we not only would want our preference curve to increase
smoothly as the probability of the better consequence increased, but also
would want our curve to have a property called *decreasing positive risk
aversion*. If we add this requirement, our three assessments should usually suffice to tie our preference curve down quite tightly.

If in our attitude toward risk we believe that we would never want to
value an uncertain situation at greater than its expected monetary value,
then we would have *positive risk aversion*. There is no theoretical reason
why we *should* have positive risk aversion over any particular range of
consequences. It has been observed, however, that almost all decision
makers who have considered this problem state that they would *want* to
have positive risk aversion in any decision problem they regard as nontrivial.

If we are faced with two strategies, one giving an even chance at $0 or
$1 million, the other giving an even chance at $10 million or $11 million;
most responsible decision makers will in fact assess a smaller risk premium for the second profile than for the first. Try it yourself. What are
your two risk premiums?

More generally, if we add a fixed substantial amount to every possible
consequence of a strategy, it is almost certain we would want to have a
smaller risk premium for the augmented profile than for the original pro-

file. As the added amount becomes greater, we would want our risk premium to get smaller and smaller (but never negative). If we wish an attitude toward risk to have that characteristic we would be specifying a desire for *decreasing positive risk aversion.*

One way to obtain a partial check on whether the preliminary assessments for our preference curve were in substantial violation of the desire for decreasing positive risk aversion is to look at a series of proposals in which the two consequences differ by a fixed amount. Then for each proposal we compute and compare the certainty equivalent, the expected monetary value, and the risk premium. If departures from decreasing positive risk aversion are observed, we may wish to rethink our original assessment of the certainty equivalents.[3]

From the preference curve developed in Figure 4–1, we could develop Table 4–11. At least in the choices shown, the curve did not obviously violate the desire for positive decreasing risk aversion. Had they not had that characteristic, we might want to modify our preliminary assessment and recheck.

Table 4–11
Risk premiums from preliminary preference curve

Consequences with 50/50 probability ($)	Expected monetary value ($)	Certainty equivalent based on preference curve in Figure 4–1 ($)*	Risk premium, EMV − CE ($)
−10,000,000 or 0	−5,000,000	−6,500,000	1,500,000
0 or +10,000,000	+5,000,000	+4,000,000	1,000,000
10,000,000 or 20,000,000	+15,000,000	+15,000,000	0
20,000,000 or 30,000,000	+25,000,000	+25,000,000	0
30,000,000 or 40,000,000	+35,000,000	+35,000,000	0
40,000,000 or 50,000,000	+45,000,000	+45,000,000	0

* Limited by accuracy of reading from Figure 4–1.

Stability of preference curves over time and the selection of a criterion

If we attempt to assess our preference curve for the cash flows potentially involved in a specific decision problem, our degree of risk aversion would undoubtedly be affected by our financial strength at the time of the assessment. If, as an entrepreneur, we had substantial liquid assets, we

---

[3] To check to see if the curve possesses the desired characteristics of positive decreasing risk aversion for *all possible* fixed spreads almost certainly requires a computer program which can (1) check whether our assessments are consistent throughout with decreasing positive risk aversion; (2) explain how they might be employed if they are not consistent; and (3) provide preference values for any other certainty equivalents consistent with our assessments. One such program is described in Robert Schlaifer, *Computer Programs for Elementary Decision Analysis* (Boston: Division of Research, Graduate School of Business Administration, Harvard University, 1971).

would almost certainly demand a different risk premium than we would if we were in a very weak position with relatively low liquid assets. If we were managers in a large, publicly held corporation at a time when anticipated earnings looked very good, we would almost certainly be more aggressive (demand smaller risk premiums) than if our assessment took place when our anticipated earnings were less optimistic.

Rather than assessing our preference curve for a single current decision, we may wish to develop such a curve to describe our policy about risk taking and hope that the policy (and the curve) will remain relevant over some extended period of time. If we assess our preference curve for the cash flows from decisions at a time when we have a given level of financial strength, it will almost certainly be too aggressive in periods of relative financial weakness and not aggressive enough in periods of relatively greater financial strength.

One way by which we might hope to obtain greater stability for our preference curve would involve changing our criterion for evaluating potential consequences of our decisions from cash flows to one which includes our total relevant financial picture. Then, if we were an entrepreneur, we might evaluate the potential consequences of a decision by determining what our net liquid assets would be at each of the possible outcomes and take into account our risk aversion by assessing our preference curves over a range of possible net liquid assets. As our financial fortunes ebbed and flowed, we could take that into account, with the different starting assets which we would add to the relevant cash flows in our risk profiles. We could then still use our same preference curve for various liquid asset positions to incorporate our desired degree of risk aversion into the decisions.

Similarly, if we were a professional manager in a publicly held corporation, we might adopt year-end earnings or year-end earnings per share as our criterion, assess our preference curve for various possible earnings, convert the risk profiles of our strategies to reflect the possible impact on earnings, and evaluate the comparable certainty equivalents for the alternative strategies in that way. Again, as our year-end earnings prospects become brighter or dimmer, we could take that into account, through the impact on our criterion, without requiring the assessment of new preference curves.

OPERATING DECISIONS: EXPECTED MONETARY VALUE AND LINEAR PREFERENCE

In our analyses up to this point, we have argued that when faced with an operating decision, one in which the range of consequences is not "too large," our certainty equivalent for uncertain results could be obtained by calculating the expected monetary value. This value then becomes an appropriate guide to action. We can now look a little more closely at this situation.

If in assessing our CEs for various reference profiles, we always set them equal to their EMV, when we plotted our curve it would turn out to be a straight line. In such a case, we could say that our preference curve was linear over all values between the worse and the better result.

Linear preference is of interest because it can be proven that when preference is linear over all consequences involved in any actual risk profile, then computing our CE for the actual risk profile by the methods described above will yield a result exactly equal to the EMV of the profile. It follows then that if our preference is linear over all the payoffs involved in the actual risk profiles of a decision problem, the certainty equivalents for each profile developed from the preference curve will be equal to the EMV of the various strategies. Noting this, there would be no need in this decision to construct or use a preference curve.

We could then say in a sense that an operating decision is one where, over the range of all the consequences involved, our preference curve would be essentially a straight line. A range of consequences is not "too large" if over that range the preference curve is or would be so close to a straight line that it could be treated for practical purposes as linear.

PREFERENCE ANALYSIS AND THE EVALUATION OF A DECISION DIAGRAM

Up to this point, we have thought of preference analysis and a preference curve as a way of deciding among risk profiles in nonoperating decisions—those in which risk aversion plays a role. If rather than specifying the contending strategies and their risk profiles we wished to select a "best" strategy by analyzing and folding back through a decision diagram, we could incorporate the attitude toward risk shown in our preference curve by a procedure equivalent to that used to determine our certainty equivalent for an actual risk profile. Specifically, we could substitute for the monetary consequence found at each end point on the diagram our preference value read from our preference curve. We could then work backward through the diagram in the usual way, except that we would use the preferences rather than the monetary consequences. Hence we would be calculating expected preference at event nodes and selecting the act with the highest preference (and thus the highest CE) at every act node. The optimal strategy, developed in such a way, is thus also the strategy for which the risk profile has a higher CE than for any other strategy. The mechanics of this procedure are shown in Figure 4–2, using preference values from Figure 4–1.

FIGURE 4–2

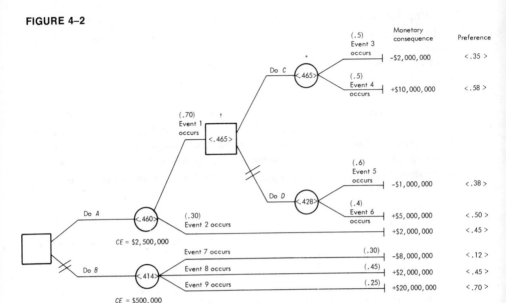

* .465 is .5(.35) + .5(.58), or the expected preference at this event node.
† .465 is the larger of .465 and .428; at a decision node we choose the larger of the preference values.

EXERCISES

4.1. Construct the preference curve for an individual who gave the following as a certainty equivalent for the stated uncertainties:

  a. A certainty equivalent of $1,500 for a 50 percent chance at $6,000 and a 50 percent chance at $0.

  b. A certainty equivalent of $500 for a 50/50 gamble at $0 or $1,500.

  c. A certainty equivalent of $3,500 for a gamble in which there is a 50 percent chance of obtaining $1,500 and a 50 percent chance of obtaining $6,000.

4.2. Determine whether the preference curve constructed in Exercise 4.1 displays decreasing risk aversion.

4.3. Which of the two risk profiles shown in Table A should be preferred by the individual whose preference curve was constructed in Exercise 4.1? What is that individual's certainty equivalent for each option?

Table A

Option A		Option B	
Possible final results ($)	*Probability*	*Possible final results ($)*	*Probability*
200	0.10	1,000	0.20
2,000	0.25	3,000	0.40
4,000	0.50	4,000	0.25
6,000	0.15	5,000	0.15
	1.00		1.00

4.4. Analyze the decision diagram in Figure A, using the preference curve from Exercise 4.1.

FIGURE A

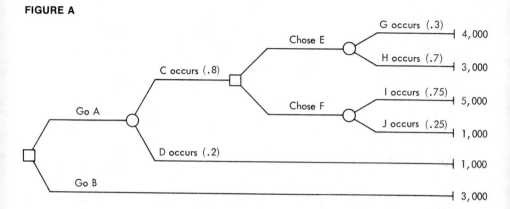

What is that decision maker's desired strategy? What is the decision maker's certainty equivalent value for that strategy?

Case 4–1

Farris Associates

In late December 1969, Mr. Robert Farris had just decided to sell his company, Farris Associates, to General Aeronautics, a large aerospace firm. As the founder and sole owner of Farris Associates, he had been negotiating the sale with General Aeronautics over the last several months. All that remained was to decide which of the three compensation alternatives offered by General Aeronautics would be most attractive to him. Briefly, the three alternatives were to receive all of the compensation in cash, all of the compensation in the stock of General Aeronautics, or a 50–50 combination of the two.

Company background

Robert Farris had worked for 14 years in the aerospace industry, primarily as a systems analyst on large aerospace contracts. Over that span of time he had developed a considerable expertise in applying various analytic techniques to the planning of military and civilian aerospace projects. Discouraged by the narrow focus of his work and eager to strike out on his own, he left his employer in 1966 and became an independent consultant on project planning for several large defense contractors. In 1967 he formally founded Farris Associates and hired several of his previous acquaintances in the industry. In the following years, Farris was successful in landing small government contracts of his own, and his company grew steadily. He continually attempted to shift the focus of his work away from the aerospace industry and toward the civilian programs of other government agencies. His efforts coincided with a widespread public optimism that the sophisticated technology of aerospace programs could be transferred to other fields of endeavor, and he was very successful in obtaining small contracts to study problems of urban housing, mass transportation, and the applications of "systems techniques" to urban and social problems. By late 1969 Farris Associates had established a growing reputation as a small professional consulting firm engaged in "systems analysis" of government-funded public sector programs. The recent sales and earnings record of Farris Associates is shown in Exhibit 1.

126

Exhibit 1
Approximate sales and earnings of recent years

Year	Sales	Earnings
1967	$ 78,000	$ 3,560
1968	385,000	21,820
1969*	1,400,000	61,000

* Estimated figures for the 1969 fiscal year, which will end December 31, 1969.

The offer from General Aeronautics

Meanwhile, the aerospace industry, from which most of Farris' professional staff had come, had fallen upon hard times. The military procurement requirements of the Vietnam War had been winding down; NASA's budget had been severely reduced following the Apollo moon landings; the SST had been delayed; and most commercial airlines were headed for loss years because of reduced passenger travel. Thus, most of the aerospace industry was faced with a severely limited and declining market, with little reason for optimism about the future. Several of the aerospace firms felt that diversification was the only answer to their dilemma, and several firms had already made substantial moves in this direction. General Aeronautics (GA) had decided that it should diversify into several areas, including the application of aerospace technology to other fields of endeavor, notably public sector programs. Because GA had little experience in this area, it decided, as part of its strategy, to acquire several small firms which had already developed the necessary contacts with funding sources in Washington. Because these contacts were so critical to operating in the public sector, it was willing to pay an appreciable premium over what would otherwise be the value of a small consulting firm. This strategy led General Aeronautics to Robert Farris, with whom it began discussions in November 1969. General Aeronautics offered to acquire the ownership of Farris Associates from Robert Farris, provided he would stay on for at least one year as the manager of what would be its new subsidiary. Because it was reasonably short of funds, it preferred to give Mr. Farris stock in General Aeronautics, in exchange for the sole ownership of Farris Associates. In particular, it offered him 60,000 shares of General Aeronautics common stock, which was then selling at $10 per share, paying no dividend. Farris would be legally obligated to hold the stock for almost one year (until December 20, 1970), after which he was free to leave the company, sell the stock, or both. In addition, he would be required to agree not to trade in General Aeronautics stock during the year.

From Farris' point of view, the deal seemed very attractive, except that he perceived an appreciable risk that the value of the stock would decrease substantially in the year before he could sell it. He thus preferred a cash transaction, and had negotiated with General Aeronautics to replace the $600,000 of common stock with an equal amount of cash. As the final outcome of these negotiations, General Aeronautics had offered Farris three alternatives:

1. 60,000 shares of common stock.
2. $500,000 in cash.
3. $250,000 in cash and 30,000 shares of common stock.

Mr. Farris had consulted his accountant, who explained the tax ramifications of these transactions. Assuming that the sale to GA occurred after January 1 and that Mr. Farris sold the stock before December 31, 1970 (which he planned to do), he would have to pay taxes at the end of 1970 on both transactions. In particular, since he would be in a 50 percent tax bracket, he would have to pay the 25 percent capital gains tax on essentially the total of the cash received in the original transaction and the sale of stock. Thus, Mr. Farris' net after-tax cash from the sale of Farris Associates, evaluated on December 31, 1970, would amount to 75 percent of the total of the original cash received and the value of the GA stock when sold in one year, plus whatever after-tax interest was accrued on the original cash during 1970. Mr. Farris was concerned that he would be required to pay installment-estimated tax payments, but his accountant assured him that this would not be necessary due to his low tax liability of the previous year.

Mr. Farris' decision

If Mr. Farris chose to accept the cash, he would not need it for any anticipated transactions during the year; indeed, he planned to invest the cash in tax-exempt municipal securities which matured in one year and yielded 5 percent. The real disadvantage of accepting the common stock was that Mr. Farris had to hold it for almost one year. The market value of the stock would fluctuate during this year, and he felt that its value could be substantially changed by the time he sold it. At $10 per share, the stock was actually very cheap compared to its value in the past five years, so that the price could easily rise. On the other hand, the overall prospects of the aerospace industry were not good. General Aeronautics had already suspended its dividend payments because of its tight cash situation, and some stock market analysts believed that things could easily get worse rather than better. On balance, and after assimilating as much information as possible about the prospects for GA's stock, Farris thought that the stock price was equally likely to go up or down and that the possible price movements were large. As a "first cut," he assessed the equiprobable values shown in Exhibit 2 for the value of GA's stock in one year.

Exhibit 2
Probability of stock price in one year

Percent increase or decrease	Stock value	Probability
+50%	$15	0.20
+20	12	0.20
+ 0	10	0.20
−20	8	0.20
−50	5	0.20

After assessing the probabilities of various stock price movements, the dimensions of Mr. Farris' decision became a little clearer to him. On an expected value basis, the value of the stock was greater than the cash, even after including the interest that the invested cash would accumulate over the year. Thus on an expected value basis, he should certainly favor the offer of common stock. On the other hand, the common stock offer entailed a substantially greater risk, and the real question was whether this undesirable risk outweighed the greater expected value.

Mr. Farris recalled that on several occasions he had used preference theory to evaluate risks for several of the clients of Farris Associates. He therefore decided to use this same technique to help him with his current problem. Removing the various probabilities from his mind, he attempted to discern just how much relative value he would ascribe to the possible ''personal net cash positions'' he might find himself in after taxes, as of December 31, 1970. His current available cash was balanced by a bank loan he intended to repay, so that his net cash position one year later would be essentially equal to the after-tax proceeds of the sale to GA plus any accrued interest. After the one year, he intended to invest the cash in safe long-term investments, perhaps utility bonds. He hoped that the yield of these investments would allow him to live in the style to which he had grown accustomed, thus leaving him free to pursue other interests. While it obviously would not be a complete disaster if this were not possible, Mr. Farris thought it would be a substantial disadvantage if he lost a major portion of the stock value. To assess his preference for various uncertain levels of cash assets, Mr. Farris considered, first, a 50/50 gamble between $200,000 and $800,000 receivable in one year, and estimated the certain amount of cash for which he would just be willing to trade this gamble one year later. Continuing the process, he considered the other 50/50 gambles shown in Exhibit 3. Using these data, he then constructed his preference function for cash assets one year later. This preference function is shown in Exhibit 4.

Gathering his probability estimates and the preference curve which expressed his attitude toward risk, Mr. Farris sat down to determine which of the three alternative terms of sale seemed most desirable to him.

Exhibit 3
Mr. Farris' assessments of certainty equivalents for 50/50 gambles

Gamble	*Mr. Farris certainty equivalent*
50/50 gamble between $200,000 and $800,000	$320,000
50/50 gamble between $200,000 and $320,000	$240,000
50/50 gamble between $320,000 and $800,000	$470,000

Note: All of these assessments apply to Mr. Farris' net cash position on December 31, 1970, one year after his decision. The "certainty equivalent" is that amount of cash which he would just be willing to trade, on that date, for the gamble described on the left.

Exhibit 4
Mr. Farris' preference curve on the basis of his certainty equivalent assessments

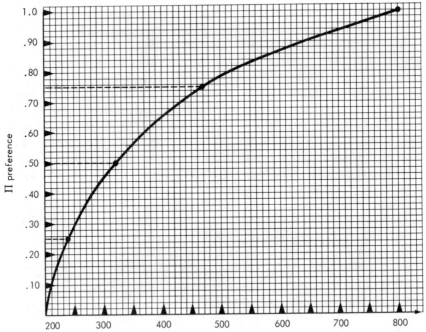

Net cash assets as of December 31, 1970 ($000)

Case 4–2

Waterman Engineering Corporation

On August 14, 1969, Mr. L. E. Waterman had only a few more days in which to make up his mind whether or not to sign a proposed contract with a syndicate in the city of Norwood. The contract provided that the Waterman Engineering Corporation, of which Mr. Waterman was president, should build a community television antenna according to certain specifications on a site some distance from the city and link it to a distributing point near the center of the city; the local syndicate would then pay Waterman in cash for the complete system and take over its operation.

The Waterman Engineering Corporation's sole business was the design and construction of community antenna systems to service towns and small cities beyond the reach of existing television broadcast facilities. The company had been founded by Mr. L. E. Waterman in 1965, after he had received a master's degree in civil and electrical engineering from Georgia Tech in June 1963 and then spent two years working in the Broadcasting Facilities Department of a major television network. Its initial capital had consisted of $15,000 paid in by Mr. Waterman's father, a successful construction contractor. Since the founding of the company, all of its stock had been held by members of the Waterman family. The company's assets on August 14, 1969, amounted to $90,000,[¹] of which $57,000 represented cash, while the remainder represented the net book value of the construction and office equipment. The firm's profit to date for the 1969–70 fiscal year (Waterman's fiscal year was May 1–April 30) was $89,000, of which $40,000 had been used to repay the Waterman family for loans made in the 1968–69 fiscal year.

In order to conserve working capital,[1] Waterman had a firm policy of avoiding involvement in the ownership and operation of any antenna system once it had been completed and tested. In developing a new location, the company obtained a franchise from the city government and then, before committing any resources to actual construction, tried to interest local business executives and investors in forming a local company to purchase and operate the system as soon as it was completed and proved out. When Waterman failed to organize a local group which would contract for purchase of the system on satisfactory terms, he invariably preferred to forfeit the franchise rather than tie up his capital for an indefinite period of time. On August 14, 1969, Waterman held only one franchise,

---

[1] Working capital, also called net current assets, is equal to net liquid assets plus inventories at the lower of cost or market.

Adapted from *Analysis of Decisions Under Uncertainty* by Robert O. Schlaifer (New York: McGraw-Hill Book Company, Inc., 1968), pp. 81–83, 196–198.

the one in the city of Norwood, and saw no prospect of getting another one within the next several months. The Norwood franchise would become invalid unless construction "begins not later than September 1 and continues thereafter with no unnecessary or undue delays."

The only suitable location for the antenna at Norwood was at a very substantial distance from the city, and therefore it would be more economical to transmit the television signals from the antenna to the distributing point in the center of Norwood by microwave relay than by coaxial cable. Such microwave transmission required a license from the Federal Communications Commission (FCC), however, and because there was a local television station in Norwood, it was not at all certain what action the FCC would take concerning Waterman's application for a license. The license might be granted without restrictions, but in similar circumstances in the recent past the FCC had sometimes restricted the license to prohibit transmission of programs that the local station wished to rebroadcast by use of kinescope recordings and had sometimes refused to grant any license at all. The examiner's report on the Waterman case was not to be rendered until December 15, and Waterman knew of no way of getting any advance indication of the examiner's conclusion; he felt sure, however, that the commission would accept the examiner's recommendation in this case, whichever way the examiner ruled.

The granting of a restricted license would be disadvantageous to Waterman because the proposed contract with the Norwood syndicate specified a price of only $120,000 for a system with a microwave connection and a restricted license, whereas it specified a price of $150,000 for a system with a microwave connection and an unrestricted license. The syndicate would also pay $150,000 for a system with connection by coaxial cable, over which the FCC would have no control, but whereas construction of the system would cost only about $110,000 if a microwave link was used, it would cost about $180,000 if a cable connection was necessary. Although no money would have to be spent on equipment for either type of connection until after the examiner's report was received on December 15, the terms of the franchise meant that the antenna itself, which accounted for about $80,000 of the total cost, would have to be nearly if not quite completed before that date.

On August 15, 1969, before he had made up his mind whether or not to sign the contract with the local group in Norwood, Mr. L. E. Waterman learned quite unexpectedly that a competitor, the Electronics Service Corporation, was willing to sell him a franchise and contract held by Electronics in the city of Prescott; the price would be $10,000 cash. Waterman had offered to buy the franchise and contract at that price some months before, but at that time Electronics had flatly refused to sell. Electronics now indicated that it had another offer for the franchise and contract, in the amount of $9,000, which it would accept if Waterman did not close the deal within one week. Although the Prescott Franchise had come along unexpectedly, Waterman felt quite sure that the chances of his being offered still another franchise within the next several months were virtually nil.

The contract with the local operating group at Prescott called for an antenna to be erected on a hill just outside the city and to be connected by cable with a distributing point in the city. The price to be paid by the group for the completed system was $140,000, and from the investigation he had conducted before making his original offer, Waterman had concluded that he could build the complete system for about $90,000, provided that he could get by with an antenna 100 feet high, as he hoped he could. There was some risk, however, that an antenna only 100 feet high would not receive a signal of the strength and clarity required by the contract, since a mountain range partially obstructed the antenna's reception. If the 100-foot antenna did prove insufficient, Waterman was certain that for an additional cost of $70,000 he could increase its height to a point where the signal was not obstructed; virtually none of this extra cost could be saved by building the higher antenna to begin with.

The local group and the city government had agreed to allow Electronics to sell the franchise and contract to Waterman. The franchise was valid, provided that the system was in operation on April 1, 1970, and Waterman felt absolutely sure that construction would take less than three months even if he had to work on the Norwood job at the same time and even if the height of the antenna at Prescott had to be increased. Waterman would, however, have to deposit $5,000 with the operating group within one week of taking over the contract, and he would have to agree that if he should fail to complete the system, the deposit would be forfeited in lieu of any suit the operating group might have brought.

On August 16, 1969, Mr. L. E. Waterman decided to make a systematic analysis of the decision problem he faced regarding the proposed contract with a syndicate in the city of Norwood and the offer he had received from the Electronics Service Corporation. To do so, he first assessed the following probabilities:

License for microwave connection at Norwood:

Granted without restrictions 0.5
Granted with restrictions 0.2
Refused 0.3
                                           ───
                                           1.0

Increase in height of antenna at Prescott:

Necessary 0.4
Unnecessary 0.6
                                       ───
                                       1.0

After thinking more carefully about the possible consequences of his possible courses of action, Mr. Waterman decided that his certainty

Exhibit 1
L. E. Waterman's preference assessments (certainty
equivalents for 50/50 gambles for net liquid assets)

Gamble consequences		*Certainty equivalent*
1. $110,000	$25,000	$40,000
2. $150,000	$40,000	$60,000
3. $ 40,000	$25,000	$30,000

equivalents for some of the gambles he might face would not be at all close to his corresponding mathematical expectations. After some further thought he decided to base his analysis on his preferences for net liquid assets on April 1, 1970, and after selecting $110,000 and $25,000 as his reference terminal values, he stated his certainty equivalents as shown in Exhibit 1 and the preference curve which is shown in Exhibit 2. In doing so,

Exhibit 2
L. E. Waterman's preferences for net liquid assets relative to $110,000 and $25,000 in
the presence of his base nonmonetary assets

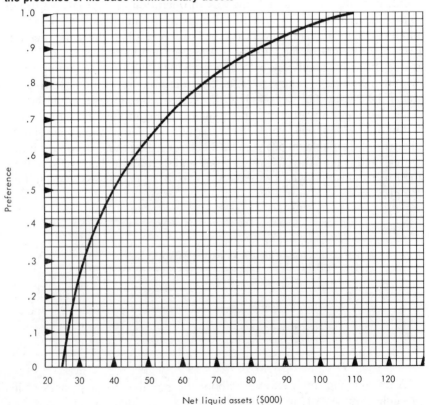

Net liquid assets ($000)

he took his current nonmonetary assets as his base, assuming that none of the acts or events in the decision problem he was facing would in any way alter this base. Mr. Waterman expected that in the coming fiscal year, as in the previous one, the Waterman Engineering Corporation would be taxed at 48 percent.

Case 4–3

Retlon Division

The Midwest Corporation
Retlon Division
Chicago, Illinois
November 3, 1968

John:

As you know, since I left the Business School in 1958 I have worked for the Midwest Corporation at various locations. You may not know that I've been made the General Manager of our newly formed Retlon Division. Retlon is a chemical product we sell to another company which uses it in producing a more complex product for the paint industry. Retlon aids substantially in maintaining pigments in suspension and all but does away with the need for shaking. It's a great product, and I plan to do everything I can to make this division a profitable one.

Right now I have a particularly sticky decision to make on the pricing of Retlon. I feel that the problem is amenable to quantitative analysis, but I'm just not sure how to go about it. I'll try in this letter to describe the essential features of the problem and give you odds on certain outcomes. However, I know that such an analysis can get complex quickly, so I've arbitrarily cut down on the number of things I can do and things that can happen, etc. The essence is maintained, and once I see how to solve this simplified problem, I'm sure I can do it in more detail.

Midwest has a standing policy not to enter the retail business. We manufacture raw inputs and sell to converters. We do, however, a very thorough job of marketing. Retlon, for instance, was test-marketed in several cities last fall. We go to the converter and say, "Here's the market; here's the product; here's how to convert it; what do you say?" What the converter says, of course, depends on our pricing decision. Right now I'm trying to figure that one out.

Retlon is good, but initially it's not going to sweep the paint market. I figure from the marketing reports that the market is somewhat elastic in the high-volume end. A lower price will probably mean that we can replace more of the existing products. A few paint manufacturers will probably try it as long as the price to them is within reason. Actually it represents a relatively small portion of their total costs.

Right now the Retlon Division is in its pilot stage. We are selling to only one converter this year. If the division makes a satisfactory return, we will expand it and develop more converters so as to be able to go after the market in a big way. My own position can be substantially affected by the outcome of this pilot operation. If we get a high return, I'll be in a good position to request capital for an expansion. If not, the division may be closed down, and I'll return to the corporate staff.

The essence of the pricing decision is that the price we set to the converter will be fixed by contract throughout the year. The converter's price to the manufacturers is based on our price, and generally this doesn't change during the year. Naturally, the converter's price affects the demand for the converter's product and, ultimately, for ours. We would like to set a high price to the converter and have the converter quote a low price to the manufacturers. Then we would have both high volume and high margin. It just isn't going to work out that way!

To make sure that there are no problems of antitrust action, our Counsel has directed all divisions to bend over backward to avoid any charge of dictating selling prices for a converter's product. Thus, we cannot tell the converter what price to set for the converted product. We have, however, in our sales pitch given the converter our market forecasts based on several prices. These were drawn up by a reputable market research firm and are as unbiased as can be expected. Since the volume-price forecasts are not certain, we asked that the consultant's report reflect this by using probability distributions over the possible volumes, conditional on a given price. The converter is a shrewd operator and can be expected to do a pretty thorough analysis of the price question before setting a price for the year.

I've arbitrarily assumed, for the purposes of the trial analysis, that there are only two prices we can charge for Retlon: $1 and $1.50 per pound. This can be changed later to include many other possibilities. Also, I've arbitrarily set the price the converter will charge to $5 and $6.50 per pound.

Our variable cost in the coming year should be about $0.50 per pound, and our fixed costs around $300,000. If we expand in the future, they could get to be ten times their present size.

Our engineers, in estimating the production costs in the initial proposal to the converter, calculated the converter's fixed costs to be $1,000,000 and the converter's variable cost to be $2 per pound in addition to the cost of Retlon. I feel that these estimates are accurate, and I believe that the converter thinks so too.

I've really used the ax with regard to the volume of the converter's final product at a given price. There are a multitude of possible volumes. I've trimmed it down to two possible volumes for each of two prices, as shown in Table 1.

Table 1
Distribution of volume given converter's price

Price = $5 per pound		Price = $6.50 per pound	
Probability	*Volume*	*Probability*	*Volume*
0.6	600,000	0.5	350,000
0.4	1,200,000	0.5	550,000

The way I see it, we set a price to the converter, the converter sets a price to the manufacturers, and a sales volume occurs that gives both the converter and ourselves a profit (or a loss). The essence of the problem is that the converter doesn't set a price until after we do and that the converter does this in the face of uncertain volume.

Now the converter does other business than Retlon conversion, so a loss does not mean bankruptcy. On the other hand, the converter is far from being an out-and-out gambler. I suppose an insurance agent who was willing to underwrite some of the risks could make some money from the converter. Following this line of reasoning, I asked my production manager, who used to do some conversion work, to help me by simulating with paper and pencil the position of the converter. I asked the production manager to be the converter while I was the Retlon Division. We spent several hours just bargaining with each other and going over the pricing problem. In particular, we tried to obtain a preference function that the converter might have in this particular situation. We used year-end before-tax profit from Retlon conversion as the variable of interest. I've enclosed in Exhibit 1 the preference function that we feel best represents the converter's attitude toward risk.

Exhibit 1
Preference curve of simulated converter

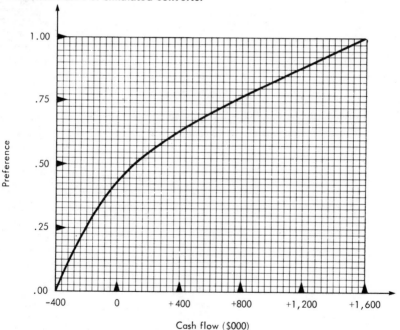

Cash flow ($000)

Since I, myself, am making the decisions on Retlon's price and must live with the consequences, I thought for a while and came up with my own preference for year-end reported profits (before tax), shown in Exhibit 2. While I absolutely do not want to report a loss on this venture, I am willing to gamble in order to show a large return on investment.

Exhibit 2
My own preference for year-end profit

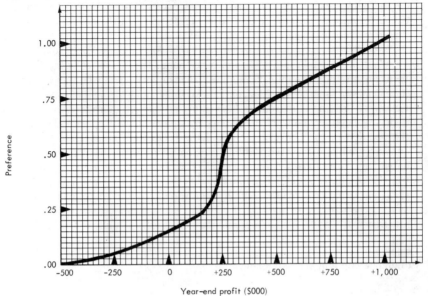

Year-end profit ($000)

Now the question is, How do I systematically go about analyzing this problem, assuming that I have captured the true preference of the converter and that the converter views the possible outcomes and probabilities the way that I have presented them?

I would appreciate your ideas on this problem and hope to hear from you at your earliest convenience. I have attached graphs of the preference curves we came up with.

Yours truly,
Earl J. Williams
General Manager
Retlon Division
Midwest Corporation

Case 4–4A

The National Machine Company (A)

On an afternoon in June 1968, Dan Ellsworth left the office of the Corporate Treasurer, Mr. Edward Holland, armed with what he hoped would be enough information to analyze one of the company's foreign exchange decisions. Dan believed that he could lend some insight into this particular decision, but he also hoped that he could suggest a general framework for considering these foreign exchange decisions in the future.

The company background

The National Machine Company was a large established manufacturer of heavy capital equipment. Though its product line was partially diversified across a number of different types of equipment, it tended to specialize in heavy equipment of an electrical nature, for example, large electric motors, generators, turbines, and electrically powered industrial equipment. Its sales were primarily directed to domestic industrial corporations and utilities, although in recent years it had begun to expand its international sales, particularly to the developed countries of Western Europe, Japan and Australia. National's balance sheet as of December 31, 1967, is shown in Exhibit 1 and its sales and earnings for the past 12 years are shown in Exhibit 2. Like most companies in the cyclical capital goods

Exhibit 1

THE NATIONAL MACHINE COMPANY
Balance Sheet
As of December 31, 1967
($000 omitted)

Assets		Liabilities and Equity	
Cash	$ 4,944	Accounts payable	$ 6,502
Marketable securities	5,892	Accrued income taxes	10,206
Accounts and notes receivable, net.	27,455	Other accrued liabilities	4,744
Prepaid expenses	571		
Inventories	49,263		
Total Current Assets	$ 88,125	Total Current Liabilities	$ 21,452
Miscellaneous investments	1,059	Common stock ($8 Par)	27,528
Property, plant and equipment	48,262	Capital surplus	1,868
Less: Reserve for depreciation	25,436	Retained earnings	65,864
Net Property Account	$ 23,885	Total Stockholder's Equity	$ 95,260
Goodwill, patents	218	Less: Treasury stock at cost	4,484
Total Assets	$112,228	Net Stockholder's Equity	90,776
		Total Liabilities and Equity	$112,228

Exhibit 2
Sales, earnings, and earnings per share

Year	Sales ($ million)	After-tax earnings ($000)	Reported earnings per share
1956	55.3	7,764	2.22
1957	60.1	7,826	2.40
1958	45.2	5,399	1.16
1959	53.9	5,619	1.80
1960	57.3	6,667	1.94
1961	53.2	6,471	1.37
1962	59.9	7,589	1.71
1963	63.3	8,706	2.05
1964	75.4	9,844	2.45
1965	88.6	11,378	3.28
1966	104.3	13,305	3.86
1967	96.4	10,426	3.03

industries, National had generated substantial sales and earnings growth in the economic expansion of the middle 1960s, and its management was optimistic about the prospects for its industry as a whole, and for its own earnings growth in particular, over the next several years.

International sales and the foreign exchange markets

As the small but growing proportion of its sales to foreign customers had increased, several new and different problems were raised for National. Most of the firm's senior managers were executives who had progressed upward through the company, largely on the basis of their experience in established domestic markets. Most of them were just learning of the special problems involved in marketing capital equipment abroad. At several times in the past, outside consultants had suggested that National reorganize its management and establish a separate International Division. As of the year 1968, however, the company was still organized along traditional functional lines, with Vice Presidents of Engineering, Sales, and Production, a Controller, and a Treasurer, all of whom reported to the President. The international marketing problems were handled in the same manner as domestic sales problems, and the Treasurer was responsible for any special problems of international finance.

This raised particular problems for Mr. Holland, the Corporate Treasurer, who was responsible for National's decisions in the foreign exchange markets. Most of the company's sales in a foreign country resulted in a net balance receivable in the local currency of that country. Typical terms of sale of a large electrical generator in Great Britain, for example, might be a significant deposit at the time the contract was signed, and the balance due in pounds sterling 60 days after the final installation of the generator. Mr. Holland's problem arose from the time delay after the contract was signed but before the final payment. If the British pound sterling were devalued in this intervening period, then the sale would result in the contractual revenue in pounds, but a significantly smaller number of dollars. It was possible, therefore, to actually lose money on an ostensibly profitable sale, due to a devaluation. Several large U.S. corporations had sustained severe losses in the British devaluation of 1967, amounting in some cases to a very significant proportion of their net income. Needless to say, the prospect of these losses, in connection with what should have been profitable opportunities, worried National's management and also Mr. Holland.

As Mr. Holland knew, the foreign exchange markets allow corporations to eliminate or reduce these risks of international sales. The foreign exchange markets are places where corporations, governments, or individuals can buy or sell foreign currencies for U.S. dollars. In practice, a large U.S. corporation will generally conduct foreign exchange transactions through its primary banking connections, usually a large bank in New York City. If on a given day, a corporation would like to buy or sell British pounds, it may do so at the "spot rate" continuously quoted in the foreign exchange markets, for example, 2.4183 dollars to the pound, plus a very small transaction charge. Most foreign governments effectively value their currency relative to the U.S. dollar, and attempt to control its value within narrow limits surrounding the official exchange rate. These narrow limits are formed by what are called the "upper peg" and "lower peg" of the exchange rate; and except for unusual crises, a government will buy and sell its own currency in the foreign exchange markets to guarantee that the "spot rate" does not diverge from these limits.[1] When this practice becomes either impossible or too costly for a country, that is, when it concludes that its currency is in some fundamental way "overvalued" relative to the dollar, it may devalue its currency to a lower level where it hopes to be able to maintain an equilibrium.[2] These devaluations are the source of concern to U.S. business executives.

In addition, there is a "forward market" for foreign exchange, where it is possible to buy or sell currencies to be delivered and paid for at some future date. For example, it is usually possible to buy or sell a 90-day forward contract for pounds sterling at a continuously quoted "90-day forward rate," say, 2.4141 dollars to the pound. In 90 days, the seller is obligated to deliver the specified number of pounds to the buyer for the certain exchange rate of 2.4141. This forward foreign exchange market is one method that business executives use to reduce their risks. If

---

[1] Generally speaking, the value is controlled within 1 percent on either side of the explicitly announced value. For example, the pound sterling's nominal exchange rate is $2.40, and the corresponding upper and lower "pegs" are $2.424 and $2.376, respectively.

[2] On the other hand, a currency may be "revalued" upward, if conditions warrant.

a corporation has an account receivable in a foreign currency which is due in 90 days, the corporation may elect to "sell forward" the amount of the payment, thereby removing the risk of devaluation and substituting a certain future revenue in U.S. dollars. This is often called "hedging" the foreign exchange risk. As might be expected, in times when the devaluation of a foreign currency appears imminent, many business executives "hedge" their risks in the forward market, driving the forward rates significantly below the spot rate of the currency. There can thus be a significant "cost" of hedging, particularly at times when a devaluation seems imminent.

Mr. Holland had become familiar with the operation of these foreign exchange markets, and used them on occasion to reduce the risks of National's international business. His policy had generally been to hedge some or all future receivables denominated in a particular foreign currency at a time when a devaluation of this currency seemed relatively likely, but to avoid the costs of hedging at most other times.

The problems in France

National had recently completed a large sale of electric generators to a French firm, and the balance on the terms of sale of 25 million francs (about 5 million dollars at the current rate) was receivable in a little under 30 days. The riots and related events in France in recent weeks had shaken people's confidence in the franc, and the foreign exchange markets reflected this crisis. In particular, the "spot" rate for the franc was 0.2011 U.S. dollars, just marginally above the "lower peg" of $0.2010 where the French government was committed to buy francs rather than let the price fall further. In addition, francs could be bought or sold "forward" 30 days at $0.2000, significantly below the "lower peg."

Mr. Holland believed that people were behaving very irrationally, and that a devaluation was highly unlikely in the existing circumstances. On the other hand, if a devaluation did occur, National was going to lose a significant sum of money. For example, a devaluation of 20 percent would result in a loss of about a million dollars, throwing this particular sale of generators "into the red," but moreover reducing National's annual income by almost 5 percent "overnight." Because of this dire prospect, Mr. Holland was tempted to hedge his risk by selling the 25 million francs in the 30-day forward market and obtaining a sure $5 million. He was troubled, however, by the apparent costs of this step. Assuming that he did not sell the francs forward and that the rather unlikely devaluation did not occur, he could surely exchange the francs in 30 days for at least the "lower peg" value of $0.2010. Selling them forward was therefore going to "cost" National a pretty penny, about $25,000 he figured, which would have to be deducted from the profits of the sale. He wondered whether this wasn't an exorbitant price for protection from what was after all a very unlikely event.

Mr. Holland recalled an occasion earlier that year when the corporate planning staff had helped the senior managers of National with a "probability analysis" of a large investment decision that was then under consideration. Although he wasn't quite sure what to expect in this situation, Mr. Holland believed that some of the ideas used in that analysis might be helpful in sorting through the issues of this foreign exchange decision. He made arrangements to meet later in the day with Dan Ellsworth, a member of the planning staff.

The meeting between Ellsworth and Holland

Dan Ellsworth arrived early in the afternoon and patiently listened while Mr. Holland explained his problem. As the Treasurer talked, Dan observed that the foreign exchange problem was similar in many respects to other uncertainty problems which he had encountered before. When Mr. Holland had finished explaining, Dan jotted down a few quick notes presenting his view of the problem. Excerpts from the ensuing conversation are presented below:

Ellsworth: As I see it, we can analyze this foreign exchange decision, and others like it, using a fairly simple form of probability analysis. The basic problem is that there is substantial uncertainty surrounding the future value of the francs in this sale. What we need to do is estimate the chances that the future value of the franc will be at or near several representative levels, and then see what this means for National.

Holland: That sounds like the same kind of probabilities that you had several of us estimate for sales in that last capital investment decision. I guess that we can give it a try.

Ellsworth: OK, let's take a first cut at the probabilities or chances from the bottom up. What do you think the chances are that the franc will be worth $0.10 in 30 days?

Holland: There's no chance of it. They'd never devalue by that much.

Ellsworth: How about $0.15?

Holland: [After a pause] I think that $0.15 is within the realm of possibility, but it's still highly unlikely. First of all, a devaluation is unlikely, and second of all, it's unlikely that it would be a full 25 percent even if it did occur.

Ellsworth: Let's separate the problem into two parts: the chances that a devaluation will occur and the possible size of a devaluation if it indeed does occur. Assuming that a devaluation occurs, how big is it likely to be?

Holland: Well, that's the easier part of the problem. It seems to me that if it occurs, a devaluation is not likely to be less than 5 percent, for anything less is just not worth the trouble, embarrassment, and political problems it would cause. On the other hand, it is certainly quite unlikely to be as large as 25 percent because I think in everyone's view the franc is not fundamentally that overvalued. I'd say, therefore, that the range of likely devaluation is 5–20 percent. Within this range, it could fall just about anywhere, I suppose.

Ellsworth: Why don't you pick a small number of possible values for the franc which you think are fairly representative of this range?

Holland: [After a pause] As I said, it could fall just about anywhere, but the round numbers 0.16, 0.17, 0.18, and 0.19 dollars to the franc are "representative," I suppose, if I understand the question.

Ellsworth: OK, let's use those four values. Of the four, which do you believe is the most likely, and which is the least likely?

Holland: [After a pause] Now you've got me. I'm really not sure. I think that I'd have to call them all equally likely.

Ellsworth: Let's suppose that you will get a prize of $10,000 if your prediction for the size of the devaluation is very close to the actual value. Would you be willing to base your prediction on a random draw from a hat containing these four estimates?

Holland: I think so, yes.

Ellsworth: Now, on a different aspect, suppose that the franc is not devalued, what do you suppose the "spot rate" will be in 30 days?

Holland: Well, it's not likely to budge much from the "lower peg"; I think $0.2010 is a reasonable estimate.

Ellsworth: OK, let's go on to the harder part of the problem. What is the chance that de Gaulle will devalue the franc at all?

Holland: Well, I think you've skirted the real problem. It seems to me that de Gaulle himself would be extremely unlikely to devalue the franc, at least for two or three months. The real problem in France, I think, is that the de Gaulle government might resign or fall, and who knows what his successor might do?

Ellsworth: Let's assume for the sake of argument that de Gaulle remains in power. What are the chances of a devaluation?

Holland: I'd say virtually zero, at least in the next 30 days.

Ellsworth: And if the de Gaulle government resigns or falls?

Holland: I don't know; just about anything could happen. Politically it's always easier to devalue when you first take office, blame it on the other person, and start with a clean slate yourself. On the other hand, I suppose any successor would realize that the worst time to devalue is when people are expecting it. I'd rate the chances 50/50.

Ellsworth: And what are the chances of the de Gaulle government resigning or falling?

Holland: That's the tough one. I must admit I probably know more about French politics than the average person on the street because I've spent some time in France, and because of my job I follow the political situation pretty closely. But somehow that still leaves me a little uneasy, maybe more uneasy than if I knew nothing. [At this point, Mr. Holland discussed the political situation in France in some detail. This detail is omitted here for the sake of brevity.] I'd say it is quite unlikely that de Gaulle would either resign or be thrown out in a pinch. I'd say the chances are less than one in ten. On the other hand, it's a possibility, isn't it? I'd have to say greater than 1 in 100. I suppose my best guess would be 1 chance in 20 that his government would not remain in power.

Ellsworth: OK, I think that's all I need.

Holland: What are you going to do with these probabilities?

Ellsworth: As a first cut, I'd like to lay out the possible values of those 25 million francs in 30 days and attach some probabilities to them. Then I can compute the average or expected value of the francs in 30 days and compare it to the certain $5 million you could get now in the forward market. That should at least tell us where to go from here on this particular decision. How about getting together again early tomorrow morning?

Holland: Fine, I'll be interested in hearing what you come up with.

As Dan Ellsworth left Holland's office, he thought he had a good idea of how to analyze Mr. Holland's decision. He hoped that he would also be able to present the analysis in a way that could be used as a basis for other future decisions in the foreign exchange markets.

Case 4–4B

The National Machine Company (B)

On a morning in June 1968, Dan Ellsworth returned to the office of Mr. Holland, the Corporate Treasurer, with his suggested analysis of the foreign exchange decision described in National Machine Company (A). The following is a series of excerpts from their conversation, which characterizes the major issues they discussed.

Ellsworth: After some thought, I decided that a reasonable analysis of this problem could be obtained by using your assessments to compute an "expected value" for the future value of the franc. Essentially this expected value is a kind of average value for the franc, where the possible values are weighted by the probabilities you assessed. If this expected value for the franc is greater than the amount we can get for certain today in the forward market, then we would be better off in the long run if we do not hedge. If, on the other hand, the expected value is less than the forward rate, then we should hedge or sell forward the entire 25 million francs. My calculations show that the expected value of the franc is 0.20035, or $5,008,750 for the 25 million francs. This compares with the 5 million we could obtain now in the forward market. Thus, in the long run we would be $8,750 further ahead if we wait 30 days and hope the franc is not devalued.

Holland: What do you mean in the long run? It seems to me that we're either going to lose a pretty penny in the next 30 days or not. There's no long run beyond those 30 days in this decision.

Ellsworth: But there really is, at least implicitly. Over the next several years, you are going to have many forward exchange decisions to make, and we can establish a long-run policy for considering them. This expected value method, if used consistently for all those decisions, will result in the lowest average losses per foreign exchange crisis. In the long run, we'd be further ahead by hedging only when the certain returns in the forward market exceed the expected value of the currency.

Holland: But every foreign exchange crisis is really quite different, and involves different currencies, values, and probabilities. In certain situations, we may have good estimates for the probabilities, but more often than not these estimates will be very speculative. I gave you some probabilities yesterday because I knew we needed them for the analysis. But I honestly have very little faith in them.

Ellsworth: I'm sure it's true that the probabilities for this decision are very difficult to assess. But the only hope we have for making rational decisions in uncertain situations is to assess the uncertainties as best we can, and this is what we tried to do yesterday. It's difficult to feel secure with assessments in this kind of situation, but at least we know that we can make the best decision on the basis of the information we have. Suppose you were to make the decision without the analysis; you would still have to implicitly use some notion of probabilities or chances for devaluation. Don't you think it is better to assess these explicitly, and examine their rational implications?

Holland: Well, maybe, but I am bothered by the kinds of decisions that this proposed analysis recommends. If I understood you correctly, we should either "hedge" the entire amount of the transaction or none at all, depending on this expected value calculation. Somehow that doesn't intuitively seem right. It seems to me that if we're very sure of the currency's value we should not hedge, and if we're very worried about the risk of a devaluation we should hedge everything. But shouldn't there be a large middle ground where we hedge some fraction of the total sum, depending on just how risky the situation seems. I think the reason your proposed policy yields an "all or none" decision is that it ignores the degree of risk in the situation. Somehow that can't be right. It seems to me that the whole purpose of hedging is to decrease the risk in a devaluation; the more risk there is, the more it should be reduced. Your formulation seems to ignore this reduction of risk.

Ellsworth: Well, the analysis doesn't really ignore the risk; it tries to quantify it with probability estimates. Your intuition about the "all or none" decision rule is very perceptive, though. These decisions come about because we have really assumed that National is not "risk averse" in this situation, that is, that National is willing to play the long-run averages. That is a crucial assumption that I've worried about, and I thought a lot about what our attitude toward risk should be in these situations. In the worst case of a devaluation of $0.16, we would lose about $1 million, or 5 percent of our projected annual earnings. That seems like a huge risk at first glance, but I'd suggest that it really isn't that great relative to the other risks we take. For example, several of the capital investment decisions that were made by the executive committee lately have involved potential increases or decreases in earnings at least that large, in fact probably larger; and the chances of the decreases were substantially larger than the chances of a devaluation. Furthermore, just being in a cyclical industry, we're constantly subjected to the risk that the economy will enter a recession and that our sales and earnings will fall drastically. Relative to these other risks. a 5 percent decrease in earnings doesn't seem quite so bad.

Holland: Yes, but this foreign exchange risk is different. We're in business to take those other risks; they're a necessary part of being in the capital equipment industry. We're not in business to speculate on foreign exchange risks, not if we can help it.

Ellsworth: I'm not sure I understand the distinction. It seems to me that we should be interested in the earnings of National, and the possible effects of decisions on those earnings. A 5 percent decline in earnings is a 5 percent decline in earnings, regardless of the source of the problem. Similarly, the risk of a 5 percent decline is the same risk, no matter what the source of uncertainty.

Holland: I think there is a difference, though. It seems to me that, over the years, we've developed a good deal of expertise in the capital goods industry, and we understand the uncertainties which are a necessary part of our business. I'm not afraid to take a risk on a new production facility or a new product, because we're paid to at least implicitly consider those risks and make rational judgments about them. If we couldn't judge those uncertainties, we'd have been out of business a long time ago. But the foreign exchange markets are a whole different ball game; and we're probably playing that game against others who have much more experience than we do. I don't feel that confident of my ability to estimate the chances of a French devaluation, but I'm sure others do. I think we should take risks where our expertise is, and avoid them otherwise as long as the cost is not too great.

Ellsworth: That's what we're trying to determine: When is the cost too great? Or alternatively, what is a reasonable cost for avoiding these uncertainties?

Holland: Yes, I agree. And your comments about our cyclical industry brought to mind another problem. It seems to me that, in a good year like some of our recent years, we might be quite willing to take significant risks as long as we knew our decisions were rational in some long-run sense. On the other hand, in a poor year when our earnings were already depressed, I'm not sure we'd be willing to take extra risks. It seems to me that it is going to be difficult to formulate hard-and-fast methods of analysis or rules of thumb which make any sense, because I think the acceptable level of risk will vary from year to year.

Ellsworth: I think year-to-year variability could be a problem. There is a formal and explicit way to evaluate our company's attitude toward risk, though—it's called a preference function. Basically, by probing the company's choice between hypothetical gambles and certain amounts of earnings, we could construct a "preference curve" which could be used to consistently evaluate the risks. We could ask the President, or perhaps the Board of Directors, to assess this preference curve for us. If it became necessary to include the year-to-year variability, I'm sure we could do this too. Then this preference curve could be used both for foreign exchange decisions and other decisions under uncertainty.

Holland: I'm not sure that I know what you mean by a preference curve, but I do know that I'm not interested in making my decisions according to the Board of Directors' attitude toward risk, however it's explicitly or implicitly measured. If a devaluation occurs, it's my neck, not theirs. The division managers who handled this French contract will be very upset if their tidy profit becomes a huge loss overnight; and they'll come to me, not the the Board of Directors. I would have a good deal of explaining to do. And I doubt that they'd be too impressed by my assurances that we had acted in National's best long-run interest. Somehow the long-run interest of the company has a very hollow ring to it when your head is on the chopping block.

Ellsworth: I suppose that's true; but do you think we should let the rather narrow personal problems of managers be the basis of our decisions?

Holland: Phrased in those terms, I'd have to say no. But still, let's face it; this company is really just a collection of individuals, and we're rewarded and punished with promotions raises, etc., as individuals. Do you think that our division managers really have the company's best interests at heart, that they really want exactly what the Board of Directors wants. Not on your life they don't; and they'd be foolish if they did. Basically they have their own personal and career interests foremost in mind, and they'll act accordingly. Luckily, their interests and the company's usually coincide; but not necessarily, and certainly not on the subject of risk. What may be a tolerable, perhaps almost negligible, risk for the company is likely to be intolerable for a particular division manager, or for me for that matter.

Ellsworth: But if we all made our decisions that way, the sum total of them would be consistently too conservative. I'm not sure that's desirable.

Holland: I'm not sure it is either. But I think it's realistic. How many managers of large corporations do you know who have taken significant risks? Not too many, and certainly not National's managers, it seems to me. At least, we shy away from the kinds of risks we could take from the viewpoint of the company as a whole. I'm all for changing the way we view risks, but I'm not sure I want to be first in line with these foreign exchange decisions. You see, it's not just the amount of the loss that bothers me. If any devaluation occurs, no matter how small, it reflects badly on me. One of my jobs is to make sure we don't get caught by a devaluation, and if we do, I've failed in some sense. At least that's the way it looks to everyone, including the President and the Board of Directors, even if I claim that I was making decisions which properly reflected their attitude toward risk. It seems to me it's worth a great deal to me to avoid the risk of any devaluation, regardless of the expected value or risk to the company as a whole.

Ellsworth: Well, we could attempt to measure your own attitude toward risk in these situations and codify it into a preference curve for devaluation decisions. That wouldn't be too difficult. Or we could more informally try to infer some of the characteristics of your attitude toward risk by looking at your certainty equivalents in particular decisions.

Holland: What would that latter method consist of?

Ellsworth: Well, suppose that before-tax earnings for this year were going to be in the vicinity of $20 million, as we're currently projecting. Now suppose that you as Treasurer were offered the following hypothetical gamble: 97.5 percent of the time, or 39 chances out of 40, the earnings will be increased by $25,000; but with 1 chance out of 40, the earnings will be severely reduced by some amount which is equally likely to be $250,000, $500,000, $750,000, or

$1,000,000. How much is it worth to you to obtain that gamble? If you were willing to play the long-run averages, it should be worth its expected value of $8,750. But presumably it will be worth something less than that to you, both because the company might be willing to pay some extra amount to insure itself against the risks involved, and because the loss, if it actually occurred, would reflect badly upon your decision.

Holland: You've asked me a difficult question. Basically, I don't think the gamble would be worth anything to me.

Ellsworth: Would you sacrifice some small amount of corporate earnings to avoid having to take the gamble?

Holland: Yes, I believe I would.

Ellsworth: Then I guess we can conclude that your aversion to the risks involved is sufficient to warrant hedging the entire sum of 25 million francs in this present foreign exchange decision.

Holland: Yes, I was pretty sure that's what you would conclude. Somehow, I don't feel too comfortable with the decision, though. Your hypothetical gamble wasn't hypothetical enough, if you know what I mean. I knew what you were going to conclude from my answer, and I just followed my "gut feel," which has been to hedge this contract all along. I'm not worried that this particular decision would be so bad, but I would like to somehow find a more rational and consistent framework for making these decisions, as you suggested in our first meeting.

Ellsworth: Well, I think we've opened up a number of important issues here that I haven't thought through very clearly. Why don't we both give those problems some further thought, and get back together again late this afternoon for a while?

Holland: Fine, let me think about the company's attitude toward risk and my own, and whether these can and should be made explicit. I'll be interested in discussing your suggestions again late this afternoon, Dan.

PART II

Judgmental assessment and limited information

Chapter 5

Assessment and use of continuous probability distributions

In Part I we used probabilities as a language for expressing beliefs about relevant uncertainties in decision problems. In the problems considered so far, the event forks in the decision diagrams have been very simple, with only a limited number of branches to represent possible outcomes at each fork. For example, in the Warren real estate agency problem in Chapter 1, each event fork had only two branches, one representing the outcome that Warren was able to sell the particular property and the other representing his failure to do so. In some of the other problems discussed the event forks have had more than two branches, but they have all had very few. Experience with real-world uncertainties, however, should make it obvious that many of the uncertainties decision makers would like to include in decision analyses have many rather than few possible outcomes: demand for a cereal in units of boxes for next year, the price of a particular stock on the New York Stock Exchange next January 15, or the amount a major competitor will bid for a particularly attractive contract. The techniques developed so far in this book cannot handle such problems; this chapter shows how continuous probability distributions can do so.

In the first section of this chapter we expand the terminology available for describing distributions, using only event forks with few branches, so we will be able to discuss more complicated distributions easily in the following sections. The second main section addresses the difficult task of assessing meaningful probability distributions for uncertain quantities even if they can have any of a large number of outcomes. In the third section we discuss the problems of handling event fans which represent uncertainties with many possible values in the process of evaluating decision diagrams.

In the final section we consider how more than one probability distribution can be combined into a single distribution. In some situations the techniques discussed in the final section make it possible to assess distributions in the most natural way and then, if they are not in the form required for a decision analysis, to manipulate them into an appropriate form. Throughout this chapter we consider only the judgmental assessment of distributions; a discussion of the uses of historical data in procedures for assessing probability distributions is presented in Part III.

DESCRIBING PROBABILITY DISTRIBUTIONS

A probability distribution for the possible outcomes of some uncertainty is a quantitative statement of the likelihood assigned to each possible outcome. In assigning probabilities to the outcomes, the decision maker is distributing a set of weights among possible events in a way which reflects his or her judgments about their relative likelihoods. Thus, if the decision maker estimates that one possible outcome is twice as likely as another outcome, the probability assigned to the first outcome is twice the probability assigned to the second.

There are two common ways of presenting a probability distribution: the probability mass function and the cumulative distribution function. Both types of functions will be described below. First, however, it is worthwhile to recall that the set of possible outcomes at an event fork must be defined carefully; they must be collectively exhaustive (so that they include all possibilities) and also mutually exclusive (so that no two outcomes overlap). In the discussion below we assume that the decision maker has identified a collectively exhaustive and mutually exclusive set of possible outcomes and then consider ways to describe the probabilities assigned to such a set.

The probability mass function

For many uncertainties (or uncertain quantities) it makes sense to consider the likelihood that the actual event or outcome is exactly equal to a particular value. A probability mass function assigns to each possible outcome the likelihood that the decision maker attaches to having exactly that outcome occur. For example, consider a low-volume item sold by a small hardware store. The retailer might have 12 of the items in stock and might be trying to predict next week's sales. If no further items will be received by the store that week, then sales cannot exceed 12. The retailer can probably think intelligently about the likelihoods of various sales figures which do not exceed 12 and, after some careful thought, might assign them the weights given in Table 5–1. Note that these weights are all between 0 and 1 and that they sum to 1.0; thus they comprise a proper probability mass function.

Table 5–1
Probability mass function for sales

Number of units sold	Probability
0	0.10
1	0.15
2	0.15
3	0.12
4	0.10
5	0.10
6	0.08
7	0.07
8	0.05
9	0.03
10	0.02
11	0.02
12	0.01
	1.00

Probability mass functions are sometimes presented in graphical form. The mass function for sales given in Table 5–1 is also shown in Figure 5–1. By custom, the y-axis (the vertical axis) in a graph of a probability function gives the probability values, while the x-axis (the horizontal axis) gives the possible values of the uncertain quantity (UQ). A probability mass function has the value zero for values of the uncertain quantity which the decision maker considers impossible. Thus, for example, the graph in Figure 5–1 is zero at 1.5 and at 13 units of sales. In fact, the function is zero everywhere except at the integers from 0 through 12, and so the graph below is simply a row of vertical lines at these integers. The

Figure 5–1
Probability mass function for sales

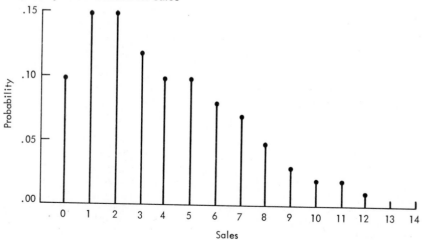

height of each line is the probability assigned to that particular sales value.

The cumulative distribution function

Frequently, instead of considering the probability that an uncertain quantity will assume a particular value exactly, the decision analysis considers the probability that the UQ will be less than or equal to a specific value (i.e., that it will not exceed that value). The cumulative distribution function assigns to each value the probability that the value will not be exceeded (that the UQ will be less than or equal to that value).[1] For example, in the probability mass function in Table 5–1 above, the retailer believes that there is a .1 chance that sales will be 0 and a .15 chance that sales will be 1. The retailer could also have said that there was a .25 probability that sales would not be more than 1 (because sales not more than 1 means sales must be 0 or 1). Thus, the cumulative distribution function, which gives the probabilities that the UQ will not exceed the various possible values, can easily be constructed from the probability mass function. To find the value assigned by the cumulative function to a specific value, simply add up the values assigned by the probability mass function to all values not exceeding the specific value. The cumulative distribution function corresponding to the distribution given in Table 5–1 is shown in Table 5–2. Notice, for example, that the cumulative probability for sales of four units is .62, which is simply the sum of the individ-

Table 5–2
Cumulative distribution function for sales

Number of units sold	Cumulative probability
0	0.10
1	0.25
2	0.40
3	0.52
4	0.62
5	0.72
6	0.80
7	0.87
8	0.92
9	0.95
10	0.97
11	0.99
12	1.00

---

[1] It makes just as much sense to talk instead about the probabilities that the UQ will *not be less than* specified values, but it is conventional to discuss the probabilities of *not exceeding* specified values.

ual probability mass values for zero, one, two, three, and four units (or .10 + .15 + .15 + .12 + .10 = .62).

Cumulative distribution functions are often presented in graphical form. By convention, such graphs have the cumulative probability values on the vertical axis and the possible values of the UQ on the horizontal axis. Such a graph for the distribution in Table 5–2 is shown in Figure 5–2.

Figure 5–2
Cumulative distribution function for sales

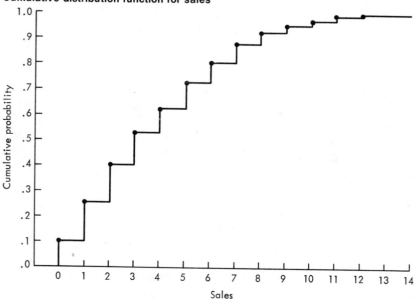

Notice that the cumulative distribution function is nonzero for every number above 0. Even for a value which is impossible (such as 1.5), it still makes sense to ask for the probability that that number will not be exceeded. (For example, 1.5 will not be exceeded if sales are 0 or 1, and the probability of one or the other of those outcomes is .25). Similarly, even though sales could not be 13, the probability is 1.0 (certainty) that sales will not exceed that value.

As shown above, the probability mass function can be used to obtain the cumulative distribution function. It is also possible to go in the reverse order and use a cumulative distribution function to find the corresponding probability mass function. For example, suppose that a hardware store owner has assessed the cumulative distribution function in Table 5–3 for sales of a specific part. The cumulative distribution function gives the probability that sales will not exceed 5 as .90 and the probability that sales will not exceed 4 as .80. If you recall how cumulative probabilities are calculated from mass probabilities (by adding a set of probabilities), it

Table 5-3
Cumulative distribution function
for sales of a part

Number of units sold	Cumulative probability
0	0.25
1	0.45
2	0.60
3	0.70
4	0.80
5	0.90
6	0.95
7	1.00

should be clear that the difference between the cumulative probability at 5 and that at 4 is simply the mass probability that sales are exactly 5 (which is the value of the probability mass function at 5). Similarly, the cumulative probability at 7, minus the cumulative probability at 6, is the value of the probability mass function at 7. Thus we can calculate the probability mass function in Table 5-4 corresponding to the cumulative distribution function in Table 5-3.

Table 5-4
Probability mass function for
sales of a part

Number of units sold	Probability
0	0.25
1	0.20
2	0.15
3	0.10
4	0.10
5	0.10
6	0.05
7	0.05
	1.00

Continuous and many-valued uncertain quantities

Suppose that a meteorologist is trying to forecast the likely amounts of rain which will fall in a particular area over the next three months. A great many outcomes are possible for this uncertainty; for example, the rainfall might be 1.00347528 inches. In fact, there are infinitely many possible outcomes, and even if we limit our discussion to numbers with no more than two or three decimal places, there are still very many. The meteorologist will find it virtually impossible to assign probability mass values to individual values in an intelligent way.

The problem in this situation is that the uncertain quantity (inches of rain in the next three months) is continuous: that is, it can take any value between zero and some large amount. Because there are infinitely many outcomes, the probability that the UQ will take a specific value exactly is very small indeed. Thus it does not make sense to consider the probability of specific outcomes. Instead, we speak in terms of the probabilities that the UQ will take values in different ranges (such as the range between 0 and 1 inches, or the range of values which are greater than 1 but not larger than 2). Very often probabilities are considered for the ranges of values not greater than specified numbers (such as the probability of no more than 3 inches of rain or no more than 5 inches); these numbers are simply cumulative probabilities. Thus, for the continuous uncertain quantities, cumulative distribution functions are often used to describe a decision maker's belief about the possible outcomes.

The meteorologist might, for example, give the cumulative probability function in Figure 5–3. This figure shows that the probability that rain will not exceed 11 inches is .9, while the probability that it will not exceed 9 inches is .75. Thus, the probability that rain will be between these two values can be calculated (using logic similar to that we used in going from a cumulative function to a probability mass function above) as .90 − .75, or .15. It is a property of cumulative distribution functions that their graphs rise more steeply above ranges of values which are more likely to occur than above ranges which are less likely. For example, notice that the curve in Figure 5–3 rises more steeply over the range between 7 and 9 inches (which has a .25 probability) than it does over the range from 9 to 11 inches (which has a .15 probability).

Figure 5–3
Cumulative distribution function for rainfall

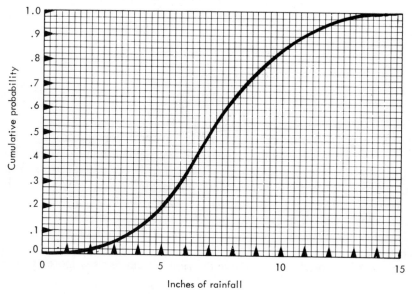

Inches of rainfall

It is also possible to construct and graph an analog of a probability mass function for a continuous uncertain quantity. Such a function is called a probability density function; we will not consider these functions in detail, but it is worthwhile to consider their relation to cumulative distribution functions. We noted above that in constructing a cumulative distribution function, ranges such as the range of values less than 3 or the range of values less than 5 are considered. To explain in intuitive terms how probability density functions describe distributions, intervals, such as the interval from 0 up to 1, from 1 up to 2, from 2 up to 3, and so on are considered instead. As explained above, the probabilities that the rain in the next three months will lie in these ranges can be found by subtracting pairs of values from the cumulative distribution curve. Table 5–5, which gives the ranges and their probabilities, can be thought of as describing a few-valued UQ. Figure 5–4 is a probability mass function corresponding to Table 5–5. In the figure, the bar giving the probability for a particular range is above the range; the bar for the range from 4 to 5 inches is .09, for example.

Table 5–5
Probabilities corresponding to ranges

Inches of rainfall	Probability
0 and under 1	0.01
1 and under 2	0.02
2 and under 3	0.04
3 and under 4	0.05
4 and under 5	0.09
5 and under 6	0.13
6 and under 7	0.16
7 and under 8	0.14
8 and under 9	0.11
9 and under 10	0.09
10 and under 11	0.07
11 and under 12	0.04
12 and under 13	0.03
13 and under 14	0.01
14 and under 15	0.01

Now, suppose that you constructed a table like Table 5–5 but with intervals half as wide (from 0 to ½, etc.). The corresponding graph would have twice as many bars, but it would still be true that the relative heights of the bars were proportional to the relative likelihoods of the ranges. You can think of a probability density function as the curve you would get if you considered a very large number of ranges for the UQ and drew a curve whose relative heights above different ranges were proportional to the likelihoods of those ranges. An example of the graph of a probability density function is given in Figure 5–5.

As we have noted, a cumulative distribution curve rises more steeply

Figure 5–4
Probabilities corresponding to ranges

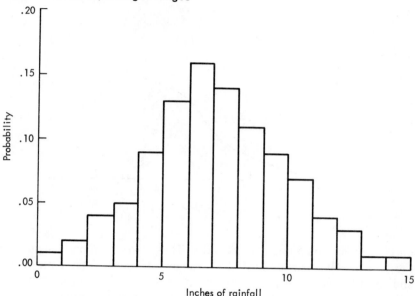

Inches of rainfall

above regions with a higher likelihood of occurrence and less steeply above less likely ranges. For the density function, the graph is higher above likely values, lower above less likely ranges. Thus it is particularly easy to find most likely values from such graphs. As an example of the relationship between the shapes of the graphs of the cumulative distribution function and the probability density function of a continuous UQ; consider Figures 5–6 and 5–7. Figure 5–6 is the graph of a cumulative distribution function; notice that the curve has two particularly steep

Figure 5–5
Probability density function

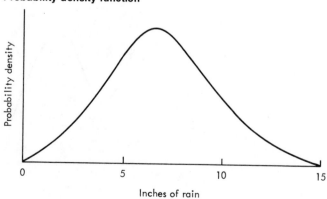

Inches of rain

Figure 5–6
Cumulative distribution function

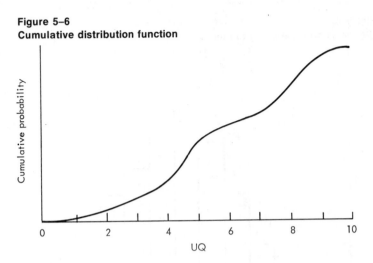

parts—one around 5 and one around 8. These two steep parts signal that the UQ has two particularly likely ranges of values. The same fact is shown in the graph of the probability density function in Figure 5–7, in which the curve has two humps, one around 5 and one around 8, corresponding to the two steep parts in Figure 5–6. Whenever you assess or derive a distribution with a cumulative graph shaped like the one in Figure 5–6 (or, equivalently, with a density function shaped like the one in Figure 5–7), you should be sure to try to determine whether that general shape makes sense. For example, for the UQ in Figures 5–6 and 5–7, you should try to understand why values around 5 and 8 should be likely, while values between 6 and 7 are much less likely. It might be that Figures 5–6 and 5–7 actually describe a mixture of two different processes, one of which gives rise to values around 5 and the other of which gives values around 8; if so,

Figure 5–7
Probability density function

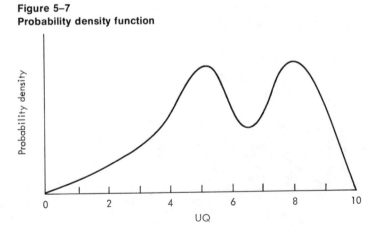

in many cases it would be better to consider the two processes separately rather than in a combined distribution.

In the future we will use cumulative distribution functions almost exclusively for continuous UQs, for two reasons. It turns out in practice that such functions are easier for decision makers to determine (either judgmentally or from historical data) than are probability density functions. In addition, the cumulative curves are better suited for use in the techniques we will consider in this book, for incorporating distributions into decision problems.[2]

The preceding discussion introduced distribution functions for an uncertain quantity which was in fact continuous (*ANY* number of inches of rain—such as 3.342594—could in fact occur). In practice, more often quantities which are not in fact continuous are encountered. For example, consider the sales of quarts of milk by a supermarket during one week. The store sells hundreds of quarts. Surely it sells an integral number of quarts (not 652.2, for example), yet the decision maker usually will not be able to think intelligently about the probability that sales will exactly equal some specified value, such as 425 quarts. Instead, she or he will generally find it much more natural to make judgments about cumulative probabilities, such as the likelihood that sales will not exceed 500 quarts. This type of uncertain quantity, which can assume many different values but which is not strictly continuous, is called a *many-valued UQ*. In practice, many-valued UQs are far more common than are truly continuous ones. In assessing probability distributions for many-valued UQs, it is convenient to treat them as if they were continuous and deal with cumulative distribution curves for them just as we did for the truly continuous rainfall example above.

Describing a distribution using measures of central tendency

The probability mass functions and cumulative distribution functions discussed above provide rather complete descriptions of probability distributions. Instead of or in addition to these functions, it is often useful to have various summaries of the properties of a probability distribution. This section describes three such summary measures, all of which are called measures of location of the distributions, or measures of central tendency.

The most commonly used summary of a distribution is the *mean* or expected value. The mean is calculated from a probability mass function as follows: For each outcome, multiply the value (the outcome) by its probability, and add all of the products; the mean is the resulting sum.

---

[2] We will discuss these techniques later in this chapter and also in Part III.

Table 5–6
Calculating the mean of the distribution in
Table 5–1

Value	Probability	Value × Probability
0	0.10	0.0
1	0.15	0.15
2	0.15	0.30
3	0.12	0.36
4	0.10	0.40
5	0.10	0.50
6	0.08	0.48
7	0.07	0.49
8	0.05	0.40
9	0.03	0.27
10	0.02	0.20
11	0.02	0.22
12	0.01	0.12
		3.89 Mean

Table 5–6 shows how to calculate the mean of the probability distribution in Table 5–1.[3]

A second summary measure of a probability distribution is the *mode,* which is defined as the most likely value of the uncertain quantity. Thus, for the distribution in Table 5–4 the mode is 0 (which has a .25 probability). In the distribution in Table 5–1, there are two values which have the highest probabilities (1 and 2 each have a .15 probability). We say that that distribution has two modes (or is bimodal). Similarly, a distribution may have more than two modes.

For continuous or many-valued UQs, the mode (or modes) is the highest point (or points) on the probability density function; alternatively, modes can be found (though usually not so easily) as the values above which the cumulative distribution function rises most steeply.

A third commonly used measure is the *median,* which can be defined in graphical terms using the cumulative graph of the distribution. To find the median, start on the probability (vertical) axis at .5. Move straight across, parallel to the x-axis, until you hit the distribution curve; then read straight down until you hit the horizontal axis at some value. That value is the median.

Verbal definitions of the median tend to be rather awkward: The median of a probability distribution is the value for which it is true that (1) there is at least a .5 probability of that value or a smaller one, and (2) there is at

---

[3] The mean is the average value of the UQ, with the probabilities used as weights. You calculate it as you would any other weighted average: First you take a sum of weights times values. Then you would normally divide by the sum of the weights, but because the probabilities sum to 1.0, this step is unnecessary in calculating a mean from a probability distribution. The mean of a continuous or many-valued UQ also can be calculated, as explained below.

least a .5 probability of that value or greater. In less precise but less awkward terms, the median can be thought of as the middle value on the cumulative distribution curve.

Actually, the median is just a special example of a class of measures called *fractiles*. The median is the .5 fractile; other fractiles are also defined as values read from the cumulative graph. For example, to find the .4 fractile, start at .4 on the vertical axis, move across to the curve and then straight down; the value at which you hit the horizontal axis is the .4 fractile.

Similarly, you could calculate the .25 or the .75 or other fractiles. Figure 5–8 shows how to find several fractiles for the distribution also shown in Figure 5–2.

Figure 5–8
Reading fractiles from a cumulative distribution

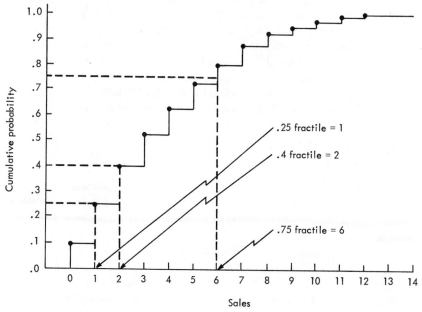

ASSESSING PROBABILITY DISTRIBUTIONS FOR UNCERTAIN QUANTITIES

The preceding section has developed terminology and summary measures for describing probability distributions. In this section we turn to the question of how to assess probability distributions for many-valued or continuous uncertain quantities. We will consider a method appropriate for situations in which a decision maker must assess the probabilities for outcomes of some event for which there are no readily available relevant historical or survey data. Such a problem may arise when a decision maker wants to assess a distribution for the demand for a new product. It might be worthwhile to try to collect data on the uncertainty; as a first cut, the decision maker could make a judgmental assessment of the uncertain quantity in an attempt to decide whether to undertake data collection efforts. If it were impossible to collect any data, the decision maker would have to rely solely on judgmental assessment. This section gives a description of how to conduct such judgmental assessments.

We saw in Chapter 1 that when there are only a very small number of possible outcomes of an uncertainty, the decision maker can assign probabilities to all possible outcomes. For example, a manager worried about whether or not a given piece of equipment will fail can reasonably try to select a probability, p, that the equipment will fail (and the complementary probability $1 - p$ that it will not). In many cases, however, there are many possible outcomes of an uncertainty; for example, a decision maker might be concerned with this year's demand for a product where the demand could conceivably be any value between 1,000 and 10,000. It would be extremely difficult for the decision maker to assign a probability to each possible outcome—such as the probability of exactly 4,120 units of demand. Instead, it is more natural to consider the probabilities that the UQ falls within specified ranges—for example, that the demand is between 5,000 and 7,000 units, or is less than 4,000 units. The assessment procedure described in this section is just a systematic way of finding and using such judgments about the probabilities that UQs will fall in certain ranges.

The essence of this procedure is to make the decision maker concentrate on a few special ranges of the uncertain quantity of interest. The first value the decision maker selects is the median, also known as the .5 fractile. (The median and other fractiles were defined in the preceding section.) For a continuous UQ, the definition of a fractile given above is equivalent to the following: If the decision maker thinks that the UQ will be less than or equal to a certain value with probability .X then that value is defined as the .X fractile of the assessed probability distribution. Thus the decision maker specifies as the median that number which, in her or his opinion, divides the possible values of the UQ into two equally likely ranges; the UQ, in the opinion of the decision maker, is equally likely to be above or below the median. Note that the median is not necessarily the single most likely value of the UQ. Rather, the emphasis in this discussion is on ranges, and the median divides all possible values of the UQ into two equally likely ranges. One way to select the median is to think about being faced with a choice of gambles. Assume that in the first gamble you will receive $50 if, and only if, the UQ turns out to be less than or equal to some specified value. In the second gamble you will receive $50 if, and only if, the UQ turns out to be greater than that value. If you are entirely indifferent between the first gamble and the second, then the specified value of the UQ is the median of your assessed distribution. If you find the first gamble more attractive, then the specified value is above the median, while if you find the second gamble more attractive, the chance of the UQ being above the specified value is more than 50/50, and so the specified value is less than the median.

Next in this assessment procedure, the decision maker selects other points which divide the range of the UQ into other ranges of interest. In particular, the .25 fractile is that possible value of the UQ which divides the range of possible values into two parts: the chances are 1 in 4 that the actual value of the UQ will be in the left-hand (or smaller) part of the range, and 3 in 4 that it will be in the right-hand or larger part. Again, it may be useful to think of a choice between gambles. Assume that we know for certain that the UQ is below the median. Now think of a gamble in which you will receive $50 if, and only if, the UQ is less than or equal to a specified value. Alternatively, think of a second gamble in which you win $50 if, and only if, the UQ has a value between the specified value and the median. If you are entirely indifferent between these two gambles, then the specified value is the .25 fractile of your assessed probability distribution for the UQ. If you prefer the first gamble, then you must think that the chances are greater than 1 in 4 that the UQ will be less than or equal to the specified value, and so your .25 fractile is smaller than the specified value. Similarly, if you prefer the second gamble, then your .25 fractile is larger than the specified value.

The .75 fractile of a probability distribution is the number which divides the range into two parts such that the chances are 3 in 4 that the UQ value will be less than or equal to the .75 fractile and 1 in 4 that it will exceed that value. A choice between gambles can again be used in selecting the .75 fractile; you should be indifferent between a gamble in which you win if the UQ is between the median and the .75 fractile and another gamble in which you win if, and only if, the UQ is greater than the .75 fractile.

In addition to the .5, .25, and .75 fractiles, the decision maker is asked to assess what are called *extreme fractiles* of the distribution. Most people feel that it is not difficult to make judgments about the extreme values of a distribution, but experience has shown that assessors do have considerable difficulty in making such judgments consistently. For example, you will probably find it very difficult to differentiate between the .99 fractile (which should be exceeded with a probability of .01) and the .999 fractile (which should be exceeded with a probability of .001). In fact, most people do not intuitively distinguish among the .99 fractile, the .999 fractile, and the "highest possible outcome." In addition, experiments with large numbers of people have shown that many give distributions which are too "tight," in the sense that the distribution of possible outcomes for the UQ of interest is not wide enough. You can think about this problem as follows. If you assess the .01 fractile for some UQ, then you are stating that you believe the chances are 1 in 100 that the actual value of the UQ is below this value. Thus, if you assess distributions for many UQs, you would expect each to have a .01 chance of falling below its .01 fractile or, on average, only 1/100 of the UQs should be below their respective .01 fractiles. Most beginning assessors find that when they are told the actual value of the UQ, they are surprised by values below their assessed .01 fractiles considerably more than once in 100 times. Most assessors find that they must concentrate on spreading out their assessed distributions.

Some people feel that they can better assess UQs if they first assess the median, then assess the .25 and .75 fractiles, and then assess extreme fractiles. Others prefer to start with the median, proceed to the extremes, and then concentrate on the .25 and .75 fractiles. Still others might want to select the extreme fractiles first and then select the .25, .5, and .75 fractiles. In fact, you may find one procedure best for one UQ and another preferable for another. No one procedure is correct, and you should use whichever you find most comfortable—but remember the warning about distributions which are too tight. If, for example, selecting the extremes first makes you select narrow ranges for the UQs, do not use that procedure.

Once you have a preliminary list of fractiles (for the .01, .25, .5, .75, and .99 fractiles, for example) you can proceed to think about the values some more in order to check that they really incorporate your best judgment about the UQ. For example, since the chance is 1 in 4 that the UQ will be below the .25 fractile, in your opinion, and 1 in 4 that it will exceed your .75 fractile, you should believe that it is equally likely that the value will be in the interval between these two fractiles (called the interquartile range) as that it will lie outside that interval. Another aid in examining your judgments is to plot the cumulative distribution implied by your assessments. For example, you might have selected the five fractiles shown graphically in Figure 5–9. Note that the cumulative distribution does not rise smoothly in that figure. You may want such irregularity in your distribution but, if you do not, you should proceed to revise your estimates to remove it.

This procedure of assessing distributions will probably leave you feeling somewhat uncomfortable. Remember that the procedure is predicated on uncertainty—we are merely trying to give you a systematic way of thinking about your uncertainty about some UQ. Also, remember that any distribution is correct if it adequately and accurately describes *your* feelings about some UQ. Even the warnings about spreading your distribution are intended to help you to express well and consistently your feelings about the value of some UQ—they are not intended to force you to accept anyone else's best judgment about that UQ. In business (and other) situations, it will be true, of course, that some people have better intuition or more knowledge about certain UQ's than do others. Therefore, a decision maker calls in experts to provide information about parts of a decision problem. The process of training assessors is a separate one, aimed not at giving you intuition but at helping you express the intuition that you have.

Example of assessing a probability distribution

A person who has to meet a plane at Logan Airport in Boston one Friday afternoon might go through the following thought process to assess the UQ—which is the difference, in minutes, between the scheduled arrival time and the actual arrival time, where it is assumed that late arrivals correspond to positive differences.

> Well, the plane is scheduled to come in at 4:00 and it is coming from New York . . . the airport is probably awfully crowded at that time of day, especially on Fridays . . . people who travel on business are probably trying to get home for the weekend . . . so my best guess is that the plane will be late . . . it could conceivably be early, but I think that's less likely . . . and also, since it's coming from New York and it wouldn't have taken off early, there's a limit as to how early it could be . . . I suppose I'd guess that the plane is as likely to be 5 minutes or less late as not . . . if I had to gamble on whether or not the plane would be 5 minutes or more late, I don't know which to choose . . . so I'll call 5 minutes the median of my distribution . . . I really don't think it's too likely that the plane will be early . . . but if the plane makes good time, they might want to get it out of the way before the real crunch . . . maybe 1 chance in 4 that it wouldn't be late, I'd say . . . so that would make 0 my .25 fractile . . . and I really couldn't believe a New York flight would be more than 10 minutes early . . . well, maybe once in a blue moon . . . call it 15 minutes to be conservative and I'll

Figure 5–9
Preliminary distribution

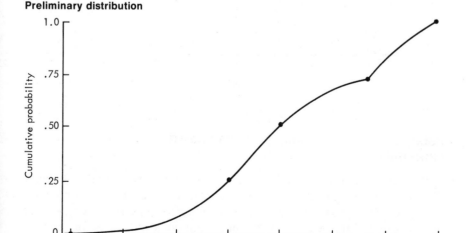

call that my .01 fractile . . . now about the .75 fractile, I really don't know
. . . they do try to get the planes in, at least . . . 10 minutes? . . . that's
probably too generous an assessment of their ability to make things work
. . . I'll try 13 . . . and I suppose 20 minutes might be the .99 fractile.

These values give the cumulative probability function shown in Figure
5–9.

What's that wiggle in the graph . . . it says that the graph rises considerably more steeply above 13 than it does just below 13 . . . I'm not sure I
believe that . . . and, in fact, I think I've been too generous on the high end
. . . airline performance is probably worse than that . . . I'd bet 1 flight in
100 is at least 25 minutes late . . . or maybe 30. And my .75 fractile should
probably be 12 rather than 13. (I seem to think in round numbers like 0 and 5
and 25 . . . I wonder how much of a difference that makes . . .)

Figure 5–10 gives the second cumulative distribution.

Figure 5–10
Revised distribution

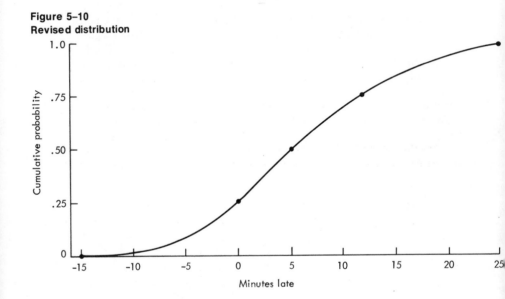

USING BRACKET MEDIANS TO APPROXIMATE
PROBABILITY DISTRIBUTIONS

We have shown in the preceding sections that most of the probability
distributions that arise in business problems are continuous or many-
valued ones; that is, they assign probability to large (or even infinite)
numbers of different values for the uncertain quantity. As we have seen,
such distributions are most easily described by cumulative distribution
functions which assign probabilities to outcomes of the uncertainty in
various ranges (in particular, in ranges of the type "all values less than or

Figure 5–11
Forecast of demand

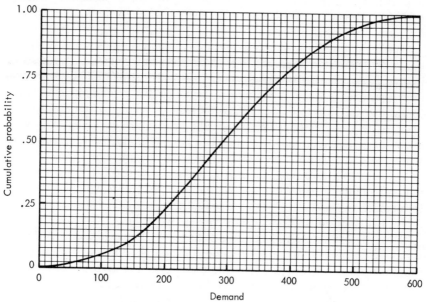

equal to some specified value"). Figure 5–11 gives an example of such a cumulative distribution function for forecasting demand.

In drawing decision trees, the presence of a continuous uncertainty is indicated by drawing a fan, as shown in Figure 5–12. While a fan can be used to indicate the presence of a continuous distribution, it is really not

Figure 5–12
Simple decision tree

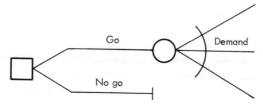

adequate for use in evaluating a decision tree. When averaging out and folding back in such a tree, as described in Chapter 1, the decision maker considers nodes one at a time; for event nodes, the values at the ends of all of the branches leading from them are averaged out. An event fan, how-ever, indicates an infinite number of possible branches[4]—that is, an infin-

---

[4] Actually, a fan indicates either an infinite or else simply a very large number of branches; as we have seen, many-valued UQs are treated, for practical purposes, as if they were infinite; hence this section considers the case of infinite numbers of possible values.

ite number of possible values of the UQ, and it is not possible to calculate and average an infinite number of values, one for each of the possible branches. Hence, to average out at an event fan, a new method for analyzing trees must be developed.

The technique for evaluating trees involving event fans is a very simple one. Continuous *event fans*, with their *infinite* possible values, are approximated by essentially equivalent *event forks* with *limited* numbers of values (and branches). Once the fans are replaced by essentially equivalent forks, the decision tree is analyzed by simply averaging out and folding back, as in trees without fans. Thus the problem of handling trees with event fans is reduced to that of finding a limited number of representative values to place on an event fork to replace a specific event fan.

Suppose that as a decision maker, we must select five representative values from the distribution, shown in Figure 5–11, that we have assessed for demand.[5] One way to do this is to find what are called *bracket medians* of the distribution. In finding such values, we argue as follows:

If we choose five representative values, we would like each value to stand for (or represent) a set of values of the uncertain quantity that are reasonably like one another and like their representative. As a first step we divide the entire range of possible values into mutually exclusive subranges—such as all values less than or equal to 100 or all values greater than 100 and less than or equal to 200, for example. Next, we must decide how to select the values that divide all possible values of the UQ into the ranges. Again, it should seem reasonable to select the dividers in such a way that the resulting ranges are all equally likely. Thus, if we are choosing five representatives (and hence five ranges), we would want five ranges each of which has a .2 probability. In the graph in Figure 5–11 we can find such ranges by finding the 0, .2, .4, .6, .8, and 1.0 fractiles. Thus, there is a .2 chance that the UQ will assume a value between the 0 and the .2 fractile (or between 0 and 185), there is also a .2 chance that the UQ will fall between the .2 and .4 fractiles (or 185 and 255), and so on.[6]

Having divided the possible values of the UQ into the desired number of ranges, we have only to select one representative value from each range. To do so, we suggest taking the middle of the range (in a probability sense) as a good representative. By this we mean that the range from the 0 to the .2 fractile would be represented by the .1 fractile (or 140 in Figure

---

[5] In actual problems computers are generally available to help with the number work, so we can use large numbers of representative values and hence obtain very good approximations to the continuous distributions. For illustrative purposes in hand-worked exercises we will use five or perhaps ten values. The approximations provided with such limited numbers of values are not very good in many cases, but the number pushing is kept within reasonable limits. We settle for the small numbers of values because the hand examples are intended primarily for illustrative purposes, anyway.

[6] To be very precise, we would specify which range contains the dividing points (such as the .2 fractile). For example, we might put each dividing point into the left-hand range of the two ranges it separates.

5–11), the range from the .2 to the .4 fractile would be represented by the .3 fractile (or 220), and so on. These representatives are called *bracket medians*. Table 5–7 shows the ranges and the representative values selected when Figure 5–11 is approximated by five bracket medians.

Table 5–7
Determining bracket medians

Cumulative probabilities defining range	Corresponding fractiles	Cumulative probability of representative value	Representative value
0.0 and 0.2	0 and 185	0.1	140
0.2 and 0.4	185 and 255	0.3	220
0.4 and 0.6	255 and 325	0.5	290
0.6 and 0.8	325 and 405	0.7	360
0.8 and 1.0	405 and 600	0.9	460

When we let the representative of a range of values stand for the values in that range, we assign to the representative a probability equal to all of the probability assigned to the range in the original distribution. Thus the first bracket median of 140 in Table 5–7 represents all values from 0 to 185 in the original distribution. Those values had a total probability of .2. Hence, we will assign a .2 probability to the first bracket median. Similarly, we find that each bracket median should be assigned a probability of .2 when it represents its entire range of values. Thus we have arrived at the distribution in Table 5–8 for use in approximating the continuous distribution in Figure 5–11.

Table 5–8
Bracket medians and probabilities

Value	Probability
140	0.2
220	0.2
290	0.2
360	0.2
460	0.2

Next we consider how to use these bracket medians in analyzing a decision tree. Suppose that the distribution from Figure 5–11 appears at the event fan in the decision tree in Figure 5–12. Suppose further that the end-point value for the no-go branch is 0, while the end-point value for a branch with a specific demand level is $2 for each unit of demand up to 250, plus $1.50 for each additional unit of demand, minus $400 in fixed costs. To evaluate the decision tree, we first replace the event fan by an event fork with a limited number of branches, each corresponding to a

Figure 5–13
Placing bracket medians on the decision tree

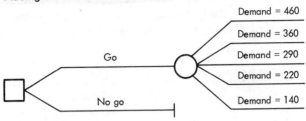

bracket median. With five bracket medians, we would obtain the results shown in Figure 5–13.

We then proceed to put the end-point values on the tree and evaluate it by averaging out and folding back. The results are shown in Figure 5–14. For an EMV analysis, these results indicate that the go decision is preferable and has an expected value of 152.

Figure 5–14
Analyzing the decision problem

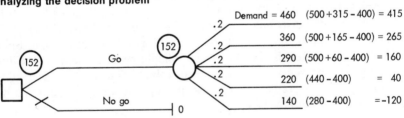

Finally, we should note a procedural shortcut. Recall that we used the 0, .2, .4, .6, .8, and 1.0 fractiles to define equally likely ranges, and then selected the middles of these ranges, in a probability sense, or the .1, .3, .5, .7, and .9 fractiles. Once you have understood the reasoning behind this process, you can take the .1, .3, .5, .7 and .9 fractiles at once and use them as five bracket medians, without first reading off the 0, .2, .4, .6, .8, and 1.0 fractiles.[7]

Thus, to handle continuous or many-valued uncertainties which are represented by event fans in decision diagrams, we replace each event fan with an event fork, each of whose branches corresponds to one of a set of representative values from the distribution represented by the fan. To pick bracket medians as our representatives, we divide the total range of the UQ into a number of equally likely ranges. We then select a representative

---

[7] Similarly, if you wanted ten brackets, the equally likely ranges would be between the 0 and .1 fractiles, the .1 and .2 fractiles, and so on, and the bracket medians would turn out to be the .05, .15, .25, . . . , .95 fractiles.

of each range by taking the middle of that range, in a probability sense. Each such bracket median is assigned the same probability. We put the bracket medians and their probabilities on the branches of an event fork, replacing the event fan, and proceed to average out and fold back in the tree.

OBTAINING PROBABILITY DISTRIBUTIONS FROM OTHER PROBABILITY DISTRIBUTIONS

Often a decision maker wants a probability distribution for a UQ which is most naturally thought of as a combination of two or more other UQs. For example, suppose that, as a decision maker, we want a distribution for the sales of a manufacturing company which serves two basic markets: an industrial market and a consumer market. Suppose further that we would assess the distributions for industrial sales and consumer sales *independently* because we believe that knowing the industrial sales level

Figure 5–15
Industrial sales

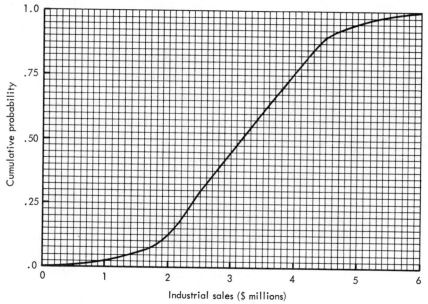

Industrial sales ($ millions)

would not alter our beliefs about what consumer sales are apt to be, and vice versa. Therefore we have assessed a probability distribution for industrial sales, as shown in Figure 5–15, and one for consumer sales, as shown in Figure 5–16. Now we want to combine the two distributions into a distribution for the total sales.

Figure 5–16
Consumer sales

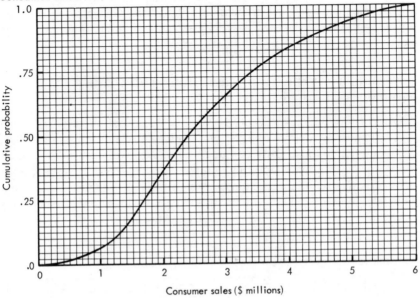

Consumer sales ($ millions)

A portion of a tree showing these two distributions is given in Figure 5–17. We want to combine the two fans in this figure into a single fan for total sales. To do so, we first replace each fan by a set of bracket medians from the appropriate distribution. We then label each end point with the total sales figure corresponding to the industrial and consumer figures on the path to that end point. This step is shown in Figure 5–18.

Figure 5–17

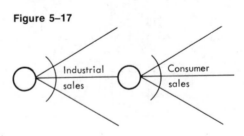

Next, note that each of the five brackets for industrial sales has a .2 probability and that each of the brackets for consumer sales has a .2 probability. Recall that we assumed that the distributions for the two types of sales are independent. Therefore, in our judgment, the probability of the joint outcome of a pair of one industrial bracket and one consumer bracket is .2 × .2, or .04. In other words, the 25 end-point values in Figure 5–18 are equally likely figures for total demand. To create

Figure 5–18
Finding values for total sales

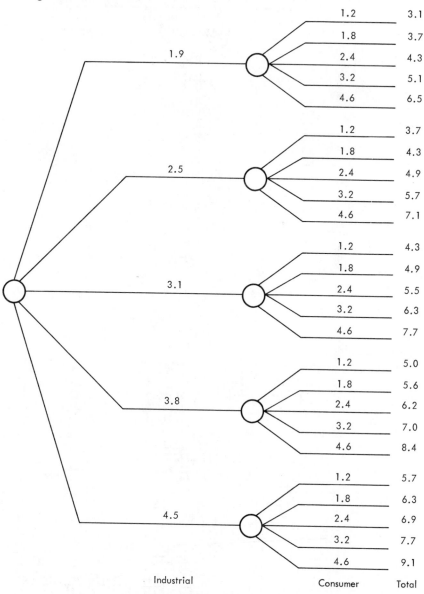

a distribution for total demand, we use those 25 values as an approximation of the distribution. First, we sort the end points into increasing order
and list the different values with their respective probabilities, as shown in
Table 5–9. (Note, for example, that the value 3.7 occurs at two end points.
Each end point has a .04 probability; therefore, 3.7 has a .08 probability.)

Table 5–9
Finding the distribution for total sales

Value	Probability	Cumulative probability
3.1	0.04	0.04
3.7	0.08	0.12
4.3	0.12	0.24
4.9	0.08	0.32
5.0	0.04	0.36
5.1	0.04	0.40
5.5	0.04	0.44
5.6	0.04	0.48
5.7	0.08	0.56
6.2	0.04	0.60
6.3	0.08	0.68
6.5	0.04	0.72
6.9	0.04	0.76
7.0	0.04	0.80
7.1	0.04	0.84
7.7	0.08	0.92
8.4	0.04	0.96
9.1	0.04	1.00

Figure 5–19
Combined distribution

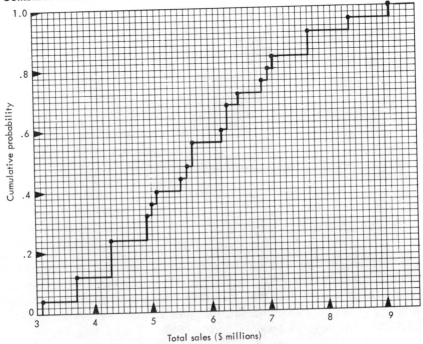

Total sales ($ millions)

Then we plot the cumulative distribution function as shown in Figure 5–19. The graph in this figure is irregular rather than smooth. Had we used many more bracket medians for each uncertainty (as we certainly would have done if the work were being done by computer), we would have obtained an essentially smooth curve.

Once we have this cumulative distribution function, we can use it as we would any other such function. For example, for the distribution in Figure 5–19 we can read the median (5.7) or the .25 and .75 fractiles (4.9 and 6.9).

Dependent UQs

Next, consider what happens if the decision maker wants to calculate the distribution of one UQ from two other distributions but does not believe that these two distributions can be assessed independently. For example, a company sells its product in two geographic markets. Suppose it is believed that the sales in market A are determined in part by national factors and in part by local factors and, similarly, the sales in market B are caused by a combination of factors. If the sales in market A are known, the decision maker cannot be sure of the sales in B, for the two are affected by different local factors. Still, if sales in A were low, relatively low sales would be expected in B. In technical terms, the conditional distributions for sales in B are different for various levels of sales in A, and vice versa.

Suppose that market A is the company's traditional market, and its executives find it natural to think of sales in market A as a base and to think of sales in market B in relation to the base sales. To derive a distribution for total sales in this case, if the decision maker finds it appropriate to find total sales by adding sales in A and sales in B, it may be appropriate to assess a distribution for sales in market A and conditional distributions for sales in B, given different sales in A. For example, suppose that as a decision analyst we assess a distribution for sales in A and find five bracket medians of 1.0, 1.3, 1.6, 1.8 and 1.9. We then assess five conditional distributions for sales in B, one of which would apply if sales in A were 1.0, the second for A sales of 1.3, and so on. We would then read bracket medians from each of those distributions to fill in the appropriate part of a diagram, as shown in Figure 5–20. We then label each end point in that diagram with the total sales figure corresponding to it, just as we did in Figure 5–14.

We note that each of the end points in Figure 5–20 is equally likely (and has a .04 probability). Hence, we can use the 25 representative values on those end points as an approximation of the distribution of total sales, and we can set up a table (like Table 5–9) listing those values in increasing order, and then graph the cumulative distribution function as shown in Figure 5–21.[8]

---

[8] Again, if we had used more bracket medians we would have obtained a smoother curve in Figure 5–21.

Figure 5–20
Finding the distribution of total sales

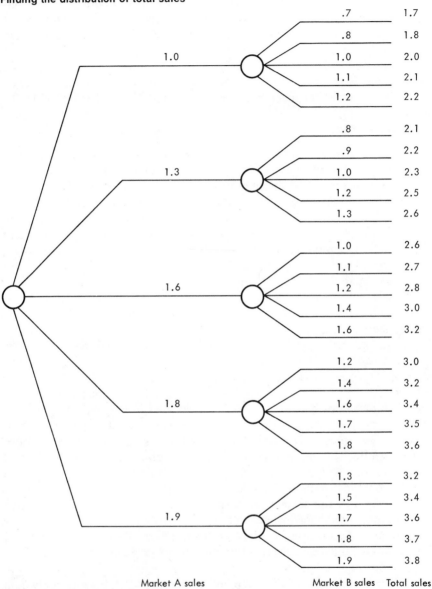

	Market A sales		Market B sales	Total sales

In finding the distribution in Figure 5–21, we had to assess six different distributions (one for sales in market A and five conditional distributions for sales in market B). If we had used more bracket medians we would have had to assess more distributions, so this method of combining probability distributions is cumbersome and difficult to use effectively. Often

Figure 5–21
Combined distribution

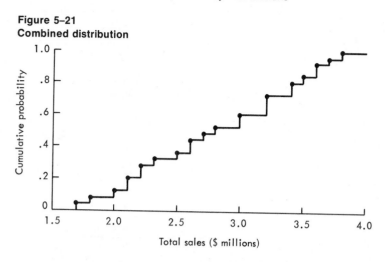

Total sales ($ millions)

we try instead to define UQs for which it is natural to assess distributions and which, at the same time, we think we can assess independently. Then we can use the simpler method, involving only two assessments, which was used in finding the distribution in Figure 5–19. For example, the decision maker might think that sales in market A and the ratio of sales in B to those in A were independent (market A was not apt to have a larger share in a good than in a bad year) and, moreover, that distributions for sales in A and for the ratio of B to A could be obtained. If so, then we could use the two independent UQs and would have to assess only two distributions. Then we would take bracket medians (perhaps five for hand calculations) for sales in A and bracket medians for the ratio of sales in B to sales in A. Each pair of these values for A sales and for the ratio would be equally likely. To find the corresponding total sales figure, we could first find the market B figure for each pair (by multiplying the A sales by the ratio) and then add this figure to the A sales to find the total sales, which is the figure we want.

As an example of this procedure, consider Figures 5–22 and 5–23, in which distributions for sales in market A and for the ratio of B to A are used to find a distribution for total sales. The bracket medians for the ratio are .65, .74, .85, .96, 1.06—regardless of the level of sales in market A. We should note, of course, that a decision maker who finds it possible or natural to obtain the total sales distribution directly would certainly do so; the procedures discussed here are for the other cases in which the decision maker prefers to assess distributions other than the one required.

Finally, we should consider what happens if the UQ of interest depends on three or more other UQs. Suppose, for example, that a company's sales are of three types (I, II, and III) and that its managers believe that the three types of sales are independent. They want a distribution for total sales. If you were the decision analyst you could proceed much as we did

Figure 5–22
Finding the distribution of total sales

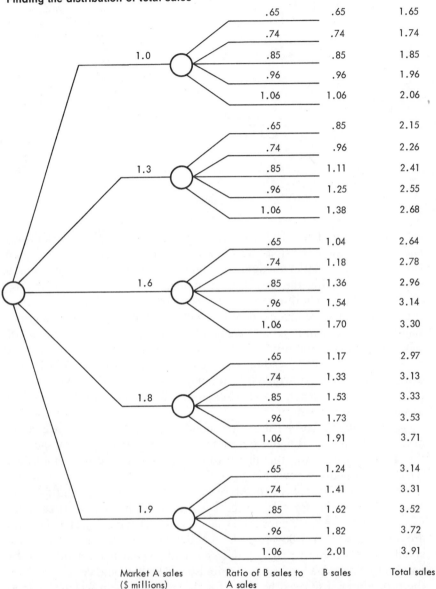

Market A sales ($ millions)	Ratio of B sales to A sales	B sales	Total sales
1.0	.65	.65	1.65
	.74	.74	1.74
	.85	.85	1.85
	.96	.96	1.96
	1.06	1.06	2.06
1.3	.65	.85	2.15
	.74	.96	2.26
	.85	1.11	2.41
	.96	1.25	2.55
	1.06	1.38	2.68
1.6	.65	1.04	2.64
	.74	1.18	2.78
	.85	1.36	2.96
	.96	1.54	3.14
	1.06	1.70	3.30
1.8	.65	1.17	2.97
	.74	1.33	3.13
	.85	1.53	3.33
	.96	1.73	3.53
	1.06	1.91	3.71
1.9	.65	1.24	3.14
	.74	1.41	3.31
	.85	1.62	3.52
	.96	1.82	3.72
	1.06	2.01	3.91

with two independent UQs. That is, you obtain a distribution for each type. You take bracket medians of each of the distributions (five each for hand calculations) and then think of a tree with one end point for each combination of values (125 end points if each fan is replaced by five bracket medians). You then calculate 125 values of total sales, one at each

Figure 5–23
Distribution of total sales

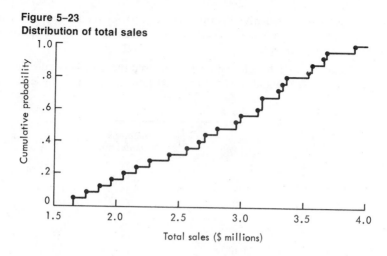

Total sales ($ millions)

end point. You use those values as an approximation of the distribution of total sales; each of the 125 values is equally likely.

Similarly, if the three or more UQs were not independent, you could in principle use the methods described for such UQs above, but it should be clear that you would have to assess a very large number of conditional distributions and that doing so would be difficult, at best. Instead, it would be much easier if you could use three or more UQs which were carefully defined so that you were willing to assess them independently and then combine the distributions (using the method for independent UQs) to obtain a distribution of the UQ of interest.

EXERCISES

5.1. The director of fund raising for a worthy cause has given the probability mass function shown in Table A for the amounts of individual contributions this year. The pledge cards used in fund raising show amounts of $5, $10, $15, $20, $25, $35, $50 and $100. Virtually all contributions are for one of these specified amounts, so the director has decided to use a discrete UQ which takes only these values.

Table A

Amount	Mass probability
$ 5	0.3
10	0.2
15	0.1
20	0.05
25	0.15
35	0.05
50	0.1
100	0.05

What is the cumulative distribution function for the amounts of donations? Graph this function. What are the mean and mode? What are the .25, .6, and .75 fractiles?

5.2. Last year, the director of fund raising assessed the cumulative distribution function for the amount of last year's donations as shown in Table B.

Table B

Amount	Cumulative probability
$ 5	0.25
10	0.5
15	0.55
20	0.6
25	0.8
35	0.85
50	0.93
100	1.0

What is the probability mass function?

5.3. The director of fund raising has assessed the .01, .25, .5, .75, and .99 fractiles of the number of contributors this year as 2,000, 4,000, 5,000, 6,500 and 10,000, respectively. Construct a graph of the cumulative distribution function and find the .1, .3, .7 and .9 fractiles.

5.4. Figure A gives the cumulative distribution assessed by the president of a small company for the company's sales for next year. Find five bracket medians that can be used to approximate this distribution. What probability should be assigned to each bracket median?

Figure A

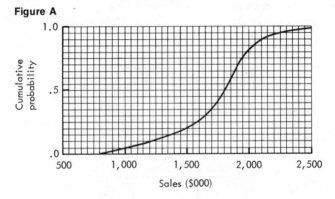

5.5. Mrs. I. J. Kresge is the sole proprietor of Kresge Home Comforts, Inc. She has an exclusive franchise for operating the lunch counter at the Felton Lumber Company, located just outside Dayton, Ohio. She must decide how many of her renowned *soufflés maison* to prepare for her 20 customers at lunch today. They must all be prepared well before the customers arrive for lunch. The out-of-pocket cost of producing each soufflé is 50 cents; its price to a customer is 90 cents. Members of the Kresge staff with sturdy household pets are always happy to pay 10 cents each for any soufflés left over after lunch.

In order to keep expenses down, Mrs. Kresge has an established policy of offering a limited menu of only two luncheon selections. Since Kresge Home Comforts has the exclusive noontime meal concession, and Felton employees do not have time to drive to other eating facilities during their one-half-hour lunch break, the policy of limited menus has never resulted in any of the 20 customers refusing to order one or the other of the two entrees offered.

Today Mrs. Kresge is offering, as the alternate selection, her *paté froid,* a staple item which finds its way onto the menu with striking regularity. Experience has shown that the paté can be stored for a considerable number of days without any noticeable deterioration in taste, a fact which has led to a policy of producing it in batches of 50 servings; there is presently nearly a full batch on hand. A serving of paté is, unfortunately, a low-profit item, having an out-of-pocket cost of 40 cents and selling for only 60 cents.

Mrs. Kresge realized that the physical appearance of her soufflés had a strong impact on the demand for this item. If the preparation was not carefully monitored, the soufflés were unappetizing in appearance. When this happened, demand was almost nonexistent. If the soufflé was prepared correctly, there was usually some demand; however, in no case had she ever sold more than five soufflés in one day when paté was the other item on the menu. After much thought, Mrs. Kresge decided the probability distribution of demand for soufflés shown in Table C was her best estimate.

How many soufflés should Mrs. Kresge prepare for today's lunch?

Table C
Distribution of demand for soufflés maison

Number of soufflés	Probability of that number being demanded
0	0.10
1	0.20
2	0.05
3	0.10
4	0.25
5	0.30
6 or more	0.0

Case 5–1

American General Films

In August 1973, Mr. Henry Mott, President of American General Films, was considering which of two financial arrangements he should adopt in connection with the rights to a new film, *New Zealand Safari*. During the previous 12 months American General had test-marketed this film, and now it had to decide which of two alternative financing arrangements it should make with the New Zealand government, the owner of the film.

American General Films was a privately-owned firm that specialized in the mass marketing of family-oriented films. Its normal method of operation was to obtain the rights to a film, such as *New Zealand Safari,* from a private producer and then to market it throughout the United States and Canada by offering limited engagements at several theaters in each major population center. The showings of a given film in a major market were scheduled for a two-week period, so that TV time could be purchased and used to advertise those theaters at which the movie would play. This program would then be repeated each year for three or four years, or until American General felt that the marginal cost of marketing the film exceeded the marginal revenue. The film was then generally placed in the firm's inactive film library. During the past five years, this method of operation had been very successful, resulting in the firm's adoption of a hurdle rate of 18 percent.

The situation facing American General in connection with *New Zealand Safari* was a typical one. It had obtained the rights to run a market test on the film early in 1972. That test had now been completed, and from its results Mr. Mott felt that he could estimate what the gross receipts would be on the film during its first full year of showings. He thought it equally likely that these receipts would be greater or less than $3,000,000. He also felt that there was a 25 percent chance that the receipts would be less than $2,500,000 and a similar likelihood that they would exceed $3,600,000. In no case did he feel that the first year's gross receipts on the film would exceed $5,500,000 or fall below $1,200,000. Mr. Mott felt certain that American General would want to market the film extensively during the coming year because the film was by far the most promising of those which it had tested, and its initial agreement with the New Zealand government required that it promote the film on a nationwide basis during the coming year.

By September 1, 1973, American General had to sign an agreement with the New Zealand government on the terms of payment for exclusive rights to the film. Two options were available. The first was that American General could make a single cash payment of $690,000 on October 1, 1973. The alternative was to make a down payment of $200,000 on October 1, 1973, and then to make five payments at one-year intervals thereafter. The amount of each of the additional payments was to be 5 percent of the gross receipts of the film during its first full year of promotion (October 1, 1973–September 30, 1974), subject to a minimum payment of at least $140,000 per year. Although the thought of accepting this second set of terms and then only promoting the film in a limited fashion during the coming year had occurred to Mr. Mott, he had ruled it out both because of the previous agreement with the New Zealand government and because of the company's need to include the film as a major part of the coming year's product line.'

Case 5–2

New Mexico Health Insurance Institute

In 1966 the New Mexico Health Insurance Institute (NMHII), a large nonprofit health insurance corporation based in Albuquerque, became an intermediary for the federal Medicare program. Within six months, employee rolls doubled, as did space needs. The Institute's office building, just 6 years old, had originally been built to last 20 years—it was now not large enough.

In July 1967, a Committee on Space Requirements was formed and charged to investigate the real estate, tax, and legal considerations of a new building. In November 1968, the committee received the recommendations of a special study group of planners and architects. Shortly thereafter, on the recommendation of the committee, the Board of Directors decided to buy the property that the study had recommended, a site named Pleasant and Grove Streets. The site is in a very strategic location as it forms the shortest link between the financial district and the central retail-commercial district, is adjacent to the current offices, and is convenient for either automobile or public transit. The State Insurance Commissioner approved the vote in that same month. Within the next several months, adjacent lots were also acquired. The final parcel's deed was registered in March 1970. During this period, the Institute had been advised by its legal counsel that certain restrictions existed which clearly prohibited it from owning property and buildings other than those directly related to the conduct of its business. These restrictions were exceptionally broad and, in fact, prohibited NMHII from investing in any security more risky than long-term government bonds.

It was thus impossible for the Institute to gradually develop the property as its needs developed, nor could it build a building adequate to meet its greatest needs and then rent any unused space. It was clear that it would have to enter into a joint effort with some development firm. Three developers were invited to make proposals for the planned site. In April 1971, the Abbot Corporation was selected as the developer, dependent upon the decision to build. The criteria by which Abbot was selected are given in Exhibit 1. Although the exhibit attributes equal weight to the eight dimensions, the management viewed the criterion of maximum flexibility to buy space as being the most important.

The desire for flexibility grew out of the rather widespread acceptance of the concept of National Health Insurance. In 1971 there were 14 propo-

Exhibit 1
Criteria for selection of a developer (with rating of developers)

Criteria	*W. R. Collins*	*Abbot Corp.*	*Winston Development*
1. Recent successful management of building programs for high-rise offices.	1	3	2
2. Financial capacity to undertake building of this size and others concurrently.	2	3	1
3. Ability to supervise the entire project, including reasonable backup of key personnel.	2	3	2
4. Demonstrated ability to hold project to the budget; likelihood of accomplishing the same thing with our project; minimum open-ended financial risk for NMHII.	1	3	1
5. Contractor, architects, engineers proposed should be of highest qualifications.	2	2	3
6. Ability to coordinate work with Metro developers and other government agencies.	1	3	2
7. Maximum flexibility allowed to NMHII to buy space.	1	3	2
8. Willingness on the part of the developer to expend his own money to continue developing his proposal up to the point of our final decision.	1	3	1
	11	23	14

Rating scale:
 3 = High.
 2 = Medium.
 1 = Low.

sals on the subject introduced in Congress. Judging from the numbers alone, it seemed clear that legislation would be forthcoming in the future, but probably not until 1973. A congressional aide, who had watched the emergence of the health insurance issue, felt that "the great health care sweepstakes is on. It's pure political cynicism, but every congressman has to have a bill with his name on it to show to the voters."

Most of the bills were based on an insurance concept and could be classified as employing four rather distinct approaches. The majority of the bills seek solution through a mixed public-private endeavor. At the other end of the spectrum, a few others, notably the Kennedy-Griffiths bill, follow an exclusively public approach, based on the social security concept that eliminates the existing private health insurance industry. Remaining proposals are distinguished by their respective emphasis on catastrophic illness or tax credit as a financing mechanism. The impact of these bills on the Institute as a health insurance agent range from essentially exclusion from the market to a widely expanded role (far greater than its projected growth of 2 to 3 percent per year, if there were no change). Thus, the management required a space plan that would be adaptive.

The major national health insurance plans

Although 14 health insurance plans had been submitted in Congress, the Institute considered four of them as serious contenders. On August 9, 1971, the *New York Times* summarized three of these proposals as follows:

The Administration Plan. The Nixon Administration's plan, called the National Health Insurance Partnership Act, provides mandatory insurance for the employed and federally financed coverage for the poor. Private insurance companies would underwrite and administer the plan, subject to Government regulation. Subscribers to the workingman's plan would receive unlimited hospital and physician services and laboratory and X-ray services, subject to deductibles and coinsurance. There are provisions for catastrophic coverage. Insurance for the poor is limited to 30 hospital days, all in-patient doctors' services and eight outpatient visits a year. Employees and employers would pay for the general plan; insurance for the poor would be paid out of general tax revenues. Federal officials estimate the Government's share of the cost at $5.5-billion. Employer-employee premiums would rise, they say, from the present voluntary $13-billion to a compulsory $20-billion by 1974.

Medicredit. Under Medicredit, a plan endorsed by the American Medical Association, the Federal Government would pay insurance premiums for the poor and would allow income tax credits to all others toward the purchase of approved private insurance. Benefits would include 60 days' hospitalization, all emergency and outpatient services, all physician services, dental and ambulance services, drugs, blood, psychiatric and physical therapy, subject to deductibles and coinsurance. Catastrophic illness coverage would also be available. Everyone under the age of 65 would be eligible, based on their tax liability. Those who pay no income taxes would receive certificates redeemable for 100 percent of the cost of approved basic coverage. The A.M.A. estimates the cost at $14.5-billion.

The Kennedy Plan. The Health Security Act, sponsored by Senator Edward M. Kennedy, Democrat of Massachusetts, seeks to establish "cradle-to-grave" nationalized insurance coverage for every United States resident. The plan would provide all physician and institutional services without limits and dental care, drug treatment, nursing-home care, and private psychiatric care with some limitations. Fifty percent of the cost of the plan would be paid from general tax revenues. The rest would come from a series of payroll taxes. Cost estimates vary from $53-billion to $77-billion by the fiscal year 1974.

The fourth major plan is:

The Long Plan. The Comprehensive Health Insurance Program, sponsored by Senator Long, Chairman of the Senate Finance Committee, extends Medicare protection to persons under 65. Private carriers would serve as administrative agents, and the program would be supervised by HEW through Medicare, with the state agencies setting quality standards. The coverage would be a basic-type insurance program with no upper limits on benefits. Financing would be through payroll taxes. HEW cost for the first year of operation is estimated at $2.5 billion.

Reactions to these bills might be described as highly emotional and wildly dissimilar. The medical profession was unhappy with those plans that relied heavily on governmental involvement. One physician described her lack of enthusiasm as follows: "Government control has never been successful in anything. What makes them think it's going to be successful in medicine, one of the most difficult fields of all?" A poll conducted by *Medical Economics* indicated that 11 percent of doctors would abandon medicine and 35 percent would retire sooner than otherwise if national health insurance were enacted. At the other extreme, organized labor, main contributors to the writing of the Kennedy Plan through Walter P. Reuther's Committee for National Health Insurance, stood firm on its position that the country needed a comprehensive, publicly administered health program.

Within Congress there had been a tremendous amount of lobbying, bickering, and criticism of the plans ever since the first set of bills was introduced in January 1971. The Nixon proposal had been attacked for being too complicated and for not offering the same benefits to the poor and the middle class. The Kennedy concept was faulted as being too expensive, the AMA idea as not containing cost controls. There had been considerable talk about a compromise, but proponents of each of the major bills insisted that they would not back down. Senator Wilbur Mills, Chairman of the House Ways and Means Committee, had suggested that he might submit a bill incorporating what he felt to be the best aspects of

Exhibit 2
Impact of NHI plans on departmental areas

	Percent of current requirements	Administration Plan	Medicredit	Long Plan
Policyholder relations	5	++	0	--
Cost and Quality Control	10	+	0	0
Records	20	+	-	0
Internal	5	0	0	-
Accounting	10	0	0	--
Claims	30	++	+	0
Marketing	5	--	-	++
Actuarial/underwriting	5	-	-	--
Computer applications	10	++	0	-

Rating scale:
++   Large increase .... +50%
 +   Moderate increase .... +25%
 0   No change 0
 -   Moderate decrease .... -25%
--   Large decrease .... -50%

The rating scale was judged inappropriate for the Kennedy Bill since the changes would be so dramatic. If this bill were to be enacted, NMHII would be approximating 15 percent of its current size.

existing proposals. By late 1971, he had not specified any details of his compromise bill.

By the fall of 1971, the Institute had completed two analyses directed at a better understanding of the national health insurance scene. The first of these examined the impact of each major NHI bill on various departmental areas within the Institute. By necessity, the evaluations were subjective, since many of the bills' provisions were vague, but utmost care was taken to assure objectivity. The results are summarized in Exhibit 2. The second study was essentially an opinion poll of experts in the field of health insurance. One of the main inquiries of that survey was the respon-

Exhibit 3
Survey results

Responses to the question: Let the following four bills represent their class of NHI plans. How would you rank these classes with regard to their chances of passage? Let 1 be the lowest chance and 4 the highest chance.

Participant	Administration Plan	Medicredit	Kennedy Plan	Long Plan
1	1	2	4	3
2	2	3	1	4
3	4	3	1	2
4	4	1	2	3
5	3	2	1	4
6	4	3	1	2
7	2	3	1	4
8	3	4	1	2
9	4	2	3	1

dent's ranking of the four major NHI proposals, with regard to their chances of passage. Although the number of participants was limited, the breadth of their outlooks and the prominence of their positions were considerable. To encourage candor in their responses, the participants were guaranteed anonymity. The results from this particular question are in Exhibit 3.

Proposed Pleasant Street Building

The Abbot Corporation submitted in mid-November 1971 a firm proposal concerning the Pleasant Street Building. It offered two options, rental or purchase, for a total NMHII occupancy of 546,460 square feet. This total commitment represented a January 1, 1975, initial occupancy of 428,948 square feet (all usable areas in the basement through 14th floor with the exception of a small amount of retail space on the lobby floor) and five-year expansion space of 57,754 (floors 15 and 16) and eight-year expansion space of 59,758 square feet (floors 17 and 18). The initial occupancy would be sufficient to house the entire NMHII operation (estimated at 282,000 square feet in 1971) and thus permit sale of the current building, whose estimated 1975 value was $5 million. A decision concerning the Pleasant Street Building had to be reached within the next few months.

NMHII and Abbot Corporation agreed that an equitable rental rate could be calculated according to a formula that included an allocation of the building's operating expenses, of the construction costs for NMHII's share of the building (about 60 percent), and of city taxes. This would amount to $11.30/square foot with provisions for escalating operating costs and taxes. Under this arrangement Abbot would rent the land at Pleasant and Grove Streets from NMHII at 6.5 percent of the total, cleared-land costs of $4,600,000, with payments commencing at completion of the building. The expansion space would be handled in the following manner: NMHII would lease its total 546,460 square feet under a Master Lease for a term of 35 years. Abbot Corporation would sublease back from NMHII 57,754 square feet (floors 15 and 16) for five years at a rate of $7.97/square foot and 59,758 square feet (floors 17 and 18) for eight years at a rate of $9.08/square foot. Abbot would then have the responsibility and risk of leasing the 117,512 square feet of short-term space in the open market. If Abbot were successful in leasing this space at rates above $7.97 and $9.08, it would attempt to make NMHII "whole" by crediting to it any incrementally higher rates (net of actual leasing costs) up to the total rent of $11.30. This method of handling the hard-to-lease short-term expansion space would reduce NMHII maximum exposure on the expansion space to an average of about $2.78/square foot, while assuring the five- (1980) and eight-year (1983) expansion areas. The expansion options could be exercised early if the need arose. Exhibit 4

Exhibit 4
Schedule of new building costs ($000)*

	1974	1975	1976	1977	1978	1979	1980	1981	1982	1983	1984
Lease option											
Initial space	—	$4,847	$5,070	$5,336	$5,606	$5,928	$6,288	$6,619	$7,185	$7,691	$ 8,284
Five-year expansion	—	192	192	192	192	192	847	891	967	1,035	1,115
Eight-year expansion	—	133	133	133	133	133	133	133	133	1,071	1,154
Total	—	5,172	5,395	5,661	5,931	6,253	7,268	7,643	8,285	9,797	10,553
Purchase option											
Purchase costs	$25,775	—	—	—	—	—	3,470	—	—	3,591	—
Credit for land	−4,600	—	—	—	—	—	—	—	—	—	—
Expenses											
Initial space	—	1,398	1,484	1,583	1,690	1,810	1,939	2,080	2,235	2,402	2,591
Five-year expansion	—	—	—	—	—	—	261	280	301	323	349
Eight-year expansion	—	—	—	—	—	—	—	—	—	335	361
Total	$21,175	$1,398	$1,484	$1,583	$1,690	$1,810	$5,670	$2,360	$2,536	$6,651	$ 3,301

* Assumes that NMHII exercises expansion options at end of the fifth and eighth years and that operating costs escalate at 5 percent per year and city taxes at 15 percent per year. The figures are year-end costs.

gives the schedule of costs to NMHII for the least option. Abbot suggested that "if recent history were an accurate guideline, in all probability it would be successful in leasing most of this space at rates that would come close to making NMHII 'whole' on the expansion space."

The alternative offered to NMHII was the purchase of the 546,460 square feet at the price of $60.09/square foot in a condominium form of ownership. It was specified that NMHII would have to purchase the full 428,948 square feet of initial occupancy on January 1, 1975, but could delay the purchase of any expansion space under the following conditions. The 57,754 square feet of floors 15 and 16 would be available up to the end of year five at the price of $60.09. This purchase could be exercised before year five, but if it were delayed past year five, the price would increase at 5 percent/year thereafter. The purchase of the 59,758 square feet of floors 17 and 18 was similarly specified, but with an eight-year constant price. The operating costs to be borne by NMHII were estimated to be $3.26/square foot in 1975, escalating at about 7 percent annually. Exhibit 4 gives the ten-year projected costs of this option. The purchase option price considered only the developed building and did not include any imputed value of the land. It was specified that at the time of formation of the condominium (January 1, 1975), NMHII would transfer the land into the condominium entity at the value of $4,600,000 as part of its payment for its purchased space.

NMHII had inquired as to the feasibility of a lease-then-buy arrangement. The Abbot Corporation emphatically rejected such a proposal since it could shift the entire risk of the venture onto Abbot, and Abbot's management was unwilling to subject itself to the resultant risks.

The multiple-location alternative

The Institute also had the option of leasing small office buildings or floors in larger buildings to augment, as its needs arose, the 239,000 square feet of its current building. This would give the Institute far more flexibility than either of the two alternatives for the new building, since it was felt that there would be no difficulty in locating suitable space as the Institute's precise needs became apparent. Real estate agents estimated that general office space could be found in 1972 for about $8/square foot per year, with an operating cost clause of $1/square foot and a real estate tax clause of $0.75/square foot. It was also estimated that the base rental would annually increase at about $0.50/square foot, the operating costs at 5 percent, and the real estate taxes at 15 percent. The smallest amount that could be rented at these prices was 25,000 square feet. The current building costs approximately $2.3 million to operate. These expenses have been increasing at a rate of nearly 10 percent per year.

The multiple-location operations would incur certain additional costs due to the duplication of personnel (e.g., Xeroxing facilities at different locations) and to lost time (e.g., transferring documents between operating departments located in various buildings). These costs were estimated to be $117,000 and $105,000, respectively. They were assumed to increase at 5 percent annually.

Case 5–3

J. B. Richards Fertilizer & Explosives, Inc.

J. B. Richards Fertilizer & Explosives, Inc., manufactures and sells fertilizers and explosives in the southeastern United States. The company was founded in 1910 by J. B. Richards to sell fertilizer in Alabama. Through the years sales expanded, and gradually the company found itself serving customers in all the southeastern United States.

Throughout its history, ownership of Richards was closely held. Its management also stayed within the company, the current president being J. B. Richards III, grandson of the founder. The Richards family was a prominent one, active in community affairs where the company's headquarters were located.

History relating to J. B. Richards' involvement in explosives

Like that of many fertilizer companies, J. B. Richards' entry into the explosives business came as a result of a major disaster in the late 1940s. In April 1947 a ship containing ammonium nitrate (AN) fertilizer caught fire at its berth in Texas City, Texas. After attempts to extinguish the fire failed, the captain ordered the hatches to be battened down in the hope of smothering it. Instead of the fire going out, the ship exploded, resulting in a disaster that took over 400 lives and did millions of dollars in property damage.

The repercussions of this explosion were soon to rock the entire explosives industry. Prior to the disaster, most explosives were based on nitroglycerin and TNT, mixed with limited amounts of AN; explosives were then selling at $20–$30 per 100 pounds. Subsequent to the explosion various parties attempted to develop an AN-based explosive. Among them was Robert L. Akre, a blasting foreman for Maumee-Collieries Coal Company. In 1955 he and Hugh B. Lee were issued a patent[1] for an

---
[1] U.S. Patent 2,703,528, March 8, 1955.

explosive consisting of "ammonium nitrate and carbonaceous fuels." Referring to the Texas City fire, part of their patent read:

> The theory of the cause of this explosion which we developed is that the gases generated by the raging fire which were trapped beneath the hatches caused the ship itself to explode and that this explosion, owing to the high pressure inside the ship, caused the detonation of the ammonium nitrate. It was conceived that, if the conditions of this Texas City explosion could be duplicated in the blasting of rock strata and the like, it would be possible to make substantial savings in the cost of blasting explosives since the company with which we are associated had been purchasing blasting explosives at a price several times that at which ammonium nitrate was being sold to farmers as fertilizer, for example. This conclusion led to an extensive series of experiments during the course of which the present invention was developed.

The resultant new products offered users at least a 50 percent cost reduction. In the late 50s, companies that had not previously been in the explosives business, such as fertilizer and oil companies, rushed in, and the traditional explosives manufacturers scrambled to adapt to these new competitive and technological developments. The original patent proved to have narrow coverage, and within a few years of its issue most manufacturers found a way to get around it. In the meantime royalties of close to $500,000 were collected on it.

Richards entered the explosives market in 1956. As it overcame distribution problems and succeeded in hiring technical personnel to solve customers' individual blasting problems, its business grew. By the early 60s, however, the industry began to be plagued by overcapacity and competition grew intense. Success then hinged on getting a technological or service edge on competition. In 1964 the company's chief blasting engineer, J. A. Dawes, developed a formulation of AN-based explosives and a detonation system which offered a temporary edge in certain market segments. The firm marketed the system under the trade name DIREX. A new system, developed in 1966, superseded DIREX.

Threat of a patent suit

In early 1967 Saunders Explosives, one of the larger independent manufacturers, had been sued for patent infringement by American Explosives. American's suit alleged that Saunders had been infringing a patent, granted to American six months previously, that covered an AN-based formulation and detonation system. Examination of American's patent revealed that the patent application predated Dawes' development and that DIREX fell under the claims of the patent. This caused great concern to Mr. Richards.

He asked Mr. Robert Mather, Executive Vice President, to consider the patent question, assemble expert opinion, and suggest a course of action which the company should take regarding this potential threat. In assigning this responsibility to Mr. Mather, Mr. Richards suggested that the company's attorney on retainer be brought into the situation as early as possible, rather than after things were out of the company's hands entirely.

As Mr. Mather saw the problem, American's move on Saunders was a strategic one. After talking to his marketing manager, he found that Saunders had had sales second only to American in products related to the patent. If American could get a ruling against Saunders, it would be armed with a powerful precedent when it came to other firms infringing the patent. If American won its case, there was little doubt that J. B. Richards would be the next target.

Conversation with the firm's counsel

Mr. Mather next consulted the firm's counsel, Mr. Arthur Grant, on the possible consequences to J. B. Richards should it be pursued by American. Mr. Grant's answer was that American would set a tough initial bargaining position. It would seek to collect substantial back royalties based upon the gross sales of DIREX. If no agreement satisfactory to both parties could be reached, the case would then go to court. Unless the amounts were quite large, the case usually terminated with the decision of the court. The total cost of any of these possible outcomes would depend on the legal fees and court costs as well as the final payment, if any.

When asked about the chances of any of the outcomes, Mr. Grant replied that he had not had time to survey the related patents, laws, and precedents sufficiently, but that certain generalizations could be made about this type of situation. The most important consideration in how to deal with a case like this was timing.

For instance, Mr. Grant continued, if Richards were to initiate negotiations with American before the outcome of the Saunders case was clear, it could probably get a lower payment than if it waited and the Saunders case was decided unfavorably. On the other hand, if American couldn't prove patent infringement, Richards might have settled needlessly. By waiting for the Saunders decision, Richards would be in a position of either having no problems if American lost or of having an almost certain suit, with a high probability of losing its case if American won. If American lost the Saunders case, it probably would not make further attempts to enforce the patent, whereas if it won, its bargaining position would be considerably stronger.

In the eventuality that Richards waited for the outcome of the Saunders case and the decision went against Saunders, Richards could pursue its case in court if it felt that American was asking too much in direct settlement. Once in court, Richards could either contest the validity of the patent or merely fight the amount of the settlement. If it contested the patent decision, the consequence of losing would probably be more stringent a settlement than if it did not. If it won, no back royalties would be paid.

The advantages of going to court, not to contest the decision but to fight the payment, were that Richards might get a lower settlement than American was willing to offer out of court. While it was possible to appeal the court ruling if it turned out unfavorable to Richards, Mr. Grant advised against this. His advice was based on the fact that the costs of proceeding, weighed against the chances of a reversal of the decision, were generally justified only for very large amounts of money.

Given this information, Mr. Mather asked the counsel to review the existing laws in matters similar to this, and to think about the chances that various events could occur. In addition, he scheduled a meeting where Mr. Grant, Mr. Cooper (the Controller), and he would be present to discuss the possible actions and consequences of the problem.

Conversation with the Controller

After discussing the matter with Mr. Grant, Mr. Mather next contacted Mr. Cooper, the company's Controller, to apprise him of the situation and to suggest a data-gathering plan which would provide the information needed to describe the consequences of various outcomes.

He asked Mr. Cooper to prepare a schedule of yearly sales of DIREX. Mr. Cooper said that it would take a little time but that he could have the schedule ready for the meeting with Mr. Grant. He also hoped that he could come up with a few more numbers that would be of interest in deciding what to do.

Meeting of Messrs. Richards, Mather, Cooper, and Grant

In preparing for the proposed meeting, Mr. Mather realized that he could avoid much needless work by including Mr. Richards in the early stages of the analysis. Consequently, Mr. Richards was present when the three men met in the company's boardroom.

At the meeting Mr. Cooper presented figures (see Exhibit 1) showing DIREX sales, and pointed out that this had been a very profitable line. Variable production and distribution costs had averaged about 50 percent

Exhibit 1
Schedule of revenues received from DIREX sales

	DIREX sales revenues	Richards sales	Richards after-tax profits
1964...........	$120,000	$13,387,000	$1,080,000
1965...........	430,000	11,290,000	257,000
1966...........	390,000	15,713,000	1,241,000
	$940,000		

of sales. He remarked that the amounts concerned were substantial but that they constituted less than 10 percent of this year's revenue, and presented additional figures on Richards' corporate sales and profits. He concluded by saying that the company's cash balance was $500,000, which appeared to him to be more than enough to handle even the worst possible outcome.

The estimates of legal fees for different possible actions were then given by Mr. Grant. (These estimates are shown in Exhibit 2.) Upon being questioned about the very high cost if Richards contested the patent decision (approximately $25,000), he replied that court costs would be higher and that outside legal help would be necessary to prepare the case properly.

Exhibit 2
Estimates of legal fees and court costs for different preparations*

1.	Settle out of court now	$ 3,600
2.	If Saunders loses case—settle with American out of court	4,000
3.	If Saunders loses case—prepare Richards case for contesting decision	25,000
4.	If Saunders loses case—prepare for fighting amount of settlement payment .	13,000

* All figures include $600 already expended for preliminary legal search to draw up these estimates.

At this point Mr. Richards interrupted to comment on the various outcomes. He was quite concerned that an adverse court ruling might reflect on his personal reputation. Settling out of court, he went on, was bad enough, but the stigma associated with a court-directed settlement was worse, and fighting the decision and losing was the worst possible outcome. He stated that the monetary costs did not really reflect the undesirability of these various events.

After they had all agreed that they wished the whole thing had not come up, Mr. Mather proceeded to try to get a feeling for the strength of Mr. Richards' opinions about different outcomes. For some time there was some confusion over how this might be done. Mr. Mather suggested fictitious payments which might be made in lieu of certain of the outcomes. He asked Mr. Richards to think hard about what he would be willing to pay to have the stigma completely removed.

After thinking some time about this, Mr. Richards decided that, although he would prefer having Saunders win its case, he could assign costs he would just be willing to pay to avoid any "patent infringer" black eye. For instance, he said that he would be willing to pay $5,000 to avoid the reputation damage associated with settling out of court now.

After more questions Mr. Richards was able to give the following as the amounts he would be willing to pay to avoid reputation damage if various events occurred.

1.	Settle out of court now	$ 5,000
2.	Saunders loses—Richards settles out of court	12,000
3.	Saunders loses—Richards fights payment	15,000
4.	Saunders loses—Richards contests patent—loses	20,000

The meeting then turned to Mr. Grant's analysis of the possible strategies and chances of various events. The men used the concept of a lottery to think about chances of outcomes. First, Mr. Grant spoke to what he called the two-outcome events. These events included for/against verdicts, and the chance that American would pursue Richards if it won the Saunders case. His assessments are given in Exhibit 3. When asked why it was not a virtual certainty that Richards would be pursued if American won, Mr. Grant replied that the cases were not exactly the same. There was enough difference to make it possible that American would not.

Exhibit 3
Assessed probabilities of two outcome events

1. Probability of American pursuing case with Richards should it lose its case against Saunders 0
2. Probability of Saunders losing case 0.6
3. Probability of American pursuing case against Richards given that it wins case against Saunders 0.9
4. Probability of Richards winning its case, given that Saunders loses and that Richards contests decision 0.25

Mr. Cooper asked why Richards shouldn't include the possibility of taking its case to court before the outcome of the Saunders case was known rather than limiting itself to an out-of-court settlement. To this, Mr. Grant said that Richards had not yet been contacted by American. American would have to initiate the proceedings. Richards could settle out of court with the sufferance of American, however.

Mr. Grant went on to point out that the sums of money involved, based on the position taken by American in the Saunders case and in similar cases, American would start with an initial demand that Richards pay back royalties equal to 10 percent of DIREX sales. This position would probably soften as the bargaining proceeded, however. "As their bargaining position changes, so does their settlement amount," was Mr. Grant's summary.

In order to analyze the problem further, Mr. Mather realized that he needed some estimates of the amount of the settlement that would be finally reached under the various possible outcomes of these proceedings with American; for example, what the amount might be if Saunders lost and Richards then settled with American out of court. Accordingly, Mr. Mather thought long and hard, and assessed .01, .25, .50, .75, and .99 fractiles of several distributions of settlement percentages, which are shown in Exhibit 4.

The remainder of the meeting was spent on explanations of the various figures and on the implementation procedures necessary if different strategies were adopted.

Exhibit 4

Fractiles of settlements as a percentage of sales revenues, given various outcomes

		Fractiles	Settlement percentage
1.	If Richards settles out of court now	0.01	1.5
		0.25	4
		0.50	5
		0.75	6
		0.99	8.5
2.	If Saunders loses and Richards settles out of court	0.01	3.5
		0.25	6.5
		0.50	8
		0.75	9
		0.99	9.5
3.	If Saunders loses and Richards goes to court, contests decision, and loses	0.01	5.5
		0.25	8
		0.50	9
		0.75	9.5
		0.99	10
4.	If Saunders loses and Richards goes to court and fights payment	0.01	4
		0.25	5.5
		0.50	6.5
		0.75	7
		0.99	9

Mr. Mather's problem

Armed with the various judgments and evaluations, Mr. Mather felt that he had all the information necessary to proceed with an analysis of the problem.

Case 5–4

The "Stephen Douglas"

William Babcock,[1] a successful Philadelphia real estate entrepreneur, was excited—yet concerned—about a venture in which he had recently become involved. This venture had nothing to do with real estate and was considerably riskier than any of his previous business dealings. On the other hand, the potential rewards were substantial and the enterprise

[1] This case was made possible by a businessman ("William Babcock") who prefers to remain anonymous and who requested that some case information be disguised.

appealed to his sense of adventure. He was considering the feasibility of salvaging cargo from a sunken Victory ship at a 240-foot depth in the Irish Sea.

Victory ships were used in World War II for convoy duty. They were relatively fast for their day (capable of 15 knots). They had a length of approximately 455 feet, beam of 62 feet, loaded draft of 28 feet, and deadweight tonnage of 10,850. Together with the Liberty ships, they provided a vital link in sustaining the logistics of the Allied effort.

During the war, a number of these ships were torpedoed en route to England from Canada and the United States. As a result, the British government took over several tugboat companies to tow damaged vessels to the nearest friendly port. Frequently, vessels were so badly damaged that they sank while in tow. Of particular interest to Mr. Babcock was the *Stephen Douglas,* one of seven vessels lost in the period of 1942–44 while under tow by the tug *Christopher J. Lovelock.* To the best of his knowledge, no successful major salvage operations had been conducted on these vessels.

Mr. Babcock had learned about the *Stephen Douglas* during a business trip to the Bahamas in November 1969. He had struck up a friendship with Andrew Greer, a salesman for a Bahamian land company, and during the week that they jointly investigated a property, they became well acquainted.

The salesman mentioned that he had been in the underwater salvage business for several years prior to moving to the Bahamas. As he described some of his salvage operations, he mentioned the story of the seven vessels which sank in international waters while under tow by the *Christopher J. Lovelock.* One of the seven, the *Stephen Douglas,* had the most attractive cargo. According to Mr. Greer, when it left New York for Liverpool it contained some $3 million worth of planes, tanks, and ammunition. In his opinion, subsequent saltwater corrosion and changing technology made these items valueless. In addition, however, it reportedly contained bismuth metal, chrome ore, and blister copper which, if fully salvaged at 1970 market prices, would be worth approximately $6 million; these metals would not be affected by corrosion. (Vessels frequently carried such a mixed cargo in wartime to minimize risk to the war effort as a result of the loss of any individual vessel.)

Salvage rights to this vessel had been purchased from Lloyd's of London in 1945 by a British firm. Its salvage ships had traveled back and forth across the area where the vessel allegedly sank, but never were able to locate its position. Subsequently, the firm had made no further attempts at salvage operations. Its difficulties in locating the ship, according to Mr. Greer, resulted from the vagueness with which the coordinates of the sinking were registered in the Ministry of Transport. Virtually all of the detailed reports and other records of World War II sinkings had been destroyed in a fire in the Archives a number of years earlier.

Mr. Greer claimed that he knew more about the location of the ship than the salvage company because he had located Captain Wiley, who was in command of the tug *Christopher J. Lovelock* at the time of the sinking. Wiley had kept a private diary during World War II which contained, among other things, the precise coordinates of all vessels under his tow at the time of sinking. He had kept the diary for the purpose of writing a book, something he had never done. Nonetheless, he turned the diary into personal profit when Mr. Greer persuaded him to sell it for $5,000.

Using the coordinates provided by Captain Wiley, Mr. Greer had located three of the ships—including one at the location where the *Stephen Douglas* was alleged to have sunk—and had salvaged a safe from one of them. Because of the high cost involved in conducting a salvage operation at 240 feet in an area known for its severe currents, Mr. Greer had been unable to continue. Eager to begin again, he asked whether Mr. Babcock wanted to join him by backing a salvage venture. A detailed background check of Mr. Greer revealed that, while he had had mixed financial success in past ventures, he was considered to be of unquestioned integrity. Subsequently, Mr. Babcock paid him $6,000 to form a partnership, the terms of which gave Mr. Babcock 90 percent of the first million dollars of net revenue, 85 percent of the second million, 80 percent of the third million, 75 percent of the fourth million, and 50 percent of everything else..Net revenue was to be adjusted for legal expenses but not for the salvage expenses, which were to be borne by Mr. Babcock.

At this point Mr. Babcock was concerned about how to proceed, since there was substantial uncertainty associated with many aspects of the proposition. First, he was not sure that the ship had in fact left New York with the indicated cargo of metals. In a book written in the mid-1950s describing the history of the British tug and steamship companies, the *Christopher J. Lovelock* was written up in some detail. Reference was made to the $3.million worth of planes, ammunition, and tanks on the *Stephen Douglas,* but no mention was made of the ore. Mr. Babcock felt that this was an oversight due to incomplete research on the part of the author.

Exact copies of the manifests of the seven Victory ships were available from the British Ministry of Transport; however, Mr. Babcock was reluctant to contact.the Ministry, since this might draw renewed attention from other salvage firms and particularly the firm that owned salvage rights to the *Stephen Douglas*. The query might also raise some uncomfortable questions from the Ministry of Transport, which might claim that he was unlawfully withholding vital information from the Crown (i.e., the coordinates in the diary). This could lead to protracted legal proceedings, which he wished to avoid at this early stage of his venture. Weighing all these factors, he decided to proceed without seeing the manifest. He believed that there was an 80–20 probability that the vessel had left New York with the ore and metal aboard and that the cargo on the vessel in 1943 had either contained the $6 million worth of ore and metal or had contained none at all.

He decided that his first action should be to hire a boat with divers to relocate the sunken vessel and to put the divers on the deck. They would be instructed to recover the wheel or some other vital element of the boat to ensure positive identification. In early December, he made a quick half-day trip out to sea aboard a fishing vessel, but the sea had been so rough that the fathometer of the fishing vessel was unable to work with sufficient precision to spot any unusual formation on the bottom. Mr. Babcock was encouraged, by an offhand remark during the trip by the owner of the fishing vessel, who did not know the purpose of the trip. The owner had mentioned that some large object seemed to be submerged nearby, as his deepwater fishing nets had repeatedly snagged in this vicinity.

Weighing the evidence, Mr. Babcock assessed a 95 percent chance of being able to locate a sunken vessel near the coordinates given in the diary. This discovery probability referred to finding a Victory ship near these coordinates. Given discovery, the odds of its being the *Stephen Douglas* were in his opinion roughly .75 in favor and .25 against. He did not anticipate that the cargo from any ship other than the *Stephen Douglas* would be worth salvaging. Further, he felt that the probability of two Victory ships being sunk in this area was infinitesimal.

The cost of the search designed to locate and identify the ship could vary from $1,000 to $5,000 because of uncertainty about the time required to locate the ship and the high daily cost of the search vessel and divers. If it was not on the precise coordinates, a grid search pattern would be used to cover the general area. A fathometer and grappling irons would be employed to locate the ship; once an object was snagged by the irons, a diver would be sent down the line to investigate. The minimum cost of the search would be $1,000, but Mr. Babcock felt that there was a 25 percent chance of its costing $1,500 or less, a 50 percent chance of its costing $2,000 or less, a 75 percent chance of its costing $3,000 or less, and absolute certainty that the cost would be $5,000 or less. Thus, the cost of conducting a thorough search and not finding a vessel would be $5,000.

Because of the weather conditions, even this initial search could not commence until April. If he located the *Stephen Douglas,* he then would retain a larger team of divers to survey the ship. The survey would reveal whether the ship contained metal, whether the cargo was intact, and how much of the cargo could be salvaged. It would also allow an estimate of the salvage cost.

This survey would cost between $8,000 and $16,000, with amounts in between judged to be equally likely. The large expense was due to the need for a series of complicated dives. At 240 feet a diver can work on the bottom for only ten minutes without going through a complex decompression sequence. Further, divers would have to breathe a special mixture of oxygen and helium. Because the tidal currents were so strong, the dives could take place only twice a day during periods of one-hour duration. It was also very difficult to place explosives on the deck of the ship to open it for examination to determine the position of the cargo, assess the difficulty of getting the cargo out and the cargo's physical condition, etc. Finally, this work would be further hampered by the 15-foot visibility at this depth.

Of particular concern was whether the cargo was intact. The tides and the currents in this particular location were among the swiftest and most complex in the world, and even small cracks in the vessel could have resulted in the contents being scattered over the bottom of the ocean in the course of 27 years. Mr. Babcock thought that there was about a 15 percent chance, given that the ship originally contained metal, that none would appear to be salvageable.

Mr. Babcock next turned his attention to forecasting the value of the cargo that would actually be salvaged if the *Stephen Douglas* were located and the survey reported that there was ore and metal on board that appeared to be salvageable. He recognized that divers were notoriously optimistic and that in this situation particularly serious problems could be encountered in any salvage attempt. Babcock therefore indicated that in his judgment there was a 20 percent chance that even if the divers reported salvageable ore and metal from the survey, none would be recoverable during the attempted salvage. Taking into account his uncertainty about the value of the original cargo as well as the uncertainty of what percentage would be recoverable, Babcock assessed the distribution shown as Exhibit 1. More specifically, this exhibit shows his distribution for the value of the cargo recovered, given that at least some of the cargo was salvaged.

In Babcock's opinion, conducting the actual salvaging operation would be relatively expensive. He would have to commit in advance approximately $125,000 for the necessary diving and dredging equipment and about $50,000 in salaries during a two-month period to conduct the operation. He felt that he could raise $75,000 of the $125,000 for equipment from outside leasing companies which would be willing to take the equipment as security, and that he would be able to dispose of the equipment at the end of the operation for about $75,000.

If he were able to raise the cargo, Mr. Babcock expected a legal battle from the company that owned salvage rights to the ship. Lawyers informed him that salvagers had strong claims on salvaged material, even if they did not own the salvage rights, but that they could be successfully sued for as much as 10 percent of the salvage revenue minus expenses. Mr. Babcock felt that there was a 15 percent probability that the lawsuit

Exhibit 1
**Cumulative probability distribution for the amount of cargo recovered, given that
some were salvaged from the *Stephen Douglas***

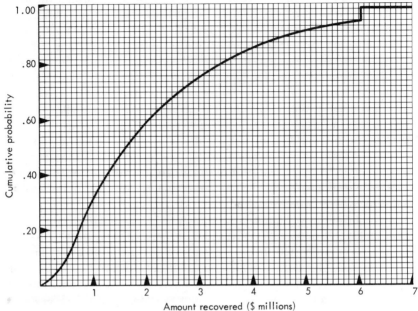

Amount recovered ($ millions)

would be thrown out entirely, since the owners of the salvage rights had,
in effect, abandoned search for the vessel. If he did have to pay a percentage, he indicated that his uncertainty could be described by a symmetrical
probability distribution with median 5 percent and with lower and upper
quartiles at 4 percent and 6 percent, respectively. He stated, however,
that "this set of estimates is really off the top of my head." He further
noted that the tax consequences of the operation would be negligible since
he and his partner could set up a Bahamian corporation to handle the deal.

Because of the risk involved in the salvage operation, he considered the
possibility, if he relocated the ship, of selling its coordinates to the company that owned the salvage rights or to another salvage company. Being
in possession of a part of the ship that clearly established its identity, such
as its wheel, would make his claim to knowledge credible to a potential
buyer. It was his opinion that he might get as much as $50,000 for the
coordinates or as little as $5,000, with the values in between being equally
likely. Without evidence of credibility, he thought he could get very little
for the information.

Another way of reducing the risk of a salvage operation was to enter
into an agreement with a large salvage company. He wondered whether,
given credible evidence of the ship's location, a salvage company would
accept the job on a contingency basis, charging nothing if no cargo were

salvaged and taking a percentage if cargo were salvaged. He had no idea what percentage a firm would want, but he suspected that a larger firm could recover a greater percentage of the cargo than he could by his own efforts. Such a firm would probably want to conduct its own survey of the wreck, rather than rely on the information of others.

In examining the proposition in terms of his personal financial position, Mr. Babcock felt some concern about the amount of financial risk to which he was exposing himself. He thought preference theory might be useful, but what he had learned about the subject at an executive program in a nearby university was a bit rusty. After a 30-minute discussion with the casewriters, during which Mr. Babcock learned a great deal more about preference theory, the data labeled "first assessments" in Exhibit 2 were collected. Mr. Babcock felt uncomfortable about the results, and when some of the implications of his initial assessments were pointed out, he apologetically asked to start over again. The discussion continued for another half hour and resulted in the data listed under "second assessments" in Exhibit 2.

Exhibit 2
William Babcock's two preference curves

First assessments—certainty equivalents for 50–50 gambles with the following incremental cash flows:

	Gamble consequences		Certainty equivalent
1.	+$6,000,000	−$ 200,000	$ 500,000
2.	+ 6,000,000	+ 500,000	3,500,000
3.	+ 500,000	− 200,000	− 75,000
4.	+ 500,000	− 75,000	100,000
5.	+ 6,000,000	+ 3,500,000	5,000,000

Second assessments–certainty equivalents for 50–50 gambles with the following incremental cash flows:

	Gamble consequences		Certainty equivalent
1.	+$6,000,000	−$ 200,000	$ 300,000
2.	+ 6,000,000	+ 300,000	1,400,000
3.	+ 300,000	− 200,000	− 100,000
4.	+ 300,000	− 100,000	0
5.	+ 6,000,000	+ 1,400,000	2,400,000
6.	− 100,000	− 200,000	− 160,000

Some of the more interesting comments made by Mr. Babcock during the conversation are quoted below.

Real estate may sound like a high-risk business, but it really isn't. By using a good lawyer, selecting appropriate deals, using personal contacts, and carefully studying situations, I am able to eliminate most of the uncertainty. I have only been in on a losing proposition once in the last seven years. That was when I went into a partnership with a recent graduate of the Harvard Business School. I lost $5,000, and he lost $30,000. I won't make that type of mistake again.

The frustration of this deal is that I don't know the subject well. If I had been in the salvage business as long as I have been in real estate, I would be more comfortable with my ability to size up the situation.

I don't want to be known as someone who made it and then blew it. I know too many of that type. On the other hand, it would be a real feather in my cap if I could pull this one off.

Chapter 6 _____

Updating probability assessments with additional information

A decision tree lays out the component parts of a decision problem in the order in which the actions are taken or the outcomes of the uncertainties are revealed to the decision maker. We can think of decision makers as standing on some node of the tree. Everything that has already happened lies behind them, while everything on the path (or possible paths) ahead lies in the future. The time sequencing of the tree also applies to the probabilities placed on the event nodes. On a particular event node, the probabilities are for the outcomes of the uncertainty after everything on the path to that node has already occurred; in technical terms, they are *conditional probabilities,* conditional on what has come before in the tree.

One of the problems faced in decision analysis is that the probabilities that can be assessed may not be exactly the ones needed for use in decision diagrams. This problem occurs often when decision analysis is used to update probability assessments with additional information—for example, in attempts to use the results of a consumer survey to update probability assessments for the sales of a product. The first section of this chapter develops techniques for updating probability assessments. The second section describes the use of these techniques in the important practical problems of determining whether or not to collect additional information.

CONDITIONAL PROBABILITIES AND BAYES THEOREM

To illustrate the idea of conditional probabilities we will start by considering a procedure for testing components of some sort. We assume that the test is not perfect and may at times indicate that a component is good

when it is in fact bad, and vice versa. We also assume that the test is
entirely consistent for any individual component; a second test on a component which the first test said was good will always produce another
good reading, while a bad test result on the first test will always be
followed by another result of bad if the component is retested.

In Figure 6–1, which describes this test, the probabilities for the
component-is-good-or-bad event nodes should be conditional probabilities, for when one of these nodes is reached in the decision tree, either the
test-good or the test-bad branch will already have been traveled. Therefore
node 1 should be labeled with the probability that the component is good
after the test says good and the probability that the component is bad after
the test says good. Similarly, node 2 should be labeled with the probabilities for the actual state of the component after the test says bad.

Figure 6–1

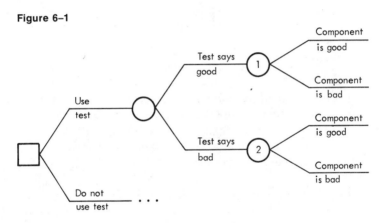

In many decision problems, the analyst is given, or finds it more natural
to assess, probabilities which are not in the order in which they must be
put into the tree. In this example, an attempt may have been made to
calibrate the component test to see how accurate it is. A natural way to do
this is to subject to the test a batch of components which includes some
known to be good and some known to be bad. The results obtained give
measures of how often the test correctly or incorrectly identifies good and
bad components. The resulting probabilities are called the conditional
probabilities that the test says good when the component is in fact good,
that the test accurately identifies a bad component, and so on. Thus, the
calibration provides probabilities of good or bad reports from the test
conditional on (i.e., after knowledge of) good or bad components. On the
other hand, the tree requires the probabilities of good or bad components
conditional on (after knowledge of) good or bad test results. This section
considers how to transform one such set of probabilities (such as the calibration information), together with some other necessary information, into
the set of conditional probabilities needed for the tree.

As a further illustration of the task to be tackled, consider the two event nodes in the order in which they occur in the calibration test, where the good and bad components are first identified and then subjected to the test (Figure 6–2). Note that the order of the event nodes in the original tree (Figure 6–1) is the opposite of what it is in Figure 6–2. The aim of this discussion is to teach you how to flip the order of the nodes and label the new nodes with correct probabilities; this process is sometimes called *probability flipping,* or tree flipping. We begin with a very simple example in which all the probabilities of interest can be found simply by counting and then proceed to the problem of flipping probabilities in a more general context.

Figure 6–2

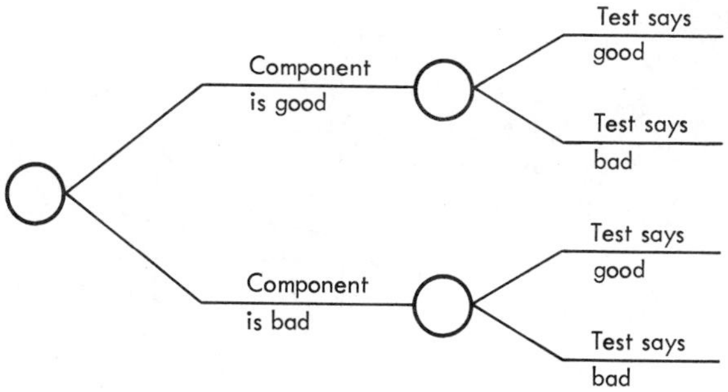

For the initial example, consider a roulette wheel like the one shown in Figure 6–3. Note that the wheel has 25 marks, each with a number on it. Each of the numbers between 1 and 25 appears on exactly one of the divisions of the wheel. Assume that the wheel is fair or, in other words, that on any particular spin the marker is equally likely to stop on any of the marks. We will use this simple roulette wheel to illustrate the different types of probabilities that are used in decision trees.

As we work out the problem together, we first might want to ask questions such as: What is the probability that the next spin of the wheel will end with the marker pointing to a red mark? In asking this question, we do not assume any prior knowledge about any other result; hence, such probabilities are called *unconditional probabilities,* because they are not conditional on any other information. Similarly, we can ask for the probability of black, odd or even.

By convention, such unconditional probabilities are written symbolically in forms like the following:

$P(R)$ = Probability of a red mark on the next spin.
$P(O)$ = Probability of an odd number on the next spin

In the roulette wheel example we can find the unconditional probabilities by counting. We know that there are a total of 25 marks on the

Figure 6–3
Roulette wheel

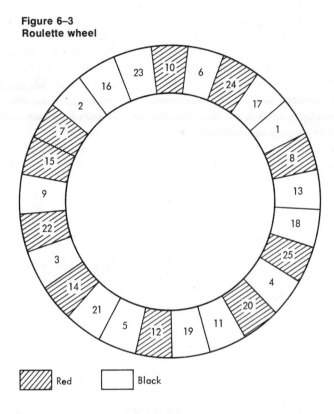

wheel. Of these, we can see that 24, 8, 25, 20, 12, 14, 22, 15, 7, and 10 are red; thus, 10 of the 25 marks are red and, since we are assuming that every mark is equally likely to turn up on the next spin, the probability of a red mark is just 10 in 25, or 10/25. Similarly, we can see that 6, 17, 1, 13, 18, 4, 11, 19, 5, 21, 3, 9, 2, 16, and 23 appear on black, so the probability of black is 15/25. Also, we can count 12 even numbers and 13 odd numbers, so that the probabilities of even and odd are 12/25 and 13/25, respectively. Thus,

$$P(E) = 12/25 \qquad P(R) = 10/25$$
$$P(O) = 13/25 \qquad P(B) = 15/25$$

Joint outcomes and joint probabilities

There are other ways we could frame questions about the next spin of the wheel. For example, we might be interested in the probability that on the next spin the marker points to an even number on a black mark. Such a result (even *and* black) is called a joint outcome, and its probability is called a *joint probability*. Joint probabilities are conventionally written in forms such as:

$P(E,B)$ = Probability of even and black

Note that the order of the E and B within the parentheses does not matter, because if a mark is even and black, then it is surely also black and even. In other words, $P(E,B) = P(B,E)$.

For the simple roulette wheel example, we found the unconditional probabilities by counting, and we can find the joint probabilities in the same way. For example, we know that there are 15 black marks on the wheel. Of these, we count five with even numbers (18, 4, 2, 16, 6) and ten with odd numbers (17, 1, 13, 11, 19, 5, 21, 3, 9, and 23). Therefore, of the 25 marks on the wheel, exactly 5 are both black and even; the joint probability of black and even is 5/25. In a similar way, we can find all four joint probabilities:

$$P(E,B) = P(B,E) = 5/25$$
$$P(O,B) = P(B,O) = 10/25$$
$$P(E,R) = P(R,E) = 7/25$$
$$P(O,R) = P(R,O) = 3/25$$

The equations above say that the joint probability of black and even, $P(B,E)$, is the same as the joint probability of even and black, $P(E,B)$. Surely this idea seems reasonable, for we are saying that the two outcomes occur together; the order in which we list them should not matter. As an example, we can calculate this probability in a second way. Above we first found the black marks and then counted how many of them were even. Now, we start by noting that there are 12 even marks (2, 4, 6, 8, 10, 12, 14, 16, 18, 20, 22, 24). Of these, five are also black (2, 4, 6, 16, 18). Thus, we find a joint probability of 5/25, just as we did above.

Conditional probabilities

Conditional questions about the outcome of the next spin of the wheel yield conditional probabilities, which are of particular use in decision trees. For example, we might ask for the probability that the marker is pointing to an odd number if we already know that it is pointing to a red mark. This probability is a conditional one; it is conditioned on the knowledge that the mark is red. In considering conditional probabilities what we are really doing is limiting our attention to some subset of the outcomes we had originally considered possible; in this example, we have limited ourselves to the results which involve red marks. Within that subset of the outcomes, we then ask what fraction satisfies some other condition—in this example, the additional condition that the number is odd.

Symbolically, conditional probabilities are written with an upright line within the parentheses of the probability symbol. The outcomes which are already known are written to the right of the line, and the symbol for the event whose conditional probability is wanted is written to the left of that line. Our example of the probability of an odd number if we know that the mark is red would be written $P(O|R)$ and read "the probability of an odd number, given a red mark." Thus, "given" is short for "conditional on the knowledge that." Examples of conditional probabilities for the roulette wheel are:

$P(E|R)$ = The probability of an even number, given a red mark
$P(O|R)$ = The probability of an odd number, given a red mark
$P(R|O)$ = The probability of a red mark, given an odd number

Note the difference between the second and third probabilities above. In the second, we already know that the mark is red and want the probability that it is also odd. In the third, we already know that the mark is odd and want the probability that it is also red.

The values of the conditional probabilities for the roulette wheel can be found by counting. For example, we know that there are 15 black marks on the wheel; to find $P(O|B)$ we first limit our attention to the 15 black marks. Of these marks, exactly ten are odd numbers. Therefore, the fraction of black marks which have odd numbers is 10/15; this number is $P(O|B)$. (Note that we used 15, not 25, in the denominator because we are considering only black marks, not all marks on the wheel.) Similarly, we can count marks on the roulette wheel to obtain other conditional probabilities:

$$P(O|B) = 10/15 \qquad P(B|O) = 10/13$$
$$P(E|B) = 5/15 \qquad P(R|O) = 3/13$$
$$P(O|R) = 3/10 \qquad P(B|E) = 5/12$$
$$P(E|R) = 7/10 \qquad P(R|E) = 7/12$$

Probability calculations without counting

In most situations in which probabilities are used, the straightforward expedient of counting to obtain the various probabilities is not possible. In addition, usually some but not all of the probabilities are given or immediately available. For these situations, there must be a method of calculating some probabilities from other probabilities which are known. As an example, we will use the roulette wheel discussed above, but we will pretend that we have available only the probabilities given in Tables 6–1 and 6–2.

Thus we assume we have the set of unconditional probabilities for color as well as the probabilities for odd or even, conditional on color. We

Table 6–1
Unconditional probabilities for color

Red	10/25
Black	15/25

Table 6–2
Conditional probability for odd or even,
given color

	Odd	Even
Red	3/10	7/10
Black	10/15	5/15

will assume that we need the other set of conditional probabilities (those for color conditional on odd or even) for use in a decision tree; hence, we will use the information in Tables 6–1 and 6–2 to calculate $P(R|E)$, $P(B|E)$, $P(R|O)$, and $P(B|O)$. The next two sections explain two entirely equivalent methods of finding the needed probabilities: one using tables and the other using trees. In both methods the general idea is to start with one set of unconditional probabilities and the corresponding conditional probabilities (such as those given in Tables 6–1 and 6–2). We will calculate the joint probabilities, then the set of unconditional probabilities, and finally the second set of conditional probabilities.

The tabular method

In the tabular method we first calculate the joint probabilities, using a rule that states that the joint probability of two outcomes is simply the product of the unconditional probability of one of the outcomes times the conditional probability of the second outcome, given the first. To make this statement more clear with an example, the rule could state that the joint probability of red and even is the product of the probability of red with the conditional probability of even, given red: $P(R,E) = P(R) * P(E|R)$. Intuitively, we can explain this rule as follows: to find the probability of red and even, first consider the fraction of all possible outcomes which are red, which, in this example, is simply $P(R)$, or 10/25. Then ask what fraction of that subset is also even: $P(E|R)$, or 7/10. Finally, note that if 7/10 of the 10/25 are red and even, then $7/10 * 10/25 = 7/25$ is the fraction of all outcomes which are red and even, or $P(R,E)$. Using this rule, we can form the joint probabilities shown in Table 6–3.

Table 6–3
Joint probabilities

	Odd	Even
Red	3/10 * 10/25 = 3/25	7/10 * 10/25 = 7/25
Black	10/15 * 15/25 = 10/25	5/15 * 15/25 = 5/25

Next we calculate the second set of unconditional probabilities by using another rule. We argue that if we consider the joint probabilities in Table 6–3, then we can identify two of the four outcomes which involve an even number (the red and even outcome and the black and even outcome). To find the probability of even, we simply add all of the joint probabilities which involve even numbers, or $P(E,R)$ and $P(E,B)$, to find $P(E) = 12/25$. Note that this operation is the same as adding all the probabilities in the even column of Table 6–3. Similarly, we can add the probabilities in the odd column to find the unconditional probability of odd, as shown in Table 6–4, which is simply Table 6–3 with the columns and rows summed.[1]

Table 6–4
Joint and unconditional probabilities

	Odd	*Even*	
Red	3/25	7/25	10/25 = $P(R)$
Black	10/25	5/25	15/25 = $P(B)$
	13/25 = $P(O)$	12/25 = $P(E)$	

At this point in our calculation we have found the joint probabilities and the second set of unconditional probabilities. Next, we proceed to find the second set of conditional probabilities. To do so, we simply divide the joint probabilities by the unconditional probabilities of the outcomes which appear to the right of the upright lines in the probabilities that we are seeking. For example:

$$P(R \mid O) = \frac{P(O,R)}{P(O)} = \frac{3/25}{13/25} = 3/13.$$

In intuitive terms, what we have done is to take the fraction of all possible outcomes which are odd, $P(O)$, and then ask what portion of that fraction is also red, $P(O,R)$. This calculation is entirely analogous to the equation $P(R \mid O) = 3/13$ which appeared in the section above in which we used counting to find the conditional probabilities. The only difference is that we used 3 and 13 (which are *numbers* of outcomes) in one equation and 3/25 and 13/25 (which are *fractions* of all outcomes) in the other.

In terms of the tables of probabilities, the procedure is to take each of the second set of unconditional probabilities, $P(O)$ and $P(E)$, and to divide it into each joint probability involving that outcome (i.e., into each joint probability in its column in Table 6–4). The result is the set of conditional probabilities shown in Table 6–5.[2]

---

[1] The table gives the results of applying the formulas $P(E) = P(E,R) + P(E,B)$ and $P(O) = P(O,R) + P(O,B)$.

[2] The table shows the results of applying the formulas $P(R \mid O) = P(O,R)/P(O)$, $P(B \mid O) = P(O,B)/P(O)$, $P(R \mid E) = P(E,R)/P(E)$, and $P(B \mid E) = P(E,B)/P(E)$.

Table 6–5
Conditional probabilities of color,
given odd or even

	Odd	Even
Red	3/13	7/12
Black	10/13	5/12

At this point we have accomplished what we set out to do: we started with the probabilities in Tables 6–1 and 6–2. Using only that information, we calculated the joint probabilities and then the second set of unconditional probabilities in Table 6–4. Finally, we then found the second set of conditional probabilities in Table 6–5 (note that the probabilities in this table are the same as the ones we found earlier by counting). The principle embodied in this set of steps is generally called *Bayes theorem*.[3]

The tree method

In the alternative method for manipulating probabilities, trees rather than tables are used. With this method, we would represent the information in Tables 6–1 and 6–2 on a probability tree instead, as shown in Figure 6–4. Note that in this tree the probabilities in the first set (reading from the left) are unconditional, for when we reach the first node in the tree we do not have any information about the outcome of a spin of the roulette wheel. When we reach node *A* in the figure, though, we already know that the mark is red (remember that when we stand on a node of a decision tree, everything behind us has already happened). Hence, we should label the branches leading from that node with conditional probabilities for odd and even, given red.

As in the tabular method, in the tree method we follow a sequence of calculating first joint probabilities, then the second set of unconditional probabilities, and finally the remaining conditional probabilities. First, to

---

[3] To derive the usual form for Bayes theorem, we would use the following steps:

1. $P(R|O) = P(O,R)/P(O)$, as shown above.
2. For $P(O,R)$ we substitute $P(O|R)P(R)$.
3. For $P(O)$ we substitute $P(O,R) + P(O,B)$, which can then be replaced by $P(O|R)P(R) + P(O|B)P(B)$.
4. Thus we arrive at

$$P(R|O) = \frac{P(O|R)P(R)}{P(O|R)P(R) + P(O|B)P(B)}.$$

Entirely similar steps could be used to find $P(R|E)$, $P(B|O)$, and $P(B|E)$. For example,

$$P(B|E) = \frac{P(E|B)P(B)}{P(E|B)P(B) + P(E|R)P(R)}.$$

These formulas are specific examples of Bayes Theorem.

Figure 6–4
Initial probability tree

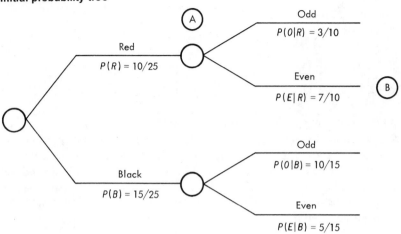

find the joint probabilities, notice that each end point denotes a joint outcome; for example, the end point labeled *B* in Figure 6–4 represents the joint outcome red and even. We will label each end point with the joint probability of the joint outcome that it represents. To do so, we simply multiply together all of the probabilities on the path, from the root of the tree to that end point; for end point *B*, we multiply 10/25 and 7/10 to obtain 7/25. The other joint probabilities are found in an analogous manner, as shown in Figure 6–5.

Next, to find the unconditional probability of odd, or *P(O)*, we simply add the probabilities of all of the end points which represent joint outcomes involving odd numbers. We find the unconditional probability of even in the same way. Thus *P(O)* = 3/25 + 10/25 = 13/25, and *P(E)* = 12/25.

Figure 6–5

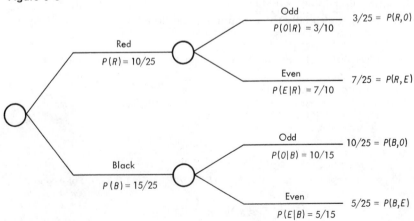

Finally, we must obtain the second set of conditional probabilities; $P(R \mid E)$, and so on. Notice that to represent these probabilities in a probability tree, we should draw the tree with the node for odd or even first, as shown in Figure 6–6. On that tree the joint probabilities and the second set of unconditionals, all of which were calculated just above, have also been entered.

Figure 6–6

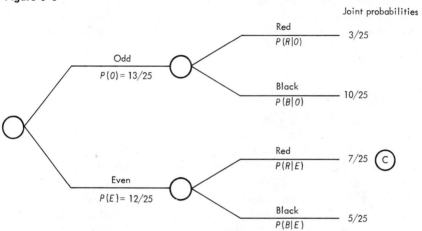

Our final job is to find values for the conditional probabilities in the tree in Figure 6–6, or what we have been calling the second set of conditional probabilities. Doing so is straightforward. For example, we know the joint probability at end point C (red and even) in Figure 6–6. In addition, we know $P(E)$, the probability on the first branch on the path to that node.

Figure 6–7

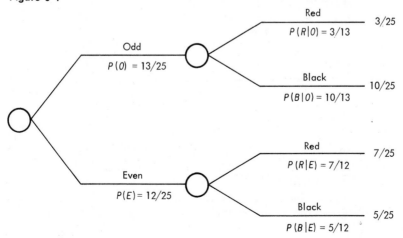

Finally, we know that the probability at the end point must be the product of the probabilities of the branches on the path leading to the end point. Hence, *P(E)*, or 12/25, and *P(R |E)* must multiply to give *P(R,E)*, or 7/25. Therefore, *P(R |E)* is just *P(R,E)* divided by *P(E)*. *P(R |E)* = (7/25)/(12/25) = 7/12. Similarly, we can divide the other end points by the unconditional probabilities in Figure 6–6 to obtain the conditional probabilities shown in Figure 6–7. Note that these probabilities are just the same as the ones obtained with the tabular method (and, in fact, the arithmetic we did was really the same in both cases). As noted above, the process of reversing the order of nodes in a probability tree (as we did in going from Figure 6–4 to Figure 6–7) is called tree flipping.

Another example

In the preceding sections we demonstrated two methods for starting with one set of unconditional and corresponding conditional probabilities, calculating joint probabilities, finding the second set of unconditional probabilities, and finally finding the second set of conditional probabilities. As a second example of these methods we return to the test for good and bad components which was described at the beginning of this chapter. Recall that a component could be either good or bad and also that the test *could say* either good or bad. Assume that one third of the components are bad and two thirds of them are good. Further, assume that the test correctly identifies three fourths of the good components, but it says that one fourth of them are bad. Thus, *P* (test says good | component is good) = ¾. Similarly, assume that the test correctly identifies four fifths of the bad components but it calls one fifth of those components good. Thus, *P* (test says good | component is bad) = ¹/₅. We will use the following notation: *TG* means test says good, *TB* means test says bad, *CG* means component is good, and *CB* means component is bad.

Table 6–6
Unconditional probabilities

CG	CB
2/3	1/3

If we use the tabular approach, we start with Tables 6–6 and 6–7. We then multiply to find the joint probabilities in Table 6–8 and add the columns and rows to find the unconditional probabilities. Finally, we use the numbers in Table 6–8 to find the second set of conditional probabilities, *P(CG |TG)*, and so on, in Table 6–9.

Table 6–7
Conditional probabilities
(given CG or CB)

	TG	*TB*
CG	3/4	1/4
CB	1/5	4/5

Alternatively, we could start with the probability tree in Figure 6–8. Then we could calculate the joint probabilities as shown at the end points in Figure 6–9. Finally, we could add to find the second set of unconditional probabilities, fill in the end points on the flipped tree, and divide to find the second set of conditional probabilities, as shown in Figure 6–10.

Table 6–8
Joint probabilities

	TG	*TB*	
CG	2/3 * 3/4 = 6/12	2/3 * 1/4 = 2/12	8/12 = P(CG)
CB	1/3 * 1/5 = 1/15	1/3 * 4/5 = 4/15	5/15 = P(CB)

6/12 + 1/15 = 34/60 = P(TG)   2/12 + 4/15 = 26/60 = P(TB)

Thus we have found in this section that in a few situations (such as the roulette wheel example) we can simply count to find all the probabilities which we might want to use. In most cases, however, counting is not feasible, and so we use alternate methods to start with some of the probabilities in a situation and calculate others. In general, the procedure is to start with one set of unconditional and conditional probabilities, find the joint probabilities, find the second set of unconditionals, and finally obtain the second set of conditionals. Either the tabular method or the tree method can be used. These techniques are especially useful for problems

Table 6–9
Probabilities conditional on test result

	TG	*TB*
CG	30/34	10/26
CB	4/34	16/26

Figure 6–8

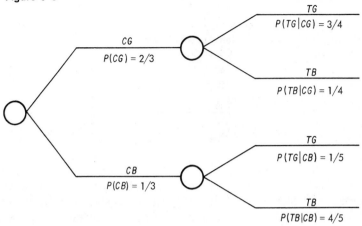

Figure 6–9

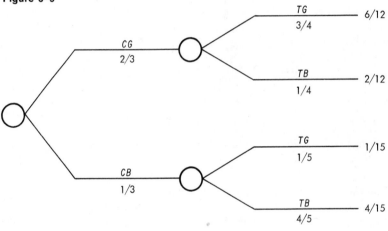

Figure 6–10

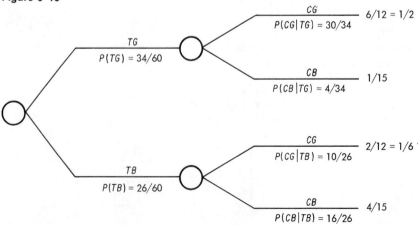

(such as the component-testing problem considered here) in which the probabilities which are available or most natural to obtain are not in the order in which they must be used in a decision diagram.

THE EXPECTED VALUE OF PERFECT INFORMATION AND THE EXPECTED NET GAIN FROM SAMPLING

We have seen that the mechanics involved in deriving probabilities for tests which are not perfect can be quite involved. In general, it is also true that evaluation of potential sources of additional information in decision problems is a complicated task. Accordingly, the question of whether or not to collect additional information about some uncertainty in a particular problem is often evaluated in two stages. First, decision makers ask for the expected value to them of obtaining *perfect* information about the uncertainty; second, if necessary, they consider the actual *imperfect* information that it is actually possible to collect. They do not believe that, in most situations, it is possible to obtain perfect information, but the fiction of perfect information is used to help screen out potential sources of real information. Basically, the idea is first to perform the relatively less difficult job of finding the expected value of perfect information. The argument then is that imperfect information can never be worth any more than the corresponding perfect information would be worth. Hence, if the imperfect information would cost more to obtain than the perfect information would be worth, the idea of obtaining the imperfect information can be immediately ruled out. Only if the imperfect information passes the first hurdle by being less expensive than the expected value of perfect information is the imperfect information analyzed further.

To see how this process works, we return to the component tester example used earlier in the chapter. Suppose that we are running a business and that we receive $60 in contribution for each component shipped but must pay a $90 penalty to our customer for each bad component shipped. The customer then repairs and uses the component, so there is no net increase in the number of components ordered if a bad component

Figure 6–11

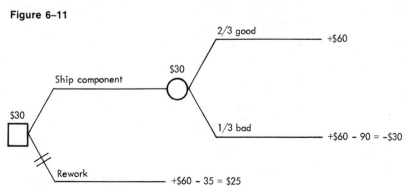

has been shipped. If we catch a bad component before it is shipped, we can rework it ourselves for $35; the component is certain to be good after reworking. In addition, suppose that there is a $10 cost per component for testing. If no test were available, the decision problem for each component would be as shown in Figure 6–11; we should ship the component.

To decide whether or not the test is worthwhile, as the decision analyst, we would begin with the fiction of a perfect test at zero cost. If we could obtain perfect information about a component, the decision tree would look like Figure 6–12, with the event node for information about whether

Figure 6–12

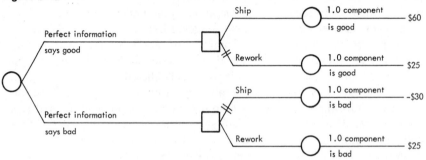

the component is good or bad *preceding* the decision on whether to ship the component. To put probabilities on this tree we argue as follows: The perfect information will say that the component is good in exactly those cases in which the component is in fact good. Hence, in our best judgment, the probability that the information will say the component is good is just 2 in 3, the probability that the component is in fact good. Similarly, the information will say that the component is bad with a probability of 1 in 3. Putting these values on the tree and solving gives an expected value of $48⅓ as shown in Figure 6–13.

The expected value for the original problem in Figure 6–11 was $30. The difference, or $18⅓, is called the expected value of perfect information (or EVPI), for it tells how much better we are, in an expected-value sense, if we know for sure whether the component is good in time to act on that information. In general, in larger and more complicated decision trees

Figure 6–13

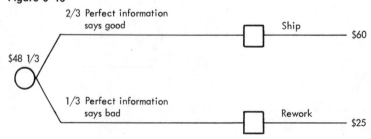

several different EVPI values can be calculated to consider the expected value of perfect information about particular uncertainties at particular times. The procedure is to solve the original tree and then redraw and evaluate a tree with the nodes reordered to reflect the new order of events and decisions if a particular piece of information is obtained at a particular time. The EVPI for the particular uncertainty at the specified time is the difference in expected value between the two decision trees.

Now consider the question of whether or not to obtain real (and thus imperfect) information. It can be argued that the value of any information lies in its ability to allow decision makers to make better decisions than they would have made without the information. Further, it can be argued that real-world information cannot be worth more to them than would be the corresponding perfect information. Hence, the analyst can use EVPI as a screen. In considering whether or not to collect some real-world information, we first calculate the corresponding EVPI. We then argue that if the EVPI is less than the cost of obtaining the real information, the real information should not be considered further. If, on the other hand, the real information costs less than the EVPI figure, we can proceed to evaluate the gain in expected value provided by the real-world or sample information (called the ENGS, for expected net gain from sampling).

In the tester example, the proposed test has passed the EVPI screen, because $10 is less than $18⅓, so we go on to consider the actual test. First we redraw the tree to consider the decision problem if we use the test and we evaluate the new tree, usually using Bayes theorem to obtain some of the probabilities that we need. Figure 6–14 shows the tree for the current problem, including some of the probabilities derived earlier in this chapter.

Figure 6–14

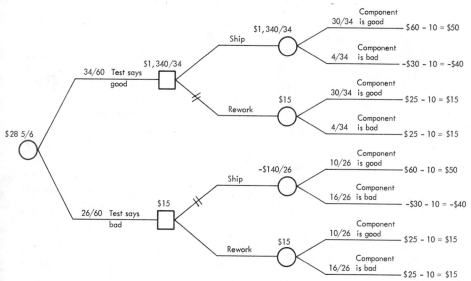

The difference in expected value of the best decisions in the problem without additional information and the best decisions with additional information is the ENGS.[4] In this case the ENGS is $28\frac{5}{6} - 30$ or $-\$1\frac{1}{6}$; hence, we should not use the test. Even though the EVPI was positive, the fact that the real test costs money, coupled with the fact that it is not entirely reliable, makes the test unattractive.

Thus, EVPI and ENGS are useful concepts for evaluating potential sources of additional information for use in decision problems. In general, the value of information lies in its ability to allow better decisions than would have been made without the information. We use the EVPI as a screen in considering what it would be worth to obtain perfect information about a particular uncertainty at a particular time. If potential sources of real or sample information cost less than the EVPI for the corresponding information, then we proceed to evaluate the real-world information, finding the ENGS. If the ENGS is positive, the real-world information is attractive. For either EVPI or ENGS, we redraw the decision tree to reflect the situation we would face with the additional (perfect or imperfect) information, evaluate the tree, and compare the resulting expected value with the expected value for the original tree, the one for the problem in which we proceeded without additional information.

EXERCISES

6.1. Analysis, Inc., a small West Coast consulting firm, is currently negotiating for two contracts. Management believes that its chance of winning the first contract is 60 percent, and that the winner will have a definite advantage in the negotiations for the second contract. It believes that if Analysis wins the first contract, it will have a 70 percent chance of winning the second, but that, if it loses the first contract, its chances for the second would drop to 1 in 10.

What is the probability that Analysis will lose both contracts? What is the probability that Analysis will win the second contract?

6.2. A large department store's experience indicates that customers who have sufficient funds in their checking accounts postdate a check by mistake once in a thousand times, whereas checks written on insufficient funds are postdated about half the time. Checks written on insufficient funds constitute 2 percent of the total. A cashier receives a postdated check from a customer. What is the probability that the customer has insufficient funds?

6.3. An outdoor carnival is scheduled to appear in a city on a given date. Experience indicates that its profit depends heavily on the weather. If it rains, the owners expect to lose $15,000; if not, they expect to make $10,000. A provision for cancellation before setup begins is written into their contract,

---

[4] Some of the literature in decision analysis also considers the EVSI (or expected value of sample information if the information were to cost nothing to obtain). In the tester problem, the EVSI is $8\frac{5}{6}$, and the ENGS is the EVSI minus the test cost of $10.

but the carnival is required to forfeit the $1,000 deposit in the event of cancellation.

Three days before the appearance, setup is scheduled to begin, and the weather bureau is predicting rain. The carnival manager hastily collects data on past weather and past predictions. Past weather data indicates that the chance of rain is .15 at this time of year, and the information on past weather bureau predictions indicates that 80 percent of the sunny days were correctly predicted, but the weather bureau prediction was correct on only half of the rainy days.

What course of action would you recommend to the carnival manager?

6.4. Bertrand's Box Paradox: Each of three boxes has two drawers. As shown below, in box A each drawer contains one gold coin; each drawer of box B contains one silver coin; while in box C, one drawer contains a gold coin, the other a silver coin.

Box A	Box B	Box C
Gold	Silver	Silver
Gold	Silver	Gold

A box is chosen at random; one of the two drawers is chosen at random and it is found to contain a gold coin. What is the probability that the coin in the other drawer of that box is also gold? One possible answer is the following: The box we picked must be either A or C. If it is A, the unopened drawer contains a gold coin; if it is C, a silver coin. Since it was just as likely that we would pick box A as that we would pick C, the probability of finding a gold coin in the unopened drawer must be 50 percent. Do you agree with this answer?

6.5. Technometrics, Inc., a large producer of electrical components, was conducting a study of its manufacturing process for a particular component with which it was having some difficulty. Under its current process, 25 percent of the units produced were defective. The contribution for this component was $40. According to the contract the company had with its customers, Technometrics refunded $60 for each defective component. The customers would then regrind the components to make them usable.

Recently, a simple tester had been developed to evaluate this particular component before shipping. For each unit, the tester would register positive, negative, or, on occasion, inconclusive. While the test was not perfect, it was consistent for a given component. That is, the same reading would be obtained for a component regardless of the number of times it was tested. To calibrate the testing instrument, it was run on a batch of known good components and a batch of known bad components. The results are shown in Table A.

Table A

	State of components	
Instrument reading	*Good*	*Defective*
Fraction positive	0.80	0.05
Fraction inconclusive	0.10	0.20
Fraction negative	0.10	0.75

For example, of the known defective components tested, 75 percent tested negative, 5 percent read positive, and for 20 percent the tester was unable to reach a verdict. The test cost $2 per component tested.

Technometrics could rework any components thought to be defective at a cost of $30 per component (regardless of whether the part was in fact defective). The reworked items could then be sold at the normal price and would definitely *not* be defective.

Management was undecided on the question of this proposed test. What would you recommend?

Case 6-1

Monitor Systems, Inc.

Monitor Systems, Inc. (MS), is a small- to medium-sized electronic systems development firm. Most of its business consists of contracts from the U.S. Department of Defense or subcontracts from large aerospace firms. In early 1967 MS's volume of orders had leveled off and MS sales personnel were instructed not to overlook any promising contract that could possibly be profitable. At this time sales came up with several small contracts, one of which was a systems monitor for a large prime contractor's development work. The remainder of this case is concerned with MS's appraisal of the merits of the systems-monitor contract.

* * * * *

Mr. Robert Bowen, President of MS, and Mr. Samuel Allen, production engineer, were discussing the systems monitor.

R. Bowen: What if we install the systems monitor at the customer location and it doesn't perform up to their specifications?

S. Allen: The contract is pretty explicit about payment and performance. We would have to rip it out, bring it back here, and rebuild it. Then ship it back to them and reinstall it.

R. Bowen: Can't we rebuild it at their location?

S. Allen: No. We use some fairly sophisticated gear in the rebuilding that can't easily be moved around.

R. Bowen: Is there a chance that it won't work after we rebuild it? I mean, this kind of thing could go on forever.

S. Allen: No, not really. We can build a near perfect system if we spend enough money. In the same way we will make sure the rebuild is perfect.

R. Bowen: Why not build it expensively initially? That would solve the problem.

S. Allen: Sure, we could do it. But it would be pretty expensive, say $84,000 installed.

R. Bowen: Well, the contract is for $100,000; we'd have a sure profit of $16,000.

S. Allen: What about your rule that a project should show a 20 percent return on the contract amount?

R. Bowen: I don't know about that. Let's think about it and come back to it later. What's the alternative to building it expensively?

S. Allen: We could use normal care and manufacture it for about $60,000.

R. Bowen: A $40,000 profit would be nice. Let's do it that way.

S. Allen: The problem is that if we did it with normal expense there would be a significant chance that the system wouldn't perform up to specifications.

R. Bowen: Oh. That's why we might have to rebuild it.

S. Allen: Exactly.

R. Bowen: Isn't there some way for us to test and iron out the bugs before we ship and install?

S. Allen: Well, every situation seems to have its little quirks. We used to think that we could simulate customer conditions and test our equipment perfectly before shipment. We've found out that it isn't quite so easy. What happens is that we can devise a test with low probability of a bad system showing favorable results, but just because the test is unfavorable, we don't know that the system is bad.

R. Bowen: That's rather confusing.

S. Allen: I've worked up some figures that should help explain it. I'll show them to you in a minute.

R. Bowen: What will it cost to test?

S. Allen: I figure that $5,000 ought to cover all costs, including sending a man to visit the customer to analyze the conditions and to build the test equipment here.

R. Bowen: What if the tests shows unfavorable results? Do we rebuild it here?

S. Allen: I really don't know if we should or not, yet. I haven't done any analysis. On the surface it seems foolish to test, get unfavorable results, then do nothing about it. If we were not planning to rebuild, then why suffer the test expense?

    The advantage in testing is that we *can* rebuild it here before shipping, and thereby avoid the expense of shipping it back and forth and the reinstallation cost.

R. Bowen: What will it cost to rebuild?

S. Allen: $25,000 is my estimate.

R. Bowen: That hurts. Is there a chance of failure after a rebuild?

S. Allen: No.

R. Bowen: As I see it, the excess cost of having the installed system turn out bad is the freight cost to bring it here, rebuild it for $25,000, freight to them again, and reinstall it.

S. Allen: That's it except for them being plenty mad about the delay.

R. Bowen: How much will the excess freight and reinstallation cost?

S. Allen: I figure about $11,000 in total. What do you think about the loss in goodwill? That is, how much would you be willing to pay not to have that happen?

R. Bowen: We do other work from time to time for them, and I'd hate to get on their bad side. About $10,000 would be my limit.

    Now about the chances of these various events happening, you know more about them than I, and you've had good judgment in the past. What do you think about them?

S. Allen: I'm glad you asked. I sat down with my design engineers yesterday, and we talked over this problem in detail. Here are my judgments as I developed them at that meeting. [At this point he handed Mr. Bowen a sheet of paper containing the information reproduced in Table 1.]

First, if we go the expensive route, there is really no chance of failure. But if we produce by the normal-expense production method, the odds are only 50–50 that the installed system will perform to specifications.

Table 1
If normal-expense production

P (system good)	0.50 .6
P (system bad)	0.50 .4
P (favorable results⎮good)	0.64 .7
P (favorable results⎮bad)	0.16 .1
P (favorable results)...................	0.40
P (unfavorable results⎮good)	0.36
P (unfavorable results⎮bad)	0.84 .9
P (unfavorable results)	0.60
P (good⎮favorable results)	0.80
P (bad⎮favorable results)	0.20
P (good⎮unfavorable results)	0.30
P (bad⎮unfavorable results)	0.70

In our meeting yesterday we talked for a long time about what the possible causes of failure could be and what kinds of tests we could perform. It became clear that there were three or four places where things could go wrong in the mating process, but we all felt that the strain gauge was crucial. It has to read at the same accuracy over a very wide range of stresses. Given the test apparatus we can put together for this job, we think the odds are eight to two that if we get a favorable report from the test, the monitor will perform to specifications. However, if we get an unfavorable report, we still think that there is a three in seven chance the monitor will perform.

This will give you an idea of the sort of thing we mulled over. After the meeting I sat down and reassessed the probabilities. You will notice in the table I've given you every probability I thought you could be interested in. A lot of them, you know, are interrelated; the reason I did so many was so that I could check on the consistency of my assessments.

By the way, if you are having trouble reading the table the vertical bar in the table is shorthand I've used to get one statement per line. You read the last line of the table like this: Given that the result of the test turns out unfavorable, the probability that the system will not perform is 0.7.

R. Bowen: Do we need all those probabilities to do an analysis?

S. Allen: No, I suppose not. I just got carried away when I drew them up.

R. Bowen: My feeling is that our best strategy is to build the inexpensive model and test it.

S. Allen: Wait a minute. Hadn't we better analyze the problem and decide whether or not to accept the contract? In addition, what about your 20 percent rule?

R. Bowen: You do whatever analysis you think is necessary and make a recommendation. That goes for the 20 percent rule, too.

Case 6–2

Hawthorne Plastics, Inc.

Hawthorne Plastics, located in Hawthorne, California, specialized in the fabrication of plastic parts as a subcontractor to companies marketing plastic products, such as manufacturers of toys, kitchenware, fishing tackle, etc. Most of its production involved the molding or extrusion of plastic raw materials, and over half of its production was for two major manufacturers of toys, located nearby. The vast majority of its customers were located in southern California, with a few in Arizona, Nevada, and northern California. In its market area the company was known for its high-quality, low-cost products. Its low cost was based on extremely efficient production methods, so efficient that on some items it produced at prices lower than the costs of the company for which it was subcontracting. Other items were produced for companies lacking their own production facilities. Still others (about 40 percent of total dollar volume) were produced as "overflow" for companies whose own production facilities were operating at capacity.

The high percentage of overflow sales had always been a matter of concern to William Campanella, Hawthorne's President and founder. His concern was based on the fact that in economic downturns the overflow business tended to decline quickly, making Hawthorne's sales revenue more cyclical than he desired. Mr. Campanella and his Marketing Manager, John D. Stein, had lately been considering the possibility of developing several proprietary lines which Hawthorne could produce and market. This would eliminate some of the uncertainty that resulted from being exclusively a subcontractor. It would also, however, require expansion of the company's three-person sales force.

The polypropylene strapping subcontract

On October 10, 1969, Mr. Stein had just completed negotiations on a subcontract proposed by the David F. Pynes Strapping Co., located in nearby Gardena, California. Pynes produced and sold a line of plastic strapping, the fastest growing part of which was used for bundling such items as magazines and newspapers. Plastic was rapidly displacing baling wire in this segment of the strapping market. The costs of wire and plastic were comparable, but plastic was more flexible than wire. Its use resulted in fewer newspapers or magazines being torn by the strapping material when the bundles were thrown during shipment.

Pynes had discovered that in spite of the obvious advantages of plastic strapping over baling wire, few newspapers and magazines were aware of it. However, with an aggressive personal selling effort the company had succeeded in converting many users to plastic. So successful was its marketing effort that sales were running nearly twice what had been projected, with the result that Pynes' plant was operating three shifts and orders were being turned down. Pynes had sought to advance the starting date on a plant expansion originally scheduled to be completed in a year, but the best that could be done was completion by April 10,1970. Consequently Pynes contacted Hawthorne to see if it could handle some of this "overflow" production.

The request came at an opportune time for Hawthorne, since capacity had just been freed up after heavy production for the Christmas toy season. The negotiations proceeded to the point where Hawthorne agreed to deliver 100,000 pounds of polypropylene plastic strapping per month to Pynes for the next six months; capacity problems at Hawthorne prevented larger shipments, although Pynes would have liked to buy more.

The price per pound that Pynes would pay depended on the quality of the strapping that Hawthorne delivered. The industry distinguished between "low camber" and "high camber" strapping: low-camber strapping was much straighter and thus was suitable for use in automated bundling machines; high-camber strapping would cause automated equipment to jam and thus was suitable for use in manual equipment only. Because low-camber strapping was sold at a higher price on the market, it was frequently referred to as "high quality," whereas the high-camber strapping was referred to as "average quality."

Pynes had agreed to pay Hawthorne 60 cents per pound for high-quality strapping and 50 cents per pound for average quality. It did not matter to Pynes which quality strapping it received, because by adjusting its own production process it could provide itself with relatively more high-quality strapping if Hawthorne provided average-quality strapping in a given month, and vice versa. Pynes would provide the production dies, and Hawthorne would deliver the strapping on spools bearing the Pynes trademark.

After consultation with his Production Engineer, Ralph Nelson, Mr. Stein signed a contract agreeing to the above terms on behalf of Hawthorne.

Mr. Stein was also influenced in his decision to take the contract by the apparent attractiveness of plastic strapping as a potential proprietary line for Hawthorne; for example, Pynes' selling price was about $1 per pound for high-quality strapping and about 75 cents per pound for average-quality strapping, which, given Hawthorne's production efficiency, would yield a nice markup. While Pynes seemed to have a strong position in the magazine and newspaper market, Stein had read of other applications of plastic strapping pioneered by other companies; for example, the Signode

Corporation of Chicago, Illinois, had developed a scheme for compressing and bundling automobile tires with plastic strapping. Mr. Stein felt that with an imaginative applications engineer other markets might be opened.

The production decisions

During the contract negotiations Mr. Nelson was considering how he would produce the polypropylene strapping. It would have to be produced by extruding polypropylene resin, which cost between 20 and 25 cents per pound, and in 100,000 pound batches because of scheduling considerations.

One of the most important unanswered questions was what production equipment to use. This issue was clouded by the fact that the quality of the strapping produced depended on what extrusion equipment was utilized and on a key characteristic of the raw material. If the average length of the chemical chain forming the molecules of the raw material exceeded a critical length, then production of high-quality strapping was possible if the right equipment were used. From raw material with shorter chains it was impossible to obtain high-quality strapping with any process available to Hawthorne.

Nelson had three manufacturing processes available to him, whose production costs increased with their ability to produce high-quality strapping. Process 1 involved the use of a simple extruding machine, and produced average-quality strapping, regardless of the raw material. Process 2 used a different machine which could utilize better temperature controls than Process 1, but which had no means of controlling pressure. Consequently Process 2 was capable of producing high-quality strapping from long chain raw material, but only if the extrusion pressure remained above 150 pounds per square inch during the processing of a batch. Process 3 involved adding pressure controls to the temperature controls used in Process 2, which guaranteed that long-chain raw materials would be converted into high-quality strapping. The capabilities of the three processes are summarized in Table 1.

Any one of the three processes could be used on any batch of raw

Table 1
Type of finished strapping for various combinations of chain length and process

	Process 1	*Process 2*	*Process 3*
Long-chain molecule	Average quality	High quality if pressure maintained above 150 psi Average quality if pressure not above 150 psi	High quality
Short-chain molecule	Average quality	Average quality	Average quality

material, but Mr. Nelson knew that once he decided on the process for any given batch, the other machine would be used for other production processes. He planned to decide on the process for the Pynes job first, since the equipment had equal costs on the alternative jobs coming up in the next six months, jobs which were far less demanding than the strapping job. However, because of scheduling problems, he knew that it was impossible to use more than one process on a given batch of strapping; further, because of the continuous nature of the process, once started it was expensive to stop and restart.

Process 1 had a variable cost of 13 cents per pound of finished strapping plus a $200 setup cost per batch, whereas Process 2 cost $700 setup plus 15 cents per pound variable cost. The most expensive process, Process 3, cost $1,200 setup plus 17 cents per pound variable cost. The difference in operating costs was due to a difference in the number of operators required in each case, and differences in the costs of setting up dies, sensing devices, and control equipment. These costs excluded the cost of raw materials; all three processes required one pound of raw material per pound of strapping. However, the Process 2 and Process 3 setup costs did include an allocation of $200 per production run, which Mr. Nelson had added to recover $1,200 that was spent in experimenting with the sensing devices and controls on the two processes. Further, the setup figures included an allowance for the nominal cleanup costs for each process. However, Mr. Nelson knew that on a few types of products, the machine used for Processes 2 and 3 required considerably more cleanup labor—up to $250 more than nominal. He was not sure whether extra cleanup would be required in the production of strapping.

Nelson had pressure data from other production runs of polypropylene on Process 2 for conditions nearly identical to those required to produce the Pynes' strapping. These data are summarized in Table 2.

Table 2
Minimum pressures observed on ten production runs using Process 2

Date of run	Minimum pressure (psi)	Date of run	Minimum pressure (psi)
2/7/68	153	9/12/68	154
3/17/68	147	12/1/68	146
4/30/68	153	3/5/69	153
6/19/68	151	3/13/69	148
7/25/68	146	8/21/69	154

Mr. Nelson planned to purchase raw material in batches large enough to produce 100,000 pounds of strapping. To him, the choice of production process would be an easy one if the chain length of the particular batch of raw material were known for sure at the time of choice. Unfortunately, this was not the case; although the manufacturer of the polypropylene resin could assure uniformity within a given batch of raw material, he could only tell Hawthorne that the chances were 50–50 that any batch of raw material would be of the long-chain variety. Since the manufacturer made no claims that the chain length of a particular batch was long, polypropylene that turned out to be short-chain could not be returned.

Accurate determination of chain length required a series of very expensive chemical tests. However, using a standard piece of test equipment in the Hawthorne lab, it was possible to perform a rough measurement of average molecular weight which would be an indicator, albeit imperfect, of chain length. It was only possible to tell from the test whether the molecular weight was "large" or "standard."

As a service to its customers, the manufacturer of the test equipment distributed various technical bulletins about the accuracy of its test equipment. One bulletin described the results of a series of experiments on samples of polypropylene that had been subjected to the elaborate and expensive chemical tests necessary to determine molecular weight accurately. The following results were obtained:

1. For batches known to be of long-chain material, 96 percent tested out as "large molecule" and 4 percent tested out as "standard molecule."
2. For batches known to be of short-chain material, 24 percent tested as "large molecule" and 76 percent tested out as "standard molecule."

Performing the test would cost $200 per batch; its inaccuracy was an inherent feature of the test which could not be improved by repeated testing of a given batch.

Mr. Nelson felt that the pressure resulting in Process 2 was unrelated to both molecular weight and chain length.

Case 6–3A

Wilson Plastics, Inc.

Wilson Plastics, Inc., manufactured metal and plastic specialty items to order. The company had moved into plastics after a quarter of a century of manufacturing small metal parts, about half by die-casting and half by stamping from sheet metal. Almost all of the plastic items were made by injection molding, using pelletized raw material.

Throughout 1969, Wilson had been experimenting with metal plating on plastic. While it was not a pioneer in the process (larger firms, such as Amerace, had used a plating process to chrome-plate such items as radio knobs for automobiles for some years), Wilson had, nonetheless, developed some unusual applications. Most of its applications relied on the fact that plastic was a strong, lightweight material that could be formed into intricate shapes at a much lower cost than most alloys, and that plating by such hard metals as chromium could then provide an exterior hard enough for bearing and mating surfaces.

Among the items the company had developed was a quick-acting butterfly valve. The valve parts were chrome-plated molded plastic; however, to get sufficiently good fits it was always necessary to do a lapping operation on the mating surface. This involved rubbing the surfaces of the valve together in the presence of an abrasive material so that a tight fit was achieved.

In the completed parts, two identifiable types of faults were evident. One was inherent to the plating process, namely, the lack of uniform adhesion of the metal to the plastic. For items such as radio knobs this was of no concern because the strength of the plating was sufficient to keep it intact, but in the valve, lack of adhesion was a primary concern. The other fault was that the plating sometimes was deposited at nonuniform thicknesses. It was felt that the two faults tended to occur together and that they resulted from irregularities in electric current flow during plating.

It was clear to the management that the plating process was not well understood; in fact, the whole operation was regarded as an art. This annoyed Wilson's chief engineer, Jon Ender, no end; he kept experimenting with the operating conditions of the process. He disliked being told by the operator that the next batch would be a good one, as if the operator were "divining" the result of the plating. But everyone referred to the batches as either 90 percent ones or 60 percent ones, these being the yields of good parts in the batch. The operator had kept careful records of all the batches she had processed. From these Mr. Ender concluded that the odds were seven in ten that a given batch would contain 10 percent defectives; otherwise it would contain about 40 percent defectives.

Mr. Ender thought that it would take him somewhere between a year and 18 months to find out enough about the process to improve it, and that after that time all batches would be of the 10 percent-defective variety. The improvement of the process, in his opinion, would come as a sudden breakthrough rather than by gradual development, because, he thought, there was something critical about the process which caused adverse electric current conditions about 30 percent of the time. Once this critical condition was discovered and understood, it could be eliminated.

His immediate problem involved deciding what to do in the interim. He considered the following alternatives:

1. He could send each batch directly to the assembly operation, as

was the present practice. The records showed the cost of delays and of the adjustment required to make an entire batch usable to be about $1,500 for each batch with 10 percent defectives, and $4,000 for each one with 40 percent.

2. He could test and rework the whole batch. He estimated that reworking would cost $2,500 per batch, and would eliminate all defectives, regardless of whether a batch was originally a 90 percent batch or originally a 60 percent one.

3. He could, for approximately $250, add a fixture to a dynamic balancing device and test a small sample drawn randomly from each batch. Because of time allocation problems in the Test Department, he decided that if he sampled, the sample size would be three. Depending upon the outcome of the sample test, he would either send the entire batch to assembly or rework it. Testing a sample of three would cost $15.

One further piece of information seemed relevant to him. Wilson supplied this valve for only one customer, and Ender obtained a prediction that he could expect orders for two batches a year. He was told that the sales revenue per order was $13,500.

Case 6–3B

Wilson Plastics, Inc. (supplement)

Mr. Ender obtained the probabilities shown in Table 1 for the number of good items in a sample of three, given knowledge of the batch from which the sample was drawn. These probabilities were read from a table of binomial probabilities, as shown in Table 2 and explained in the Appendix.

Table 1
Probability distributions for the number of good parts in a sample of size 3 for 60 percent batches and for 90 percent batches

			Outcome = Number of good units			
		0	*1*	*2*	*3*	*Total*
	90%	0.0010	0.0270	0.2430	0.7290	1.00
Type of batch	60%	0.0640	0.2880	0.4320	0.2160	1.00

Table 2

Excerpt from a binomial probability distribution

N = 3

R	P	01	02	03	04	05	06	07	08	09	10	
0		9703	9412	9127	8847	8574	8306	8044	7787	7536	7290	3
1		0294	0576	0847	1106	1354	1590	1816	2031	2236	2430	2
2		0003	0012	0026	0046	0071	0102	0137	0177	0221	0270	1
3		0000	0000	0000	0001	0001	0002	0003	0005	0007	0010	0
		99	98	97	96	95	94	93	92	91	90	P R

Probabilities of various sample outcomes given a 90 percent batch

R	P	11	12	13	14	15	16	17	18	19	20	
0		7050	6815	6585	6361	6141	5927	5718	5514	5314	5120	3
1		2614	2788	2952	3106	3251	3387	3513	3631	3740	3840	2
2		0323	0380	0441	0506	0574	0645	0720	0797	0877	0960	1
3		0013	0017	0022	0027	0034	0041	0049	0058	0069	0080	0
		89	88	87	86	85	84	83	82	81	80	P R

R	P	21	22	23	24	25	26	27	28	29	30	
0		4930	4746	4565	4390	4219	4052	3890	3732	3579	3430	3
1		3932	4015	4091	4159	4219	4271	4316	4355	4386	4410	2
2		1045	1133	1222	1313	1406	1501	1597	1693	1791	1890	1
3		0093	0106	0122	0138	0156	0176	0197	0220	0244	0270	0
		79	78	77	76	75	74	73	72	71	70	P R

R	P	31	32	33	34	35	36	37	38	39	40	
0		3285	3144	3008	2875	2746	2621	2500	2383	2270	2160	3
1		4428	4439	4444	4443	4436	4424	4406	4382	4354	4320	2
2		1989	2089	2189	2289	2389	2488	2587	2686	2783	2880	1
3		0298	0328	0359	0393	0429	0467	0507	0549	0593	0640	0
		69	68	67	66	65	64	63	62	61	60	P R

Probabilities of various sample outcomes given a 60 percent batch

R	P	41	42	43	44	45	46	47	48	49	50	
0		2054	1951	1852	1756	1664	1575	1489	1406	1327	1250	3
1		4282	4239	4191	4140	4084	4024	3961	3894	3823	3750	2
2		2975	3069	3162	3252	3341	3428	3512	3594	3674	3750	1
3		0689	0741	0795	0852	0911	0973	1038	1106	1176	1250	0
		59	58	57	56	55	54	53	52	51	50	P R

N = 4

R	P	01	02	03	04	05	06	07	08	09	10	
0		9606	9224	8853	8493	8145	7807	7481	7164	6857	6561	4
1		0388	0753	1095	1416	1715	1993	2252	2492	2713	2916	3
2		0006	0023	0051	0088	0135	0191	0254	0325	0402	0486	2
3		0000	0000	0001	0002	0005	0008	0013	0019	0027	0036	1
4		0000	0000	0000	0000	0000	0000	0000	0000	0001	0001	0
		99	98	97	96	95	94	93	92	91	90	P R

R	P	11	12	13	14	15	16	17	18	19	20	
0		6274	5997	5729	5470	5220	4979	4746	4521	4305	4096	4
1		3102	3271	3424	3562	3685	3793	3888	3970	4039	4096	3
2		0575	0669	0767	0870	0975	1084	1195	1307	1421	1536	2
3		0047	0061	0076	0094	0115	0138	0163	0191	0222	0256	1
4		0001	0002	0003	0004	0005	0007	0008	0010	0013	0016	0
		89	88	87	86	85	84	83	82	81	80	P R

R	P	21	22	23	24	25	26	27	28	29	30	
0		3895	3702	3515	3336	3164	2999	2840	2687	2541	2401	4
1		4142	4176	4200	4214	4219	4214	4201	4180	4152	4116	3
2		1651	1767	1882	1996	2109	2221	2331	2439	2544	2646	2
3		0293	0332	0375	0420	0469	0520	0575	0632	0693	0756	1
4		0019	0023	0028	0033	0039	0046	0053	0061	0071	0081	0
		79	78	77	76	75	74	73	72	71	70	P R

R	P	31	32	33	34	35	36	37	38	39	40	
0		2267	2138	2015	1897	1785	1678	1575	1478	1385	1296	4
1		4074	4025	3970	3910	3845	3775	3701	3623	3541	3456	3
2		2745	2841	2933	3021	3105	3185	3260	3330	3396	3456	2
3		0822	0891	0963	1038	1115	1194	1276	1361	1447	1536	1
4		0092	0105	0119	0134	0150	0168	0187	0209	0231	0256	0
		69	68	67	66	65	64	63	62	61	60	P R

R	P	41	42	43	44	45	46	47	48	49	50	
0		1212	1132	1056	0983	0915	0850	0789	0731	0677	0625	4
1		3368	3278	3185	3091	2995	2897	2799	2700	2600	2500	3
2		3511	3560	3604	3643	3675	3702	3723	3738	3747	3750	2
3		1627	1719	1813	1908	2005	2102	2201	2300	2400	2500	1
4		0283	0311	0342	0375	0410	0448	0488	0531	0576	0625	0
		59	58	57	56	55	54	53	52	51	50	P R

Appendix: Mr. Ender's use of a binomial probability distribution

A binomial probability distribution applies to a situation where a random sample of size n is drawn from a population, a proportion p of which has a certain property of interest. It indicates the probability that r items of the n in the sample will have the property of interest.[1]

The property of interest in this case is that an item is good. Mr. Ender was contemplating taking a sample of size 3 (thus $n = 3$) and needed to know the probability that his sample would contain 0, 1, 2, or 3 good items. Thus the possible values of $\bar{r}$ range from 0 to 3. The probability distribution of $\bar{r}$ clearly depends on the proportion p of good items in the population being sampled. In this case Mr. Ender was interested in two values of p, namely, $p = .6$ and $p = .9$, corresponding to 60 percent and 90 percent batches, respectively.

Tables of binomial probabilities are readily available; for example, one appears on pp. 655–71 of *Analysis of Decisions under Uncertainty* by Robert O. Schlaifer.[2] (Part of such a table is reproduced as Table 2.) As indicated above, Mr. Ender was interested in a probability distribution for $\bar{r}$ with sample size $n = 3$, given that $p = .6$ [written symbolically as $P(3 \rightarrow r \,|\, p = .6)$] and for $\bar{r}$ with sample size $n = 3$, given that $p = .9$ [i.e., $P(3 \rightarrow r \,|\, p = .9)$]. He obtained the probabilities in Table 1 by reading from the portion of the binomial table for $n = 3$ for the situations $p = .6$ and $p = .9$, as marked in Table 2.

If Mr. Ender had used a computer, he could have computed the binomial probability distributions easily. The formula is

$$P(n \rightarrow r \,|\, p) = \left[\frac{n!}{r!(n-r)!} \right] p^r (1-p)^{n-r},$$

where

$$n! = n(n-1)(n-2) \ldots 1,$$
$$r! = r(r-1)(r-2) \ldots 1,$$

and

$$(n-r)! = n-r)(n-r-1)(n-r-2) \ldots 1.$$

Most computer time-sharing libraries contain programs for computing the binomial distribution, where the user specifies n, r, and p.

---

[1] It should be noted that the binomial probability distribution applies to random sampling where the fraction p remains constant during sampling. In practice this is true if the sample size is small compared to the size of the population from which the sample is taken. It is also true if sampling is done with replacement; that is, after an item is drawn from the population, it is replaced in the population before the next item is drawn, but this is rarely done in practice.

[2] Robert O. Sehlaifer, *Analysis of Decisions under Uncertainty* (New York: McGraw-Hill Book Company, Inc., 1968).

Case 6–4

Caroline Development Corporation

On the morning of May 4, 1965, Mr. Robert Barker, President, chief operating executive, largest stockholder, and a director of the Caroline Development Corporation, was about to reach a final decision as to whether the company should reduce its working interest in a field with proven natural gas reserves in eastern Montana in order to acquire a working interest in an unproven tract of land in a natural gas–producing region in the bayous of southern Louisiana. The company had hitherto devoted itself to the purchase of undeveloped leaseholds containing proven reserves of natural gas, oil, or distillate,[1] and the subsequent development, production, and marketing of the product; the eastern Montana field, though larger than any in which the company had as yet acquired a working interest, was otherwise typical of the kinds of properties in which Caroline had invested and by which it had prospered in the past.

The southern Louisiana leasehold had been appraised by Mr. John Hubbell, Caroline's chief geologist and a director of the company, as a favorable location for drilling an exploratory wildcat well with the hope that if reserves were found, the rest of the field could be developed in the same fashion as any of Caroline's other properties. The lease in which the company could acquire a working interest specified that the operator (Caroline) would have the right to drill on the property for as long as gas, oil, or distillate would be produced in economic quantities, provided that drilling operations commenced by June 30, 1965; the lease would terminate automatically if drilling had not started by that date.

The decision was an extremely difficult one because each dollar already invested in the development field would produce marketable reserves in an amount which could be forecast now with reasonable accuracy, while each dollar which could be diverted to the wildcat field *might*, on the one hand, produce no reserves at all, but *could*, on the other hand, produce reserves in an amount which, though very hard to forecast now, might be very much greater than the reserves from the development field.

The problem facing Mr. Barker was complicated by the fact that most of the capital which had been used to finance the acquisition of the development field or would be used to finance the acquisition of the wildcat field was supplied by a syndicate; Caroline was to act as operator in carrying out drilling, production, and marketing, with Caroline and the syndicate sharing subsequent costs and profits in proportion to their origi-

---

[1] Distillate is a petroleum product consisting primarily of gasoline. It is found in gas wells and is separated from the gas at the wellhead.

nal shares of capital invested. Although Caroline had already invested all of its available cash in the development field, the members of the syndicate, who were eager to invest in both properties, had offered the company the opportunity to reallocate its funds in any way it desired, subject to a minimum commitment in each field acquired. Thus the alternative of diverting funds from the development into the wildcat field was not a simple one, but required a decision as to *how much* of the funds to divert.

The problem was further complicated by the fact that, even if Mr. Barker did decide to invest in the wildcat field, it was still his company's prerogative to decide what additional geologic information, if any, should be acquired before a decision was made whether or not to drill. To induce Caroline to invest in the wildcat field and to earmark funds for exploration purposes, the syndicate had agreed that if for any reason Caroline should deem it advisable to stop short of full development of reserves in that field, any such funds which had not been consumed could be used to repurchase shares in the development field from the syndicate at a slight premium over the present price.

Mr. Barker had spent the previous afternoon with Mr. Hubbell and with Mr. Victor Cass, the Vice President, Treasurer, principal financial officer, and a director of the company. He was about to meet with them again this morning in order to get the final figures which would permit him to reach a decision regarding the wildcat field by 10:00 A.M. the next day.

Company history

Caroline Development Corporation had been founded in 1959 by Mr. Barker, until then Operations Vice President of the Prometheus Petroleum Company. An energetic and enthusiastic entrepreneur, Mr. Barker had left his $40,000-a-year position at Prometheus in order to "make money for myself instead of for others," purchased the charter of a defunct oil and gas well drilling company, opened an office in downtown Denver, and invested his life savings to provide the initial capital for the company.

Mr. Hubbell and Mr. Cass, who had been colleagues of Mr. Barker's, had agreed to join in his new venture and had resigned their positions at Prometheus shortly after Mr. Barker did. John Hubbell, a geological engineer, had been responsible at Prometheus for finding and recommending to management promising sites on which to acquire drilling rights. He had developed a reputation as an extremely astute judge of locations for both wildcat and development fields, and he welcomed the opportunity to join a small company where his expertise would more directly affect his personal fortunes. Victor Cass, who had a master's degree in economics, had started in the controller's office at Prometheus, and was Assistant Treasurer there at the time of his resignation.

Mr. Barker had stated at the outset that he hoped that the company would be able to operate successfully by taking the right kinds of risks at the right times. "I'm looking forward to the time when we can take the kinds of gambles that, with a little luck, can really make this company, but right now we're just too small to do anything but play it real conservatively and try to build up our capital."

The three officers agreed to limit their activities initially to leasing and developing properties with already proven reserves. To conserve capital and to permit the company to undertake projects in widely separated geographic regions, it was agreed that all drilling and completion rigs would be supplied and operated by independent drilling contractors under routine industry contractual terms, and that all testing procedures, including seismic surveys, core drilling, and magnetometer and gravimeter studies, would similarly be contracted out.

Sources of capital

Although the initial capitalization of the company was not sufficient to provide the cash needed for the purchase or lease of any properties in which Caroline was interested, Mr. Barker was acquainted with a number of private investors who had expressed interest in providing some of the capital needed for the development of such properties in exchange for a share in the net revenue to be produced from them. One of these potential investors, Mr. H. Wentworth Moore, a New York financier, was willing to provide capital for Caroline's first venture, the development of a 320-acre plot in eastern Oklahoma. This proved to be an extremely profitable development, as several of the oil wells drilled were exploitable as dual producers, producing not only from the formation in which reserves had already been found, but also from a hitherto undiscovered shallower formation.

Mr. Moore participated several more times with Caroline in development well ventures, obtaining satisfactory returns each time. He approached Mr. Barker one day in September 1964 with a proposal that he, Mr. Moore, establish a syndicate to raise capital which could be used by Caroline to finance the acquisition and development of some really large fields on which the profit per dollar invested was higher, on the average, than on the smaller fields to which Caroline had heretofore been restricted. Mr. Moore stated that a number of his business acquaintances would be ready and willing to join such a syndicate.

As proposed by Mr. Moore, the syndicate would raise $2,500,000 by January 1965, after which time Caroline would give the syndicate right of first refusal on all investment opportunities in which the company was interested but which it could not finance internally. If the syndicate decided to invest, it would share, in proportion to its percentage participation, both in additional direct costs to be incurred and in the proceeds of the development. Caroline would be free to make whatever operating decisions were necessary without consultation with or agreement by the syndicate, but the syndicate's consent would have to be obtained before the company could in any way alter either its participation or the syndicate's in any joint deal. Mr. Moore also stated that if the company accepted his proposal, he would like to be named as a director of the company.

Mr. Cass and Mr. Hubbell argued against Mr. Moore's proposal on the grounds that Caroline would have to bear all the fixed overhead costs and that the members of the syndicate, as private investors, would have tax advantages which would not be available to the company. At the very least, they maintained, some overhead costs should be allocated to each operation in which the syndicate participated. Mr. Barker replied that he had already discussed this problem with Mr. Moore, but that the deals in which the latter had already participated had been carried out on a direct-cost basis and that he could not be persuaded to accept a less favorable basis now. He pointed out that the Moore syndicate did provide important services for Caroline, in that it permitted the company to choose among a larger variety of projects than had heretofore been possible. He emphasized that Caroline had no obligation to see to it that all of the syndicate's funds were invested, and that this worked to Caroline's advantage, since the syndicate, not the company, would absorb the difference between the funds needed for a project and the funds available, thereby permitting the company to exercise much better cash control. Finally, he argued that what the syndicate might gain was no loss to Caroline, that the availability of capital on the terms proposed by Mr. Moore was vital to the growth of the company, and that there were very few, if any, alternative sources of capital supplied on these terms. Messrs. Cass and Hubbell then agreed with Mr. Barker to accept the terms of Mr. Moore's proposal.

By January 1965, the syndicate's $2,500,000 of capital had been raised. At about the same time Mr. Cass, with Mr. Barker's approval, decided to earmark $500,000 of the company's funds for acquisition of undeveloped but proven reserves; these funds would be obtained in part from cash that had been thrown off from the company's operations, but principally from cash which had not yet been acquired, but could readily be acquired by selling "production payments." The sale of production payments, a common means of financing in the industry, was a form of loan whereby in exchange for cash the seller pledged unrecovered but proven reserves as collateral, the outstanding cash balance bearing interest and being repaid out of production from these reserves. The $500,000 to be raised in this fashion would virtually exhaust the company's present sources of ready cash; funds for developing the planned acquisitions would be largely generated by sale of production payments, using the newly acquired reserves as collateral.

Because of the availability of capital through the syndicate, Mr. Hubbell was instructed to review prospects which involved larger commitments than the company had been accustomed to making. At the urging of Mr. Moore, who spoke for the majority of the members of the syndicate, with Mr. Hubbell's enthusiastic concurrence, and in spite of Mr. Cass's heated objections, Mr. Barker authorized Mr. Hubbell to consider exploratory drilling prospects as well as development opportunities. "We're hocked up to the eyeballs with production payments," Mr. Cass protested. "If we sink this $500,000 into a wildcat and don't find reserves—and we all know that there's a pretty slim chance of hitting pay dirt on a wildcat—we'll really be in the soup. The cash flow from our existing wells, after deducting royalties, overrides, and production payments, is barely enough to pay for our current operations and overhead, with just a thin margin for profit. The results which we can get by using this $500,000 for development can really spell the difference between having a successful company and one which is just scraping by." Mr. Barker acknowledged that a wildcat venture would be risky, but argued that Mr. Cass's protest really amounted to an admission that the company *could* sustain a complete loss on a wildcat; such a loss would be very painful, he granted, but not utterly catastrophic. He agreed that it would be foolish to plunge into an exploratory venture without first giving very careful thought to the risks involved, but said that he was at this time merely authorizing Mr. Hubbell to bring interesting prospects to management's attention. He also remarked that he was confident, as a result of Mr. Hubbell's record on wildcat acquisitions at Prometheus, that Caroline would not act amateurishly in evaluating wildcat prospects.

The Elsemore field

In March 1965, after reviewing several dozen development field and wildcat opportunities, Mr. Hubbell was approached by a broker who advised him that leases could be acquired on a package of property including two natural gas and distillate wells in eastern Montana. The package consisted of the 640-acre tract on which the Elsemore Drilling Company had drilled a successful new-field wildcat in December 1963 and an adjacent 640-acre tract, on which a successful development well had been drilled. Because the field was remote from other proven reserves, there was as yet no way to utilize the potential production from these wells, but the Great Western Gas Transmission Company had guaranteed that a pipeline connection would be made by June 1966 if a major development program were begun on the property by December 1965. A contract had already been drawn whereby all gas to be produced from the property would be sold to Great Western at 15 cents per MCF (thousand cubic feet) on the basis of a 20-year depletion contract. The going price of distillate at the wellhead was $3.05 per barrel.

The package could be obtained at a cost of $2 million, with the added stipulation that if oil, gas, or distillate were found on the property the landowner would receive a one-sixth royalty, while the two present leaseholders would split a 10 percent overide[2] on the pooled production. Independent consulting engineers had estimated that the reserves obtainable through a well-conducted development program on this property would be 80 million MCF, plus about 15 barrels of distillate per 1,000 MCF.

Mr. Hubbell studied the maps of the area, the results of the seismic surveys that had been taken prior to the drilling of the Elsemore wildcat well, and the well logs, and finally paid a brief visit to the region to examine the surface geology at first hand. Upon his return to Denver, Mr. Hubbell reported enthusiastically on the prospect. His independent appraisal of the natural gas and distillate reserves coincided with the consulting engineers', and he foresaw no problems or unusual expenses in carrying out a standard development program. Mr. Barker made a few telephone calls to make sure that money could be raised through sale of production payments on the field if this were desired; he was assured by the potential lenders that as far as they were concerned the two wells on the property constituted proven reserves, even if they were not yet producing. With this assurance he then telephoned Wentworth Moore in New York. Mr. Moore expressed his interest in the proposal, and, after contacting the two other members of the executive committee of the syndicate and obtaining their approval, called Mr. Barker back to say that $1,500,000 of the syndicate's money was available for investment in the Elsemore field. Caroline's $500,000 was quickly obtained, and the transaction was completed three days later.

The directors' meeting of April 5

At the April 5 directors' meeting, Mr. Barker described plans for beginning development of the Elsemore field in December. Contracts for drilling rigs had already been signed, and discussions had been held with the President of Great Western, who stated that he was satisfied that Caroline's plans constituted a major development commitment, so that he in turn would commit his company to completing the pipeline by the following June.

Mr. Moore stated that he and the members of the syndicate were pleased with the new acquisition, but were somewhat disappointed to have uncommitted funds remaining with very little possibility of investing them in the near future in any joint venture with Caroline. Mr. Cass agreed that such a possibility was remote since no cash was to be generated from the investment in the Elsemore field for some time, and the cash throw-off

---

[2] Though technically a royalty and an override differ slightly, they both entitle the holder to receive a certain proportion of the production from a lease free from any expenses of operation.

from other operations would not be sufficient to permit him to earmark funds for additional acquisitions in the foreseeable future.

Mr. Moore replied that in order to induce Caroline to seek additional investment opportunities both on its own behalf and on the syndicate's, the members of the syndicate had agreed that if Caroline were to find an additional prospect—preferably a wildcat—in which both parties were interested, the syndicate would permit the company to withdraw some portion of the $500,000 which it had allocated to the Elsemore field and to invest these funds in the new prospect. "Of course, we'd like you to *keep* some share of the Elsemore deal—a minimum of $100,000, let's say—and if you did decide to go along on another acquisition, we'd like you to put up a minimum of about $100,000 on *it,* but except for those restrictions you could split your $500,000 any way you liked," Mr. Moore explained. "We'd like not to get into any deals where cash needs greatly exceed our present uncommitted funds, but we can always raise modest amounts of additional funds if needed."

Mr. Barker remarked that between now and December, when the development work on the Elsemore field was to begin, there was some slack time available, so that if anything interesting were to cross Mr. Hubbell's desk he thought that it should be brought to the attention of the other officers of the company and of Mr. Moore. "Another development field wouldn't cause any problem," Mr. Barker stated, "but one difficulty that I can anticipate with a wildcat field is that for any of a number of reasons we might stop short of full development; we might actually drill a dry hole, or we might even acquire some acreage and then decide not to drill at all if subsequent testing suggested that the chances of finding reserves were not as good as we originally thought. I'm sure Vic Cass will agree with me that we'd be crazy to touch a wildcat proposition unless we had set aside funds in advance to do whatever testing is necessary to drill and complete a wildcat, and to drill enough development wells to de- lineate the field and prove out the reserves; we couldn't get any outside financing until we had gotten at least that far. But if we were stopped short of that stage, we'd have cash on our hands and nothing to invest it in."

"That kind of situation would be as bad for the syndicate as it would be for Caroline," Mr. Moore commented. "However, if your concern about this problem would make this kind of investment unattractive to you, I think I could get approval from the syndicate to let you reinvest any excess cash in Elsemore. They might insist that you pay some nominal penalty—for each dollar reinvested, for instance, you might get only 90 percent as much as you got for each dollar of original investment. If that sort of arrangement sounds reasonable, I'll see if I can work it out."

Mr. Barker replied that as far as he was concerned this sounded like a fair and sensible proposal which he would like to see approved by the syndicate, and Messrs. Cass and Hubbell concurred.

The Black Star property

On the morning of Tuesday, April 27, 1965, Mr. Raymond Atwood, a broker, advised Mr. Hubbell that Black Star Petroleum, one of the major oil companies, had a lease on 3,840 acres in the bayou region of southern Louisiana which would expire on June 30 if the lessee (or a sublessee) failed to commence drilling operations on the tract by then; Black Star, though optimistic about the possibility of finding reserves, was heavily engaged in other operations, and would prefer to farm out the lease at a small profit to an operator prepared to drill at once than to devote its already taxed resources to this operation with a possibly high but also risky profit. The farmout could be obtained for a cash payment of $50 an acre, which was the bonus originally paid by Black Star to the owners of the property, provided that Caroline would provide a royalty of one eighth to the lessee and a 5 percent override to Black Star on all gas or oil discovered on the property.

The property was located six miles to the northwest of a field in which three gas distillate wells had been drilled, with reserves estimated at 144,000,000 MCF of gas plus 3,100,000 barrels of distillate. Preliminary gravimetric surveys by Black Star had indicated a structural high near the center of the property in the "Miocene Trend" around 13,000 feet below the surface. (The Miocene Trend is a geologic layer containing oil, gas, and distillate, with exceptionally high reserves and unusually high reservoir pressures, permitting wells in this layer to produce for long periods of time.) Oil and gas were often found in geologic traps located in structural highs of the sort indicated by the gravimetric survey. In the particular region in which the Black Star plot was located, oil was seldom, if ever, found; producing wells practically always contained gas and distillate only, with very close to 20 barrels of distillate per 1,000 MCF of gas. The high demand for natural gas in the industrial areas along the lower Mississippi usually resulted in rapid connections to existing pipelines; the fact that the sale of gas was intrastate permitted the buyer and seller to negotiate terms of sale without regulation by the Federal Power Commission.

Although access to the region in question might be exceedingly difficult, Mr. Hubbell nevertheless felt that the Black Star property was by far the most attractive exploratory drilling proposition that he had encountered since he began examining proposals in January. To be sure, there were many uncertainties which would have to be resolved under severe time pressure if Caroline were to make a major commitment in this deal, but no deals of this kind were without uncertainty, and the potential benefits of this one were far better than any that he had seen so far. He decided to examine the prospect at first hand, and spent the rest of the week on the site, making a geologic appraisal and contacting local drilling and seismic survey contractors. He returned to Denver over the weekend and assembled his information.

On Monday, May 3, Mr. Hubbell called Mr. Atwood to ask whether the Black Star field was still available, and whether he could have three days in which to discuss and analyze the proposition with his colleagues and the syndicate. Mr. Atwood replied that the property had not yet been farmed out, but that time was of the essence, since several other companies were extremely interested in the proposition. A $10,000 deposit would, however, hold it for two days, that is, until 10:00 A.M. on May 5. Mr. Hubbell walked across the hall to explain the situation to Mr. Barker, who immediately telephoned Wentworth Moore. Mr. Moore first told him that the syndicate had approved the terms for reinvesting funds that were tentatively proposed at the April 5 directors' meeting. Mr. Barker then described the Black Star property and asked whether the syndicate would be sufficiently interested in the proposition to risk the $10,000 deposit. "We need a couple of days to analyze this deal, and although our interests pretty generally coincide with yours, we'll obviously do what's best for us, even if it means that the syndicate will lose its deposit—but it does look like a very interesting possibility, and if you're willing to take this much of a chance we'll do the necessary pencil pushing."

Mr. Moore, replying that he would have an answer within an hour, called back 35 minutes later to say that the members of the syndicate's executive committee had authorized Caroline to make the deposit on behalf of the syndicate, which would reimburse the company forthwith. Mr. Barker, after depositing the $10,000 with Mr. Atwood, scheduled a meeting with Victor Cass and John Hubbell for 2:00 P.M. that day to discuss what Caroline should do.

The meeting of May 3, 1965

At 2:00 P.M. on May 3, 1965, Messrs. Barker, Cass, and Hubbell met in the President's office to discuss whether Caroline Development Corporation should exercise the option which had been acquired by the syndicate to sublease 3,840 acres in southern Louisiana from Black Star Petroleum for the purpose of undertaking exploratory drilling.

Mr. Barker, after announcing that a check for $10,000 reimbursing Caroline for the deposit made on the syndicate's behalf had been received that morning, asked Mr. Hubbell to present the geologic data which had stimulated his interest in the property. After reviewing the results of the gravimetric survey and the status of nearby fields, and briefly summarizing the inferences he was able to make in his on-the-spot survey, Mr. Hubbell stated that he would recommend that a wildcat well be drilled to 13,000 feet; actual production might occur between 11,000 and 13,000 feet. He said that although he would be willing to start drilling tomorrow, based on the results of the gravimetric surveys, the surface geology, and the proven reserves nearby, it would, nevertheless, be possible and perhaps prudent to see first whether a seismic survey would confirm the structural high which already existing information led him to believe was there.

Mr. Barker next asked Mr. Hubbell for his estimates on the cost of the property, of drilling, and of taking seismic tests. At $50 an acre, Mr. Hubbell replied, the property would cost $192,000, the brokerage fee being paid by Black Star. Because of the inaccessibility of the property, it would be extremely hard to move in a drilling rig by conventional methods. He had contacted a number of contractors, and all had agreed that the only feasible way to deliver a rig to the property and ready it for drilling by June 30 would be to bring in the components by helicopter, a very expensive method of delivery, but one that was often used for this kind of inaccessible location. The first well drilled would have to bear the cost of delivery as well as ordinary drilling costs; for a 13,000-foot well, this would total $450,000, although $50,000 of this amount was completion cost which could be avoided if the well were dry. To try to confirm the indicated structural high would, according to Mr. Hubbell, require a seismic survey costing about $20,000; under less time pressure it would have been possible to spend an initial $10,000, analyze the results, and cancel further expenditures if the results were conclusive, but under the existing pressures it was agreed that the issue was only whether to spend the full $20,000 or to bypass the seismic survey entirely.

When asked how certain these estimates were, Mr. Hubbell replied that the least certain one was the drilling cost, but that even this estimate would, he felt practically sure, be within a few thousand dollars of the true cost—"nothing worth worrying about in relation to the really big uncertainties we're confronted with."

Turning next to the question of the actual drilling operation, Mr. Barker first asked whether seismic information would help in the location of a drilling site. Mr. Hubbell replied that he knew right now where he would like to have the first well sunk; if the seismic survey would confirm the gravimetric survey results, he would be more certain of finding reserves, but it would not provide any additional information to guide him on *where* to drill.

"Suppose we went ahead and drilled our first well and were lucky and found natural gas and distillate reserves," said Mr. Barker. "Where would we stand?"

"We still wouldn't be out of the exploratory phase," Mr. Hubbell answered. "We'd have to drill a couple of additional wells in order to be able to evaluate our reserves with reliability comparable to our evaluation of the Elsemore field. There's a chance that one or even both holes might be dry, in which case we would be able to save the completion cost on the dry holes, but it's such a slight chance that I think it would be better to negotiate a fixed-fee contract to drill down to 13,000 feet and to complete the wells if they are successful. Using the rig already on the property, we could negotiate a contract to drill two wells for a total of $350,000, give or take a few dollars. Of course, once *those* wells were drilled, I guess we'd be essentially out of the wildcatting business and back in the development business again. We could treat this situation just as we treated the Elsemore field or any other properties in which we invest funds for development. We could take well logs, monitor the flow, evaluate the reserves, sell production payments, and begin a regular development operation. If we *didn't* succeed with the first well, though, we'd have a tough problem deciding whether and where to drill another well."

"That's not going to be a tough problem at all," Mr. Cass interrupted. "Between the syndicate and us we are certainly not going to earmark sufficient funds on this deal to include the possibility of a dry hole, a second wildcat, and two development wells, to say nothing of the cost of a seismic survey, if we decide to get seismic information first. But without funds nominally set aside for these purposes, we would have to re-negotiate with the syndicate if we wanted to try again after a dry hole. You know as well as I do that under those circumstances the syndicate wouldn't play ball with us except on terms which would be so disadvantageous to us that we wouldn't consider them. Let's make up our minds now that if we drill this one, and it's dry, we'll just chalk up our loss and go on to other things. I doubt if we'd be able to farm out the property for a nickel after drilling a dry hole on it."

"I certainly agree with you, Vic, on that issue," Mr. Barker said. "Now let's get down to brass tacks. Suppose we do find reserves, drill two additional wells, and then have the reserves in the field evaluated by some independent engineering consultants—say the outfit that evaluated the Elsemore field reserves. What do you think their evaluation will be, John?"

"Forecasting the figure which the engineering consultants will give us isn't easy, Bob, but aren't you really after something that's even harder to guess: the actual reserves in the field? After all, that's what will determine the ultimate profitability of this whole venture. Of course, we won't know that figure until 20 years or so from now, but it may turn out to be very different from the consultants' evaluation of our reserves."

"I recognize that the evaluations made at the beginning of the development phase are far from being sure things," Mr. Barker acknowledged, "but we make all of our development decisions on the basis of these evaluations, we borrow money on them, and in general we know how to live with the uncertainties associated with them. You have suggested that when we begin the development phase of the Black Star property we'll have evaluations that are of roughly the same reliability as those on our other properties, and that's all we can ask for. What's really hard about analyzing this proposal is that there's so much *more* uncertainty *now* than there is when we acquire development fields. This kind of uncertainty never bothered us so much at Prometheus because we had the resources there to more or less average out our gains and losses, but the swing on *this* deal can *really* have a big effect on us."

At this point Mr. Cass entered the discussion. "I agree that we need to forecast what the evaluation of reserves at the beginning of the development phase might be; let me ask John a couple of questions to see if we can get at something meaningful. John, suppose you had to make a bet today, which would be operative if and only if we find reserves on the Black Star property, about how the engineering consultants who evaluated the Elsemore field reserves would evaluate the reserves on the property after three wells had been drilled. Suppose you could take either side of a 50–50 bet that the reserves would be greater than 100 million MCF; which side would you take?"

"I'd certainly bet that the evaluation would be above 100 million," Mr. Hubbell replied without hesitation. "It looks to me as if all 3,840 acres could be productive; with a pay of 40 feet and a density of, say, 2,000 MCF per acre-foot, which seem to be not too unrealistic numbers, we'd have about 300 million MCF. I guess I'd find it pretty hard to answer your question if you asked me what side I'd take on a bet that the evaluation would be above 300 million. In fact, I really don't know what answer I'd give to that one. Even so, my forecast could easily be off by a factor of two."

"Do you think there's as much as a 50–50 chance that your forecast is within a factor of two?" Mr. Cass inquired. "In other words, which side of a 50–50 bet would you take—that the evaluation of reserves will be between 150 million and 600 million MCF, or that they'll be outside that range?"

"I'd bet that they'd be within that range. If you narrowed it a little— say to a factor of 1.5, that is, between 200 million and 450 million MCF—I guess I'd have a tough time deciding which side of the bet to take, and if I knew that the evaluation would be in this range I'd have trouble deciding whether it was more likely to be above 300 million than below. But I could be off by a really big amount. There's maybe about 1 chance in 100 that we'll really strike it rich—that the final evaluation will be at least four times my present forecast; and there's about an equal chance that even if we find reserves with the wildcat, the development wells will reveal that only a fraction of the property will be productive, in which case the evaluation might be no greater than one fourth of my forecast. I'm in favor of analyzing everything you can, but when you're *this* uncertain, I guess there's nothing to do but take a gamble and pray."

"If we do take the gamble we'll certainly pray," Mr. Barker interjected, "but these answers of yours may help us to decide whether to gamble or not—and how much to gamble if we do. Let me change the subject for a moment, John, and ask you what you think the chances are that we'd hit natural gas reserves if we went ahead and drilled right now."

"That's a hard one to answer directly, Bob," Mr. Hubbell replied. "You see, what I'm really betting on is that there's an anticlinal structure beneath this field that would trap the natural gas in the Miocene Trend. This kind of structural formation is common in southern Louisiana, and most of the large natural gas fields in the vicinity are formed in this way.

The well logs from nearby fields, their surface geology, and the results of Black Star's gravimetric survey all indicate that this site is an unusually good bet. We should also remember that this whole region is a particularly good one for drilling discovery wells: the historical success ratio on wildcats has been almost double that of the country as a whole—around one success in every five wildcats drilled. All in all, I'd guess that there's something better than a 50–50 chance—maybe around six chances in ten—of the structure actually being there."

"But that doesn't mean that the chances of actually finding gas are six in ten, does it, John?" Mr. Barker asked.

"No, it certainly doesn't. Even with a structure there may not be an effective seal, in which case any gas which may have been trapped would leak out. But if the structure is closed, we're in good shape. In this region about 35 percent of the anticlinal structures of this type are closed, and there's nothing about this particular site that distinguishes it from any other as regards the chances of closure."

"Tell me, John," Mr. Barker said, "whether in this region you could find natural gas where there was no structure. And are you sure to find gas if there's a closed trap?"

"The answer to your first question is almost certainly no. As far as closure is concerned, I guess it's possible for there just never to have been gas in a perfectly developed closed structure, but if we drill into a structure and don't find anything we invariably chalk up our failure to lack of closure. I suppose that what we really do is say there's closure whenever we find gas."

"OK," said Mr. Barker, "as I understand it, there's about a six-tenths chance of this site having a structure, and about a 35 percent chance of closure if there is structure. We're sure to find gas if there is both structure and closure, and sure not to otherwise. Now tell me what you think the chances of having a structure would be if we took a seismic and it confirmed your hunches."

"Well, obviously they'd be higher than six in ten, but how much higher is awfully hard to judge. What I *can* tell you is that this kind of structure is not too hard to detect with a seismic survey. If there *is* structure, there's quite a good chance—maybe 85 in 100—that the seismic will confirm it; what's really bothersome is that even if there's no structure, we may still get reflections off various intermediate layers which would result in a misleading confirmation; I guess that the chances of *that* happening are about three in ten."

"We've pulled together a lot of loose ends this afternoon," Mr. Barker remarked. "Let me just try to summarize what's been said so far. Looking at the Black Star property itself, we and the syndicate together would have to commit funds now not only to acquire the land, but also to drill and complete a wildcat and two development wells; if we were to decide to have a seismic survey taken, we'd have to commit funds for that too. If we *do* decide to go into this, we can withdraw between $100,000 and

$400,000 from our commitment in the Elsemore field, reducing our share there proportionately; and whatever we withdraw from the Elsemore field, taken as a fraction of the total cash commitment needed to go into the Black Star exploration, will determine our share in Black Star. If we quit before three wells are drilled, any cash remaining can be reinvested in the Elsemore field, though each dollar will buy only 90 percent as much as it did initially. The syndicate's $10,000 deposit will be credited against the funds which it will be required to commit if we go ahead with Black Star, but we're under no obligation to undertake the deal at all, and if we should decide against it, the syndicate loses the deposit, while we lose nothing.

"In analyzing our problem, I guess we can say that diverting funds from Elsemore to Black Star will cause us to give up objectively estimated reserves for a chance at maybe nothing or maybe some reserves, though if we *do* get reserves, it's pretty hard to pin down even what the evaluation of reserves will be, much less what the actual reserves which will materialize over the next 20 years will be. But just suppose we diverted, say, $250,000 from Elsemore to Black Star; that means we'd be giving up half of our share, or an eighth of the *total field's* reserves, or our rights to an estimated 10 million MCF of reserves. Now suppose that we *found* reserves on the Black Star property, and suppose that our share of *those* reserves turned out to be an estimated 10 million MCF. Would our diversion of funds be of no consequence, or would we be better off or worse off with this result?"

"We'd certainly be better off," Mr. Cass responded. "To begin with, after royalties and overrides we and the syndicate will be entitled to only 73.3 percent of the production from Elsemore, while the comparable figure for Black Star is 82.5 percent. The going rate is 22 cents per MCF in Louisiana, while the rate in Montana is only 15 cents. We have a 20-year depletion contract for the Elsemore field, and that's standard in Louisiana too. The cost of development per estimated MCF will be higher initially in the Louisiana fields, but if we did find reserves we'd soon have other people drilling in the vicinity; as a group we could clear and drain the land at a reasonable expense and lick the accessibility problem. The *rate* of development will be roughly the same in the two fields, and the lifting costs will be similar. The Black Star field will probably contain about 30 percent more distillate per MCF than the Elsemore field. Taking into account tax considerations, I would say that an estimated 10 million MCF of reserves in Black Star is worth about as much as an estimated 14 million MCF in Elsemore. But I certainly hope this appraisal won't tip the balance in favor of our going into this deal; even if reserves were *twice* as valuable as in Elsemore, I wouldn't favor trying it. But I think that in order to keep our thinking straight we ought to talk about the reserves in the two fields in comparable units; and since we've become accustomed to evaluating Elsemore field reserves, I suggest we talk about the possible reserves in Black Star in these units. That means we should jack up John's forecast to 420 million MCF in terms of reserves comparable to Else-more's.

"If you're satisfied with these figures, let me turn to another problem which has been bothering me. We've never really pinned down the question of whether we have time to get going before the lease expires; I gather that we'd be able to make the deadline if we didn't get seismic information, but how about if we did? Of course the seismic wouldn't be worth two hoots in hell unless we could postpone our decision to spend an initial $400,000 for the wildcat until we have the results of the test; but if we postpone the decision *too* long, we won't meet the lease deadline."

Mr. Hubbell replied that he had a seismic crew ready to start operations on Monday, May 10, if notified to do so within the next three days, and that the seismic survey and analysis would take four weeks. He had already received a guarantee from a drilling contractor that with helicopter delivery a rig would be set up to permit Caroline at a minimum to satisfy the legal definition of "commencing drilling operations" by June 25 if the contractor were notified by June 7 of Caroline's intention to drill. "It's cutting things pretty close," Mr. Hubbell admitted, "but these are reliable men, they're looking for work, and they've given their guarantees; I'm absolutely sure that it can be done."

Once drilling operations began, according to Mr. Hubbell, the success or failure of the wildcat would be known before December, when the development of the Elsemore field was to begin. "If we fail," he said, "we can devote our full resources to Elsemore; if we succeed, we'll be kept pretty busy with *two* fields being developed, but we can handle it, and under these conditions I don't think any of us would mind being kept busy." He said that by June 1966 the two development wells would be completed and that reserves could then be estimated with reasonable accuracy.

At this point Mr. Barker said that if there were no further questions or comments, he would suggest adjourning the meeting and reconvening the next day in his office at 9:00 A.M. "I'd like to mull this over and sleep on it, and I suggest you do the same. It's awfully hard to pass up this opportunity, but I just get cold feet whenever I think of where we might be if we try and fail. I think with a fresh start we'll be able to make some progress."

The meeting of May 4

On the morning of Tuesday, May 4, 1965, with one day remaining for Mr. Barker to decide whether to commit Caroline and the syndicate to exploratory drilling in the Black Star field or to forfeit the syndicate's $10,000 deposit, Messrs. Barker, Hubbell, and Cass met in the President's office at 9 o'clock to present their points of view.

Mr. Barker started off by saying that he had absolutely convinced himself that the company and syndicate should exercise the option and that Caroline should take as large a share as it could obtain. "I wish they'd let us put in all $500,000, but since they won't, let's put up the full $400,000 that they will allow. Just look at what we can get: John forecasts 300 million MCF, and in terms of Elsemore reserves that's equivalent to having more than 400 million MCF. With a maximum investment we could get a chance at close to a half share of the field, or nearly 200 million MCF of reserves comparable with Elsemore's, by giving up less than our 25 percent share, or 20 million MCF, in Elsemore. Even if we did no better than the average wildcatter in the area, we'd have one chance in five of getting these reserves, and *that* looks like a pretty attractive proposition to me. To make matters even better, though, we have the possibility of basing our decision on a seismic survey, which certainly ought to increase our chances; and in addition, if we *don't* find reserves, we not only don't lose our whole investment, but have a way of reinvesting our remaining cash immediately in a perfectly attractive venture. With added reserves of nearly 200 million MCF we'd really make our friends at Prometheus stand up and take notice of us. Vic, you've been the prophet of gloom; I hope a good night's sleep has laid your doubts to rest."

"I'm afraid not, Bob," Mr. Cass responded. "You always like to look at the bright side, but let's face facts: no matter how clever we are, the chances are *against* our finding reserves, and *then* where will we be? Sure, we won't be broke, but remember how long it took to build up our capital to the point where we could earmark this $500,000 for new acquisitions? We're in a position now where, once the Elsemore field becomes productive, we can really move ahead fast. In a couple of years we might very well be in good enough shape so that I'd be as enthusiastic about a proposition like Black Star as you are. But if we lose on this deal, it will be a long time before we're ready to try another exploratory venture.

"As far as our chances of finding reserves are concerned, the fact that we can take a seismic certainly doesn't *improve* them, as you suggested. We can decide whether to drill the wildcat or not after examining the seismic results, but don't forget there's a pretty good chance of the seismic confirming a structure which isn't there, in which case it's just been a waste of money; and there's an even worse problem: there's also a chance that the seismic will tell us not to drill when there is structure, in which case we lose not only the cost of the seismic but also abandon $200,000 worth of property on which, under *those* circumstances, even *I* would want to drill. The seismic might be worth something if we were able to base our decision to acquire the lease on its outcome, but of course Black Star wouldn't lease the property to us at only $50 an acre if they knew that a seismic had confirmed structure. As the situation stands, if $192,000 *is* committed to lease acquisition, lack of confirmation of structure by the seismic wouldn't convince me *not* to drill.

"One other thing bothers me: you talk about John's forecast of the equivalent of around 400 million MCF of Elsemore reserves as if it were a sure thing. Even if the drilling succeeds, we may find a lot less than that, in which case the picture isn't as rosy as you suggested. Of course, the reserves may also be above John's forecast, but let's remember that simply finding reserves doesn't necessarily mean that we've hit the jackpot. My position boils down to the conviction that if we do go into this deal we should not get seismic information, but if we just go ahead and drill, our chances of success are too low, our loss if we fail is too serious, and our gain if we succeed may not be great enough for me to view this whole proposition with any enthusiasm at all."

Mr. Hubbell remarked that he had come to the meeting feeling exactly as Mr. Barker did, but that he could not help being somewhat swayed by Mr. Cass's argument. "I agree that we shouldn't go into this to the tune of $400,000," he conceded, "but if we split our $500,000 between the two fields we won't be set back too far if we fail, and we still stand to do very well if we succeed. As far as the seismic goes, Vic, your argument sounds reasonable in principle, but I think we should look a little more closely at the chances that the seismic will give us erroneous information. I suggest that we take a more careful look at the consequences of diverting $250,000 from the Elsemore field to Black Star."

"That sounds like an excellent idea, John," Mr. Barker said. "Vic also made me feel uncomfortable about investing up to the limit in Black Star, and I certainly would like to consider backing off a bit. It's awfully hard to know *how much* to back off, though, and the issue of the seismic seems to add to the confusion. Why don't we take a coffee break, sharpen our pencils, and come back with some bright ideas about how to put all of these numbers and estimates together so that we can decide what to do."

_____ PART III

Using historical data to develop
probabilities

Chapter 7

Elementary forecasting

Most decision problems involve the selection of actions or sets of actions which, in some sense, lead to the best expectations for the future. In evaluating possible actions in such problems, decision makers must quantify their judgments about what is likely to occur in the future—or, more accurately, about the likelihoods of the various possible outcomes of the uncertainties which will affect the values to them of possible decisions. One way to quantify judgments about the future (the only method we have considered to this point) is through the direct judgmental assessment of probability distributions. Managers who are familiar with a particular product might use their accumulated knowledge and intuition to assess fractiles for the demand for that product the coming year; presumably, they would use all the information they knew about, such as past performance of the same or similar products or likely decisions of competitors. In the direct assessment procedure it is assumed that such information is incorporated in some unspecified way into the decision maker's knowledge and judgment and is thus involved in the assessment procedure somewhat indirectly.

Frequently it is preferable to use data from the past in some more formal way in arriving at probability distributions to be used in decision making. For example, suppose that a retailer has past weekly demand information for a particular product from the past year. Rather than asking the retailer to digest all of the demand figures and incorporate them into a judgmental probabilistic forecast for sales the coming week, for example, more systematic ways of using the past data can be suggested.

This chapter considers methods for using such data in elementary forecasting. In the first section, we consider cases in which the past and future situations are sufficiently similar in all important respects that the past data can be used directly in preparing a probabilistic forecast. In the second section we consider methods that can frequently be used in cases in which the past and future situations are not sufficiently similar to allow direct use of the data, but a human or mechanical forecaster has been providing predictions. The past predictions can be used to make the past data useful in forecasting the future situation.

HISTORICAL DATA FROM INDISTINGUISHABLE SITUATIONS

At the outset of this discussion about using historical data, you should be aware that even the more systematic methods of using data which are discussed here involve large measures of judgment. The decision makers must specify which data are useful and which are reliable, and in doing so, they use their own judgment and knowledge about the decision situations. We are suggesting ways to use past data as an indication of what is likely to happen in the future, but doing so is advisable only when the decision maker is convinced that the particular data being used are a good guide for the future.

With that warning in mind, we can proceed to consider the question of when data from the past can be used in planning for the future. Suppose that a decision maker who is concerned with some uncertain event which will occur in the future has available data from similar situations in the past. If the past data can reasonably be used to draw inferences directly about the future event, then the past data are defined as data which arose from *indistinguishable situations* (or occasions). Indistinguishable situations thus are those that, in the best judgment of the decision maker, are sufficiently alike that the results of some of them can be used to make statements about the likely results of another. The problem, of course, is in deciding when a particular set of data meets the definition of having come from indistinguishable situations.

In identifying indistinguishable situations, we are concerned with the decision maker's beliefs about an uncertainty *before* the event, not after the result becomes known. Thus the decision maker is asked to state whether, before learning about the outcomes of the various uncertainties, there was no reason to differentiate one from another. If so, for the decision maker the situations are indistinguishable. Note that this question does *not* ask whether, after the outcomes of the uncertainties, the decision maker could have explained the differences in the actual results. It focuses on the decision maker's beliefs and knowledge *before* the outcomes became known and asks if the decision maker would have given the same forecasts in each of the situations *before the fact*.

Note that this definition of indistinguishable situations relies very heavily on the judgment of the decision maker. In some cases, it is relatively easy for a decision maker to decide that data arose from indistinguishable occasions; consider, for example, the artificial example of the throw of a die. If a decision maker has past data on the results of throwing that die many times, and if the same die is to be thrown in the same manner in the future, then it certainly seems reasonable to use past information (for example, with regard to the question of the fairness of the die) in planning for the future. The past throws and the future throws are not identical, of course (they occur at different times, at the very least), but most people would consider them close enough to identical, in all ways that matter, that the past data can be used in forecasting.

Unfortunately, in most real-life cases it is possible to find some characteristics to distinguish any two situations. As an example, consider a newspaper dealer who must predict sales of a specified paper. If the dealer has available demand figures from the past several weeks, they are candidates for use in predicting tomorrow's demand. But, on further reflection, the retailer will probably worry about using demand information from last Sunday to predict tomorrow's demand if tomorrow is a Wednesday; that is, the demand pattern for Sunday papers may well be different from that for weekday papers. In this case, the decision maker might feel that each day of the week had to be considered separately. Alternatively, the retailer might believe that Saturday and Sunday were different, but that the forces giving rise to demand for papers on any of the five weekdays were sufficiently similar that these days could be considered indistinguishable. The conclusion would be that the past figures on weekday demand could be considered to come from indistinguishable situations and, hence, that they could be used in forecasting future weekday demands.

When first confronted with the problem of deciding when historical data can be used, most people tend to one extreme or the other. They may try to use all conceivable data (presumably looking for strength in numbers) and throw in data from situations which are clearly distinguishable, or they may become so concerned with the differences in the situations from which the individual items of the data have come (it is always possible to find *some* differences) that they despair of finding any useful historical results. Hence, the process of identifying useful data is a rather difficult one; the decision maker or analyst must try to decide which types of distinguishing differences matter for the particular forecasting problem and then label as indistinguishable all historical situations which did not differ in those characteristics. Data from situations which are indistinguishable from one another (and from the situation for which a forecast is needed) can be used directly in preparing a forecast (as will be shown below). Intuitively, we can think of two situations as indistinguishable if we believe that the forces that generated or will generate the outcomes of the two are comparable.

Once a decision maker has selected the useful set of historical data (i.e., the results of indistinguishable situations), the next problem is how to use that information. The appropriate methods generally differ, depending on how much past information there is. To see this point, suppose you were tossing coins. You are asked to accept a gamble whose payoff to you depends on the outcomes of tossing ten pennies, and you are allowed to experiment with the coins before the gamble in order to decide if you think they are fair (and, if any of them is not fair, what you think its probabilities are of turning up heads or tails). Suppose you throw each coin 1,000 times and the results are as listed in Table 7–1 (assume that the

Table 7–1
Results of 1,000 tosses of each coin

Coin	Heads	Tails	Coin	Heads	Tails
A	494	506	F	498	502
B	512	488	G	504	496
C	503	497	H	215	785
D	506	494	I	510	490
E	486	514	J	501	499

pennies have been designated A, B, C, . . . , J for convenience). We assume that you believe the 1,000 tosses of any one of the coins are indistinguishable (and therefore can be used in predicting the outcome of the next toss of the *same* coin), but you think there may possibly be significant differences between coins. Thus you would not, for example, predict the results of the next toss of coin J from the results of the 1,000 tosses of coin F.

On the basis of these results, most people would agree that coin H is indeed unfair. Moreover, most would be comfortable using the historical information in Table 7–1 on past tosses to assign the probabilities of heads in Table 7–2 to the outcomes of the next tosses. Thus, given enough data

Table 7–2
Probabilities of heads

Coin	Probability	Coin	Probability
A	0.5	F	0.5
B	0.5	G	0.5
C	0.5	H	0.2
D	0.5	I	0.5
E	0.5	J	0.5

from situations that seem indistinguishable to us, we are usually willing to take past values of the *relative historical frequencies* of the possible outcomes and to use those frequencies as a probability distribution.

Our willingness to do so generally depends, however, on the amount of data available. To see this point consider how you would have felt if instead of tossing each coin 1,000 times you had tossed each only 10 times, obtaining the results given in Table 7–3. If you were required to assess your probabilities of heads for each of the ten pennies without conducting any more trials, what would you do? Many people would assign a probability of tossing heads of .5 for each coin. They would reason that most pennies are fair, that fair pennies *could* give the results in Table 7–3, and that ten trials were not enough to make them believe that a coin was biased. Thus, they would have started with the notion that coins are generally fair and would have concluded that the data in Table 7–3 are not sufficiently at odds with that belief to warrant discarding it.

Table 7–3
Results of ten tosses of each coin

Coin	Heads	Tails	Coin	Heads	Tails
A	4	6	F	3	7
B	6	4	G	4	6
C	5	5	H	1	9
D	5	5	I	5	5
E	6	4	J	6	4

However, you might feel that the results in Table 7–3, together with any presumptions you might be willing to make about the fairness of the coins, had led you to conclude the coins were not all fair. In that case, what probabilities should you assign to the outcome of the tosses of the coins? One possibility is to assume that the relative frequencies observed in the ten test trials are equal to the underlying probabilities of the two possible outcomes (a similar assumption to the one made above with 1,000 trials). This assumption implies the probabilities given in Table 7–4.

Table 7–4
Probabilities of heads

Coin	Probability	Coin	Probability
A	0.4	F	0.3
B	0.6	G	0.4
C	0.5	H	0.1
D	0.5	I	0.5
E	0.6	J	0.6

Even if the results of the ten test throws have made you unwilling to accept the probability distribution that assigns equal weight to each of the two outcomes for each coin, you are probably not quite ready to accept the distributions in Table 7–4 either. Most people would argue that it might be reasonable to believe that coin H is not really fair, but surely the results of ten trials need not mirror exactly the underlying probability distribution. How often, they would ask, do ten tosses of a truly fair coin result in exactly five heads?

Note the distinction in this discussion between cases in which there is relatively little data and cases in which there is copious information. With only ten tosses per coin in the data, we would usually be reluctant to assume that results such as those in Table 7–3 were caused by an underlying unfairness of the coin rather than simply by what are called *small-sample variations* (the deviations in small samples from the expected long-run average results, caused by the very randomness of the process). In such cases, it does not seem at all appropriate to use the relative frequencies of possible outcomes directly as a probability distribution. With copious data from indistinguishable situations, on the other hand, we would generally assume that the underlying probabilities will show through, and we would be willing to use the relative frequencies as probabilities.

When decision makers have scanty historical data which they nevertheless want to use, they will be considerably less certain as to how to use the data than they would be if the data were plentiful. Unfortunately, in a real decision situation it is far more likely that they will be in the less desirable position of having some data, but not plentiful amounts. Therefore, we must consider an appropriate method for using data in such situations.

Consider the example of a newspaper dealer who has saved the figures for demand for the morning paper from the last 20 weekdays. These figures are shown in Table 7–5 and, in a different form, in Table 7–6. To forecast

Table 7–5
Past demand

Day	Demand	Day	Demand
1	55	11	46
2	47	12	49
3	54	13	52
4	61	14	44
5	51	15	59
6	48	16	50
7	50	17	41
8	54	18	56
9	59	19	54
10	43	20	46

demand for the morning paper on the 21st weekday, the dealer must first decide whether the situations giving rise to the demand on each of the 21 days can be considered to be indistinguishable (i.e., whether the data in Table 7–6 can be used directly in predicting the next demand figure). If not, then it will be necessary to assess the probability distribution for the next demand judgmentally.[1]

---

[1] Unless the dealer can somehow adjust the data to remove the effects of the distinguishing factors. This section does not discuss how to do so, but the following section will consider the question.

Table 7–6
Past demand

Number of papers	Number of days that number were demanded	Number of papers	Number of days that number were demanded
40	0	52	1
41	1	53	0
42	0	54	3
43	1	55	1
44	1	56	1
45	0	57	0
46	2	58	0
47	1	59	2
48	1	60	0
49	1	61	1
50	2	62	0
51	1		

Assume, however, that the dealer does decide that the 21 occasions are indistinguishable. One way to proceed is to assign the historical relative frequencies as a probability distribution, as was done for the probabilities of heads in Table 7–2. The result would be the probability mass function shown in Table 7–7.

Table 7–7
Probability mass function for demand on 21st day

Demand	Probability	Demand	Probability
40	0.00	52	0.05
41	0.05	53	0.00
42	0.00	54	0.15
43	0.05	55	0.05
44	0.05	56	0.05
45	0.00	57	0.00
46	0.10	58	0.00
47	0.05	59	0.10
48	0.05	60	0.00
49	0.05	61	0.05
50	0.10	62	0.00
51	0.05		

Table 7–7 does give a proper probability distribution, and it certainly corresponds closely to the historical record, but on careful examination it will very likely not be satisfactory. For one thing, the distribution in Table 7–7 implies that while demand could very well be a number between 50 and 55, there is no chance at all that demand will be 53 on the next day. Most people would feel that a demand of exactly 53 papers is certainly possible, even though none of the 20 historical figures was exactly 53. In addition, the distribution in Table 7–7 implies that demand must be be-

tween 41 and 61, the lowest and highest figures which occurred during the 20-day history. Most people would believe, on the contrary, that the lowest or highest figure which occurred during a particular 20 days of history is not the lowest or highest figure which could *ever* occur, and a better probability distribution would reflect the possibilities of more extreme values. Thus, most people would want to use the historical record as a guide in drawing a probability distribution but would not want to assign the exact historical frequencies without very large amounts of data.

To use historical data when only limited amounts are available, we suggest first calculating the historical cumulative frequencies as shown for the demand data in Table 7–8. Recall, from Chapter 5, that we can give the values of this cumulative function at *all* points, for even if a specific value did not occur (53, e.g.) or could not occur (53.5), it still makes sense to say what fraction of the outcomes did not exceed that value. The cumulative relative frequencies can then be plotted on a graph. Such a graph for the data in Table 7–8 is shown in Figure 7–1.

Table 7–8
Historical cumulative relative
frequency of demand

N = Number demanded	Fraction of days with demand not exceeding N	N = Number demanded	Fraction of days with demand not exceeding N
41	0.05	52	0.60
42	0.05	53	0.60
43	0.10	54	0.75
44	0.15	55	0.80
45	0.15	56	0.85
46	0.25	57	0.85
47	0.30	58	0.85
48	0.35	59	0.95
49	0.40	60	0.95
50	0.50	61	1.00
51	0.55	62	1.00

Our next step as a decision analyst is to go from the cumulative frequency graph in Figure 7–1 to a cumulative probability function which we can use as the distribution for demand. As argued above the unevenness of a graph like Figure 7–1 is most likely caused by the particular characteristics of the small sample of data available to us. In proceeding from Figure 7–1 to a probability distribution, we would like to smooth away some of the roughness caused by the small size of our sample. In doing so, we would certainly want to use our best judgment about what the underlying probability distribution is. One issue we must decide is how large a range to use for values of the uncertain quantity on the probability graph. In most cases, we believe that the worst or the best outcome which actually occurred in a small sample of results is definitely not the worst or the best outcome which is possible. Hence, we would want the range of possible

Figure 7–1
Historical cumulative frequencies

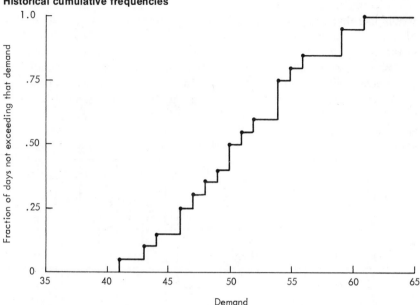

Demand

outcomes in our smoothed probability distribution to be wider than the range of outcomes in our data; because they are not based on data, these extreme points for the curve must therefore come from the best judgment of the decision maker.

In addition, especially because we are usually dealing with small amounts of historical data, it is important to apply our best judgment to the entire curve-drawing procedure. Subject to these warnings about using judgment, the following procedure is suggested for fairing in (or smoothing) a curve: try to draw a smooth curve which, insofar as possible, passes through the centers of the flats (the flat steps) in Figure 7–1. Do try to make the curve smooth; try to go through or close to the centers of the flats to the extent that you can do so without making the curve very uneven. We can justify this procedure as follows. First, we want a smooth curve because in most situations we expect probabilities to change smoothly as the values of the uncertain quantity change. We do not expect the many short alternating regions of high and then low probabilities that would be implied by a jagged curve. As for going through the flats, we can argue that for this particular example we find that for any number between 52 and 54 we can say that 60 percent of our data items were less than or equal to this number. When we draw the step graph in Figure 7–1, we show the cumulative probability of .6 for all of those values (the numbers between 52 and 54). When we draw a smooth curve, we will remove the flats and, therefore, there will be only one value at which the smoothly rising cumulative probability function takes the exact value of .60. We would like that value to be in some sense representative of the range from 52 to 54; the midpoint of the range, 53, (which is also the horizontal value at the center of the flat) is suggested as such a representative value.

Another consideration in drawing the curve is the shape it should assume near the high and low extremes. In general we suggest that the end pieces curve as shown in Figure 7–2, giving the curve a general S shape.

Figure 7–2
Constructing a cumulative probability function

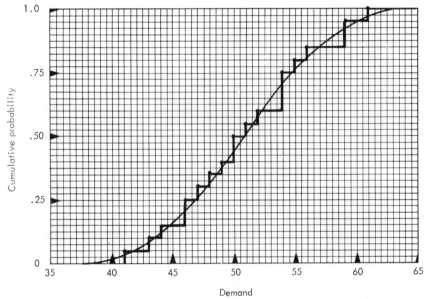

We reason that if we have identified two numbers as the highest and lowest possible (say 35 and 68 in this example), we probably think that these numbers and numbers very close to them must be quite unlikely to occur (otherwise we have probably not chosen sufficiently wide extremes). Since, as noted in Chapter 5, cumulative probability functions rise more steeply above more likely outcomes and less steeply above less likely outcomes, we argue that the tails of the cumulative curve should generally be quite flat, as they are in Figure 7–2. In addition, often we believe that a probability distribution should be unimodal, with one most likely region of values and with the curve smoothly becoming less and less steep as we move away from the most likely region. The result of all of these assumptions is an S shape.

By plotting the historical cumulative frequencies as shown in Figure 7–1 and then smoothing through a cumulative probability curve, using a judicious blend of judgment and curve fitting, we have found a distribution function which is based in a systematic way on a relatively small supply of historical data. Once we have that curve, we can use it in any of the ways we would use a probability distribution we had obtained from any other method (such as from judgmental assessment). We could take bracket medians, or we could read off fractiles of particular interest. For example, the median value in Figure 7–2 is just under 51.

Thus, to use historical data directly in constructing a probability distribution for a future uncertainty, we must first be sure that we believe that the situations from which the past data came are indistinguishable from one another and from the future situation for which we want to forecast as well: that is, we must be sure we believe that the mechanisms that caused the past results and those that will cause the future result are sufficiently similar so that we are willing to use the past results as a partial basis for our judgments about the future result. If we do have data from occasions which we feel are indistinguishable, then what we do next depends on how much data we have. In the unlikely event that we have large amounts of data, we can assign the past relative frequencies as a probability mass function for the outcomes of the future uncertainty. Alternatively, we can plot a cumulative probability graph; the copious data will result in very short flats and, hence, an almost smooth curve. In the more likely case that we have a small or moderate amount of data, we can first construct a graph of the historical cumulative frequencies, such as the one in Figure 7–1. Next, we should think about what we judge should be the extremes and the general shape of a curve through our step graph. Using those judgments and, in most cases, smoothing through the flats, we can construct a cumulative probability function such as the one shown in Figure 7–2.

DEVELOPING PROBABILITY DISTRIBUTIONS FROM POINT FORECASTS

The method developed in the preceding section is useful only when we judge that the available data came from indistinguishable situations. In most real decision situations, however, we can find one way or another to distinguish any situations from which the available data came. While some of the distinguishing characteristics can safely be ignored, there frequently remain distinguishing characteristics which must be considered explicitly. The problem is that in many cases the factors influencing the outcomes of uncertainties change so rapidly or vary so widely that it is virtually impossible to find historical data from situations which the decision maker can consider sufficiently close to indistinguishable for the results to be useful.

For example, a forecaster who is helping Susan Lee, retailer, forecast demand for the next quarter has available the past demand data shown in

Table 7–9
Past demand data

Quarter	Demand	Quarter	Demand
1	500	7	545
2	650	8	700
3	495	9	490
4	805	10	655
5	608	11	510
6	620	12	720

Table 7–9. Lee is convinced that the demands from these 12 quarters cannot be considered to come from indistinguishable occasions. First, the seasonal pattern is apparent (with particularly high demand in the 4th, 8th, and 12th quarters, for example). In addition, she knows that the marketing decisions of her company and those of its competitors have not remained constant over the 12-quarter period for which the data were gathered. In particular, she knows now (and, moreover, she knew before the fact) that the major competitor would spend proportionately less on promotion during the first six quarters than during the final six. Consequently, if she had tried to predict each of the demand figures *before* it occurred, she would have expected higher market shares for her company during the first year and a half than during the second six quarters. Because she would have forecast these values differently, we can conclude that she considers the occasions to be distinguishable.

In some cases in which only data from distinguishable occasions are available, there is not much the decision maker can do except try to digest the information contained in the data and then assess a probability distribution entirely on a judgmental basis. In other cases, however, options are available. This section considers one of them: methods that can be used on historical data from distinguishable situations when a human (or even mechanical) forecaster has been preparing single-number forecasts for the situations. Because such forecasts are commonly available in businesses, the techniques developed here are applicable in many decision problems.

Suppose the forecaster in the above example is an employee who prepares forecasts for demand of the various products the retailer sells. The forecaster does not assess an entire probability distribution (or probabilistic forecast) for each demand figure but gives only a single number (called a *point forecast*) for each. The past point forecasts the employee has prepared are as shown in Table 7–10.

The retailer believes that the forecaster has been consistent in the past in the method used to prepare the projections; moreover, she believes that the forecaster has considered all major elements which make the individual quarters distinguishable from the forecaster's point of view (so that the uncertain errors in the forecasts reflect only indistinguishable elements). Thus, for example, Lee assumes that the employee has not been

Table 7–10
Past demands and forecasts

Quarter	Forecast demand	Actual demand	Quarter	Forecast demand	Actual demand
1	510	500	7	540	545
2	620	650	8	750	700
3	500	495	9	475	490
4	840	805	10	680	655
5	635	608	11	480	510
6	600	620	12	750	720

learning to forecast more accurately (or else the forecasts would improve over time), that the forecaster does not swing regularly back and forth between high and low forecasts in an attempt to compensate for past errors (or else the forecast errors would form a regular pattern of pluses and minuses), and so on. If she is willing to make all of these assumptions (and they are substantial ones), then a probability distribution can be constructed using a *forecasting model*. The effects of distinguishing elements (in this case, the effects contained in the forecasts) are removed from the data. Then, a distribution is constructed from the residuals (or leftovers), treating them as if they had arisen from indistinguishable occasions. Finally, appropriate distinguishing elements (in this case the current forecast) are factored back in to give a probability distribution for the next uncertain quantity.

There are two main types of forecasting models. Both require a consistent forecasting procedure, so they would usually be inappropriate if, for instance, different forecasters with different methods had prepared various past forecasts or if a single forecaster had been improving over time. In addition, both models require an assumption that the forecast accounts for all major distinguishing elements in the situations (i.e., all of the factors which would have led to different expectations of their outcomes *before* the results occurred). The two models, the *absolute-error* model and the *relative-error* model, are discussed in the next sections.

Absolute-error model

Table 7–11 gives the past forecasts, together with the actual-demand figures which occurred for the forecast periods and the absolute errors, which are defined as the differences between the actuals and their respective forecasts (or the $A - F$ values). If Lee believes that the absolute errors can be assumed to come from indistinguishable situations, then the absolute-error model is appropriate. If she feels instead that the forecaster is improving with time or that the sizes of the errors in the forecasts depended on the sizes of those forecasts, with larger errors for larger forecasts, then the use of this model would not be appropriate. (In the first

Table 7–11
Absolute errors

Quarter	Forecast F	Actual A	Absolute error (A − F)	Quarter	Forecast F	Actual A	Absolute error (A − F)
1	510	500	−10	7	540	545	5
2	620	650	30	8	750	700	−50
3	500	495	− 5	9	475	490	15
4	840	805	−35	10	680	655	−25
5	635	608	−27	11	480	510	30
6	600	620	20	12	750	720	−30

of these cases *neither* forecasting model would be appropriate; in the second, the relative-error model discussed below might be useful.)

To use the absolute-error model, we (the decision analyst) first remove the effects of the distinguishing elements, which are all contained in the forecasts, by subtracting the forecasts from their corresponding actuals, as has already been done in Table 7–11. We treat the resulting error quantities as if they were data from indistinguishable occasions; hence, we can turn those errors into a probability distribution just as we would any other set of data from indistinguishable situations. Figure 7–3 shows

Figure 7–3
Absolute-error distribution

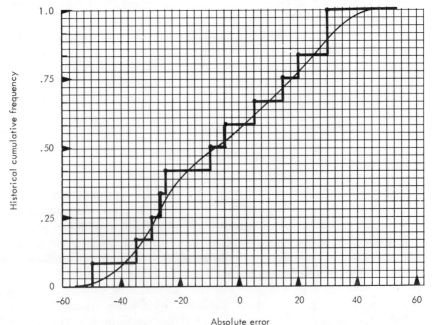

Absolute error

the probability distribution obtained from the absolute errors in Table 7–11. To construct this figure, the errors were put into size order, the historical cumulative frequency distribution (the stair steps in the figure) was constructed, and then a smooth-shaped curve was drawn through the flats. The result is a cumulative distribution function for the errors in the point forecasts made by the retailer's forecaster.

The first step in using a probability distribution such as this one is to examine the shape of the curve to see if it seems reasonable. The curve in Figure 7–3 seems to indicate bimodality (that is, it shows two regions of relatively high probability, reflected by relatively steep parts of the curve, separated by a region of lower probability, shown by a flatter part of the curve). Probability curves that seem to show bimodality should always serve as a red flag. In this case, we would ask Lee whether the forecasting process is particularly likely to give errors between −40 and −20 or else likely to give errors larger than −10 but relatively unlikely to give errors in between those two ranges. Such behavior of the errors might occur, for example, if the forecaster used one of two forecasting methods, the first of which gave negative and the second of which gave positive errors. If Lee believes that there are in fact two forecasting processes, then we would try to consider the two processes separately. We would want to identify the differences between the situations in which the first process was used from those in which the second was used. We would forecast separately for the two types of situations.

If, on the other hand, Lee determines that there does seem to be a single forecasting procedure after all, and the errors should be treated as arising from indistinguishable situations, despite the shape of the curve, she can proceed to try to use the distribution. If the errors are truly indistinguishable, however, it is very likely that the curve will be S shaped, and she should try to determine why any other type of shape has arisen.

For purposes of illustration in this case, we will proceed to use the distribution in preparing a probabilistic forecast for demand in the next quarter. To do so, we must also have the forecaster's point forecast for the next quarter, which will contain (by assumption) the effects of all factors which make that quarter distinguishable from the past quarters. Assume that the forecaster has predicted a demand of 500 units for the next quarter. Our next task is to combine this point forecast with the distribution for absolute errors to obtain a probabilistic forecast or distribution for demand in the next quarter. Since the absolute error is simply the actual minus the forecast, we want to use such errors to find possible values of the actual. To do so we merely add the current forecast to each entry on the horizontal axis in Figure 7–3; thus we obtain the distribution in Figure 7–4 for the next actual. (The errors are $A - F$; we add F to them to obtain A.) Thus Figure 7–4 is really the same as Figure 7–3, except that the horizontal axis has been relabeled. Once we have the distribution in Fig-

Figure 7–4
Distribution for next actual

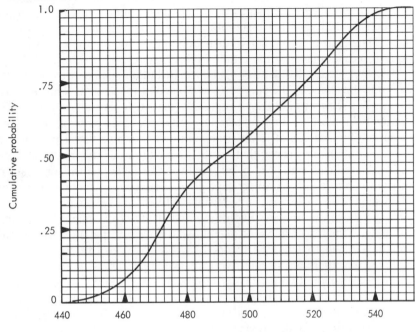

Next quarter's demand

ure 7–4 we can use it in any of the ways we use other cumulative distribution functions for demand—taking bracket medians or fractiles, for
example.

The absolute-error model (like the relative-error model described below) is useful even in situations when the forecaster is not very accurate.
If the forecaster's predictions have been consistently high, for example,
this bias will be included automatically in the error distribution, which
will show a better than 50/50 chance of a negative $A - F$ value. Similarly,
if the forecaster's past record has contained substantial errors (although
not consistently positive or negative ones) the resulting error and forecast
distributions will be spread out to indicate uncertainty in the predictions.
Thus, the absolute-error model requires only a consistent forecaster
whose absolute errors can be treated as if they were the outcomes of
indistinguishable occasions; it does not require an accurate or unbiased
forecaster.

Relative-error model

Table 7–12 gives the past forecasts and actuals together with the ratio
of each actual to the corresponding forecast. The actual to forecast (or

Table 7–12
Relative errors

Quarter	F	A	A/F	Quarter	F	A	A/F
1	510	500	0.980	7	540	545	1.009
2	620	650	1.048	8	750	700	0.933
3	500	495	0.990	9	475	490	1.032
4	840	805	0.958	10	680	655	0.963
5	635	608	0.957	11	480	510	1.063
6	600	620	1.033	12	750	720	0.960

A/F) ratios are used as measures of what are called relative errors.[2] The .980 A/F value for the first quarter indicates that in that quarter the actual (500) was 98 percent of the forecast (510). Stated differently, the actual was 2 percent below the forecast. The 1.048 for the second quarter indicates that in that quarter the actual (650) was 4.8 percent above the forecast (620).

Use of the relative-error model is extremely common, based on a belief that people tend to make larger absolute errors for larger forecasts and smaller errors for smaller forecasts; they seem to make errors of around the same *percentage* values. Thus, for example, a forecaster who tends to make errors of a hundred dollars or so in forecasting dollar figures on the order of $10,000 would not be likely to make the same magnitude of errors in predicting much larger or much smaller amounts. Rather, such a forecaster might make errors on the order of tens of dollars in predicting amounts near $1,000 but errors of tens of thousands in making predictions in the millions. These errors vary with the size of the forecasts (and the corresponding actuals), but note that they are all the same in percentage terms. Such percentage errors seem so natural and so common in human predictions that we generally have a strong initial inclination to select the relative-error model rather than the absolute-error model. Of course, if the decision maker believes that the absolute errors and not the relative ones should be treated as coming from indistinguishable situations, then the absolute-error model should be used. The relative-error model is often appropriate, but there are some situations in which the absolute-error model agrees better with the judgments of the decision maker.

The use of the relative-error model involves steps similar to those used in the absolute-error model. First, we remove the effects of distinguishing factors from the past record; to do so, we form the A/F values, as has already been done in Table 7–12. Next, we use those measures of past

---

[2] Actually, a more correct definition of the relative error would be the error $(A - F)$ divided by the actual, or else the error divided by the forecast. In order to be able to use the current point forecast in constructing a probabilistic forecast, we choose to use the error divided by the forecast, or $(A - F)/F$. Noting that $(A - F)/F$ is equal to $A/F - F/F$, or $A/F - 1$, we argue that we can use the A/F figures rather than the errors relative to the forecasts (A/F minus the constant 1).

relative errors, which we have assumed can be treated as if they arose from indistinguishable occasions, to construct a probability graph for *A/F* ratios, as shown in Figure 7–5. To construct this graph, we put the ratios into size order, plot the historical cumulative frequencies, and then smooth an S-shaped curve through the flats. We examine the curve for reasonableness and note, for example, that it does not appear bimodal (as did the curve in Figure 7–3).

Figure 7–5
Relative-error distribution

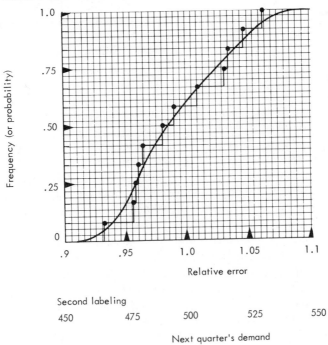

Next, we must combine the distribution in Figure 7–5 with the current forecast (assumed to be 500) to obtain a distribution for the next actual. To do so, we simply multiply each entry on the horizontal axis in the figure by the current forecast. Because the axis was originally labeled with *A/F* values, multiplying by the current *F* value gives values for the current *A* (actual) along that axis. The new labeling is shown in Figure 7–5 in the row marked second labeling at the bottom of the figure. The result of this process is a distribution for the next demand figure, which can be used with any method for manipulating probability distributions.

As was true for the absolute-error model, the relative-error model does not require a good forecaster. The distributions produced with this method will automatically be shifted left or right to account for bias and will be spread out to account for substantial error in the forecasts. The relative-error model requires only a consistent forecaster whose relative errors can be treated like the outcomes of indistinguishable occasions.

Adjusting data for one distinguishing factor

A simple extension of the methods discussed in this section can sometimes be useful when we have data which we cannot consider to have come from indistinguishable situations and when, moreover, we do not have point forecasts prepared by an appropriate person. In some of these situations we are willing to make the assumption that the occasions giving rise to the data would have been indistinguishable if it were not for the effects of a single factor.

For example, consider a chain of five retail stores. We might decide that the stores have different average sales levels but that the sales of one store relative to its average level would be indistinguishable from the sales of the second store relative to the second store's average. We might believe, for example, that the first store was just as likely to experience sales of 110 percent or less of its average as the second store was to experience sales of 110 percent or less of the second store's average, and so on. In cases for which we can make this type of assumption, there is an easy way to use the data, even though they come from distinguishable situations. Basically, the idea is to define some measure as a forecast for each data point. For the five retail stores, we would use the store averages as forecasts; the average for the first store would serve as the forecast for all sales figures for that store, the average for the second store would be considered the forecast for that store, and so on. Having identified such forecasts we could proceed to apply one of the forecasting models discussed in this chapter. For the five retail stores, our assumption about percentage changes means that the relative-error model would be appropriate. We could then prepare probabilistic forecasts for the future just as we would have if the forecasts had come from a human forecaster rather than from a mechanical process (averaging, in our example).

The two forecasting models discussed in this section can sometimes be used to render useful historical data from distinguishable occasions. For their use to be appropriate, there must, of course, be a consistent set of past point forecasts, and, in addition, the decision maker must be willing to make the necessary indistinguishability assumptions about the errors (either absolute or relative) in those forecasts. The first step in using this approach is to select one of the two models. We generally start with a strong bias in favor of the relative-error model, which uses percentage errors, but the absolute-error model is preferable in some situations. After selecting the model, we form the error terms from the past information on forecasts and actuals. We then use those numbers to create a distribution for errors. Finally, we use the current point forecast to transform this distribution to a probabilistic forecast for the next actual and use the resulting forecast in a decision problem.

EXERCISES

7.1.   The frozen food division of a large food-processing company has had quarterly sales to distributors of two firmly established product lines—peas and strawberries—as shown in Table A.

Table A

		Sales in thousand lbs.	
Year	*Quarter*	*Peas*	*Strawberries*
1969	2	439	386
	3	644	496
	4	709	728
1970	1	626	807
	2	681	589
	3	786	462
	4	572	754
1971	1	521	676
	2	843	432
	3	603	525

Based on this historical record, develop a probability distribution for the next quarter's sales for each product.

7.2.   For the past two years, Bob Cohen and J. B. Sullivan have been serving as timber estimator apprentices under Al Beers, one of the two master estimators presently retained by Shasta Timber, a moderately large wood products firm in northern California. The timber estimator is a crucial link in maintaining a steady flow of logs from the forests to the mill, for, based on his estimates, logging decisions are made and the flow is thus established. If the flow is too low, the milling operations are disrupted, and if too high, excessive waste will result. Consequently, a good estimator is a highly valued asset to any company. Shasta will soon begin developing several new areas, and a third master estimator will be required to cover these tracts. Cohen and Sullivan are prime candidates for this assignment.

A timber estimator surveys the tracts by foot and by helicopter, estimating the forest density, the average height of the trees, and their average diameter. From this data and a certain feel that is developed over many years of close association with logging operations, an estimate of the number of cubic feet of usable timber is made. This estimate is given to the manager of the Forest Operations Division, where it is locked and stored in his safe. The division manager is the only person in the company who has access to the estimate as well as to the actual yield from each of the surveyed tracts. The yield is roughly measured when the cut logs are transported from the tract to the mill.

The estimator works in an environment of little feedback, for Shasta does not inquire as to how he made his prediction, nor do they tell him the actual yield. In addition, two master estimators are never assigned to survey the same tracts. Thus the estimator does not have a standard against which he can compare his performance. In fact, the only indication that he has been performing well is that he has retained his job, since, when an estimator goes bad, he is transferred to another area.

The training program operates in precisely the same way except that the master estimator assists in the apprentice's estimates. For the past six months the two apprentices have been operating without Beers's assistance, and the performance shown in Table B has resulted.

Table B

Cohen		Sullivan	
Estimate*	Actual*	Estimate*	Actual*
1,500	1,410	1,425	1,570
1,625	1,940	1,625	2,000
1,225	1,660	1,400	1,330
1,375	1,140	1,100	1,250
1,850	1,200	1,500	1,780
1,450	1,550		

* Cubic feet per acre.

Based on these records, the division manager must decide which apprentice is to be retained.

Case 7–1

Consolidated Pulp and Paper Ltd.

Desmond O'Hara wiped the perspiration from his forehead, looked out of his window at the green countryside on this the first warm day of early summer, and thought how the cold of the northern Quebec winters seemed always to affect his world. Today, with the temperature in the high 80s, he was worrying about the river freezing over later in the year, and its effect on planning for his mill at Ste. Josette.

Supplying wood to the mill

The Consolidated Pulp and Paper Ltd. paper mill in Ste. Josette, Quebec, was the largest of the company's seven mills. It produced newsprint, operating continuously throughout a seven-day week. It had an annual capacity of 250,000 tons.

Wood to supply the mill was cut 120 miles north of the mill in the company's timber holdings or purchased from owners of timberlands near those of Consolidated. After the trees were felled they were cut into four-foot lengths and floated down the Moneskeg River to the mill. During the open season on the river, logs were caught in a boom and moved directly into the mill as needed. The location of the timberlands and the mill made this an extremely efficient form of transportation. Recent studies had indicated that the transportation was performed at a variable cost of $8 per cunit.[1]

The problems with this form of supplying the mill began when the river froze over in the fall and did not end until the spring thaw. To supply the mill during that freeze period an inventory of wood—the Block Pile—had to be built up before the freeze to last until the regular flow resumed. Every year, it seemed, there were extended and sometimes heated discussions of how big The Block Pile should be. He sat thinking through what his position would be at tomorrow's meeting when this would again be the topic for discussion.

---

[1] A cunit is a unit of measurement corresponding to 100 solid cubic feet of wood.

The meeting—June 28, 1973

O'Hara, as the mill manager at Ste. Josette, held this year's meeting in his office at the mill. The other participants in the meeting were Jacques Leveque of the Woodlands division and Harvey Wilson, an assistant treasurer from the home office in Montreal. Each participant had before him the information contained in Exhibit 1. This indicated the size of The Block Pile at the beginning of the freeze in each of the last six years and the size of the pile, if any, at the time the river opened again in the spring (this automatically became the start of the pile to be built for the following winter). O'Hara began the discussion.

Exhibit 1
Size of Block Pile at beginning and end
of freeze

Year	Size of pile in fall (000 cunits)	Size of pile in spring (000 cunits)
1967–68	100	12
1968–69	100	*
1969–70	125	40
1970–71	113	27
1971–72	110	5
1972–73	110	28

 * The pile was exhausted—12,000 cunits of wood were purchased locally.

"You both remember, I am sure, the terrible problems we had in 1969 when we exhausted the Block Pile and had to buy wood locally to keep the mill operating. The same factors which caused us to run out—high paper demand and a long freeze—affected a number of other mills the same way. With that demand our local farmers were able to charge us an effective price of about twice what it costs to buy and ship logs from the North Country—and we had no alternative but to pay or shut down the mill. In fact, that's no alternative at all because the cost of stopping our operation and then restarting makes even purchase at those costs more attractive. But the point is this: the increased cost of wood wiped out all of the mill's profit contribution that year and in fact made the mill a drain on the company. I hope we can all agree at the outset that we will build the Block Pile big enough this year so that we won't have a repetition of that fiasco."

Harvey Wilson frowned, tugged at his mustache, and finally said, "We all recognize the problem and in fact sympathize with you on it, Desmond, but remember there is another side to the coin too. Sixty-nine was really bad luck. Not only did we pick up much more newsprint business than we had forecast, but it was a devilishly long winter. It's not likely that we'll run into that combination again. Certainly we can't do all of our planning to protect ourselves against every extreme contingency. Don't forget, that Block Pile really costs big money, and we're not the old cash-cow we used to be. Our current diversification and expansion program has turned up a number of good opportunities that will yield about 20 percent before taxes on our investments. Every extra dollar you tie up in the Block Pile is one less we can use for these programs.

"I'm not quite sure what you're driving at, Harvey. Surely the cost of making the woodpile an adequate one is very small." O'Hara paused to make a few quick calculations and then continued. "We can always use any wood left over early the next winter. There would only be a cost for the added bleaching chemicals for the older wood of about $1 per cunit, and I suppose you fellows would want interest on the money tied up in shipping the wood a year too early. Since I remember the Woodlands people always have cut logs they haven't shipped at the end of the season, I know you wouldn't want to charge me on the cutting costs."

Harvey broke in and said, "That's not really the point, Desmond. It's not whether there is still cut lumber lying on the ground in the North during the winter, but whether Woodlands cuts more because of our decision on the Block Pile. Not only that, but my boss has told me that when he was involved in this he used to argue that if we cut a year too early, not only have we lost the use of those funds, but we give up a year's growth on the tree, probably somewhere between a 5 percent to 10 percent increase in wood. And don't forget, for every additional $1,000 value of the Block Pile our fire insurance cost[2] goes up by $7.50. By the way, Jacques, what kinds of costs are we looking at in Woodlands now?"

"Well, we feel pretty comfortable with evaluating our full cost for cutting a cunit at $27.50. About $23 of that is variable cost. The variable shipping cost when the log goes directly into the mill runs about $8. Of course, when you have to put a log on the top of the pile and then later send it into the mill by conveyor from the bottom, it adds about $2 per cunit to the cost."

After examining some notes, Jacques finally added, "The only other factor I might point out is that for the last few years Woodlands has been operating full out, cutting all we can and even buying from the landowners near us. Our plans for the next few years call for the same all-out operations. In fact, we have already agreed to a three-year contract with some of our regular suppliers to buy as much of their wood as we need cut into four-foot lengths at the river for $35 per cunit. No matter what decision we make here, we will need to buy some wood from them this year. By the way, what kind of demand do you fellows at Ste. Josette plan to place on us this year?"

"Demand and our backlog are such that we are almost certain we will

---

[2] For insurance purposes the Block Pile was valued at $40 per cunit.

operate through the entire winter at full capacity. That means each week we will use up 4,800 cunits of wood.

"The thing that bothers me is that how much wood I will need in the Block Pile depends not only on my rate of consumption of wood but on how long the bloody river will stay frozen. Even the Farmer's Almanac doesn't give me the answer to that one, and it really makes a difference.

"When I looked back in our files I was able to piece together the length of the freeze in each of the past ten years. For each of the years I was able to get a good fix on the last day in the fall when we moved logs directly from the boom into the mill. From our operating records I could also learn the earliest date in each year on which logs from the river were again used in production."

As O'Hara passed a sheet to each of the others (see Exhibit 2) he added: "Here is the record I was able to come up with. As you can see, there are tremendous differences from year to year."

Exhibit 2
Length of freeze of Moneskeg River by year, 1962–1973

Year	Freeze (number of days)*
1963–64	142
1964–65	151
1965–66	120
1966–67	148
1967–68	144
1968–69	170
1969–70	138
1970–71	146
1971–72	159
1972–73	130

* Number of days between last day on which logs could arrive in the fall and the first day on which logs arrived in the spring.

Case 7–2

Malaysian Tourist Development Corporation

In May 1974, M. S. R. Burhanuddin, Chairman of the Malaysian Tourist Development Corporation (MTDC), conferred with his Marketing Director, Lillian Too, on how best MTDC could present its request for increases in its promotional budget to members of the government's Treasury Committee.

Background information

Although MTDC functioned as a corporation, it was, in reality, a statutory body operating as an extended arm of the government. Technically, it was under the purview of the Ministry of Trade and Industry, and as such, all major policy matters required approval of the ministry. At the same time, MTDC operated with funds provided by the Treasury (Ministry of Finance). Each year budget estimates for the following fiscal year were presented at a meeting with officials from the Treasury. The level of funding obtained depended on how effectively senior MTDC officials could justify budgetary requests to the Treasury representatives.

The meeting scheduled for the following week was one such budget meeting. Under consideration would be MTDC's request for funds for advertising and promotional purposes for fiscal 1975. Burhanuddin and Too viewed the meeting as crucial to the success of MTDC's efforts at increasing tourism in Malaysia. This meeting was particularly crucial, since the Ministry of Finance had recently announced that budgetary increases would be limited to 5 percent unless it could be demonstrated that proposed expenditures had a definite productive impact on the economy.

Tourism and economic development in Malaysia

Although tourism was not currently a significant sector in the Malaysian economy, it was regarded by the government to be potentially significant in terms of meeting the objectives of its economic development program, the New Economic Policy. Quantitative support for this judgment was derived from the fact that visitors to Malaysia had been increasing at an annual rate of 22 percent, twice the rate of growth of GNP.

One of the central objectives of the New Economic Policy was to "generate employment opportunities at a rate sufficient to reduce current levels of unemployment and eventually bring about full employment of the whole labour force." In practice the government was engaging in activities designed to attract labor-intensive industries to Malaysia in combination with programs designed to increase the skills of the labor force as a means to achieve this objective.

Tourism was considered to be significant in terms of expanding employment opportunities, since:

1. It was highly labor intensive.
2. It provided a vehicle for the injection of foreign financial resources into the Malaysian economy.
3. Its very high growth rate showed no signs of diminishing.

MTDC's activities consisted primarily of endeavors designed to increase the flow and length of stay of visitors to Malaysia. To date, MTDC's activities had included:

1. Assisting in the development of tourist sites and facilities.
2. Implementing extensive tourist promotion activities in areas with promise as tourist sources, including the United States, Japan, Europe, and the ASEAN countries.[1]
3. Establishment of MTDC offices in areas with high tourist source potential.
4. Implementation and design of more efficient data collection systems on the flow of tourists.
5. Actively promoting Malaysia as a tourist area to members of the tourist trade.
6. Planning for orderly development of the tourist industry in Malaysia.

In addition to the activities cited above, MTDC would also be engaging in joint ventures with the private sector to develop and expand suitable tourist projects, such as hotels and resort areas. Negotiations were under way with a number of international firms and hotel chains in the industry.

The promotional budget

Promotion was but one segment of the MTDC budget. Other categories included advertising, overseas operations, MTDC operations, development projects, sales missions, public relations activities, etc. Promotional expenditures were, however, an important part of MTDC's budget. The great bulk of these funds was spent on the design, printing, and distribution of posters and brochures.

The brochures had been printed at an average cost of M$0.85[2] for 1974. MTDC was expecting a 60 percent increase in printing costs for 1975, primarily due to the skyrocketing cost of paper. It was expected that design and distribution costs would increase by about 20 percent and that other expenses would remain constant. Thus the expected per brochure costs for 1975 were:

	M$
Printing	1.36
Design	0.07
Distribution	0.05
Other expenditures	0.02
Total	1.50

---

[1] ASEAN countries included Thailand, Indonesia, the Philippines, Malaysia, and Singapore.

[2] One Malaysian dollar (M$1) equals approximately $0.44 U.S.

There were four main channels of distribution for the brochures:

1. Visitors entering Malaysia, to advise them of opportunities for tourism in Malaysia and to make their stay more pleasant. It was hoped that this would influence some individuals to make repeat visits and/or extend their stay in Malaysia.
2. The MTDC's overseas offices for foreign promotional activities.
3. The trade, i.e., travel agencies, tour operators, and airlines.
4. Journalists, to provide basic information on Malaysia to those writing stories for tourist and holiday publications.

In the past, Lillian Too had found that producing brochures based on the assumption of visitor demand consuming 70 percent of production and the other categories 30 percent had been a surprisingly accurate rule of thumb. In other words, if there was an insufficient quantity of a particular brochure, it seemed that all of the channels of distribution ran out of brochures at the same time. Thus she planned that incoming visitors would receive 70 percent of the brochures produced for 1975.

The problem of estimating the quantity to be produced was further complicated by the fact that all copies of a particular edition had to be printed at one time. This was necessitated by cost considerations as well as scheduling difficulties. Thus, once a brochure's supply was exhausted, it could not be replenished until the following year's budget made funds available. On the other hand, excess brochures were of little value. While they could be distributed in the following year, there was great reluctance to do so since the rapid growth of tourist facilities rapidly dated a particular edition. Thus excess brochures were generally recycled. Lillian Too had arbitrarily decided to set the value of an excess brochure at M$0.15, one tenth of the total production cost.

Burhanuddin and Too had decided that their best strategy for the upcoming meeting would be to develop a systematic method of estimating optimal brochure production. They decided that the best approach would be to use the data available to decide on the production level for one of MTDC's 25 publications, "Kuala Lumpur: Capital City of Malaysia." The Kuala Lumpur (KL) brochure was chosen because a substantial portion of Malaysia's visitors entered through Kuala Lumpur's airport; because it was one of the more attractive brochures in the portfolio; and because nearly all of Malaysia's visitors eventually visited Kuala Lumpur during their stay. As such, the KL brochure was included in all of the visitor information kits provided to each visitor during the entry process.

The data at Burhanuddin and Too's disposal are presented in the exhibits. Exhibit 1 summarizes the forecast and actual annual visitor arrivals to Malaysia. Exhibit 2 lists the information available on the economic impact of the brochure program.

The mechanism derived in the analysis of the KL brochure would then be applied to the other MTDC brochures. Burhanuddin and Too hoped

Exhibit 1
Estimated and actual visitor arrivals

Year	Forecast	Actual
1964	n.a.	180,686
1965	175,000	169,526
1966	300,000	335,139
1967	327,000	310,964
1968	356,000	369,255
1969	388,000	387,380
1970	473,000	555,609
1971	577,000	585,793
1972	720,000	725,883
1973	864,000	869,559
1974	1,080,000	1,097,383*
1975	1,296,000	—

* Projected total for the year on the basis of the results through September 1974.

that they could convince the Treasury of the economic impact of the brochures with their method. They realized that one measure of the brochure program's success which would be acceptable to the Treasury officials would be the tax receipts to the Treasury attributable to the program. They were also hopeful that a standardized approach would greatly increase the chances of having their proposed budgetary increases approved by the Ministry of Finance.

Exhibit 2
Economic benefits from distribution of brochures

It was estimated through the use of data on tourist spending rates and an MTDC survey on visitor reactions to brochures that each KL brochure given to a tourist entering Malaysia would induce additional spending by tourists of M$4.72.

Government economic planners estimated that consumer spending would account for M$14,254 million of estimated 1975 GNP of M$17,705 million. This can be shown to imply that each additional M$4.72 spent by tourists would produce total spending of M$24.21.*

The estimated government receipts for 1975 as a percentage of the GNP was 28.3 percent.† This meant that each brochure distributed to a visitor would yield tax receipts to the government of M$6.85.

* Computed as follows:

$$14.254/17.705 = \text{Spending as a percent of GNP} = 80.5\%$$

It is then assumed that each person (or organization) receiving M$1 will spend 80.5 percent of the M$1. The next person in the chain, who receives M$0.85, will spend 80.5 percent of that amount (or M$0.65), and so forth. Thus, the series of spending would be:

M$s:	1.00 +	0.805 +	0.648 +	0.521 +	0.420 +	0.338 +	0.272 + . . .
	↑	↑	↑	↑	↑	↑	↑
Person:	1st	2d	3d	4th	5th	6th	7th . . .

The series can be proven to sum to 5.13. Thus the total impact of the additional tourist spending + M$4.72 × 5.13 = M$24.21.

† Estimated by the following equation:

$$\frac{\text{Total government expenditures} - \text{Government deficit}}{\text{Projected GNP}}$$

Case 7–3

The Davison Press, Inc.

In early June 1961, the General Manager of the Davison Press, Mr. Frank Davison, called in his Sales Manager, Mr. Leroy Jervis, to discuss a production order soon to be sent to the firm's Printing Department for the next year's winter specialty line of diaries and calendars. It was Davison's policy to process in one lot an entire season's supply of each item of the line, since the selling season was so brief that it was impossible to foresee running out of any item before it was too late to produce a second batch without jeopardizing the company's ability to meet other commitments. Each spring, the Sales Manager prepared sales forecasts for all the items of the following winter's specialty line, taking into account the quantity of the same and similar merchandise sold in previous years by Davison and its competitors, the number and the volume of business of the retailers expected to be carrying the Davison line in December, and the general economic outlook. Mr. Davison's ordinary practice had been to go over Mr. Jervis' estimates with him, make revisions by agreement, and then produce a quantity equal to the forecast sales of each item.

Background

The Davison Press had been founded in 1921 in Cleveland as a small printing job shop, selling mainly to local small businesses. Letterheads, cards, price lists, and catalogs were produced to meet orders solicited by salespersons who visited nearby firms. During the next several years Davison did an increasing trade in special-purpose forms designed in collaboration with large manufacturers to meet their special control and record-keeping needs. Acquisition of modern, high-speed machinery in the late 20s made possible the speedy and inexpensive handling of a large volume of relatively small individual orders. Setup costs (which ordinarily accounted for more than half of the production cost of such orders) were tightly controlled. Ambitious advertising brought in customers throughout the Midwest, and revenue increased to several hundred thousand dollars per year, although competitive conditions held profit margins very low.

After barely surviving the depression under the burden of debts contracted in the purchase of the new equipment, Davison in the mid-30s sought a line of business that would tie its fortunes less tightly to the ups and downs of the business cycle, and this led to the firm's entry into the retail stationery field. Sample books were compiled and taken by salespersons to variety, drug, and department stores within a few hundred miles of Cleveland. Customers could order personalized letter paper and envelopes, making their own choice of design and paper stock and buying as few as 60 sheets. This division of the business became increasingly profitable just before and during World War II. It involved little selling cost or effort on the part of Davison, demanding only the accurate and efficient handling of orders.

After the war, attention was given to the marked seasonal character of the business. At that time, only a trickle of orders came in during the four summer months, and most of those orders were small ones. It was under these circumstances that the winter specialty line was marketed for the first time in 1951, by direct selling to the outlets that had been handling the sale of stationery. The line, originally consisting of two diaries and two appointment books, was a quick success. By 1960, sales of the line had grown to nearly $250,000 per year and were yielding a net profit of about $70,000.

Sales of the company's other lines, however, had also grown very rapidly during the decade of the 50s. Distribution area and sales volume expanded in each succeeding year, and by 1960 Davison was marketing its goods throughout the eastern half of the country. Total sales of the firm that year were over $3,100,000, yielding a net profit of about $410,000, and the seasonal pattern in sales had virtually disappeared. In fact, overtime operation of most of the company's facilities had been necessary through a great part of 1960. Although a move to larger quarters was planned, it seemed clear that overtime operation would be called for continuously until early 1962; it was estimated that about 20 percent of all direct labor hours worked during the remainder of 1961 would be performed on overtime. Mr. Davison did not believe that he would actually have to refuse any orders, or that the effort to obtain them should be slackened, but he did believe that it was important to estimate sales closely enough to avoid any serious overruns, since the loss arising from the printing of one diary or appointment book too many would be far greater than the profit which would be forfeited if one too few to satisfy demand were printed.

Jervis' record and recommendation

In the summer of 1958 the whole winter specialty line had been redesigned and Jervis had been hired as Sales Manager, with responsibility for all lines except the custom-designed business forms. During the past three years, the items in the winter specialty line had been as follows: No. 1 was a large (8 × 11), handsomely laid out diary, with a simulated leather cover, selling at retail for about $7.50; No. 2 was a smaller (5 × 8) diary and daily appointment book, of somewhat less sumptuous appearance, retailing at around $3.00; No. 3 was a weekly memorandum book, with spaces for notations relating to each hour (9:00 through 4:00) and each day of the week, which sold for $1.75; Nos. 4 and 5 were pocket diaries, one bound in Leatheroid and the other in paper, selling for $1.00

and $0.65, respectively. Mr. Davison felt that uniformity and continuity were better buying incentives than novelty, and the 1962 line was to differ from its predecessors only to the extent necessary to accord with the change in the calendar. In general, Mr. Davison was quite satisfied with the rate of growth of winter specialty sales; the greatest potential for future growth, he felt, was in other directions, but winter specialty production would keep the expanded facilities fully employed, and on high-margin goods at that.

As regards sales forecasts, Mr. Davison felt that Jervis' record in predicting sales of the winter specialty line (Exhibit 1) was amazingly good, much better than that of his predecessor and much better than Jervis' own record in predicting sales of stationery. But even though he was impressed with the small percentage error in Jervis' predictions, Mr. Davison had noticed that the predictions were frequently on the high side, where errors were more expensive; and he wondered whether the sales forecast should not be revised downward in determining the number of units to be ordered into production. His reasoning was that "producing a lot too few is no worse than producing a few too many."

Exhibit 1
Winter specialty sales and forecasts (hundreds of units)

	No. 1	No. 2	No. 3	No. 4	No. 5
1959 estimate	82	199	388	174	585
Actual to 11/15	68	134	218	130	413
Actual total	82*	189	301	174*	584
1960 estimate	128	316	564	261	915
Actual to 11/15	88	236	370	162	673
Actual total	123	316*	552	225	915*
1961 estimate	136	320	589	273	972
Actual to 11/15	92	294	369	191	627
Actual total	134	320*	539	273*	892
1962 estimate	176	435	770	360	1,175

  * Sales limited by stockout.

Jervis disagreed strongly with this view. He pointed out that when a store or a consumer wanted to buy an item and could not do so, bad will was likely to be created that would endure and make future selling more difficult. In the first place, he said, someone who bought a diary this year was far more likely to buy one next year than someone who did not; hence, failure to make a sale should be considered to entail a far greater loss than the forfeited profit on one diary. Furthermore, a store owner who was disappointed or annoyed by the situation might stop pushing the line or might even refuse to handle it at all. Therefore, Jervis concluded, it was actually *worse* rather than better to produce too little rather than too much. Because of the marked dissimilarity of the prices and uses of the various items in the line, it was unlikely that a person wishing to buy one of them would be willing to take another instead; he would buy a competitor's product, or none at all.

Mr. Davison acknowledged that Jervis had made out a good case for a generous production order, but he argued that at least as good a case could be made out on the other side. For instance, many of those who bought diaries and appointment books used them only during the earliest months of the year and then neglected them, and such people could not be considered as likely sales prospects in the following year. It might even be claimed that if such a person had *wanted* to buy an item in 1962, he would buy one in 1963 only if he had *not* actually bought one in 1962; in these cases, no money, except possibly a small amount of interest, would be lost as a result of the undersupply. In addition, regular users of Davison products would almost surely buy their new books soon after these appeared on the market, from the first shipment their retailers received from Davison, and even when Davison did run out of stock, this never prevented filling the retailers' *initial* orders, virtually all of which were received before November 15.

As to the matter of goodwill, Davison said that the primary objective of the Press was not to increase the respect or affection it received from customers; this was a pleasant incident, not to be confused with practical, dollar-and-cent considerations. If goodwill implied potential for future profits, it should be considered, but if it referred to a state of mind not closely connected with willingness to buy, it should be ignored. In this instance, his judgment was that Jervis' case was overstated. Davison had enjoyed good relations with most of its present outlets over a period of some years, and most of them handled the lucrative stationery sales the year round. They would regard an inability to fill orders at the tag end of the season as entirely understandable and forgivable. After all, they were themselves conservative in their stocking policy, preferring as a rule to run out and have to reorder rather than have to scrap surplus or sell it at a loss. For a retailer to hide the diaries behind the counter next year would be stupidly self-destructive; the retailer had more to lose by this than Davison. The retailer's profits from the Davison line were sufficient, even if lower than they might be, to dissuade him from trying to switch to a competitor, and in any case there was no reason to think that either of Davison's chief competitors in the field of diaries and appointment books was superior to Davison as regards out-of-stocks. On balance, Mr. Davison felt that while the total loss resulting from insufficient stock was perhaps a little greater than the foregone immediate profit, the difference was almost certainly negligible. He was satisfied to treat it as zero and, if this proved wrong, to learn from the experience. This seemed better than to assume the contrary and never be able to check the validity of the assumption. Damage done would not be permanent, especially on the retailer level, where it could be excused if necessary as a single year's aberration rather than the result of any change of policy. And since overtime was being incurred this year but would probably not be needed next year, the present seemed an unusually good time to try the experiment of producing below Jervis' sales forecast.

Jervis did not contest further the matter of "goodwill" losses, but he reacted quite strongly to Davison's mention of costs. "It's no wonder these diaries look expensive when the boys down in accounting are finished with us; we're charged for everything from the watchman's salary to the paint on the back fence. It's ridiculous; they could be printed in gold ink for the costs that they've got on the books. When are we going to get a fair deal on this? And another thing, why is work charged at the overtime rate just because the company was making business forms before it got into the diary business? Davison Press makes a much higher profit margin per press hour on diaries than it does on forms and catalogs; if we had to choose between making diaries and making forms, we would certainly choose diaries. It's the *forms* that should be charged the overtime rate. The only real expense in producing more diaries is material and labor, but instead of recognizing this, accounting is even charging diaries with depreciation on the presses that are going to be sold for scrap when we move next year. And anyway, even if the costs *were* figured right, I don't understand this business of producing some number other than the number we expect to sell. Just because one kind of mistake is cheaper than another, why commit one of the cheaper mistakes on purpose?"

What are the costs?

Before trying to make up his own mind about Jervis' last question, Mr. Davison decided to clear up the cost question, and with this in view he asked Mr. Herman Lewis, his Chief Accountant and Assistant Treasurer, to prepare a detailed cost breakdown for each item of the winter specialty line, showing how much it would cost per unit to produce a lot of the size recommended by Jervis for each item. The next day, Lewis came to Mr. Davison's office with the information requested of him (Exhibit 2). Mr. Davison raised the questions brought up by Jervis the previous day, with particular emphasis on the matter of overtime charges and undue overhead allocations, and Lewis vigorously defended his department's methods and results.

In the first place, Lewis said, every penny of expense incurred by Davison had to be attributed or allocated to some product. "The reason why there is a back fence to be painted and a janitor to be paid is that we are making and selling printed pieces of paper of one kind or another. These costs wouldn't exist if we weren't here doing printing, and they are just as much a part of the total cost of the work we do as electricity and labor are. They appear on our income statement, and unless the prices we set and the revenue we receive take account of them, we will be operating in the red and going broke. Nobody is smart enough to know what part of

Exhibit 2

Estimated costs for 1962 winter specialty production (dollars per 100)

		No. 1	No. 2	No. 3	No. 4	No. 5
1.	Setup labor	4.38	1.34	0.69	0.31	0.31
2.	Pressroom labor	5.03	1.97	1.01	0.79	0.79
3.	Total direct labor	9.41	3.31	1.70	1.10	1.10
4.	Supervisory labor	3.51	1.23	0.63	0.41	0.41
5.	Overtime premium	6.46	2.27	1.16	0.76	0.76
6.	Payroll taxes, etc.	2.33	0.82	0.42	0.27	0.27
7.	Setup materials and plates	12.14	4.08	2.13	0.82	0.82
8.	Pressroom materials and stock	25.33	13.40	4.35	2.11	2.11
9.	Power	0.78	0.64	0.61	0.42	0.42
10.	Press maintenance	0.47	0.19	0.11	0.09	0.09
11.	Press depreciation	2.46	0.98	0.51	0.40	0.40
12.	Other plant overhead	27.67	9.73	5.00	3.23	3.23
13.	Binding, fixed charge	3.41	1.15	0.65	1.11	0.08
14.	Binding, per 100 units bound	81.17	29.94	20.25	12.63	3.23
15.	Total manufactured cost	175.14	67.74	37.52	23.25	12.92
16.	Winter specialty S and A	40.81	15.78	8.74	5.44	3.01
17.	General overhead	128.20	49.59	27.46	17.09	9.46
18.	Total cost	344.15	133.11	73.72	45.78	25.39
19.	Price to dealers	485.00	187.50	105.00	65.00	37.50

Row

1, 7	Total cost divided by estimated units produced.
4	37.3 percent of line 3.
5	50.0 percent of lines 3 and 4.
6	12.0 percent of lines 3, 4, and 5.
11	Straight-line depreciation allocated to products by press hours.
12	294 percent of line 3; includes insurance and property taxes.
13, 14	Binding done by outside contractor who charges a fixed amount for each style plus an amount proportional to the number of units produced.
16	23.3 percent of line 15.
17	73.2 percent of line 15.

some of these overhead charges should be viewed as being due to production of business forms, which to stationery, and so forth, and I don't pretend that we can calculate the precise cost of each piece of paper that we sell. But the total amounts we allocate come from an overhead budget that has been very carefully prepared, and the formulas we use in allocating these amounts are consistent, reasonable, and fair. The manufacturing overhead we incur in the plant is divided among our products in proportion to direct-labor hours because the reason we have a plant is so that direct labor can be performed. Executive salaries and general office expenses are charged in proportion to what it costs us to make the products, the same as we would do if we bought the products outside, except, of course, that any expense that we can trace directly to a particular line, like the salaries of the stationery salespeople, is charged to that line. As to depreciation of buildings and equipment, it appears on our income statement as a cost, and it *is* a cost, just the same as the ink we use up is a cost, whether we buy it in the same period we use it or not. Our method of cost accounting is entirely modern and accepted. Naturally, we'd all like to see the costs as low as possible; I don't blame Jervis for that. But he should see the effects beyond his own department. If we report a lower cost for one of his babies, we'll have to pile it onto someone else's, and he'll complain the same way that Jervis does now. I can't see that there's a suggestion here for a better *system* than the present one—just one person trying to get an advantage over someone else."

Lewis felt less certain about the proper handling of the overtime charges. Historically, of course, the winter specialty line had been taken on mainly to keep the presses running during the slack season; business forms were the bread-and-butter line. Hence, on those few occasions prior to 1961 when overtime had been necessary during the summer, its cost had been charged to winter specialties. It was true that diary sheets and appointment book pages were produced steadily throughout the working day (during both regular and overtime hours), whereas business form orders, which often could be run off in only a couple of hours of press time, might be printed at any time, regular or not. The plant usually ran with a reduced work force after the regular closing time; in particular, the setup people almost never worked overtime. It would be possible to calculate costs on the basis of actual press-hour charges (orders run wholly or partly after 5:30 being charged at time and a half); or he could average out the costs and charge the average rate to all lines alike, whether run on overtime or not. Basically, Lewis felt that this was a policy question that should be settled by Mr. Davison rather than by himself.

Case 7–4

Palo Alto Products, Inc.

Palo Alto Products, Inc., a producer of digital equipment which specialized in supplying the automobile industry, had received an informal invitation to bid on the purchase of a batch of transistors from the Fairway Instruments Company, a large semiconductor manufacturer. Pamela Cannon, a purchasing agent for Palo Alto, was analyzing the question of how much Palo Alto should bid on the batch of 70,000 transistors.

Palo Alto needed 50,000 of the special transistors for use on a contract for controllers for the assembly lines of one of the automobile manufacturers. Palo Alto dealt very often with that auto company and was one of its regular suppliers of digital equipment. The auto company had a policy of maintaining multiple suppliers whenever possible, however, and so had not awarded Palo Alto the contract for all of the controllers which were needed. Instead, it had contracted for half of the work with Palo Alto and for the other half with Sunnyvale Systems, Inc., a nearby firm which was very much like Palo Alto Products in size, market, and capabilities. Ms. Cannon knew that Sunnyvale would also be bidding on the batch of transistors; she believed that Sunnyvale and Palo Alto would be the only two bidders.

Requests to bid on components from Fairway Instruments were common; often Palo Alto bid on several batches in one month. Fairway did large amounts of defense contract work, and the specifications for components for use in building equipment for defense contracts were very tight—considerably stricter than the specs for components for commerical use. All of the semiconductor manufacturers rejected many of the components which came off their production lines; a manufacturer producing for military applications rejected a particularly high percentage of the units started. For example, on the transistor currently being offered by Fairway, if 10,000 good components were needed for military use, Fairway might start as many as 100,000 in production. Large numbers would be rejected at the various intermediate production steps, before reaching final testing. At the end of the production process, Fairway tested every component individually against the military specs; for 10,000 units meeting those specs, there would also be several thousand units which had reached the final testing stage but were not suitable for the defense contracts. Fairway offered those rejects for bid to commercial users. The company knew that the rejects did not meet the military specs, but it did not know at all accurately how many of the units would meet the looser commercial specs. Fairway was able, however, to give a rough estimate of the fraction of a batch of rejects which would meet Palo Alto's commercial specs; its estimate on the current batch was 0.75 usable by Palo Alto.

The semiconductor industry and the industries which built equipment from semiconductors were changing rapidly. The technologies of these industries changed very often, and prices had been dropping rapidly. In addition, there were large numbers of similar but not interchangeable parts available. For these reasons, Fairway was always anxious to sell its components rapidly and to keep inventories low. For the same reasons, Palo Alto had a firm policy of not buying most parts for inventory; only the most commonly used parts would be held in inventory. The type of transistor then needed by Palo Alto was not likely to be required again in the near future, and so Cannon knew that any transistors left over after the controllers had been built would be dumped.

If Fairway had not been offering the batch of rejects, Palo Alto would have bought the transistors from the regular supply of commercial-quality components at 16 cents apiece. (Similarly, it would buy those regular commercial units if it bid on the rejects but lost.) These components would have been individually tested by the supplier against the commercial standard and verified as acceptable. The minimum order for the commercial-quality components was 30,000 units.

If Palo Alto did bid and win on the batch of military rejects, the 70,000 units would be tested by Palo Alto as a normal part of the production process for the controllers. Cannon was willing to assume that since the normal commercial units would also have to be tested in that same way, the testing of the rejects would not involve extra expense. However, there was always the possibility that the 70,000 rejects would not yield 50,000 good components. If not, Palo Alto could purchase somewhat higher commercial quality units in a small batch at 25 cents each; the minimum order was 2,000 such units.

In thinking about the problem of how much Palo Alto should bid, Ms. Cannon realized that the value of the batch of rejects was dependent on how many of the transistors were actually good. Moreover, she knew that because Fairway tested the components against the higher defense standard only, the estimate of the fraction meeting Palo Alto's commercial specs was rough. (Fairway was quite frank about this fact; it told prospective bidders that its estimates were not precise and, moreover, that it suspected that the estimates which came from its testing procedures tended to give too high a figure for the fraction meeting commercial standards.) Palo Alto had bid on many batches of rejects of similar but not identical products in the past year.[1] Cannon decided that the testing procedures for the different batches were very similar even though the transistors differed slightly. Consequently, she considered the data in Table 1 on the actual fractions good in batches which Palo Alto had won in the

---

[1] The transistor technology had not changed during that period.

Table 1
Fractions of good components

Estimate by Fairway	Actual fraction	Batch size
0.60	0.59	80,000
0.65	0.39	65,000
0.60	0.50	75,000
0.80	0.94	60,000
0.75	0.58	50,000
0.50	0.55	50,000
0.70	0.50	80,000
0.60	0.67	70,000
0.70	0.58	75,000
0.50	0.47	80,000

past year to be a good basis for inferences about the likely fractions good in the current batch.

In addition, Ms. Cannon was concerned with what Sunnyvale Systems would bid for the 70,000 rejects. She had collected information on the most recent 20 occasions on which Palo Alto and Sunnyvale had bid on batches of units which were similar to the current transistors. The transistors involved had differed in some technical design details from one another and from the present 70,000 components. However, while the different batches would not have been interchangeable in use, Cannon felt that the bidding processes in the different situations had been very similar.

Table 2
Bidding history

Batch size	Fairway's estimate of fraction good	Sunnyvale's bid	Palo Alto's bid
70,000	0.70	$5,000	$4,500
80,000	0.60	4,600	4,800
65,000	0.65	3,400	4,200
70,000	0.50	4,600	3,900
75,000	0.60	4,000	4,800
85,000	0.75	6,400	5,800
55,000	0.55	3,400	3,200
60,000	0.80	4,700	5,300
50,000	0.75	3,900	4,500
50,000	0.50	2,000	2,200
70,000	0.60	4,600	4,100
80,000	0.70	4,800	5,100
70,000	0.60	3,900	4,000
65,000	0.70	4,100	4,000
50,000	0.75	4,100	3,900
60,000	0.55	2,900	2,700
75,000	0.70	5,500	5,800
70,000	0.80	4,600	4,400
80,000	0.50	4,800	4,900
60,000	0.60	3,800	3,600

Moreover, the standard prices for the different components were the same. Thus, she was willing to base the current analysis on those 20 bids from the past year. Table 2 gives the information on the past bids as well as the batch sizes and Fairway's estimates of the fractions of good components in the batches. Cannon felt that Sunnyvale had been bidding about 10 cents per estimated unit good, on average, but there was considerable variability in the actual bids. She also knew that Palo Alto's bidding procedure had not been entirely systematic in the past, and she hoped on the current bid to work out some more systematic procedures which Palo Alto could use in setting bids in the future.

Case 7–5

Cronin Dairy Company

It was Wednesday, August 20, 1975, and Harry Horne had to decide how many gallons of vanilla ice-cream mix should be produced by the Cronin Dairy Company for use during the week from August 21 through August 27. Cronin was a large regional dairy firm which made a variety of products, including milk, cheese, yogurt, and ice cream. The ice-cream mix which Horne was considering was the basis of a soft ice cream which was sold through a group of company-owned stands in a large resort area. The mix was a high-quality product; the marketing for it stressed its good taste and its "naturalness."

All ice-cream mix had a short code life (the period which the health codes allowed between production and use), so that it was not easy to avoid having to dump extra out-of-date product. Thus, Horne's problem was to try to meet demand without causing excessive wastage from such dumping.

The Cronin Dairy Company had a regular production schedule, with each product made on one or more days each week; the vanilla ice-cream mix was produced every Wednesday during the summer. The operators of the stands placed orders for the product late in the day on Wednesday for delivery on Thursday. Those deliveries used up only part of the Wednesday production run; the remainder was put into cold storage in what was called the chest. The stand operators placed a second set of orders on Sunday morning for delivery on Monday. Any ice-cream mix which had been produced on Wednesday and was not needed for either the Thursday or the Monday delivery was thrown away. If, on the other hand, the supply in the chest was not sufficient to fill the orders for Monday delivery, a special overtime run was made on Sunday.

In trying to predict what demand would be during the following week, Horne knew that the orders from the stands closely matched the retail demand (for the stands would not inventory so perishable a product). Moreover, he knew that the popular wisdom in the company linked sales levels on the various ice-cream products very closely to the weather conditions. The people responsible for the storage chest and for actually shipping the products tended to categorize various week's demands for ice-cream products by the weekend weather, both because about half of the sales occurred over the weekends and also because they felt that the weekend weather forecasts were the basis on which vacationists made their travel plans. Weekends were classified as sunny and warm, sunny and cold or rainy. According to the accepted rule of thumb, sales on a sunny and warm summer weekend would be one and a half times as high as those on a comparable rainy weekend. Each Wednesday morning the weather forecaster on the local television station made long-term forecasts for the weekend, and Horne had kept track of the forecasts, the actual weather conditions, and the orders from the stand operators during the past two summers. Table 1 summarizes that information.

Table 1
Past demand and weather data

Week starting (Thursday)	Demand†	Weather forecast*	Actual weather*
1974			
June 27	4,219	SW	SW
July 4	4,390	R	R
July 11	3,410	SC	SC
July 18	4,938	SW	SW
July 25	3,388	SW	R
August 1	3,144	R	R
August 8	4,775	SC	SW
August 15	5,200	SW	SW
August 22	2,304	R	R
August 29	5,967	SC	SW
1975			
June 26	2,616	R	R
July 3	7,045	SW	SW
July 10	3,988	SW	SC
July 17	6,194	SW	SW
July 24	3,960	SC	SC
July 31	4,040	SC	SC
August 7	4,225	SW	SW
August 14	3,684	R	R

* SC = Sunny but cold.
  SW = Sunny and warm.
   R = Rainy or cloudy.
† Total orders from stand operators during that week.

The practice of the dairy was to meet demand and not to turn down requests for its products. Thus, the production department made a special run of ice-cream mix if the Sunday orders were higher than the supply in the chest at that time. Horne suspected that a policy of bending over backward to meet demand, without a thorough accounting for the costs (in overtime premiums, extra start-up and cleanup costs, and disruption to the normal work schedule), was not necessarily wise, especially for perishable products like the ice-cream mix, but he knew that the policy would not be changed in the immediate future.

Thus, for the time being there would be an initial production run on Wednesday, and then the orders would come in and the first shipments would be made on Thursday. If the Sunday orders were higher than the supply left from the Wednesday run, another run would be made on Sunday. That run would involve setup costs of $200 (as opposed to the $50 setup costs for the regular run) and variable costs of $1.68 per gallon (as opposed to the $1.48 costs on the regularly scheduled run). The minimum possible production batch size was 300 gallons. Above that amount, production could be increased in units of 100 gallons. Because production had to be in a batch of some multiple of 100 gallons (and could not be less than 300 gallons), even Sunday runs could not be matched exactly to demand, even though demand was known; if, for example, 450 extra gallons were needed, the Sunday run would have to be for 500 gallons. The excess production was not wasted however; it was just put into storage and became part of the next week's normal Wednesday supply.

At present, the storage chest held no ice-cream mix. Horne had checked and had found that the long-term forecast was for sunny and cold weather the next weekend.

Chapter 8

Developing forecasts with the aid of time series decomposition

The data available for the development of a forecast often take the form of a sequence of dated observations, generally referred to as a time series. This consists of observations made at regular intervals of time on the variable to be forecast; for example, the data may be the annual sales of a specific product ten years ago, nine years ago, eight years ago, and so on. This chapter will present one method for using time series data in the development of a probabilistic forecast.

In almost all business or economic situations a forecaster looking at a relevant time series would not consider the data as arising from indistinguishable situations. Such data would thus provide an inappropriate basis for developing a distribution directly from the raw data.

For example, a decision analyst faced with the problem of forecasting the sales of new automobiles in the United States for the final quarter of the year to come (in this example, 1976) would have available as an aid the quarterly data shown in Table 8–1 and plotted in Figure 8–1. A quick inspection of the figure should indicate one reason why most forecasters would not be willing to consider the data as arising from indistinguishable situations. It appears that there has been a long-term growth in sales, perhaps due to long-term growth in population and increases in the standard of living. Recognizing this trend, most forecasters would, before the fact, have forecast higher sales in 1975 than in 1958.

Further inspection of Figure 8–1 shows a recurring pattern in sales within each year. Quite regularly, quarter 2 has higher sales than quarter 3, with the sales of the first and fourth quarters somewhere in between. The occurrence of such a seasonal pattern, traditionally related to climate or custom, forms still a second basis for "distinguishability" in the data.[1]

---

[1] If the series had been made up of monthly data, a recurring 12-month pattern within the year would have constituted the seasonal pattern in the series. Similarly, a series of weekly figures per year might be marked by a seasonal pattern which recurred every 52 weeks.

Table 8–1
New car sales of U.S. franchised dealers,
by quarter, 1958–1974

Year and quarter	Sales (thousands of cars)	Year and quarter	Sales (thousands of cars)
1958		**1967**	
1st	1,069	1st	1,744
2nd	1,142	2nd	2,235
3rd	927	3rd	1,692
4th	1,151	4th	1,897
1959		**1968**	
1st	1,323	1st	2,021
2nd	1,613	2nd	2,321
3rd	1,289	3rd	1,934
4th	1,263	4th	2,349
1960		**1969**	
1st	1,515	1st	2,030
2nd	1,739	2nd	2,347
3rd	1,330	3rd	1,927
4th	1,559	4th	2,161
1961		**1970**	
1st	1,212	1st	1,782
2nd	1,550	2nd	2,189
3rd	1,180	3rd	1,654
4th	1,624	4th	1,490
1962		**1971**	
1st	1,559	1st	1,977
2nd	1,887	2nd	2,281
3rd	1,360	3rd	1,988
4th	1,946	4th	2,676
1963		**1972**	
1st	1,721	1st	2,078
2nd	2,056	2nd	2,537
3rd	1,498	3rd	2,165
4th	2,059	4th	2,541
1964		**1973**	
1st	1,844	1st	2,473
2nd	2,171	2nd	2,742
3rd	1,753	3rd	2,247
4th	1,895	4th	2,208
1965		**1974**	
1st	2,196	1st	1,771
2nd	2,381	2nd	2,166
3rd	1,822	3rd	1,949
4th	2,366	4th	1,562
1966			
1st	2,207		
2nd	2,209		
3rd	1,744		
4th	2,218		

Source: Constructed from data from several issues of *Ward's Automotive Yearbook*.

Figure 8–1
New car sales of U.S. franchised dealers, 1958–1974

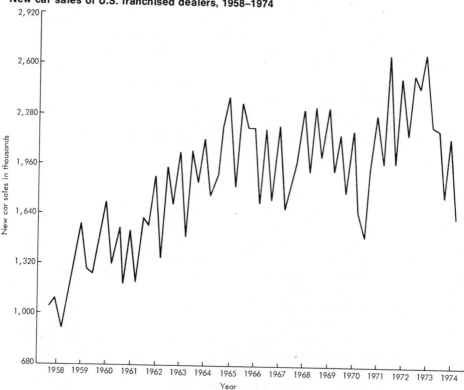

Further observations of the series reveal the existence of wavelike fluctuations around the trends which have duration greater than a year but which do not have the strict periodicity that characterizes the seasonal pattern. Identification of the historic dates at which the peaks and troughs of these waves occurred suggests their relationship to fluctuations in general business activity—the so-called business cycle. This cyclical pattern is still a third basis for distinguishability in the factors affecting sales.

After allowance for trend, seasonal, and cyclical factors, there are still residual fluctuations. If appropriate allowance can be made for the trend, seasonal, and cyclical factors, the forecaster might consider these residuals as arising from indistinguishable situations, and thus they would provide a basis for developing a probabilistic forecast. This view of a time series suggests a model of the form

$$A = T \times S \times C \times U,$$

where:

A = Actual value of the variable of interest
T = Trend level of the series

S = Effect of the seasonal factors

C = Relative effect of the cyclical factors

U = Effect of the unexplained factors which the forecaster may wish to consider as arising from indistinguishable situations

In the procedure described in this chapter, a time series of past values will be decomposed into these components. The components will then each be extrapolated into the future to form the basis (through recombination) for a probabilistic forecast.

MEASURING THE COMBINED EFFECT OF TREND AND CYCLE

Annual data display no seasonal variations—no variations from a pattern which unfold completely within a year. The relative amplitude of any unexplained fluctuation should also be substantially less in annual data than in monthly or quarterly data.[2] Thus if the values of data for the 12 months or four quarters within a year are added to obtain a series of annual totals, these totals will not be affected by seasonal variations or, to any great extent, by the unexplained fluctuations. Differences among these annual totals will thus provide a measure of the effects of trend and most of the cycle. For example, the annual total sales of cars in 1972 differs from the annual total sales in 1973 because of the long-term growth in the series and because the two years may be in different phases of the business cycle. Since both the annual totals contain one first-quarter, one second-quarter, one third-quarter, and one fourth-quarter value, differences in the quarterly patterns will not be reflected. In addition, unexplained variations in each quarterly sales total will tend to balance out over the four quarters.

In order to compare these annualized values to the original quarterly observations, they must be made comparable in both magnitude and timing. The annualized values can be made comparable in size by converting the annual total to a monthly or quarterly average (dividing the total by 12 or 4). The steps in the following procedure assure that the annualized values and the original observation are comparable in timing.

1. Calculate a 12-month or four-quarter moving average. This is found, for quarterly data, by averaging the first four quarters, then quarters 2 through 5, 3 through 6, and so on.[3] Each average is placed in time at the midpoint of the dates of the included observations. Thus, the first average refers to a point in time midway between the dates of the second and third quarterly observations, the second is a point between the third and fourth quarters, and so on.

Table 8–2 illustrates this procedure when applied to the quarterly data on new car sales in the United States in 1958–1974. The plot of these data

---

[2] The unexplained variations that make one month or quarter higher and another month or quarter lower tend to cancel out when averaged over a year or multiple of years.

[3] In monthly data the first average would come from the data of months 1 through 12, then 2 through 13, and so on.

and the properly centered moving averages are shown in Figure 8–2. The first number in Column (3) of Table 8–2 was found by averaging the first four values in Column (2):

$$\frac{1,069 + 1,142 + 927 + 1,151}{4} = 1,072.$$

This value was located between the second and third observations.

Table 8–2
Computation of centered moving averages for new car sales, 1958–1974

Year and quarter	Actual sales (thousands of cars)	Four-period moving average	Centered moving average
1958			
1st	1,069		—
2nd	1,142	—	—
3rd	927	1,072	
4th	1,151	1,136	1,104
1959			1,195
1st	1,323	1,254	
2nd	1,613	1,344	1,299
3rd	1,289	1,372	1,358
4th	1,263	1,420	1,396
1960			1,436
1st	1,515	1,451	
2nd	1,739	1,462	1,456
3rd	1,330	1,536	1,499
4th	1,559	1,460	1,498
1961			1,436
1st	1,212	1,413	
2nd	1,550	1,375	1,394
3rd	1,180	1,391	1,383
4th	1,624	1,478	1,435
1962			1,521
1st	1,559	1,563	
2nd	1,887	1,608	1,585
3rd	1,360	1,688	1,648
4th	1,946	1,729	1,708
1963			1,750
1st	1,721	1,771	
2nd	2,056	1,805	1,788
3rd	1,498	1,834	1,819
4th	2,059	1,864	1,849
1964			1,879
1st	1,844	1,893	
2nd	2,171	1,957	1,925
3rd	1,753	1,916	1,936
4th	1,895	2,004	1,960
1965			2,030
1st	2,196	2,056	
2nd	2,381	2,073	2,065
3rd	1,822	2,191	2,132
4th	2,366	2,194	2,192
1966			2,172
1st	2,207	2,151	
2nd	2,209	2,131	2,141
3rd	1,744	2,094	2,113
4th	2,218	1,979	2,037
			1,982

Table 8–2 *(continued)*

Year and quarter	Actual sales (thousands of cars)	Four-period moving average	Centered moving average
1967		1,985	1,979
1st	1,744	1,972	1,932
2nd	2,235	1,892	1,927
3rd	1,692	1,961	1,972
4th	1,897		
1968		1,983	2,013
1st	2,021	2,043	2,100
2nd	2,321	2,156	2,157
3rd	1,934	2,158	2,162
4th	2,349		
1969		2,165	2,164
1st	2,030	2,163	2,140
2nd	2,347	2,116	2,085
3rd	1,927	2,054	2,035
4th	2,161		
1970		2,015	1,981
1st	1,782	1,947	1,863
2nd	2,189	1,779	1,803
3rd	1,654	1,828	1,839
4th	1,490		
1971		1,851	1,892
1st	1,977	1,934	2,082
2nd	2,281	2,231	2,243
3rd	1,988	2,256	2,288
4th	2,676		
1972		2,320	2,342
1st	2,078	2,364	2,347
2nd	2,537	2,330	2,380
3rd	2,165	2,429	2,455
4th	2,541		
1973		2,480	2,490
1st	2,473	2,501	2,459
2nd	2,742	2,417	2,330
3rd	2,247	2,242	2,170
4th	2,208		
1974		2,098	2,061
1st	1,771	2,024	1,943
2nd	2,166	1,862	
3rd	1,949	—	—
4th	1,562		

Source: From *Ward's Automotive Yearbooks.*

2. To obtain averages that correspond in timing with the original observations, a two-period moving average of the four-quarter moving average is then taken. Since the first moving average refers in time to a point
midway between the second and third quarters, and the second to a point
midway between the third and fourth quarters, the average of these two
averages is located *at the same point* as the third-quarter observation.
Similar centering makes each of these averages correspond in time to an
original observation in the series.

Figure 8–2
Actual new car sales and centered four-quarter moving averages, 1958–1974

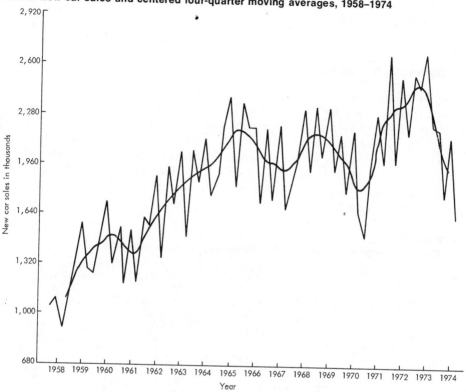

The first value in Column (4) of Table 8–2 was obtained by averaging the first two values of Column (3). Thus:

$$\frac{1,072 + 1,136}{2} = 1,104.$$

This value corresponds in time to the third-quarter observation of 927.

You should note that the moving average contains both trend and cyclical movement[4] but does not have the regularly recurring seasonal patterns of the original data, and the unexplained, irregular movements have been substantially canceled out.

SEPARATING THE EFFECTS OF TREND AND CYCLE

During the first phase of this analysis we noted that the moving averages contain trend and cyclical movements, and did not contain the

---

[4] Strictly speaking, the moving average does not contain all of the cyclical movements, since it tends to undercut the peaks and overcut the troughs.

seasonal swings or most of the unexplained variations.[5] We will now show how to take this measure of the combined effect of trend and cycle and split it apart into the two separate effects.

Determination of trend

Since by definition *trend* is the smooth, long-term movement which underlies a series, data covering a relatively long period of time (perhaps 15 to 20 years) are usually required in order to allow the identification of the trend. With such a series, there are a number of methods that can be used to arrive at a description of trend. Perhaps the most straightforward method is the one that will be used here. It involves the free-hand fitting of a smooth line which, in the judgment of the forecaster, is a good fit to the moving averages.[6]

Figure 8–3
Moving average of car sales and a free-hand trend line, 1958–1974

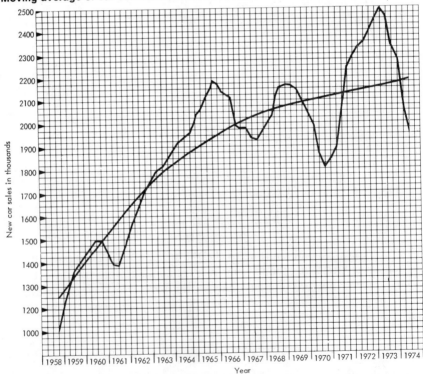

---

[5] Symbolically, moving average $= T \times C$.

[6] More mechanical methods of determining a line which is in some sense the "best" fitting line are also available. Some of these methods will be considered in Chapter 9, on regression analysis.

A free-hand fit of a trend to the moving averages in the example of new car sales is shown in Figure 8–3. It should be noted that such a method for identifying trend rests heavily on the judgment of the forecaster. If projections of the trend are to be made, small differences in the descriptive judgments might result in substantial differences in trend estimates for distant future periods.

Describing cyclical variations

When the moving-average values containing trend and cyclical movements are expressed as a percentage of the trend, the fluctuations around 100 percent should reveal a pattern of the cyclical movements.[7] This reasoning can be shown through the following relationships:

$$\frac{\text{Moving average}}{\text{Trend}} = \frac{T \times C}{T} = C.$$

Table 8–3 shows the calculation of these cyclical relatives in the new car sales example. The trend values were read from Figure 8–3, and the resulting measures of cyclical variation are plotted in Figure 8–4. It should

Table 8–3
Computation of relative cyclical residuals for new car sales, 1958–1974

(1)	(2)	(3)	(4) = (2) ÷ (3)
Year and quarter	Centered moving average (thousands of cars)	Trend (thousands of cars)	Relative cyclical residuals (moving average/trend) × 100
1958			
1st	—	—	—
2nd.................	—	—	—
3rd	1,104	1,250	88.3%
4th	1,195	1,280	93.3
1959			
1st	1,299	1,310	99.1
2nd.................	1,358	1,340	101.3
3rd	1,396	1,370	101.9
4th	1,436	1,400	102.5
1960			
1st	1,456	1,430	101.9
2nd.................	1,499	1,460	102.6
3rd	1,498	1,490	100.5
4th	1,436	1,520	94.5
1961			
1st	1,394	1,550	89.9
2nd.................	1,383	1,580	87.6
3rd	1,435	1,610	89.1
4th	1,521	1,640	92.7

---

[7] Since, as previously noted, the moving average has dampened out some of the within-year cyclical variations, the peaks may be understated and the troughs overstated. Methods for overcoming this difficulty are available but are beyond the scope of this text.

Table 8–3 (continued)

(1) Year and quarter	(2) Centered moving average (thousands of cars)	(3) Trend (thousands of cars)	(4) = (2) ÷ (3) Relative cyclical residuals (moving average/trend) × 100
1962			
1st	1,585	1,670	94.9
2nd	1,648	1,695	97.2
3rd	1,708	1,720	99.3
4th	1,750	1,745	100.3
1963			
1st	1,788	1,765	101.3
2nd	1,819	1,785	101.9
3rd	1,849	1,805	102.4
4th	1,879	1,823	103.1
1964			
1st	1,925	1,840	104.6
2nd	1,936	1,857	104.3
3rd	1,960	1,874	104.6
4th	2,030	1,890	107.4
1965			
1st	2,065	1,906	108.3
2nd	2,132	1,922	110.9
3rd	2,192	1,938	113.1
4th	2,172	1,954	111.2
1966			
1st	2,141	1,970	108.7
2nd	2,113	1,985	106.4
3rd	2,037	1,998	101.9
4th	1,982	2,010	98.6
1967			
1st	1,979	2,021	97.9
2nd	1,932	2,030	95.2
3rd	1,927	2,038	94.5
4th	1,972	2,046	96.4
1968			
1st	2,013	2,054	98.0%
2nd	2,100	2,061	101.9
3rd	2,157	2,068	104.3
4th	2,162	2,074	104.2
1969			
1st	2,164	2,080	104.0
2nd	2,140	2,085	102.6
3rd	2,085	2,090	99.8
4th	2,035	2,095	97.1
1970			
1st	1,981	2,100	94.3
2nd	1,863	2,105	88.5
3rd	1,803	2,110	85.5
4th	1,839	2,115	87.0
1971			
1st	1,892	2,120	89.3
2nd	2,082	2,125	98.0
3rd	2,243	2,130	105.3
4th	2,288	2,135	107.2
1972			
1st	2,342	2,140	109.4
2nd	2,347	2,145	109.4
3rd	2,380	2,150	110.7
4th	2,455	2,155	113.9

Table 8–3 (concluded)

(1)	(2)	(3)	(4) = (2) ÷ (3)
Year and quarter	Centered moving average (thousands of cars)	Trend (thousands of cars)	Relative cyclical residuals (moving average/trend) × 100
1973			
1st	2,490	2,160	115.3
2nd	2,459	2,165	113.6
3rd	2,330	2,170	107.4
4th	2,170	2,175	99.8
1974			
1st	2,061	2,180	94.5
2nd	1,943	2,185	88.9
3rd	—	—	—
4th	—	—	—

Source: From *Ward's Automotive Yearbooks*.

be noted that the trend is now represented by the horizontal 100 percent line, that the recurrent seasonal pattern of the actual series is no longer present, and that the unexplained, irregular variations have been substantially canceled out. The cyclical measure for the second quarter of 1970 of 88.5 indicates that in that quarter new car sales were 88.5 percent of the trend, or 11.5 percent below the trend, due essentially to cyclical factors.

Figure 8–4
Relative cyclical residuals in new car sales, 1958–1974

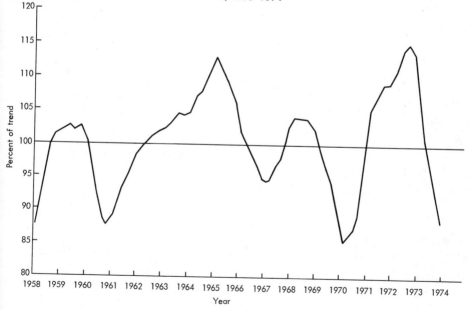

MEASURING THE COMBINED EFFECTS OF SEASONAL AND UNEXPLAINED MOVEMENTS

The original observations in new car sales data series contained trend, cyclical, seasonal, and unexplained variations. We have seen that the moving averages measure trend and cycle. If we divide each original observation by its moving average (multiplying the ratio by 100 to convert it to the more common form of a percentage), the variations from 100 percent reflect variations due to seasonal and unexplained factors. Symbolically, the elimination can be looked at in terms of the following equation:

$$\frac{A}{\text{Moving average}} = \frac{T \times C \times S \times U}{T \times C} = S \times U.$$

Table 8–4 shows the original data expressed as a percentage of the corresponding moving average.

Table 8–4
Actual new car sales expressed as a percentage of the four-quarter moving average

(1)	*(2)*	*(3)*	*(4) = (2) ÷ (3)*
		Centered four-quarter	
	Sales	*moving average*	*Ratio of actual sales*
Year and quarter	*(thousands of cars)*	*(thousands of cars)*	*to moving average*
1958			
1st	1,069	—	—
2nd	1,142	—	—
3rd	927	1,104	0.840
4th	1,151	1,195	0.963
1959			
1st	1,323	1,299	1.018
2nd	1,613	1,358	1.188
3rd	1,289	1,396	0.923
4th	1,263	1,436	0.880
1960			
1st	1,515	1,456	1.040
2nd	1,739	1,499	1.160
3rd	1,330	1,498	0.888
4th	1,559	1,436	1.086
1961			
1st	1,212	1,394	0.869
2nd	1,550	1,383	1.120
3rd	1,180	1,435	0.823
4th	1,624	1,521	1.068
1962			
1st	1,559	1,585	0.984
2nd	1,887	1,648	1.145
3rd	1,360	1,708	0.796
4th	1,946	1,750	1.112
1963			
1st	1,721	1,788	0.963
2nd	2,056	1,819	1.130
3rd	1,498	1,849	0.810
4th	2,059	1,879	1.096

Table 8–4 (continued)

(1) Year and quarter	(2) Sales (thousands of cars)	(3) Centered four-quarter moving average (thousands of cars)	(4) = (2) ÷ (3) Ratio of actual sales to moving average
1964			
1st	1,844	1,925	0.958
2nd	2,171	1,936	1.121
3rd	1,753	1,960	0.894
4th	1,895	2,030	0.934
1965			
1st	2,196	2,065	1.063
2nd	2,381	2,132	1.117
3rd	1,822	2,192	0.831
4th	2,366	2,172	1.089
1966			
1st	2,207	2,141	1.031
2nd	2,209	2,113	1.045
3rd	1,744	2,037	0.856
4th	2,218	1,982	1.119
1967			
1st	1,744	1,979	0.881
2nd	2,235	1,932	1.157
3rd	1,692	1,927	0.878
4th	1,897	1,972	0.962
1968			
1st	2,021	2,013	1.004
2nd	2,321	2,100	1.105
3rd	1,934	2,157	0.897
4th	2,349	2,162	1.087
1969			
1st	2,030	2,164	0.938
2nd	2,347	2,140	1.097
3rd	1,927	2,085	0.924
4th	2,161	2,035	1.062
1970			
1st	1,782	1,981	0.900
2nd	2,189	1,863	1.175
3rd	1,654	1,803	0.918
4th	1,490	1,839	0.810
1971			
1st	1,977	1,892	1.045
2nd	2,281	2,082	1.095
3rd	1,988	2,243	0.886
4th	2,676	2,288	1.170
1972			
1st	2,078	2,342	0.887
2nd	2,537	2,347	1.081
3rd	2,165	2,380	0.910
4th	2,541	2,455	1.035
1973			
1st	2,473	2,490	0.993
2nd	2,742	2,459	1.115
3rd	2,247	2,330	0.964
4th	2,208	2,170	1.018
1974			
1st	1,771	2,061	0.859
2nd	2,166	1,943	1.115
3rd	1,949	—	—
4th	1,562	—	—

Source: From *Ward's Automotive Yearbooks*.

SEPARATING THE EFFECTS OF SEASONAL AND UNEXPLAINED VARIATIONS

Seasonal variations, as we have noted, are periodic movements in a time series which repeat over a specific time period, usually a year, and are typically brought about by factors associated with climate or custom. The traditionally higher sales of ice cream and lower sales of fuel oil in summer are extreme examples of climatic causes. Two examples of seasonal patterns affected by customs are the lower end-of-year inventories associated with the closing of financial accounts and the high retail sales in December encouraged by the tradition of gift-giving.

Strictly speaking, the term "seasonal variation" can apply to any repetitive pattern in a time series where the interval of time to completion of the pattern is one year or less. Thus the term could be used to describe not only a monthly or quarterly pattern within a year but also a weekly pattern within a month, a daily pattern within a week, or even an hourly pattern within a day. In this section we will deal with the more usual annual repetitive patterns observed in series of quarterly or monthly observations.

Measuring the seasonal pattern

The very regular pattern ascribed to seasonal variations provides a basis for separating them from irregular, unexplained variations. If the ratios of the observations of actual sales to their corresponding moving averages are regrouped by period (i.e., all first quarter together, all second quarter, and so on), the effect of the unexplained variation becomes apparent. In series with stable seasonal patterns,[8] each first-quarter figure, for example, would be the first-quarter seasonal effect times variation brought about by unexplained factors. Each first quarter would have the same seasonal effect, and so the year-to-year differences in the percent of moving average figures for the first quarter must be brought about by the unexplained movements.[9] Since these unexplained variations by their very nature may arise from indistinguishable situations and have an expected or average difference of zero, averaging the ratios of a given period (such as for the first quarters) should eliminate, or at least substantially dampen, these fluctuations. The resulting averages, one for each period, measure the effect of the various seasons. These numbers are usually called *seasonal indices*.

The type of average usually used in eliminating the irregular

---

[8] If we believe there is a changing or shifting seasonal pattern, there are variations on this method that can be applied. These go beyond the scope of this text, however.

[9] Also, any small part of the cycle not contained in the original moving averages would cause differences here.

movements is referred to as a *modified mean*. Since some of the unexplained variations may have a very major impact, arising from factors such as strikes and fires, and since a large deviation can distort a straight average, it is often considered best to eliminate extreme values before calculating the seasonal indices. Thus, a modified mean is found by discarding the low extreme and high extreme and then calculating an average of the remaining values. Table 8–5 shows the calculation of the four modified means, one for each of the four quarters, from the data on automobile sales in the new car sales example. Figure 8–5 is a series of four graphs (one for each quarter) showing the percent of moving averages and the modified mean as a horizontal straight line.

Table 8–5
Calculation of quarterly seasonal indices, new car sales, 1958–1974

Year	*Percent of moving averages, quarter*			
	1st	*2d*	*3d*	*4th*
1958...................	—	—	84.0	96.3
1959...................	101.8	~~118.8~~	92.3	88.0
1960...................	104.0	116.0	88.8	108.6
1961...................	86.9	112.0	82.3	106.8
1962...................	98.4	114.5	~~79.6~~	111.2
1963...................	96.3	113.0	81.0	109.6
1964...................	95.8	112.1	89.4	93.4
1965...................	~~106.3~~	111.7	83.1	108.9
1966...................	103.1	~~104.5~~	85.6	111.9
1967...................	88.1	115.7	87.8	96.2
1968...................	100.4	110.5	89.7	108.7
1969...................	93.8	109.7	92.4	106.2
1970...................	90.0	117.5	91.8	~~81.0~~
1971...................	104.5	109.5	88.6	~~117.0~~
1972...................	88.7	108.1	91.0	103.5
1973...................	99.3	111.5	~~96.4~~	101.8
1974...................	~~85.9~~	111.5	—	—
Modified Mean	96.5	112.4	87.7	103.6

Total of modified means = 400.2
Adjustment factor = 400/400.2 = .9995

Seasonal Indices

1st	*2nd*	*3rd*	*4th*
96.4	112.3	87.7	103.6

Source: From *Ward's Automotive Yearbooks*.

If the elimination of all the nonseasonal factors had been precise, the resulting four seasonal indices would average 100 percent. In most cases, the average at this stage will be very close to but not exactly equal to 100 percent. As a final step, the preliminary indices are adjusted to average 100 percent. It is usually assumed that the adjustment should be proportional for each index. Thus, an adjustment factor is found by taking the

Figure 8–5
Ratio to moving average values and quarterly seasonal indices, new car sales,
1958–1974

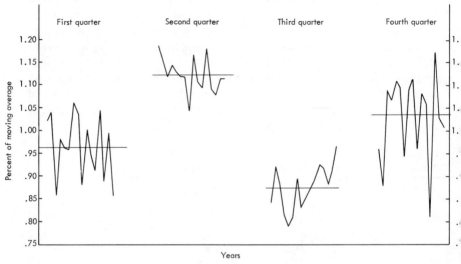

ratio of the desired average (100) to the actual average (in this example, 100.05). Each of the preliminary indices is multiplied by this factor to give a final set of indices which now will average 100 as desired. The calculations are shown in Table 8–5.

Measuring the unexplained variations

Once the seasonal indices have been developed, they can be used to eliminate the seasonal effect from any series through simple division. Recall that the ratio of actual sales to moving-average values contains the effects of seasonal and unexplained variations. Therefore we can measure the unexplained variations by dividing the ratios to moving-average values by their corresponding seasonal indices (in decimal form). Thus each first-quarter ratio to moving average can be divided by the first-quarter index (in this example, .964), each second-quarter ratio by the second-quarter index, and so on. Symbolically this can be shown in the following equation:

$$\frac{A/\text{Moving average}}{S} = \frac{S \times U}{S} = U.$$

For the example of new car sales, the unexplained variations are developed in Table 8–6. If the forecaster is willing to consider these variations as arising from indistinguishable situations, they could be used to construct a cumulative probability distribution which would describe

Table 8–6
Calculation of unexplained variations for new car sales, 1958–1974

(1) Year and quarter	(2) Actual sales (thousands of cars)	(3) Centered moving average (thousands of cars)	(4) = (2) ÷ (3) Ratio to moving average	(5) Seasonal index (decimal form)	(6) = (4) ÷ (5) × 100 Unexplained variations (%)
1958					
1st	1,069	—	—	0.964	—
2nd	1,142	—	—	1.123	—
3rd	927	1,104	0.840	0.876	95.8
4th	1,151	1,195	0.963	1.036	93.0
1959					
1st	1,323	1,299	1.018	0.964	105.6
2nd	1,613	1,358	1.188	1.123	105.8
3rd	1,289	1,396	0.923	0.876	105.3
4th	1,263	1,436	0.880	1.036	84.9
1960					
1st	1,515	1,456	1.040	0.964	107.8
2nd	1,739	1,499	1.160	1.123	103.3
3rd	1,330	1,498	0.888	0.876	101.3
4th	1,559	1,436	1.086	1.036	104.8
1961					
1st	1,212	1,394	0.869	0.964	90.1
2nd	1,550	1,383	1.120	1.123	99.8
3rd	1,180	1,435	0.823	0.876	93.9
4th	1,624	1,521	1.068	1.036	103.1
1962					
1st	1,559	1,585	0.984	0.964	102.0
2nd	1,887	1,648	1.145	1.123	102.0
3rd	1,360	1,708	0.796	0.876	90.8
4th	1,946	1,750	1.112	1.036	107.4
1963					
1st	1,721	1,788	0.963	0.964	99.8
2nd	2,056	1,819	1.130	1.123	100.6
3rd	1,498	1,849	0.810	0.876	92.5
4th	2,059	1,879	1.096	1.036	105.8
1964					
1st	1,844	1,925	0.958	0.964	99.3
2nd	2,171	1,936	1.121	1.123	99.8
3rd	1,753	1,960	0.894	0.876	102.0
4th	1,895	2,030	0.934	1.036	90.1
1965					
1st	2,196	2,065	1.063	0.964	110.3
2nd	2,381	2,132	1.117	1.123	99.4
3rd	1,822	2,192	0.831	0.876	94.8
4th	2,366	2,172	1.089	1.036	105.1
1966					
1st	2,207	2,141	1.031	0.964	106.9
2nd	2,209	2,113	1.045	1.123	93.1
3rd	1,744	2,037	0.856	0.876	97.7
4th	2,218	1,982	1.119	1.036	108.0
1967					
1st	1,744	1,979	0.881	0.964	91.4
2nd	2,235	1,932	1.157	1.123	103.0
3rd	1,692	1,927	0.878	0.876	100.2
4th	1,897	1,972	0.962	1.036	92.9

Table 8–6 (continued)

(1) Year and quarter	(2) Actual sales (thousands of cars)	(3) Centered moving average (thousands of cars)	(4) = (2) ÷ (3) Ratio to moving average	(5) Seasonal index (decimal form)	(6) = (4) ÷ (5) × 100 Unexplained variations (%)
1968					
1st	2,021	2,013	1.004	0.964	104.1
2nd	2,321	2,100	1.105	1.123	98.4
3rd	1,934	2,157	0.897	0.876	102.3
4th	2,349	2,162	1.087	1.036	104.9
1969					
1st	2,030	2,164	0.938	0.964	97.3
2nd	2,347	2,140	1.097	1.123	97.6
3rd	1,927	2,085	0.924	0.876	105.4
4th	2,161	2,035	1.062	1.036	102.5
1970					
1st	1,782	1,981	0.900	0.964	93.3
2nd	2,189	1,863	1.175	1.123	104.6
3rd	1,654	1,803	0.918	0.876	104.7
4th	1,490	1,839	0.810	1.036	78.2
1971					
1st	1,977	1,892	1.045	0.964	108.3
2nd	2,281	2,082	1.095	1.123	97.5
3rd	1,988	2,243	0.886	0.876	101.1
4th	2,676	2,288	1.170	1.036	112.9
1972					
1st	2,078	2,342	0.887	0.964	92.0
2nd	2,537	2,347	1.081	1.123	96.2
3rd	2,165	2,380	0.910	0.876	103.8
4th	2,541	2,455	1.035	1.036	99.9
1973					
1st	2,473	2,490	0.993	0.964	103.0
2nd	2,742	2,459	1.115	1.123	99.3
3rd	2,247	2,330	0.964	0.876	110.0
4th	2,208	2,170	1.018	1.036	98.2
1974					
1st	1,771	2,061	0.859	0.964	89.1
2nd	2,166	1,943	1.115	1.123	99.3
3rd	2,949	—	—	0.876	—
4th	1,562	—	—	1.036	—

Source: From *Ward's Automotive Yearbooks*.

the uncertainty surrounding forecasts based on the trend, cyclical, and seasonal effects. Figure 8–6 shows a cumulative probability distribution of these relative errors.

DEVELOPING A PROBABILISTIC FORECAST

We have shown how a series of past values can be decomposed into trend, cyclical, seasonal, and unexplained residuals. If it is assumed that the past patterns of these individual components will continue into the future, future values of the time series can be forecast by projecting the

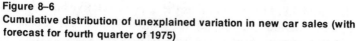

Figure 8–6

Cumulative distribution of unexplained variation in new car sales (with forecast for fourth quarter of 1975)

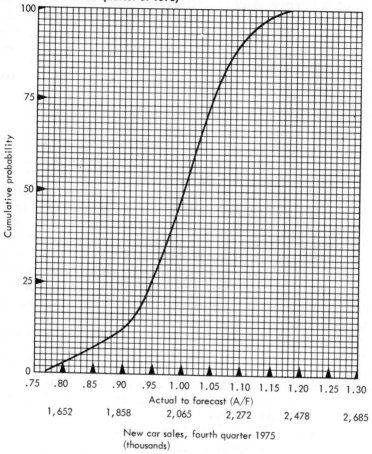

individual components and then combining the projections. Thus the forecast for a future period can be made by projecting the trend, cyclical, and seasonal movements individually, combining these projections, and then superimposing a distribution which describes the uncertainty around the projection.

An extrapolation of the trend to the desired future period forms the foundation of the forecast. Perhaps the most difficult judgment is required in predicting the cyclical relative for the forecast period. Based on information from general economic predictions and perceptions of the relationship between these conditions and the series being forecast, a projection for the cycle as a percent of trend (or a probability assessment of this quantity, if the uncertainty is substantial) must be made. The forecasts for trend and cyclical movements are then multiplied together.

After the product of the trend times the cyclical relative has been found for the forecast period, multiplying it by the appropriate seasonal index yields a point forecast. A point forecast of new car sales for the fourth quarter of 1975 could involve a trend extrapolation of 2,215,000, judgmental projection of the cycle as a percent of trend of 90 percent, with a fourth-quarter seasonal index of 103.6 percent. These values would yield a forecast of 2,065,000 cars.

If the forecaster is willing to consider the unexplained relative variation as arising from indistinguishable situations, the point forecast for the fourth quarter of 1975 can be combined with the cumulative distribution of the unexplained variation to develop a probabilistic forecast of sales for that period. The lower scale of Figure 8–6 is obtained by multiplying each value on the upper scale by the point forecast of 2,065,000 cars.

It should be noted that the uncertainty in such a distribution would almost certainly be an understatement of the real uncertainty in the situation. This distribution would be appropriate if it was believed that the projections of trend, cyclical, and seasonal movements were as good for the future period to be forecast as they had been retrospectively for the past. It would also have to be assumed that the factors and forces generating these patterns of movement in the past would continue, at least in significant ways, into the future until the time of the forecast. These assumptions are questionable in general and particularly bothersome in relation to the projection of the cyclical movements.

One way to deal with this concern would be to adjust judgmentally the distribution of the quantity being forecast, bearing in mind that the cumulative distribution obtained previously is a lower limit on the uncertainty in the probability distribution of the quantity. A more formal adjustment which would be useful if the forecaster were willing to assess a probability distribution of the cyclical effect in the forecast period would involve combining point values for trend and seasonal movements with the distributions of the cyclical effect and the unexplained variations.[10]

The resulting probability distribution gives a probabilistic forecast which can be used by a manager in analyzing a decision situation in which uncertainty about the quantity forecast is a relevant factor.

OTHER USES OF SEASONAL INDICES

Although this chapter deals primarily with the task of developing probabilistic forecasts using time series data, there are other purposes for which some of the results, particularly the seasonal indices, are often

---

[10] See the section, "Obtaining Probability Distributions from Other Probability Distributions," in Chapter 5. Theoretically the same procedure could be used for the trend and the seasonal movements. Generally by far the greatest concern, however, centers on the cyclical projection.

used. This section will consider a very common use of seasonal indices: the seasonal adjustment of a series of observations, or the so-called deseasonalizing of a series.

Suppose the decision maker wants to compare the sales of new cars in the fourth quarter of 1974 with those in the third quarter of that year to get an indication of whether car sales went up or down after allowance has been made for the normal seasonal differences in the two quarters. In order to accomplish this it would be necessary to eliminate the differing seasonal effects from the actual sales volumes before the comparison was made. This could be accomplished by dividing each of the actual values by its appropriate seasonal index (in decimal form). Thus the sales in the fourth quarter of 1974 would be divided by the fourth-quarter index. The actual sales in the fourth quarter of 1974 were 1,562,230. This value, divided by the fourth-quarter seasonal index of 103.6 percent, or 1.036, gives a seasonally adjusted value for that period of 1,507,944. Similarly the third quarter 1974 sales of 1,949,025, divided by the third-quarter index of 87.6 percent, gives a seasonally adjusted value of 2,224,914 cars for the first quarter of 1975. The seasonally adjusted drop is thus more severe than would be seen in a comparison of the actual data.

The desire to compare values in a series, net of the seasonal effect, is so common that almost all economic and business series published by the government appear not only as the actual observations but also in a seasonally adjusted form, that is, with each actual value having been divided by its appropriate seasonal index. The reasoning behind this deseasonalizing can be seen in the following relationships:

$$\frac{A}{S} = \frac{T \times C \times S \times U}{S} = T \times C \times U.$$

EXERCISES

8.1. The procedure described for decomposing a time series to develop a forecast is fairly complex. Often simpler procedures will give adequate forecasting results. For example, the method of *moving averages* is sometimes used to produce a forecast directly. In this method, the forecast for the next period F_{t+1} is simply determined by averaging a number of the previous observations A_t, A_{t-1}, etc. The forecast is then given by

$$F_{t+1} = \frac{A_t + A_{t-1} + A_{t-2} + \ldots + A_{t-N+1}}{N}$$

here N is the number of previous observations used in determining the forecast.

The Chamber of Commerce and Industry of Paris has been asked by several of its members to include a forecast of the French index of industrial production in its monthly newsletter. Using the monthly data given below

a. Computer a forecast for periods 13 through 29 using the method of moving averages with 12 months of observations in each average.

b. Compute the error $A_t - F_t$ in each forecast. How accurate would you say these forecasts are?

c. Now compute a new series of moving averages using six months of observations in each average and again compute the errors.

d. How do these two moving average forecasts compare? Which seems most accurate? Why do you think this is so?

Period	French index of industrial production	Period	French index of industrial production
1	108	15	98
2	108	16	97
3	110	17	101
4	106	18	104
5	108	19	101
6	108	20	99
7	105	21	95
8	100	22	95
9	97	23	96
10	95	24	96
11	95	25	97
12	92	26	98
13	95	27	94
14	95	28	92

8.2. The treasurer of a publicly traded firm has been asked by the directors to include a forecast of the trading price of the company's stock in his monthly report to the board.

Using the method of moving averages and the data given below, answer parts (a) through (d) asked in Exercise 8.1.

e. Does the method of moving averages seem to work better in this case than in the situation given in Exercise 8.1? Explain why or why not.

Period	Average stock price	Period	Average stock price
1	72	13	73
2	71	14	75
3	73	15	75
4	72	16	68
5	70	17	68
6	74	18	71
7	76	19	72
8	76	20	69
9	78	21	72
10	71	22	75
11	73	23	72
12	70	24	74

8.3. Although the method of moving averages appears to be a reasonable forecasting procedure, two difficulties are often cited for not applying it in practice. First, why should all observations included have equal weight in determining the forecast? It would seem more reasonable to have older observations weighted less than more recent observations. Second, in making forecasts for a large number of items employing a computer, the method of moving averages requires a great deal of data storage. For example, 3,000 inventory items using 12-month moving-average forecasts requires 36,000 pieces of information to be stored.

The method of *exponential smoothing* is very commonly used to overcome these difficulties. This method is based on averaging (smoothing) past values of a time series in a decreasing (exponential) manner. It requires storing for each item only the most recent forecast and observation. The usual formula for exponential smoothing is

$$F_{t+1} = \alpha A_t + (1 - \alpha) F_t$$

where α is chosen between zero and one. By repeatedly substituting for F_t, F_{t-1}, F_{t-2}, etc., we can rewrite the forecast in terms of the observations as follows:

$$F_{t+2} = \alpha A_t + \alpha(1 - \alpha)A_{t-1} + \alpha(1 - \alpha)^2 A_{t-2} + \alpha(1 - \alpha)^3 A_{t-3} + \cdots$$

This form illustrates the decreasing nature of the weights applied to the past observations.

Another way to view exponential smoothing is to rewrite the usual formula as follows:

$$F_{t+1} = F_t + \alpha(A_t - F_t)$$

Calling $(A_t - F_t)$ the error E_t in the forecast at time t, the forecast at $t + 1$ may be given by

$$F_{t+1} = F_t + \alpha E_t$$

is just the forecast at t corrected by a weighting α of the error in the forecast at t. Because of the ease of implementing the exponential smoothing method on a computer and its relatively good performance, the method of exponential smoothing is often used in practice.

a. Apply the forecasting method of exponential smoothing to the data given in Problem 8.1 using $\alpha = .3$ and $\alpha = .6$.
b. Compute the error $A_t - F_t$ for each period of each of the two sets of forecasts.
c. Which value of α gives the best results? What does this imply about the basic pattern in the data?

8.4. Answer the three parts of Exercise 8.3 using the data given in Exercise 8.2.

8.5. Now compare the two moving average forecasts and the two exponential smoothing forecasts prepared for the data given in Exercise 8.1. Which of these forecasting approaches would you recommend be used in this situation? Why?

8.6. Answer Exercise 8.5 for the forecasts prepared on the data contained in Exercise 8.2.

Case 8–1

Perkin Elmer Instrument Division[1]— Operating plans and forecasts

In October 1974, Gaynor Kelley, vice president and manager of Perkin Elmer's Instrument Division, perceived disgruntling differences among three plans central to his division's operations.

The first plan was the division's annual business plan. This plan, dated July 1974, was the result of the division's annual planning activities. It was based on a projected division sales level of $93.4 million. The second plan had just reached Kelley. It was an updated forecast of orders received made by the product managers in early October 1974. It forecast 1974–75 fiscal year orders at $103.1 million. The third plan, also recently received by Kelley, was a manufacturing plan, which forecast the sales value of the product which was to be manufactured during the 1974–75 year. This "build plan" indicated that manufacturing planned to build $111.8 million worth of product for sale in the year. Inventories had already increased by over $1 million since August in anticipation of the increase in sales projected by the product managers.

Kelley was more troubled by the high volumes indicated by the later two plans than by the discrepancies between them. Division sales had almost doubled in the previous three years, but signs that the economy was weakening had long been expected and were already appearing in other major industries. Moreover, the corporate financial staff had indicated that they had not planned to provide funds to meet the unexpected surge in business predicted by the marketing and build plans, and that they would have difficulty in obtaining them economically on such short notice.

Company background

Perkin Elmer was an international developer and producer of high technology scientific instrumentation. The company was founded in 1938 to design and produce ultra-precise optical equipment. Growth in this area was rapid as these optical instruments found wide application in defense and space programs. In the 1970s under the leadership of chair-

---

[1] To protect the confidentiality of company data, certain figures in this case have been disguised.

man Chester W. Nimitz, Jr., and president Robert H. Sorensen, the company began to emphasize the development of other types of laboratory analytical instrumentation, which were marketed to researchers in college and hospital clinical laboratories, and to research and process control groups in a variety of industries. The rapid growth of the Instrument Group, which was responsible for manufacturing and selling these nonoptical instruments resulted in a decrease in the percentage of the company's business that went to U.S. government agencies. This percentage fell to only 27 percent of total sales in 1974. By this time, Instrument Group's sales accounted for more than one half of the sales of the total company.

The company emphasized research and development to maintain its position as a company on the leading edge of rapidly expanding optical and electrical technologies. In 1974, the company spent $16.7 million on research and development, not counting a much larger amount spent on government contract research (see Exhibit 1 for financial data). Almost 15 percent of the company's 8,600 employees were graduate scientists and engineers.

The Instrument Group, under the guidance of senior vice president Horace McDonell, had sales of $150 million in 1974, a 17 percent increase over 1973 sales levels. This group also emphasized research and development as an integral part of their competitive strategy. Historically, research and development expenses had averaged 8 to 9 percent of instrument sales. Over 70 percent of the orders taken by the group in 1974 were for products that had not existed in 1969.

The Instrument Division

The Instrument Division headed by Gaynor Kelley was the largest organizational entity in the Instrument Group. Kelley had profit and asset responsibility for the marketing and manufacture of eight product lines. Reporting to him were eight product managers, the director of manufacturing, and the technical director who was responsible for engineering and development. Kelley also worked closely with the vice president of the Instrument Marketing Division, which was responsible for field sales and service.

Instrument Division products were sold through the field sales and service representatives of the Instrument Marketing Division. These people called on and advised potential customers, attended trade shows, and provided spare parts and technical service advice to users of Perkin Elmer equipment.

Marketing strategy, product line selection, and promotional strategy were the responsibility of the eight product managers in the Instrument Division. Each product manager had profit responsibility for an entire line of instruments and associated accessory items.

Exhibit 1

Ten year financial summary (dollar amounts in thousands except per share amounts)

	1974	1973	1972	1971	1970	1969	1968	1967	1966	1965
Financial operations (years ended July 31)										
Net sales	$272,042	$233,323	$216,813	$202,550	$232,948	$227,104	$171,962	$128,542	$103,511	$78,383
Cost of sales	161,524	141,286	136,864	129,818	159,049	157,814	114,428	80,199	62,466	46,380
Research and development	16,727	13,120	10,772	10,076	10,814	10,394	8,869	8,135	6,357	4,747
Marketing	43,191	35,178	30,240	28,053	27,052	23,754	20,409	18,025	14,878	11,699
General and administrative	21,681	17,455	16,365	14,892	16,197	15,244	13,009	10,546	8,992	7,018
Interest expense	1,385	919	1,575	1,443	1,563	1,628	1,564	1,146	732	764
Other income—net	(3,082)	(1,867)	(1,912)	(1,729)	(1,843)	(570)	(541)	(440)	(576)	(613)
Income before provision for income taxes	30,616	27,232	22,909	19,997	20,116	18,841	14,224	10,931	10,662	8,388
as a percent of sales	11.3%	11.7%	10.6%	9.9%	8.6%	8.3%	8.3%	8.5%	10.3%	10.7%
Net income	$ 17,159	$ 15,698	$ 13,133	$ 10,122	$ 9,647	$ 9,297	$ 6,601	$ 5,193	$ 5,486	$ 4,201
as a percent of sales	6.3%	6.7%	6.1%	5.0%	4.1%	4.1%	3.8%	4.0%	5.3%	5.4%
Net income per share	$ 0.98	$ 0.90	$ 0.77	$ 0.60	$ 0.58	$ 0.57	$ 0.42	$ 0.34	$ 0.38	$ 0.33
Dividends per share	0.225	0.214	0.206	0.15	—	—	—	—	—	—
Return on shareholders' equity at year-end	11.9%	12.4%	11.9%	10.6%	11.1%	12.3%	10.7%	9.9%	12.4%	11.1%
Financial condition (at July 31)										
Working capital	$109,085	$ 91,233	$ 86,179	$ 79,548	$ 71,540	$ 60,002	$ 47,368	$ 37,778	$ 29,860	$27,051
Fixed assets at cost	71,206	65,577	58,503	57,249	55,284	52,169	47,929	39,181	31,186	24,256
Long-term debt	4,295	5,704	7,072	16,015	18,213	19,055	19,718	13,681	8,274	8,605
Shareholders' equity	144,390	126,493	110,814	95,750	86,996	75,858	61,876	52,331	44,318	37,725
General										
Average number of common shares outstanding including common stock equivalents (in thousands)	17,667	17,514	17,305	16,740	16,621	16,445	15,890	15,081	14,441	12,899
Employees	8,627	7,933	7,334	7,509	7,827	8,204	7,623	6,978	5,769	4,417
Shareholders	10,668	10,559	10,087	10,176	10,925	9,562	9,510	8,118	6,427	5,588

The above data include Interdata, Incorporated on a pooling of interests basis. Interdata results included for the fiscal years 1974 and 1973 are for the 12 months ended July 31 and for the fiscal years 1967 (its first year of operations) through 1972 are for the 12 months ended December 31. In addition, certain other amounts have been included to conform with the 1974 presentation.

Exhibit 1 *(continued)*

PERKIN ELMER INSTRUMENT DIVISION
Consolidated Balance Sheet
At July 31

Assets	1974	1973
Current Assets:		
Cash, including time deposits	$ 7,554,375	$ 9,727,595
Marketable securities, at cost (approximate market)	17,535,029	16,608,661
Accounts receivable, less allowance for doubtful accounts of $608,630 ($583,809 in 1973)	62,787,044	55,732,439
Inventories, at lower of cost or market	75,287,832	54,857,102
Prepaid expenses and other current assets	6,612,049	4,426,662
	169,776,329	141,352,459
Marketable securities maturing beyond one year, at cost (approximate market)	5,753,005	6,598,684
Property, Plant and Equipment, at cost		
Land	4,285,966	4,499,384
Buildings	36,207,139	34,540,674
Machinery and equipment	30,712,593	26,536,833
	71,205,698	65,576,891
Accumulated depreciation and amortization	(34,625,214)	(31,290,702)
	36,580,454	34,286,189
Other Assets		
Excess of purchase price over net assets of companies acquired	4,207,142	4,194,168
Other investments, patents, deferred charges, etc.	3,534,311	3,873,891
	7,741,453	8,068,059
	$219,851,241	$190,305,391

Liabilities	1974	1973
Current Liabilities		
Loans payable, United States	$ 7,500,000	$ 3,385,994
Loans payable, foreign	7,220,911	3,828,395
Accounts payable, including advances from customers	17,671,796	16,023,352
Accrued salaries and wages	11,347,676	10,041,667
Accrued taxes on income	7,086,132	7,745,084
Other accrued expenses	9,865,276	9,095,211
	60,691,791	50,119,703
Long-Term Debt		
United States	—	—
Foreign	4,294,631	5,704,420
Other Long-Term Liabilities	8,957,309	6,677,774
Minority Interest	1,517,760	1,310,986
Shareholders' Equity		
Capital stock		
Preferred stock, $1 par value: Shares authorized 1,000,000	—	—
Common stock, $1 par value Shares authorized 20,000,000 Shares issued 17,435,881 (17,264,034–1973)	17,435,881	17,264,034
Capital contributed in excess of par value	28,386,472	24,284,280
Retained income	98,567,397	84,944,194
	144,389,750	126,492,508
	$219,851,241	$190,305,391

The price of an instrument varied from \$3,000 to \$35,000, while the price range for the accessory items used to operate the instrument was from \$200 to \$5,000. Price was not the primary basis for competition, however. Perkin Elmer's product managers claimed that the most important selling points were the features of their products. Perkin Elmer customers tended to be highly sophisticated from a technological standpoint. Thus, new instruments which could perform new tests or measurements with a high or greater degree of accuracy and reliability were preferred by them. Most major competitors tended to compete on the same basis.

A secondary selling point was delivery time and service. In the words of Jack Kerber, product manager for the atomic absorption instrument line, "A customer may take up to a year deciding whether he needs an instrument or in obtaining funds to purchase it, but once they decide and have the money, they want immediate delivery. And a lot of times, if they can't get it, they'll turn to our competitors if they have a comparable instrument."

Because the mechanical or electrical failure of an instrument could delay the completion of a research project, or shut down the production of industrial customers, rapid customer service was also felt to be important. To respond rapidly to these customer service needs, over 60 domestic field sales and service offices were maintained by the U.S. Sales Division.

The Instrument Division dealt with delivery lead times in two ways. First, they maintained an informal standard delivery lead time of 4 to 6 weeks. In other words, they attempted to maintain enough components in parts inventory or in-process, to be able to assemble, inspect, package, and ship an instrument within 4 to 6 weeks after it was ordered. During 1974, the average delivery lead time had slipped to about 12 weeks, however. According to Bill Chorske, General Manager, U.S. Sales Division, "We just haven't been able to catch up with our orders. The purchase lead times on some of the critical parts and materials we use have gone out to 10 to 12 months from an average of three months. Add to that the manufacturing time required to assemble parts into an instrument and you've got an impossible planning horizon. Couple that with an unexpected increase in demand and the result is inevitable."

The second way that the Instrument Division coped with delivery lead times was to keep the field sales force constantly informed of changes in them. This was partially accomplished with a monthly "Export Instrument Shipment Schedule" for export items and sales. In the United States, delivery lead times for an item could be supplied to the field sales force almost instantaneously if they called the marketing service department at Perkin Elmer's home office in Norwalk, Connecticut. Marketing service representatives queried computerized files from the centralized production control system on video display units to determine if enough parts were on hand to assemble the item immediately, or to determine the length of time required to obtain unavailable parts. This information was relayed to the field representative. If a firm order was made, parts were reserved for that order and an assembly order issued.

The planning process

The total planning process at Perkin Elmer's Instrument Division involved the coordination of the plans of the four major functional entities: engineering, marketing, manufacturing, and finance. The degree of coordination in these individual efforts was most apparent in the annual business and financial planning cycle.

The business plan. The annual business plan started off with a detailed instrument-by-instrument forecast of order receipts. This forecast was made from a "bottom up" sales forecast from the field sales and service personnel in the Instrument Marketing Division, and a top down forecast by the product managers. Differences between these two forecasts were resolved by further investigation and negotiation between the two groups. These forecasts specified orders by month for the two immediately following quarters, and projected orders by quarter for the last half of the fiscal year (Exhibit 2).

Exhibit 2
Instrument orders forecasts (fiscal year ends July 31)

Instru- ment	Actual and (forecasts)* for fiscal year			Fiscal year 1975 (forecasts)								12- month total†
	1972	1973	1974	Aug.	Sept.	Oct.	Nov.	Dec.	Jan.	3d Q	4th Q	
874X	—	—	78 (101)	19	33	51	27	29	48	133	129	469
90475Z ..	174 (169)	235 (214)	153 (160)	8	8	18	15	8	14	18	20	109
9903751..	177 (185)	122 (111)	110 (85)	2	3	9	—	2	3	11	—	30
4753ZY ..	22 (15)	14 (21)	15 (15)	—	—	2	1	—	1	—	1	5
976427 ...	3 (5)	14 (10)	18 (20)	—	—	7	1	—	2	1	3	14
74678 ...	—	4 (0)	33 (45)	4	7	12	2	6	11	29	26	97

* For each product in each year the actual sales are given. The corresponding forecast is given below in parentheses.

† Annual forecasts are simply the sum of the forecasts for six single months plus two quarters prepared as a part of the business plan just prior to the start of each fiscal year.

In addition to the forecast of orders for instruments, the sales of spare parts for technical service and accessory items were also forecasted. Since these items were generally stocked in inventory for immediate delivery, sales rather than orders were forecasted. A computer program incorporating some simple smoothing methodologies was used to forecast most of these items. All in all, accessories and spare parts sales accounted for about 20 percent of the division's annual sales. Instruments accounted for only a small percentage of the total number of saleable items, but made up 80 percent of sales.

Yet a third source of forecast information was Gaynor Kelley himself. He reserved the right to make "management stock orders." These were essentially hedges on major products with long lead times. For example, one new product which was still partially in the preproduction design stage was expected to be completely ready for manufacture by February 1975. Since the procurement and manufacturing lead times for this item were in excess of a year, and the company wished to be in a position to promise six weeks delivery when it was introduced, Kelley, after weighing both the market and engineering risks, might wish to forecast sales for this item in April. This would serve as an authorization to purchase or start manufacturing the long lead-time parts that went into the instrument. Similarly, if a major sale to a single customer (such as the government) of a particular high value, long lead-time instrument was expected (over and above regular sales), a management stock order might be placed to ensure that a reasonable delivery lead time could be offered to the prospective customer, or to make sure that the sale could be made within the current fiscal year.

Management stock orders were collected together in a special "Z" plan. In general, the Z plan served to ensure that the major risks of the division were handled and monitored by the highest levels of management. In October 1974, the sales value of the instruments in the Z plan for fiscal year 1975 was $4.3 million, while the product manager's forecast plus the forecast for spare parts totaled $72.2 million.

The three forecasts—the product manager/marketing forecast of major instrument orders, the computer generated forecast of accessory and spare parts sales, and the "Z" plan for management stock orders—were given to manufacturing. The production planning group then proceeded to project the manufacturing function, and the business as a whole. This was accomplished with the help of a computerized material and capacity requirements planning system.

First, the forecasts were used to construct a series of master plans. At least a part of the forecast data was forecasted order receipts. To construct the "exploded" master plan, which showed forecasted shipments, the standard delivery lead times were added to the forecasted order receipt dates. For example, instrument number 874ZX had sales orders for 51 systems projected for October. The "exploded" master plan broke this monthly forecast down into a weekly forecast for 13 units in each of the four weeks of the month. Then, since the Instrument Division tried to maintain a four-week position on this part, that is, be able to deliver four weeks after an order, the forecast orders for 13 units in each week in

October were translated into forecast shipments of 13 in each week of November.

Parts and accessories which were stocked for immediate shipment were transposed directly into a "sales" master plan without adding lead times. The Z plan, which already reflected delivery time hedging, was the third type of master plan used by the Instrument Division.

The business plan was formulated in the manner described above at the beginning of each fiscal year. The process was repeated at midyear in what was called the phase II plan. Thus, the company maintained a rolling six-month plan.

Short-term planning. Between the business planning cycles, the process of forecasting and replanning was carried out on a continual basis. Sales and orders forecasts for major items were reviewed monthly by product managers. Sales and orders forecasts for less important items were reviewed bimonthly or every quarter. These changes in forecasts meant that changes in the master plans were made monthly.

Preparing for a business turndown

Gaynor Kelley felt that the differences between the forecasts in the annual business plan, the product manager forecast, and the build plan were largely due to differences in the perceptions of the people involved in making these forecasts. The product managers, after having been caught short during the 74 boom, were bullish. Many manufacturing people, and especially the product planners, after having lived through a period of shortages, extended lead times, and vendor unreliability, were cautious. They were attempting to gain back the four- to six-week delivery position lost earlier in the year, and were still projecting protracted lead times for use in timing orders in the material requirements planning system.

Kelley felt that fiscal year 1975 sales would actually turn out to be very close to those projected in the original business or financial plan. The Instrument Division had generally followed a cyclical pattern close to that of the national economy. Some lead times were falling and purchase commitments for the division were rising. Order cancellations threatened in other industries. But, he was at this point undecided as to whether the Instrument Division should position themselves to handle the upside or downside risks.

The upside risks of losing sales and market position would be felt if they cut back, and a recession did not materialize. The downside risks of large inventories and a high fixed cost position would be felt if they increased production and a recession did materialize.

Case 8–2

Kool Kamp Inc.

One cold, snowy day in mid-January 1975 Fred Clark, president and chief
stockholder of Kool Kamp Inc., sat in his office in Melrose Park, Illinois
considering the topics that had been covered in a recent seminar he had
attended. While the seminar was aimed at short- and long-range planning
for smaller manufacturing companies, a good part of it had dealt with the
problem of forecasting and the available methods that might be used. Fred
realized that there was substantial opportunity to use forecasting as part
of the planning operation in his own firm and was anxious to pursue such
an application. As a first step, he wanted to focus on the selection and
application of one or more forecasting methods to the problem of predicting monthly sales for Kool Kamp Inc. Fred had collected the historical
sales data for the company's past four years as shown in Table 1 and
Exhibit 1. However, he was still at ground zero in terms of applying any
formal forecasting technique to his situation.

Company background

The Kool Kamp company had been founded in 1970, shortly after Fred
had completed an MBA degree at the Harvard Business School. He had
chosen the general Chicago area as a plant location site because of its
ready access to a nationwide distribution network and the fact that many
of his customers were either headquartered in Chicago or were regularly
passing through the area.

Fred had started the business after extensive discussions with a close
family friend who owned a small chain of sporting goods stores. This
friend had informed Fred that there appeared to be a substantial market
for inexpensive styrofoam ice chests and coolers and at that time there
were no major manufacturing concerns involved in that segment of the
business. Seeing this as an opportunity to get in on the ground floor, Fred
had formed the company to manufacture and sell as its first product a
styrofoam camp cooler which retailed for less than $7. Since its initial
production run, the company had added a couple of sizes and alternative
models but had not yet extended its product line to any other segment of
the cooler market or the leisure product field. (Fred did hope to be able to
expand into other related product lines in the near future.)

Distribution and sales for the company were handled through three
manufacturing reps and by Fred himself. Most of the sales went to major
discount chains and to retail sporting goods chains. Thus there were only
a couple of dozen customers that accounted for 90 percent of the firm's

Table 1
Actual sales 1971–1974 (in $000s)

Fiscal year and month	Actual sales	Fiscal year and month	Actual sales	Management estimates
1971		**1973**		
1. October	$ 1.3	25. October	$ 18.8	
2. November	0.1	26. November	13.2	
3. December	0.5	27. December	11.6	
4. January	9.5	28. January	53.4	
5. February	37.2	29. February	126.2	
6. March	81.1	30. March	153.9	
7. April	87.3	31. April	188.2	
8. May	59.5	32. May	206.1	
9. June	72.9	33. June	168.9	
10. July	58.6	34. July	97.6	
11. August	28.1	35. August	35.2	
12. September	14.1	36. September	33.7	
1972		**1974**		
13. October	$ 6.4	37. October	$ 20.4	
14. November	12.7	38. November	13.5	
15. December	13.3	39. December	22.8	
16. January	20.9	40. January	92.7	
17. February	65.5	41. February	161.7	
18. March	124.5	42. March	316.8	
19. April	144.0	43. April	372.8	
20. May	137.8	44. May	272.4	
21. June	156.0	45. June	181.0	
22. July	89.2	46. July	92.1	
23. August	36.9	47. August	39.9	
24. September	25.2	48. September	34.2	
		1975		
		49. October	$ 15.8	21.0
		50. November	13.1	13.0
		51. December	23.0	22.0

business. Since price seemed to be the most important criteria in sales of this product, most of the company's emphasis had been placed on maintaining low cost through effective purchasing of materials and efficient manufacturing.

As indicated by the figures in Table 1 and Exhibit 1, sales had grown dramatically since 1970 and Fred now felt that he had a substantial share of the low cost styrofoam cooler market. Unfortunately one of the problems with the demand for the company's product was that it was extremely seasonal both at the final consumer level and in terms of retail store purchases from Kool Kamp's reps. The latter was the case because of the substantial storage space required for holding more than a few dozen units of the product in any single location. While Fred was aware that some steps might be taken to try to spread peak demand over a longer period of time, so far he had not attempted to do so.

The company's general production policy was to work two full shifts in the late winter and spring months and then to work a single shift through-

Exhibit 1
Graph of sales results, 1971–1974 (from Table 1)

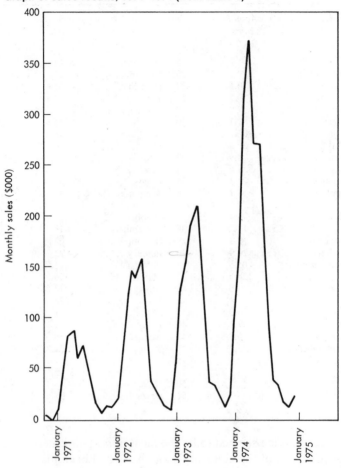

out the remainder of the year. Thus substantial inventories were built up in the late summer and fall periods until demand began to pick up in midwinter. Because of these production requirements, Fred was most anxious to prepare aggregate plans for the company that would be based on the best available information concerning demand. It was in this regard that Fred saw the first use of the sales forecasts whose preparation he was presently contemplating.

Even before Fred had attended the recent seminar, he had asked his three manufacturing reps to help him prepare sales estimates for the first three months of fiscal 1975. These estimates, along with the actual results for those first three months, are shown in Table 1. Fred had found it extremely difficult to obtain these estimates and even when he did, he had been told by all three reps that they were simply ball park figures and that they (the reps) certainly wouldn't put too much faith in them. The reps had pointed out that one of the problems was that the company's sales were becoming even more seasonal than they had been in the past. This made it extremely difficult to forecast sales for individual months although the reps felt they could do a reasonably good job in forecasting annual demand.

Forecasting issues to be considered

One of the things that Fred had learned at the recent seminar was that there were a number of issues that needed to be considered in applying formal forecasting techniques in any particular situation. One of these that he felt was particularly important in the case of Kool Kamp was selecting one or more techniques that appeared to be appropriate for the situation and then developing a procedure that could be used in testing to determine which one should be used in the future. From his discussions with the reps, he also felt it would be important to decide whether the initial forecast should be of total annual demand which could then be broken down into forecasts for individual months or whether he should first forecast each month and then simply aggregate them to obtain an estimate of annual demand.

While he wanted accurate forecasts immediately, he realized that there would be a period of time over which he would need to use two or more techniques in order to build up experience with them and to determine their strengths and weaknesses in his situation. One of the things he wanted to do was be sure that he designed his initial procedures in such a way that he could obtain that experience as quickly as possible and build up confidence in his own mind and for others in the organization concerning the reliability of the forecasts.

Fortunately Fred had a close friend who owned a small time-sharing service bureau and he was certain that he could buy time from that friend at a very reasonable price (perhaps $5 to $8 per terminal hour). In addition he felt that he could impose upon his friend to write him some simple forecasting programs and/or to supply more elaborate programs (such as regression analysis) from the library package supplied by the computer manufacturer. Thus for a rather modest cost Fred was certain that he could gain access to a computer to help him in this forecasting situation.

Case 8–3

Perrin Frères

Late in the fall of 1972, the champagne-making firm of Perrin Frères, located in Epernay, France, was preparing its financial plan for the coming calendar year. The impetus behind the preparation of this plan was a request from the company's banker, Société Générale, although obviously such a plan would be of general use to the management of Perrin Frères as well. Because the demand for champagne followed a marked seasonal pattern during the course of the year, most champagne companies relied on banks to finance their fluctuating working capital needs. Such was the case at Perrin Frères. Due to the recent financial difficulties of some other companies in the industry, Société Générale had requested a set of pro forma cash flow, profit, and balance sheet statements (for each of the next 12 months) before formally approving Perrin's request for a working capital loan for parts of the coming year.

The Director of Finance at Perrin Frères had asked his assistant, Michel Cunche, to prepare the necessary statements for the bank. After some initial thought, Michel decided that once he had accurate monthly forecasts for sales, the delay in cash receipts for actual sales, and the various operating costs, it would be primarily an accounting matter to combine these into the proper pro forma statements. From Michel's familiarity with the French champagne industry, and especially Perrin's operations, he felt that the most appropriate method for predicting the company's monthly cash operating expenses and the time delay in cash receipts would be to take the average values for each calendar month over the past three years and use that as the basis of a forecast. Of course, Michel realized that there might be a few instances in which he would want to modify one of these forecasts because of new information that was available, but he did not foresee any major problems in doing this.

The task of forecasting the company's champagne sales for each of the next 12 months appeared to be much more difficult. After considerable thought Michel decided that one approach for doing this would be to obtain a monthly industry forecast of champagne sales and then to apply the market share figures of Perrin Frères to this to determine the level of sales his firm could expect to achieve. Besides helping to meet the requirements of the company's bank, this approach had an additional benefit in that the industry forecast could serve as a basis for some of the other planning activities of the firm, particularly in the marketing area.

As an initial step in developing a forecast of monthly French champagne sales, Michel contacted the Association of French Champagne Firms, to which Perrin Frères belonged. While the association did not

Exhibit 1
Monthly champagne sales—France (millions of bottles)

(1)	(2)	(3)	(4)	(5)	(6)	(7)
						Ratio of
		Obser-	Actual	12-month moving	Centered moving	actual to moving
Year	Month	vation	sales	average*	average	average
1964	January	1	2.815	—	—	—
	February	2	2.672	—	—	—
	March	3	2.755	—	—	—
	April	4	2.721	—	—	—
	May	5	2.946	—	—	—
	June	6	3.036	—	—	—
	July	7	2.282	3.478	3.467	0.658
	August	8	2.212	3.455	3.447	0.642
	September	9	2.922	3.439	3.450	0.847
	October	10	4.301	3.462	3.485	1.234
	November	11	5.764	3.507	3.542	1.627
	December	12	7.312	3.576	3.585	2.040
1965	January	13	2.541	3.593	3.624	0.701
	February	14	2.475	3.655	3.636	0.681
	March	15	3.031	3.617	3.645	0.832
	April	16	3.266	3.673	3.680	0.887
	May	17	3.776	3.688	3.732	1.012
	June	18	3.230	3.777	3.821	0.845
	July	19	3.028	3.864	3.888	0.779
	August	20	1.759	3.912	3.934	0.447
	September	21	3.595	3.956	3.998	0.899
	October	22	4.474	4.041	4.051	1.104
	November	23	6.838	4.062	4.069	1.681
	December	24	8.357	4.076	4.107	2.035
1966	January	25	3.113	4.139	4.148	0.750
	February	26	3.006	4.158	4.150	0.724
	March	27	4.047	4.142	4.140	0.978
	April	28	3.523	4.137	4.168	0.845
	May	29	3.937	4.198	4.231	0.931
	June	30	3.986	4.263	4.300	0.927
	July	31	3.260	4.338	4.432	0.736
	August	32	1.573	4.526	4.530	0.347
	September	33	3.528	4.533	4.519	0.781
	October	34	5.211	4.506	4.547	1.146
	November	35	7.614	4.588	4.612	1.651
	December	36	9.254	4.637	4.660	1.986
1967	January	37	5.375	4.683	4.700	1.144
	February	38	3.088	4.716	4.719	0.654
	March	39	3.718	4.722	4.773	0.779
	April	40	4.514	4.823	4.832	0.934
	May	41	4.520	4.841	4.870	0.928
	June	42	4.539	4.900	4.958	0.916
	July	43	3.663	5.016	4.943	0.741
	August	44	1.643	4.871	4.921	0.334
	September	45	4.739	4.971	4.989	0.950
	October	46	5.428	5.008	4.991	1.088
	November	47	8.314	4.975	4.980	1.669
	December	48	10.651	4.985	4.994	2.133

Exhibit 1 (continued)

(1)	(2)	(3)	(4)	(5)	(6)	(7)
				12-month	Centered	Ratio of actual to
		Obser-	Actual	moving	moving	moving
Year	Month	vation	sales	average*	average	average
1968	January	49	3.633	5.003	5.016	0.724
	February	50	4.292	5.028	5.032	0.853
	March	51	4.154	5.035	5.048	0.823
	April	52	4.121	5.061	5.123	0.804
	May	53	4.647	5.185	5.250	0.885
	June	54	4.753	5.314	5.342	0.890
	July	55	3.965	5.371	5.387	0.736
	August	56	1.723	5.403	5.389	0.320
	September	57	5.048	5.375	5.389	0.937
	October	58	6.922	5.404	5.411	1.279
	November	59	9.858	5.417	5.431	1.815
	December	60	11.331	5.444	5.441	2.083
1969	January	61	4.016	5.438	5.419	0.741
	February	62	3.957	5.401	5.405	0.732
	March	63	4.510	5.409	5.416	0.833
	April	64	4.276	5.423	5.421	0.789
	May	65	4.968	5.419	5.459	0.910
	June	66	4.677	5.498	5.606	0.834
	July	67	3.523	5.713	5.656	0.623
	August	68	1.821	5.599	5.555	0.328
	September	69	5.222	5.511	5.463	0.956
	October	70	6.872	5.416	5.393	1.274
	November	71	10.803	5.371	5.286	2.044
	December	72	13.916	5.201	5.172	2.691
1970	January	73	2.639	5.143	5.172	0.510
	February	74	2.899	5.201	5.198	0.558
	March	75	3.370	5.194	5.194	0.649
	April	76	3.740	5.194	5.175	0.723
	May	77	2.927	5.157	5.117	0.572
	June	78	3.986	5.077	5.042	0.791
	July	79	4.217	5.007	5.061	0.833
	August	80	1.738	5.115	5.125	0.339
	September	81	5.221	5.136	5.175	1.009
	October	82	6.424	5.213	5.252	1.223
	November	83	9.842	5.291	5.378	1.830
	December	84	13.076	5.464	5.501	2.377
1971	January	85	3.934	5.538	5.556	0.708
	February	86	3.162	5.573	5.570	0.568
	March	87	4.286	5.566	5.597	0.766
	April	88	4.676	5.627	5.650	0.828
	May	89	5.010	5.674	5.674	0.883
	June	90	4.874	5.674	5.658	0.862
	July	91	4.633	5.641	5.658	0.819
	August	92	1.659	5.675	5.692	0.291
	September	93	5.951	5.709	5.721	1.040
	October	94	6.981	5.733	5.738	1.217
	November	95	9.851	5.742	5.726	1.720
	December	96	12.670	5.710	5.728	2.212

Exhibit 1 (concluded)

(1)	(2)	(3)	(4)	(5)	(6)	(7)
						Ratio of
				12-month	Centered	actual to
		Obser-	Actual	moving	moving	moving
Year	Month	vation	sales	average*	average	average
1972	January	97	4.348	—†	—†	—†
	February	98	3.564	—	—	—
	March	99	4.577	—	—	—
	April	100	4.788	—	—	—
	May	101	4.618	—	—	—
	June	102	5.312	—	—	—
	July	103	4.298	—	—	—
	August	104	1.431	—	—	—
	September	105	5.877	—	—	—

* These 12-month moving average figures are centered on the seventh observation. Thus the first value of 3.478 which is listed opposite observation 7 is the average for observations 1 through 12; the value opposite observation 8 is the average for observations 2 through 13; etc.

† The two types of moving averages and the ratios of the actual to the centered moving averages *could* be found for the first few months of 1972 from these data. The calculation of those values has been left as an exercise for the reader.

Exhibit 2

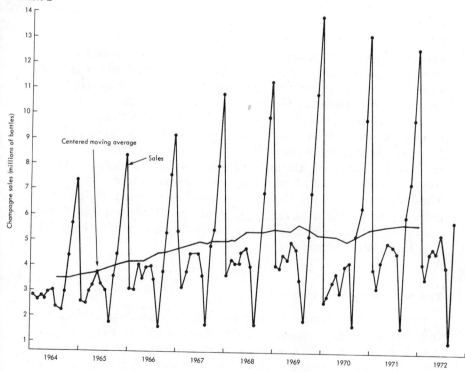

have an accurate set of monthly forecasts that would meet Perrin's needs, it did have available the historical data in Exhibit 1. In addition, it had computed a 12-month moving average for these data at the request of another member of the association. It was very happy to supply Perrin Frères with this information.

To help him in determining what forecasting technique might be appropriate for this situation, Michel plotted the historical data of Exhibit 1 as shown in Exhibit 2. While he was not surprised to see a strong seasonal pattern in French champagne sales, he was surprised to find what looked like a fairly consistent pattern over each calendar year. Because of this apparent consistency, he felt that some time series approach to forecasting that adequately considered seasonal factors would be most appropriate, and he set out to determine what that technique might be and how he might use it in this situation.

Case 8–4

Tempo, Inc.

Louis De Rosa, the president of Tempo, Inc., had just acquired a new computer for his firm's data processing needs. Tempo was a medium-sized temporary help company operating throughout the New York–New Jersey metropolitan area. The new computer was intended primarily for payroll work (a particularly complex task for Tempo, which used a large number of part-time and occasional workers), but De Rosa had read enough about the uses of computers to realize that he should also consider the potential for having the machine contribute to the business in other ways. In the past, he had personally taken charge of forecasting the demand for workers in the 25 different categories supplied by Tempo; he prepared such forecasts several days in advance. He hoped that the new computer system could simplify this forecasting task and, perhaps, take over the bulk of the forecasting work.

The temporary help industry

In 1974 the U.S. temporary help industry was only about 25 years old. It had grown from a volume of $100 million in 1960 to one of a billion dollars in 1973. Initially, most of the workers provided by the temporary help agencies were clerical workers, but as the industry grew it had begun to provide a much wider range of employees, including some with specialized technical skills. The industry was dominated by Manpower, Inc., a 25-year-old company which accounted for a quarter of the industry's business in 1973. There were other large firms (Kelly Services, Inc., and Olsten Temporary Services) and also several thousand smaller (and more localized) firms in the field. Altogether, temporary workers comprised approximately 3 percent of the U.S. labor force in 1973; the fraction of temporary workers was expected to rise markedly.

Customers of these temporary help firms hired temporary workers for varied reasons. Some firms used temporaries to staff once- or twice-a-year efforts, such as the mail work associated with special promotions. Other firms used temporaries to fill in for regular workers who were on vacation. Sometimes employees who had reached the mandatory retirement age of their employer company were transferred to a temporary help agency and then hired through the agency by their original employer so that they could continue to work while technically not violating the retirement rules.

The conservative business climate and the inflationary pressure in 1974 had provided a particularly good opportunity for a more widespread and more sophisticated use of temporary help. Instead of maintaining personnel at the levels needed for times of maximum or near-maximum work load, companies whose work loads varied over the year were beginning to maintain their permanent staffs at lower levels, nearer the minimum required levels, and to fill in during peak times with temporary help. Such temporary workers generally cost the customer companies more than would their own permanent workers on a per hour basis, but the temporaries were nevertheless useful because they could be hired (and hence paid) for only the hours which they worked. The customers' own permanent help, on the other hand, had to be paid both wages and fringes during both the times when they were badly needed and the times when they were largely superfluous. The *total* cost of the temporaries turned out to be lower because the temporaries were not paid when they were not needed.

Another factor aiding the growth of the temporary work industry was the fact that workweeks in many industries were being shortened at the same time that the hours of stores and banks were being extended. Part-time and sometimes temporary help was used to provide staffing for the stores and banks over their extended working days.

Competition among temporary help firms was based primarily on the quality of the workers and on the ability of the agencies to respond to customer needs; most of the agencies charged comparable rates, and so price competition was not important.

In 1974 the industry had been growing at more than 20 percent a year and its firms were finding it more difficult to find high-quality employees. Manpower's vice president for marketing was quoted in *Business Week*

(August 3, 1974) as saying that past marketing efforts had been concentrated on generating job orders but that the current problem was to build up Manpower's pool of workers. The industry was spending more effort on recruiting and training its employees and was also working to reduce its extremely high turnover rates (75 percent each year for Manpower, with many employees working only a few months) and to establish closer ties with its customer firms.

Tempo, Inc.

Tempo operated 12 different offices scattered throughout the New York–New Jersey metropolitan area. The company prided itself on (and advertised strongly) its high-quality personnel and its ability to fill many customer requests for help on extremely short notice—often within a matter of hours. Each of the 12 offices maintained a call list of workers in each of the 25 diverse fields in which the company claimed competence. These areas included secretarial work, typing, outdoor maintenance, janitorial work, electrical wiring, bookkeeping, drafting, driving, and moving. Normally each office would receive most of the requests for workers at least one day early, although some of the requests came in at the last minute. The company was not always able to meet last-minute requests for workers but, especially if the requests came from regular customers, the managers did try to provide the requested help. For orders for help placed at least a day early, the managers of the individual offices had orders to meet the demands, even if doing so involved unusual effort; for example, if there were an unusually high demand for outdoor maintenance workers, one office might exhaust its own call list in this area and might have to try to call up workers from other offices' lists.

De Rosa had established a system under which the work orders were reported from the individual offices to his office so that he could examine them as they came in. He also kept the demand figures for each office for each category of worker for the past several weeks to use in his forecasting. With this information, he tried to anticipate the demand figures a full week in advance so that the individual offices could have early warning of abnormally high or low demand levels. In addition, he knew that the early demand estimates were important to his managers in maintaining the particularly high quality work force which was extremely important for Tempo's business. Many of the workers on Tempo's lists were particularly good workers who, for one reason or another, chose to work part time and, often, required advance warning so that they could make arrangements to work on any given day. Many of the other temporary help firms in the metropolitan area refused to hire such people because managing them required extra effort, but De Rosa's policy was to encourage such arrangements if the workers were particularly good. His theory was that the workers would be likely to remain with Tempo much longer than was common in the industry, simply because the company was willing to arrange for their needs. He saw the policy as a way of making Tempo's work force significantly better in quality than were those of some of the competitors.

Tempo had a policy for all of its workers that they would be paid in full for every day for which they were called to work, even if a job did not materialize for them on some days. Thus, the company could not afford to call up enough workers to be certain to meet all of the last-minute requests which came in. On the other hand, De Rosa did ask the office managers to call in a few workers for filling such requests.

De Rosa felt that the business benefited in several ways from the demand forecasts which he prepared. The forecasts gave the branch managers advance warning of their labor needs so that they could call up appropriate numbers of workers; often a manager used the forecasts to call up workers before firm orders for those individuals had been received. In some cases, the early warning allowed managers to call on workers who could work only on advance notice. In other cases, a manager was warned by the forecasts of an impending particularly heavy demand in time to be able to ask for names from the lists of other branch offices to fill the demand. De Rosa believed that without the forecasts his managers would have been reluctant to call up large numbers of workers to meet any anticipated heavy load of last-minute requests for workers; he feared that without forecasts the managers would not have wanted to go out on a limb before substantial numbers of firm orders were received. With the forecasts, on the other hand, De Rosa had himself taken responsibility for such orders and his managers were far less reluctant to plan in anticipation of demand.

The forecasting problem

As a first step in setting up a forecasting system, De Rosa sat down with a consultant in the field to discuss the important characteristics of his business which any worthwhile system would have to consider. He explained:

> I do my planning in half-day time periods. Full-day periods just aren't fine enough, and I've never had the time to consider more than two periods per day. Actually, though, I really don't think more than two slots per day would make sense.

> It's essential to keep track of the figures for the separate offices rather than to try to guess at total figures for the business. The whole pattern of demand at the office near Wall Street is fundamentally different from the one in Long Island City and also different from the various Jersey offices. The offices have different busy days, different patterns of demand for the various categories of workers—I guess I'd just call them basically different.

> I have to keep the figures for the 25 different worker categories separate, too. In fact, if I had the opportunity, I'd really like to break the categories

down more finely than I have in the past. I think it would help to match workers to jobs more effectively. Anyhow, the categories behave differently, in terms of demand. Some are higher at one time of the year, others are higher at other times. Also, the pattern of use of the various categories over the year isn't the same at all 12 of our offices.

There are real differences in the demand pattern over the course of an individual week, too. Demand is particularly high on Mondays, for example, and there is often a rush of last-minute orders at the end of the week as our customers try to finish one job or another. I don't think that the pattern within a week depends on the time of the year for any one of our offices, but I'm pretty sure that the patterns at the different offices are different.

There's another set of problems which complicates the forecasting process. They're what I call special events—a bad snowstorm which raises the demand for outdoor maintenance help, for example. I can predict some of these special events (conventions, for example) but not others. And after one of those things, it's never quite clear to me how to use the demand figures which were affected by a special event.

There are, as I see it, two main sources for information for my forecasting. One is the demand information from the past few weeks. Unfortunately, I haven't kept good demand information over the years, but I do always have reasonable information from the past month or so, and I use that information, together with any hunches I have based on the time of year or special events or something, to come up with a preliminary set of demand figures a full week in advance. I use those figures to give the managers a really early indication of what to expect a week later.

There's a second set of numbers which I've decided should be used separately from the demand numbers. Those are the actual work orders as they come in. I know, for example, that work orders for a given day straggle in over the week or maybe two weeks preceding. If I see an unusually high number of orders for five days from now, I can do some work to try to find out whether something unusual is happening and has to be prepared for, or whether there's just a fluke in the timing. I'm pretty certain that I want the forecasts prepared from the past demand kept separate from the forecasts prepared from the early orders because I wouldn't want to have to look at a single high figure, say, and try to decide which of the two factors (past demand or early orders) made it high. Also, I'd like the computer system to generate the figures based on past demand automatically. Maybe it should consider the early orders and also check whether those orders look unusual. It could send out a warning only if something strange is happening which needs my attention.

I've been assured that there is computer time available for doing some forecasting. We'll probably need to buy some extra storage space of one type or another for the data. I'm anxious to keep the costs of the computer installation down, but I do think some kind of automated forecasting would be worthwhile.

Chapter 9

Developing forecasts with the aid of regression analysis

When historical data are to be used to aid in the assessment of a probability distribution, either the forecaster must believe the data come from indistinguishable situations, or adjustments must be made in the data to remove the effects of the causes which make the situations distinguishable from one another. Forecasting with regression analysis is essentially a process of identifying factors which bring about relevant distinguish ability, evaluating their influences, and allowing for them in the development of a forecast.[1]

AN ESTIMATING PROBLEM

To explore the reasoning involved in this process, consider the following estimating problem. A number of single-family dwellings located in a particular metropolitan area have been sold over the past year. A house will be selected at random from the list. Our task as a forecaster is to provide a point estimate and a probability distribution for its selling price. At this first stage no other information about the house, other than that it comes from the list, is provided. What information would we try to obtain before making a forecast? How would we use the information to make a point estimate? How would we develop our probability distribution?

A moment's reflection will indicate the desirability of obtaining a complete list of the selling prices of the houses, or at least a sample of them. Since we will have no additional information, the situations at each of the

---

[1] There are other uses of regression analysis which raise issues not considered in this chapter.

sales were indistinguishable occasions to us, and the distribution of the selling prices provides us with data for assessing our probability distribution.

If we were asked, along with others, to make point estimates of the prices for a series of randomly selected houses from the list, the value we would select from the distribution to be our point estimate would depend upon the criterion by which the winner would be selected. If the winner would be the individual with the most estimates exactly correct, the mode of the distribution should be selected. If the winner would be the individual with the estimates with the smallest error, on the average, the median would be the desired point estimate.[2] If the criterion for judging the winning set of estimates would be the set with the smallest average square error, then the arithmetic mean would be chosen.[3] In most situations in which regression is used, this last criterion, the so-called least squares criterion, is used. In this chapter it will be assumed that the least squares criterion is being employed in judging a series of estimates.

In this estimation task, as we are asked to estimate the selling price for one house after another, we would make the same point estimate for each house, namely the mean of the selling prices for all the houses on the list (or at least from some representative sample of houses from the list). At the end of our task we could then get a measure of how well we had done in our estimates by comparing our estimates to the actual selling prices and calculating the average squared error. The larger the average squared error, the poorer our set of estimates. The smaller the average squared error, the better our estimates would have been under our criterion.

As a second estimating task we will be asked again to estimate the selling price of a house selected from the list. This time, however, we will be given some additional information, namely, the size of the house. This house has 1,500 square feet of living area measured to the nearest 100 square feet. Again our task is to develop a point estimate and assess a probability distribution of its selling price. What data would we now seek from a list of all (or a sample) of the sales? The entire list of sales no longer arises from occasions which are indistinguishable to us. Those situations in which a large house is sold are now distinguishable from those in which smaller houses were sold, so the entire list as it stands would not provide us with our probability distribution for the selling price of the house, nor would the mean of all the selling prices provide us with a desired "best" estimate. If, however, we select from the total list all of the sales in which the house sold was 1,500 square feet in size, these sales would contain data from situations which in our view are indistinguishable from the one we wish to forecast. The distribution of these selling prices would provide

---

[2] It can be easily demonstrated that the median is the value in a distribution from which the sum of the deviations, without regard to sign, is a minimum.

[3] The mean can be shown to be that value in a distribution from which the sum of the squared deviations is at a minimum.

us with a basis for assessing our probability distribution for the selling price of the selected house. The mean of the distribution would provide us with our point estimate.

If we expected to be faced with making a series of such estimates for a number of houses of various sizes, we would classify the basic data on the list by house size and record the distribution of selling prices for each size. The average selling price in each size category would provide us with our point estimates. The variability within each distribution would give our assessment of the uncertainty. We may have found, for example, that houses with 1,500 square feet of living area sold on the average for $30,000, and those with 1,700 square feet sold on the average for $32,000. We would then take $30,000 as our point estimate for a house with 1,500 square feet of living area, but $32,000 for our estimate for any house with 1,700 square feet.

After a series of such estimates have been made we can go back and check on how well we have done. If, in fact, selling price is related to the size of houses, then the average squared error in this later set of estimates should be smaller than those from our estimates developed when we had no other data. The stronger the relationship, the greater the reduction in the average squared error.

Our third estimating task will be again to estimate the selling price of a house selected at random from the list. This time we will have as information on which to base our estimate not only the size of the house but also its type of construction. All houses on the list have been classified as either (1) frame, (2) mixed frame and brick, or (3) all brick.

An extension of the preceding idea should suggest that we could simultaneously cross-classify all houses within the list by these two characteristics: size and type of construction. If the house for which we want to make the estimate is a brick house of 1,800 square feet, then the distribution of the selling price for all brick, 1,800-square-foot houses provides us with relevant data for assessing our probability distribution on the sales price. The mean of the distribution would, under the least squares criterion, provide our point estimate.

To make a series of point estimates for a variety of houses, a table of the average selling price cross-classified by size and type of construction would provide the relevant data. If the average price of 1,500-square-foot brick houses was $40,000 and the average price of 1,500-square-foot frame houses was $30,000, then our point estimate for a brick house of 1,500 square feet would be $40,000. Our point estimate for a frame house of the same size would be $10,000 less.

In concept this same procedure can be expanded to take into account other hopefully related pieces of information. If we were asked to estimate the selling price of a house from the list and were told the size of the house, type of construction, and size of lot on which the house is located, a series of distributions of price—each conditional on a particular size of house, type of construction, and size of lot—would provide data for the appropriate probability assessment. A table of mean selling prices cross-classified simultaneously on all three dimensions (size of house, type of construction, and size of lot) would provide the basis for a series of point estimates. As information on additional factors which we believe constituted distinguishable features in the situations is made available for our estimating, we could take them into account by simultaneously cross-classifying on the basis of the added factors as well as the previously considered ones.

If data were free in cost and unlimited in the amount available, estimating methods would never involve more than the use of the conditional averages and distributions described above. The successful application of the methodology would, however, require for most situations a huge amount of data—in some cases more than conceivably could be obtained; in others, more than could be justified economically. If we had only four factors which made situations appear distinguishable to us (four so-called explanatory variables), and if each of these factors could take on only ten values, we would have 10,000 cells (or categories) in our cross-classified table. If we needed, for example, 50 observations in each cell to get an approximation of the distribution of values in the cell, we would need a total of half a million observations to provide the basis for our estimates. If we want to add additional explanatory variables, the number expands rapidly. Thus, although this idea of basing estimates on distributions conditional on a given level of each of a number of explanatory variables provides us in concept with a powerful aid in estimating, in practice we rarely have, or could obtain, enough data to implement it directly. Regression analysis, as we will consider it, is a method for approximating what we would have gotten from the cross-classification analysis without demanding the voluminous amount of data that a direct application of that approach would have required. In such analysis a combination of relatively sparse data and some strong judgment on the part of the forecaster substitute for the extensive data otherwise needed.

The following example gives a rough idea of how judgment and sparse data can substitute for more extensive data. Imagine that in preparing for our estimates of selling price we have gone through the total list and selected a sample of 50 houses which were all 1,500 square feet in size. We calculated the average selling price and found it to be $30,000. We then took a second sample of 50 houses, all of which were 1,700 square feet in size. The average selling price of these houses we found to be $32,000. Before we have time to perform any additional analysis we are required to make an estimate for a house selected from the master list. We learn that the size of this house is 1,600 square feet (a size we have not specifically studied). What will we do? Although we have no direct data, most people's judgment would suggest that as the size of the houses increases, their average selling price would increase, and thus we would expect to find our estimate of the selling price for this house somewhere between $30,000 and $32,000.

Depending on the estimator's judgment of how selling price and size are related, a number of interpolations could be made. We might believe that from size group to size group of houses, each group differing from the previous one by 100 square feet, the average price increases by a constant amount (a linear relationship). Then we would make a linear interpolation and estimate $31,000 as the mean price, conditional on a size of 1,600 square feet as our point estimate. On the other hand, if we believed there were some sort of diminishing returns in the relationship between selling price and size, we would interpolate a value greater than $31,000, for we would expect a greater difference between the average price of houses of 1,600 square feet compared to those of 1,500 square feet than between the 1,600-square-foot and 1,700-square-foot houses. A statement of the specific form of the relationship we believe to hold would allow us to obtain a specific value. Whether the value thus obtained would be very close to what we would have obtained had we had the extensive data depends primarily on how perceptive we were in understanding the nature of the relationships. If our perceptions correspond closely to what is actually going on, then our approximation will be close to what would have been obtained with extensive data, and the forecast will be a useful one. If our judgments are poor, we can still interpolate, but our forecast may be quite different from what would have been obtained from the extensive data and therefore misleading. In a sense we will be conducting regression analysis as a procedure for combining some relatively sparse data with our judgments about the nature of relationships, to approximate the conditional distributions and conditional means we could have obtained by cross-classification if voluminous data had been available directly.

The arithmetic involved in developing regression estimates in any realistic problem is so extensive that it is almost essential that a computer be employed. Fortunately, almost every computer system has as part of its regular library a regression program. Programs may differ in the way in which information is to be provided and the exact form of the output, but all require the same kind of inputs from the user, and all provide in general the same information in the output. The next two sections will look at the kinds of information the computer requires of the user before it can perform regression analysis, and the kind of output the computer can usually provide to the user to convey the results of the analysis.

INPUTS TO A REGRESSION ANALYSIS

There are five kinds of information the user must supply to the computer before it can do its job. They are:

1. Identify the "dependent" variable. We have put quotation marks around the word "dependent" because it does not really refer to any characteristic of the variable itself. Rather, it is the customary way of identifying the variable that is being estimated or forecast. In the example above in which we attempted to estimate the selling price of a house based on its size and type of construction, selling price would be referred to as the dependent variable. With exactly the same data, if we wished to estimate the size of a house given knowledge of its selling price and type of construction, size would be the dependent variable. This requirement therefore states that if we wish to estimate or forecast some variable located in the computer data base, we must be able to indicate to the computer which variable it is we wish to estimate or forecast.

2. Specify the explanatory variable or variables. The explanatory variables[4] are those factors which, in the judgment of the forecaster, form the potential basis for distinguishability among the situations giving rise to the past data, and distinguishability from the situations for which estimates or forecasts are required. They are in essence the factors which it is hoped are related to the dependent variable and which will be used to "explain" differences among the values of the dependent variable. Selecting the explanatory variables to include in an estimating process is one of the important judgmental inputs required from the forecaster. The issues involved in these judgments are described in more detail in a subsequent section of this chapter, "Developing the Model."

3. Specify the relevant group of observations for the analysis. If the data base contains data on a set of observations larger than the group for which the analysis is desired, the forecaster must specify the subgroup of interest for the current analysis. If in the example above we were interested only in the selling price of single-family houses located in the metropolitan area, and if the total data base contained all property sales of that area, we might want to give the computer instructions to select for the analysis only that part of its total data base which refers to single-family houses.

4. Specify the nature of the relationship between the dependent variable and each of the explanatory variables. In the example of estimating the selling price for a house of 1,600 square feet, we saw that different estimates would result from different judgments regarding the nature of the relationship between size and price. A belief that the relationship was essentially a linear one led to a point estimate of $31,000. If we believed that the relationship was such that a difference in size of 100 square feet would have a greater effect on price if it were the difference between 1,000 square feet and 1,100 square feet than if it were between 2,000 square feet and 2,100 square feet (a retarding form of relationship), our point estimate would have been greater than $31,000. If we state the specific form of the mathematical relationship, a unique value can be

---

[4] These variables are also referred to as "independent" variables.

obtained. In a similar sense, if we believed that the relationship between size and price was one which accelerated (i.e., the average difference in price for the difference between 1,000 square feet and 1,100 square feet was *less* than the average difference in price between 2,000 square feet and 2,100 square feet), our point estimate for the house of 1,600 square feet would be less than $31,000. Again, a statement of the specific mathematical relationship assumed would allow the calculation of a unique value. Before the computer can perform the calculation necessary to provide us with regression output, we must therefore specify a particular functional form of relationship between each explanatory variable and the dependent variable. The issues involved in deciding upon such relationships, the choices that are available, and the manner by which those choices can be communicated to the computer will be discussed in more detail in the subsequent section dealing with developing the model.

   5.   Provide data on the dependent variable and the various explanatory variables from all or a sample of observations from the relevant group.   The basic goal of the regression process has been described as to combine judgments of the forecaster with relatively sparse data to obtain an approximation of results that would have required much more extensive data to obtain directly. This fifth requirement states that the appropriate relatively sparse data must be provided to the computer in the form of a data file. In the example in which we wished to estimate the selling price of houses based on their size and type of construction, a file containing the selling price, size, and type of construction for all or a sample of the single-family houses sold during the past year in the metropolitan area would have to be provided.

OUTPUTS FROM A REGRESSION ANALYSIS

If the forecaster provides the inputs mentioned above, the computer can do the arithmetic required for the regression analysis and provide the output. The various kinds of outputs from regression programs can be thought of as belonging to one of three categories: regression coefficients, measures of goodness of fit, and estimates or forecasts.

Regression coefficients

In the example of the estimate of selling price based on knowledge of the size of the house, if we were willing to specify that the relationship between price and size were linear, there are two numbers we would need to know to reproduce the entire cross-classified table of average selling prices for each size category. We would need, as a starting point, the average price in any one cell, and in addition, the constant change in the average price as the size of the house changed by a unit. If we were told that the average selling price of houses of 1,500 square feet was $30,000, and that for every 100-square-foot increase in size the average price increased by $1,000 (i.e., that in our judgment the relationship was *linear* between 1,000 square feet and 3,000 square feet), we could reproduce any entry in the table of average selling price conditional on size over that range. For example, we would estimate that the average selling price for houses of 2,000 square feet was $35,000 with this procedure: Starting with recognition that the average selling price for houses of 1,500 square feet was $30,000, and recognizing that a house of 2,000 square feet was 500 square feet larger and that the average selling price increased by $1,000 for every additional 100 square feet of floor area, we would conclude that houses of 2,000 square feet would have an average price $5,000 greater than houses of 1,500 square feet or $35,000. Similar reasoning could allow us to estimate all of the conditional means of the table. The calculated values of the average change in the dependent variable per unit change in a given explanatory variable are known as *regression coefficients*.

Regression programs inevitably provide the user with a regression coefficient for each of the independent variables, as well as a starting point. Conventionally, the starting point is the average value for a dependent variable when each of the independent variables is set at zero. Thus, in the example the conventional starting point reported would be $15,000 (you can check to see that such a starting point would be consistent with a change of $1,000 per hundred square feet and a price of $30,000 for a house of 1,500 square feet). It should be noted that in many situations the starting point or constant does not have any interpretive significance. (In the example on selling prices, it does not make much sense to talk about houses with 0 square feet). The starting point merely provides an agreed-upon and convenient value to which the changes can be added to get the point estimate.

When there is only a single explanatory variable, a graphic depiction of the data and a geometric interpretation of the coefficients are possible.

Table 9–1
Selling price and size from a
sample of ten houses

Selling price (y) ($ thousands)	Size of house (x) (hundreds of square feet)
33.0	15
30.0	24
37.5	19
42.0	29
44.5	22
34.0	21
40.0	20
24.5	18
48.0	27
36.5	25

Suppose, for example, we wished to predict selling price of houses and we had foreknowledge of only the size of the house before we must make the prediction. Suppose also we had past data on the selling price and house size of a sample of ten houses, as shown in Table 9–1 and graphed in Figure 9–1.

Figure 9–1
Scatter diagram of selling price (y) and size of house (x)

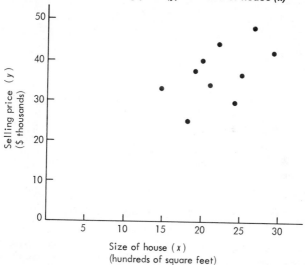

In Figure 9–1, called a scatter diagram, each dot represents the size of the particular house *(x)* and its sales price *(y)*. The points show that the sales prices of the houses generally increased with increased size. Although the data are so sparse that we cannot calculate an average sales price for each size house, we might ask whether we believe the average relationship might fairly well be described by a straight line like the one shown in Figure 9–2. How this particular line was chosen will be described later. For the moment it is sufficient to note that such a line may be thought of as describing the average house value *(y)* for any house size *(x)* and thus it provides a reasonable forecast of the selling price of a house given any house size. This line represents a forecasting formula of the form

$$\text{Est } y = 17.39 + .8916x.$$

The slope of the line in Figure 9–2 is the regression coefficient. If the line had been projected back to where the size of house was 0 square feet, it would have corresponded at that point to a selling price of $17,390. Thus, geometrically the starting point corresponds to the point where the

Figure 9–2
Geometric interpretation of regression coefficients

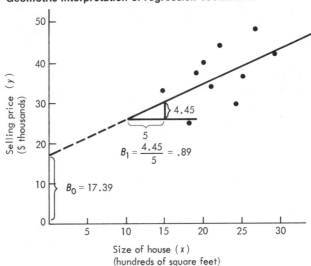

Size of house (x)
(hundreds of square feet)

line intersects the y axis and the regression coefficient to the slope of the line when a linear relationship is specified.

In the regression program we will use, and in fact in most regression programs, the constant and the regression coefficients are symbolized as B values. Thus, in an example with selling price as the dependent variable and with two explanatory variables—for example, size of house (in hundreds of square feet) and size of lot (in hundreds of square feet)—the computer output[5] might be of the following type:

y = Selling price
x_1 = Size of house in hundreds of square feet
x_2 = Size of lot in hundreds of square feet

$B_0 = \$10,000$ Constant
$B_1 = +\$1,000$ Change in y associated with a unit change (100 square feet) in x_1, the size of house
$B_2 = +\$500$ Change in y associated with unit change (100 square feet) in x_2, the size of lot

The regression coefficients reported are those that, if used to estimate retrospectively in the data base, would provide a series of estimates which would have a smaller average squared error than any other comparable set of values. Although the coefficients are not actually calculated

---

[5] This could be expressed as a linear equation of the form:

$$\text{Est } y = B_0 + B_1x_1 + B_2x_2.$$

this way, we can think of it as following this procedure: In the example, with the two explanatory variables there are three coefficients (one constant and two slopes). The computer could pick three numbers, any three, for these coefficients and then use them to make estimates of selling price for all the observations contained in the analysis. When the estimates have been made they can be compared to the actual prices and the average squared error calculated and remembered. Then a second set of three numbers can be chosen for the coefficients and a similar procedure followed. If the computer swept through all possible sets of numbers, it could then report to us that set of values which provided the "best" set of estimates: the one with the smallest average squared error.

In many situations the data used in the analysis comprise a sample of the complete set of data that could have been analyzed. In such cases the sample regression coefficients are approximations of the coefficients that would have been obtained had the complete set of data been analyzed. Most regression programs, in addition to reporting the regression coefficients themselves, also provide information which allows the user to evaluate how good an approximation each sample regression coefficient is of the coefficient that would have been obtained had the complete set of data, or at least a very large sample, been analyzed. When the regression program[6] used to provide the computer output in this book was applied to the data from Table 9–1, the following results were obtained:

	Estimated regression coefficient	UNC	P(SGN)
B_0	17.39	10.81	0.927
B_1	0.89	0.48	0.949

The information in the column under the heading UNC reports the amount of variability that would occur in a large number of regression coefficients obtained from samples of the same size drawn from the complete set of data. The smaller this value, the less sampling error we anticipate; the larger the value, the less accurate we would fear our sample approximation would be. In the final column the heading P(SGN) is to be read: the probability that the sign of the sample regression coefficient (+ or −) is the same as the sign of the sample regression coefficient that would be obtained if the complete set of data, rather than only a sample of this size, had been analyzed. The results in this column are obtained by comparing the size of the regression coefficient to the size of its potential sampling error, to indicate the probability we should be willing to assess that the "true" regression coefficient has the same sign (+ or −) as the one reported from the sample. In an analysis when a regression coefficient

---

[6] This program is part of a collection of statistical computer programs developed by Robert O. Schlaifer of the Harvard Business School. The collection of programs is called the AQD collection.

is reported as $+0.89$ and the P(SGN) is 0.95 we would recognize that in the sample there was a positive relationship (increases in the explanatory variable were accompanied by increases in the average value of the dependent variable, decreases by decreases). We would assess only 5 chances in 100 that if we ran an analysis with the complete set of possible data (or with a huge sample) we would find the true relationship was a negative one (increases in the values of the explanatory variable were associated with decreases in the average of the dependent variable).

In contrast, if a sample regression coefficient were reported as $+0.89$ but the P(SGN) was given as 0.52, we would believe that it was almost as likely that the true relationship was negative (with increases in the explanatory variable associated with decreases in the dependent variable, and vice versa) as that it was the positive one indicated by our sample.

In most other regression programs the same information is provided, but other terms are sometimes used. The measures of uncertainty for the regression coefficients are often labeled as *standard errors*. Information with the same potential use as that provided under P(SGN) is provided by some programs in the form of the t statistic. In this context t is defined as the ratio resulting from dividing the regression coefficient by its uncertainty (or standard error). If t is evaluated under the appropriate number of degrees of freedom with a Student's t distribution, the resulting probability has essentially the same meaning and use as P(SGN).

When the interest is solely in forecasting, the principal use of the regression coefficients is as a check on the sensibleness of the results. Potential explanatory variables are introduced in the analysis because the forecaster anticipates they will bear some relationship to the dependent variable and thus will increase predictive power and give a smaller average squared error and a less dispersed probability distribution. The reason for their inclusion will usually also suggest whether the relationship would be anticipated to be positive ($+$ sign for regression coefficient) or negative ($-$ sign for the regression coefficient). Discovery of a sign or magnitude contrary to that anticipated by the analyst should at least raise a red flag and encourage further investigation before the results are used to make forecasts.

You may develop, or be provided with, a very complex regression model and wish to determine whether the results make sense to you. In such cases, a simple interpretation of a coefficient and through it a simple test of "sensibleness" may not be possible. You can, however, make a series of forecasts in which you place all of the explanatory variables but the one under consideration at a fixed level and vary the value of the explanatory variable for which the reasonableness of the relationship is being considered. From the series of forecasts you can trace out the behavior of the forecasts as the explanatory variable takes on successively larger values and determine whether this pattern is a sensible one in the light of your knowledge of the factors involved.

Measures of goodness of fit

A second type of output provides measures of how good estimates using these regression coefficients were when the estimates and actuals were compared retrospectively in the data base. The magnitude of the errors that would have been made in the past if such an estimating procedure were used gives the analyst some indication of the uncertainty that could be anticipated around new point estimates or forecasts made by this procedure. This type of information is reported in a number of different ways and using a number of different terms which largely reflect the preferences of the individual who wrote the particular computer program. In some cases, the *average squared error* is reported and referred to by that name. In others, the same value is used, but it is called the *unexplained variance*. Because the units of the averaged squared error are cumbersome, many people prefer to report the square root of this value, which is expressed in the original units of the dependent variable. The square root of the average squared error is referred to either as the *standard error of estimate* or the *residual standard deviation*. This latter term is employed in the regression program used in this book.

In the numerical example of the sales price and size of a sample of ten houses shown in Table 9–1 above, a measure of goodness of fit can be calculated by the procedure shown in Table 9–2. The average squared

Table 9–2
Calculation of average squared error (unexplained variance)

	Sales price (y)	Size of house (x)	Estimated selling price* (Est y)	Error (y − Est y)	Squared error (y − Est y)²
	33.0	15	30.76	2.24	5.02
	30.0	24	38.78	−8.78	77.14
	37.5	19	34.33	3.18	10.08
	42.0	29	43.24	−1.24	1.54
	44.5	22	37.00	7.50	56.25
	34.0	21	36.11	−2.11	4.45
	40.0	20	35.22	4.78	22.88
	24.5	18	33.43	−8.93	79.81
	48.0	27	41.46	6.54	42.80
	36.5	25	39.67	−3.18	10.08
Average	37.0	22	37.00	0	31.00

* Based on the forecasting formula Est $y = 17.39 + .8916x$.

error, or unexplained variance, is shown to be 31. The standard error of estimate, or residual standard deviation, is the square root of this number, or $\sqrt{31} = 5.568$ or \$5,568.

Whether we are considering the average squared error or its square root, the interpretation is such that the larger the value, the poorer the set of point estimates; the smaller the value, the better the set of point estimates. If we were comparing two sets of estimates made for the same group of dependent variables, and if the basis for the two sets of estimates made equally good sense to us, we would probably prefer the estimating procedure with the smaller residual standard deviation. The interpretation of these measures is always a relative one. Is a residual standard deviation of $500 good or bad? If we have available an alternative procedure with a residual standard deviation of $50, then $500 is large, but if the next best forecasting procedure had a residual standard deviation of $1,000, then $500 would signal a considerably better forecasting process.

A second set of measures closely related to those described above is also customarily included in regression output. When the average squared error for a set of estimates based on a regression is compared to the average squared error from a set of estimates based only on the unconditional mean of the dependent variable (in the example above, the average selling price for all houses in a sample), a measure of the degree of improvement in the point estimates accomplished through the regression is obtained. The customary comparison involves determining the percentage reduction in the average squared error from the set of estimates found without regression (based solely on the average of the dependent variable) to the set of estimates determined by the regression process. For example, if the average squared error in the set of estimates based on estimating selling price of every house at the mean selling price was 200,000 squared dollars and the average squared error in the set of estimates of the prices of the same group of houses based on a regression, taking into account a number of explanatory variables, was 60,000 squared dollars, you could indicate that there had been a 70 percent (or 140/200) reduction in the average squared error. This percentage reduction, traditionally symbolized as R^2, is called the *coefficient of determination,* or the *percent variance explained.* Since this value is a percentage reduction, it varies between 0 and 100 percent. It is usually expressed as a decimal between 0 and 1. The greater the improvement brought about by the regression, the closer will this value be to 100 percent; the less the improvement, the closer to 0 percent.

Again referring to the numerical example involving the sales price and size of the house in the sample of ten houses, we listed from Table 9–2 an average squared error around the estimates of sales price based on the linear relationship with size of house of 31,000 squared dollars. If we had developed estimates of the value of each house *without* knowledge of size of house, we would have been forced to base our estimate on the average sales prices of the houses. Table 9–3 shows the calculation of the average squared error from such a forecast.

In this example, had we been forced to estimate solely on the basis of the average selling price, an average squared error would have been 44,200

Table 9–3
Calculation of the total variance

	Selling price (y)	Estimated selling price (Avg y)	Error (y − Avg y)	Squared error (y − Avg y)²
	33.0	37	− 4.0	16.00
	30.0	37	− 7.0	49.00
	37.5	37	0.5	0.25
	42.0	37	5.0	25.00
	44.5	37	7.5	56.25
	34.0	37	− 3.0	9.00
	40.0	37	3.0	9.00
	24.5	37	−12.5	156.25
	48.0	37	11.0	121.00
	36.5	37	− 0.5	0.25
Average	37.0	37	0	44.20

squared dollars.[7] Referring back to Table 9–2, recall that the average squared error from a forecast made by taking into account the linear relationship between sales price and size was 31,000 squared dollars. The percent variance explained is the percentage reduction in the average squared error, in this case, from 44.2 to 31.0. This percentage reduction becomes $(44.2 − 31.0)/44.2 = 0.30$. Thus in the example, 30 percent of the variance in selling price is "explained" by its linear relationship with the size of the house: $R^2 = 0.30$.

Although this measure is on a standard scale from zero to one, its interpretation is still a comparative one. Does an $R^2 = 0.8$ indicate a regression we would want to employ? Not if we have an equally sensible process with an $R^2 = 0.9$. Is an analysis with an $R^2 = 0.2$ useful? Certainly, if the next best alternative for estimating has an $R^2 = 0.08$.

In most cases, the same comparative conclusions will be reached from any of the above sets of measures.[8] The set of estimates with the larger average squared error or residual standard deviation will usually be the set with the smaller percent variance explained.[9] If we wish to choose among any number of estimating methods that seem equally sensible to us on substantive grounds, the selection of that particular procedure with the smaller average squared error (or residual standard deviation), or, in the same sense, the one with the larger percent variance explained would

---

[7] The average squared error around the mean is, in this context, called the total variance.

[8] It is possible that an estimate of a population R^2 obtained from a sample may yield a negative number. For practical purposes, this should be interpreted as zero.

[9] This does not hold true necessarily if a transformation of the dependent variable is made for one of the sets of estimates. Such a situation will be described in the section on specification of the dependent variable below.

allow us to pick the method that, at least in the past, would have done best.[10]

The estimates or forecasts

Once the regression analysis has been run, we may wish to develop point estimates and probability distributions with the results. Such estimates and distributions constitute the third type of output provided by regression programs. In order to obtain a point estimate from the regression we must provide a known or estimated value for each of the explanatory variables. The computer does the arithmetic to provide the estimate of the mean value of the dependent variable, conditional on the stated level of each of the explanatory variables. In the example in which we wished to estimate the selling price of houses based on the size of the house (x_1) and size of the lot on which it is located (x_2), we had the following regression coefficients:

$B_0 = \$12,000$
$B_1 = +\$10$ per 100 square feet
$B_2 = +\$0.50$ per 100 square feet

If we now wish to have a forecast made, it is necessary to indicate the characteristics (in terms of the explanatory variables) of the house for which we wish to estimate the selling price. If we indicated interest in a house of 1,500 square feet located on a lot of 20,000 square feet, the computer would calculate the point estimate by carrying out the following calculation:

Estimated selling price $= \$12,000 + 10\,(1,500) + 0.50\,(20,000)$
$= \$37,000.$

The regression program used to prepare output in this book will also provide a cumulative probability distribution which takes into account two sources which contribute to uncertainty in the estimate or forecast. Even when used to develop point estimates for the observation in the data base from which the coefficients have been determined, there are errors in individual estimates. If we are willing to consider these variances as arising from indistinguishable situations, then, in a manner comparable to our previous use of an $A - F$ forecasting model, we can introduce this form of uncertainty around our new point estimate. If our regression coefficients had been developed from data on the entire relevant group of observations, or from an extremely large sample, this form of uncertainty alone would provide us with our probability assessment. When the regression coefficients are based on a relatively small sample, however, we have seen that the coefficients themselves are subject to uncertainty arising from

---

[10] If, based on a sample, we employ the model with the larger *estimated* percent variance explained, it provides us with the regression that promises to do best in the future.

potential sampling error. Uncertainty that the sample regression coefficient may differ from the "true" regression coefficient that would have been found if a huge sample had been taken thus introduces an increase into the amount of uncertainty surrounding a given forecast. The standard deviation of the forecast is determined, taking into account both of these sources of uncertainty. The computer programs used to provide the computer output in this book offer a summary measure of the uncertainty in the form of the standard deviation of the forecast. It also provides the entire probability distribution of the forecast in either graphic or tabular form. Such a distribution might then be used as a probability distribution in a relevant decision analysis.

The following output was obtained for the example of Table 9–1, in which selling price and size of house were related for a sample of ten houses. The forecast is for a house that has 2,600 square feet of living area.

Distribution of selling price (in thousands of dollars)

Mean: 40.566

Standard deviation: 7.858

Fractiles:

.01	.1	.25	.50	.75	.90	.99
20.8	31.0	35.8	40.6	45.4	50.1	60.3

Use of the resulting distribution as our forecast would still rely on our willingness to assume that the future situations for which the forecasts are required are indistinguishable from the situations that gave rise to the observation under analysis, in terms of their effect on the variations between the actual values of the dependent variable and the point estimate from the regression. This would only hold true if, among other things, we were willing to assume that the forces and factors which gave rise to the relationship of the past would continue to operate in the same way in the future.

DEVELOPING THE MODEL

As we have seen, three important sets of specifications are required in preparing to use regression as an aid in forecasting. It is necessary to specify the dependent variable, to indicate the set of explanatory variables to be used as a basis for the forecasts, and to indicate the nature of the relationship between each of the explanatory variables and the dependent variable. The determination of these three inputs constitutes the construction of a regression model. This section deals with the issues and problems involved in making the required choices.

Selection of the dependent variable

We have noted that the dependent variable is the variable which is directly estimated by a regression model. It might appear, therefore, that knowing what we want to estimate or forecast automatically allows us to specify the dependent variable. In a sense this is true, and yet the scale and form in which we consider the dependent variable may have a major effect on the reasonableness of the assumptions underlying the analysis and thus on the usefulness of the results.

To return to the example in which we wanted to estimate the selling price of each of a group of houses, in addition to the selling price of each house in our data base, we might have information on size (square feet) and age (years). In the type of regression model we are considering here, an assumption is made that a given change in one explanatory variable adds a fixed amount to an estimate of the dependent variable when all of the others are held constant. It further assumes that this amount is the same regardless of the level at which the other explanatory variables are held constant.[11] If we were to use selling price as our dependent variable with size and age as two explanatory variables, the underlying assumption would be that a five-year difference in age, say, would add the same amount to our estimate of selling price for very large houses as for very small houses. We would almost certainly prefer an assumption that the average change in the price associated with a given age differential was greater for larger houses than for smaller houses. One way to accomplish this would be to specify our dependent variable not as sales price but as sales price *per square foot*.

In a similar way, if we were interested in estimating the sales of a particular product among various sales territories, we might have information on sales, population, median income, and percent urban population for each of the territories. If we were to select sales as our dependent variable, the assumption that a given difference in median income would bring about the same absolute difference in total sales in territories with large populations that it would in territories with small populations would almost certainly seem unreasonable. If we were to specify *per capita sales* as the dependent variable, the assumption that the effects of median income and percent urbanization are additive is much more reasonable.

We should be aware that if we convert the dependent variable from *selling price* to *selling price per square foot* or from *sales* to *sales per capita* it will have a major effect on some measures of goodness of fit. The coefficient of determination (R^2), for example, compares the average squared error around the regression estimates with the average squared error around the mean of the dependent variable. Since the scaling of the dependant variable in the manner decided above almost certainly reduces the total variance (the average squared error around the mean) more than the variance around the regression estimates, a much smaller R^2 would result. This is an inevitable consequence of the definition of R^2 and should not concern us in our choice of models.

---

[11] There are other types of models possible (e.g., the multiplicative regression model). These go beyond the scope of this discussion, however.

If our real goal is to forecast *sales* but, in order to employ a model where the assumptions make more sense, we have used as a dependent variable *sales per capita,* we must convert the forecast made from the model to the form needed for the forecast. Developing a forecast of sales in a given territory from a model that generated a forecast of per capita sales requires only multiplication by the population of the territory.[12]

In thinking through the specification of the dependent variable, we ought to think carefully about the nature of the additivity assumption under the various alternatives for expressing the dependent variable. Selection of a form for the dependent variable which makes the additivity assumption most reasonable to us should provide a model in which we have greater confidence and forecast distributions which we would be more willing to incorporate into the analysis of our decisions.

Selection of explanatory variables

If the number of observations available to us is very large relative to the number of potential explanatory variables, the selection is rather straightforward. We ought to include in our model all of the potential explanatory variables which we believe make sense in terms of our knowledge of the substantive area involved, and for which we will either know the value or have a good estimate of the value at the time we will be using the model to make a forecast. In some cases we may include variables which in our judgment do not themselves bear a relationship to the dependent variable but are related to an explanatory variable whose value is not known. In that context the included variable is brought into the analysis as a proxy for the unknown but related explanatory variable. When time is introduced as an explanatory variable, it is almost always in the role of a proxy variable. If we include an explanatory variable but it in fact does not improve our ability to forecast, nothing is lost as long as the number of observations is substantial.

Only variables which we will know or have a good estimate of at the time we need to make forecasts belong in our regression model. For example, it may well be true that historically the price of beef bears a close relationship to the price of pork. In a regression model designed to forecast the price of pork, it would not be useful to include the price of beef as an explanatory variable if we would not know beef prices, or at least have a better estimate of them than we could have of pork prices, at the time we had to make the forecast. It would not be sensible to include the original asking price of the house in forecasting the selling price even though they may be highly correlated if we are going to make forecasts of selling price before the original asking price has been established.

If the number of observations available for our analysis is not very large

---

[12] The standard deviation of the forecast of sales can also be determined by multiplying the standard deviation of the forecast for per capita sales by the given population.

relative to the potential number of explanatory variables, a question of priority for including explanatory variables becomes important. If two or more potential explanatory variables are themselves closely related, it would make sense to include only one in the restricted group of explanatory variables. At the extreme, if we had two measures of the size of a house, one in square feet and the other in square meters, although either one may be closely related to selling price, it would not make sense to include both. In a less extreme example, but based on the same reasoning, if because of sparse data we were limited in the number of explanatory variables, we would not want to include both the per capita disposable income of the area in which the house is located and the median family income of the area. Although they are not identical measures, they are so closely related that most of the predicting power of one is contained in the other.[13] We would want to select the one that we thought made more sense and eliminate the other from our model. If the number of remaining potential explanatory variables, all of which have a sensible claim for inclusion, is still large, we may wish to select for inclusion in our forecasting model the subset that produces the lowest estimated residual standard deviation.

Lagged variables

When the data available for the regression analysis are in the form of a time series, where observations refer to different points in historical time, we may wish to use information from one period as an explanatory variable to help us forecast the value of the dependent variable in another period. If we were making an annual sales forecast for a given product for 1975, we might use the 1974 sales as an important explanatory variable. We can think of the original data base as a table, the columns of which

Table 9–4

Year	Sales (thousands of units)	Advertising expenses ($ thousands)	Average price ($)
1970	872	250	6.10
1971	915	275	6.25
1972	950	290	6.30
1973	1,020	320	6.30

refer to the variables and the rows to the observations. Table 9–4 shows a part of a data base in which the annual sales and other characteristics of a given product are recorded.

If we wished to include the previous year's sales as an explanatory variable in our model, we would have to instruct the computer to construct a

---

[13] In technical terms, the two variables are said to be collinear.

fifth column in the data base. In the fifth column would be entered the sales of the previous year. Thus, in this column opposite 1971 we would find the sales of 1970; opposite 1972, the sales of 1971, and so on. Table 9–5 shows a segment of this expanded data base derived from Table 9–4.

Table 9–5

Year	Sales (thousands of units)	Advertising expenses ($ thousands)	Average price ($)	Previous year sales (thousands of units)
1970	872	250	6.10	—
1971	915	275	6.25	872
1972	950	290	6.30	915
1973	1,020	320	6.30	950

Dummy variables

In some situations a potential explanatory variable we wish to include in our model may not be measured in units like dollars, square feet or years but instead may describe a qualitative category into which an observation can be classified. In the example of developing a procedure to estimate the selling price of houses, the type of construction (frame, mixed, or brick) illustrates such a situation. We do not say that a house is some number (such as 1.75) on a "construction *scale*"; rather we think of a house as falling exactly into one of the three *categories*. This type of explanatory factor can be incorporated into our model by the establishment of a "dummy variable" system. A dummy variable system requires the addition to the data base of a number of variables which is one less than the number of categories in the classification. In our example with the three categories (frame, mixed, or brick) two new variables would have to be established. Values for a variable in a dummy variable system are either 0 or 1. The 0 indicates that the observation does not possess the characteristic described by the particular variable. The value 1 indicates that the observation does have the characteristic described by the variable.

In introducing the type of construction into our model to predict selling price, since there are three categories (frame, mixed, or brick) we would add two dummy variables to our data base. The first dummy variable could refer to frame construction. In the data base the number 1 would be put under that variable for every house of frame construction. A zero for that variable would indicate that the particular house was *not* of frame construction (and was either mixed or brick). A second additional variable might refer to mixed construction. Observations relating to houses with mixed construction would have a 1 recorded for this variable. A house that was either all frame or all brick would have a 0 recorded under this variable.

To put a third variable in this system relating to brick construction would be redundant. Any house that had values of 0 under both the frame and the mixed variables *must* have a 1 under brick. Any house that had a 1 under either frame or mixed variables *must* have a 0 for a brick construction variable.

When a dummy variable is used, the resulting regression coefficients indicate the difference between the average value of the dependent variable for the category identified by that variable and the average value of the dependent variable for the category not explicitly included in the system. In our example, if the regression coefficient relating to the dummy variable called frame was −$3,000, it would indicate that, on the average, frame houses sold for $3,000 less than brick houses (the category not explicitly included in the system). Had we arbitrarily chosen to form a variable for brick but not explicitly included one for frame, we would have obtained a regression coefficient for brick of +$3,000 to show that brick houses sold for $3,000 more than frame (the excluded category). Similarly, in a system where we chose to eliminate brick from explicit inclusion, we might have obtained a regression coefficient for the mixed variable of −$1,000. This would indicate that for two houses identical in all other characteristics included in our model, but where one was brick and the other of mixed construction, we would have an estimate for the latter that was $1,000 lower than for the brick house.

To review: the procedure to follow to include qualitative classifications as an explanatory factor in a model involves establishing *one less dummy variable* than the number of categories in the classification. Under a given variable the value of 0 is given if the observation does *not* have the indicated characteristic, and the value of 1 if it does. The resulting regression coefficients will then indicate the difference in the average value of the dependent variable from those observations that have the characteristic *not* explicitly included as a variable in the system.

Determining the nature of relationships

Once we have specified the set of explanatory variables we wish to include in our model, we must further specify the way in which we believe each of these variables relates to the dependent variables. The decision regarding the nature of a particular relationship springs largely from our knowledge of the substantive area in which we are forecasting. Our choice of the type of relationship we wish to specify between the selling price and size of house would come largely from our perception of what goes on in the real estate market. If we think of a group of houses that are the same in all characteristics considered by our model other than size of house, we might ask ourselves questions about what we would anticipate in terms of differences in the average selling price which will accompany differences in size.

If we believe that when houses differ by 100 square feet of floor space their average selling price will differ by a given amount, and that this amount will be the same regardless of where in the range of possible sizes we find the two groups of houses (e.g., 1,000 v. 1,100, or 2,000 v. 2,100), then we should specify a linear relationship between size and average selling price in our model.

In contrast, if we believe that a given difference in size (e.g., 100 square feet) would be accompanied by a larger difference in price if the difference were between 1,000 and 1,100 square feet than if it were between 2,000 and 2,100 square feet, we would specify some form of retarding or diminishing return relationship. There are a large number of mathematical functions of this general shape that could be specified. Within the scope of this book, we will have one such function available, the square root. If we believe, based on our knowledge of the subject matter involved, that the relationship we are dealing with, net of all the other explanatory variables in the model, is of one of either of the general shapes described in Figure 9–3, we should specify a square root relationship between the dependent and that particular explanatory variable.

Figure 9–3

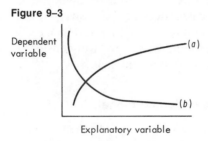

Explanatory variable

On the other hand, if we felt, based on our knowledge of the real estate market, that a given difference in size would, on the average, be accompanied by a larger difference in price for large-size homes compared to small-size homes, then we would want to specify some form of accelerating relationship or one of increasing returns to scale. Again, there are a large number of functions which would allow us to specify this general shape. For the purpose of this book, however, we will be provided with one such function, namely the square function. When we believe the particular relationship is of one of the shapes shown in Figure 9–4, we should specify this form of relationship.

In both Figures 9–3 and 9–4, a positive relationship that is retarding (9–3) or accelerating (9–4) is shown as the a curve. The retardation of a negative relationship is shown by curve b in Figure 9–3. The acceleration of a negative relationship is shown by curve b in Figure 9–4.

Figure 9–4

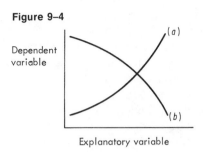

Using the data under analysis, the computer will determine the values and the sign, positive $(+)$ or negative $(-)$, of the relationship. But we must specify our judgment on the nature of the relationship (linear, retarding, or accelerating) before the analysis can be made.

There are, of course, a number of different mathematical functions or types of forecasting formulas which would depict nonlinear relationships. Each equation embodies a bundle of assumptions about behavior at extremes and patterns of change. A refined analysis would attempt to select the particular nonlinear form which embodied assumptions closest to those the forecaster was willing to make about the net relationship under analysis. If the forecaster does not have strong beliefs about the relationship, nonlinear functions are often selected merely to obtain a "good fitting" curve. For simplification, we will consider only the two (square and square root) previously mentioned.[14]

Two warnings in developing models

There is a natural tendency to look for help in making the often difficult choices involved in specifying the nature of each relationship. However, there are difficulties to be encountered in looking at the data in order to get such help.

The fishing expedition. One suggestion that might come to mind, particularly since a computer is available to do all of the calculation involved, is to try out all the possible explanatory variables in all possible combinations of forms. If we had five potential explanatory variables and, let us say, seven different functions which could be used to express each relationship, we could run the 16,807 different regressions and select, for example, the one with the highest percent variance explained.[15] The form of each relationship in this "best-fitting" model would constitute the forms we would then use in our final model. There are a number of studies that show that such a procedure runs a grave risk of suggesting a model

---

[14] Some commonly used nonlinear functions include: $\log x$, $1/x$, e^x, x^a, $ax + bx^2$, and higher order polynomials.

[15] Since each of the five variables could be specified with each of the seven forms, the total number is $(7)^5$

which does not make sense and which does *not* have predictive power. A common experiment sets up a dependent variable and a number of explanatory variables, all from a table of random numbers. Regressions are run for all combinations of the various functions for the explanatory variables. Inevitably, by the vagaries of chance, some peculiar combination just happens to give a set of estimates close to the values in the data base and a large value for R^2 results. How much use would that model be to us in forecasting the next value of the dependent variable? Since the next value of the dependent variable is determined from the next random number, none. The explanatory variables and their relationships must make sense to us in the light of our knowledge of the area in which we are forecasting before we would be willing to use the model to help provide our assessment of the uncertain future.

The two-dimensional graph.   Another common tendency, in trying to decide on the nature of the relationship between a given explanatory variable and the dependent variable, is to plot a graph in which the explanatory variable is shown on the horizontal axis and the dependent variable is shown on the vertical axis. For each observation a point is made at the intersection of its value on each scale. The shape of the cluster of points on such a graph (called a scatter diagram) could then be used to suggest the nature of that relationship. The scatter diagrams shown in Figure 9–5 indicate this procedure.

Figure 9–5

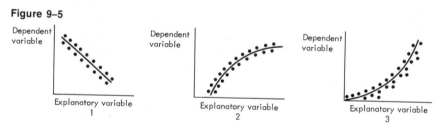

Observing scatter diagram 1 would lead us to specify a linear relationship. Having observed scatter diagram 2, we would probably specify a retarding relationship (square root). Scatter diagram 3 would suggest that an accelerating relationship (square) was called for.

There is a danger in following this procedure too literally. The nature of the relationship we are required to specify is that of a *net* relationship between the explanatory and dependent variables. The term "net" in this context means that all other explanatory variables contained explicitly in our model are held constant. In our example relating to the selling price of homes we would have to specify the nature of the relationship between selling price and size of home for houses of the same type of construction, located on lots of the same size, and so on.

The relationship that is observed in direct plotting of an explanatory and dependent variable is in contrast a *gross* relationship. In this context the term "gross" indicates that the relationship is depicted while the other explanatory variables are not controlled and can take on a variety of values. If the explanatory variables are not only each related to the dependent variable but related to one another, it is possible that the gross relationship might be of a quite different nature than the net relationship which is desired. A rather extreme example may illustrate this point. Assume we know for certain that there is no net relationship between the selling price of a house and the number of windows in the house. That is, for houses of exactly the same size, type of construction, and type of lot, the average selling price is the same for varying number of windows. If we were to plot a scatter diagram of selling price against the number of windows we would find a direct relationship in the diagram, since houses with a small number of windows typically are small houses, and the smallness of the house is, in general, associated with a low selling price. Large houses, on the other hand, have a large number of windows in general, and thus through the mechanism of the size relationship, the number of windows is positively related to the selling price. If, as in this example, a scatter diagram of a gross relationship could show a strong positive relationship when we know there was no net relationship, it should also be clear that the gross relationship could look like one shape while the net relationship was of some other form.

The results from plotting two-variable gross scatter diagrams may be suggestive but should not be followed too strongly. If the shape suggested does not make sense in the context of the problem, it would be unwise to use that relationship merely because of the scatter diagram. On the other hand, if we believed that the particular explanatory variable was essentially independent of the other explanatory variables, the plot of the scatter diagram may stimulate our thinking and improve our understanding of the phenomena we are attempting to model.

Protection against overfitting. It is, of course, difficult and in fact undesirable not to have some aspects of the data affect our choice of model. The patterns we observe as we run preliminary analyses with our data often suggest some "sensible" forms of relationship. Preliminary results frequently suggest what variables we wish to include and exclude from our final model. If we follow this natural procedure there is a danger we may be *overfitting;* that is, we may be selecting a model that matches the idiosyncrasies of the *particular sample of observations* under analysis but does not perform in nearly the same way when applied to new sets of observations from.the same population.

If we have an adequate amount of data, one way to guard against overfitting is to develop the model and determine the regression coefficients from one part of the data and then apply the results to obtain forecasts from the other part. We can divide, in an appropriate way, all of the observations into two sets. The first set can be used to determine a preliminary model and its coefficients. The second set of observations can be used to determine the results obtained when using that model to make estimates for a new set of observations.

If overfitting has taken place and the preliminary model takes into account primarily the peculiar characteristics of the particular sample of observations from which it has been developed, this should show up in a comparison of the estimating errors from the two sets of observations. The fitting procedure guarantees that the average error for the set of observations used to determine the coefficients will equal zero. We can now use that same model to make an estimate of the dependent variable for each observation in the second set (the set not involved in developing the model or determining the coefficients). If the average error from this set of observations is substantially different from zero, it would show an undesirable bias in the model when used in estimating new observations. If a comparable measure of the average *squared* error is substantially larger from the second set than from the set that suggested the model and provided the regression coefficients, we would know that overfitting had occurred.

If evidence of overfitting occurs either through a nonzero average error or a poorer goodness of fit, or both, the preliminary model should be abandoned and the search for a better model continued. Our goal is to develop a model which has the best fit of those models that give consistent results when applied to the second set of observations. Once this model has been found, the final coefficients can be determined by fitting the model to the combined set of observations.

The key to developing a model useful to us in assessing probability distributions for uncertain quantities lies in our perception of the factors that relate to changes in the variable that are being forecast. A regression analysis merely develops and quantifies the implication of the assumptions and judgments we introduce into the model. In the last analysis, the usefulness of the forecasts that result will depend not on the mechanics of the regression but on the soundness of our assumptions and judgments.

EXERCISES

9.1. Al Jones is the marketing manager of the Cape Dairy Products Company. Cape has experienced some difficulties in the past in producing ice cream products at levels consistent with demand; they have sometimes over-produced and sometimes produced too little. In an attempt to remedy this situation, Jones has agreed to try to provide the production department each week with forecasts for demand two weeks in advance. If Jones uses a regression analysis as an aid in preparing forecasts, what variables would you suggest that he use in trying to predict ice cream demand two weeks in advance?

9.2. Grace Smith is an analyst on the corporate planning staff (in fact, she *is* the corporate planning staff) of a rapidly growing company in a labor-intensive industry. At present, she is helping the personnel and production departments with their planning for how many new workers will have to be hired and trained during each month of the coming year. The marketing department is preparing forecasts of demand for each of those months. Smith feels that the next step is to estimate the output of the current work force (many of whom are recent hires). To estimate the future productivity of current personnel, she would like to develop a regression equation relating a worker's productivity to his or her length of service with the firm and to any other important variables. What specific regression equation would you suggest Smith try?

9.3. Bert Black is analyzing the automobile industry. In particular, he is interested in predicting the market for replacement parts for used cars for next year. He has collected data on the following variables for each quarter of the past ten years:

Sales of used cars.
Sales of new U.S.–made cars.
Sales of new foreign-made cars.
Gross national product.
Cost-of-living index.
Price of gasoline.
Dow Jones industrial average.
Per capita disposable income.
Prime interest rate.

What regression equation would you suggest that he try for his prediction? How would you suggest that he choose among alternative possible equations?

9.4. The Cambridge Company is a large chemical company with five major divisions. One of these divisions manufactures and sells house paint. The data in Table A had been collected by the marketing department for the paint division. The data were to be used to forecast paint sales for 1965.

Table A

Year	Paint division's sales (millions of dollars)	Home improvement loans granted (billions of dollars)	Index of building construction started in U.S.
1948	$280.0	$3.909	9.43
1949	281.5	5.119	10.36
1950	337.2	6.666	14.50
1951	404.2	5.338	15.75
1952	402.1	4.321	16.78
1953	452.0	6.117	17.44
1954	431.0	5.559	19.77
1955	582.0	7.920	23.76
1956	596.6	5.816	31.61
1957	620.8	6.113	32.17
1958	513.6	4.258	35.09
1959	606.9	5.591	36.42
1960	628.0	6.675	36.58
1961	602.7	5.543	37.14
1962	656.7	6.933	41.30
1963	778.5	7.638	45.62
1964	827.6	7.752	47.38

a. How well can you explain the sales numbers, using only a time variable?

b. Can you improve your regression by using the construction index? How?

c. Is there a relationship between the construction index and time? What is it?

d. Does the information on home improvement loans help? Why?

e. What forecast would you give for paint sales in 1965 if you predicted that the construction index would be 50.0 and that home improvement loans would be $8.5 billion in that year?

9.5. At the end of 1972, Dale Williams, the production manager for the Allston Manufacturing Company, was analyzing a decision about the timing of the purchase of a new piece of equipment for the firm. The machine would replace another machine at Allston, whose performance, as expected, deteriorated over time, and Williams had to decide when the replacement should be bought. The machine (old or new) would be especially important in the work Allston would be doing on a large contract in the last quarter of 1973. While the production department knew that the failure rates with the old machine would be appreciable, they felt that they could live with those rates as long as they didn't become too high. The company preferred to defer the purchase of the new equipment until 1974, but Williams had the assurance of the financial vice president that the replacement *could* be brought in earlier if it was needed.

For the analysis of the problem, Williams wanted a probabilistic forecast of the failure rate (the proportion of the output which would be defective) for the older machine for the crucial fourth quarter of 1973. The past failure rates had been calculated for each quarter for the past five years, as shown in Table B.

Table B

Quarter		Rate in percent	Quarter	Rate in percent
(first quarter — 1968)	1	0.1	11	5.0
	2	0.5	12	9.1
	3	0.2	13	7.2
	4	0.8	14	7.5
(first quarter — 1969)	5	0.9	15	16.0
	6	1.4	16	20.0
	7	1.8	(first quarter — 1972) 17	13.5
	8	1.3	18	18.1
	9	2.5	19	20.5
	10	3.0	20	22.9

Prepare a probabilistic forecast for failure rate for Williams to use in analyzing the decision.

9.6. The Burlington Press publishes textbooks, primarily texts for junior high schools (seventh and eighth grade). As part of an analysis the company was carrying out in order to try to understand the market for their texts, the data in Table C had been collected on total purchases of texts for seventh grades by one city. (The figures give total purchases, not just Burlington's share.) Each seventh-grader received a set of texts from the school, used

Table C

Year	Number of texts purchased (total for all subjects)	Number of 7th-grade students
1940–41	2,111	2,000
1941–42	2,083	2,027
1942–43	2,264	2,050
1943–44	2,025	2,052
1944–45	2,303	2,061
1945–46	2,149	2,075
1946–47	2,177	2,079
1947–48	2,023	2,089
1948–49	2,178	2,091
1949–50	2,057	2,093
1950–51	2,371	2,131
1951–52	2,368	2,162
1952–53	2,439	2,194
1953–54	2,457	2,250
1954–55	2,764	2,292
1955–56	2,783	2,363
1956–57	2,596	2,412
1957–58	2,500	2,447
1958–59	2,598	2,470
1959–60	2,756	2,488
1960–61	2,457	2,502
1961–62	2,713	2,525
1962–63	2,748	2,567
1963–64	2,773	2,585

the books for the year, and then returned them. When new editions were brought out or when the schools conducted curriculum reviews, the texts for a particular subject might all be replaced at one time.

How might you use this information to predict purchases of texts for 1964–65 if the seventh grade population (which was known quite closely six months before the start of school) was expected to be 2,600?

9.7. Robin Keller of the Synergistic Systems Corporation was preparing a forecast of the total sales of Synergistic's industry for the first quarter of 1976. Keller had collected the past data on actual national GNP, on a forecast of GNP, and on seasonally adjusted industry sales, as shown in Table D. The GNP forecast for first quarter 1976 was $1,600 billion.

a. How good a job has the GNP forecaster done?

b. How might Keller use regression in preparing a sales forecast? Would you suggest using the actual GNP or the GNP forecast in your regression model? Why?

look at forecast change vs. actual change

Table D

Year	Quarter	Actual GNP (billions)	Forecast GNP (billions)	Industry sales (millions)
1966	1	$ 725.9	$ 705.7	$ 77.6
	2	736.7	770.7	72.8
	3	748.8	742.8	75.2
	4	762.1	821.8	68.3
1967	1	766.3	814.2	76.8
	2	775.1	767.7	84.6
	3	800.4	817.3	79.4
	4	816.1	808.3	92.4
1968	1	835.3	825.7	86.4
	2	858.7	847.0	94.4
	3	876.4	920.0	102.5
	4	892.5	965.5	95.7
1969	1	908.7	929.3	94.7
	2	923.7	954.4	82.8
	3	942.6	1,023.6	93.6
	4	951.7	972.0	89.0
1970	1	959.5	991.5	95.1
	2	970.1	1,012.6	92.0
	3	985.5	1,015.0	95.4
	4	990.9	1,009.2	93.4
1971	1	1,027.2	1,068.7	108.1
	2	1,046.9	1,081.1	100.0
	3	1,056.9	1,051.9	94.9
	4	1,078.1	1,067.5	112.0
1972	1	1,109.1	1,122.5	111.9
	2	1,139.4	1,153.6	108.7
	3	1,164.0	1,144.1	113.1
	4	1,195.8	1,221.0	126.3
1973	1	1,265.0	1,283.8	126.3
	2	1,287.8	1,354.8	122.9
	3	1,319.7	1,303.8	139.2
	4	1,352.7	1,346.8	130.8
1974	1	1,370.9	1,382.0	135.1
	2	1,391.0	1,387.3	143.0
	3	1,424.4	1,508.4	138.4
	4	1,441.3	1,432.8	155.0
1975	1	1,433.6	1,437.4	142.9
	2	1,460.6	1,447.1	149.8
	3	1,528.5	1,490.9	147.6
	4	1,572.9	1,550.7	155.9

9.8. The president of the Brighton Catering Company was attempting to analyze data on labor costs of meals which the firm had prepared and served. Brighton's standard dinner included an appetizer, a main course, and a dessert. Customers could choose any one of three appetizers (fruit cocktail, shrimp cocktail, or melon with prosciutto). The firm also offered other options. Customers might add a salad course, and they might include after-dinner drinks. The president wanted to adjust the firm's prices and, as a first step, wanted to understand the labor costs for different combinations of options. (Food costs would be considered separately.) Accordingly, careful cost studies had been conducted to determine the per guest labor costs of 35 different meals (with 100 to 150 guests each). The results are given in Table E.

How could regression analysis be used to help predict the labor costs of a meal with shrimp cocktails, salad, and liqueurs?

Table E

	Cost per person (cents)	Appetizer: (1 = fruit cocktail 2 = shrimp cocktail 3 = melon + prosciutto)	Salad (1 = yes)	Liqueurs (1 = yes)
1	110.8	1	1	0
2	120.7	1	1	1
3	103.0	1	0	0
4	103.5	1	0	1
5	115.3	1	1	0
6	95.3	1	0	0
7	120.1	1	1	1
8	120.3	1	1	0
9	122.9	1	0	0
10	95.1	1	0	0
11	115.4	1	1	0
12	113.7	1	0	1
13	119.8	1	1	1
14	120.1	1	1	0
15	128.1	2	0	1
16	133.1	2	1	0
17	152.0	2	1	1
18	125.4	2	0	1
19	108.8	2	0	0
20	140.4	2	1	0
21	124.1	2	0	0
22	145.1	2	1	1
23	148.3	2	1	1
24	129.3	2	1	0
25	124.7	3	1	0
26	99.7	3	0	0
27	143.4	3	1	1
28	130.6	3	1	1
29	125.5	3	0	1
30	102.6	3	0	0
31	95.6	3	0	0
32	118.9	3	1	0
33	117.2	3	0	1
34	124.3	3	1	1
35	103.4	3	0	0

Case 9-1

The avocado

In the late 50s, the Israel Agriculture Export Company (Agrexco) began the gradual introduction of an essentially unknown fruit, the avocado, into the European marketplace. France was the first target area and limited distribution was begun in 1957. Shipments that year amounted to 18 tons. Avocados slowly spread to other countries and by 1972 the Agrexco avocado shipments to Europe had grown to 6,100 tons. Of this total, 3,038 tons were to France, 1,266 to England, and 533 to Germany.

Early in 1972, Germany was selected as a major target market and a wide promotional campaign was proposed. In order to design and direct such an effort effectively, Agrexco began to collect detailed data on the current market penetration of avocados and the potential customers for avocados. Specifically, a consumer research study was undertaken with the objectives of identifying (1) the level of penetration of the avocado in the market and the target groups for the promotion, (2) the stages of the customer's decision-making process in eating and purchasing foreign fruits and vegetables, and (3) the most effective channels of communication and the appropriate messages to influence the target groups. The preliminary results of this project had just become available and Agrexco began to evaluate their significance for the German promotion.

The consumer research study

It was felt within Agrexco that the avocado was viewed by the public as an "innovative" and unfamiliar fruit and, due to its high price, it was also considered a luxury product. As a result, it was more likely to be consumed by the high-income, high-education groups within the population. These judgments and a relatively small budget for research led Agrexco to target its German study on the high-income, high-education group and to limit the effort to a small geographical area.

The study was designed to take a sample of 300 Munich housewives of the upper and upper-middle classes, between the ages of 20 and 50. The respondents were chosen by means of quota sampling in which the selection criteria were age, social grouping, size of household, and whether or not the respondent left the house to work. The interviews, conducted in all parts of Munich from April 4 to April 21, 1972, were based on a structured questionnaire designed by the Institut für Verbrauchs-Und Einkaufsforschung EmbH, Hamburg. The questionnaire sought responses in the three principal areas of recognition and usage of the avocado, attitude toward the avocado, and factors contributing to the purchase of fruits and vegetables. The specific questions in each of these areas were the following:

Recognition and usage

a. Which are your favorite vegetables and fruits? (Open-ended question.)
b. Which of the following foreign vegetables and fruits (a list of names) do you know, have you eaten, or have you purchased?
c. How many times have you purchased avocado in the last six months?

Attitude

a. How strong is your intention to buy oranges, bananas, eggplants, avocado? (Each indicated on a scale of 1 to 7.)
b. How much do you think you and your family will enjoy eating oranges, bananas, eggplants, avocado? (Each indicated on a scale of 1 to 7.)

Purchasing Factors

a. How important in making your purchasing decision are the following 12 attributes of fruits and vegetables? (Each indicated on a scale of 1 to 7.) The list of attributes included criteria such as "always fresh in the shop," "has high vitamin content," "obtainable everywhere and always," and "can be served to guests with high standards."

Preliminary survey results

Shortly after the interviews were conducted, Agrexco received tabulations and preliminary analyses of the responses to the three questions dealing with recognition and usage. The data is presented in Exhibits 1, 2, and 3. Agrexco was particularly eager to review this information, for it would offer an indication of the current level of penetration of the avocado in the German marketplace and would form the basis for their future discussions.

It was suggested by the market research consultants that the data supported the following conclusions:

1. Avocado is conceived to be a vegetable rather than a fruit.
2. In an unaided, open-end question avocado has a low preference, as compared to other vegetables and fruits.
3. Among foreign (imported) vegetables and fruits, the relative level of awareness and usage of avocado is medium, but the absolute level is

quite high for a new product (known—84 percent; eaten—62 percent, bought—48 percent).

4. There is a gap between knowing and using avocado, since only 73 percent of those who know about avocado have eaten it, and less than 50 percent have bought it in the last six months.

It was proposed that the significance of the gap between knowledge and use of the avocado could be better evaluated by comparing the avocado to the other fruits and vegetables in the study. Based on all the fruits and vegetables, relationships could be established between the percent of the respondents who had eaten (or, alternatively, bought) the product and the percent of the respondents who were aware of the product. This would give norms against which the avocado's actual "performance" could be judged. Regression analysis was used in conjunction with the data of Exhibit 2 to calibrate these relationships with the following results:

$$\begin{pmatrix} \text{Percent who} \\ \text{have eaten} \end{pmatrix} = -15.4 + 1.06 \times \begin{pmatrix} \text{Percent who} \\ \text{are aware} \end{pmatrix} \quad \begin{array}{l} R^2 = 0.92 \\ SEE = 10.3 \end{array}$$

$$\begin{pmatrix} \text{Percent who} \\ \text{have bought} \end{pmatrix} = -21.2 + 1.04 \times \begin{pmatrix} \text{Percent who} \\ \text{are aware} \end{pmatrix} \quad \begin{array}{l} R^2 = 0.82 \\ SEE = 15.6 \end{array}$$

The market research analysts suggested that these relationships demonstrate that "the potential of the examined segment of the population is not fully exploited." They based their conclusion on the observation that the first equation predicts that 73.6 percent[1] of the sample population should have eaten avocado but in fact only 62 percent had. Likewise, the second equation predicts that 66.2 percent of the population should have bought avocado, but only 48 percent actually had. The poor performance

Exhibit 1
Preference of vegetables and fruits

Vegetables		Fruits	
Asparagus	41%	Apples	51%
Cauliflower	30	Oranges	43
Carrot	26	Strawberries	40
Beans	21	Cherries	21
Peas	20	Peaches	19
Cabbage	20	Pears	16
Fennel	18	Grapes	15
Brussels sprouts	16	Citrus	10
Kohlrabi	10	Apricots	8
Avocado	3	Grapefruit	8

---

[1] Since 84 percent of the population were aware of avocado, the equation predicts that $-15.4 + (1.06 \times 84) = 73.6$ percent of the population would have eaten avocado.

Exhibit 2
Recognition and usage of foreign fruits and vegetables

Fruits or vegetables	Aided awareness	Eaten	Bought
Oranges	100%	100%	100%
Lemons	100	100	100
Grapefruits	100	100	99
Bananas	100	100	99
Olives	100	99	95
Melons	100	99	94
Green paprika	99	99	97
Red paprika	99	99	97
Dried figs	99	97	94
Chicory	99	97	96
Dried dates	99	95	92
Sweet corn	99	88	72
Artichokes	98	88	73
Fennel	98	79	68
Raw, fresh figs	93	75	58
Aubergines	95	77	63
Pomegranates	85	62	42
Avocado	84	62	48
Zucchini	79	63	50
Fresh raw dates	76	48	37
Mangos	75	37	23
Kakis	68	50	41
Broccoli	56	43	34
Cactus figs	50	26	16
Papayas	24	11	7
Guavas	21	7	3
Lychees	17	14	8
Kivis	14	5	3
Maracuya	8	4	2

of the avocado relative to the other fruits and vegetables in the study meant that there was indeed substantial potential for improvement.

These conclusions were encouraging and Agrexco eagerly awaited the tabulations of the other questions, for they would give more specific information on how to tap the potential of this market.

Exhibit 3
Recognition and usage of avocado

Known (unaided recall)	14%
Known (aided recall)	84
Eaten	62
Bought	48
Bought in the last 6 months	40
1–2 times	20
3–5 times	10
More than 5 times	10
Correct identification of photo	65

Case 9–2A

Harmon Foods, Inc.

John MacIntyre, general sales manager of the Breakfast Foods Division of Harmon Foods, Inc., was having difficulty in forecasting the sales of Treat. Treat was a ready-to-eat breakfast cereal with an important share of the market. It was also the major product in those company plants where it was manufactured. Mr. MacIntyre was responsible for the sales forecasts from which production schedules were prepared.

In recent months, actual Treat sales had varied from 50 percent to 200 percent of his forecast. Most of his difficulty in preparing forecasts arose from the great variability in historical sales; that variability can easily be seen in Exhibit 1. Since sales were debited on the day of shipment, Exhibit 1 represents unit shipments as well as sales.

Exhibit 1
Sales of Treat (standard cases)

	Year			
Month	1966	1967	1968	1969
January........	425,075	629,404	655,748	455,136
February	315,305	263,467	270,483	247,570
March	432,101	468,612	429,480	732,005
April	357,191	313,221	260,458	357,107
May..........	347,874	444,404	528,210	453,156
June	435,529	386,986	379,856	320,103
July	299,403	414,314	472,058	451,779
August	296,505	253,493	254,516	249,482
September	426,701	484,365	551,354	744,583
October	329,722	305,989	335,826	421,186
November	281,783	315,407	320,408	397,367
December	166,391	182,784	276,901	269,096

Manufacturing problems

Accuracy in production forecasts was essential for the health of the entire business. The individual plant managers received these forecast schedules and certified their ability to meet them. Acceptance of a schedule by a plant manager represented a "promise" to deliver; crews and machines were assigned, materials ordered, and storage space allocated to meet the schedule.

Schedule changes were expensive. On the one hand, the lead time on raw material orders was several weeks, so that ordering too little caused shortages which were expensive in lost production time and disappointed customers. After schedule reductions, on the other hand, the raw material could not be used as fast as it arrived. Storage space was short, and so some of the material had to be left on the truck, railroad car, or barge in which it had been shipped. The resultant tie-up of these vehicles was extremely expensive in demurrage charges.[1]

Even more important than the storage problem was the problem of efficient manpower utilization. Production schedules were kept tight to avoid unnecessary costs. Overtime was avoided because it was expensive and interfered with weekend maintenance. The labor force was highly skilled and difficult to increase in the short run. Layoffs, on the other hand, were avoided to preserve the skills of the crew. This job security resulted in a high level of employee morale and was an important part of the company's labor policy. Thus, the production manager had to try to make production schedules efficient for a constant-size work force and to use as little overtime as possible.

Advertising expenditures

Inaccuracy of sales forecasts also led to a reduction in the effectiveness of Treat advertising expenditures. Most of the advertising dollars for Treat were spent on Saturday morning network shows for children, time for which was purchased up to a year or more in advance. This time was relatively expensive, costing $20,000 per one-minute commercial, but it was the opinion of all the brand managers in the Breakfast Food Division that these network programs delivered the best value for each advertising dollar spent. This opinion was based upon cost per million messages delivered, viewer-recall scores, and measures of audience composition.

It was the policy at Harmon Foods, as at many companies, to budget advertising expenditures at a fixed amount per unit sold. Each year monthly budgets for advertising were established, based on forecast sales. Brand managers tended to contract for time on network programs to the limit of their budget allowance. When shipments ran high, however, brand managers tended to increase advertising expenditures to the level warranted by the actual sales. In such circumstances, they would seek contracts for time from other brand managers who were shipping below budget. Failing this, they would seek network time through the agencies, or if such time were unavailable, they would seek spot advertising as close to prime program time as possible. Thus, unplanned advertising expenditures could result in the use of time which gave lower value per advertising dollar spent than did the best network time.

Budgets and controls

The errors in forecasts were also the subject of complaints from the controller of the Breakfast Foods Division. Each brand prepared a budget

---

[1] Demurrage charges are assessments made by a carrier against a consignee for delays in unloading (or the initiation of unloading) of a transport vehicle. Typically, there is an allowance of one free hour in excess of normal unloading time for trucks. Rail cars and barges have typical allowances of three days and one day respectively, including unloading time. Typical charges for delays beyond these allowances range from as low as $5 per hour for a truck and $8 per day for a rail car to as high as $1,000 per day for a large barge.

based on forecasted shipments. This budget "promised" a contribution to division overhead and profits. Long-term dividend policy and corporate expansion plans were based in part on these forecasts. Regular quarterly increases in earnings over prior years had resulted in a high price-earnings ratio for the company. Since the market value of the common stock was a chief interest of the owners, profit planning was an important part of the management control system.

The discretionary "overspending" on advertising noted earlier tended to amplify the problems of profit planning. These expenditures did not have budgetary approval, and until a new "budget base" (sales forecast) for the fiscal year was approved at all levels, such overspending was merely borrowing ahead on the current fiscal year. The controller's office charged only the budgeted advertising to sales in each quarter and carried the excess over, since it was unauthorized. This procedure resulted in spurious accounting profits in those quarters with sales in excess of forecast, with counterbalancing reductions in profit in subsequent quarters.

The extent to which profits could be affected by deferred advertising expenditures had been demonstrated in the past fiscal year. Treat, along with several other brands, had overspent extensively in the early quarters, and as a result divisional earnings for the fourth quarter were more than $1 million below corporate expectations. The division manager, as well as his sales manager, brand managers, and controller, had felt very uncomfortable in the meetings and conferences which had been held as a result of this shortage of reported profits. The extra profits reported in earlier quarters had offset shortages of other divisions, but in the final quarter there had been no division to offset the Breakfast Foods shortage.

The brand manager

Donald Carswell, the brand manager for Treat, prepared his brand's "budget base," or the set of monthly, quarterly, and annual forecasts which governed monthly advertising and promotional expenditures. These forecasts, along with forecasts from the division's other brand managers, were submitted to Mr. MacIntyre for his approval. This approval was necessary because, in a given month, the sales force could support the promotions of only a limited number of brands. Once approved, the brand managers' forecasts served as the basis of the "official" forecasts made by Mr. MacIntyre.

The use of the brand managers' forecasts as the basis for the sales manager's official forecasts (and thus, the basis for production scheduling) required mutual confidence and understanding. From the sales manager came information on Harmon's, and also the competitors', activity and pricing at the store level. From the brand manager came knowledge of market trends for his brand and its competitors. The brand manager also kept records of all available market research reports on his and similar brands, and was aware of any package design and product formulations under development.

As brand manager, Mr. Carswell knew that the responsibility for improving the reliability of sales forecasts for Treat rested with him. After talking to analysts in the Market Research, Systems Analysis, and Operations Research Departments, he concluded that better forecasts were possible, and Robert Haas of the Operations Research Department offered to work with him on the project. Carswell received enthusiastic support for his planned undertaking from both the sales manager and the controller. Although such projects were outside the normal scope of a brand manager's duties, Carswell recognized the opportunity to find a solution to his forecasting problem that would have company-wide application.

Factors affecting sales

Carswell and Haas discussed at great length the factors that influenced sales. A 12-month moving average of the data in Exhibit 1 indicated a long-term rising trend in sales. This trend confirmed the A. C. Nielsen store audit, which reported a small but steady rise in market share for Treat, plus a steady rise for the commodity group to which Treat belonged.

In addition to trend, Carswell felt that seasonal factors might be important. In November and December, sales slowed down as inventory levels among stores and jobbers were drawn down for year-end inventories. Summer sales were often low because of plant shutdowns and sales vacations. There were fewer selling days in February. Salespersons often started new fiscal years with a burst of energy in order to get in a good quota position for the rest of the year.

Nonmedia promotions, which represented about 25 percent of the advertising budget for Treat, were known to have a very strong influence on sales. Such promotions were of two main types. Promotions targeted directly at the consumer were called "consumer packs," so named because the consumer was reimbursed in some way for each package of Treat which was purchased. Promotions which sought to increase sales by increasing the degree to which the brand was "pushed" by dealers were called "dealer allowances," so called because allowances were made to dealers to compensate them for expenditures incurred in promoting Treat. Consumer packs and dealer allowances were each offered two or three times per year during different canvass periods. (A sales canvass period is the time required for salespersons to make a complete round of all customers in their assigned areas. Harmon Foods scheduled ten five-week canvass periods each year. The remaining two weeks, one at midsummer and one at year-end, were for holidays and vacations.)

Consumer packs

Consumer packs usually took the form of a five-cent-per-package reduction in the price paid by the consumer. The offer could also take the form of a coupon, an enclosed premium, or a mail-in offer; but based on the results of consumer-panel tests of all such offers, Carswell was confident that each of these forms was roughly equivalent to the five-cent price reduction in its return to the brand. Consequently, he decided to group all forms of consumer packs together.

Consumer packs, along with supporting advertising material and special cartons, were produced ahead of the assigned canvass period for shipment throughout the five-week period. Any packs not shipped within this period would be allocated among salespersons for shipment in periods in which no consumer promotion was officially scheduled. From a study of historical data covering a number of consumer packs, Haas found that approximately 35 percent of a consumer-pack offering moved out during the first week, 25 percent during the second week, 15 percent during the third week, and approximately 10 percent during each of the fourth and last weeks of the canvass period. Approximately 5 percent was shipped after the promotional period was over. (See Exhibit 2.) Since they saw no reason for this historical pattern to change, Haas and Carswell were confident that they could predict with quite reasonable accuracy the monthly consumer-pack shipments that would result from a given promotion undertaken in the future.

Exhibit 2
Consumer packs (standard shipping cases)*

Month	1965	1966	1967	1968	1969
			Year		
January	−15	75,253	548,704	544,807	299,781
February	−47	15,036	52,819	43,704	21,218
March	−7	134,440	2,793	5,740	157
April	−1	119,740	27,749	9,614	12,961
May	15,012	135,590	21,887	1,507	333,529
June	62,337	189,636	1,110	13,620	178,105
July	4,022	9,308	436	101,179	315,564
August	3,130	41,099	1,407	80,309	80,206
September	−422	9,391	376,650	335,768	5,940
October	−8	942	122,906	91,710	36,819
November	5	1,818	15,138	9,856	234,562
December	220	672	5,532	107,172	71,881

* Negative shipments are returns of consumer packs by customers.

The impact of consumer packs on total shipments was, of course, favorable in the month in which the consumer packs were actually shipped; but since the consumer ate Treat at a more or less constant rate over time, Carswell was convinced that part of this increase in total shipments was the result of inventory buildups on the part of jobbers, stores, and consumers. Thus it seemed reasonable to expect that consumer packs might have a negative impact on total shipments as these excess inventories were depleted in the first and possibly the second month after the packs were shipped.

Dealer allowances

Sales seemed even more sensitive to allowances offered to dealers for cooperative promotional efforts. These allowances were provided to participating dealers via a $1 to $2 per case discount on their purchases during the canvass period of the allowance.

The total expenditure for dealer allowances during a given promotional canvass period was budgeted in advance. As with consumer packs, any "unspent" allowances would be allocated to salespersons for disbursement after the promotional period was over. The actual weekly expenditures resulting from these allowances were found to follow approximately the same pattern as was found for the shipment of consumer packs, and consequently Carswell felt that the monthly expenditures resulting from any given schedule of future dealer allowances could also be predicted with reasonable accuracy.

Promotional efforts by dealers took the form of "giant spectacular end-of-aisle displays," newspaper ads, coupons, or fliers, among others. The extent to which such efforts could effect sales is illustrated by the fact that an end-of-aisle display located near a cash register could give an average of five weeks' business in a single weekend. As with special packs, however, Carswell believed that much of the resulting sales increase was attributable to inventory buildups, and therefore he expected reactions to these buildups as late as two months after the initial sales increase.

Actual expenditures made for dealer allowances over the past five years are shown in Exhibit 3.

Exhibit 3
Dealer allowances (dollars)

	Year				
Month	*1965*	*1966*	*1967*	*1968*	*1969*
January	·99,194	114,433	0	166,178	8,133
February	38,074	63,599	78,799	134,206	5,867
March	39,410	64,988	175,906	137,890	1,125,864
April	61,516	66,842	49,616	37,520	125,226
May	83,929	39,626	119,720	145,200	0
June	81,578	107,503	114,293	108,770	0
July	65,821	97,129	177,370	90,286	11,526
August	122,169	56,404	11,345	24,461	23,063
September	8,482	260,576	7,020	7,593	1,217,488
October	56,007	243,523	27,880	37,581	94,139
November	76,001	75,473	66,800	73,261	94,139
December	88,218	19,037	88,576	40,697	138,134

Conclusion

Carswell and Haas felt that they had identified, to the best of their ability, the most important factors affecting sales. They knew that competitive advertising and price moves were important but unpredictable, and they wished to restrict their model to those variables which could be measured or predicted in advance.

Haas agreed to formulate the model, construct the data matrix, and write an explanation of how the solution of the model could be used to evaluate promotion strategies, as well as to forecast sales and shipments. Carswell and Haas would then join in planning a presentation to divisional managers.

Case 9–2B

Harmon Foods, Inc. (supplement):
Regression analysis of historical data

This supplement presents the results of several computer runs applying regression analysis to the forecasting problem described in Harmon Foods, Inc. (Case 9–2A). The historical data used on each of the variables are listed in Exhibit 1. Section A of Exhibit 1 defines the variables used in this situation and presents the results of a regression model which forecasts monthly case shipments, based on the 18 explanatory variables that are listed. Section B shows the use of regression to investigate a possible relationship between consumer promotions and dealer promotions. The final three sections—C, D, and E—show the results of regression models using as explanatory variables only the consumer promotion variables (C), only the dealer promotion variables (D), and only trend and seasonal variables (E).

Exhibit 1

Historical data on Harmon Foods used in regression analysis

1*	2	3	4	5	6	7	8	9	10	11	12	13	14	15	16	17	18	19	20	21
13	425,075	75,253	114,433	1	1	0	0	0	0	0	0	0	0	0	0	0	220	5	88,218	76,001
14	315,305	15,036	63,599	2	0	1	0	0	0	0	0	0	0	0	0	0	75,253	220	114,433	88,218
15	432,101	134,440	64,988	3	0	0	1	0	0	0	0	0	0	0	0	0	15,036	75,253	63,599	114,433
16	357,191	119,740	66,842	4	0	0	0	1	0	0	0	0	0	0	0	0	134,440	15,036	64,988	63,599
17	347,874	135,590	39,626	5	0	0	0	0	1	0	0	0	0	0	0	0	119,740	134,440	66,842	64,988
18	435,529	189,636	107,503	6	0	0	0	0	0	1	0	0	0	0	0	0	135,590	119,740	39,626	66,842
19	299,403	9,308	97,129	7	0	0	0	0	0	0	1	0	0	0	0	0	189,636	135,590	107,503	39,626
20	296,505	41,099	56,404	8	0	0	0	0	0	0	0	1	0	0	0	0	9,308	189,636	97,129	107,503
21	426,701	9,391	260,576	9	0	0	0	0	0	0	0	0	1	0	0	0	41,099	9,308	56,404	97,129
22	329,722	942	243,523	10	0	0	0	0	0	0	0	0	0	1	0	0	9,391	41,099	260,576	56,404
23	281,783	1,818	75,473	11	0	0	0	0	0	0	0	0	0	0	1	0	942	9,391	243,523	260,576
24	166,391	672	19,037	12	0	0	0	0	0	0	0	0	0	0	0	1	1,818	942	75,473	243,523
25	629,404	548,704	0	1	1	0	0	0	0	0	0	0	0	0	0	0	672	1,818	19,037	75,473
26	263,467	52,819	78,799	2	0	1	0	0	0	0	0	0	0	0	0	0	548,704	672	0	19,037
27	468,612	2,793	175,906	3	0	0	1	0	0	0	0	0	0	0	0	0	52,819	548,704	78,799	0
28	313,221	27,749	49,616	4	0	0	0	1	0	0	0	0	0	0	0	0	2,793	52,819	175,906	78,799
29	444,404	21,887	119,720	5	0	0	0	0	1	0	0	0	0	0	0	0	27,749	2,793	49,616	175,906
30	386,986	1,110	114,293	6	0	0	0	0	0	1	0	0	0	0	0	0	21,887	37,749	119,720	49,616
31	414,314	436	177,370	7	0	0	0	0	0	0	1	0	0	0	0	0	1,110	21,887	114,293	119,720
32	253,493	1,407	11,345	8	0	0	0	0	0	0	0	1	0	0	0	0	436	1,110	177,370	114,293
33	484,365	376,650	7,020	9	0	0	0	0	0	0	0	0	1	0	0	0	1,407	436	11,345	177,370
34	305,989	122,906	27,880	10	0	0	0	0	0	0	0	0	0	1	0	0	376,650	1,407	7,020	11,345
35	315,407	15,138	66,800	11	0	0	0	0	0	0	0	0	0	0	1	0	122,906	376,650	27,880	7,020
36	182,784	5,532	88,576	12	0	0	0	0	0	0	0	0	0	0	0	1	15,138	122,906	66,800	27,880
37	655,748	544,807	166,178	1	1	0	0	0	0	0	0	0	0	0	0	0	5,523	15,138	88,576	66,800
38	270,483	43,704	134,206	2	0	1	0	0	0	0	0	0	0	0	0	0	544,807	5,532	166,178	88,576
39	429,480	5,740	137,890	3	0	0	1	0	0	0	0	0	0	0	0	0	43,704	544,807	134,206	166,178
40	260,458	9,614	37,520	4	0	0	0	1	0	0	0	0	0	0	0	0	5,740	43,704	137,890	134,206
41	528,210	1,507	145,200	5	0	0	0	0	1	0	0	0	0	0	0	0	9,614	5,740	37,520	137,890
42	379,856	13,620	108,770	6	0	0	0	0	0	1	0	0	0	0	0	0	1,507	9,614	145,200	37,520
43	472,058	101,179	90,286	7	0	0	0	0	0	0	1	0	0	0	0	0	13,620	1,507	108,770	145,200
44	254,516	80,309	24,461	8	0	0	0	0	0	0	0	1	0	0	0	0	101,179	13,620	90,286	108,770
45	551,354	335,768	7,593	9	0	0	0	0	0	0	0	0	1	0	0	0	80,309	101,179	24,461	90,286
46	335,826	91,710	37,581	10	0	0	0	0	0	0	0	0	0	1	0	0	335,768	80,309	7,593	24,461
47	320,408	9,856	73,261	11	0	0	0	0	0	0	0	0	0	0	1	0	91,710	335,768	37,581	7,593
48	276,901	107,172	40,697	12	0	0	0	0	0	0	0	0	0	0	0	1	9,856	91,710	73,261	37,581
49	455,136	299,781	8,133	1	1	0	0	0	0	0	0	0	0	0	0	0	107,172	9,856	40,697	73,261
50	247,570	21,218	5,867	2	0	1	0	0	0	0	0	0	0	0	0	0	299,781	107,172	8,133	40,697
51	732,005	157	1,125,864	3	0	0	1	0	0	0	0	0	0	0	0	0	21,218	299,781	5,867	8,133
52	357,107	12,961	125,226	4	0	0	0	1	0	0	0	0	0	0	0	0	157	21,218	1,125,864	5,867
53	453,156	333,529	0	5	0	0	0	0	1	0	0	0	0	0	0	0	12,961	157	125,226	1,125,864
54	320,103	178,105	0	6	0	0	0	0	0	1	0	0	0	0	0	0	333,529	12,961	0	125,226
55	451,779	315,564	11,526	7	0	0	0	0	0	0	1	0	0	0	0	0	178,105	333,529	0	0
56	249,482	80,206	23,063	8	0	0	0	0	0	0	0	1	0	0	0	0	315,564	178,105	11,526	0
57	744,583	5,940	1,217,488	9	0	0	0	0	0	0	0	0	1	0	0	0	80,206	315,564	23,063	11,526
58	421,186	36,819	94,139	10	0	0	0	0	0	0	0	0	0	1	0	0	5,940	80,206	1,217,488	23,063
59	397,367	234,562	94,139	11	0	0	0	0	0	0	0	0	0	0	1	0	36,819	5,940	94,139	1,217,488
60	269,096	71,881	138,134	12	0	0	0	0	0	0	0	0	0	0	0	1	234,562	36,819	94,139	94,139

* The original data started with January 1965, which was labeled month 1. The data in this table (and in the following regression analyses) start with January 1966, which was month 13.

Exhibit 1 *(continued)*

A.
```
      PROGRAM? REGRES     Full linear regression
      WORKFILE NO. ? 3
      INDICES? 2 1 3 18 19 4 20 21 6 7 8 9 10 11 12 13 14 15 16
        2 SHIPMENTS-CASES   ← dependent variable
        1 MONTH T
        3 CONS PACKS        ⎫
       18 CONS PACKS(T-1)   ⎬
       19 CONS PACKS(T-2)   ⎭
        4 DEAL ALLOW   .    ⎫
       20 DEAL ALLOW(T-1)   ⎬
       21 DEAL ALLOW(T-2)   ⎭
        6 JAN                    ⎫
        7 FEB                    ⎪
        8 MAR                    ⎪
        9 APR                    ⎪   Explanatory variables
       10 MAY                    ⎬
       11 JUN                    ⎪
       12 JUL                    ⎪
       13 AUG                    ⎪
       14 SEP                    ⎪
       15 OCT                    ⎪
       16 NOV                    ⎭


      OPTION? 1
      NAT     EST         UNC       P(SGN)
      B0    1.609E+05   2.688E+04   1.000  ← constant
      B1    1.045E+03   5.525E+02   0.966  ← trend
      B3    4.180E-01   6.952E-02   1.000  ⎫
      B18  -2.158E-01   6.641E-02   0.999  ⎬ consumer packs
      B19  -1.717E-02   6.540E-02   0.603  ⎭
      B4    2.974E-01   3.404E-02   1.000  ⎫
      B20   1.103E-02   3.449E-02   0.624  ⎬ dealer allowances
      B21  -7.261E-02   3.669E-02   0.971  ⎭
      B6    1.840E+05   3.736E+04   1.000  ⎫
      B7    1.282E+05   3.552E+04   0.999  ⎪
      B8    2.113E+05   3.642E+04   1.000  ⎪
      B9    9.631E+04   3.000E+04   0.998  ⎪
      B10   2.082E+05   2.975E+04   1.000  ⎬ seasonals
      B11   1.491E+05   2.861E+04   1.000  ⎪ (base is December)
      B12   1.646E+05   2.876E+04   1.000  ⎪
      B13   6.272E+04   2.807E+04   0.983  ⎪
      B14   1.823E+05   3.263E+04   1.000  ⎪
      B15   1.272E+05   3.197E+04   1.000  ⎪
      B16   1.174E+05   3.153E+04   1.000  ⎭
      EST. RES. SD        3.912E+04

      SAM. RES. SD        3.040E+04
      SAM.  R SQR         0.943
      (29 DEGREES OF FREEDOM)
```

Exhibit 1 (continued)

B.   OPTION? 7
       INDICES? 3 4
          3 CONS PACKS
          4 DEAL ALLOW

       OPTION? 1
       NAT:
       B0   1.188E+05   2.259E+04   1.000
       B4   -1.434E-01   8.728E-02   0.946
       EST. RES. SD   1.372E+05

       SAM. RES. SD   1.343E+05
       SAM. R SQR   0.055
       (46 DEGREES OF FREEDOM)

Checking the relationship between consumer packs and dealer allowances

C.   OPTION? 7
       INDICES? 2 3 18 19
          2 SHIPMENTS-CASES
          3 CONS PACKS
         18 CONS PACKS(T-1)
         19 CONS PACKS(T-2)

       OPTION? 1
       NAT:
       B0   3.384E+05   2.540E+04   1.000
       B3   4.598E-01   1.114E-01   1.000
       B18   -2.729E-01   1.087E-01   0.992
       B19   2.737E-01   1.114E-01   0.991
       EST. RES. SD   1.045E+05

       SAM. RES. SD   1.001E+05
       SAM. R SQR   0.382
       (44 DEGREES OF FREEDOM)

Explaining shipments using only the consumer packs variables

} consumer packs

D.   OPTION? 7
       INDICES? 2 4 20 21
          2 SHIPMENTS-CASES
          4 DEAL ALLOW
         20 DEAL ALLOW(T-1)
         21 DEAL ALLOW(T-2)

       OPTION? 1
       NAT:
       B0   3.356E+05   2.170E+04   1.000
       B4   3.436E-01   6.759E-02   1.000
       B20   -1.855E-02   6.707E-02   0.608
       B21   6.108E-02   6.755E-02   0.815
       EST. RES. SD   1.053E+05

       SAM. RES. SD   1.008E+05
       SAM. R SQR   0.373
       (44 DEGREES OF FREEDOM)

Explaining shipments using only the variables for dealer allowances

} dealer allowances

Exhibit 1 (concluded)

```
E.     OPTION? 7
       INDICES? 2 1 6 7 8 9 10 11 12 13 14 15 16
          2 SHIPMENTS-CASES
          1 MONTH T   ← trend
          6 JAN  ⎫
          7 FEB  ⎪
          8 MAR  ⎪
          9 APR  ⎬  seasonals
         10 MAY  ⎪
         11 JUN  ⎪
         12 JUL  ⎪
         13 AUG  ⎪
         14 SEP  ⎪
         15 OCT  ⎪
         16 NOV  ⎭
```

Explaining Shipments using only trend and seasonals

```
       OPTION? 1
       NAT:
       B0    1.296E+05    5.031E+04    0.993
       B1    2.242E+03    8.032E+02    0.996
       B6    3.422E+05    5.353E+04    1.000
       B7    7.283E+04    5.340E+04    0.909
       B8    3.119E+05    5.329E+04    1.000
       B9    1.161E+05    5.318E+04    0.982
       B10   2.353E+05    5.309E+04    1.000
       B11   1.703E+05    5.301E+04    0.999
       B12   1.968E+05    5.295E+04    1.000
       B13   4.867E+04    5.289E+04    0.818
       B14   3.347E+05    5.285E+04    1.000
       B15   1.289E+05    5.282E+04    0.990
       B16   1.072E+05    5.280E+04    0.975
       EST. RES. SD        7.466E+04

       SAM. RES. SD        6.375E+04
       SAM.  R SQR        │ 0.749 │
       (35 DEGREES OF FREEDOM)
```

Case 9–3

Crocker Coupler Corporation

During the summer of 1972 Mr. James Everly, President of Crocker Coupler Corporation (CCC), returned from an industrial convention that brought him in contact with the executives of several of his competitors and many of CCC's customers. The tenor of the meeting was optimism—possibly cautious optimism, but at least optimism. This was a particularly good feeling for Everly, since the past few years had been difficult ones for CCC. It barely had been able to break even in five out of the past six years. Since its gross margin had been running between 5 and 6 percent of sales, its depressed sales volume had made it difficult to cover its overall

Exhibit 1
Quarterly historical orders (four-quarter moving average)

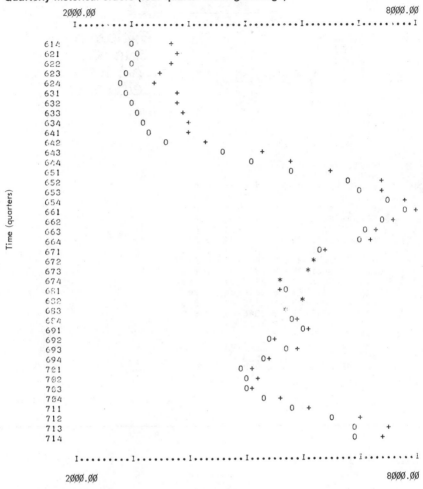

Dollars (thousands)

0 = Orders, total external market in actual dollars
+ = Orders, total external market in constant dollars (1st quarter 1967)
* = Approximately same value for 0 and +

selling and administrative expenses and its other indirect costs. The past
two years had shown substantial increases in orders (Exhibit 1), but many
feared that this might be a repeat of the 1964–66 period. However, if this
newly found optimism could be translated into a continued increase in
machinery investment in CCC's markets, Everly knew that he would have
to look seriously at the expansion of his plant or change his marketing
strategy. If the decision were to expand the plant, he wanted to be sure

that the continued upswing was really there, since the last thing he needed was a large amortization cost eating away his earnings with the new capacity going unused. On the other hand, he did not want to be too cautious, since the experience of 1965, when he brought new equipment on line just as the boom ended, was very fresh in his mind. This investment had yet to pay back even though his criterion for undertaking investments was a three-year payback. He wasn't prepared to change the marketing strategy at this point in time, since it depended to a large degree on CCC's potential in its various markets, and right now he simply didn't have reliable information on that.

Company background

The Crocker Coupler Corporation, founded in 1934, had grown from rather modest beginnings to a position of strength in the gearbox and coupling industry. CCC supplied the link between relatively large motors (from several hundred horsepower to 10,000 horsepower) and the machinery they drove. It had built its reputation in the industry through a wide variety of skills—engineering, marketing, and manufacturing.

The firm had remained relatively small until World War II, when it grew rapidly to meet the demands of the expanding war industry. After the war, CCC continued to grow as the economy adjusted to peacetime and began to satisfy the pent-up desire for consumer durables. Just as this effect was slackening, the Korean Conflict brought increased sales to the defense-related industries. During CCC's expansionary period, the bulk of its sales were a result of new-equipment investment decisions on the part of its customers. Although there was another consumer boom following the Korean Conflict, CCC did not benefit substantially from it, since most manufacturers did not require new equipment. This heralded the first really serious setback for CCC when business declined abruptly in 1956 and 1957. The firm's financial position was weak, and in late 1957 it was acquired by one of the emerging conglomerates.

In the early 1960s, there was another boom, again linked to the general condition of the economy. CCC had not foreseen this accelerated growth and was caught short of capacity. Not until late 1965 was it able to bring the new capacity on line. Shortly thereafter the market turned down, and it had leveled off at this lower level until recently. In 1966, CCC was caught completely unprepared for the downturn, with substantial unused capacity and large inventories, and in poor financial shape from the cash flow point of view. As a result of this, there had been several large turnovers in management. In each case, Mr. Everly just barely avoided the guillotine. There were also several reorganizations. One of the major developments was the expansion, both in scope and personnel, of the marketing research department. Recently, it had been charged with the responsibility for the establishment of an early warning system of business change, for the creation of a medium-range forecasting procedure tied directly to the economy, and for a better understanding of the characteristics of the end-use markets for couplers and gearboxes.

The marketplace and the competitors

The gearbox and coupler industry had become mature. The technology was slow to change. There had been no fundamental design changes in the past ten years. The only advances had been along the lines of material substitution and the minor design changes that resulted from it. On the other hand, 30 years earlier engineering expertise had been the industry's hallmark. Gearboxes and couplers were designed to fit precisely the needs of each individual task. Crocker had always been and still was a leader in the industry in this respect. In fact, many of the engineers who had helped establish CCC in this field were still with the company, most of them in middle- and upper-management positions. With increases in costs and improvement in materials, the industry had been gradually shifting to the production of high-volume, general applications products. Crocker had not yet begun to reap the potential benefits of this change in the times. Many of its contracts still involved the more complex applications requiring large engineering inputs, oftentimes more than were anticipated, and frequently resulting in poor profits.

During the growth period of the industry, Crocker competed with three mirror images of itself. In fact, the history of these firms closely paralleled the history of CCC. Now all of them were owned by conglomerates, had strong engineering expertise, and were in an earnings pinch. With the maturing industry and the resultant technological slowdown, several new firms had been able to enter the market by concentrating on high-volume, minimally complex products for general applications. These applications generally had required standard gearboxes to which steady loads were applied, with nominal shock at startup. They enjoyed high sales volume and low production cost. This had allowed the recent entrants in the industry to compete aggressively on price. As a result, the old-line firms had been watching their margins shrink even on the special engineering contracts. In general, the older firms, particularly Crocker, had not yet taken advantage of the potential cost reductions afforded by the highly standardized general-purpose lines.

Due to the changing environment, CCC had lost considerable market share in the past six years. It was currently running about 25 percent. In recent years it had bid on approximately 10,000 items per year. These bids had resulted in 500 to 600 contracts, with a production of 5,000 items per year. The bidding was by sealed bid. The outcome seemed to be more dependent on price than on reputation, provided that the bidders met the specifications, although customer loyalty did seem to exist in the specialized products. Crocker had been beneficiary to this, but unfortunately the margin on these contracts had been low due to the overall price suppression and the higher costs.

Current forecasting methods

For the past several years, the Market Research Division of CCC had conducted its forecasting along the following general lines. The problem was first segmented into internal sales, i.e., sales to other firms within the conglomerate, and external sales. The external sales market was further subdivided into sales to the utilities (electric power generation industry) and sales to general industrial markets. For each of these categories, the following forecasts were made:

1. Total market orders in constant dollars.
2. CCC's orders received in constant dollars.
3. Price index.
4. CCC's orders received in period dollars (derived from the above forecasts).
5. CCC's sales in constant dollars.
6. CCC's sales in period dollars (derived from the above forecasts).

The constant dollars forecasts were in first-quarter 1967 dollars, and thus the price index for the first quarter of 1967 was 1.00.

The internal sales forecasts were taken from the forecasts of each of the other companies within the conglomerate. It was a simple job count. Internal sales had historically represented approximately 15 percent of CCC's business.

The utility market was identified as a separate segment of external sales since the mechanism that triggered its sales had been fairly well understood. The total market was tied directly to megawatt additions to the national electric power generating capacity. This dependency was intuitively appealing and had been proven by several in-depth studies. CCC then forecast market share, using the historical record and its current marketing policies. From this, CCC's utility sales were calculated. Orders received did not follow megawatt additions, due to varying lead times in the placement of orders by the customer. These lead times were forecast, and the orders received calculated. Of late, the predicting power of the single indicator, megawatt additions, had been deteriorating since environmental concern was beginning to change plant design and was also causing plant alterations that were not directly linked to increases in generating capacity.

The forecasting of the external industrial market (excluding utilities) was a particularly important aspect of the problem since this market had historically represented approximately 60 percent of CCC's annual orders. Following the example of the utilities market forecasts, total industrial orders (excluding utilities) were forecast from the economic indicator "plant and equipment expenditures: total manufacturing industries." A regression model was used to estimate the quantitative relationship (see Exhibit 2). Market share was then forecast, and the remaining forecasts were made by assessing a price index for the period and a lag for converting orders into sales. The lag had been running approximately 9 to 12 months. Subsequently, the aggregate forecasts were broken down into

Exhibit 2
Regression model for external industrial market

ANALYSIS INTERVAL   61   71

**** STEP   1 ****   DEPENDENT VARIABLE INDUS

VAR IN	F-RATIO	R-SQUARE	SE EST	CONSTANT
PMF	96.300	0.915	6571.921	-20582.293

VAR	COEFF	SE COEFF	T VAL
PMF	2964.023	302.043	9.813

(1) PERIOD	(2) INDUS	(3) ESTIMATE	(2)-(3) RESIDUAL
61	22106.9456	21840.2800	266.665527
62	20418.2756	23974.3765	-3556.100830
63	23343.8767	27323.7219	-3979.845215
64	36986.1313	36504.7822	481.349121
65	60132.2622	48546.1230	11586.139160
66	72418.5020	62714.1509	9704.351074
67	55071.8652	64114.6519	-9042.786621
68	65577.8564	63469.9771	2107.879395
69	66532.0049	73214.2021	-6682.197266
70	73461.6680	74259.0186	-797.350586
71	68339.2051	68427.3047	-88.099609

(1) PERIOD	(2) INDUS	(3) ESTIMATE	(2)-(3) RESIDUAL
72	-NA-	70838.1719	-70838.1719
73	-NA-	79142.6836	-79142.6836
74	-NA-	87044.3779	-87044.3779
75	-NA-	94263.5020	-94263.5020

INDUS = Total industrial orders (excluding utilities).
PMF = Plant and equipment expenditures: total manufacturing industries.

forecasts by individual product classifications for use in production scheduling. The aggregate forecast was also subdivided into forecasts by market for use in directing the sales effort. CCC was currently using the market segmentation of Exhibit 3. The industrial market forecasts had been considerably less successful than the utility forecasts. While plant and equipment expenditure was certainly a causal factor in gearbox and coupler orders, it seemed that it might be too "macro"—that many of the subtleties that induced gearbox and coupler orders were lost in the aggregation.

One way to avoid this problem was to do the forecasting by market segment and then to combine these forecasts into a forecast of total indus-

Exhibit 3
Market segmentation

Market	Percent of CCC annual orders			CCC's gross margin (percent of sales)
	1961	1970	1971	
Utility	15.4	19.5	37.4	8.8
Pumps and compressors	15.0	25.2	17.6	0.6
Metals	4.4	5.9	2.2	8.3
Machinery—machinery, material handling, metalworking, industrial processing equipment	17.1	7.0	4.2	11.0
Stone, clay, and glass	3.5	0.6	0.5	10.1
Mining..............................	8.2	3.7	2.7	8.3
Construction	2.2	1.0	0.8	8.5
Paper—paper and wood machinery	10.2	6.9	5.0	3.9
Chemical	2.1	0.7	0.8	9.7
Petroleum—refineries, pipelines	n.a.	10.0	4.4	6.1
Other external	10.7	4.0	5.2	2.1
Total external (including utilities).......................	89.2	84.5	80.6	
Total internal	10.8	15.5	19.4	
Grand Total	100.0	100.0	100.0	

trial orders. In effect, this procedure would be building the forecasts in a direction that was exactly opposite to that of the current method or its predecessor, trend analysis of total industrial orders. The forecasts would now be from the bottom up rather than from the top down. It was hoped that good causal indicators could be found for each market segment, just as CCC had been able to do with the utility market.

The major problem with this proposed shift in technique was the availability, collection, and accuracy of the market segment data that were required to make the system work. Crocker had recorded its quarterly orders by market for the past 11 years (Exhibit 4 shows the annual figures) and felt fairly confident of the accuracy of these data. The quarterly sales data had been saved for only seven years—the annual figures are shown in Exhibit 5. To assist in making the market-oriented forecasts, CCC had signed a contract with a distinguished economic forecasting firm to supply it with forecasts of economic indicators that were market segment–directed. A partial list of the indicators that were available are shown in Exhibit 6. Through the gearbox and coupler industry organization (National Association of Coupler Manufacturers—NACM) total market data were available on an annual basis (Exhibit 7). The data were collected on a volunteer basis from the membership, and thus suspect. But even so, the industry information allowed Crocker to estimate its market share in each of the market segments (Exhibit 8). Unfortunately, they were the only industry-wide figures available.

Exhibit 4
Annual orders in actual prices ($000) by markets

Year	Construction	Paper	Chemical	Petroleum	Metals	Machinery	Pumps and compressors	Stone, clay, and glass	Mining	Electrical utility	Other external	Crocker internal
1961	289	1,362	278	n.a.	591	2,292	2,004	468	1,102	2,053	1,434	1,441
1962	306	1,093	303	n.a.	673	2,588	1,596	261	1,646	2,128	634	1,848
1963	363	1,110	558	n.a.	667	2,261	3,355	296	1,024	1,937	2,213	4,127
1964	511	2,927	860	n.a.	1,347	2,692	5,027	873	1,168	3,022	1,261	2,735
1965	570	4,225	960	n.a.	4,484	2,714	6,477	951	1,316	2,439	2,013	4,405
1966	1,169	3,865	758	1,916	918	3,599	5,923	163	1,340	5,674	2,517	2,947
1967	527	1,559	391	1,527	888	2,370	6,436	122	588	5,891	1,997	3,253
1968	731	1,999	398	1,752	1,666	2,182	4,892	148	579	6,860	1,922	2,130
1969	338	1,656	348	846	1,137	2,161	5,457	374	623	6,515	1,537	2,682
1970	255	1,738	166	2,577	1,481	1,770	6,327	149	927	4,883	1,100	3,730
1971	256	1,682	256	1,481	731	1,433	5,969	177	910	12,663	1,761	6,560

Exhibit 5
Annual sales in actual prices ($000) by markets

Year	Construction	Paper	Chemical	Petroleum	Metals	Machinery	Pumps and compressors	Stone, clay, and glass	Mining	Electrical utility	Other external	Crocker internal
1961 to 1965	n.a.	n.a.	n.a.	n.a.	n.a.	n.a.	n.a.	n.a.	n.a.	n.a.	n.a.	n.a.
1966	615	2,314	590	1,615	1,648	3,180	3,843	791	1,030	2,347	1,547	1,806
1967	1,149	3,426	696	1,376	1,048	3,248	5,877	142	1,230	4,585	2,541	2,696
1968	683	1,733	430	1,905	995	2,538	5,105	118	517	4,720	2,276	3,635
1969	399	1,828	366	1,037	889	1,527	6,176	374	587	5,506	1,761	2,151
1970	286	1,530	114	1,374	1,543	2,424	5,008	152	1,054	6,440	1,469	2,781
1971	222	2,068	311	2,718	1,514	1,726	6,033	173	725	8,007	1,317	4,314

Exhibit 6
Economic indicators available from outside firm

Gross national product and selected indicators
   Gross national product
   Personal consumption (various categories)
   Private investment (various categories)
   Government expenditures (various departments)
   Demographic data

Plant and equipment spending, FRB Index, and construction
   Plant and equipment (categories similar to CCC's markets)
   FRB Index (categories similar to CCC's markets)
   Construction

Selected industry indicators—production and sales
   Production and sales (some market segments)
   Inventories

Selected industry indicators—shipments and investment
   Shipments (categories similar to CCC's markets)
   Purchases of durable equipment

The opportunity for an increase in capacity

James Everly could see the recent increases in orders as an opportunity (or possible necessity) to install a new semiautomated line in his plant. The smallest technically feasible set of equipment would cost between $1 and $1.5 million and could be on line in about one year. It would have a long useful life but would be depreciated over ten years. Everly's greatest concern was whether or not the increases in orders that had been recently experienced would continue. He knew that the increases would have to continue for the new equipment to be a sound investment. He felt that the current plant could adequately handle the current orders volume plus the anticipated increases in the utilities market. This implied that the investment would have to be based on whatever increases might occur in the external, nonutility markets.

Exhibit 7
Industry orders in actual prices ($000) by markets

Year	Construction	Paper	Chemical	Petroleum	Metals	Machinery	Pumps and compressors	Stone, clay, and glass	Mining	Electrical utility	Other external	Crocker internal
1961	714	2,095	807	958	2,165	2,910	4,121	2,507	1,799	6,259	2,232	1,441
1962	634	2,042	693	808	2,959	3,204	3,242	2,026	2,144	5,542	1,854	1,848
1963	519	2,276	859	745	2,303	2,818	6,979	1,785	1,587	4,138	3,619	4,127
1964	866	4,665	1,502	1,053	4,960	3,607	10,517	3,440	1,907	6,884	3,187	2,735
1965	1,051	7,788	1,786	4,493	5,732	7,093	16,303	7,216	2,605	9,204	5,070	4,405
1966	1,658	6,184	2,365	2,838	9,691	11,957	13,573	11,325	2,838	15,171	6,328	2,947
1967	901	4,021	1,187	3,181	6,120	6,447	17,879	7,022	1,925	21,899	3,249	3,253
1968	1,293	4,914	1,659	3,996	8,073	9,387	16,675	10,148	1,820	18,899	4,719	2,130
1969	1,249	5,817	1,633	2,866	6,248	9,792	19,654	11,596	2,346	19,105	5,002	2,682
1970	1,542	6,825	1,819	3,775	6,218	12,047	15,582	12,804	3,061	15,118	5,335	3,730
1971	2,206	5,523	2,332	3,678	4,131	12,330	15,676	12,740	3,668	30,961	5,628	6,560

Source: National Association of Coupler Manufacturers.

Exhibit 8
Crocker market share by markets $\left[\dfrac{\text{Crocker orders (Exhibit 4)}}{\text{Industry orders (Exhibit 7)}}\right]$

Year	Construction	Paper	Chemical	Petroleum	Metals	Machinery	Pumps and compressors	Stone, clay, and glass	Mining	Electrical utility	Other external
1966	0.71	0.63	0.32	0.68	0.09	0.30	0.44	0.01	0.47	0.37	0.40
1967	0.58	0.39	0.33	0.48	0.15	0.37	0.36	0.02	0.31	0.27	0.61
1968	0.57	0.41	0.24	0.44	0.21	0.23	0.29	0.01	0.32	0.36	0.41
1969	0.27	0.28	0.21	0.30	0.18	0.22	0.28	0.03	0.27	0.34	0.31
1970	0.17	0.25	0.09	0.68	0.24	0.15	0.41	0.01	0.30	0.32	0.21
1971	0.12	0.30	0.11	0.40	0.18	0.12	0.38	0.01	0.25	0.41	0.31

Case 9–4

J. L. Hayes & Sons

Early in April 1963, the Western States Power Company (WESTCO) announced plans to sell at public sealed bidding a new $5 million series of its first mortgage bonds. WESTCO would accept bids for the bonds, which were to mature on May 1, 1988, at its offices in Denver, Colorado, until 11:00 A.M. MDT on Tuesday, May 7, 1963. Bidders were required to stipulate a coupon rate on the bonds in a multiple of one eighth of 1 percent of par value; the price offered to Western States for the bonds was required to be between 99 percent and 102 percent of par value. Western States proposed to award the bonds to the bidder whose combination of coupon rate and bid price represented the lowest annual cost of money to it. It reserved the right, however, to reject all bids if none of them were considered acceptable. The sale was subject to receipt of necessary approvals and clearances from federal and state regulatory agencies. The bonds had been rated Aa, the second highest quality rating, by Moody's Investors Service.[1]

The announcement by Western States was not unexpected at the La Salle Street headquarters of J. L. Hayes & Sons in Chicago. Hayes & Sons, as a leading securities firm, engaged in a variety of financial activities. As a member of the principal securities and commodity exchanges, it offered brokerage services to institutional and individual investors; it also dealt in the over-the-counter securities markets. The buying department, directed by Mr. Francis E. Hayes, a partner in the firm and grandson of the founder, provided financial services to corporations raising funds through new issues of securities. Mr. Hayes was aware that the recently announced plant expansion program of Western States would require funds in excess of those being generated by the company internally. He also knew that the company had a relatively low debt to equity ratio for the electric utility business, and so he had anticipated that the company would decide to finance the deficiency in its funds through a new debt issue. Hayes had already decided that, should his anticipations prove correct, Hayes & Sons would submit a bid on the new bond issue of Western States.

Most new securities issues are brought to market by what is called the "syndicate method," under which a number of investment banking firms join in a temporary partnership or "syndicate" for the purpose of buying the issue from the corporation and carrying it in inventory until it is finally

---

[1] For a brief description of the bond market, investment banking, and public sealed bidding, see Appendix.

placed with investors. Because of the relatively small size of the Western States issue, however, Hayes decided not to attempt to form a syndicate to bid on the issue, but rather to bid individually on behalf of Hayes & Sons only.

On April 24, Western States conducted an information meeting for prospective bidders at its offices. At this time, copies of the various documents related to the new bond issue were distributed to the prospective bidders and discussed with them. The treasurer of Western States presided at this meeting and answered questions raised by the bidders regarding the financial plans and prospects of the company. Five other investment banking firms were represented at this meeting in addition to Hayes & Sons. In the subsequent week, however, Mr. Hayes learned that four of these firms had decided against bidding on the Western States issue, leaving Hayes & Sons with only a single competitor, the Continental Securities Corporation.

On Monday evening, May 6, 1963, Mr. Hayes was reviewing the information he had obtained on Western States Power Company, the new bond issue, and the previous record at competitive bidding of Continental Securities Corporation. Prior to 10:45 A.M. MDT the next morning (11:45 A.M. CDT), Mr. Hayes had to decide on the terms of the Hayes & Sons bid. He would then phone these terms to an employee in his department who would be at the Western States office for the purpose of submitting the final bid of Hayes & Sons.

Determination of price

The first step in Mr. Hayes' analysis was to determine the price at which Hayes & Sons would reoffer the Western States bonds to investors if it should win the bidding. To assist him in reaching this decision, Mr. Hayes had asked Mr. Edward Bowman, a young financial analyst in his department, to prepare a "spread sheet" listing comparative data on the WESTCO bond issue and on outstanding bond issues with similar characteristics, such as quality rating, interest coverage, maturity, and call provisions. Since the outstanding bond issues were traded on the over-the-counter market, it was possible to get price quotations for them which, Mr. Hayes felt, would give him some feel for the price at which the Western States bonds could be sold to the public. Mr. Hayes felt that considerable judgment was required in evaluating this comparative information. No two bond issues were ever exactly alike, even if they came from the same issuer; differences in maturity, coupon rate, and so forth, could have an effect on the price which the public was willing to pay for the bonds of a particular issuer. Investors might also tend to favor securities of one issuer over those of another for qualitative reasons which were not reflected in conventional financial statistics. Even if corrections were made for these factors of noncomparability, it was necessary to consider the fact that the price quotations from the over-the-counter market represented trades of relatively small quantities of bonds, generally less than $100,000 in par value. It was reasonable to expect that lower prices would have been necessary in order to sell as much as $5 million of bonds.

It would, of course, be possible for Hayes & Sons to buy the entire WESTCO bond issue for its own portfolio and to hold it indefinitely, earning interest on it. This would, however, have been against the firm's normal policy of disposing of any new issue within two weeks of acquisition. The partners believed that it was more profitable to turn the firm's limited funds over relatively rapidly in its main line of business, buying and selling securities, rather than permitting them to be tied up for extended periods of time in a small number of issues; the firm deviated from this policy only when there was a prospect of substantial capital gains, which could not be said of a public utility bond issue. For this reason, Mr. Hayes was concerned with setting a price which, in his opinion, would succeed in clearing the entire Western States issue out of inventory within one to two weeks. Any of the bonds remaining in inventory at the end of two weeks would probably have to be sold at whatever price could be obtained for them.

In addition to the comparative data prepared by Mr. Bowman, Mr. Hayes had available to him reports of telephone calls placed by the firm's retail salespeople to a number of large institutional investors—pension funds, trust funds, and insurance companies. Under the regulations of the Securities and Exchange Commission (SEC), it is illegal for an investment banker to accept firm orders for new securities before the SEC has given its final clearance to the issue, a clearance which is granted only after the bids have been opened. For this reason, the salespeople were permitted to obtain only "indications of interest" in the issue from their customers, which could not be construed as firm orders. Further detracting from this source of information was the inevitable tendency of potential customers to try to talk down the price of the new issue in order to make it a more attractive buying opportunity when the final price was set. Thus, this information contributed to Mr. Hayes' "feel" for the market but was by no means definitive.

After reviewing all of the information bearing on price that he had accumulated, Mr. Hayes decided that, if Hayes & Sons won the bidding on the next day, the WESTCO bonds would be reoffered to the public with a 4⅝ percent coupon at a price of 101.25 percent of par value, for a yield of slightly less than 4.54 percent to the investor. If a single large institutional investor offered to buy the entire issue from Hayes & Sons immediately after the bidding, Mr. Hayes felt that he would be willing to lower this price to 100.75, since such an offer would immediately eliminate virtually all of the costs and risks which Hayes & Sons might otherwise expect to incur in carrying the issue and in selling it publicly. The exception would be $15,000 in legal fees that would still have to be paid.

From the reports received from the sales department, however, it did not seem to Mr. Hayes that there was any possibility that a large institutional investor would be interested in acquiring the entire issue at anywhere near this price.

Considerations affecting spread

Having decided on a public offering price, Mr. Hayes' next concern was to arrive at a "spread" which would be subtracted from the public offering price to determine the bid which would be submitted to WESTCO. The spread would clearly have to be large enough to cover anticipated costs if it was to be worthwhile submitting a bid at all. Hayes & Sons would also expect compensation for its risks in carrying the bonds until sold. Beyond that, however, the primary determinant of the spread was probably the intensity of the competition for the issue. Even were there no other bidders, of course, Hayes & Sons would have to be reason-

Exhibit 1
Bidding history of Continental Securities Corporation

Issue number*	Par value ($ millions)	Moody's quality rating†	Number of bidders‡	Hayes' proposed offering price§	Continental's bid§
1	27.5	Aa	4	99.036	97.970
2	16.0	Baa	5	103.356	102.152
3	100.0	Aa	3	99.886	98.955
4	12.5	Baa	3	97.542	96.057
5	20.0	Baa	2	99.028	97.176
6	9.0	Baa	4	101.716	100.484
7	2.0	Aa	5	99.018	96.947
8	17.5	A	3	98.017	97.274
9	20.0	Aa	3	94.340	92.910
10	7.5	A	7	99.524	98.856
11	27.5	Aaa	2	100.526	99.176
12	3.5	Baa	3	103.224	101.463
13	17.0	A	3	99.704	98.770
14	13.5	Aaa	2	100.766	99.739
15	45.0	Ba	4	97.986	96.284
16	22.0	Aa	4	99.172	98.236
17	8.5	A	3	101.276	99.514
18	3.0	Aa	5	99.628	98.260
19	35.0	Baa	4	101.014	99.571
20	25.0	Baa	3	97.248	95.878
21	2.5	Baa	4	99.700	97.276
22	12.5	Aa	3	102.712	101.041
23	5.0	Aaa	7	98.878	97.699

* For identification only; not relevant to characteristics of issue.

† See Appendix for description.

‡ Including Hayes and Continental.

§ As a percentage of par value. To permit comparability, Hayes' price and Continental's bid have been adjusted to a common coupon rate for each issue. The prices and bids given in this exhibit, taken in conjunction with the common coupon rate, result in the same yield to investors or cost of money to the issuer, respectively, as the actual prices and bids taken in conjunction with the actual coupon rates.

able on its spread, since WESTCO had reserved the right to reject all bids in the event that none of them were considered acceptable. Beyond that, the fact that Continental Securities Corporation was also expected to submit a bid exerted a further tempering influence on the size of Hayes' contemplated spread.

Mr. Hayes knew Bob Gordon, his counterpart in Continental Securities, and was aware of the fact that he had a reputation in the business for a "sharp pencil" when it came to figuring prices and bids. Mr. Hayes checked his files and discovered records of 23 previous occasions when both Hayes and Continental had submitted bids on the same issue. The information from his files on these 23 issues is given in Exhibit 1.

Appendix

A *bond* is a contract between a corporation and an investor, under which the investor pays a certain sum of money to the corporation in exchange for the corporation's commitment to pay definite sums of money to the bondholder at specified times in the future. While each bond is a separate contract, it is customary for corporations to enter into a large number of such contracts at the same time; the complete collection of such contracts is called a *bond issue*. As a rule, the individual bond contracts in an issue are supplemented by a trust agreement, called the *bond indenture,* running between the corporation and a trustee or trustees. The individual bondholders are the beneficiaries of this agreement, which spells out in somewhat greater detail the rights of the bondholders under their individual contracts.

Major provisions covered in the bond and/or indenture are as follows:

1. *Conditions of payment.* The corporation's promise to make future payments to the bondholders usually involves two parts. First, at a future time known as the *maturity* of the bond, the corporation promises to make a lump-sum payment to the bondholder which will serve to extinguish the contract and the corporation's liability under it. The amount of this lump-sum payment is called the *par value* or principal amount of the bond and serves as a basis for the reckoning of other payments which will or may be made under the contract. It is not required, however, that the amount paid to the corporation by the bondholder be equal to the par value, although some states prohibit the issuance of bonds at less than par value. When bonds are issued at less than par value, the difference between par value and the amount received by the corporation is called a *discount;* the corresponding difference if the issue price is greater than par value is called a *premium*. It is common for bonds to be issued in denominations of $1,000 par value.

Second, during the life of the bond (the period from issue to maturity), the corporation promises to pay interest to the bondholder at stated intervals, generally semiannually. The interest is calculated at an interest or *coupon rate* which is to be applied to the par value to determine the amount of the payment. For example, 5 percent interest on a bond of $1,000 par value would require the corporation to pay $50 interest annually, or $25 semiannually. On many bonds, the corporation's obligation to pay interest is evidenced by coupons attached to the bond which may be detached and presented to the corporation or its agent for payment on the specified date; hence the term *coupon rate*.

The bond contract may also include a *sinking fund* requirement, which compels the corporation to repay some of the bonds in an issue prior to maturity or to provide for repayment by setting aside a fund of money. The contract may also permit the corporation, at its option, to *call* or repay any or all of the bonds prior to maturity. If these provisions are included, the bond contract will generally state the prices and other conditions which are to govern these repayments.

2. *Security.* Many bonds, particularly those of railroads and public utilities, are backed by a mortgage on specified property of the issuing corporation. In the event of default on any of the corporation's obligations under the bond contracts or the indenture, the trustee may foreclose on the mortgage for the benefit of the bondholders. If the bonds are secured by a mortgage, the indenture will usually set forth its provisions, including a description of the property subject to the mortgage. Unsecured bonds are commonly called *debentures*.

3. *Protective covenants.* Since purchasers of bonds are looking for a high degree of certainty that payments will be made to them as scheduled, the indenture frequently includes covenants by the corporation to avoid certain specified actions which, it is believed, might endanger its ability to make these payments. For example, the corporation may be restricted in its right to sell assets or to pay dividends on its common stock. These limitations will be set forth in the indenture.

Investors attempting to determine which of two bonds to purchase are thus presented with a wide variety of different features, to say nothing of the inherent differences in the characteristics of the two issuing corporations. Somehow they must be able to cut through this mass of detail in order to determine which of the two bonds is the better for their purposes.

Regarding the payments to be made by the corporation, it is customary to reduce the entire sequence of payments to a single number, called the *yield*. The yield is the annual return on investment, expressed as a percentage, which the investor would earn by purchasing the bonds at the offering price and holding them until maturity. Published bond value tables are available which make it a relatively easy matter to determine the yield on any bond, given its current price, its maturity date, and its coupon rate.

As a means of summarizing the factors bearing on the certainty with which payments called for under the bond contract will be made, several investment advisory services prepare and publish *bond ratings*. The best known of these are issued by Moody's Investors Service, Standard and Poor's, and Fitch's. The essential features of these three rating systems are quite similar, and we will use the Moody's rating system merely for illustrative purposes. Further details on each of the systems may be found by consulting publications of the issuing service.

Moody's analysts classify bond issues into nine categories on the basis of a judgmental estimate of the quality of each bond issue, arrived at by consideration of the issuer's financial position and history and other factors. The highest quality rating is Aaa, which is assigned only to bond issues when, in the opinion of Moody's analysts, there is virtual certainty that payments will be made as scheduled. The next highest quality rating is Aa, and the ratings range down to C. Bonds of the lowest ratings are considered to be highly speculative, with relatively low probability that the contractual payments will be made as scheduled. In many states, banks and trust funds are not permitted to invest in bonds of the lower grades, usually those below Baa.

When a business enterprise wishes to obtain new funds through sale of stocks or bonds, it is customary for it to employ an *investment banking firm* to assist it in determining terms of the new issue, setting the price, and performing the merchandising functions of carrying the securities in inventory from the time of issue until the time of sale and of finding buyers. Since the fees charged by investment banking firms are usually small relative to the price of the issue being distributed, even relatively small price fluctuations in an issue during the period of distribution can more than wipe out the entire profit expected by the investment banker in entering into the deal. In an issue of substantial size, these market risks might be more than is tolerable for a single investment banking firm. In addition, a substantial amount of capital may be necessary to carry the issue in inventory until final placement with investors, and no single investment banking firm may have adequate resources for this purpose. For these reasons, it has become customary in the investment banking industry for firms to form temporary partnerships, known as *syndicates* or *buying groups,* for the purpose of purchasing or distributing a particular issue. These syndicates are strictly *ad hoc;* a firm might be a co-member of one syndicate with another investment banking firm at the same time that it is competing against that firm for another issue. One of the firms in a syndicate, generally the one which took the initiative in organizing the syndicate, is designated as the manager, and has the primary decision-making role within the group.

Whether a single investment banking firm or a syndicate handles the distribution of a new issue, the price to be paid to the company for the issue may be determined in one of two ways: by *negotiation* between the issuer and a single-purchase syndicate the issuer has invited to handle the issue; or by the solicitation of *sealed bids* from any syndicate which cares to submit such a bid.

The method of negotiation is almost universally used in the sale of new securities issues by industrial companies. Railroad and public utility companies, on the other hand, are required by the regulatory authorities in many states to offer new security issues at public sealed bidding. If the issue is to be offered competitively, the company will publish an invitation for bids in the financial press. This invitation will specify the terms of the prospective issue in some detail and will also give the time and place for the submission of bids. Investment banking firms which specialize in managing issues may respond to this invitation by organizing syndicates to bid on the issue.

Prospective bidders on a competitively offered issue, whether individuals or syndicates, will generally start by determining a *public offering price* which they intend to quote to prospective investors should they succeed in winning the bid. The next step will be to determine their spread, or the margin they wish to retain on the issue to cover their expenses and profits. Finally, by subtracting their spread from their proposed public offering price, the bidders will arrive at the bids they will make to the issuer.

When bonds are offered at competitive bidding, the bidding groups will specify the coupon rate on the bonds as well as the price to the company. Since it is possible that two different bidding groups will specify different coupon rates, the issuer must stipulate some way of standardizing bids for purposes of awarding the bonds. The method commonly followed is to award the bonds to the bidder whose combination of coupon rate and bid represent the lowest annual cost of money to the company. Cost of money is defined as the annual rate of interest paid by the company calculated on the amount it receives from the investment bankers. It is calculated in a manner similar to the investor's yield although, of course, it is somewhat higher than the yield because of the investment banker's spread. The same bond value tables used in determining yield can also be used to determine cost of money to the issuer.

Case 9–5

Korvettes Department Stores

During the 1974–75 school year, Michael Weingarten, a first-year student at Harvard Business School, had begun to wonder whether regression analysis could be used to help with a problem that had faced him in his former job at Korvettes Department Stores. Specifically, he wondered whether regression could be used to predict sales in new stores, using sales and characteristics of existing Korvettes stores as a guide. By 1976 Mr. Weingarten had done some preliminary analysis showing that the approach looked promising and Korvettes executives wanted to use it to evaluate several proposed sites for new stores.

Company background

Korvettes was started in 1948 by Eugene Ferkauf and Joe Zwillenberg, two men from Brooklyn, New York, who had served together on a corvette (boat) during World War II. The two took their first initials, changed the c in corvette to a K to avoid confusion with the Corvette car, and opened the first "E. J. Korvettes" on 48th Street in New York. It was one of the first two discount stores in New York and was a huge success from the start, selling branded merchandise at 20 to 22 percent off. Within the next two years the firm began opening additional stores in the suburbs of New York, where again it met great success. Its customers were largely middle-class people with money to spend and strong price sensitivity. For the time, its stores were large in size; their image was that of full-line discount stores with exceptionally good prices.

In its early years, the operation style at Korvettes was distinctly entrepreneurial in flavor and was marked by an absence of controls and procedures. The offices were marked by enthusiasm and confusion. But Korvettes had a very salable idea and business was excellent. The firm was turning its goods so fast that it was receiving its customers' money well before it had to pay the distributors from whom it purchased most of its goods.

The period from 1950 to the mid-1960s saw strong years for the company. Its sales expanded to about $600 million. By 1965 it had over 40 stores, mostly in the New York metropolitan area but also in Philadelphia, Baltimore, Washington, Chicago, Detroit and St. Louis. During the 1950s other discount chains had started, among them Zayre, Topps, Two Guys, and others. In addition, during the 1950s and 1960s the major department stores began moving to the suburbs, often to large shopping malls with many stores. An example was Roosevelt Field Shopping Center on Long Island, not far from Korvettes' Westbury suburban store. Roosevelt Field had a million square feet of store space, including a Macy's, a Gimbel's, and many smaller stores. Korvettes' early suburban stores, on the other hand, were all freestanding along the side of major roads.

As the pressure from department stores and from other discounters grew, Korvettes faced new pressures. It began to promote its merchandise considerably more than it had in the past, emphasizing special price promotions rather than normal day-to-day prices in some cases. The problem of the shopping malls was a difficult one, especially considering the fact that the department stores would not allow discounters into many of the new malls. Many of the discount chains formed during the 1950s had serious problems in the late 1960s and early 1970s. Those stores were generally smaller than Korvettes (perhaps 100,000 square feet versus 150,000 to 200,000 for Korvettes stores). They began and remained supermarketlike in their operation, with front-end checkouts. They were basically self-service stores, with low service, low fashion, low markup, low expense—and low prices. Some of these chains survived the difficult period, but a number, such as Arlans and Interstate, went into bankruptcy in the early 1970s.

During the 1960s and early 1970s Korvettes' image changed somewhat from what it had been in the chain's early history. The firm began to build a few two-story stores that were more like department stores than the early one-story Korvettes had been. Stores included more fashion goods in clothes and related departments and, in general, moved to a position somewhere between the low-end discounters and the more quality- and service-conscious chains like Sears and J. C. Penny. At the same time that some of the early low-end discounters went out of business, in the 1970s, other chains started, often arising from existing retail organizations. For example, K Mart was started from Kresge, while Venture discount stores came from the May Company. This second generation of discounters was considerably more professional than had been the first, and their stores were marked by lower expenses and lower prices.

Between 1960 and the mid-1970s Korvettes went through several significant ownership and management changes. In the mid-1960s it merged with Spartan Industries, a firm that produced and sold shirts and sportswear. It also operated a chain of 100 discount stores under the name of Spartan-Atlantic. Eventually Charles Bassine, who had come into the firm with the Spartan merger, emerged as the dominant force in the company and Eugene Ferkauf, the founder, left. In 1971 the firm merged with a real estate development firm called Arlen to form Arlen Realty and Development Company; Korvettes was a division of that firm. Several years later Korvettes was made a separate corporation, although it was still wholly owned by Arlen.

By the end of 1974 Korvettes was the fifth largest general merchandise discount store chain in the United States. Annual sales were $700 million, coming from 52 stores in 12 different advertising markets. (Since certain metropolitan areas like New York or Washington extend over multistate areas, it is more useful to consider advertising markets than simple political boundaries.) Twenty-two of the stores were in the New York metropolitan area. The company's plans for growth included new store expansion.

In the mid-1970s Korvettes stores continued to sell both hard goods (such as housewares, appliances, stationery, drugs) and soft goods (such as clothing), as they had from the start. The hard goods were still generally name brands; the soft goods sold in discount stores were generally not well-known brands. Discounters in general sold perhaps 40 to 45 percent soft goods at the time, while department stores sold more like 70 or 75 percent soft goods. Margins on soft goods, where fashion was an important factor, were generally better than those on hard goods, and Korvettes' management was anxious to encourage further growth in the proportion of soft goods sold.

Korvettes' customers had changed somewhat from its clientele in its early period. It still had some of the early middle-class, relatively affluent, but very price-conscious customers with whom it had had such success at the outset; such customers were particularly interested in Korvettes' hard goods. In addition, however, Korvettes had many lower- and lower-middle-income customers, including many members of minority groups who, it seemed, were particularly apt to shop at the chain. These customers were by and large the ones who bought the stores' soft goods.

Korvettes' executives saw their competition coming from both department stores and other discounters. In the main market area in New York and New Jersey, there were Two Guys discount stores and some small regional discounters, but Korvettes tended to see the department stores as much stronger competition than the relatively few other discounters in the area.

Store location analysis at Korvettes

Mr. Weingarten had worked as a staff assistant at Korvettes for two years before entering the MBA program at Harvard. In that position, he had had several opportunities to observe the site selection process at Korvettes and had had several prolonged talks with Ray Blank, Vice President for new store sites, about some of the problems involved in store site selection. The traditional method by which retailers predicted sales of new stores started with demographic analyses and site visits and studies by the firm's (or others') real estate experts. They would consider the degrees of current and expected future competition, the ease of highway access, the costs of the site, and other factors. They would also consider the average sales per square foot of space for all existing stores. The real estate experts would judgmentally combine demographic information, site information, and overall average sales rates to come up with an estimate of sales for the new store.

In an effort to make the estimation procedure more accurate, Korvettes also considered the fact that different stores had different trading zones, or zones from which they drew their traffic. For a given size of store, the more people in the trading zone, the greater should be the sales figure, all else being equal. More specifically, Korvettes executives knew that for a typical suburban Korvettes store, 75 percent of all customers came from within a five-mile radius (or a ten-minute drive, when road access was not equal in all directions). Thus, sound forecasting of store sales should, they felt, consider the characteristics of the population of the store's trading zone.

The method of analysis then in use at Korvettes did attempt to consider the trading zone. When a new site was being considered, its trading zone (perhaps a five-mile radius) was drawn on a map. Using computerized census data from a time-sharing service, the firm would obtain income data for the zone and from that information would estimate the zone's expenditures for what was called GAFO (general merchandise, apparel, furniture, and other department store–type merchandise). In doing so, Korvettes planners used figures for GAFO as a percent of income that were published for various geographic areas; they might in some cases commission studies to check on the validity of those percentages. Then, Korvettes' overall share of GAFO for all of its markets was applied to give the projected Korvettes sales in the market area under study. For example, if Korvettes had an overall 3 percent share of GAFO in the overall market, the sales estimate for the new store would be 3 percent of the GAFO for its trading zone, subject to judgmental adjustment in light of real estate analyses.

Korvettes executives had become more and more aware that even this more sophisticated approach was inadequate, for sales for new stores had been significantly different from what had been projected on the basis of share of GAFO. Looking at the results of the store planning to date, Mr. Weingarten felt that the GAFO scheme ignored the fact that Korvettes attracted lower- to lower-middle-income people, while higher-income groups were more likely to shop in full-line department stores. Thus, it was important to realize that a trading zone with 100,000 households and a median disposable income of $10,000 would represent more business for Korvettes than would a zone with exactly the same GAFO but with 50,000 households and a median disposable income of $20,000. Other characteristics of the trading zone might also influence Korvettes' sales. Korvettes executives believed that members of minority groups (particularly blacks and Spanish-speaking people) were particularly likely to shop at Korvettes. Similarly, since families often bought children's clothing in discount stores (since the clothing would soon be outgrown), family sizes in a trading zone might be important. When he first worked on the problem, Mr. Weingarten did not know how to take the various factors into account and so he did not pursue the matter.

While taking first-year Managerial Economics at HBS, however, he realized that regression analysis provided a method that might be applicable to the problem. He contacted Ray Blank, who had by then left Korvettes to start his own consulting company (R. M. Blank Associates). Mr. Blank was in the process of doing some site location work for Korvettes and was able to make available computerized census data for the trading zones of ten specific Korvettes stores. Mr. Weingarten proceeded to work on those data, despite the small number of observations, with the idea that if the results looked promising, Korvettes might find it worthwhile to pay for the collection of data on additional stores. (Such data collection would cost a few thousand dollars.) His preliminary results were encouraging, and in 1976 the firm hired Mr. Blank's company to provide data on a larger set of stores. All of these stores were in the general New York area and, in particular, in the suburban parts of the region. Exhibit 1 gives some of the census tract data provided by R. M. Blank Associates for those stores. Exhibit 2 gives characteristics of the stores themselves as well as past sales figures. Korvettes divided sales into home furnishings and mercantile sales (everything else). Furnishings had been phased out of some of the stores outside of New York and were not being

Exhibit 1*

| Store | Population (percent)† | | Family income distribution (percent) | | | | | | | Median family income |
| | Black | Spanish | 0–5 | 5–7 | 7–10 | 10–15 | 15–25 | 25–50 | 50+ | |
			(thousands of dollars)							
1	1.4	1.2	17.1	10.6	19.5	28.2	19.6	4.2	0.6	$10,480
2	23.9	22.4	28.0	14.0	20.0	22.4	13.1	2.3	0.2	8,204
3	11.1	0.9	8.7	6.6	14.5	28.8	28.8	10.2	2.3	13,495
4	5.3	1.3	10.7	8.2	17.0	29.6	26.3	7.0	1.0	12,362
5	26.0	1.3	11.8	7.9	16.1	27.9	25.9	8.7	1.8	12,563
6	4.4	0.4	7.8	5.0	14.9	35.2	29.6	6.7	0.6	13,151
7	7.7	1.0	8.1	5.4	11.3	30.4	33.6	10.2	0.9	14,142
8	8.4	1.1	9.9	6.7	17.3	32.6	27.4	5.5	0.6	12,474
9	6.3	1.3	9.6	7.1	16.4	31.1	27.1	7.8	1.0	12,730
10	14.4	7.8	17.3	10.6	18.9	26.6	19.7	5.7	1.2	10,610
11	5.1	0.7	8.5	6.2	12.8	23.7	25.6	15.5	7.8	14,771
12	6.7	0.4	7.9	5.3	11.8	23.7	29.2	16.4	5.7	15,413
13	6.4	1.6	11.1	7.6	17.4	34.2	24.8	4.4	0.5	12,036
14	11.2	0.3	7.4	5.5	13.8	30.1	30.2	11.2	1.8	13,873
15	5.9	2.9	9.0	6.3	17.6	37.9	24.0	4.5	0.7	12,251
16	9.8	0.4	8.3	6.2	17.1	35.2	26.3	6.0	0.9	12,617
17	1.4	1.0	5.8	4.2	12.2	33.8	35.1	8.1	0.8	14,117
18	8.3	0.6	7.9	5.6	13.5	29.8	31.3	10.2	1.6	13,851
19	4.1	0.3	4.5	3.6	10.4	28.9	35.4	14.4	2.7	15,710
20	2.8	0.6	5.8	4.4	10.9	27.6	35.1	14.0	2.1	15,347
21	0.6	0.7	8.0	5.5	16.3	35.8	28.9	5.1	0.5	12,821
22	28.9	1.1	10.5	7.7	16.1	29.9	27.2	7.4	1.1	12,618
23	7.1	3.4	11.7	7.7	16.8	29.8	25.9	7.1	1.1	12,318
24	6.6	0.4	7.0	4.9	12.0	27.8	31.8	13.2	3.2	14,690
25	18.4	1.9	13.3	8.8	17.0	27.4	22.9	8.6	1.9	11,972

* The census tract data reported here cover a circular area around the store, with a three-mile radius used for stores closer to New York City's center and a five-mile radius used for stores farther from the city. The only exception to this rule is that the data do not include areas within the specified radius but separated from the store by a water barrier.
 † In the census tract data, the population is divided into white, black, and other (totaling 100 percent). The classification Spanish-speaking can include members of the white or black group. Thus, black and Spanish are *not* mutually exclusive categories.

Exhibit 1 *(continued)*

| | Home rental and ownership | | | | Car ownership (percent) | |
| | *Median rent paid* | *Median home value* | *Percent homeowners* | *Percent own second home* | *No car* | *One car* |
Store						
1	$ 94	$27,768	10.6	1.8	47.1	46.1
2	70	24,063	7.0	1.4	61.2	33.6
3	146	30,107	52.6	2.5	20.9	53.3
4	141	29,153	19.3	2.5	39.3	51.0
5	127	26,801	62.9	1.6	21.8	48.2
6	154	25,121	85.5	1.5	6.1	44.7
7	147	35,519	67.0	2.0	8.5	40.4
8	123	24,767	61.4	2.3	12.4	43.7
9	124	29,675	58.7	2.0	13.2	45.3
10	90	31,942	13.8	1.9	44.5	43.6
11	136	46,883	50.7	3.1	13.2	44.1
12	147	44,132	47.5	2.4	14.2	48.2
13	110	26,560	52.4	1.3	19.6	55.7
14	131	30,382	71.5	3.0	7.4	40.2
15	154	22,625	82.3	1.0	6.9	45.7
16	134	25,193	64.9	1.8	8.1	43.1
17	154	29,644	91.4	3.5	3.1	37.1
18	150	28,477	76.8	4.5	10.5	47.4
19	161	31,519	90.4	4.3	4.1	34.9
20	138	32,805	88.8	5.0	4.5	34.1
21	158	26,885	85.1	3.1	4.6	43.1
22	130	25,744	69.9	4.0	20.4	50.2
23	111	29,973	55.9	4.2	16.7	40.4
24	155	30,331	81.0	4.8	8.3	43.7
25	123	27,593	38.7	5.3	26.1	44.4

Exhibit 1 (continued)

Store	Households with appliances (percent)					
	With TV	With washer	With dryer	With dishwasher	With air conditioner	With freezer
1	91.7	40.6	9.8	8.2	32.7	5.4
2	90.2	36.8	4.8	3.3	16.6	4.8
3	93.5	58.5	28.4	25.9	43.2	13.7
4	92.3	36.6	12.9	14.0	43.0	6.2
5	93.6	62.7	32.2	24.3	33.3	17.4
6	94.4	77.2	52.5	32.0	32.3	24.5
7	92.6	69.5	52.1	41.2	39.3	21.0
8	93.1	69.4	39.8	22.6	47.6	16.7
9	93.1	69.0	37.7	21.4	45.1	14.8
10	91.8	40.7	10.8	9.7	28.1	7.0
11	92.8	65.4	39.0	36.2	37.5	19.1
12	92.1	58.5	36.7	36.7	41.0	16.9
13	92.7	69.4	33.3	16.9	37.9	9.9
14	93.5	73.7	50.2	33.1	47.4	19.4
15	93.1	74.8	48.7	27.2	21.3	22.3
16	93.3	68.4	42.1	21.5	49.7	16.3
17	99.1	88.4	69.2	55.3	38.6	29.1
18	98.6	77.7	43.8	32.8	54.0	20.3
19	98.3	85.4	64.4	51.8	57.3	32.0
20	98.0	85.1	66.4	55.4	45.8	28.7
21	98.7	84.6	63.2	44.2	33.0	26.2
22	98.1	68.6	32.3	23.1	46.8	18.1
23	97.3	71.2	40.2	23.9	48.7	15.4
24	98.5	80.5	51.2	40.9	56.7	24.5
25	96.7	61.0	30.4	21.6	46.4	13.4

Exhibit 1 *(concluded)*

	Education of adults over 25 (percent)					Total population and family size	
Store	With 0–8 years school	With 9–11 years school	With 12 years school	With 13–15 years school	With 16+ years school	Total population	Average family size
1	37.3	19.0	29.2	7.4	7.2	642,990	3.2
2	40.9	22.4	27.2	5.0	4.5	742,557	3.5
3	22.2	16.9	34.4	11.4	15.0	872,388	3.4
4	26.6	16.2	32.3	10.9	14.1	720,417	3.1
5	24.2	19.1	34.5	10.7	11.5	490,775	3.6
6	19.6	21.4	39.4	9.9	9.7	286,402	4.0
7	18.8	14.6	33.9	12.9	19.8	159,397	3.9
8	25.9	17.4	33.0	8.8	15.0	189,767	3.7
9	26.9	18.5	32.7	9.7	12.3	529,803	3.4
10	32.9	18.9	30.5	7.6	10.1	1,113,180	3.3
11	20.7	13.7	29.9	12.1	23.6	132,749	3.5
12	16.5	13.1	31.8	13.0	25.6	336,557	3.4
13	27.7	22.5	34.4	7.6	7.9	308,776	3.7
14	18.1	14.1	33.8	12.0	22.0	229,714	3.6
15	21.4	23.6	38.6	8.8	7.6	243,626	4.0
16	21.5	17.6	36.2	9.6	15.1	280,040	3.6
17	16.8	16.1	38.0	12.8	16.4	216,949	4.2
18	21.7	18.0	36.4	10.9	13.0	517,503	3.7
19	14.9	16.2	38.0	12.8	18.1	201,518	3.9
20	14.8	13.6	35.7	14.0	22.0	179,826	3.9
21	16.6	18.2	37.6	12.1	15.5	165,542	4.0
22	24.4	20.2	34.9	10.1	10.4	647,149	3.7
23	30.7	18.6	29.1	8.7	12.9	210,112	3.6
24	19.1	16.7	36.0	11.9	16.3	421,851	3.7
25	26.1	18.6	30.4	9.8	15.1	607,050	3.4

Exhibit 2

Store	Selling area (thousands of square feet)	Annual sales ($ thousands)	Percent hard goods
1	122.5	$19,221	53.3
2	111.7	23,637	52.9
3	123.4	15,607	63.9
4	106.0	13,326	51.5
5	116.9	10,161	59.5
6	85.0	8,640	51.2
7	90.3	10,811	55.9
8	74.9	7,371	54.6
9	122.8	14,877	58.6
10	120.9	24,194	54.0
11	120.3	14,797	58.6
12	64.4	14,843	60.5
13	112.6	11,673	54.7
14	93.8	11,203	51.1
15	49.1	4,684	54.3
16	118.1	11,009	51.2
17	104.5	9,674	43.7
18	110.1	7,985	46.9
19	105.0	9,011	50.0
20	77.2	7,271	55.1
21	85.7	8,757	48.7
22	100.0	13,238	51.1
23	116.1	8,441	52.6
24	74.1	8,109	66.0
25	113.2	13,416	53.6

emphasized by Korvettes. Accordingly, the main interest was in predicting mercantile sales. In an attempt to consider the competitive forces on the various stores, Mr. Robert Warner, Senior Vice President at Korvettes, had given the competitive information summarized in Exhibit 3.

New store sites

Korvettes planners hoped to use the past data from the first three exhibits to study the relationship between sales and possible explanatory factors. They then hoped to use their new information in evaluating potential new sites. Two possible sites seemed good candidates for consideration. The first was in Town A, New York. Exhibit 4 gives census tract information for the trading zone for the site and also proposed characteristics of the store. The site was in a densely populated area with good access and little competition. Korvettes believed that GAFO dollars from the trading zone were being spent in significant amounts outside of that zone, which was "understored".[1] The store would have adequate parking

---

[1] In deciding whether an area was understored, Korvettes planners first found the estimated GAFO for the area, as described earlier. They divided that figure by $60, an estimate of retail volume per square foot. Comparing the result with the estimated actual retail square footage in the area, they determined the relation between supply and demand for department store–type sales space.

Exhibit 3

Competitive type	Stores	Description
1	1, 2, 10	Densely populated areas, particularly good store sites with relatively little direct competition
2	3, 11, 12, 25	Good locations in relatively high-income areas, with little direct competition
3	7, 9, 13, 16, 19, 20, 21, 23	Locations near major shopping centers
4	4, 18	Stores in downtown areas of suburbs
5	5, 14, 17	Stores with competition from discounters only (not from department stores)
6	6, 22	Stores in shopping centers
7	8, 15, 24	Old stores located along the sides of major roads

Exhibit 4
Town A site

Store size:
  170,000 gross square feet
  125,000 selling square feet
Competitive group (see Exhibit 3): 1
Population:
  40.0% black
  10.8% Spanish
Family income ($000):

$ 0–5	....	26.6%
5–7	....	14.0
7–10	....	19.9
10–15	....	23.9
15–25	....	13.3
25–50	....	2.0
50+	....	0.3

Median family income: $8,419
Median rent: $80
Median home value: $23,395
Homeowners: 10.1%

Cars
  0: 57.0%
  1: 36.3
Households with:

TV	....	90.0%
Washer	....	41.8
Dryer	....	9.0
Dishwasher	....	6.0
Air conditioner	....	17.9
Freezer	....	6.1
Second home	....	1.6

Education (adults over 25):

0–8 years	....	37.4%
9–11 years	....	24.1
12 years	....	29.0
13–15 years	....	5.6
16+ years	....	3.9

Total population: 955,000
Average family size: 3.7

space; it could be increased in size from 170,000 to 200,000 square feet gross if sales warranted.

The second potential site was in the Town B Shopping Plaza in New Jersey. The area was densely populated. A new Korvettes store would face competition from some low-end discounters but not from department stores, which were considered more of a threat. Exhibit 5 provides information on the trading zone and proposed new store in Town B.

Exhibit 5
Town B site

Store size:
   160,000 gross square feet
   120,000 selling square feet
Competitive group (see Exhibit·3): 5
Population:
   13.8% black
   6.6% Spanish
Family income ($000):

$ 0–5	19.2%
5–7	13.0
7–10	22.2
10–15	27.1
15–25	15.7
25–50	2.5
50+	0.3

Median family income: $9,401
Median rent: $83
Median home value: $18,029
Homeowners: 10.7%

Cars:
   0: 44.0%
   1: 45.7%
Households with:

TV	93.6%
Washer	53.6
Dryer	12.2
Dishwasher	4.6
Air conditioner	39.3
Freezer	5.0
Second home	4.6

Education (adults over 25):

0–8 years	40.1%
9–11 years	23.5
12 years	25.5
13–15 years	5.2
16+ years	5.7

Total population: 431,285
Average family size: 3.5

Simulation in the analysis of complex decisions

Chapter 10

Simulation as a decision aid

Most people have experienced or witnessed a simulated environment at some time or other. A classroom session in which cases are analyzed and discussed is a simulation of the development and presentation of recommendations for resolving a business problem. Other examples include such models as the production lines used by industrial engineers, the taste panels conducted during the development of a new consumer product, and the models of bridges, dams, and aircraft used in the testing of new designs. A simulation model may be completely non-mathematical and full size, such as the aircraft mock-ups used in the early stages of pilot training. Or the model may be a set of mathematical equations which describe the relationships among different quantities, such as the algebraic representation of a firm's balance sheet for use in financial pro forma analyses. There is a broad range of applications for the simulation approach to the analysis of problems, and there is a variety of forms in which simulation models may be designed.

The simulation of business systems has developed into one of the more powerful of the tools available for the analysis of business decisions. The construction and use of a simulation model permits the performance of a system or strategy to be observed within a simulated environment. This gives a better understanding of how the system or strategy might behave when confronted with a real-world environment. Of course, the more closely the model resembles reality, the more closely the model results will resemble the performance eventually exhibited by the system in the real world. Thus, through simulation, the decision maker has a means of experimenting with a situation and its possible future environments without disrupting the present conditions. In this way, the performance of changes in current conditions can be observed without actually implementing any change. This avoids the cost of implementing the new strategy, the disruption that would occur if the change proved to be an undesirable one, and the time lag before it is possible to observe actual performance in real time.

In most business applications, simulation requires extensive numerical calculation. As a result, computers play an important role in the implementation of business simulation models. But business simulation should not be thought of as being synonymous with computers, nor should it be viewed as being dominated by computer technicians. In addition to any computer programming that may be necessary, the development and use of a simulation model requires the conceptual design of the model, the assessment of the input data, and the interpretation of the output. These are crucial steps in the analytical process. They are the primary determinants of the success or failure of the simulation model as a useful managerial tool, and for this reason the manager must play an active role in their conduct.

This chapter introduces the concept of simulation, more specifically computer simulation, as an aid to business decision making.

AN OVERVIEW OF THE SIMULATION APPROACH

Although simulation will not be given a precise definition, it can be described as involving the following steps:

1. Formulating a model of the process or problem under study.
2. Designing a set of experiments to be carried out using the model, that is, the strategies to be tested or the "what if" questions to be answered.
3. Carrying out these experiments and recording the model's behavior under the experimental conditions.

In the decision context, simulation also involves:

4. Analyzing the results of these experiments, making judgments about how the real situation (to the extent that it is represented by the model) would behave under the experimental conditions, and formulating a plan of action.

These steps present simulation as an analytical tool, and it must be determined when this tool should be selected rather than some other. The main justification for simulation is that it offers an opportunity to observe *in detail* the dynamic behavior of the situation under study. Frequently, problems arise where the necessary details and interactions are so complex that either more formal mathematical methods cannot provide adequate models or, if the models are formulated, they defy solution. Many of these situations are those for which the appropriate decision diagram is very "bushy," due either to many levels of uncertainty in the problem or to the need to consider individually the outcomes of several successive, many-valued uncertainties. For these cases, simulation may be the only alternative. In addition, simulation provides the flexibility to easily alter assumptions with regard to the input data, the level of detail in the model, and the measures of performance used in judging the strategies to be evaluated. The degree of flexibility offered by simulation generally exceeds that of other analytical techniques.

Along with these benefits, however, are the nonnegligible costs of designing, programming, and running a simulation model. Since simulation is deceptively easy to conceptualize, these costs are often underestimated. In addition, the inherent flexibility of the simulation technique makes it very tempting for the model to evolve to something much more detailed than initially envisaged or required. Each of these tendencies can lead to surprisingly large developmental costs. The introduction of specialized simulation computer languages, lower per unit computer costs, and the accumulation of experience and skills in constructing simulations are contributing to a general reduction in simulation costs. It remains, however, a potentially expensive tool of analysis, and careful consideration must be given to the tradeoff between the benefits and the costs.

Perhaps the broadest dichotomy that we can make in classifying simulation models is mathematical models v. physical models. We will concentrate exclusively on the former. Within the category of mathematical simulations, there is the further classification of *deterministic* (those simulations where all factors are known for sure or at least assumed to be known for sure) and *probabilistic* (those where the uncertainty is treated explicitly). We will discuss in detail probabilistic simulations after briefly illustrating deterministic models.

DETERMINISTIC SIMULATION MODELS

Deterministic models are characterized by the assumption that all factors included in the model are known with certainty. The models are principally used to evaluate the answers to "what if" questions concerning the impact of changes in the model's inputs or changes in strategy. In some business situations, certainty may in fact be present, but more often it is an assumption whose importance must be checked as a part of the analysis. In this context the deterministic model and the "what if" evaluations of the uncertain elements become a first step in the analytical process, and this may lead to a probabilistic model in which the important uncertainties of the problem are modeled explicitly.

As an illustration of a situation in which a deterministic simulation might give valuable insights, let us examine the performance of an electronic firm's inventory control system for a commonly used, but expensive, electrical component. The current inventory policy is to replenish the stock whenever the month-end inventory is below 150 units. In this case, the order is made for the difference between 500 units and the ending inventory. It takes approximately a month for the order to be placed, filled, and delivered. Each order costs $1,200 in fixed costs and $90 per unit ordered. The firm estimates that its inventory-carrying costs are $1 per unit per month, computed on the average inventory for that month. Since stock is taken only at the end of the month, the average is approximated by the average of the starting inventory and ending inventory. Stockouts are viewed with disdain since, in addition to disrupting the orderly production process, it costs $120 per unit to purchase the shortages on an emergency basis with immediate delivery. In recent months, management has felt that the parts inventories have generally been too high, and it is interested in evaluating this particular component because of its high per unit cost.

A first step in making this evaluation might be to examine the performance of the current policy against the demand experience of the past 12 months. The results of this evaluation are shown in Table 10–1. The inventory levels have indeed been high, but how can they be reduced? What if the inventory level that triggers the reorder decision were reduced? What if the order size were made smaller? What if demand is 10 percent higher in the future than it has been in the past? Answers to these questions involve the complex interaction of the various inventory costs, the particular inventory control strategy, and the demand patterns being considered. Each question can be answered by examples similar to those in Table 10–1. We might keep the same reorder point and monthly demands as in this table but reduce the size of the orders that are placed. This study would indicate the potential for cost savings by reducing the size of the orders. Similarly, the other "what if" questions can be answered. Finally, based on these single-variable studies, several new strategies might be tested and the one with the lowest total cost selected as being the best policy.

In the above model, all behavior was assumed to be known with certainty. In reality, there is uncertainty and some of the inputs will vary within a range, but this is not explicitly allowed for in the model. The most obvious area in which the uncertainty is ignored is the demand for the component. The range of variations may be broad, and the assumption of certainty may be questionable. Sensitivity analysis is one method for investigating the importance of the variations in such an input to the model. By running the model with different levels of demand (say an optimistic, pessimistic, and several intermediate values) and different sequences of monthly demand, the impact and importance of the uncertainty can be partially analyzed.

When the number of parameters for which variations must be examined grows, the number of different combinations of values for these parameters increases at an exponential rate. Thus there will be a great number of sensitivity runs, which might be costly. More important, however, is the

Table 10-1
Deterministic inventory control example

	Sept.	Oct.	Nov.	Dec.	Jan.	Feb.	Mar.	Apr.	May	June	July	Aug.
Starting inventory	386	268	176	73	427	345	223	127	418	306	199	114
Demand	118	92	103	108	82	122	96	82	112	107	85	99
Ending inventory	268	176	73	0	345	223	127	45	306	199	114	15
Normal orders	—	—	427	—	—	—	373	—	—	—	386	—
Emergency orders	—	—	—	35	—	—	—	—	—	—	—	—
Costs												
Holding*	$327	$222	$ 124	$ 25†	$386	$284	$ 175	$86	$362	$252	$ 156	$64
Ordering	—	—	34,630	—	—	—	34,770	—	—	—	35,940	—
Shortage	—	—	—	4,200	—	—	—	—	—	—	—	—
Total	$327	$222	$34,754	$4,225	$386	$284	$34,945	$86	$362	$252	$36,096	$64

* Costs have been rounded to the nearest dollar.
† Due to stockout, inventory was carried for only a fraction of the month.

difficulty in interpreting the results. It is likely that many of the runs will give widely varying results and, before any conclusions can be drawn, the relative importance of each of the different combinations must be decided upon. This task is at best difficult and is the main drawback of the sensitivity approach to the treatment of uncertainty. The remainder of this chapter will discuss probabilistic simulations, in which the uncertainty is explicitly treated in the model.

PROBABILISTIC SIMULATION MODELS

The probabilistic class of simulation models involves not only a model of the structural aspects of the system, as in deterministic simulation models, but also the explicit treatment of the uncertainty. Almost all models of this type can be depicted as large, complex decision diagrams, and probabilistic (Monte Carlo) simulation can be thought of as an alternative to "folding back" the tree.

The situations we have examined so far in decision analysis have not involved many levels of uncertainty, nor have they required the detailed consideration of the outcomes of several successive many-valued uncertainties. The result was that our analyses required the consideration of relatively few possible outcomes. We saw how, for each course of action being evaluated, the probabilities of the possible outcomes are combined with the values associated with those outcomes to yield an expected value (or weighted average).

There are a large number of complex problems involving many sources of uncertainty for which it is impractical to consider all possible outcomes in the computation of the expected payoff value of each strategy. Decision diagrams for problems of this sort would have end points numbering in the thousands. The following conditions would bring about such complexity:

1. The problem may contain a large number of uncertainties, each of which has many or even an infinite number of possible outcomes.
2. The probabilities of the events in the problem may be influenced by a course of action previously selected or the outcomes of previous uncertainties.
3. The value of the final outcome to the decision maker may depend on the detailed sequence of events that lead to the final result, not simply the final result itself.
4. There may be combinations of points 1, 2, and 3 above, which are typical of most planning problems, particularly those involving evaluations over an extended period of time.

The Weatherburn example to be discussed below will illustrate these situations. The complexities of these problems arise in the interrelations among the probabilities of the events and in the vast number of possible ending positions. Such complications make both the decision diagram approach and deterministic simulation with sensitivity analysis inappropriate. The decision diagrams become unmanageable, and the deterministic simulation with sensitivity analysis becomes uninterpretable.

Sampling the possible consequences

The essence of probabilistic simulation is the selection of a *representative sample* of the possible consequences for each of the strategies under evaluation. For a given strategy, a particular value is selected for each of the uncertain quantities affecting that strategy. The selection of the specific value of an uncertain quantity makes use of the probability distribution for that quantity. When a value has been specified for each of the uncertainties, the criterion (result) is calculated. This constitutes one simulation *trial*. Equivalently, it is one of the end points of the decision diagram, had you drawn the diagram. Since this is only one of the many possible results of the strategy under evaluation, a representative sample on which to base an estimate of the expected payoff value would require many trials. After many trials, that is, when there has been an adequate opportunity for a "representative" sample of results to be collected, the average of the payoff from the trials gives an estimate of the expected payoff for the strategy. In addition, the collection of trials can be used to estimate the risk profile for the alternative.

There are no general rules as to how many trials constitute an adequate sample, although in many business simulations we frequently see 100 trials. Of course the number of trials may range from just a handful in complex military simulations, where a single trial is very costly, to several thousand trials in the simulation of chemical processes, where very precise results are important. The determination of the appropriate number of trials involves the interaction of the cost per trial and the precision of the simulation estimations. This difficult problem has received considerable interest and attention but will not be discussed here.

The selection of a representative sample hinges on an appropriate procedure for the selection of specific values of the uncertain quantities within each trial. In probabilistic simulation models, this selection is usually achieved through the use of a *random number generator* in conjunction with the decision maker's probability distributions. A random number generator is a device or a computer program which is, for example, equally likely to produce any combinations of two digits (such as 09, 54, 00, 72) each time it operates, irrespective of the chain of numbers it has already generated. The chance of it producing a 77 as the next two-digit pair is the same whether the last number was 32 or 96 or even 77. Such a random number generator could be a bag of 100 poker chips. On each of the chips one of the digits 00 to 99 is inscribed, and each digit appears on one chip. Whenever a random number is required, a chip is drawn from the bag, its number noted, and the chip returned to the bag. On each draw, each two-digit number has an equal chance of occurring. Technically, this is a *two-digit random number generator*. Since there are 100 possible two-digit combinations (00–99), each has a probability of .01 of occurring each time the random number generator operates. Similarly, one of any pair of these two-digit combinations (i.e., 54 *or* 85, 00 *or* 01, 72 *or* 91) has a probability of .02 of occurring each time the random number generator operates. It is therefore possible to specify a collection of two-digit combinations whose occurrence will have the same probability as an outcome of one of the uncertainties in the situation being modeled. For example, an outcome which has a probability of occurrence of .03 could be represented by the occurrence of the random numbers 00, 01, *or* 02 each time the random number generator operates. Since all triplets of two-digit numbers are equivalent in terms of their probability of occurring, the outcome in the model could be represented equally well by the occurrence of the numbers 57, 74, or 98.

In the following example we will expand on these notions and develop in detail a procedure for applying them to the development of a probabilistic simulation model.

EXAMPLE OF A PROBABILISTIC MODEL: THE WEATHERBURN AIRCRAFT COMPANY

The Weatherburn Aircraft Company manufactures a gear by means of a two-stage production process. Stage 1 (hobbing) has a setup cost per order of $1,000 plus a variable cost per piece of $100. Stage 2 (finishing and heat treating) has a setup cost per order of $500 and a variable cost per piece of $80. The anticipated average reject rate in the first stage is 4 percent (of the pieces put into the first stage), and in the second stage it is 20 percent (of the pieces put into the second stage). Rejects are not detected until the end of each stage. How many pieces should be ordered into production if the customer requires that exactly ten good gears be shipped? If the process results in less than ten good gears, the shortfall will be "hand-crafted" at a cost of $1,200 per gear. For purposes of simplicity, let us assume that:

1. All good pieces coming out of the first stage will be processed in the second stage.
2. Even if the number of rejections in the first stage is large, a rerun of the first stage will not be made until after the good parts are processed in Stage 2.
3. At the end of the second stage, all good gears in excess of the required ten will be scrapped at zero value.

Decision diagram for the Weatherburn problem

Even this overly simplified problem would require a cumbersomely large decision diagram to fully represent the possible outcomes for each of the alternative starting quantities. For example, the alternative "Start 14" would have possible outcomes such as "12 good pieces out of Stage 1 and 11 of those being good when finished with Stage 2". There are 120 such possible outcomes, and this is just for the alternative "Start 14" The evaluation of several alternate starting quantities would result in many more end positions. Figure 10–1 is a partial decision diagram for this problem.

Figure 10–1
Decision diagram for Weatherburn Aircraft Company

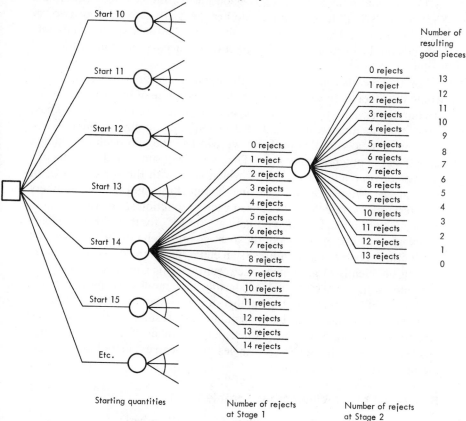

Not only is the appropriate decision diagram cumbersome, but associated with each ending position is the probability assessment for the results of Stage 1 and the results of Stage 2. These assessments are not trivial. The probabilities related to the number of good pieces resulting from Stage 1 depend on the number that are started. For example the probability of having "12 good pieces out of Stage 1" will be different if you start 12 than if you start 13. In the same fashion, the probabilities associated with the results of Stage 2 depend on the number of good parts that enter Stage 2, that is, the number of good parts that leave Stage 1. While these probabilities can be explicitly computed from the data in the case, the implication is that there are as many probability assessments at Stage 2 as there are end points, and in addition the Stage 1 probabilities must also be assessed.

The problem is complicated further by the fact that it is important to record the stage at which rejects take place. This is needed not only for the assessment of the probability distribution for the Stage 2 results, as observed above, but also for the computation of the results. With an input of 14 units and a final output of 12 good pieces, the cost may be $4,020, $3,940, or $3,860, depending on whether there are zero, one, or two rejects in Stage 1. Thus the value of the criterion for a specific outcome depends on the fashion in which that outcome occurs, not simply the final results.

For the Weatherburn example, the explicit use of decision diagrams would be difficult. In fact, this example has all three of the characteristics of complex situations in which decision diagrams are impractical. Thus, rather than dealing with the entire decision diagram and all the possible outcomes, in solving this problem we will use the approach of taking a sample of the potential outcomes. That is, we will simulate the results of a number of production runs, all of which start with the same number of input pieces. We will do this by using the reject rate and random numbers to determine the rejects that occur in each production stage. In this simulation, each trial becomes a hypothetical "future" for this problem, which is governed by our estimates of the average rejection rate in each stage of production. Each of these futures is an end point on the decision diagram. After a sufficiently large sample, the resulting costs can be averaged as an estimate of the expected cost of starting that number of pieces. Other strategies (in this example, the number of pieces started in Stage 1) can be evaluated in a similar fashion: simulate the results of that particular number of starting pieces and, after a large number of trials, average the resulting costs. After several strategies have been evaluated in this way, the best one can be selected.

Simulation of the Weatherburn problem

To carry out in detail a simulation of the Weatherburn example, we represent the rejections of the hobbing operation (Stage 1) by a random number generator with rejections occurring whenever the numbers 00, 01, 02, *or* 03 are generated, since there is a 4 percent chance of rejection for any one piece.[1] If 14 are started into hobbing, then 14 two-digit random numbers (one for each starting piece) are generated, and those pieces with random numbers 00, 01, 02 *or* 03 are rejects at the end of Stage 1. The probability that a 00, 01, 02 *or* 03 will occur when we examine any two-digit random number is .04; this is the same as the probability that any

---

[1] The choice of 00, 01, 02, and 03 is purely arbitrary. Any other set of four two-digit numbers—say, 11, 37, 86, and 92—would have done equally well, but this is a senseless complication of the process.

piece will become a reject in hobbing. Similarly, the 20 percent reject rate in the finishing operations can be simulated by the occurrence of a 00, 01, 02, 03, 04, 05, 06, 07, 08, 09, 10, 11, 12, 13, 14, 15, 16, 17, 18, *or* 19 in the output of a two-digit random number generator. In Stage 2, we would generate a new random number for each of the pieces which were not rejected in Stage 1, and all those with random numbers between 00 and 19 would be rejects in Stage 2.

Appendix B is a table of random digits, arranged in five-digit groups, which are the output of someone else's experiments to generate random digits. For convenience, the columns and rows have been labeled across the top of the table and down the sides. The random digit in Row 5, Column 63 is a 1, that in Row 30, Column 2 is a 3. Any procedure which is systematic and not biased against any digit or combination of digits is permissible in using the table as a source of random digits. To generate two-digit random numbers, we start at some randomly chosen position and proceed down a column or pair of columns or across a row, selecting successive pairs of digits.[2] Thus, a starting position of Row 5, Column 63 would give us the two-digit random numbers 11, 00, 12, 93, 82, and so on if we went down Columns 63 and 64 beginning in Row 5. If we went across Row 5, beginning in Column 63, and used successive pairs of digits, we would get the digits 11, 14, 53, 03, 30, and so on. Either procedure results in an equally "good" set of random numbers.

Since we were going to identify rejects in the first stage of Weatherburn's production process by the occurrence of the numbers 00, 01, 02, *or* 03, and those in the second stage by 00, 01, 02, 03, 04, 05, 06, 07, 08, 09, 10, 11, 12, 13, 14, 15, 16, 17, 18, *or* 19, the following simulation trial for the act "Start 14" would result from selecting random numbers in Columns 63 and 64, starting at Row 5 and working downwards:

Stage 1

Gear no.	*Random no.*
1	11
2	00 (reject)
3	12
4	93
5	82
6	89
7	78
8	69
9	81
10	83
11	43
12	15
13	73
14	91

Cost: $1,000 + 14 ($100) = $2,400

---

[2] If it were necessary to generate three-digit random numbers, as it would be if probability were measured in thousandths, successive triplets of digits would be taken from the table.

One piece is rejected in Stage 1 (gear no. 2), so 13 pieces are put into the second stage, and 13 new random numbers (one for each piece entering Stage 2) are generated by continuing down Columns 63 and 64.

Stage 2

Gear no.	*Random no.*
1	46
2	(rejected in stage 1)
3	21
4	34
5	69
6	34
7	57
8	51
9	37
10	85
11	01 (reject)
12	27
13	38
14	78

Cost: $500 + 13 ($80) = $1,540

The result of this one simulation trial for 14 starting pieces is 12 pieces good, with one reject in each stage, and a total cost of $3,940. This is one of the end points in the decision diagram given in Figure 10–1. To estimate the expected cost of "Start 14," many more trials (samples) would have to be performed and the results averaged. In this larger sample, many of the other possible end positions would occur; in fact, the particular one experienced in this example may even reoccur. For a very large sample, the percentage of times a particular end point appears is approximately the same as the probability of occurrence that would be used in the decision diagram. This is very much like the repeated flipping of a coin to simulate an event whose probability is .50. After many flips, approximately 50 percent of the occurrences would be heads (or equivalently whatever outcome is associated with heads).

Interpreting the results of the Weatherburn simulation

Since simulation is a technique based on taking a sample of the possible outcomes of a strategy, we must be careful in our interpretation of simulation results. The basic question we must ask is whether the sample is large enough to ensure us that the conclusions we draw from this particular sample are not due to the vagaries of an unusual sample. Suppose we were to make 20 trials of the strategy "Start 14". How representative are these 20 examples? One way to answer this is to take several sets through 20 trials and compare the results. Table 10–2 shows the results of five separate sets of trials.

Table 10–2
Simulation results for 14 pieces put into production (five runs of 20 trials)

Trial no.	Rejects in Stage 1	Pieces out of Stage 1	Rejects in Stage 2	Pieces out of Stage 2	Pieces short	
Run 1						
1	0	14	2	12	0	$4,020
2	0	14	3	11	0	4,020
3	1	13	3	10	0	3,940
4	2	12	4	8	2	6,260
5	1	13	3	10	0	3,940
6	0	14	2	12	0	4,020
7	1	13	4	9	1	5,140
8	0	14	2	12	0	4,020
9	0	14	2	12	0	4,020
10	0	14	3	11	0	4,020
11	0	14	1	13	0	4,020
12	0	14	2	12	0	4,020
13	1	13	1	12	0	3,940
14	0	14	2	12	0	4,020
15	0	14	2	12	0	4,020
16	1	13	2	11	0	3,940
17	0	14	2	12	0	4,020
18	0	14	4	10	0	4,020
19	0	14	1	13	0	4,020
20	1	13	3	10	0	3,940
Average per trial	0.4	13.6	2.4	11.2	0.15	$4,168
Run 2						
1	1	13	1	12	0	$3,940
2	0	14	6	8	2	6,420
3	0	14	4	10	0	4,020
4	2	12	1	11	0	3,860
5	0	14	2	12	0	4,020
6	2	12	2	10	0	3,860
7	1	13	2	11	0	3,940
8	1	13	3	10	0	3,940
9	1	13	3	10	0	3,940
10	1	13	2	11	0	3,940
11	0	14	6	8	2	6,420
12	0	14	3	11	0	4,020
13	1	13	2	11	0	3,940
14	1	13	2	11	0	3,940
15	0	14	7	7	3	7,620
16	0	14	4	10	0	4,020
17	0	14	3	11	0	4,020
18	0	14	4	10	0	4,020
19	1	13	3	10	0	3,940
20	0	14	2	12	0	4,020
Average per trial	0.6	13.4	3.1	10.3	0.35	$4,392
Run 3						
1	0	14	1	13	0	$4,020
2	1	13	5	8	2	6,340
3	3	11	2	9	1	4,980
4	0	14	2	12	0	4,020
5	0	14	2	12	0	4,020

Table 10–2 (continued)

Trial no.	Rejects in Stage 1	Pieces out of Stage 1	Rejects in Stage 2	Pieces out of Stage 2	Pieces short	
6	0	14	1	13	0	4,020
7	0	14	1	13	0	4,020
8	1	13	2	11	0	3,940
9	0	14	6	8	2	6,420
10	1	13	3	10	0	3,940
11	1	13	1	12	0	3,940
12	2	12	2	10	0	3,860
13	0	14	2	12	0	4,020
14	0	14	6	8	2	6,420
15	0	14	2	12	0	4,020
16	1	13	3	10	0	3,940
17	0	14	2	12	0	4,020
18	1	13	4	9	1	5,140
19	0	14	3	11	0	4,020
20	2	12	0	12	0	3,860
Average per trial	0.65	3.35	2.5	10.85	0.4	$4,448
Run 4						
1	0	14	2	12	0	$4,020
2	0	14	2	12	0	4,020
3	0	14	2	12	0	4,020
4	0	14	2	12	0	4,020
5	0	14	1	13	0	4,020
6	2	12	2	10	0	3,860
7	0	14	2	12	0	4,020
8	1	13	2	11	0	3,940
9	0	14	4	10	0	4,020
10	1	13	3	10	0	3,940
11	2	12	3	9	1	5,060
12	0	14	4	10	0	4,020
13	1	13	1	12	0	3,940
14	0	14	1	13	0	4,020
15	0	14	1	13	0	4,020
16	0	14	4	10	0	4,020
17	0	14	3	11	0	4,020
18	0	14	6	8	2	6,420
19	1	13	3	10	0	3,940
20	0	14	1	13	0	4,020
Average per trial	0.4	13.6	2.45	11.15	0.35	$4,168
Run 5						
1	0	14	2	12	0	$4,020
2	0	14	5	9	1	5,220
3	0	14	5	9	1	5,220
4	1	13	1	12	0	3,940
5	0	14	3	11	0	4,020
6	0	14	2	12	0	4,020
7	1	13	4	9	1	5,140
8	0	14	1	13	0	4,020
9	1	13	1	12	0	3,940
10	1	13	2	11	0	3,940
11	0	14	2	12	0	4,020
12	0	14	3	11	0	4,020

Table 10–2 (concluded)

Trial no.	Rejects in Stage 1	Pieces out of Stage 1	Rejects in Stage 2	Pieces out of Stage 2	Pieces short	
13	0	14	2	12	0	4,020
14	1	13	4	9	1	5,140
15	0	14	1	13	0	4,020
16	0	14	1	13	0	4,020
17	0	14	2	12	0	4,020
18	1	13	3	10	0	3,940
19	1	13	2	11	0	3,940
20	2	12	3	9	1	5,060
Average per trial	0.45	13.55	2.45	11.1	0.25	$4,284

The averages for the 5 runs of 20, considered as one run of 100, are:

	0.50	13.50	2.58	10.92	0.30 *	$4,292

* The average of 10.92 pieces out of Stage 2 is not incompatible with an average of 0.30 pieces short, since extra good pieces do not count as negative shortage.

As a first step in interpreting the output of a simulation model, we will examine closely the results of the first run of 20 trials. In this sample of 20 possible occurrences, the outcome, "No rejects in Stage 1 and two rejects in Stage 2," occurs eight times (trials 1, 6, 8, 9, 12, 14, 15, and 17). Since 20 trials is a relatively small sample we do not want to jump to any conclusions, but certainly we can safely say that this particular outcome has a relatively high probability of occurring, given the reject rates specified in the problem. But this raises the question of how representative of the historical reject rate the rejections in the sample are. In Run 1, we experienced 0.4 rejections per trial in Stage 1 and 2.4 rejections per trial in Stage 2. Since 14 units were started in each trial, 0.4 rejections imply a reject rate of .029 = 0.4/14 per piece, which is lower than the historical rate. In Stage 2 the average number of starting pieces is 13.6 per trial, and of these 2.4 were rejected for a 0.176 rejection rate—again slightly lower than the historical rate. In addition, when we compare these rejection rates for each of the five runs, we notice that they are considerably different from one set to another. With just 20 samples the results are far from stable, and thus any particular set of 20 trials is not representative of the results of "Start 14." This emphasizes the need for taking a sample large enough to ensure that any sampling anomalies have had an opportunity to dampen themselves out. If we treat the five runs as one sample of 100 trials, the rejection rates in the sample are 0.036 (0.5/14) and 0.191 (2.58/13.50) for Stage 1 and Stage 2, respectively, which come reasonably close to the input rates of 0.04 and 0.20.[3]

---

[3] More formal statistical methods are available for examining the question of the appropriate number of trials, but they will not be discussed here.

If we consider the aggregate sample of 100 to be representative (in the spirit of the preceding paragraph, we should take several samples of 100 before making this judgment), we can estimate the expected cost of "Start 14" in the decision diagram of Figure 10–1 by the average of these 100 trials. The average is $4,292. The average of the samples is not the only information that we can gather from the samples. The 100 trials are really 100 examples of possible outcomes of starting 14 pieces, and thus they give us an opportunity to assess the probability distribution of the cost, that is, the risk profile. Figure 10–2 shows a histogram of the costs that

Figure 10–2
Risk profile for Weatherburn Aircraft Company (based on the 100 trials of Table 10–2)

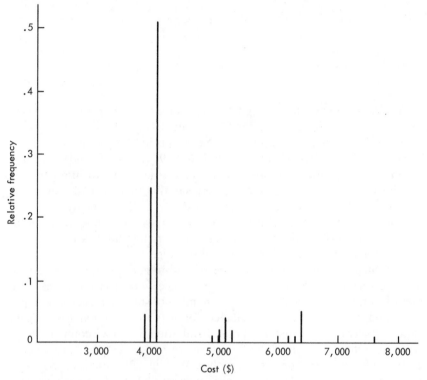

result from these trials, as well as the related cumulative distribution. Such assessments yield much more information about the process than just the estimate of the expected cost, since now we have an indication of the range over which the cost might vary and the relative likelihood of values within that range. This is the same type of information that we would have obtained had we evaluated completely the decision diagram for the problem. It should be clear that this type of information can be obtained for any variable in the model so long as the values are saved at each trial.

To find the best number of pieces for Weatherburn to start, other alternatives ("Start 12", "Start 16", and so on) would have to be evaluated using the same procedure as that described for "Start 14". For each quantity, simulation trials would be performed to estimate the expected cost. The best number of starting pieces could then be selected from among those starting quantities examined, taking into account the estimated expected cost and the estimated range of possible outcomes for each strategy.

Including continuous uncertain quantities in simulations

In Weatherburn, the uncertainty has been due to *discrete* uncertain quantities—each piece was either acceptable or not acceptable. Many problems require the simulation model to include *continuous* uncertain quantities or many-value uncertain quantities represented by continuous distributions. For example, in Weatherburn suppose that for any given production run the variable cost of the hobbing process (Stage 1) is uncertain and that the following probability assessment is available:

1. There is almost no chance that the cost will be less than $80.
2. Chances are 1 in 4 that the cost will be $90 or less.
3. Chances are 1 in 2 that the cost will be $95 or less.
4. Chances are 3 in 4 that the cost will be $105 or less.
5. There is almost no chance that the cost will be more than $125.

The cumulative probability distribution implied by these assessments is shown in Figure 10–3. This uncertainty can be included in the model in the following fashion. Each time the variable cost must be established (at the beginning of each trial), generate a two-digit random number, say 16, and take as the cost that value of cost corresponding to .16 cumulative probability, that is, $87.

This procedure is very closely related to the bracket median technique. In effect, the cost distribution has been divided into 100 sections, each having a probability of .01, and all of the possible values in each section are represented by a single value. This single value happens to be the smallest value in the section rather than the median, as in the bracket median technique. Thus there will be a slight underestimation of the cost, but the error is minor. It could be reduced by using 1,000 brackets and three-digit random numbers, but this is unnecessary.

Including more complexity in the model

The use of simulation in the Weatherburn example has been based partially on the size of decision diagram that would be required to solve the problem if we were to use such a diagram. If the situation were to be modeled without the simplifying assumptions we have made, the decision

Figure 10–3
Probability distribution for Stage 1 variable cost

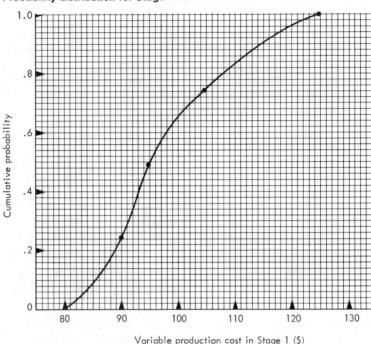

Variable production cost in Stage 1 ($)

diagram would be even more complex. One of the strengths of simulation is that it can be used to model in detail the situation under study, without making the problem unsolvable. In addition, the detail can be gradually included without requiring a complete modification of the model.

These features can be profitably put to use in the Weatherburn example. A modification that would bring the model closer to the real world would be the inclusion, after Stage 1, of a decision to make a rerun of Stage 1 before going on to Stage 2 when the number of good pieces is below some threshold. The threshold might be ten, since in that case there is no hope of obtaining ten good pieces out of Stage 2. In addition to supplying the threshold, the modification must include a decision rule (a complete strategy) for the number of pieces to rerun through Stage 1. This refinement would certainly bring the model closer to reality, since Weatherburn would never continue the production process when it is obvious that there will be a shortage. Such a change is easily implemented in a simulation model because it simply involves recycling through the Stage 1 model with the additional pieces. While the modification is easy in a simulation model, it is virtually impossible with a decision diagram analysis.

A second modification to the model that might be of interest would concern the process for making up shortages at the end of construction. Presently the model requires that all shortages be handcrafted. When the number of shortages is two or more, it may be economically attractive to rerun the normal production process, since two handcrafted pieces would cost $2,400 while the fixed costs of the normal process are $1,500 with a variable cost of $180 per unit. The analysis of this strategy would require a change to the model. Again a decision rule (a complete strategy) would have to be provided for the number of pieces to start at Stage 1, given various shortages. For example, we might want to start one more than the number short. We would then simulate the possible rejection of these pieces during the rerun. This second pass through the production model is identical to the simulation of the initial production batch, but with a smaller number of pieces. Thus it does not require a major overhauling of the model.

In addition to suggesting the adaptability of simulation models, these modifications emphasize another important feature—the models themselves do *not* optimize. The user must supply to the simulation a complete strategy, and the simulation will estimate the expected performance, given that strategy. To find the best strategy, different runs must be made using the various alternatives, and then selection is based on the simulation results.

EXERCISES

10.1.   In a group of n people, what is the probability that there is at least one pair who celebrate their birthdays on the same day? Statisticians would offer as a solution the following formula:

$$1 - \left(\frac{365}{n}\right)\frac{n!}{(365)^n},$$

but many individuals would be baffled by the complexity of the mathematical notation and the derivation of the expression. If you had an appointments calendar with a single page for every day of the year, how would you approximate by simulation techniques the probability of at least one match in a group of 25? How would you do it with a random number table?

10.2.   Using the procedure in the text, conduct one simulation trial of the Weatherburn example when the strategy is "Start 14." Where in the risk profile of Figure 10–2 does your example fall?

10.3.   Generate a set of 25 examples of the variable cost in Stage 1 using the probability distribution shown in Figure 10–3. Applying the techniques of Chapter 7, draw the probability distribution suggested by your sample of 25 examples. How closely does the sample distribution approximate the original distribution of Figure 10–3? If you increase the size of your sample to 50, what happens?

10.4. Eagle Diagnostic, Inc., a firm specializing in the diagnosis of automobile engine problems, is planning to open a new service center and is attempting to decide if one or two diagnostic bays should be built. Based on the experience at other Eagle facilities, it has been found that the service times for customers have the following frequency distribution: 1 time period (20 percent), 2 time periods (60 percent), and 3 time periods (20 percent). A time period is a 15 minute time slot. Based on its historical experience but making subjective adjustments for differing locations, Eagle feels that the probability distribution for the number of cars arriving at the proposed facility during any time period is 0.6 probability of zero arrivals, 0.3 of one arrival, and 0.1 of two arrivals. Assume that if any customers arrive, they do so at the beginning of the time interval.

    a. Simulate eight hours of operations with a one-bay facility and also with a two-bay facility, recording the following measures of performance:

        i.   Average waiting time before service.

        ii.   Maximum waiting time before service.

        iii. Average number of cars waiting for service.

        iv. Maximum number of cars waiting for service.

        v.   Number of idle hours for facility.

    b. What is the significance of those performance measures with regard to the choice between a one-bay or a two-bay facility?

    c. In evaluating the two alternatives, is it important that they be measured against the same simulated arrival sequence, or different sequences based on the same probability distributions? If it is important, which method would you use?

10.5. The local office of a national air freight transportation company maintains one pickup truck at each of four receiving centers in one of its principal cities. There is a center located in each of the city's four quadrants—NE, NW, SE, and SW. When a pickup call is received at any of the centers, the time taken for that quadrant's trucks to make the pickup, return to the center, and offload the contents varies randomly according to the following distribution:

Center		Fractiles (minutes)			
	.05	.25	.50	.75	.95
NE or NW or SE	50	70	80	95	140
SW	60	95	105	120	165

It had been found that the total time devoted to the loading and the offloading operations was 20 minutes for virtually all the pickups. The time between calls for pickup at each of the four stations is equally likely over the interval from 90 minutes to 190 minutes. At present the pickup trucks are exclusively assigned to their own sector, never traveling outside it. When a call is received, the truck responds to the call, returns to the center with the packages, and awaits another call unless one has already been received, in which case the truck responds immediately.

Due to their limited capacity, the trucks had to return to the center after each call. It was virtually impossible to fit two pickups into one of the trucks. It has been proposed that the system may operate more efficiently (with shorter delay time for the customers) if the trucks were allowed to respond to calls outside their territories. An inter-sector call would add 20 minutes to the trips if the sectors are not adjacent (that is, NE to/from SW and NW to/from SE) and 10 minutes for adjacent sectors.

a.   Simulate the operations of the current policy over an eight-hour day.
b.   What decision rule (or rules) would you propose for evaluation when inter-sector travel is allowed?
c.   Compare the performance of your new policy(s) with the existing policy.

Case 10–1

Ventron Engineering (B)*

John Warren, the Contracting Officer's Representative in the HLH project office, is reviewing the work schedule proposed by the Ventron Engineering Company for development of the Heavy Lift Helicopter blade spar.

He has been concerned about Ventron's decision to explore the extrusion process one step at a time. His concern is based on the tight scheduling of work and the total costs involved if Ventron is ultimately forced to implement the sectioning process on an accelerated basis.

Ventron's analysis showed that the expected cost of exploring the extrusion process is only slightly higher than the cost of sectioning and is worth the price. Warren feels that on the surface this is a reasonable decision, but wants more information on the risks involved.

After reviewing the elements of the project with Ventron's management, the following estimates have been agreed upon.

Sectioning is a known process which can be carried out with no risk as to length of time or level of cost. The work can be performed in anywhere from 6 to 12 months, depending on the level of effort. One month of accelerated effort is the equivalent of two months of normal effort, although the costs of overtime and shift premiums increase the cost per month to $400,000 versus $150,000.

The time to complete either material development or press modification may vary as much as two months more or less than the original six months estimate. Ventron's engineers are confident that two months is the maximum change and that the time is equally likely to be greater than or less than six months. They further feel that there is a 50–50 chance that the time will be within one month of the estimate. Since the two steps are distinct, changes in completion time for either one will not affect the completion time of the other.

Cost per month variances of working on the extrusion process could range from −10 percent to +20 percent. The following risk table was developed.

* Copyright © 1972 by Applied Decision Systems, a division of Temple, Barker & Sloane, Inc.

Cost variance (percent)	Probability of value or less
−10	0
− 5	.25
0	.50
+10	.75
+20	1.00

In considering the various alternatives, it has been decided that any sequence or combination of steps is technically possible. The only absolute requirement is that Ventron must meet the 18-month deadline.

Case 10–2

Great Western Steel Corporation

The Great Western Steel Corporation operated a dock at a port on the West Coast of the United States at which it unloaded iron ore coming by ship from Venezuela. The dock had facilities for unloading two ships at one time. The ships were all of about the same size and type. The time required to unload a ship was at least one 24-hour day, but on occasion equipment breakdowns would result in longer unloading times, as shown in Exhibit 1. Labor was readily available. When there was no ship to unload, the company did not pay for a crew's time. On the other hand, the company could go on a three-shift, seven-day basis when this was required by the number of ship arrivals.

This arrangement had worked out very well for several years. The ships radioed their arrival enough in advance so that a crew was always ready when a berth became available. Not infrequently an arriving ship found both of the dock positions occupied and had to wait before being unloaded, but it was very rarely that the delay amounted to more than a few hours. In September 1955, however, management became concerned about the fact that the approaching completion of its new steel mill would increase ore requirements and therefore ship arrivals. About 500 shiploads of ore would be required per year instead of the previous 250, and management was afraid that the ships, for which the company paid a charter rate of $1,400 a day, would sometimes have to wait a very considerable amount of time before being unloaded.

A study had been made of the possibility of making the arrivals more regular, but it appeared that the variety of conditions encountered during the voyage made this impossible. (Ships could, of course, be instructed to proceed at slow speed when normal speed would have led to arrivals producing congestion in the harbor.) A study of past records showed that ships arrived completely unpredictably—equally often at all hours and on all days throughout the year, with no apparent pattern. Exhibit 2 indicates the worksheet used in gathering observations on arrivals and dock utilization. From past observations, the best estimate for the time between arrivals of ships with the increased traffic was thought to be as shown in Exhibit 3, where the mean value of the distribution is, of course, equal to $365 \div 500 = 0.73$ days.

A study was then made of the possibility of extending the dock or of building a new dock nearby. The study showed that, using the most economical location available, the company would be obliged to spend about $1.3 million to build a one-berth dock and install all necessary equipment, such as cranes, rail spurs, etc. Maintenance of the new facilities would cost about $28,000 a year; operating expenses could be neglected because they depended on the number of ships arriving and not on the number of berths available—no premium was paid to dock crews for working nights or holidays. The life of the proposed new facilities was estimated at 25 years, and the company's policy was to make no investments which did not earn 15 percent on the investment after taxes. The construction of the dock and installation of the facilities could not be completed by the time the new mill was in operation unless it were begun almost immediately.

Exhibit 1
Unloading times

Hours	Percentage of ships
24	4
25	9
26	18
27	13
28	10
29	5
30	4
31	4
32	6
33	8
34	11
35	6
36	2

Exhibit 2
Worksheet

Time of arrival	Time spent unloading	Berth No. 1		Berth No. 2	
		Time in	Time out	Time in	Time out

Exhibit 3

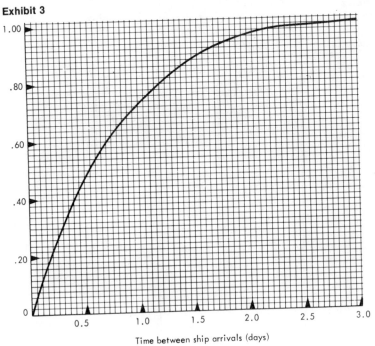

Time between ship arrivals (days)

Case 10–3A

Marsh & McLennan (A)

Marsh & McLennan are international insurance brokers[1] and employee benefit consultants. The firm is an independent contractor remunerated on a commission or fee basis. Its principal function is to assist its clients in placing risks in the insurance market at conditions and premiums equita-

---

[1] From the *Marsh & McLennan Story:* "The responsibility of the [insurance] broker is to provide for his client, through quality service by technical, administrative, and executive personnel, an expert appraisal of his insurance requirements, development of custom-made policy conditions to provide proper insurance protection, and the purchase of such coverage in the insurance markets of the world. Additionally, the broker provides during the policy term technical advice and assistance on a continuing basis to assist the client with all related problems."

ble to both insured and insurer, as well as to provide consulting, actuarial, and communication services for its clients' employee benefit plans. Marsh & McLennan's services are primarily purchased by corporate and institutional organizations which require specialized and professional counsel to assess their exposures to risk and to fulfill their insurance and employee benefit requirements.

Aircraft insurance

Early in 1969, in preparation for the renewal of coverage for a three-year policy term, Marsh & McLennan began reviewing the insurance program for one of its clients, Eastern Airlines, Inc.

Aircraft insurance received little attention until after World War I. There were no special forms to cover aviation risks, and the few policies that were issued made use of the ordinary fire and automobile forms. Initially, underwriting was characterized by a considerable element of trial and error. The volume of business was small, and values in a single risk were great. Experience upon which to predict rates was lacking. Early insurers charged high premiums, imposed heavy deductibles, and used some complicated policy conditions.

For a considerable period, insurance companies were organized into underwriting syndicates to handle the growing volume of aircraft business. Such syndicates still account for a substantial part of the business, especially the protection for the large airline transportation and aircraft manufacturing companies.

At first glance, the aircraft coverages seem to parallel the familiar automobile coverages. Each is divided into two classifications: direct loss and liability coverages. However, compared with automobile risks, aircraft insurance involves huge sums for each accident, and direct loss insurance, depreciation, and obsolescence become important factors.

Hull insurance

The specific insurance policy under study by Marsh & McLennan was hull insurance for Eastern's entire jet fleet (Exhibit 1). Premiums for aircraft hull insurance are frequently determined in a retrospective fashion and are based on the amount of losses during the coverage period. There is an upper limit on the premium amount which transfers some risk to the insurer, but generally the insurer is directly reimbursed for losses paid under the contract. There are many alternative reimbursement formulas, giving the insurer varying margins for expense and risk premiums, but Eastern was considering only two hull insurance proposals submitted by Associated Aviation Underwriters. A third alternative, self-insurance, was not being considered by Eastern at this time.

Exhibit 1
Eastern Airlines jet fleet (January 1, 1969)

Aircraft	No.	Book value Plane value	Fleet value	Insured value Plane value	Fleet value
DC–8–61	17	$ 8,709,000	$148,053,000	$ 9,000,000	$153,000,000
DC–8–63	2	11,100,000	22,200,000	11,300,000	22,600,000
	19		$170,253,000		$175,600,000
DC–9–14	15	$ 3,310,000	49,650,000	$ 3,400,000	$ 51,000,000
DC–9–21	14	2,772,000	38,808,000	3,000,000	42,000,000
DC–9–3	62	3,825,000	237,150,000	3,900,000	241,800,000
DC–9–31	5	3,825,000	19,125,000	3,900,000	19,500,000
	96		$344,733,000		$354,300,000
720	15	$ 2,455,000	$ 36,825,000	$ 3,200,000	$ 48,000,000
	15		$ 36,825,000		$ 48,000,000
727	50	$ 3,854,000	$192,700,000	$ 4,200,000	$210,000,000
727–225	1	6,092,225	6,092,225	6,200,000	6,200,000
727–QC	17	5,710,000	97,070,000	5,900,000	100,300,000
727–QC	8	5,710,000	45,680,000	5,900,000	47,200,000
	76		$341,680,000		$363,700,000
Totals	206		$896,353,225		$941,600,000

Loss Conversion plan. Eastern had been utilizing a Loss Conversion formula. Under this plan, annual premiums are equal to 135 percent of all losses incurred within that year, subject to a maximum annual rate of $1.05 and a minimum rate of $0.50 per $100 insured value. With this method of premium calculation, an incentive credit equaling 10 percent of total three-year premiums in excess of total three-year losses is given the insured if the plan runs for the full three-year term.

Profit Commission plan. John Lawton, Marsh & McLennan's Account Executive, suggested that Eastern modify its insurance program to utilize a cumulative three-year Profit Commission method of calculation. Annual premiums under this plan equal losses plus $0.25 per $100 insured, subject to a maximum annual premium of 1 percent of insured value. The incentive credit refunded at the end of the policy is equivalent to the excess, if any, of (a) premiums paid over (b) total losses plus $0.20 per $100 value per year.

When the Profit Commission plan was suggested to Mr. Peter Mullen, Eastern's Director–Insurance, he expressed some concern that it could be more expensive than the Loss Conversion plan. He pointed out that Eastern had 206 jet aircraft with a total fleet value of nearly $1 billion and an average value of $4.6 million per aircraft. If the assumption were made that one "average aircraft" was lost each year, the Loss Conversion plan would produce significant savings when compared to the Profit Commission plan. In addition, of the 206 aircraft in the Eastern jet fleet, all but two were presently valued at amounts which, in the event of loss, would produce lower costs under the Loss Conversion plan.

Mr. Lawton thought there were other factors that should be considered.

Mr. Mullen was correct in pointing out that Eastern's annual insurance premium could be less under the Loss Conversion plan provided that losses were "average." However, the alternative Profit Commission plan would cost less if there were no losses or if two or more losses occurred in a given year. Considering various possible combinations of losses over a three-year term, the Profit Commission plan produced a lower cost in eight out of ten sample adjustments. See Exhibit 2 for the sample adjustments submitted to Eastern.

Exhibit 2
Eastern Airlines hull insurance: Comparison of costs based on catastrophic losses (estimated fleet value $1 billion)

	Losses		Loss Conversion plan	Profit Commission plan
1.		$ 1,000,000	$ 5,000,000	$ 3,500,000
2.		1,000,000	5,000,000	3,500,000
3.		1,000,000	5,000,000	3,500,000
	Total	$ 3,000,000	$15,000,000	$10,500,000
	Incentive credit		1,200,000	1,500,000
	Net cost		$13,800,000	$ 9,000,000
1.		$ 1,000,000	$ 5,000,000	$ 3,500,000
2.		1,000,000	5,000,000	3,500,000
3.		6,000,000	8,100,000	8,500,000
	Total	$ 8,000,000	$18,100,000	$15,500,000
	Incentive credit		1,010,000	1,500,000
	Net cost		$17,090,000	$14,000,000
1.		$ 1,000,000	$ 5,000,000	$ 3,500,000
2.		6,000,000	8,100,000	8,500,000
3.		6,000,000	8,100,000	8,500,000
	Total	$13,000,000	$21,200,000	$20,500,000
	Incentive credit		820,000	1,500,000
	Net cost		$20,380,000	$19,000,000
1.		$ 6,000,000	$ 8,100,000	$ 8,500,000
2.		6,000,000	8,100,000	8,500,000
3.		6,000,000	8,100,000	8,500,000
	Total	$18,000,000	$24,300,000	$25,500,000
	Incentive credit		630,000	1,500,000
	Net cost		$23,670,000	$24,000,000
1.		$ 1,000,000	$ 5,000,000	$ 3,500,000
2.		1,000,000	5,000,000	3,500,000
3.		11,000,000	10,500,000	10,000,000
	Total	$13,000,000	$21,500,000	$17,000,000
	Incentive credit		850,000	0
	Net cost		$20,650,000	$17,000,000
1.		$ 1,000,000	$ 5,000,000	$ 3,500,000
2.		6,000,000	8,100,000	8,500,000
3.		11,000,000	10,500,000	10,000,000
	Total	$18,000,000	$23,600,000	$22,000,000
	Incentive credit		560,000	0
	Net cost		$23,040,000	$22,000,000

Exhibit 2 (continued)

Losses		Loss Conversion plan	Profit Commission plan
1.	$ 1,000,000	$ 5,000,000	$ 3,500,000
2.	11,000,000	10,500,000	10,000,000
3.	11,000,000	10,500,000	10,000,000
Total	$23,000,000	$26,000,000	$23,500,000
Incentive credit		300,000	0
Net cost		$25,700,000	$23,500,000
1.	$ 6,000,000	$ 8,100,000	$ 8,500,000
2.	6,000,000	8,100,000	8,500,000
3.	11,000,000	10,500,000	10,000,000
Total	$23,000,000	$26,700,000	$27,000,000
Incentive credit		370,000	0
Net cost		$26,330,000	$27,000,000
1.	$ 6,000,000	$ 8,100,000	$ 8,500,000
2.	11,000,000	10,500,000	10,000,000
3.	11,000,000	10,500,000	10,000,000
Total	$28,000,000	$29,100,000	$28,500,000
Incentive credit		110,000	0
Net cost		$28,990,000	$28,500,000
1.	$11,000,000	$10,500,000	$10,000,000
2.	11,000,000	10,500,000	10,000,000
3.	11,000,000	10,500,000	10,000,000
Total	$33,000,000	$32,500,000	$30,000,000
Incentive credit		0	0
Net cost		$31,500,000	$30,000,000

In order to prepare for an upcoming conference with Mr. Mullen and other Eastern executives, Mr. Lawton asked Marsh & McLennan actuary, Charles Porter, to evaluate the relative merits of the two alternative plans and to prepare his recommendations prior to the meeting.

Additional information

A variety of industry-wide statistics were available. Losses could be studied in detail as to type of aircraft and cause of loss, or related to the number of flights, revenue miles, flying hours, etc. In an attempt to estimate the probability that an aircraft would be lost in the course of a calendar year, Mr. Porter had found a research report of the FAA. This statistical survey had shown that the accident rate per cruise hour was essentially identical for all types of aircraft. To adjust for increased exposure during takeoff and landing, 3.7 hours of cruising were added for each flight. Thus, a flight between New York and San Francisco (flight time six hours) would be equivalent to 9.7 hours of cruising; whereas a flight between New York and Boston (flight time 45 minutes), although only one eighth as long in terms of flight time, would be equivalent to 4.45 hours of cruising.

To determine the "equivalent hours" of exposure for all jets flown by domestic trunk carriers, Mr. Porter found detailed data for both 1967 and 1968. During that period of time 15,660,000 "equivalent hours" were recorded, with total losses of jet aircraft numbering ten. While Eastern's recent experience had been much better, data relating solely to Eastern would be too scanty to provide a meaningful basis. In addition to total losses, partial hull damage (e.g., minor aircraft damage on a landing or a takeoff) might be estimated from Eastern's experience as $500,000 to $1,000,000 per year.

Information on future fleet expansion and flight schedules was not firm; but for the purposes of his analysis, Mr. Porter was told to base his evaluation of alternative plans upon the current fleet size (Exhibit 1) and an annual estimate of 10,060 "equivalent hours" per jet. The recent congestion along the eastern seaboard would eliminate any possibility of significantly higher utilization.

Armed with these data, Mr. Porter prepared to make his evaluation of the two plans.

Case 10–3B

Marsh & McLennan (B)

Charles Porter, an actuary on Marsh & McLennan's staff, decided to prepare a computer-based Monte Carlo simulation of the two alternative hull insurance plans. His objectives were to simulate the net costs of both insurance plans over the next three years, to compare these costs to determine which plan would be best for Eastern, and to ascertain whether either or both plans would provide effective protection against the excessive losses that could occur with no insurance at all.

After reviewing the information available to him, Mr. Porter constructed a computer program to simulate the possible three-year histories of aircraft losses. He reasoned that the actual losses in any one year would consist of both partial hull damage and possible total losses due to aircraft crashes. He assumed that the losses due to partial hull damage would be equally distributed between a minimum of $500,000 and a maximum of $1 million per year. He further assumed that the probability of a total loss would be the same for any aircraft in any one year, and approximately equal to the "equivalent hours" flown per year times the probability of a crash in any one "equivalent hour" based upon historical records of the

FAA. He thereby determined that the probability of losing any one aircraft in a given year was approximately 0.006424 (10,060 hours times $10 \div 15,660,000$ crashes per hour). Using these two assumptions, he structured a computer simulation program which, for each of the next three years, generated a sequence of random numbers: one to simulate the amount of partial hull damage and one random number for each of the 206 aircraft to determine if that plane would "crash." The program then added the insured values of each aircraft which "crashed" plus the partial hull damage to obtain the combined losses for each year. These yearly losses were used to determine the insurance premiums under each plan in each year; the total premiums for the three years, the combined losses for the three years, and finally the net cost after incentives of each plan for the three-year period. These basic computations formed the basis of one simulation "trial." The program was instructed to run for 200 trials, and then to offer printouts of the distributions of:

1. The net three-year cost of the Loss Conversion plan.
2. The net three-year cost of the Profit Commission plan.
3. The combined losses during the three-year period (which would be the actual cost with no insurance plan).
4. The net three-year cost of the Loss Conversion plan minus the net three-year cost of the Profit Commission plan.

In addition, the program was instructed to compute and print out the number of runs (out of 200) when the Loss Conversion plan yielded a lower net cost than the Profit Commission plan, and the number of runs when each plan yielded a lower three-year cost than the actual three-year losses. Exhibit 4 is a schematic flowchart of the operations involved in the simulation.

After checking the simulation program for validity, Porter produced the simulation results shown in Exhibit 1. He observed that the average costs of the Profit Commission plan appeared to be less than those for the Loss Conversion plan but that the standard deviation of these costs was greater. In addition, the output indicated that on 159 out of 200 runs the Profit Commission plan yielded lower net costs. This section of the output also indicated that the Loss Conversion costs were less than the actual losses on only 64 out of 200 runs and that the Profit Commission costs were less than the actual losses on only 72 of the 200 runs.

Mr. Porter wanted to make sure that he had not obtained misleading results by only using 200 trials. He therefore ran the entire simulation program again four more times, using a different sequence of random numbers each time. The results of these additional runs were compiled and compared to the original results in Exhibit 2 (only means and standard deviations were compared for the sake of brevity). Porter wanted to use these results to verify whether a run with only 200 trials could be used as a valid tool for decision making.

Finally, Porter was worried about his assumption that the FAA research data could be used as an accurate determination of the probability of a total loss. Suppose, for example, that the future probability of a crash were significantly less than the relative frequency recorded in 1967 and 1968 because of newly installed radar tracking equipment on many airport approach paths. Or suppose that this probability had increased since 1967 and 1968 because of the greatly increased congestion of major airfields and continued obsolescence of the fleet. Because of these possibilities, Porter decided to produce two more simulation runs, one with the yearly probability of a total loss increased by a factor of 1.50 to .009636 and one with this probability decreased by a factor of 0.50 to .003212. He decided to use the same sequence of random numbers that was used for the first simulation (Exhibit 1) for the sake of comparison. The results of these last two simulation runs are presented in Exhibit 3.

Armed with this collection of simulation results, Mr. Porter returned to his office to formulate his final recommendations for an insurance plan.

Exhibit 1
Simulation results for 200 trials

Costs are net three-year values in millions of dollars. The yearly probability of a total loss is .006424 per plane.

Loss conversion less than profit commission in 41 of 200 trials.
Loss conversion less than actual losses in 64 of 200 trials.
Profit commission less than actual losses in 72 of 200 trials.

	Loss Conversion	Profit Commission	Actual losses	Loss Conversion minus Profit Commission
Mean ($ millions)	22.078	20.881	20.501	1.196
Standard deviation				
($ millions)	4.030	4.721	9.104	1.431
Fractiles:				
0.001	12.91	7.60	1.96	−1.76
0.01	12.99	7.79	2.25	−1.56
0.1	16.93	15.16	9.94	−0.95
0.25	19.50	18.77	13.87	0.25
0.5	21.79	21.67	20.02	1.18
0.75	24.61	24.80	26.44	2.20
0.9	27.98	27.42	32.10	3.02
0.99	29.63	28.22	45.30	5.11
0.999	29.66	28.25	48.98	5.31

Exhibit 2
Four additional runs with 200 trials using different sequences of random numbers (the means and standard deviations are in millions of dollars)

Run 2:
Loss conversion less than profit commission in 38 of 200 trials.
Loss conversion less than actual losses in 67 of 200 trials.
Profit commission less than actual losses in 72 of 200 trials.

Run 3:
Loss conversion less than profit commission in 34 of 200 trials.
Loss conversion less than actual losses in 62 of 200 trials.
Profit commission less than actual losses in 71 of 200 trials.

Run 4:
Loss conversion less than profit commission in 47 of 200 trials.
Loss conversion less than actual losses in 65 of 200 trials.
Profit commission less than actual losses in 74 of 200 trials.

Run 5:
Loss conversion less than profit commission in 45 of 200 trials.
Loss conversion less than actual losses in 55 of 200 trials.
Profit commission less than actual losses in 74 of 200 trials.

	Loss Conversion	*Profit Commission*	*Actual losses*
Run 2			
Mean	22.004	20.944	20.469
Standard deviation	4.268	4.830	9.416
Run 3			
Mean	21.506	20.285	19.622
Standard deviation	4.195	4.837	9.583
Run 4			
Mean	22.294	21.237	20.744
Standard deviation	4.315	4.960	9.471
Run 5			
Mean	21.795	20.627	19.906
Standard deviation	4.307	5.070	10.271

Exhibit 3
Simulation results for different values of the yearly probability of a total loss

Part A: Probability decreased to .003212

Loss conversion less than profit commission in 16 of 200 trials.
Loss conversion less than actual losses in 11 of 200 trials.
Profit commission less than actual losses in 15 of 200 trials.

	Loss Conversion	Profit Commission	Actual losses	Loss Conversion minus Profit Commission
Mean ($ millions)	17.937	15.644	11.494	2.293
Standard deviation ($ millions)	3.678	4.999	6.938	1.730
Fractiles:				
0.001	12.89	7.47	1.82	−1.82
0.01	12.90	7.51	1.86	−1.58
0.1	12.99	7.92	2.26	0.28
0.25	14.76	11.78	6.14	0.95
0.5	18.36	15.63	10.80	2.62
0.75	20.27	19.41	15.49	3.21
0.9	23.61	21.94	20.79	5.02
0.99	28.27	27.51	32.53	5.38
0.999	28.41	27.69	39.19	5.42

Part B: Probability increased to .009636

Loss conversion less than profit commission in 37 of 200 trials.
Loss conversion less than actual losses in 126 of 200 trials.
Profit commission less than actual losses in 141 of 200 trials.

	Loss Conversion	Profit Commission	Actual losses	Loss Conversion minus Profit Commission
Mean ($ millions)	25.025	23.954	29.425	1.047
Standard deviation ($ millions)	3.487	3.708	10.972	1.226
Fractiles:				
0.001	12.94	7.62	2.05	−1.63
0.01	15.42	14.61	8.95	−1.51
0.1	20.40	19.57	16.55	−0.79
0.25	23.04	21.82	22.25	0.19
0.5	24.80	24.84	28.64	1.27
0.75	28.49	27.63	36.43	2.12
0.9	29.58	28.16	43.45	2.59
0.99	29.65	28.24	59.24	3.83
0.999	29.66	28.25	60.29	5.31

Exhibit 4
A schematic flowchart of the simulation structure

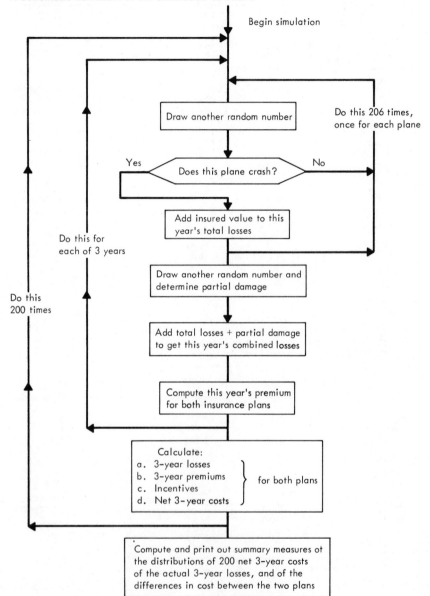

Case 10–4

Brunswick Corporation: The "Snurfer"

In mid-April 1967, Gerry O'Keefe, vice president for marketing of Brunswick Products, was trying to decide how many Snurfers he should request the manufacturing plant to produce for the 1967–68 winter season.

The Snurfer was a new item, first introduced to the consumer market by Brunswick during July and August 1966, but because of the difficulty of predicting the actual sales requirements the factory had produced more Snurfers than were eventually sold. Mr. O'Keefe was anxious to avoid the occurrence of the same situation in the 1967–68 selling season.

The Snurfer

The Snurfer was a surfboardlike device designed for use on snow. It consisted of a molded wooden plank 48 inches long by 7 inches wide upon which the rider stood and skied/surfed down snow-covered slopes. The company in its specification brochure described the Snurfer as follows:

> Snurfing is the all-new and exciting winter fun sport. Children, teens, and young adults can now combine the many thrills and skills of surfing and skiing on the new Brunswick Snurfer. It's really maneuverable, fun-filled, and easy to learn. Goes on a minimum of snow—where saucers and sleds won't go. The Snurfer is just the thing for action-packed snow outings! Also fun for sand surfing![1]

The Snurfer was produced in two types, the regular and the super. Exhibit 1 shows pictures of both versions. The regular model consisted of a molded laminated wood shell, painted yellow with black stripes, which used metal staples as foot grips. The super Snurfer was the same basic shape as the regular but incorporated a metal keel for greater maneuverability. In place of the painted finish the super had a genuine natural wood surface, included deluxe metal traction button-type Snurf-treads (foot grips), was decorated with an official red racing stripe, and was sold complete with Snurf-Wax. The wax allowed the bottom surface to be polished for even greater speeds. Exhibit 2 shows a sample of advertising material which describes the advantages of the Snurfer over other snow products, such as sleds.

---

[1] 1967 sales brochure.

Exhibit 1

Standard Snurfer

Super Snurfer

Source: Company sales brochure.

Exhibit 2
Advertising copy

Source: Company sales brochure.

The development of the Snurfer, January 1966–March 1967

The idea for the Snurfer had originated in Muskegon, Michigan, in early 1966. A plumbing supply salesman had converted a water ski for his children to use in the snow. The idea interested him, and he experimented with different sizes and shapes and coined the name Snurfer.

During February the product came to the notice of a Brunswick employee who felt that the item might be of interest to the corporation. On April 1, 1966, after some negotiation, Brunswick bought both the rights to the design and the registered name from the Muskegon salesman. The contract involved a lump-sum payment and a royalty that was based on Brunswick's gross sales of the product. The royalty was not to become effective, however, until a set number of Snurfers had been sold.

Following the signing of the contract, the Brunswick engineers commenced a careful study aimed at optimizing the shape of the Snurfer. Many samples were made, and field tests were conducted on the rapidly disappearing snow fields. By the end of April the design had been finalized and the engineers were ready to turn the project over to the production personnel.

While the engineers had been working on the design, Noel Biery, a product manager, and Mr. O'Keefe, the marketing vice president, had been attempting to determine the size of the potential market and to settle upon channels of distribution. Because the product had been proved to be more readily usable by children than adults, Brunswick had decided to distribute the product through toy channels. After making rather slow progress with the local toy stores and jobbers, the decision was made to show the Snurfer at the New York Toy Show in late March. Only one prototype Snurfer was available at that time, yet the response at the show was encouraging. During the show, manufacturers' representatives covering 38 states were appointed. The product at this time, which consisted of only a single model (which later became the regular), was sold at a factory price of $3.60 with a suggested retail price of $5.95. During the second week in April engineering prototypes together with specification sheets were sent to all representatives and Brunswick asked them to sound out the market and push for orders during the remainder of April.

By the end of April, Mr. O'Keefe had to decide whether or not to continue with Snurfer and, if so, to decide how many units he would order from the factory. The Brunswick production people were insistent that if the units were to be produced in time for the winter selling season, they must have the firm annual production requirements for the Snurfer by the end of April. With only one firm order for 3,000 units, Mr. O'Keefe decided to go ahead with the project and ordered 60,000 units from the factory for delivery during the 1966–67 winter season. Fifty thousand units were to be the regular Snurfer, and 10,000 units the super.

The tooling, capable of producing up to 150,000 units, was ordered at a cost of $50,000, and production was scheduled to commence in early September.

By June no further orders of note had been received and both Mr. Biery and Mr. O'Keefe became concerned as to what action should be taken. Brunswick's own full-time representative in New York was asked to investigate the reasons why the Snurfer was not being sold. With this assignment, and a Snurfer in hand, he visited several sporting goods stores, as distinct from toy stores, and found the reaction to be very good. By July Mr. Biery realized that the original decision to sell through toy jobbers and manufacturers' representatives had probably been a mistake; consequently the original distribution channels were closed down and Brunswick made an all-out effort to generate interest through its own dealer salespersons. However, by this time most sporting goods stores had completed their winter buying, and although a good reaction was forthcoming, many stores were unwilling to order in quantity for the current season because of the late date. During August the decision was made to retrench, and the factory managed to cut back production from 60,000 to just over 50,000 units. In addition the product mix between regulars and supers was changed.

The total number of Snurfers sold during the 1966–67 season reached only 35,000 units, with the ratio between supers and regulars being approximately 60:40. By mid-March 1967 there were nearly 17,000 Snurfers in inventory, consisting of 12,000 regulars and 5,000 supers.

The production decision—April 1967

Because of the difficulties and setbacks that they had experienced during 1966, Mr. O'Keefe and Mr. Biery were anxious to ensure that the plans for 1967 were firmly based on what they had already learned.

In reviewing the situation, they had reason to believe that most of the early problems had arisen from their decision to class the Snurfer as a toy. Experience had shown that a considerable degree of skill could be developed by Snurfer enthusiasts and that speeds in excess of 30 miles per hour were attainable. This fact, coupled with the good, although somewhat late, response received from the sporting goods shops, suggested that by careful distribution and promotion 1967 sales were potentially well in excess of the 1966 predictions. Although both Mr. Biery and Mr. O'Keefe were convinced that the immediate prospects for the Snurfer were excellent, they were uncertain as to the actual market demand for the coming year and as to the share of this market that would be taken by the super Snurfer. They were certain, however, that in order to maximize the overall profitability of the product they would have to estimate the size of the production order in a careful and systematic manner. The factory order for the 1967–68 production run had to be in the hands of the production people by the end of April.

As a first step in determining this quantity, Mr. Biery decided to review the new cost estimates for the two Snurfer models. The production department advised him that the existing tooling, which had been purchased at a cost of $50,000, was in good shape and would be capable of producing a total of 150,000 units/year in any mix of models. To produce anywhere between 150,000 and 200,000 units would require an additional $15,000 of tooling. To increase the production above 200,000 units/year would require yet another $55,000. This latter step-up in tooling would allow the factory to produce up to 500,000 Snurfers a year. In calculating costs, Mr. Biery planned to amortize tooling completely during the year in which it was ordered.

After consultation with the salespeople it had been decided to sell the Snurfers in 1967 at an average price from the factory (quantity discounts were involved) of $4.30 for the regular and $5.50 for the super. Brunswick's direct costs for these items were $2.50 and $3.20, respectively. In addition to direct costs Mr. Biery estimated that 9 percent of the gross margin for both models would be required for selling expenses, royalties, and discounts, while a further 3 percent would be allocated to advertising and promotion. In addition there would be a penalty for overproduction in the form of an inventory-carrying cost that was charged at the rate of 2 percent per month, based on Brunswick's direct costs. Mr. Biery estimated that any excess inventory could be considered as being carried for an average of six months.

Having outlined the costs involved, Mr. Biery turned his attention to the question of demand. Although he was uncertain as to what figure he should choose, he believed it unlikely that there would be any major intrusion into the 1967 market from competitive manufacturers. In addition he realized that the Snurfer was something of a novelty item, and, as such, might follow the trend of the skateboard or the hula hoop, with sales rising extremely rapidly for one or two years and then tailing off just as quickly. Because of the extreme uncertainty arising from these factors he determined to concentrate solely on the demand for the 1967–68 season.

To help in ascertaining the demand, he called on Mr. O'Keefe, and together they considered the possible sales figures for Brunswick's Snurfers. They finally decided that the median demand was 150,000 units. They were certain that the demand would not be below 50,000 or above 300,000 units, and they believed that there was one chance in four that demand would be at least 190,000 units and that there were three chances in four that the demand would be at least 125,000 units.

In order to decide on what quantity of units to order from the factory Mr. O'Keefe felt that they should estimate how this demand would be broken down between the super and regular Snurfers. This was necessary because the factory had to order raw materials well in advance, and he didn't want to be left carrying regular Snurfers in inventory while the market was demanding supers, or vice versa. Both Mr. Biery and Mr. O'Keefe believed that this breakdown of demand between models was independent of the overall level of demand. They reasoned that the consumer would purchase either the regular or the super entirely on the basis of each one's distinctive selling features and that this decision as to which to purchase would in no way be influenced by the total number of Snurfers being sold.

Mr. O'Keefe and Mr. Biery agreed that in their judgment there was a 50 percent probability that the super model would account for at least a 40 percent slice of the total demand. They felt almost positive that the proportion preferring the super model would not be below 30 percent or above 60 percent. They further concluded that there was one chance in four that the proportion preferring the super model would be below 36 percent and one chance in four that it would be above 45 percent of the total demand for Snurfers.

Case 10—5A

Green Cap and Closure Company (A)

On December 11, 1967, the executive committee on the Green Cap and Closure Company met to discuss the possible introduction of a new plastic-lined cap for the ale bottling industry. Mr. Harrison E. White, the new products manager, met with the committee in an advisory capacity.

Green was a medium-sized firm which produced and marketed bottle caps and closures for the food and beverage processing industry. The 35-year-old company was the third largest cap and closure producer in the United States, with estimated 1967 sales of $25 million, or about 10 percent of the total cap and closure market.

The cap and closure industry

The largest cap and closure producer in 1967 was the Roberts Cap Company, with 40 percent of the market; next were the Montgomery Manufacturing Company (30 percent) and Green (10 percent). Fifteen smaller companies accounted for the remaining 20 percent of the market.

Caps and closures were classified as either standard or special. For a cap or closure to be considered standard it had to be used on standard capping equipment for standardized containers or bottles filled with contents which did not react with the standard cap materials. If any of these conditions were not met, the cap or closure was considered a special item.

The standard cap market was characterized by high volume and low profits. For example, in 1966 these items had constituted 70 percent of Green's unit volume but only 50 percent of dollar sales and 20 percent of net profits. The standard cap purchasers were extremely price conscious. Moreover, entry into the market was very easy; in fact, all that was needed to sell standard caps was a cap punch and a salesman.

The special cap market was split between two types of companies: innovators and copiers. The innovators spent considerable time and money learning about the requirements of their customers and designing new products to meet those requirements. To carry on this product innovation successfully required an experienced technical staff and large amounts of capital. Green estimated that it took an average of three years and $250,000 in research and development for each new product developed. On the other hand, copying a special product required no investment in research and development and a minimum of sales engineering activity.

To compensate for this difference in investment, the customer was usually willing to pay a somewhat higher price to the firm which had developed a product to the customer's specifications. This customer loyalty was not sufficient, however, to allow the innovator to charge arbitrarily high prices. Therefore, in introducing a new product, an innovator tried to set a price which was low enough to discourage copiers from undercutting and entering the market. (Even for the rare patentable cap or closure, the innovator avoided excessively high profit margins because these would encourage other companies to do research and development to bring out improved competitive products.)

Green's new ale cap

The executive committee was discussing an ale bottle cap with a new plastic liner on which the company had already spent $235,000 for research and sales engineering (of which $100,000 would be capitalized at the end of 1967).

The impetus for starting the research effort on this cap had been the introduction by the Roberts Company in 1964 of a new ale cap which had been such an improvement over Green's old ale cap that it had reduced Green's sales to the ale industry almost to zero. The executive committee had decided at that time that copying Roberts' cap would not be profitable and so had started a development program for a cap of their own.

Mr. White, the new products manager, believed that Roberts had not done any development work on ale caps over the past three years. Moreover, particularly because Roberts and Green had dominated the ale market for some time, Mr. White felt it extremely unlikely that any of the other cap and closure companies would try to break into the ale-cap market with developments of their own. He recommended that if the executive committee did decide to introduce the new product, the price be set at $235 per thousand dozen, the same price that Roberts charged for its ale cap. He felt that a lower price would be interpreted by Roberts as a break from the usual pattern of competing in the special closures field on the basis of product features rather than price, and he worried that Roberts might retaliate by cutting prices on other products. A price higher than $235, on the other hand, would attract copiers.

Market for the new product

Mr. White estimated that total industry sales for 1967 would total 9,700 thousand dozen, and he forecast 1968 sales at 10,000 thousand dozen. He believed that the cap was good enough to capture about 70 percent of the market: "Of course, even though we've worked with the customers and think we know what they want, introducing a new product is still a bit risky. We can't be sure that the customers will buy—although the degree of customer acceptance is pretty well established by the end of the first year after introduction. The first year there is some delay in customer acceptance, but there are also customers who try the cap once and don't adopt it, so the 70 percent figure is probably good for the first year, too."

"A 70 percent market share certainly sounds attractive," said Mr. Kenneth Lindstrom, chairman of the committee, "but how long do you think we can keep it?"

Mr. White responded, "The thing that worries me most is that, as unlikely as it sounds right now, the market for our cap might disappear completely. I understand that several of the chemical companies are trying to develop a plastic bottle with a break-off top. So far they've been unsuccessful because the prolonged contact with the plastic affects the taste of the ale, but they may be able to overcome that problem one of these days. I'm sure the market will disappear, one way or another, within ten years or so."

Mr. Lindstrom said, "I appreciate the problems of predicting the time of obsolescence, but that's certainly not our problem. Surely, if we were to get the 70 percent share which you predict, Harrison, you wouldn't expect the competition just to sit on their hands and do nothing about it would you?"

Mr. White replied, "Certainly not. I think the $235 price will protect us pretty well from copiers, but there is still Roberts to worry about. I think that what they do will depend on how successful we are. If we do achieve a 70 percent share—and remember, that figure's just my best guess and by no means a certainty—I estimate that Roberts would have a competing product on the market in five years. If we had a bust, with only 20 percent of the market on this new product, I wouldn't expect them to enter the market with a new product for ten years (if the market lasts that long). And, of course, if we take the whole market now, you can be sure that Roberts will go to work on a new cap immediately—and I'd guess they'd have one on the market in two years. Again, I'm not certain about these figures; I could be off by a year or two in either direction.

"Another thing about a new Roberts product is that we aren't sure how good it would be and, therefore, what fraction of our share it would take away. I'd bet even money that we'd keep 35 percent or so of our original share—although we might keep as much as 85 percent of what we started with, or we might lose the whole market.

"Also, remember that the total market for ale caps is likely to keep growing over the next ten years—or as long as the market lasts. Our planning people predict about 1.8 percent growth per year, but they admit that growth could conceivably be less than 1 percent or even as high as 5 percent."

Production equipment for the new cap

Mr. Lindstrom next called on Mr. Jonathan Morgan, the factory manager, to discuss the production of the new product. Mr. Morgan reported that the only equipment on the market which would be capable of producing and packaging the new ale cap was a Gordon Model K semiautomatic cap punch. Some modification of the machine would be necessary for production of the new cap, but then no other equipment would be required to make or package the new product. The total cost of the equipment, including delivery, installation and modification, would be $280,000.

The Gordon machine could produce and package 8 million dozens of caps a year if operated eight hours per day, including an allowance for expected breakdowns. (This schedule amounted to 2,000 regular hours per year.) The machine required a team of four men, each of whom would be paid $2.50 per hour. Mr. Morgan believed that the machine operators could be moved to other jobs when they were not needed for ale-cap manufacture. He also said that although the factory used overtime only infrequently, there was no reason why overtime couldn't be used to increase the workday to 12 hours, allowing a maximum total yearly production of 12 million dozen caps. He was certain that even if the maximum overtime were used for machine operation, the other work on the caps (primarily inspection and packaging) could be done during the normal workday. Workers were paid time and a half for overtime.

The cost accounting department had provided the following factory cost estimate (per thousand dozen) for caps produced on the Gordon machine at its capacity speed:

Direct materials		$180.00
Direct labor:		
Gordon machine operation	$2.50	
Other (primarily inspection and packaging)	2.00	
Total direct labor		4.50
Overhead: 100 percent of direct labor		4.50
Total factory cost		$189.00

Mr. Morgan reported that the purchasing department had told him that these cost estimates assumed that Green would be able to take full advantage of quantity discounts on some of the raw materials for the caps. If sales were to fall below 5 million dozen per year, the discounts would not be available and materials costs would increase to $183 per thousand dozen.

When asked about maintenance expenses for the Gordon machine, Mr. Morgan estimated that $6,000 would be required yearly for maintenance labor and that $10,000 would be required for maintenance materials and molds, assuming production of 8 million dozen. Of these amounts, $2,000 for labor and $2,000 for materials were fixed and the remaining sums were variable with production.

The 100 percent overhead rate was based on the relationship of overhead costs to direct labor costs in 1967. Exhibit 1 gives the breakdown of these overhead costs for 1967, including a classification of the costs by the accounting department. Mr. Morgan presented the committee with the overhead budget he had prepared for 1968 (Exhibit 2).

In 1967, the company was using a 10 percent of sales figure for research, selling, and administrative expenses; of this amount, 4 percent of the selling price was paid in sales commissions.

Green used the sum-of-the-year digits method for depreciation; it was required to depreciate equipment over no less than seven years. The Gordon machine would have a physical life of at least ten years, but once modified to produce the new cap, it would not be useful for any other purposes and, in fact, it was not expected to have a salvage value in excess of the cost of dismantling and removing it.

Finally, Mr. Jones, the treasurer, reminded the committee that new products or expanded production of old ones required additional working capital. He estimated that working capital would have to be 20 percent of sales, an amount which he felt should be considered as part of the investment. He added that the company was using a 15 percent (after taxes) hurdle rate on its investments for the next ten-year planning period and that it used a 48 percent tax rate in its investment calculations.

Exhibit 1
Breakdown of overhead expense for year ending December 31, 1967

	Amount (in thousands)	Classification
Supervision	$ 700	Variable
Indirect labor	300	Variable
Maintenance labor	500	Semivariable
Unemployment compensation, social security, pensions	1,300	Variable
Maintenance materials and molds	700	Semivariable
Supplies, heat, light and power	800	Variable
Depreciation	700	Fixed
Total overhead expense	$5,000	

Exhibit 2
Budget of overhead expenses for 1968

Class of expense	Budgeted amount at expected level of production for factory (all products)	Additional amount for each $100 of direct labor
Supervision	$ 700,000	$14
Indirect labor	300,000	6
Unemployment compensation, etc.	1,300,000*	24

Class of expense	Budgeted amount at expected level of production for factory	Additional amount for each 1,000 dozen caps
Supplies, heat, light and power	$ 800,000	$ 4.00
Depreciation	700,000	0
Maintenance labor	500,000	0.50
Maintenance materials and molds	700,000	1.00

* Twenty percent of total labor (direct labor, indirect labor, supervision, and sales commissions).

Exhibit 3

GREEN CAP AND CLOSURE COMPANY
Projected Balance Sheet
As of December 31, 1967
(in thousands)

Assets

Cash and marketable securities	$2,500	
Accounts receivable	2,500	
Inventories	5,000	
Total Current Assets		$10,000
Land..	$ 500	
Buildings, machinery, and equipment—cost $9,500		
Less: Reserve for depreciation 5,000		
Buildings, machinery, and equipment—net	4,500	
Development expenses	500	
		5,500
Total Assets		$15,500

Liabilities and Net Worth

Notes payable	$ 500	
Accounts payable	1,000	
Other accruals	1,000	
Total Current Liabilities		$ 2,500
Long-term bonds		2,500
Total Liabilities		$ 5,000
Common stock	$2,500	
Retained earnings	8,000	
Total Net Worth..........................		10,500
Total Liabilities and Net Worth		$15,500

Exhibit 4

GREEN CAP AND CLOSURE COMPANY
Projected Income Statement
For Year Ending December 31, 1967
(in thousands)

Net Sales		$25,000
Cost of Goods Sold:		
Beginning inventories.................................	$ 4,500	
Plus:		
Materials purchases	10,000	
Direct labor	5,000	
Overhead expense.................................	5,000	
	$24,500	
Less: Ending inventories.............................	5,000	
Cost of goods sold		19,500
Gross Profit		$ 5,500
Research, Selling, Administrative, and Interest Expenses:		
Research expense	$ 250	
Sales expense...	1,340	
Administrative expense	730	
Interest expense	180	
Total Research, Selling, Administrative, and Interest Expenses..		2,500
Net profits before taxes...............................		$ 3,000
Taxes		1,500
Net profits after taxes		$ 1,500
Dividends declared		500
Net Addition to Retained Earnings		$ 1,000

Case 10–5B

Green Cap and Closure Company (B)

To help the executive committee of the Green Cap and Closure Company decide on whether to introduce a new plastic-lined cap for the ale bottling industry, Mr. Harrison White, the new products manager, had engaged a consultant to develop a mathematical model of the problem. After listening to the discussion at the executive committee meeting on December 1, the consultant had suggested simulation on a computer as an appropriate way to analyze the problem. Working with the accounting department and with Mr. Morgan, the factory manager, he had prepared the summary of accounting information given in Exhibit 1. He had then had a long meeting with Mr. White to discuss the uncertainties which were relevant for the decision. Exhibit 2 is an informal memo from the consultant to his staff, summarizing the results of his meeting with Mr. White.

Exhibit 1
Summary of costs (per thousand dozen caps)

1.	Selling price	$235.00
2.	Sales commissions (4 percent)	9.40
3.	Gordon machine operation	
	Regular time (up to 8,000 thousand)	2.50
	Overtime	3.75
4.	Other direct labor	2.00
5.	Supervision (14 percent of total labor)	0.63
6.	Indirect labor (6 percent of total labor)	0.27
7.	Maintenance labor	0.50
	(Plus $2,000/year fixed)	
8.	Unemployment compensation, etc. (20 percent of items 2–7)	
9.	Direct materials	
	Less than 5,000 dozen	183.00
	More than 5,000 dozen	180.00
10.	Supplies, heat, light, etc.	4.00
11.	Maintenance materials	1.00
	(Plus $2,000/year fixed)	

Exhibit 2
Memorandum to staff

We have identified the major sources of uncertainty in this problem as:

1. Initial market share.
2. Years to obsolescence.
3. Years before a new product is introduced by Roberts.
4. Fraction of initial share kept by Green after Roberts introduces a new product.
5. Growth of the market.

   Initial market share. White believes the share will certainly be between 20 percent and 100 percent, with a 50–50 chance of its exceeding 70 percent. His .25 and .75 fractiles are about 55 percent and 83 percent.

   Years to obsolescence. We'll assume that the market will disappear after between four and ten years. White and I hammered out the following probabilities:

Last year before obsolescence	Probability
5	.10
6	.15
7	.25
8	.25
9	.15
10	.10

   Years before new Roberts product. We assessed this quantity in stages. First, White gave me his best guess for the years to competition as a function of Green's original share—the first graph shows the relationship. (To make the accounting easier, we'll want to round to an integral number of years.)

Exhibit 2 (continued)

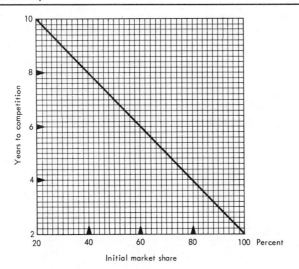

Initial market share

I've decided to use the first graph to get the median number of years to competition (five years for a 70 percent share, for example) and then to make a distribution by adding the following uncertainty:*

Error in median estimate (in years)	Probability
−2	.10
−1	.15
0	.50
1	.15
2	.10

Thus, as an example, an initial share of 70 percent gives a median of five years and the following distribution.

Years	Probability
3	.10
4	.15
5	.50
6	.15
7	.10

Fraction kept by Green. White's range runs from 0 percent to 85 percent, with a median of 35 percent. His .25 and .75 fractiles are 20 percent and 52 percent. (Thus, if Green starts with 70 percent, White's median estimate is that it will keep 35 percent of that initial amount, or 24.5 percent of the total market.) He believes that Green's new share will be established in the first year

---

* An error of −1 means that the actual years to competition are 1 *fewer* than the median estimate.

Exhibit 2 (continued)

that the new Roberts product is on the market.

Growth in the total market. White gave me a median of 1.8 percent growth per year, with a range of 0.5 percent to 5.5 percent; his .25 and .75 fractiles are 1.3 percent and 2.5 percent. I'm really not too happy about assuming a constant growth rate for the next ten years, but White has told me that growth is likely to be reasonably level (barring obsolescence) and that he really can't assess anything more accurate than a level rate.

The last three graphs give the three continuous distributions.

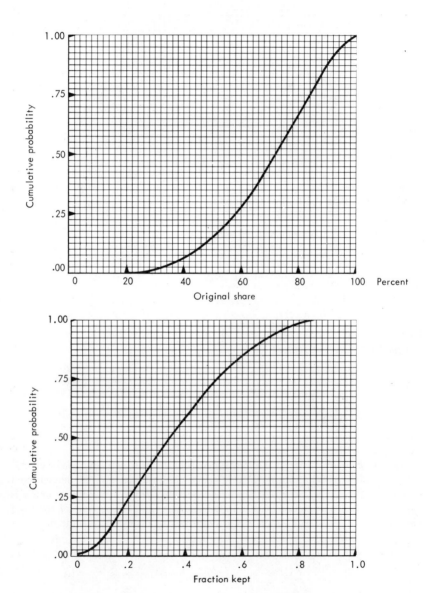

Exhibit 2 (concluded)

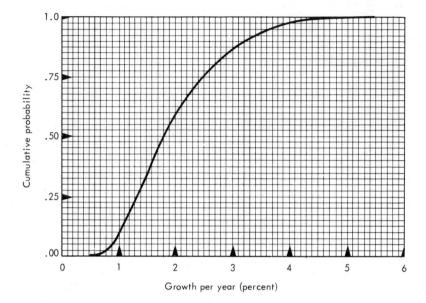

Growth per year (percent)

Case 10–5C

Green Cap and Closure Company (C)

This case describes the results of the computer simulation of Green Cap and Closure's decision on the new ale cap. Exhibit 1 gives the detailed output for one trial. Exhibit 2 gives the risk profile obtained by running 500 trials.

Explanation of Exhibit 1

1. Costs and revenues are given in Exhibit 1 of the (B) case.
2. Contribution margin = Sales revenue − Total costs.
3. Profit before tax = Contribution margin − Depreciation.
4. Total working capital = 20 percent of sales. Change in working capital is the addition or the reduction in the amount needed in a given year to bring working capital to 20 percent of sales.
5. In calculating the Net Present Value, it is assumed that changes in working capital occur at the *start* of the indicated year while profits are spread evenly through the indicated year.

Exhibit 1
Computer output for one trial

YEAR NUMBER	1	2	3	4	5	6	7	8	9	10
SALES (THOUS DOZEN)	7282	7346	7410	7475	7541	4216	4253	4290	4328	4366
SALES ($)	1711270	1726310	1741350	1756625	1772135	990760	999455	1008150	1017080	1026010
SALES COMMISSIONS	68450	69052	69653	70264	70885	39630	39978	40325	40683	41040
GORDON MACHINE OPER	18205	18365	18525	18687	18852	10540	10632	10725	10820	10915
OTHER DIRECT LABOR	14564	14692	14820	14950	15082	8432	8506	8580	8656	8732
SUPERVISION	4587	4627	4668	4709	4750	2656	2679	2702	2726	2750
INDIRECT LABOR	1966	1983	2000	2018	2036	1138	1148	1158	1168	1178
MAINTENANCE LABOR	5641	5673	5705	5737	5770	4108	4126	4145	4164	4183
TOTAL LABOR	113414	114393	115372	116367	117377	66504	67070	67637	68218	68799
UNEMP COMP ETC	22682	22878	23074	23273	23475	13300	13414	13527	13643	13759
DIRECT MATERIALS	1310760	1322280	1333800	1345500	1357380	771528	778299	785070	792024	798978
SUPPLIES HEAT ETC	29128	29384	29640	29900	30164	16864	17012	17160	17312	17464
MAINTENANCE MATRLS	9282	9346	9410	9475	9541	6216	6253	6290	6328	6366
GENERAL DEPN	0	0	0	0	0	0	0	0	0	0
TOTAL COSTS	1485267	1498282	1511297	1524516	1537937	874413	882049	889684	897526	905367
CONTRIBUTION MARGIN	226002	228027	230052	232109	234197	116346	117405	118465	119553	120642
EQUIP DEPRECIATION	70000	60000	50000	40000	30000	20000	10000	0	0	0
PROFIT BEFORE TAX	156002	168027	180052	192109	204197	96346	107405	118465	119553	120642
TAXES	74881	80653	86425	92212	98014	46246	51554	56863	57385	57908
PROFIT AFTER TAX	81121	87374	93627	99896	106182	50100	55851	61602	62168	62733
PAT + DEPREC	151121	147374	143627	139896	136182	70100	65851	61602	62168	62733
TOTAL WORKING CAP	342254	345262	348270	351325	354427	198152	199891	201630	203416	205202
CHANGE WORKING CAP	342254	3008	3008	3055	3102	-156275	1739	1739	1786	1786

```
ORIGINAL MARKET SHARE    0.728
YEARLY MARKET GROWTH     0.009
YEARS BEFORE COMPETITION   5
FRACTION OF SHARE KEPT   0.554
YEARS BEFORE OBSOLESCENCE 10
NPV AT 15. 0/0   131663
```

Exhibit 2
Risk profile

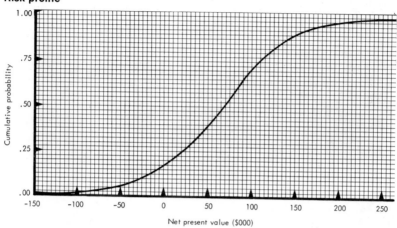

Accounting for competitive reaction

Chapter 11

Games and competitive situations

Competitive situations occur when individuals or institutions are at cross-purposes. They are situations in which there is at least some element of conflict. Two firms battling for market share are clearly at cross-purposes. So are gasoline stations waging a price war, a new car dealer and a customer haggling over price and options, a number of companies bidding for a NASA contract, the writer of an insurance contract and the insured, and an IBM representative and a customer working out the details of a multimillion-dollar computer installation.

In most of these examples the individuals or institutions are not entirely at cross-purposes, however. The car dealer and customer, for example, while at cross-purposes regarding price, share the objective of closing a mutually advantageous deal. Most competitive situations, in fact, contain elements of both mutual interest and cross-purpose. This mixture is part of what makes their analysis so challenging.

Competitive situations pervade every sphere of human activity—military strategy, diplomacy, government, politics, business, sports, and private lives are obvious examples. Because they are so pervasive, competitive situations have been studied from many viewpoints, including economics, politics, history, sociology, psychology, military strategy, and the mathematical theory of games. Depending on the administrative situation under consideration, any one or a combination of these viewpoints may aid decision making.

In deciding on which viewpoints to bring to bear on a particular situation—or, indeed, which aspects of a particular viewpoint are relevant—it helps to be aware of the dimensions on which competitive situations differ. For example, two situations may differ in the degree to which the parties have mutual interests. To facilitate thinking about competitive problems in general, it is well to be aware of the elements shared by all such situations.

This chapter addresses these issues. The first section explores the common elements of competitive situations and the significant dimensions on which they differ by describing in detail the battle among airlines for transcontinental passengers. The next section provides a framework for analyzing some competitive situations by describing how to analyze two-person zero-sum games. In the last section this framework is extended to nonzero-sum games in order to address issues of cooperation and communications.

AN EXAMPLE: THE BATTLE FOR TRANSCONTINENTAL AIR PASSENGERS[1]

Consider the airlines' battle for transcontinental passengers that has been going on since the early 1960s. The long hauls are the routes of greatest profitability, and the New York–California runs have been termed the "essence of the essence." Thus, competition has been fierce among the three largest airlines, American, TWA, and United, which collectively control about 90 percent of the market. In the days of piston aircraft, just before the battle started, TWA was the dominant transcontinental carrier. However, American, then in second place, was more aggressive than the others in introducing jet aircraft. As a result, it surpassed TWA in the early sixties, achieving 38 percent of the market by 1962. For a while TWA, awaiting delivery of its Convair jets, and United, awaiting DC–8s, emphasized services to counter American's jets. This competitive weapon continued to be used after TWA and United became competitive with aircraft. Since the industry is regulated, price competition was largely ruled out.

About 1963, TWA introduced in-flight motion pictures, and it was some two years before American and United followed suit. Later, TWA was to offer a choice of two movies. Shortly thereafter, United introduced stereo entertainment, and the others soon followed. During the mid sixties, United tried single-class service, and after several disastrous years reverted to the traditional coach and first-class service. In a series of moves and countermoves, the three competitors offered increasingly elaborate meal service, including choice of entrees or steak cooked in flight. By 1967, TWA was touting choice of seven entrees in its first-class service, all cooked in flight. United increased the number of main course choices from two to four in its coach section. Each carrier, as it introduced a new innovation, featured it in its advertising, which was constantly being used

---

[1] We are grateful to Laurence Doty of *Aviation Week and Space Technology* for providing much of the factual material for this section.

to differentiate the line's service in the eyes of the public. American was the business traveler's line, United the vacation traveler's.

Once all the carriers had sufficient jets, they began to escalate the frequency of their flights, in part in response to growing passenger demand. More importantly, the escalation stemmed from the widespread belief that the carrier with the greatest number of departures would get a share of market more than proportionate to its share of departures. This was so because many travelers initially contact the carrier offering the most flights to their destinations when they make reservations. Consequently, number of departures became one of the most competitive weapons.

By the late 1960s, just before the introduction of the wide-body jets, however, airline capacity became scarce. Nonetheless, the carriers continued their capacity war on the transcontinental routes, at some sacrifice to their less desirable routes. For instance, when American added another New York–California flight in 1967, TWA felt it had to delay the introduction of its new Cincinnati–Los Angeles nonstop service to match American's flight. By 1967, flights were so frequent from New York to California that *Aviation Week* (August 14, 1967) called them a "shuttle." American had 16 of the 43 flights a day, TWA had 14, and United had 13. Their market shares were ranked in the same order. Timing of schedules was also important; the lines constantly jockeyed with one another for the more favorable departure times.

The capacity battle intensified with the introduction of the 747s about 1970. Formerly capacity constrained, the carriers suddenly found excess capacity, because the introduction coincided with an economic recession. After load factors (percentage of occupied seats) had fallen under 40 percent, American finally tried to break the cycle by unilaterally cutting back on capacity. It hoped the others would follow. However, United stood pat and TWA increased capacity. Month by month American watched, waited for the other carriers to revise themselves, and lost market share and large sums of money. Finally, it relented and again entered the fray.

In the meantime, plane configuration became the chief competitive weapon; the "battle of the coach lounges" took place. Spurred by empty seats, in 1972 Continental Airlines removed some seats from planes on its Chicago–Los Angeles run and installed a lounge in the coach sections. The big three quickly followed suit on the transcontinental routes. Soon one carrier featured two lounges. Then came the piano bars; first American and then the others added pianos to their lounges, so passengers could gather, play the piano, sing songs, and imbibe. The battle of the lounges abated in mid–1973.

In 1972 there also was a wave of reoutfitting flight attendants, with first one carrier and then another introducing new uniforms. More moves and countermoves on food took place, with one carrier touting Trader Vic food.

Faced with excess capacity, the carriers then tried fare reductions. TWA filed an application with the Civil Aeronautics Board (CAB) for special book-ahead fares where, if the customer booked 90 days in advance, the fare paid was approximately one half. In defense, American soon filed an application for an identical plan. Not to be outclassed, United filed for similar fares with seven-days-ahead booking, but a minimum seven, maximum nine-day stay. Defensively, the others matched the United plan. The United plan met with the greatest success and finally was adopted by all carriers. The net effect, of course, was to lower the average fare collected by each carrier.

Up to this point in the battle, the carriers had been making capacity decisions independently, without consulting one another. Load factors had dropped below break-even to 36 to 38 percent; competition was so fierce that running planes through maintenance and scheduling crews was a problem. In 1972, the CAB began to encourage negotiations among the carriers to limit capacity. The negotiations started in the summer, under protest from the Justice Department and various consumer groups, and by October 1972, the first capacity reductions led to a 10 percent improvement in load factors. Starting in June 1973 fuel shortages provided further incentives to get together, and, after protracted negotiations, further capacity reductions followed. As capacity was being cut back, TWA was hit by a six-week strike, giving a major assist to the two remaining carriers. In early 1973, the carriers used advertising to vie for market share on the basis of quality of service. This was spurred by American, which was trying to recoup market share lost due to poor service stemming from a pilot slowdown in December 1972 to January 1973. Beginning in February 1973, it started touting the improvement in its service, and the others countered by praising their own.

This particular competitive battle well illustrates the richness of competitive situations: the wide variety of weapons used; the constant moves and countermoves, both offensive and defensive; the importance of timing; the uncertainty about opponents' moves, and whether they will succeed; and the great complexity of the total situation.

Elements shared by all competitive situations

Several of the elements common to all competitive situations which are illustrated by the transcontinental air passenger example are discussed below.

The rules of the game. Perhaps most important of all, there are specific rules that govern the behavior of the competitors. These competitive practices are generally agreed upon, general laws as well as specific industry regulations. For instance, the airline industry is a heavily regulated one; competitors may not change fares without prior approval of the CAB.

Potential payoffs and ultimate outcomes. There is a range of outcomes or *payoffs* that can occur for each competitor—in the case of the airlines, the various market shares, passengers carried, or profits. As a result of the actions of the competitors and possibly of events beyond their control, there is an outcome of the situation—one of the potential payoffs. Each competitor considers some outcomes to be more desirable than others—for instance, more market share is better than less. While this seems obvious, each has relative preferences for the various dimensions of the payoff: market share, immediate profits, long-range profits, cash flow, and so forth.

Outcomes determined by competitor choices and other events. Each competitor has open to it a range of potential strategies it can employ. In the airline example a strategy consists of a stance regarding number of departures, schedules, plane configurations, in-flight services, advertising, and so forth. Each competitor has some control over the situation, but it does not have full control. Some of this control is in the hands of the other competitors. American's success, for example, depends in part on its strategy, but it is heavily influenced by what TWA and United do. Furthermore, some elements may not be in the control of any competitor, such as the strike closing TWA in 1973, the economic downturn of 1970, and the pilot slowdown that hit American in December 1972.

Significant differences among competitive situations

There are also various dimensions on which competitive situations can differ significantly. The way these factors can affect the analysis of the competitive situation are noted in the sections below.

Number of competitors. The number of competitors, or distinct sets of interests, is one of the fundamental ways to categorize competitive situations. It is customary to speak of a conflict situation having two competitors as *two-person* and one with more than two competitors as *n-person,* although it may just as well be called a many-person situation. The word *person* is game-theory shorthand for a party at interest in a competitive situation; in short, one of the conflicting "sides." In this sense, a person may be an individual, a group of individuals, a corporation, or a nation.

The two-person conflict situation is the common one in which one person and an adversary have conflicting interests. Certainly the seller of a house you would like to buy does not share your interest in a lower price. Two contractors have clear conflicting interests in bidding for a construction contract.

When there are more than two interested parties, the situation becomes more complex. First, there is simply more to keep track of. Second, and more important, there is the possibility that some of the competitors might form coalitions to deal more effectively with the others. For instance, the Arab nations banded together to set a common oil policy with the developed nations in 1973, even though the individual nations had somewhat differing interests. Similarly, companies form trade associations to lobby for common interests, workers form unions, and nations sign mutual aid treaties. Sometimes the coalitions are only implicit and tacit, such as banks following common policies in setting their prime rates. Also, workers sometimes band together in informal groups to socially control "rate busters," and card players will gang up on the leader to keep anyone from amassing the number of points necessary to win the game.

When one is faced with coalitions, an important analytical issue is their stability. How likely is it that members of the coalition will break with their original coalitions to join others, form new ones, or strike out on their own? Is it advantageous to encourage or discourage this? Which group is advantageous for you to join?

Another implication of n-person situations is simply the need to recognize the number of different interests. For instance, suppose you are negotiating to purchase a small machine shop from its founders and their children. The founders want to retire and divorce themselves financially from the enterprise. The children would like to continue in its management and, if they are successful, share in the rewards. If you fail to recognize these different interests, if you consider "the owners" to be monolithic, you risk missing an appropriately structured deal which will be more in the interests of all parties—including yourself.

Degree of mutual versus opposing interest.   There are some situations in which the interests of the competitors are strictly opposed. At the end of a poker game, for example, there is usually just an exchange of assets. Since winnings are balanced by losses, their net is equal to zero. In game theory terms, this type of competitive situation is called a *zero-sum game*.

The zero-sum game may be thought of as one extreme—that of pure conflict. At the other extreme are situations of pure common interest, in which the "competitors" win or lose together, and both prefer the same outcome. For instance, in bridge the two partners do their utmost toward achieving full cooperation. Their fates are inextricably intertwined.

It is difficult to find administrative examples of either pure cooperation or pure conflict, since the vast majority of competitive situations lie between these extremes. In most situations the opponents exhibit varying degrees of common interest and competition. Formally, any game that is not strictly competitive is designated a *nonzero-sum game*.

In a labor negotiation, for instance, labor and management may not agree concerning the division of their joint profit, but both probably want to make the joint profit as large as possible. Thus they have both conflicting and common interests. Similarly, the three airlines competing for transcontinental passengers, while they would prefer gaining market share at the others' expense, would mutually prefer competitive alternatives that profitably stimulate passenger demand, or those that permit handling a given number of passengers at lower cost.

The competitive aspects of most business, political, and military conflicts can only be analyzed in a realistic way if the elements of common interest as well as conflict are taken into consideration.

Communication or agreement about actions. In the airline example, the competing carriers first made independent decisions on departures. The eventual result was that departures escalated and load factors dipped below break-even. When the carriers were permitted to decide jointly on departures, the number of flights was reduced to a profitable level.

This difference in behavior illustrates the significance of perhaps the most important distinction that can be made about competitive situations—whether or not the competitors are allowed to communicate explicitly before making their moves. If so, the situation is said to be *cooperative;* otherwise, it is designated *noncooperative.*

In general, the more the players' interests coincide, the more significant is their ability (or inability) to communicate. Where there is pure common interest, the problem is entirely one of communication. In competitive situations in which the decision makers have some common interests and some conflicting interests, communication, if permitted, plays a complex role in determining the outcome. In two-person, pure-conflict situations, communication cannot benefit either competitor.

Sometimes the competitors must take action in the complete absence of communication, as do participants in a sealed bid auction. Under such noncooperative circumstances, the analysis of a competitor's potential actions should influence the other party's actions. Sometimes competitors can communicate to a limited degree, as with public pronouncements, but must stop short of actual agreement on a mutual course of action. For example, the president of TWA might announce that TWA will match American's departures plane for plane. The purpose of this type of communication—threat, promise, or bluff—is to attempt to influence the opponent's behavior. The effect of these limited communications then enters the competitive analysis.

Finally, there is the cooperative situation where the competitors are in full communication and jointly attempt to reach agreement. Promises, threats, and bluffs continue to play a role in attempting to change each other's preferences and attitudes. However, now the adversaries, through dialogue, also attempt to create new alternatives while trying to reach agreement. This is the bargaining situation.

Before leaving the subject of communication, the role of tacit communication bears mentioning. In most marketplace competition, the law forbids collusion. Nonetheless, although competitors do not communicate directly with one another, "understandings" often develop. Price leadership in the steel industry is a good example. The kinds of understandings that emerge and their stability is an important aspect of such competitive situations. So is the way that competitors "signal" their intent to one another, without explicitly communicating. For example, American was apparently unsuccessful in signaling the other airlines to cut back capacity in 1971.

Repeating the competitive situation. Another important dimension of difference is whether the same participants will be involved in a similar situation in the future. For instance, the buyer and seller of a house most likely will not, whereas a particular union and company will be back at the bargaining table at the completion of a just-negotiated contract. Similarly, the competition between the airlines is an ongoing one.

In one-shot situations, competitors are usually out for all they can get. In an ongoing situation, they often behave much differently. All they can get is tempered by what the impact will be on what they might get in the future. If management negotiates too stringent a contract this time, the union may be more militant the next time.

Amount of information each competitor has. Information is one of the most important commodities in a competitive situation. If this were not the case, we would not see the tremendous secrecy with which Detroit's automakers treat their new designs. We would not see a petrochemical manufacturer photographing a competitor's outdoor chemical facilities from the air, so that its chemical engineers could infer the production process from the configuration of the facility and thus estimate the competitor's costs. We would not see frogmen from one oil company checking on the offshore drilling rigs of another.

Indeed, some feel that much can be gained by analyzing a competitive situation, particularly a bargaining one, in terms of exchange of information. What would you like to know about your competitor? What would you like your competitor to believe about you?

There is a host of things about which you might have relatively abundant or limited information. For instance, you may know specifically who your competitor is, or you may not. If you are building contractor submitting a bid to the city of Hartford for the construction of its proposed civic center, you may not know who your competitors are. In order to make a decision about how much to bid, you may have to hypothesize about the typical competitors facing you.

More frequently you know who your competitors are, but there may still be substantial information gaps. You may not know what competitive options your competitors are considering, much less which ones they will choose. Nor will you have a clear understanding of their objectives, or of their views—sanguine or pessimistic—of future conditions in the markets for which you are competing. You may not have information about the innermost workings of your competitor's organization, such as costs or resource allocation. (In the airline industry cost information is publicly reported, for instance, but in most industries it is not.)

Sometimes there is uncertainty about the value of the item for which you are competing. In competing for oil rights leases, for example, bidders usually do not know for certain the value of the reserves on the property. To make matters worse, some competitors may have a better idea than others about the value of the item. For instance, the seller of a company often has important information unavailable to the buyer.

Sometimes, unfortunately, you fail to have complete information about yourself and your organization. What are your objectives? Do you have the resources necessary for the competitive battle that might ensue if a particular course of action is chosen? Apparently GE and RCA did not when they announced plans to become greater factors in the computer industry and then withdrew.[2]

From the discussion and examples cited above, it is evident that decision making in competitive situations is a tricky, delicate, difficult business. In the following sections some formal structure is presented to assist in analyzing competitive situations.

TWO-PERSON ZERO-SUM GAMES

To introduce some of the key elements in the analysis of competitive situations and to put these elements as starkly as possible, we have chosen the simplest of competitive situations. This is the *two-person zero-sum game*, so named because two parties compete for the same resource; what one gains, the other loses.

Although this kind of situation is somewhat rare, many of the basic analytic ideas carry over to the more realistic nonzero-sum context. Furthermore, many people treat competitive situations that are not zero-sum as though they were. It pays to know a little about the zero-sum setting to understand what is wrong with their thinking.

We will use as examples pseudo-administrative problems in contexts with which you are familiar and will place you directly in the position of the decision maker. We use the word "pseudo" advisedly, because we have had to distort real administrative facts somewhat in order to achieve simple, zero-sum settings. First, we look at a situation in which two competitors vie for market share through television advertising. We analyze this situation only in part and then digress to consider three simpler situations which illustrate various solution techniques. We will complete the analysis of the marketing example after discussing these three situations.

---

[2] William Fruhan, "Pyrrhic Victories for Market Share," *Harvard Business Review*, September–October, 1972.

A marketing example: General Edison versus Westvania

General Edison, the largest manufacturer of electric light bulbs for home use, has as its sole competitor the Westvania Corporation. Consumers purchase their slightly differentiated products infrequently, and both brands are available widely. About three quarters of the purchases are made by consumers who are extremely loyal to one brand or the other; the other customers are not at all brand loyal. The brand these consumers select is exclusively influenced by the advertising to which they have been exposed just prior to each purchase.

The two companies vie for these uncommitted customers (whom we call *the market*) solely through television spot commercials, with advertising commitments made monthly. The Federal Trade Commission watches competition carefully and sees to it that the networks keep the advertising plans of the competitors confidential. It is a long-standing industry tradition that GE buys three spots a day on each network and Westvania purchases two a day.

The television advertising day is divided into three segments—morning, afternoon, and evening. Twenty percent of the bulbs are purchased on the basis of viewing morning advertising, 30 percent on the basis of afternoon viewing, and 50 percent on the basis of evening viewing. Whichever firm buys the most spots during a segment captures the *entire* market resulting from that period. If GE and Westvania buy the same number of spots during any one period, each gets half the purchasing audience; this is the case even if neither buys spots. Since use of bulbs is unaffected by advertising, neither company's advertising affects the size of the market—only market share is related to advertising efforts.

Suppose that you are the advertising director of General Edison and you must decide on its advertising plan for the coming month. Given the situation and industry traditions, you are in a zero-sum situation. Your interests are strictly opposed to Westvania's; what you gain in market share Westvania loses, and vice versa. What will your advertising schedule be? And how much of the coming month's market will you expect to capture as a result?

Let us speculate on how you might think about these questions. You might consider putting all your advertising in the evening. That way you are assured of at least half the market—how much more you get depends on when Westvania uses its two spots. If, for example, Westvania uses one in the morning and one in the afternoon, you will get exactly 50 percent of the market, since you have the majority of evening spots and they have the majority of morning and afternoon spots. Or, if you are lucky, Westvania will put both of its spots in the afternoon. In this case you could get all of the evening plus half of the morning, for a total of 60 percent of the market.

Your thoughts about using all your spots in the evening might tempt you to conclude that Westvania would never use its two spots in the evening. So you might decide to put two in the evening and one in the morning. That way, if Westvania puts its two spots in the afternoon, you will win both the morning and evening purchasers, for a total of 70 percent of the market. However, if Westvania splits its spots between morning and afternoon, you will get 60 percent of the market. Figuring that Westvania might do this, you then think of putting two spots in the afternoon and one in the evening; that way you get 80 percent of the market. But if Westvania knew you were thinking seriously of doing that, it might go with two in the evening—to get 60 percent of the market, leaving you with a mere 40 percent. On the other hand, you could counter their move by going back to your original idea—three spots in the evening—and thereby capture a whopping 75 percent of the market. And so it goes.

A pattern emerges. How well you do with your advertising schedule depends on what your opponent does. You must, therefore, take into account possible competitive moves in deciding on your strategy. And your competitor will take your moves into account. There is a possibility for an endless choir of "I think that they think that I think that they think . . . ." Your destinies are inexorably intertwined. How can we make progress in analyzing this problem?

Toward resolving the dilemma

There are three major steps in analyzing a game: (1) understanding the options open to you and your opponent, (2) understanding the well-being of you and your opponent in every combination of strategies, and (3) analyzing and choosing a strategy.

The first thing you need to do is get a clear picture of the choices open to you and to your opponent. It turns out that there are ten distinct options open to you and six open to your opponent in this example. Your options are for two evening spots and one afternoon spot, two evening spots and one morning spot, and so forth. Since there are 16 options for you and your opponent, you need a shorthand to list them succinctly: Let E stand for an evening spot, A for afternoon, and M for morning. Now if you want to represent two evening spots and one afternoon spot, you can simply write EEA. Using this shorthand, your options and your opponent's can be listed, as in Table 11–1. Each option is called a *strategy*.

Table 11–1
List of strategies open to you and your opponent

General Edison's strategies		Westvania's strategies
EEE	EMM	EE
EEA	AAA	EA
EEM	AAM	EM
EAA	AMM	AA
EAM	MMM	AM
		MM

In any competitive situation, you need to be aware of all the strategies open to your opponent, or your opponent could possibly slip one past you. You need to also understand your options or you might miss out on a good one, simply because you did not consider it. (Later on we will see that we really have not listed all the options open to you and your opponent in this particular situation, and failure to consider the omitted strategies can result in leaving money on the table.)

The second thing you need to do is to consider how well off you and your opponent would be for any combination of your respective strategies. For example, EEE against AA yield 40 percent market share to your opponent and 60 percent to you. There are lots of ways to indicate how well off each of you would be—tables, graphs, formulas, and words can all be used. The best way depends upon the particular competitive situation. In this case a table seems most useful. Across the top you can list your competitor's strategies, and along the side you can list yours. At each intersection you can list your market share and your competitor's, that is, the two *payoffs*.

Actually you do not have to list both your own and your competitor's payoffs, since this is a zero-sum game. If you list yours, then your competitor's payoffs will be known automatically—if yours is 60 percent, then theirs must be 40 percent. Such a table, called a *payoff table*, is presented for your problem as Table 11–2. For instance, the entry in row EEE and column EM says General Edison gets 65 percent of the market (and Westvania gets 35 percent) if General Edison follows strategy EEE and Westvania chooses EM.

Table 11–2
Market share captured by General Edison

| | *Westvania's strategies* | | | | | |
	EE	*EA*	*EM*	*AA*	*AM*	*MM*
EEE	75	60	65	60	50	65
EEA	65	75	80	60	65	80
EEM	60	70	75	70	60	65
EAA	40	65	55	75	80	80
EAM	50	60	65	70	75	80
EMM	35	45	60	70	70	75
AAA	40	40	30	65	55	55
AAM	50	50	40	60	65	55
AMM	50	35	50	45	60	65
MMM	35	20	35	45	45	60

General Edison's strategies

Now that you have a reasonably succinct statement of your problem, you can begin to analyze it in order to choose a strategy. Before doing so, we will consider a series of three simpler competitive situations that illustrate analytical approaches, then return to use them on this problem.

Situation 1: Board of directors meeting, Jimenez versus Smith

The Giant Corporation will soon have a vacancy on its board of directors, and the current 12 directors will meet early next month to choose the company's candidate for the position. Pedro Jimenez and Hamilton Smith are the only two being considered. Whoever wins the greater number of votes captures the nomination, and such a nomination is usually tantamount to election. At a subsequent meeting, the board will make a final decision about whether Giant will follow a slow, moderate, or rapid five-year growth plan.

It is thought that a nominee's position on which growth plan Giant should follow will be the biggest factor in determining the number of votes received, since the two are about equally qualified for the position. Jimenez, however, has a slight edge over Smith since he is a Mexican-American, and the board is eager to have an additional minority-group member.

You are Jimenez. After informal conversations with individual directors, you put together Table 11–3, which shows the number of votes you expect to receive if you and Smith take the positions shown. You are the Row player. If, for example, you favor moderate growth, R_M, and the Column player, Smith, favors rapid growth, C_R, then you expect to receive eight votes. Smith, of course, wins the remaining four votes, since this is a zero-sum situation.

Table 11–3
Number of votes won by Jimenez*

		Column's (Smith's) choices		
		C_S	C_M	C_R
Row's (Jimenez's) choices	R_S	7	9	10
	R_M	5	7	8
	R_R	4	5	7

* Seven votes are necessary for a majority.

You have no a priori reasons to favor one growth plan over another. Your only concern is to win the nomination. Which plan should you favor?

Analysis by dominance. Observe that you win the most votes if you favor the slow-growth plan, R_S—regardless of Column's choice. Strategy

R_S is said to be your *dominant* strategy. Your choice is easy; you would be foolish to choose a strategy other than R_S.

What will Column do? For Smith, the strategies C_M and C_R are both dominated by C_S (Remember—he likes the smaller entries.) If Smith's only concern is to maximize his own votes, and, if he perceives the situation as you do in Table 11–3, he will be acting in his best interest if he also chooses to favor the slow-growth plan. Thus, if each player chooses his dominant strategy, the final outcome is seven votes for you and five for Smith.

In this brief analysis we have assumed that each player as his sole objective wishes to maximize the number of votes received. In other words, we have assumed that both Row and Column are so-called *rational* players—that each will endeavor to choose a strategy that will maximize his own ends.

We also have assumed that each player perceived the situation in the same way. That is, we assumed Row and Column both constructed the same payoff table. Of course, there are situations in which this fundamental assumption does not hold. For example, if Smith is already a member of several other boards and feels he is too busy to hold an additional directorship, he may decide to help Jimenez win by as large a vote as possible. In such a situation, Jimenez and Smith do not have the same payoff tables. Jimenez will use Table 11–3, but Smith will construct a payoff table whose entries reflect a different utility of winning each number of votes. In other words, the entries in Smith's table must be weighted to show that he prefers to win as few votes as possible.

In our analysis of zero-sum games we will always make these two fundamental assumptions: (1) perfect rationality—each player is rational, seeking only to maximize his own gain, and (2) perfect information—both players have the same payoff table, and they both know it.

Analysis by iterated dominance.   As the date of the meeting approaches, the business outlook for the next few years is growing increasingly rosy due to unexpected events at home and abroad, and you, as Jimenez, feel that fewer of the directors will favor slow growth over the next five years. Accordingly, you decide to change your payoff table to that shown in Table 11–4.

Table 11–4
Revised number of votes won by Jimenez

		Column's choices		
		C_S	C_M	C_R
	R_S	9	5	7
Row's choices	R_M	8	7	8
	R_R	10	6	5

This time you as Row do not have a clearly dominant strategy. Neither does Column, but Column has a strategy he does *not* want to choose, his *dominated* strategy, C_S. Since every vote not cast for Row is cast for Column, Column always does better by choosing either C_M or C_R, depending on which strategy Row chose.

Assuming Column is a rational player, it follows that he will not choose C_S, so the first column can be eliminated from Table 11–4. The *reduced game* is shown in Table 11–5. In this reduced game you will do best to follow your dominant strategy, R_M, since you always do best by favoring moderate growth.

Table 11–5
Reduced payoff table

		Column's choices	
		C_M	C_R
	R_S	5	7
Row's choices	R_M	7	8
	R_R	6	5

Now, what do you think Column's position will be? Well, if he refers to Table 11–5 he will observe that he does not have a dominant strategy. However, if he notices that you do have one, R_M, and if he assumes you will follow it, then essentially Column is confronted with the reduced game shown in Table 11–6.

Table 11–6
Payoff table reduced again

		Column's choices	
		C_M	C_R
Row's choices	R_M	7	8

Now, *of course,* Column wins more votes if he favors moderate growth over rapid growth. However, you win the nomination since, in the reduced game shown in Table 11–6, you capture a majority of the votes regardless of Column's choice.

Reduction of a game by dominance is a useful first step in analyzing a game. Sometimes the reduced game can be reduced again, as in this situation. Sometimes the second reduction can be reduced still further, and so forth. This is called *analysis by iterated dominance.* In some cases, its application leads to the choice of a best strategy for each player. But usually you are not so lucky, as illustrated by the next example.

Situation 2: Selection of an advertising package, General Truck versus National Motors

General Truck and National Motors comprise a duopoly in the sale of replacement parts for diesel engines. Because of a persistent sluggishness in the U.S. economy during the past few years, replacement part sales have remained fairly constant. While neither General Truck nor National Motors has ever captured more than 65 percent of total industry sales, year-to-year fluctuations in market share have often been dramatic.

Replacement part sales have shown little sensitivity to either price increases or technological innovation. The diesel engine manufacturers supply their customers with a complete maintenance schedule specifying how often each part should be replaced. Moreover, union contracts and ICC regulations require that parts be replaced according to the maintenance schedule. Therefore, replacement part sales are a forced rather than a discretionary purchase.

Over the last ten years technological innovation has usually represented only minor changes in design or materials. These changes have not been the focus of any attempt to create product differentiation.

The principal vehicle for selling replacement parts for diesel engines is advertising. Both General Truck and National Motors advertise extensively in *Modern Diesel Design,* the largest publication devoted entirely to reporting trends and developments in diesel engines and diesel parts. Every November the editors of *Modern Diesel Design* meet with the marketing directors of General Truck and National Motors to agree on an advertising package for the next issue. Because of spacing requirements (neither General Truck nor National Motors wants their advertisements to appear within seven pages of their competitor's advertisements) and *Modern Diesel Design's* policy of limiting advertising copy to 25 pages, the editors usually submit three different package proposals to each company. Each package specifies the size, position, and page of the various advertisements in the issue.

Both General Truck and National Motors may choose any one of the three packages which the editors of *Modern Diesel Design* have proposed. While one package may offer the advantage of more advertising space at the very beginning or end of the issue, another package may propose several positions close to an editorial discussing the diesel parts replacement market.

Each firm is aware of the three packages which the editors of *Modern Diesel Design* have proposed to its competitor. Suppose that you are the marketing director of General Truck. You have just reviewed your three packages and the three packages which the editors have offered National Motors. Which package would you choose?

Several factors will influence your choice. First of all, it will depend upon your appraisal of the attractiveness of each package *Modern Diesel*

Design has offered you. Second, your choice will depend upon your perception of how well each package will fare in light of the three options open to National Motors. Finally, your choice will depend upon your estimation of which package National Motors will choose.

The choices open to each firm and the market share gain or loss which you, as the marketing director of General Truck, have assigned to each pair of choices are shown in Table 11–7. For example, if General Truck chooses package G_1 and National Motors chooses package N_3, then General Truck will gain 8 percent of the total replacement market and National Motors will lose 8 percent of the market. As we noted earlier, replacement part sales have remained relatively constant during the past few years. Thus any gain in sales for either company must come at the expense of its competitor. In other words, we have the basis of a zero-sum game—what General Truck gains (loses), National Motors will lose (gain).

Table 11–7
Payoff to General Truck

		National Motors' choices	
	N_1	N_2	N_3
G_1	−1	−4	8
G_2	0	3	6
G_3	−3	5	−7

General Truck's choices

As you survey this matrix, or payoff table, you must consider two features of the game while choosing a strategy. First, you must assume that the competition is rational; that is, no matter which package General Truck chooses, National Motors will behave in a manner which will maximize their gain and minimize their risk of loss of market share. This idea of rational behavior also points up another important feature of zero-sum games. Since this is a zero-sum game, whatever General Truck gains National Motors must lose. There is no room for bargaining in any zero-sum game, since neither player has anything to offer his opponent. (We eliminate magnanimous gestures of generosity as irrational.)

Surveying the payoff table, you first examine the matrix to determine if dominant strategies exist for either General Truck or National Motors. Since you do not find any dominant strategies, the worst possible outcomes which can result for each of General Truck's three choices are listed. In the payoff table these are the minimum values in each row—the *security level* for each strategy. Of these three minimum values, you prefer the value 0 (the minimum of G_2), which is greater than −4 (the minimum of G_1) or −7 (the minimum of G_3). This value 0, is the maximum of the minimum values, or the *maximin value*. In Table 11–8 we have reconstructed the original payoff table and have listed the three security levels

Table 11–8
General Truck's security levels

	National Motors' choices			General Truck's security levels
	N_1	N_2	N_3	
G_1	−1	−4	8	−4
General Truck's choices G_2	0	3	6	0*
G_3	−3	5	−7	−7

* General Truck's maximin value.

for General Truck in the margin. We have also placed an asterisk next to the maximin value.

You know that if strategy G_2 is chosen, then the worst outcome that can occur is neither a gain nor a loss in market share. Although strategy G_1 might result in the largest gain in market share (8 percent), strategy G_1 might lead to a loss of 4 percent.

To determine the outcome of the game, you must look at the game from the point of view of the competition at National Motors. The marketing director of National Motors will follow a plan of attack similar to the one you followed for General Truck. Since National Motors has no dominant strategies, the worst possible outcomes that can occur for each strategy are listed. However, instead of finding the minimum values for each row, the marketing director of National Motors will list the maximum value of each column. Remembering that the payoffs in the table represent the market share gain (or loss) to General Truck, the marketing director of National Motors must find the maximum value of each column. These maximum values are the maximum loss which could occur from each strategy. Table 11–9 shows that strategy N_1 could result in a maximum loss of 0, strategy N_2 in a maximum loss of 5, and strategy N_3 in a maximum loss of 8.

Of these three maximum values (security levels of National Motors), the marketing director of National Motors prefers the value 0 (the maximum of N_1), which is less than 5 (the maximum of N_2) or 8 (the maximum of N_3). This value, 0, is the minimum of the maximum values, or simply, the *minimax value*. (We have indicated with an asterisk the minimax value in Table 11–9.)

If you, as the marketing director of General Truck, play the maximin strategy (G_2), and the marketing director of National Motors plays the minimax strategy (N_1), neither player will gain nor lose any market share—the market share positions will remain the same.

This game illustrates a special case of two-person zero-sum games where the optimal strategy for each player is to select a single option: the single option is called a *pure strategy*. Row chooses Row's maximin strategy and Column chooses Column's minimax strategy. It turns out that the

Table 11–9
National Motors' security levels

		National Motors' choices			General Truck's
		N_1	N_2	N_3	security levels
	G_1	−1	−4	8	−4
General Truck's choices	G_2	0	3	6	0
	G_3	−3	5	−7	−7
National Motors' security levels		0*	5	8	

* National Motors' minimax value.

maximin value equals the minimax value; this is often called a *saddle point*. In addition, neither player has any incentive to alter its strategy as long as the other player chooses its maximin or minimax strategy. For example, if General Truck plays a maximin strategy, National Motors can only lose by playing a nonminimax strategy: N_2 would lead to a loss of 3 percent of the market, and N_3 would lead to a loss of 6 percent of the market. Similarly, if National Motors plays a minimax strategy, General Truck can only lose by playing a nonmaximin strategy: G_1 would lead to a loss of 1 percent of the market, and G_3 would lead to a loss of 3 percent of the market.

After each player has chosen the appropriate maximin or minimax strategy, both have arrived at a stable outcome. Neither player can gain from unilaterally changing strategy; the players have reached an *equilibrium point,* and the game is over. This situation, unfortunately, does not always happen this simply, as we shall see in the following example.

Situation 3: The fighter aircraft proposal, Excalibur Aviation versus Western Aircraft

For the past three decades Excalibur Aviation and Western Aircraft have dominated the military defense market for bombers, fighters, and attack aircraft. Each firm has worked closely with the Navy, Army, and Air Force in research and development projects geared to maintain U.S. air superiority.

To reduce the risk of dependence on any one company, the military allocates its aircraft demand between the two companies. It does, however, choose a primary supplier and a secondary supplier. In the past, a company's selection as primary supplier has implied a 60 to 65 percent share of the military's demands, with the balance of the total requirement accruing to the secondary supplier. Recently, the military announced that it will not be bound to any fixed allotment of aircraft between the primary and secondary suppliers.

Although Congress annually debates and approves the U.S. level of military defense spending, the effects of detente have substantially limited the number (though not the capability) of aircraft of both the United States and the Soviet Union. Since the Kiev Agreements several years ago, the aircraft arsenals of both nations have remained constant.

Over the years the aircraft division of the Navy, Naval Air Systems Command, has invited both Excalibur and Western to propose the specifications of a fighter aircraft superior to the most modern Soviet design. While the capabilities of the Soviet MIG–28 (the vanguard of their sea-to-air defense system) are well documented, the Navy's request for proposal has failed to define its basic measure of superiority.

The effectiveness of a fighter aircraft is dependent upon maximum speed and range, weapons load, and avionics gear. However, there are tradeoffs in the design of such aircraft. Because no single model can incorporate every advanced technological feature, and because no manufacturer can judge the extent of these tradeoffs until after the prototype stage, it is not unusual for a manufacturer to independently design two different aircraft.

In response to the Navy's newest request for proposal, Excalibur and Western have each developed two different aircraft. While neither company knows which aircraft its competitor will propose to the Navy, both Excalibur and Western know the general characteristics of their competitor's designs.

Suppose that you are the director of military sales for Excalibur Aviation. Your company has just completed testing the new E–11 and E–12 fighters which were developed for the Navy. Which aircraft will you propose to Naval Air Systems Command?

Even though you believe that Excalibur's fighters are superior to either of Western's two new aircraft, your choice of the E–11 or the E–12 will rest on three criteria: (1) the capabilities of each aircraft, (2) an estimation of the performance of each aircraft in comparison with Western's two aircraft, and (3) an estimation of which aircraft Western will propose.

The choices open to each company (either the E–11 or E–12 for Excalibur and either the W–7 or the W–17 for Western) and the gain in Naval fighter aircraft market share which you have assigned to each pair of choices are shown in Table 11–10. For example, if Excalibur chooses

Table 11–10
Market share gain for Excalibur Aviation

		Western's choices	
		W–7	W–17
Excalibur's choices	E–11	9	2
	E–12	3	7

strategy E–11 and Western chooses strategy W–17, Excalibur will gain a 2 percent share of the fighter market, and Western will lose a 2 percent share of the market.

Since the number of military fighters has remained constant since the Kiev Agreements, any gain (loss) in one company's market share must represent an equal loss (gain) to the other company. In other words, we have the basis of a zero-sum game.

As director of military sales for Excalibur, your first step in solving this game is to examine the payoff table for dominant strategies. However, since no dominant strategies exist, you then proceed to identify the security levels for each company's strategies and the respective maximin and minimax values. Table 11–11 lists the security levels for both companies and indicates Excalibur's pure maximin value and Western's pure minimax value.

Table 11–11
Security levels for both companies

| | | Western's choices | | Excalibur's |
		W–7	W–17	security levels
Excalibur's choices	E–11	9	2	2
	E–12	3	7	3*
Western's security levels		9	7†	

    * Excalibur's pure maximin value.
    † Western's pure minimax value.

If Excalibur plays its pure maximin strategy, E–12, and Western plays its pure minimax strategy, W–17, Excalibur will gain 7 percent of the market and Western will lose 7 percent of the market. However, the pure maximin value is not equal to the pure minimax value. If Western knew for sure that Excalibur would follow its pure maximin strategy, a rational decision would dictate that Western abandon its pure minimax strategy, W–17, and follow strategy W–7. In this way Western could reduce its loss from 7 percent of the market to only 3 percent of the market. But, on the other hand, if Excalibur knew for sure that Western would not follow its pure minimax strategy, W–17, but rather would follow strategy W–7, an equally rational decision would dictate that Excalibur follow strategy E–11, with a resulting gain of market share from 3 to 9 percent.

We can extend this type of analysis indefinitely for either company by adopting the train of reasoning "If I knew that they knew that I knew that they knew . . . ." However, before you rush to conclude that, as director of military sales at Excalibur, you have no concrete rationale for choosing either strategy, let us reexamine what we know about the characteristics of the game. We know that no dominant strategies exist and that no pure strategy will yield an equilibrium solution with maximin equal to minimax. We have also demonstrated that either company can gain from knowing which strategy its competitor will follow. Therefore, under no circumstances will either company have any incentive to reveal its strategy.

The mixed strategy. Because no pure equilibrium strategy exists, any of the four payoffs is possible. Moreover, in the absence of an equilibrium point, it might be reasonable for Excalibur to consider a different type of strategy in order to keep its opponent from guessing what it plans to do. For example, consider the following plan: You flip a coin. If heads appear, E–11, is chosen; if tails, E–12. This strategy's *expected payoffs* can be incorporated into the payoff table shown in Table 11–12. Notice that by playing this *mixed* strategy[3], Excalibur has at least an *expected* 4½ percent larger market, a higher value than either *pure strategy.*

Table 11–12
Payoff table with a mixed strategy

		Western's choices W–7	Western's choices W–17	Excalibur's security levels
	E–11	9	2	2
Excalibur's choices	E–12	3	7	3
	Mixed (½ E–11, ½ E–12)	6	4½	4½*
Western's security levels		9	7†	

* Excalibur's maximin value.
† Western's minimax value.

There is nothing sacred, of course, about a 50/50 mixed strategy. Your task is to find that combination of pure strategies which will maximize Excalibur's long-run expected payoff. You must also recognize that Western is searching for some combination of its pure strategies which will minimize its long-run loss of market share. It turns out that the optimal strategy[4] for Excalibur is to choose E–11 and E–12 in the ratio of 4 to 7, while the optimal strategy for Western is to play W–7 and W–17 in the ratio of 5 to 6. These strategies have equal expected payoffs to each company, as shown in Table 11–13. In addition, they are characterized by

---

[3] Recall that a pure strategy is one that dictates the selection of a single option. We can define a mixed strategy as one that directs the player to choose from two or more options according to some probabilistic rule which details with what probability each option is to be selected.

[4] For this simple 2 × 2 payoff table, there is an easy graphical method to compute this mix. In general, for any two-person zero-sum game, mixed strategies can be determined by formulating and solving an appropriate linear program. It is not necessary to acquaint you with the computational details of finding mixed strategies, but we want to point out that there are situations in which it is worthwhile to consider mixed strategies.

Table 11–13
Payoff table with optimal mixed strategies

		Western's choices			Excalibur's security levels
		W–7	W–17	Mixed ($\frac{5}{11}$ W–7, $\frac{6}{11}$ W–17)	
	E–11	9	2	5.18	2
Excalibur's choices	E–12	3	7	5.18	3
	Mixed ($\frac{4}{11}$E–11, $\frac{7}{11}$E–12)	5.18	5.18	5.18	5.18*
Western's security levels		9	7	5.18†	

* Excalibur's maximin value.
† Western's minimax value.

the same property found with pure strategies in the previous example: Either company will do worse if it unilaterally moves away from its optimal mixed strategy. Thus there is no incentive to do so.

Although you now know the appropriate combination mix for each player, you are still faced with the problem of choosing one strategy or the other for Excalibur. Remembering that either company can gain by knowing which strategy its competitor will follow, you must guard against any internal or external influences, preferences, or pressures which would give Western any indication of your choice of aircraft. The only fail-safe method of maintaining the secrecy of your choice and of reflecting the appropriate combination of strategies in your decision-making process is to allow some random device to make your decision for you. For example, you could place four red balls (corresponding to strategy E–11) and seven white balls (corresponding to strategy E–12) in an urn and draw one of the balls. The color of the ball will indicate which strategy you will follow. Although it may seem irresponsible to relinquish control of your decision to a random device, such a device is only a method of ensuring that your choice is made purely and exclusively on the basis of the optimal combination of strategies.

Solution to the marketing example

Earlier in this section, we began to analyze a marketing problem involving two light bulb manufacturers, General Edison and Westvania, in which you were the advertising director for General Edison. Now that we have examined the concepts of iterative dominance, minimax, equilibrium points, and pure and mixed strategies, we are equipped to finish the analysis.

The payoff table for this problem, Table 11–2, shows that some strategies are clearly bad and can be rejected immediately. Considering Table 11–2, General Edison would never want to play strategy AAA, since it is dominated by EEM; GE does better to play EEM instead of AAA, regardless of what Westvania does. EEM dominates AMM and MMM as well as AAA; and EAM dominates AAM. Thus GE's last five strategies can be effectively deleted. Once this is done, MM can be deleted for Westvania. Using iterated dominance, the table has been reduced to one in which each player has five strategies, as shown in Table 11–14.

Table 11–14
The reduced marketing game

		Westvania's strategies				
		EE	EA	EM	AA	AM
General Edison's strategies	EEE	75	60	65	60	50
	EEA	65	75	80	60	65
	EEM	60	70	75	70	60
	EAA	40	65	55	75	80
	EAM	50	60	65	70	75

Next you would analyze the reduced table by finding security levels, as indicated in Table 11–15. You, as advertising director for GE, can expect at least a 60 percent market share if you follow EEA or EEM; Westvania can expect at least 25 percent (that is, no more than 75 percent for GE) if it adopts EE, EA, or AA.

If you adopt a pure strategy and Westvania figures it out, then the best you can expect to do is to win 60 percent of the market. By appropriately choosing sometimes one strategy, sometimes another, however, you can expect to do better than this. The same is true for Westvania. The largest share it can expect to win for any choice of pure strategy is 25 percent, but by following a mixed strategy, it can gain an expected share greater than 25 percent.

Since no optimal pure strategy exists, each company can expect on average to do better than its security level if it follows a suitable mixed strategy. There is an equilibrium outcome (in between the 60/40 and 75/25 split) which is found by adopting appropriate mixed strategies. If you were to do the calculations necessary to determine the optimal mixed strategy, you would find that GE should follow each of the strategies EEE, EEA, and EAM one third of the time, and Westvania should adopt EE 6 out of 15 times, AA 5 out of 15, and AM, 4 out of 15. Then the

Table 11–15
The reduced marketing game with security levels

Westvania's strategies

		EE	EA	EM	AA	AM	Row minima
	EEE	75	60	65	60	50	50
	EEA	65	75	80	60	65	60*
General Edison's strategies	EEM	60	70	75	70	60	60*
	EAA	40	65	55	75	80	40
	EAM	50	60	65	70	75	50
Column maxima		75*	75*	80	75*	80	

* Pure strategies having positive weights in optimal mixed strategies.

expected payoff at GE will be 63⅓ percent of the market; Westvania's payoff will be 36⅔ percent.

Notice that our analysis of this and the previous example has assumed that both opponents are rational. We have said nothing about how to exploit irrational play on the part of one's opponent. It is, however, true that if you follow your optimal strategy, then having an irrational opponent (i.e., one who does not play his "best" strategy) will only increase your expected payoff over what it would have been with a rational opponent.

Summary

In this section we have taken a look at how to analyze a competitive situation, using the well-known two-person zero-sum game as a setting. In the process we have introduced the important concepts of pure strategy, payoff table, dominance, security level, equilibrium, and mixed strategy. In spite of the fact that few administrative settings are zero-sum situations, these concepts serve well in more realistic nonzero-sum situations.

In addition, we have begun to suggest a procedure for analyzing competitive situations. It consists of these steps:

1. Understand the strategies open to you and your opponent.

2. Understand how well off each of you will be for all combinations of strategies by displaying this information in a useful way.
3. Analyze the display to arrive at a preferred course of action, taking into account your opponent's likely strategy.

The particular ways of handling the last step in this procedure are quite mechanical in the case of zero-sum games. In the next section we will show that the analysis of nonzero-sum situations is not so easy.

NONZERO-SUM GAMES

In the preceding section we discussed situations in which persons or organizations were entirely at cross-purposes. In most competitive situations, however, there are elements of mutual interest as well as cross-purpose. The potential value of entering into prechoice communication and making binding agreements is a major difference between zero-sum and nonzero-sum situations. While this section will primarily consider noncooperative situations, in which the competitors may not communicate before making their moves, it will also consider cooperative situations in which the opponents are allowed to make joint decisions and the impact of communication. Threatening, promising, bluffing, bargaining, colluding, and preempting all may play a role, depending on the exact nature of the situation.

We will introduce these concepts in the context of five prototypical competitive situations. Two predominant ones are known as the Prisoner's Dilemma and the Battle of the Sexes. The others can be called no-conflict situations, threat-vulnerable situations, and force-vulnerable situations.

Games with little or no conflict

In *nonzero-sum games*, the payoff tables contain two entries in each cell; the first is the payoff to the Row player and the second is the payoff to the Column player. Game A shown in Table 11–16 is rather easy to

Table 11–16
Matrix games with Pareto-optimal outcomes

	Column				Column	
	C_1	C_2			C_1	C_2
R_1	12, 8	7, 5		R_1	12, 8	13, 5
R_2	10, 2	4, 0		R_2	10, 9	4, 0

Row (left table), Row (right table)

Game A   Game B

analyze. This game represents a *no-conflict situation* because both players do as well as possible when each maximizes his or her own return. Mutual interest is overwhelming. Notice, in this game, that by a slight extension of the concept of dominance, the outcome (12, 8) can be said to *dominate* all other outcomes. It is better, for *both* players, than any other outcome.

Now consider game B in Table 11–16. In this game, there is an element of conflict, but it is very weak. Both players still have dominant strategies, and the equilibrium outcome (12, 8) remains, in some sense, the "natural" outcome. Note, however, that Row prefers (13, 5) to the equilibrium outcome, and Column prefers (10, 9). All three of these outcomes have an important property known as *Pareto optimality*. An outcome is said to be Pareto optimal whenever it is *not* dominated by any other outcome. None of the three Pareto-optimal outcomes in game B are dominated by any other outcome. In game A, note that (12, 8) is the *only* Pareto-optimal outcome.

Threat and forcing potentials

Two similar types of competitive situations are referred to as *threat vulnerability* and *force vulnerability*. Suppose a buyer and a seller repeatedly negotiate a contract in the following way. The seller sends a written notice to the buyer indicating the selling price per unit. In reply, the buyer indicates the quantity that will be purchased at the established price. If the buyer is a retailer who must then resell the goods, a hypothetical payoff table might be Table 11–17. If each player chooses his or her

Table 11–17
Threat vulnerability game, profit to buyer and seller
($ thousands)

		Seller's price choices	
		$P_1 = High$	$P_2 = Low$
Buyer's quantity choices	$Q_1 = High$	2, 4	4, 3
	$Q_2 = Low$	1, 2	3, 1

dominant strategy, the payoff will be (2, 4). Neither player is motivated to make a unilateral shift from this outcome. However, the buyer is not satisfied with the outcome (2, 4) since (4, 3) is more attractive. If the game is to be repeated several times, the buyer would like the seller to choose P_2 to give the buyer a chance at winning 4.

If the players are allowed to communicate, the buyer can threaten the seller into lowering the price (that is, threaten the seller into giving the buyer a chance at 4) by saying he or she will only buy the smaller quantity, Q_2, if the seller does not choose P_2. The buyer's threat is effective as long as it is not carried out. Once (Q_2, P_1) occurs, however, it is not in the seller's interest to shift to P_2. Nevertheless, the seller is better off to give in rather than to suffer the consequences of the buyer's shift.

threat vulnerability [handwritten margin note]

Consider now a situation known as a force vulnerability game. As shown in Table 11–18, only Row has a dominant strategy. If Row uses this dominant strategy, the natural outcome is (0, 2). Row is less satisfied with this result than is Column. If the game is played repeatedly, Row can communicate his or her dissatisfaction and try to *force* Column into changing his or her strategy. Since Column prefers (R_2, C_2) to (R_2, C_1), Row can force Column to switch to C_2 by switching from R_1 to R_2.

Table 11–18
Force vulnerability game
($ thousands)

but how long can Row exert this "force"? [handwritten margin note]

	Column	
	C_1	C_2
R_1	0, 2	2, −1
R_2	−1, 0	1, 1

Row [label to left of table]

As you can see, threats and force are in many ways similar. The key difference is how Row tries to influence Column's behavior. In the force situation, Row tries to get what he wants by playing the strategy that leads to his best outcome, thereby *forcing* Column to do what Row wants. In the threat situation, Row must *threaten* to make a move which will punish Column if Column does not comply. The Row strategy used for threatening is not the one that leads to Row's best outcome, so Row hopes that it will not have to be used.

Opportunities for using threats and force in real-world situations are widespread. Generally, however, they are *not* obvious. The existence of threat and force potentials can be extremely subtle, and often they are noticed by only one of the players. These simple examples should increase both your awareness of such situations and your understanding of their structure. A worthwhile exercise is to try to conceive of real-world situations where threat and forcing potentials exist.

The Prisoner's Dilemma

A class of situations which are not strictly competitive is popularly known as the Prisoner's Dilemma. These are situations in which the best outcome for all concerned results when each competitor refrains from trying to maximize his own payoff. A classic example is the airline battle for a share of passengers on a particular route. As discussed in the first section of this chapter, many believe that the carrier with the largest share of departures gets a share of market disproportionately larger than its percentage of departures. For instance, 60 percent of the departures might yield 70 percent the market. Consequently, airlines have often used the number of departures as a major competitive tool, especially on the long-haul routes such as New York–California. If one of the carriers—say American Airlines—unilaterally increases capacity, hoping to increase its market share, the other carriers, United and TWA, must decide whether or not to follow suit. The nature of the dilemma is this: If they match the increase, all will be worse off, since little new demand will be stimulated, and the airlines will end up flying more empty seats. If the competitors do not match the increase, however, they will be worse off compared to the carrier that increases capacity.

Situations of this type occur so often that they have been studied in detail; in fact, a whole book has been written on the subject.[5] They all share a common structure, that of the so-called Prisoner's Dilemma.

We will first analyze the Prisoner's Dilemma in the context from which it derives its name. Two suspects, Sam and Harry, are taken into custody and separated. The district attorney is certain they are guilty of a particular crime, and the suspects know they are guilty, but the district attorney does not have adequate evidence to convict them.

Each prisoner has two alternatives, to confess to the crime or not to confess. If neither confesses, then the DA will book them on some very minor trumped-up charge, such as illegal possession of a weapon, and they will both receive minor sentences. If they both confess, he will recommend less than the most severe sentence; but if one confesses and the other does not, then the confessor will receive lenient treatment for turning state's evidence, whereas the latter will get the book thrown at him. In terms of years in a penitentiary, the situation may be described by the payoffs in Table 11–19. The problem for each prisoner is to decide whether or not to confess. Since they are in separate cells, they cannot communicate before deciding.

Let us look at the problem from Sam's viewpoint. If he could be sure Harry will not confess, perhaps he should not do so either. But on second thought, if Harry does not confess, why shouldn't he, Sam, confess and spend only a half year in prison?

In fact, no matter *what* Harry does, Sam is better off if he confesses. In other words, Sam's confess strategy dominates his do not confess strategy. The only difficulty is, Harry may reason the same way. Thus, if each chooses his dominant strategy, both prisoners end up with eight years.

---

[5] Anatol Rapoport and A. M. Chammah, *Prisoner's Dilemma: A Study of Conflict and Cooperation* (Ann Arbor: University of Michigan Press, 1965).

Table 11–19
Payoff table for prisoner's dilemma (years in penitentiary)

| | | Harry's choices | |
		H_1 Confess	H_2 Do not confess
Sam's choices	S_1 Confess	8, 8	½, 10
	S_2 Do not confess	10, ½	1, 1

This result is not the best possible, since both prisoners would be better off if neither confesses. In other words, the strategy pair (S_2, H_2) is Pareto optimal. So are the pairs (S_1, H_2) and (S_2, H_1). The final outcome, the only non-Pareto-optimal pair, is inferior for both players.

If the prisoners were allowed to communicate, they might agree to choose the Pareto-optimal pair (S_2, H_2). Notice, however, that this is not an equilibrium pair. Sam and Harry can each do better by making a unilateral change of choice, so there would be good reason for each of them to defect on their bargain. It is to everyone's advantage if no one cheats, and it is to every prisoner's advantage to cheat unilaterally—a very unstable situation. Prechoice communication cannot help in solving the dilemma unless there is some legal or moral force to bind the prisoners to their agreement.

It might be that in this situation the prisoners will choose (S_2, H_2) even if they are not allowed to communicate. Instead of each prisoner asking "When am I best off?" and assuming his opponent will do the same, each prisoner asks, "When are we *both* best off?" If the prisoners held social values that prompted each to ask this question, they then might choose (S_2, H_2).[6] In this case there is an implicit change in the entries in the payoff table, since they must now reflect both length of term and feelings about the common good.

We can apply the insight gained from studying the one-time dilemma facing the two prisoners to a Prisoner's Dilemma situation which is being repeated in time—a battle over advertising radial tires. The heavily watched Monday night NFL football games on ABC–TV represent prime advertising time for this product. For several years, Goodyear was the only tire advertiser during this time. Then Sears also began advertising during the games and continued to share the time with Goodyear for two

---

[6] Anatol Rapoport, *Fights, Games and Debates* (Ann Arbor: University of Michigan Press, 1960), p. 177.

seasons, after which the latter withdrew, leaving Sears as the only tire advertiser.

The situation facing Sears and Goodyear is shown in Table 11–20. Each manufacturer must decide each year whether (yes = Y) or not (no = N) to advertise radials during the game. Some purely hypothetical payoffs (in millions of dollars of annual contribution, taking advertising into account) are shown. Notice that if both companies advertise, each loses contribution. Apparently the message gets washed out if there is more than one advertiser in a short time period. In this case, neither Sears nor Goodyear sticks in the consumer's mind.

Table 11–20
Change in annual contribution due to TV advertising during NFL game ($ millions)

		Sear's choices	
		S_N	S_Y
Goodyear's choices	G_N	0, 0	-2, 3
	G_Y	3, -2	-1, -1

Why is this a Prisoner's Dilemma? Observe that if each manufacturer chooses his dominant strategy (G_Y, S_Y), both end up worse off than if they had made the opposite choices. The pair (G_N, S_N) is not an equilibrium pair, however. So it is to both companies' advantage if neither advertises, but it is to each company's advantage to unilaterally decide to advertise.

For several years Goodyear was the only radial tire advertiser during the game. One year Sears also advertised. This amounted to a choice of (G_Y, S_Y) for a payoff of $(-1, -1)$. The next year, Goodyear decided to stay put and continue to advertise, and so did Sears. Once again, the companies lost contribution when each tried to maximize its own return. Finally, in the third year Goodyear withdrew, the choice being (G_N, S_Y). The game is not yet over, however, since Goodyear may decide to advertise radials during a subsequent year. In the meantime, Sears has no incentive to change its strategy.

Since we do not have access to what the companies were actually thinking, we can only conjecture about what they were trying to do. Did Sears choose to advertise during the game because it knew Goodyear would be forced to withdraw after deadlocking at (G_Y, S_Y) for a few years? Or were they just lucky? Did Sears really understand the situation, or did they think that since it was profitable for Goodyear to advertise during the game it would be profitable for them to do so too?

This example serves to point out that you can go astray by assuming your opponent knows as much about the game as you do. On the other hand, you can also go astray by not ascribing this much understanding to an opponent who understands the game as well as you do—or maybe even better.

In the Prisoner's Dilemma type of competitive situation, the strategy pair that leaves both players best off is not an equilibrium pair. Thus it is to each individual's advantage to defect; but if both defect, both are worse off. If the situation is to be repeated, the competitors may wish to reach an agreement—an explicit or implicit one, depending on the rules of the game—about their respective moves. But with strong incentives to defect, such agreements may turn out to be tenuous.

The Battle of the Sexes situation: American Chemical versus Boston Pharmaceutical

Another important type of competitive situation is illustrated by the following scenario: A husband and wife have two choices for an evening's entertainment, to go to a prize fight or to a ballet. The man prefers the fight and the woman the ballet; however, to both it is more important that they go out together than that they enjoy their preferred entertainment. Any competitive situation which has a payoff table with the same properties as the one for this situation is popularly known as a Battle of the Sexes situation. The following hypothetical new product introduction is an example.

American Chemical Company must decide whether or not to introduce its newest product, so far designated only as Compound K. The company believes that its major competitor, Boston Pharmaceutical, has a very similar product ready to market. Each company has two choices—to introduce the product or not to introduce it. American's new product manager has calculated the expected payoff (present value) to each company for each alternative. The results are shown in Table 11–21. High fixed costs account for the negative entries in the lower right-hand corner. The subscript N indicates the company has decided not to introduce the product; a Y indicates that the company has decided to introduce the product.

Table 11–21
Payoff table for introduction of compound K (millions of dollars of contribution)

		Boston	
		B_N	B_Y
American	A_N	0, 0	0, 2
	A_Y	2, 0	−3, −3

Notice that both pairs of choices, American introduces and Boston does not (A_Y, B_N), and Boston introduces and American does not, (A_N, B_Y), are equilibrium pairs since for each pair American's choice is best against Boston's, and vice versa. Neither (A_Y, B_Y) nor (A_N, B_N) are equilibrium pairs. While there are two equilibrium pairs, each does not yield the same return to the players. This is in contrast to those strictly competitive situations for which there is more than one equilibrium pair, and every equilibrium pair gives identical returns to each party.

Obviously, American and Boston must make their decisions regarding the introduction of Compound K without conferring. For the sake of discussion, first let us suppose this is the only time the two companies expect to be opposing each other in this type of situation. What should American do? What will Boston do?

Both companies must realize the market is only big enough for one. If they both introduce Compound K, each will lose several million dollars. If Boston, therefore, chooses B_N to prevent a large loss, it is best for American to choose A_Y. But what if Boston expects American to give in? Then both may lose with (A_Y, B_Y) since the unhappy state of affairs is that whatever rationalization Boston has for choosing either B_Y or B_N, there is a similar rationalization for American.

Even though they may not confer, however, there are ways in which the two companies can communicate to influence the outcome. American, for example, may announce that it will introduce Compound K this coming fall. If Boston *believes* this announcement and interprets it to mean American has definitely committed itself to introducing the product, then, acting in its own best interest, it will probably not choose B_Y. Disclosing its plan ahead of time may allow American to preempt the market.

If American intends to beat Boston to the market by announcing that its product will be forthcoming, it must make its announcement credible. For instance, if American lets it be known that it has committed several million dollars to the building of facilities to produce the new product, it will be clear to Boston that its competitor has taken an irrevocable step. In that case, Boston will probably leave the market to American.

In a one-time Battle of the Sexes situation, it is all-important to preempt the other party. If, on the other hand, the companies expect to be in this type of situation repeatedly with various new products, as may well be the case, they would do well to cooperate to try to obtain either (A_Y, B_N) or (A_N, B_Y), since they are both best off with one or the other of these two Pareto-optimal pairs. *How* they would go about this is the question.

Since the two companies are prohibited from bargaining, they may not arrange to take turns (American totally capturing this market, Boston another, for example) nor may American pay Boston to stay out of the market (for example, make Boston a $1 million side payment in exchange for sticking to (A_Y, B_N). Even in the absence of prechoice agreements, however, the companies may effectively settle on a pattern of alternation between (A_Y, B_N) and (A_N, B_Y). If they are constantly introducing new products of similar profitabilities, and if each introduction involves high start-up costs, then after one company has spent several million dollars, say, it may not have the resources to introduce another new product immediately. In the meantime, Boston can seize the opportunity to do so. Once American has committed itself to producing Compound K, for example, Boston can introduce another product without immediate direct competition.

The companies might also consider using mixed strategies. Of course, each company has a host of combinations it can consider. A good way to see the complexities of this situation is to make a geometric plot of the possible payoffs, as in Figure 11–1. Along the horizontal axis American's

FIGURE 11–1
Battle of the Sexes graph for American and Boston new product introduction

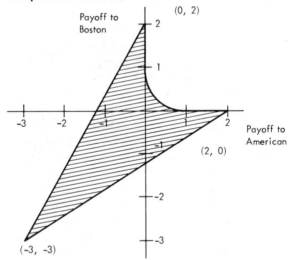

payoffs are plotted, and along the vertical axis, Boston's payoffs. Only certain combinations are possible; these are shown in the shaded region. To each point in the shaded region there is at least one corresponding pair of strategies having this point as payoffs. Conversely, to each pair of mixed strategies there corresponds a payoff which is one of the points in the shaded region.

If American follows the mixed strategy $.8A_N$, $.2A_Y$ then their expected payoff is $(.4, 0)$ if Boston chooses not to introduce its new product and $(-.6, 1.0)$ if Boston does introduce its product. If Boston has any idea American will follow this strategy, Boston would prefer B_Y. But in that case American does best to choose A_N.

If Boston follows the mixed strategy $.8B_N$, $.2B_Y$, then their expected returns are $(0, .4)$ if American chooses A_N and $(1.0, -.6)$ if it chooses A_Y. Thus, if American expects Boston to follow this mixed strategy, American should choose A_Y. But in that case, it is best for Boston to choose B_N. So if each company expects the other to follow its mixed strategy, the return is $(-3, -3)$, which is all the more reason to play the mixed strategy, which is all the more reason to defect, and so forth.

The difficulty is that this pair of mixed strategies is not in equilibrium. However for any Battle of the Sexes situation, there is a pair of mixed strategies that is in equilibrium. These mixed strategies have the desirable property that they prevent the other player from trying to get more by preempting.

In the situation facing American Chemical and Boston Pharmaceutical, the equilibrium pair of mixed strategies is $3/5 A_N$, $2/5 A_Y$ and $3/5 B_N$, $2/5 B_Y$. If American follows this mixed strategy and Boston chooses B_N, the returns are $(4/5, 0)$; if Boston chooses B_Y, the returns are $(-6/5, 0)$. Each of Boston's pure strategies is equally good against American's mixed strategy, in the sense that each has an expected return of 0. Thus, there is no incentive to preempt by Boston.

Similarly, an equilibrium mixed strategy removes American's incentive to preempt. As long as one of the companies chooses this mixed strategy, the payoff to the other company does not depend on the strategy chosen.

Regardless of the specific application, any competitive situation which can be described by a payoff table similar to Table 11–21 can be thought about in the same way as this example of new product introduction.[7] In a one-time situation, preemption is all-important. In repeated choice problems, each might also consider choosing this equilibrium pair of mixed strategies. Or, better yet, they might alternate between the equilibrium pairs through either a tacit or an explicit understanding.

Summary

This section introduced the analysis of situations that are not strictly competitive, and the approach differed significantly from that of the strictly competitive situations of zero-sum games. Whereas in the zero-sum case it is never advantageous to disclose one's strategy, in a Battle of the Sexes situation it is all-important to preempt the other party. The zero-sum case is also characterized by the fact that all equilibrium pairs yield the same return to an individual player, whereas in a Battle of the Sexes situation the return to a particular competitor depends on which equilibrium pair is selected. Furthermore, the ability to communicate and collude becomes important in some situations. In others, whether a situation will be repeated many times or is a one-shot decision makes a critical difference. The concept of Pareto optimality is useful in analyzing such situations. A Pareto-optimal outcome is such that neither player can do

---

[7] All new product introductions, however, cannot be analyzed this way; some, for instance, have a Prisoner's Dilemma character.

better, except at his or her opponent's expense. All the common ground has been squeezed out.

When a not strictly competitive, noncooperative situation is repeated many times, certain aspects change. For example, even though formal preplay communication is not allowed, the competitors may develop some form of temporal collusion. Decision makers in a Battle of the Sexes situation may settle into a pattern of choosing between the equilibrium pairs. In the Prisoner's Dilemma, the players may, after a few repetitions, repeatedly choose the Pareto-optimal strategy pair. This situation is unstable, however, since it is to each individual's advantage to cheat unilaterally.

When all is said and done, it is difficult to choose a course of action in a not strictly competitive situation, since one can never be sure what one's opponent will do. However, analysis can provide a framework for thinking about these situations, help prevent foolish moves, suggest creative moves, and give some insight into each situation.

EXERCISES

11.1. In the next classroom session you will be asked to play the role of player 1 or player 2 in a game about to be described. At this point you don't know which role you will actually play. Think hard about the problem now so that when the time comes you will be prepared to act.

The description of the game is:

1. Player 1 has 6 strategies: α_1, α_2, α_3, α_4, α_5, and α_6.
2. Player 2 has 4 strategies: β_1, β_2, β_3, β_4.
3. Each player must choose exactly one of his strategies without any knowledge of the choice made by his adversary.
4. Depending on the choice of strategies (one for each player) there will be a monetary payment from one player to the other. Table A describes the payments from player 2 to player 1. For example, if player 1 chooses α_2 and player 2 chooses β_3, then player 2 must pay player 1 an amount of \$15. As another example, if player 1 chooses α_3 and player 2 chooses β_4, then player 2 gives $-\$12$ to player 1—this, of course, means that player 2 gets a positive \$12 from player 1.

Table A
Payoffs from player 2 to player 1

	β_1	β_2	β_3	β_4
α_1	2	-1	0	13
α_2	4	0	15	-3
α_3	9	2	4	-12
α_4	3	3	4	5
α_5	3	2	12	3
α_6	1	0	10	-4

Think about the following questions in turn. Do not read the second question until you have responded to the first question, and so on. Record your initial responses.

Imagine that in the next classroom session you and another classroom participant are chosen to play. A fair coin is tossed and you happen to be chosen for *player 1's role*. The game will be played just once.

a. What strategy will you choose? (Be prepared to rationalize or justify your choice when the game is discussed in class.)

b. Before the game is actually executed, suppose that someone asks you, as the designated player 1, to sell your rights to play this game for some amount, say X. How large does X have to be before you will agree to sell?

c. What do you think player 2 will do? (Use probability assessments to reflect your judgments.)

11.2. The same instructions as in Exercise 11.1 apply, but with the payoffs given in Table B. In this exercise, each player has two strategies.

Table B
Payoffs from player 2
to player 1

	β_1	β_2
α_1	0	5
α_2	10	-2

Imagine that in the next classroom session you and another classroom participant are chosen to play. A fair coin is tossed and you happen to be chosen for *player 1's role*. The game will be played just once.

a. What strategy will you choose? (Be prepared to rationalize or justify your choice when the game is discussed in class.)

b. Before the game is actually executed, suppose that someone asks you, as the designated player 1, to sell your rights to play this game for some amount, say X. How large does X have to be before you will agree to sell?

c. What do you think player 2 will do? (Use probability assessments to reflect your judgments.)

d. Would it be worth any premium to you to be able to talk to your adversary in order to make a deal with him or her before choosing?

e. If your adversary had to announce his or her choice before you were obliged to announce yours, would you gain an appreciable strategic advantage?

11.3. Select a fellow participant to work with you on this exercise. Designate one of you as the A player, the other as the B player.

a. The A player will select either strategy a_1 or a_2. Simultaneously and without communication the B player will select either b_1 or b_2. The payoff will be shown in the cell of Table C corresponding to the two choices. For example, if A picks a_1 and B picks b_2, then the payoff is shown in the upper-right-hand corner of the table as $(-5,10)$. The first of the two numbers in the cell entry is the gain or loss $(-)$ to the A player, the second the gain or loss $(-)$ to the B player. In this example, A would lose $5 and B would gain $10.

In this part assume you will play the game only once and that your goal is *to do as well as you can for yourself*. You are neither altruistic nor vindictive with respect to your competitor.

Table C

Player A \ Player B	b_1	b_2
a_1	(5,5)	(−5,10)
a_2	(10,−5)	(−2,−2)

b.　Now play the same game assuming you will play this game an *indefinite* number of times with your competitor. The rest of the rules are the same as *(a)*. Remember your goal is to get the most in the long run for yourself. Your objective is neither to do your competitor in or to help him, *nor* is it to do well *relative* to him.

c.　Now play the same game assuming you will play the game with your competitor exactly 20 times. Remember, try to maximize *your* take.

11.4.　Compare how you behaved in part *c* of Exercise 11.3 with how you would behave in each of the following games under the same rules as Exercise 11.3 (20 plays, no communication).

a.

Player A \ Player B	b_1	b_2
a_1	(5,5)	(−50,50)
a_2	(50,−50)	(−3,−3)

b.

Player A \ Player B	b_1	b_2
a_1	(5,5)	(−4,6)
a_2	(6,−4)	(−3,−3)

11.5.   Play the following game once with no communication:

Player A \ Player B	b_1	b_2
a_1	(1,2)	(3,1)
a_2	(0,−200)	(2,−300)

11.6.   Play the game described in Exercise 11.5, but make your decision at a bargaining table with binding contracts. What happened?

Case 11–1,A

Fouraker Mining & Metals Corp.

Fouraker Mining & Metals, operator of a medium-scale molybdenum mine in the western United States, was a technically sophisticated but marginally profitable producer of molybdenum ore concentrate. In its efforts to improve operating profits, Fouraker had just entered into an exclusive supply arrangement with Siegel & Company, Inc., to purchase a biochemically produced material called "Flozyme," which greatly increased molybdenum mineral recovery from each ton of ore mined. The arrangement required Fouraker to purchase the additive weekly, in small lots, at a price set each week by Siegel. Walter Lightdale Fouraker's purchasing manager, was in the process of establishing a purchasing strategy under the new arrangement.

Fouraker Mining

Fouraker Mining was started in 1952 by a consulting geologist, Mr. L. Fouraker, and a research metallurgist, Dr. Henry Holmes. It was founded to develop a large, low-grade deposit of molybdenum ore on which Mr. Fouraker had long held mining claims, using chemical processes pioneered by Dr. Holmes.

For the next six years, they struggled to finance both the rapidly expanding pilot plant operation and the exploration and development of the ore body. By 1958 the process had been adequately tested and the mining operation had expanded to the point at which the company was almost breaking even.

In order to develop the ore body fully and to expand the plant to its most efficient size, Mr. Fouraker obtained a commitment for $16 million from a large international mining company in return for a 45 percent interest in the firm. Holmes and Fouraker personally held 10 percent each of the equity, with the remaining interest widely dispersed among individuals who had helped finance Fouraker Mining's first ten years. The balance of the $60 million capitalization was provided by banks and various equipment suppliers. In subsequent years there was a marked increase in scale of operations but the company was only barely profitable ($1.2 million before-tax profit on $37.7 million in sales in 1973.).

Siegel & Company, Inc.

Siegel & Company was a small West Coast producer of proprietary carbohydrate derivatives used in the manufacture of certain prepared foods and drugs. It had been founded shortly after World War II by a young biochemist, Sydney Siegel, in order to commercialize a number of promising new biologically active substances on which he had obtained patents.

Despite the smallness and informality of its operation, Siegel & Company had become extremely profitable in recent years as significant markets began to develop for its highly specialized, costly products. Produced in carefully scheduled and interdependent batches, most of its products were sold exclusively to single users, a consequence of Siegel's past joint-venture method of funding the majority of its research programs. Typically, the joint-venture agreements allowed Siegel to retain patents and the rights to manufacture any resulting products, while the sponsor held exclusive rights to use and/or distribute the products.

Flozyme

Although the basic extractive process for molybdenum was well known and in widespread use, Fouraker Mining had succeeded in greatly enhancing its efficiency by special techniques, including the use of special additives to increase yields. Its continuing research had revealed that use of Flozyme made for a substantial improvement in its recovery of molybdenum minerals with Flozyme was introduced into the process at rates equivalent to a few hundred pounds per week.

An extremely light and chemically unstable powder, Flozyme was a by-product of a complex, biological-organic chemical process. Dr. Holmes had learned of Flozyme's surface-activating behavior from a brief description of the process in a professional journal. On the strength of a few laboratory-scale tests, Holmes recommended that Fouraker Mining undertake large-scale process testing of Flozyme so that its precise effect on molybdenum recovery and the economics associated with its use could be accurately established.

In return for exclusive rights to buy Siegel's entire output of Flozyme—should it prove successful in this application—Fouraker Mining agreed to fund a research program in which both the production and application of the Flozyme by-product were to be investigated. After several years of sporadic activity on this program, Flozyme's effectiveness was proven to Fouraker's satisfaction.

Because Flozyme was a by-product, the yield of the main product was greatly affected by the amount of Flozyme desired. Volume production of Flozyme was possible only through extensive and costly recycling of the main product. Fouraker had learned that Flozyme production added considerably to total process costs—the cost increment becoming larger as Flozyme output increased. Prior to the sale of Flozyme, any by-product material had been disposed of as a waste product.

The purchasing arrangement

The absence of a market for Flozyme outside Fouraker Mining meant that its price would have to be established by negotiation. After lengthy discussions with Fouraker management, Siegel had decided that the simplest approach for the present was to quote weekly an appropriate unit price for the reagent and to let Fouraker place its order based on that price. Both Fouraker and Siegel hoped that prices and quantities would eventually stabilize at levels acceptable to both firms. With this procedure decided upon, Mr. Fouraker assigned the purchase responsibility to his purchasing manager, Mr. Lightdale. Mr. Lightdale was to base his weekly decisions solely on the profit contribution information (Exhibit 1) developed by Fouraker's production superintendent, the chief process engineer, and himself during the final Flozyme tests.

An equivalent tabulation of incremental profits for Siegel & Company, shown in Exhibit 2, was also available from a project report prepared by Siegel chemists at the test program's conclusion. The report was regarded as very reliable and would undoubtedly be used by Siegel in its pricing decision. The same report contained the information shown in Exhibit 1.

Because of Flozyme's great effect on the main process, Sydney Siegel had decided to handle its sale personally in order to keep close watch on the joint process and its combined economics. Weekly, Mr. Siegel would telex a price, in dollars per pound, to Fouraker and Fouraker would, in turn, transmit an order quantity, in 20-pound drums, for delivery two weeks hence. Fouraker had been advised that batches of up to 18 drums per week could be produced and that each batch had an active life of ten days at most. This meant that shipments would have to be used within ten days of manufacture or discarded.

Exhibit 1

Weekly contribution to Fouraker Mining profits resulting from use of Flozyme reagent (in dollars)

Price ($)											Quantity (drums) used per week									
Per pound	Per drum	0	1	2	3	4	5	6	7	8	9	10	11	12	13	14	15	16	17	18
20		0	570	900	1,210	1,500	1,770	2,020	2,250	2,460	2,650	2,820	2,970	3,100	3,210	3,300	3,370	3,420	3,450	3,460
40		0	550	860	1,150	1,420	1,670	1,900	2,110	2,300	2,470	2,620	2,750	2,860	2,950	3,020	3,070	3,100	3,110	3,100
60		0	530	820	1,090	1,340	1,570	1,780	1,970	2,140	2,290	2,420	2,530	2,620	2,690	2,740	2,770	2,780	2,770	2,740
80		0	510	780	1,030	1,260	1,470	1,660	1,830	1,980	2,110	2,220	2,310	2,380	2,430	2,460	2,470	2,460	2,430	2,380
100		0	490	740	970	1,180	1,370	1,540	1,690	1,820	1,930	2,020	2,090	2,140	2,170	2,180	2,170	2,140	2,090	2,020
120		0	470	700	910	1,100	1,270	1,420	1,550	1,660	1,750	1,820	1,870	1,900	1,910	1,900	1,870	1,820	1,750	1,660
140		0	450	660	850	1,020	1,170	1,300	1,410	1,500	1,570	1,620	1,650	1,660	1,650	1,620	1,570	1,500	1,410	1,300
160		0	430	620	790	940	1,070	1,180	1,270	1,340	1,390	1,420	1,430	1,420	1,390	1,340	1,270	1,180	1,070	940
180		0	410	580	730	860	970	1,060	1,130	1,180	1,210	1,220	1,210	1,180	1,130	1,060	970	860	730	580
200		0	390	540	670	780	870	940	990	1,020	1,030	1,020	990	940	870	780	670	540	390	220
220		0	370	500	610	700	770	820	850	860	850	820	770	700	610	500	370	220	50	−140
240		0	350	460	550	620	670	700	710	700	670	620	550	460	350	220	70	−100	−290	−500
260		0	330	420	490	540	570	580	570	540	490	420	330	220	90	−60	−230	−420	−630	−860
280		0	310	380	430	460	470	460	430	380	310	220	110	−20	−170	−340	−530	−740	−970	−1,220
300		0	290	340	370	380	370	340	290	220	130	20	−110	−260	−430	−620	−830	−1,060	−1,310	−1,580
320		0	270	300	310	300	270	220	150	60	−50	−180	−330	−500	−690	−900	−1,130	−1,380	−1,650	−1,940

Exhibit 2

Weekly contribution to Siegel & Company profits from sales of Flozyme reagent (in dollars)

Price ($)											Quantity (drums) sold per week									
Per pound	Per drum	0	1	2	3	4	5	6	7	8	9	10	11	12	13	14	15	16	17	18
20		0	450	660	850	1,020	1,170	1,300	1,410	1,500	1,570	1,620	1,650	1,660	1,650	1,620	1,570	1,500	1,410	1,300
40		0	470	700	910	1,100	1,270	1,420	1,550	1,660	1,750	1,820	1,870	1,900	1,910	1,900	1,870	1,820	1,750	1,660
60		0	490	740	970	1,180	1,370	1,540	1,690	1,820	1,930	2,020	2,090	2,140	2,170	2,180	2,170	2,140	2,090	2,020
80		0	510	780	1,030	1,260	1,470	1,660	1,830	1,980	2,110	2,220	2,310	2,380	2,430	2,460	2,470	2,460	2,430	2,380
100		0	530	820	1,090	1,340	1,570	1,780	1,970	2,140	2,290	2,420	2,530	2,620	2,690	2,740	2,770	2,780	2,770	2,740
120		0	550	860	1,150	1,420	1,670	1,900	2,110	2,300	2,470	2,620	2,750	2,860	2,950	3,020	3,070	3,100	3,110	3,100
140		0	570	900	1,210	1,500	1,770	2,020	2,250	2,460	2,650	2,820	2,970	3,100	3,210	3,300	3,370	3,420	3,450	3,460
160		0	590	940	1,270	1,580	1,870	2,140	2,390	2,620	2,830	3,020	3,190	3,340	3,470	3,580	3,670	3,740	3,790	3,820
180		0	610	980	1,330	1,660	1,970	2,260	2,530	2,780	3,010	3,220	3,410	3,580	3,730	3,860	3,970	4,060	4,130	4,180
200		0	630	1,020	1,390	1,740	2,070	2,380	2,670	2,940	3,190	3,420	3,630	3,820	3,990	4,140	4,270	4,380	4,470	4,540
220		0	650	1,060	1,450	1,820	2,170	2,500	2,810	3,100	3,370	3,620	3,850	4,060	4,250	4,420	4,570	4,700	4,810	4,900
240		0	670	1,100	1,510	1,900	2,270	2,620	2,950	3,260	3,550	3,820	4,070	4,300	4,510	4,700	4,870	5,020	5,150	5,260
260		0	690	1,140	1,570	1,980	2,370	2,740	3,090	3,420	3,730	4,020	4,290	4,540	4,770	4,980	5,170	5,340	5,490	5,620
280		0	710	1,180	1,630	2,060	2,470	2,860	3,230	3,580	3,910	4,220	4,510	4,780	5,030	5,260	5,470	5,660	5,830	5,980
300		0	730	1,220	1,690	2,140	2,570	2,980	3,370	3,740	4,090	4,420	4,730	5,020	5,290	5,540	5,770	5,980	6,170	6,340
320		0	750	1,260	1,750	2,220	2,670	3,100	3,510	3,900	4,270	4,620	4,950	5,260	5,550	5,820	6,070	6,300	6,510	6,700

Case 11–1B

Siegel & Company, Inc.

Siegel & Company had just entered into an unusual agreement with Fouraker Mining & Metals Corp. to supply Fouraker with a special process additive called "Flozyme." The additive had proven most effective in increasing Fouraker Mining's recovery of molybdenum minerals and was thought to offer a potentially significant contribution to the mining firm's overall profitability. However, production of Flozyme was complicated by its interference with a primary process of which it was a by-product. Costly recycling was needed to obtain the required volumes of both products. Consequently, determination of an appropriate price for Flozyme was currently a problem of some importance for Siegel.

Siegel & Company

Siegel & Company was a small West Coast producer of proprietary carbohydrate derivatives used in the manufacture of certain prepared foods and drugs. It had been founded shortly after World War II by a young biochemist, Sydney Siegel, in order to commercialize a number of promising new biologically active substances on which he had obtained patents.

Despite the smallness and informality of its operation, Siegel & Company had become extremely profitable in recent years as significant markets began to develop for its highly specialized, costly products. In 1973, the company earned almost $1.5 million before taxes from the sale of seven major products and several dozen minor products. (This profit represented nearly 60 percent of sales.) Produced in carefully scheduled and interdependent batches, most products were sold exclusively to single users, a consequence of Siegel's past joint-venture method of funding the majority of its research programs. Typically, the joint-venture agreements allowed Siegel to retain patents and the rights to manufacture any resulting products, while the sponsor held exclusive rights to use and/or distribute the products. Mr. Siegel was highly satisfied with the exclusive distribution arrangements and low-volume production, since these practices allowed him to concentrate on research and kept him free from time-consuming and uninteresting marketing duties.

Fouraker Mining & Metals Corp.

Fouraker Mining & Metals, operator of a medium-scale molybdenum mine in the western United States, was a technically sophisticated but marginally profitable producer of molybdenum ore concentrate. In its efforts to improve operating profits, Fouraker had entered into the exclusive supply arrangement with Siegel & Company to purchase Flozyme, a biochemically produced material which greatly increased molybdenum mineral recovery from each ton of ore mined. The arrangement required Fouraker to purchase the additive weekly, in small lots, at a price set each week by Siegel.

The company was started in 1952 by a consulting geologist, Mr. L. Fouraker, and a research metallurgist, Dr. Henry Holmes. It was founded to develop a large, low-grade deposit of molybdenum ore on which Mr. Fouraker had long held mining claims, using chemical processes pioneered by Dr. Holmes.

For the next six years, they struggled to finance both the rapidly expanding pilot plant operation and the exploration and development of the ore body itself. By 1958 the process had been adequately tested and the mining operation had expanded to the point at which the company was almost breaking even.

In order to develop the ore body fully and to expand the plant to its most efficient size, Mr. Fouraker obtained a major financing commitment from a large international mining company in return for a substantial interest in the firm. Holmes and Fouraker, along with the many individuals who had helped finance Fouraker Mining's first ten years, retained a controlling interest.

Flozyme

Although the basic extractive process for molybdenum was well known and in widespread use, Fouraker Mining had succeeded in greatly enhancing its efficiency by special techniques, including the use of special additives to increase yields. Its continuing research had revealed that use of Flozyme made for a substantial improvement in its recovery of molybdenum minerals when Flozyme was introduced into the process at rates equivalent to a few hundred pounds per week.

An extremely light and chemically unstable powder, Flozyme was a by-product of a complex, biological-organic chemical process. Fouraker had apparently learned of Flozyme's surface-activating behavior from an article appearing in a professional journal and had carried out some preliminary testing to ascertain the material's potential for recovery enhancement.

In return for exclusive rights to buy Siegel's entire output of Flozyme—should it prove successful in this application—Fouraker Mining agreed to fund a research program in which both the production and application of the Flozyme by-product were to be investigated. After several years of sporadic activity on this program, Flozyme's effectiveness was proven to Fouraker's satisfaction.

Because Flozyme was a by-product, the yield of the main product was greatly affected by the amount of Flozyme desired. Volume production of Flozyme was possible only through extensive and costly recycling of the main product. Flozyme production added considerably to total production costs—the cost increment becoming larger as Flozyme output increased. Prior to the sale of Flozyme, any by-product material had been disposed of as a waste product.

The purchasing arrangement

The absence of a market for Flozyme outside Fouraker Mining meant that its price would have to be established by negotiation. After lengthy discussions with Fouraker management, Siegel had decided that the simplest approach for the present was to quote weekly an appropriate unit price for the reagent and to let Fouraker place its order based on that price. Both Fouraker and Siegel hoped that prices and quantities would eventually stabilize at levels acceptable to both firms.

To guide his pricing decisions, Mr. Siegel had drawn up a table of profit contributions for Flozyme in various weekly production batch sizes (see Exhibit 1). Selling the product in weekly lots would allow Flozyme to be produced under the same schedule as the primary product. Weekly, he would telex his price, in dollars per pound, to Fouraker Mining's purchasing manager, Walter Lightdale, who would, in turn, transmit the quantity, in 20-pound drums, which Fouraker wished to order for delivery two weeks hence. Fouraker had been informed that batches of up to 18 drums per week could be produced and that each batch had an active life of at most ten days. This meant that shipments would have to be used within ten days of manufacture or discarded.

Mr. Siegel was also in possession of a profit contribution tabulation, similar to his own, which had been prepared by Fouraker Mining's engineering and purchasing groups (see Exhibit 2). This tabulation was part of the project report which summarized test program results and economics for Flozyme, a report which also contained the information in Exhibit 1.

Weekly contribution to Siegel & Company profits from sales of Flozyme reagent (in dollars)

Price ($)			Quantity (drums) sold per week																	
Per pound	Per drum	0	1	2	3	4	5	6	7	8	9	10	11	12	13	14	15	16	17	18
1 20	0	0	450	660	850	1,020	1,170	1,300	1,410	1,500	1,570	1,620	1,650	1,660	1,650	1,620	1,570	1,500	1,410	1,300
2 40	0	0	470	700	910	1,100	1,270	1,420	1,550	1,660	1,750	1,820	1,870	1,900	1,910	1,900	1,870	1,820	1,750	1,660
3 60	0	0	490	740	970	1,180	1,370	1,540	1,690	1,820	1,930	2,020	2,090	2,140	2,170	2,180	2,170	2,140	2,090	2,020
4 80	0	0	510	780	1,030	1,260	1,470	1,660	1,830	1,980	2,110	2,220	2,310	2,380	2,430	2,460	2,470	2,460	2,430	2,380
5 100	0	0	530	820	1,090	1,340	1,570	1,780	1,970	2,140	2,290	2,420	2,530	2,620	2,690	2,740	2,770	2,780	2,770	2,740
6 120	0	0	550	860	1,150	1,420	1,670	1,900	2,110	2,300	2,470	2,620	2,750	2,860	2,950	3,020	3,070	3,100	3,110	3,100
7 140	0	0	570	900	1,210	1,500	1,770	2,020	2,250	2,460	2,650	2,820	2,970	3,100	3,210	3,300	3,370	3,420	3,450	3,460
8 160	0	0	590	940	1,270	1,580	1,870	2,140	2,390	2,620	2,830	3,020	3,190	3,340	3,470	3,580	3,670	3,740	3,790	3,820
9 180	0	0	610	980	1,330	1,660	1,970	2,260	2,530	2,780	3,010	3,220	3,410	3,580	3,730	3,860	3,970	4,060	4,130	4,180
10 200	0	0	630	1,020	1,390	1,740	2,070	2,380	2,670	2,940	3,190	3,420	3,630	3,820	3,990	4,140	4,270	4,380	4,470	4,540
11 220	0	0	650	1,060	1,450	1,820	2,170	2,500	2,810	3,100	3,370	3,620	3,850	4,060	4,250	4,420	4,570	4,700	4,810	4,900
12 240	0	0	670	1,100	1,510	1,900	2,270	2,620	2,950	3,260	3,550	3,820	4,070	4,300	4,510	4,700	4,870	5,020	5,150	5,260
13 260	0	0	690	1,140	1,570	1,980	2,370	2,740	3,090	3,420	3,730	4,020	4,290	4,540	4,770	4,980	5,170	5,340	5,490	5,620
14 280	0	0	710	1,180	1,630	2,060	2,470	2,860	3,230	3,580	3,910	4,220	4,510	4,780	5,030	5,260	5,470	5,660	5,830	5,980
15 300	0	0	730	1,220	1,690	2,140	2,570	2,980	3,370	3,740	4,090	4,420	4,730	5,020	5,290	5,540	5,770	5,980	6,170	6,340
16 320	0	0	750	1,260	1,750	2,220	2,670	3,100	3,510	3,900	4,270	4,620	4,950	5,260	5,550	5,820	6,070	6,300	6,510	6,700

Exhibit 2
Weekly contribution to Fouraker Mining profits resulting from use of Flozyme reagent (in dollars)

Price ($)			Quantity (drums) used per week																	
Per pound	Per drum	0	1	2	3	4	5	6	7	8	9	10	11	12	13	14	15	16	17	18
1 20	0	0	570	900	1,210	1,500	1,770	2,020	2,250	2,460	2,650	2,820	2,970	3,100	3,210	3,300	3,370	3,420	3,450	3,460
2 40	0	0	550	860	1,150	1,420	1,670	1,900	2,110	2,300	2,470	2,620	2,750	2,860	2,950	3,020	3,070	3,100	3,110	3,100
3 60	0	0	530	820	1,090	1,340	1,570	1,780	1,970	2,140	2,290	2,420	2,530	2,620	2,690	2,740	2,770	2,780	2,770	2,740
4 80	0	0	510	780	1,030	1,260	1,470	1,660	1,830	1,980	2,110	2,220	2,310	2,380	2,430	2,460	2,470	2,460	2,430	2,380
5 100	0	0	490	740	970	1,180	1,370	1,540	1,690	1,820	1,930	2,020	2,090	2,140	2,170	2,180	2,170	2,140	2,090	2,020
6 120	0	0	470	700	910	1,100	1,270	1,420	1,550	1,660	1,750	1,820	1,870	1,900	1,910	1,900	1,870	1,820	1,750	1,660
7 140	0	0	450	660	850	1,020	1,170	1,300	1,410	1,500	1,570	1,620	1,650	1,660	1,650	1,620	1,570	1,500	1,410	1,300
8 160	0	0	430	620	790	940	1,070	1,180	1,270	1,340	1,390	1,420	1,430	1,420	1,390	1,340	1,270	1,180	1,070	940
9 180	0	0	410	580	730	860	970	1,060	1,130	1,180	1,210	1,220	1,210	1,180	1,130	1,060	970	860	730	580
10 200	0	0	390	540	670	780	870	940	990	1,020	1,030	1,020	990	940	870	780	670	540	390	220
11 220	0	0	370	500	610	700	770	820	850	860	850	820	770	700	610	500	370	220	50	−140
12 240	0	0	350	460	550	620	670	700	710	700	670	620	550	460	350	220	70	−100	−290	−500
13 260	0	0	330	420	490	540	570	580	570	540	490	420	330	220	90	−60	−230	−420	−630	−860
14 280	0	0	310	380	430	460	470	460	430	380	310	220	110	−20	−170	−340	−530	−740	−970	−1,220
15 300	0	0	290	340	370	380	370	340	290	220	130	20	−110	−260	−430	−620	−830	−1,060	−1,310	−1,580
16 320	0	0	270	300	310	300	270	220	150	60	−50	−180	−330	−500	−690	−900	−1,130	−1,380	−1,650	−1,940

Case 11–2A

Classic Greek Explosives Company (A)

Company background

Classic Greek Explosives Company (CGE) was formed during the first couple of decades of this century through the successive merger of a number of smaller local explosives companies. The smaller companies tended to have names derived from Greek mythology (e.g., Titan Powder Company, Vulcan Explosives Company, etc.); hence the name of the surviving company, which rapidly became known as CGE. By 1968 only two explosives companies were left in the United States which supplied a complete line of commercial explosives and blasting supplies nationwide: CGE and the Explosives Division of Dowpont, a major diversified chemical company. Jointly these two explosives manufacturers supply 80 percent of the industry's demand; and although the two companies' market shares fluctuate somewhat from year to year, the two have shared their 80 percent of the market roughly equally during the 60s. The remaining 20 percent of the market is divided among many small local and/or specialty explosives manufacturers. The annual domestic explosives volume is approximately $300 million. This market is growing slowly (perhaps 5 percent per year) when measured in terms of the requirements for explosive energy; however, recent years have seen the substitution of cheaper products for more expensive ones, and there has been heightened competition and a gradual erosion of prices. As a result, the annual industry volume, when measured in dollars, has remained roughly constant, and is in fact believed by some to show a slight decline. CGE sales and earnings for recent years and forecasts for 1968 are given in Table 1.

The nationwide demand for blasting supplies amounts to approximately $60 million per year. This demand is supplied entirely (except for negligible imports) by CGE and Dowpont, which are the only U.S. manufacturers of blasting supplies and share this market roughly equally.

Commercial explosives are sold either packaged (ranging from small sticks of dynamite weighing less than one pound to 100-pound bags of prills) or else supplied in "bulk." These "bulk" explosives are pumped by a pump truck directly into the hole where the explosion is to take place. Dynamites, water gels, and prills differ in many ways. The most important differences are:

1. Dynamites are the most expensive explosive, with the price typically around $20–$25 per hundredweight. They are manufactured in many different grades, corresponding to differing amounts of explosive energy,

Table 1
Recent performance of CGE

	1965	1966	1967	1968 (forecast)
Sales ($ millions)	112	123	110	114
Earnings	11.2	12.8	8.0	6.1

Product line

CGE's primary product line consists of:

1. Commercial explosives.
   a. Dynamites.
   b. Water gels.
   c. Prills and prill products.
2. Blasting supplies.
   a. Blasting caps.
   b. Detonating cord.
   c. Fuses and delays.

and can be packaged in a large variety of package sizes, ranging from a half-inch diameter on up. Dynamite will detonate in wet holes and underwater and meets all safety standards required by the government or by trade associations (e.g., dynamite won't detonate spontaneously through shock or lightning).

2. Water gels are an explosive that was introduced in the early 1960s. They are gels which can be pumped as a liquid and will then gel in the hole. They will detonate in wet holes and underwater and are available at a price that is typically between $15–$20 per hundredweight. They cannot be packaged in package sizes as small as those used for dynamite; typically water gel packages have diameters of 2½ inches or greater. Furthermore, packaged water gels don't have the mechanical rigidity of dynamites. Finally, water gels have not yet been accepted as meeting the necessary safety requirements for all applications where they might eventually be used, e.g., underground coal mining. Nonetheless, water gels have during the past eight years displaced a lot of dynamite sales.

3. Prills (ammonium nitrate granules) are the cheapest available commercial explosive, priced typically at around $5 per hundredweight. They will not detonate in wet holes unless packaged in waterproof packages which are always subject to tearing. Essentially they come in one standard grade, so that no variation of explosive power per pound is possible. They correspond in explosive power to the weaker dynamites and water gels.

Production facilities

The production facilities required vary enormously by type of explosive. Dynamite plants constitute a large investment, must be capable of making many grades and sizes, thus causing substantial production scheduling problems, and require skillful and experienced production crews in order to maintain uniform quality for the grades that are more difficult to manufacture. Because of the gradual displacement of dynamites (which were once the only commercial explosive) by water gels or prills, there is currently considerable overcapacity nationwide in dynamite production facilities.

Water gels, on the other hand, are relatively easy to manufacture and require little investment for a manufacturing facility. Most of the manufacturing costs consist of the ingredient and power costs. These are essentially the same for every manufacturer, except for the so-called sensitizers. Different manufacturers generally use different sensitizers, depending on the patents they hold or are licensed under, and these different sensitizers have greatly varying costs. The percentage of sensitizers used in a particular water gel determines the explosive power of the gel. Sensitizer percentages range from a few percent of the gel's weight to as much as 30 percent.

Prill plants constitute a high investment, and are high-volume plants. Explosive prills are essentially identical to the ammonium nitrate prills used as fertilizer. Since 1967 the fertilizer industry has had considerable overcapacity for the production of fertilizer prills and the fertilizer companies have started to dump these fertilizer prills mixed with oil on the explosives market. The essentials for keeping costs down when supplying prills are (1) to have a cheap source of ammonia, and (2) to have low transportation costs. As a result, the special logistics available to a prill manufacturer are of particular importance. Prill purchases are often local, and even CGE and Dowpont may arrange for local purchases and exchange deals with small competing manufacturers or fertilizer manufacturers in order to avoid high transportation costs from their own plants. CGE has a single prill plant with a capacity of 200 million pounds per year, enough to meet three fourths of CGEs annual demand for prills. The remainder is purchased locally for those regions far removed from the CGE plant.

Demand

Demand for commercial explosives and blasting supplies comes largely from the mining and construction industries and from seismic exploration. These are traditional industries which have been around for a long time and have often formed close relationships with their explosives suppliers. Service and reliable performance are valued highly; for although explosives are usually only a small part of the production cost of the consuming industry, they are a highly dangerous commodity, and a faulty blast can cause a catastrophe. Customers purchase their explosives either from a local explosives distributor or else directly from the manufacturer's regional sales office. The larger customers often meet their explosives requirements by issuing requests for bids to a number of explosives manufacturers. These may be bids for a delivered price/hundredweight for the estimated annual demand (this is typical for large mines), or they may be bids for the quantities required for a particular job (for example, the explosives needed for a new highway project). For CGE and Dowpont, 50 percent of the business is obtained through bids and 50 percent through general distributor sales. The smaller explosives manufacturers are more dependent on the bid business, and derive, on the average, 60 percent of their sales from bids.

CGE has its own network of distributors who sell only the CGE line of commercial explosives and blasting supplies. Although most of these distributors are independent entrepreneurs, a few distributorships are owned directly by CGE and all distributors are rather heavily financed by CGE, trained through CGE training programs, and report a substantial amount of detailed sales information back to CGE. Dowpont and all the smaller competitors sell through general explosives distributors who handle a variety of brands of commercial explosives and Dowpont blasting supplies. The usual way of ordering from a distributor is by telephone; delivery to a blasting site is generally expected the following day. Some customers buy all their explosives from one manufacturer; others spread their business to assure good service and a second source of supply. To the extent that trade relations matter, Dowpont has a superior position since its other chemical divisions can reciprocate through their purchases by favoring Dowpont Explosives customers.

The demand for explosives is spread all over the country, although there are a few regions in which particularly heavy demand is concentrated in a small area. The most extreme example of this is the Lake Superior mining district in which a substantial number of iron-mining companies operate on an iron range approximately 100 miles in length. The Lake Superior mining district alone consumes in excess of $10 million worth of commercial explosives (largely water gels) per year, and is a primary battlefield for CGE and Dowpont.

Competitive environment

The explosives industry was a profitable industry in stable equilibrium until the early 1960s. During the mid-1960s a number of events took place that greatly increased competition and reduced profitability. Water gels began to displace dynamite, and prills began to displace both dynamite and water gels in dry blasting conditions. Finally, fertilizer prills entered the explosives market. These developments did not take place uniformly across the country. There still are many areas of the country where dynamites are the principal explosive even though water gels or prills could do the job. There are other areas where competition is so fierce that certain products are being sold below the full cost of manufacturing. A number of the small manufacturers have recently closed down, and more are expected to go out of business.

In addition to this direct competition in commercial explosives, there has been "not-in-kind" competition. As mechanical rock-breaking devices have improved, they have made inroads into the explosive breaking of rock, both in tunneling and in mining. As seismic instruments and data processing improved, weaker mechanical sound sources became adequate under certain circumstances and displaced some explosives needs.

New ventures

An ongoing R&D effort in CGE produces frequent ideas for product and process improvement. Special emphasis has been given recently on finding ways of reducing manufacturing costs. In addition, numerous opportunities for entering businesses that are related to explosives are continually emerging. On the one hand, there are many natural extensions of the supply of explosives. For example, CGE could expand its services from the mere delivery of explosives in the hole to the full rock-breaking service. Similarly, CGE could acquire some seismic exploration crews and supply the seismic surveying services rather than just the explosives. On the other hand, new uses for explosives are continually emerging, for example, the production of industrial diamonds produced by the pressure from an implosion or the bonding of two different metals through an explosive blast. Some of these processes are researched in CGE's labs, and with the declining profitability of the business per se the temptation is strong to diversify into these related new ventures.

Planning Task Force

Because of the embattled condition of the explosives industry and of CGE in particular, in September 1968 the President of CGE appointed a high-level Planning Task Force to help chart CGE's future course. The four-man task force is headed by the Vice President of Market Planning, Fred Light. The other members are three Assistant Vice Presidents from the Manufacturing, the Control, and the R&D Divisions, respectively. The charter of the planning task force is: (1) to identify opportunities for increasing profits both in the short and in the long term; (2) to initiate whatever studies and analyses might appear necessary to this end; and (3) to ascertain what kind of additional long-range planning function (if any) appears desirable beyond CGE's current five-year planning activities, which consist essentially of the preparation of five-year forecasts and budgets.

Case 11–2B

Classic Greek Explosives Company (C)

The Lake Superior Mining District (LSMD) comprises the principal iron-mining areas of Michigan, Minnesota, and Wisconsin. The LSMD produces a major proportion of all U.S. iron ore, largely through open-pit mining. The iron ore is found in a long stratum of taconite, a particularly hard rock which cannot be broken on a large scale by mechanical means. The normal method of mining is therefore to drill a grid of vertical holes (typically 40 feet deep and 9–12 inches in diameter), fill them with explosives, and then blast a layer of rock. Since the holes often fill with water, the explosive has to be water-resistant, so that water gels are the principal explosive at almost all mines.

The annual volume of water gels used in the LSMD is approximately 1,000,000 hundredweight, and this volume is supplied entirely by CGE and Dowpont, each of which has a water gel plant in the LSMD, and maintains a fleet of pump trucks there to pump the gels into the holes. Both CGE and Dowpont have considerable overcapacity; in fact, either one alone could just about supply the entire needs of the District without having to add to its physical plant. Each had originally hoped to become the dominant producer in the District, which has resulted in a great intensity of competition, most recently in the form of a vicious price war. Since explosives only account for approximately 1 percent of the cost of iron production, the water gel price war in the LSMD in no way stimulates demand for water gels: it merely reduces revenues for CGE and Dowpont.

The recent price war was so severe that water gels are currently being sold at a small margin above variable cost. CGE's variable cost is $6.00/ hundredweight, and CGE estimates Dowpont's variable cost at $6.30/ hundredweight. CGE had originally hoped that this cost advantage would permit it either to drive Dowpont out of the market altogether or else to reduce Dowpont to the position of a second source of supply. In spite of CGE's aggressive price cutting, however, Dowpont has shown no signs of dropping out of the LSMD market. In fact, Dowpont has countered every price move of CGE promptly. Dowpont has not tried to underprice CGE, but has seemed intent on protecting its own contribution from the LSMD business as well as possible. At present, Dowpont's price is around $6.80/hundredweight, and CGE is trying to establish a new pricing strategy.

Although there are no significant objective differences in performance between the CGE and Dowpont water gels, it would be naive to think that the entire LSMD market will always swing to the lower-priced product. First of all, there are subjective differences in the perceptions of different mine operators: some prefer Dowpont, others swear by the CGE gels. Second, there are historical ties, recollections of credit extended (or refused!) in difficult times and personal friendships. Also, Dowpont is in a position to purchase substantial quantities of products from some of the steel companies owning certain of the mines, i.e., Dowpont has the better trade relations. And finally, many mines want to split their business in order to be assured of a second source of supply in emergencies. As a result, Fred Light, who had been in charge of the Lake Superior Mining District before becoming Vice President Sales Planning, estimated that at equal water gel prices Dowpont would take 55 percent of the market. Furthermore, Light felt that a price differential of $1/hundredweight would attract about 25 percent of the customers to the lower-price producer. In other words, if CGE were $1/hundredweight cheaper than Dowpont, CGE would take about 70 percent of the market. And vice versa, if CGE were $/hundredweight more expensive than Dowpont, CGE could expect about 20 percent of the market.

There are, of course, upper limits to price differentials that can be maintained without driving the more expensive producer out of business. Light felt that at a $2/hundredweight differential the more expensive producer would lose almost the entire market (if he continued to market the current products with the current service).

Appendix

Accepting the assumptions given in Classic Greek Explosives Company (C), the respective contributions of Dowpont and CGE, as functions of the prices asked, are as follows:

Contribution = Total Market × Market share × (Price − Variable cost)

Market share$_{Dow}$ = $0.25(P_{CGE} - P_{Dow}) + 0.55$

Market share$_{CGE}$ = $0.25(P_{Dow} - P_{CGE}) + 0.45$

Contribution$_{Dow}$ = $1,000,000[0.25(P_{CGE} - P_{Dow}) + 0.55](P_{Dow} - 6.30)$

Contribution$_{CGE}$ = $1,000,000[0.25(P_{Dow} - P_{CGE}) + 0.45](P_{CGE} - 6.00)$

Using these formulas to compute the two contributions, the construction of the following table is then straightforward.

Contribution table

Dowpont prices	6.75	7.00	7.25	7.50	7.75	8.00	8.25	8.50	8.75	9.00	9.25	9.50	9.75	10.00	10.25	10.50
10.50	750 / 0	1,000 / 0	1,250 / 0	1,500 / 0	1,750 / 0	2,000 / 0	2,250 / 0	2,375 / 210	2,441 / 473	2,475 / 735	2,478 / 998	2,450 / 1,260	2,391 / 1,523	2,300 / 1,785	2,178 / 2,048	2,025 / 2,310
10.25	750 / 0	1,000 / 0	1,250 / 0	1,500 / 0	1,750 / 0	2,000 / 0	2,138 / 198	2,219 / 444	2,269 / 691	2,288 / 938	2,275 / 1,185	2,231 / 1,432	2,156 / 1,679	2,050 / 1,926	1,913 / 2,173	1,744 / 2,419
10.00	750 / 0	1,000 / 0	1,250 / 0	1,500 / 0	1,750 / 0	1,900 / 185	1,997 / 416	2,063 / 648	2,097 / 879	2,100 / 1,110	2,072 / 1,341	2,013 / 1,573	1,922 / 1,804	1,800 / 2,035	1,647 / 2,266	1,463 / 2,498
9.75	750 / 0	1,000 / 0	1,250 / 0	1,500 / 0	1,662 / 172	1,775 / 388	1,856 / 604	1,906 / 819	1,922 / 1,035	1,912 / 1,251	1,869 / 1,466	1,794 / 1,682	1,688 / 1,898	1,550 / 2,113	1,381 / 2,329	1,181 / 2,544
9.50	750 / 0	1,000 / 0	1,250 / 0	1,425 / 160	1,553 / 360	1,650 / 560	1,716 / 760	1,750 / 960	1,753 / 1,160	1,725 / 1,360	1,666 / 1,560	1,575 / 1,760	1,453 / 1,960	1,300 / 2,160	1,116 / 2,360	900 / 2,560
9.25	750 / 0	1,000 / 0	1,188 / 148	1,331 / 332	1,444 / 516	1,525 / 701	1,575 / 885	1,594 / 1,069	1,581 / 1,254	1,538 / 1,438	1,462 / 1,622	1,356 / 1,807	1,219 / 1,991	1,050 / 2,175	850 / 2,360	619 / 2,544
9.00	750 / 0	950 / 135	1,109 / 304	1,238 / 472	1,334 / 641	1,400 / 810	1,434 / 979	1,438 / 1,148	1,409 / 1,316	1,350 / 1,485	1,259 / 1,654	1,138 / 1,822	984 / 1,991	800 / 2,160	584 / 2,329	338 / 2,498
8.75	712 / 122	888 / 276	1,031 / 429	1,144 / 582	1,225 / 735	1,275 / 888	1,294 / 1,041	1,281 / 1,194	1,238 / 1,348	1,162 / 1,501	1,056 / 1,654	919 / 1,807	750 / 1,960	550 / 2,113	319 / 2,266	56 / 2,419
8.50	666 / 248	825 / 385	953 / 522	1,050 / 660	1,116 / 798	1,150 / 935	1,153 / 1,072	1,125 / 1,210	1,066 / 1,348	975 / 1,485	853 / 1,622	700 / 1,760	516 / 1,898	300 / 2,035	53 / 2,173	0 / 2,200
8.25	619 / 341	762 / 463	875 / 585	956 / 707	1,006 / 829	1,025 / 951	1,012 / 1,072	969 / 1,194	894 / 1,316	788 / 1,438	650 / 1,560	481 / 1,682	281 / 1,804	50 / 1,926	0 / 1,950	0 / 1,950
8.00	572 / 404	700 / 510	797 / 616	862 / 707	897 / 829	900 / 935	872 / 1,041	812 / 1,148	722 / 1,254	600 / 1,360	447 / 1,466	262 / 1,572	47 / 1,679	0 / 1,700	0 / 1,700	0 / 1,700
7.75	525 / 435	638 / 526	719 / 616	769 / 707	798 / 798	775 / 888	731 / 979	656 / 1,069	550 / 1,160	412 / 1,251	244 / 1,341	44 / 1,432	0 / 1,450	0 / 1,450	0 / 1,450	0 / 1,450
7.50	478 / 435	575 / 510	641 / 585	675 / 660	678 / 735	650 / 810	591 / 885	500 / 960	378 / 1,035	225 / 1,110	41 / 1,185	0 / 1,200	0 / 1,200	0 / 1,200	0 / 1,200	0 / 1,200
7.25	431 / 404	512 / 463	562 / 522	582 / 582	569 / 641	525 / 701	459 / 760	344 / 819	206 / 879	38 / 938	0 / 950	0 / 950	0 / 950	0 / 950	0 / 950	0 / 950
7.00	384 / 341	450 / 385	484 / 429	488 / 472	472 / 516	429 / 560	341 / 604	188 / 648	34 / 691	0 / 700	0 / 700	0 / 700	0 / 700	0 / 700	0 / 700	0 / 700
6.75	338 / 248	388 / 276	406 / 304	394 / 332	350 / 360	304 / 388	276 / 416	169 / 444	31 / 450	0 / 450	0 / 450	0 / 450	0 / 450	0 / 450	0 / 450	0 / 450
CGE prices	6.75	7.00	7.25	7.50	7.75	8.00	8.25	8.50	8.75	9.00	9.25	9.50	9.75	10.00	10.25	10.50

Key: Dowpont Contribution → 956 / 707 ← CGE Contribution

Case 11–3

Maxco Inc. and the Gambit Company

PART I

Maxco, Inc., and the Gambit Company were fully integrated, major oil companies, each with annual sales of over $1 billion and exploration and development budgets of over $100 million. Both firms were preparing sealed bids for an oil rights lease on block A–512 off the Louisiana Gulf Coast. Although the deadline for the submission of bids was only three weeks away, neither firm was very close to a final determination of its bid. Indeed, management at Maxco had yet to decide whether to bid at all, let alone how much to bid. Although Gambit was virtually certain to submit a bid, the level of Gambit's bid was far from settled. This uncharacteristic hesitancy in the preparation of both firms' bids was a direct result of certain peculiarities in the situation surrounding the bidding for block A–512.

Block A–512 lay in the Alligator Reef area immediately to the south of a known oil-producing region (see Exhibit 1). Just to the north were blocks A–497 and A–498, both of which were already under lease to the Gambit Company. On its leasehold Gambit had two completed wells which had been in production for some time. In addition Gambit had an offset control well in progress near the boundary between its leasehold and block A–512. When this well was completed, Gambit would have access to direct information concerning the value of any oil reserves lying beneath block A–512. Maxco's nearest leasehold, on the other hand, was some seven miles to the southeast. Any bid submitted by Maxco, therefore, would necessarily be based solely on indirect information.

The role of information in bidding oil rights leases

In any bidding situation, information concerning either the object of the bidding or the notions of competing bidders is highly prized. This is even more the case in bidding for the rights to oil reserves lying, perhaps, thousands of feet below the surface. There are, of course, various kinds of information available to bidders for oil rights. To summarize these various types of information briefly, two categories—direct and indirect—may be established.

Information obtained by drilling on a parcel of land is called direct information. Obviously this is the most precise information obtainable concerning the subsurface structure. From core samples taken up during the drilling operation, and from careful laboratory analysis of these

Exhibit 1
Subsurface map of the Alligator Reef area

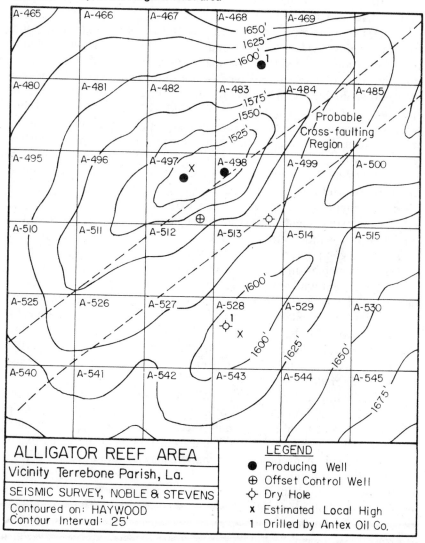

samples, considerable information may be accumulated not only about the presence or absence of oil, but also about the type, thickness, composition, and physical properties of each of the various geologic strata encountered. Such information then provides the driller with a relatively accurate estimate of the oil reserves lying beneath the parcel. Direct information concerning adjacent parcels may be obtained by drilling offset control wells. These wells are offset from the principal producing areas and are located near the boundaries of the leased parcel. Such wells may then provide a particular lessee with precise and valuable information about adjacent parcels.

Indirect information is obtained from sources other than drilling and may be roughly divided into two kinds: scouting and nonscouting. Scouting information is gained by observing the operations of other drillers. By counting the sections of drill pipe—each of known length—introduced into a hole, an observer may infer the depth of the hole. By observing the quantity of cement—required by law—used to plug the various porous strata that are encountered, the thicknesses of these strata may be determined. Normally, however, this type of scouting information will not yield nearly the precision available to the driller. It can help in the determination of whether or not oil reserves exist at a particular location, but it is much less useful in determining the size of the reserves.

More definite scouting information may sometimes be obtained by more clandestine means. Eavesdropping on informal conversations in public places, subtle forms of bribery and interrogation, even forcible entry onto a competitor's drilling site may provide much more detailed—and more valuable—information. An extreme anecdote tells of two men who were caught while inspecting a competitor's drilling log—the source document of a driller's direct information. The men were reportedly held at gunpoint for several days in anticipation of the approaching deadline for the submission of bids. Managing to escape the day before the deadline, the two men were able to report back what they had seen in the log. As a result, the operator whose log had been compromised was forced to raise his bid by $7 million.

Less melodramatic, but highly significant, sources of indirect information are available through means other than scouting. Nonscouting information is obtained, first, from published sources, such as government geologic and geophysical surveys, and from reports of previous explorations. Second, nonscouting information may be obtained from local seismic surveys conducted either by in-house personnel or by private contractors. A third source of nonscouting information is found in the trading of dry hole information. The tradition among drilling operators is to reveal their dry hole experiences. The feeling seems to be that there is far more to be gained from the reciprocal exchange of dry hole information than could be gained from watching a competitor pour a considerable investment into a site that is known to be barren. Finally, nonscouting information may also be obtained from independent prospectors, promoters, and traders who may have become familiar with certain tracts in the past and are willing to trade this information, again on a reciprocal basis.

As might be suspected in an environment where information has such a high—and immediate—value, internal security presents a clear and ever-present problem. Bank-type vaults, armed guards, and electrified fences are commonplace. On occasion, entire drilling rigs have been encased in canvas to thwart the efforts of prying eyes. Substantial slowdowns in operations, however, under almost unbearable working conditions have also resulted. Furthermore, a blanket of security must also be placed over the derivation and submission of bids. Information on the level of a particular bid can be even more valuable than information on the value of reserves. When bids were being prepared for the tracts surrounding Prudhoe Bay on Alaska's North Slope, one company packed its entire bidding organization onto a railroad train and ran it back and forth over the same stretch of track until bids had been prepared and submitted and the bidding deadline had passed.

Finally, with information such a prime concern, circulation of false information is often attempted. If operators are successful in leaking false negative information about a particular parcel, they may be able to later "steal" the parcel with a relatively low bid. On the other hand, to divert attention from a particular parcel, operators may feign interest in another one by seeming to conduct tests there.

Maxco's bidding problem

Mr. E. P. Buchanan, Vice President for Exploration and Development, had primary responsibility for preparing Maxco's bid. Mr. Buchanan's information of block A–512 was, as indicated previously, indirect in nature. Although some scouting information on Gambit's offset control well was available to him, the primary basis of his information was a private seismic survey, together with published government geologic maps and reports. Maxco had acquired the survey data, in a jointly financed effort with Gambit, through the use of a private contractor. The contractor, Noble and Stevens, had prepared a detailed survey of the entire Alligator Reef area several years previously when blocks A–497 and A–498 were up for bid. Under the joint financing arrangement, identical copies of the completed report had then been submitted to both Maxco and Gambit. Such an arrangement, while unusual, was not without precedent in known oil-producing areas. Exhibit 1 represents an updated version of a subsurface map included in Noble and Stevens' report.

Based on all of the information available to him, Mr. Buchanan's judgment concerning the monetary value of the oil reserves under block A–512 was essentially captured by the probability mass function given in Exhibit 2. Furthermore, Mr. Buchanan held that Maxco's bid should be based solely on this monetary value of the oil reserves. Since it was known that no nearby blocks were to be put up for bid for at least ten years, Mr. Buchanan did not ascribe any informational value to owning a lease on block A–512.

Mr. Buchanan also felt—for the present at least—that Gambit's uncertainty was virtually identical to his own. He was sure, however, that

Gambit's well would be completed by the deadline for the submission of bids. At that time Gambit would know the value of the reserves up to, perhaps, ±5 percent or ±10 percent.

For the past several years, Mr. Buchanan had refused to bid on any parcels of land where he felt he was at a distinct disadvantage to a competing bidder. If a competitor had superior (direct) information about a parcel while Maxco had only indirect information, then Mr. Buchanan preferred not to bid at all.

Less than five months ago, however, in an area not far from Alligator Reef, Mr. Buchanan had *lost* a bid on a block adjacent to a Maxco leasehold. Maxco had gone to the expense of drilling an offset control well on its own block and had found a reasonably large oil reserve. Maxco had then lost the bid, however, to a competitor who was operating solely on the basis of indirect information. In addition, the competitor's winning bid had still been low enough to provide for a substantial profit on the venture.

Thus Mr. Buchanan was considering a change in his policy.While he very much doubted that anyone else would enter the bidding for block A–512, he was beginning to feel that he himself should do so. If he did decide to bid, he then wondered what sort of bid might be reasonable.

PART II

Gambit's bidding problem

Mr. Buchanan's counterpart in the Gambit Company was a Mr. K. R. Mason; primary responsibility for preparing Gambit's bid thus rested with him.

Until Gambit's well on the Alligator Reef leasehold was completed, Mr. Mason's information concerning block A–512 would be indirect in nature. The primary basis of that information was still the private seismic survey, for which Gambit had contracted jointly with Maxco, together with published government geologic maps and reports.

Although Mr. Mason also had detailed production logs on the two producing wells on Gambit's leasehold, he felt that this information was not relevant to the problem of assessing the potential value of block A–512. There was almost certainly some cross-faulting in the Alligator Reef area (see Exhibit 1). Since this cross-faulting would probably terminate the producing area, the principal uncertainty surrounding the value of block A–512 was the precise location of the northernmost cross fault. Thus, Mr. Mason's judgment was also essentially captured by the probability mass function given in Exhibit 2. Although Mr. Mason's judgment certainly did not coincide precisely with Mr. Buchanan's, the facts available to the two men and the economics in the two companies were largely similar. Neither man's estimate of the situation, therefore, differed significantly from Exhibit 2.

Exhibit 2
Probability distribution of monetary values

Monetary value of oil reserves ($ millions)*	Probability
$ 1.7	.03
2.7	.06
3.7	.10
4.7	.17
5.7	.28
6.7	.18
7.7	.08
8.7	.04
9.7	.02
10.7	.01
11.7	.01
12.7	.01
13.7	.01
	1.00

Mean value = $5.83.
* Net present value at 10 percent.

This would, of course, change dramatically when Gambit's offset control well was completed. At that time Mr. Mason would be able to reevaluate the property with a much higher degree of precision.

Normally Mr. Mason would then be in a position to submit a bid relatively close to the true value of the block while still allowing a generous margin for profit. Other bidders, not knowing the true value of the block, would be unable to adopt such a strategy. If they bid at all, they would have to either bid relatively low or risk the possibility of "buying in high" to a disastrously unprofitable situation.

Over the past year, however, several operators in the Louisiana Gulf Coast had narrowly lost out when bidding for blocks on which they had direct information. Granted that in no case were extremely large reserves lost, nevertheless operators bidding with nothing but indirect information had been able to "steal away" substantial reserves from operators who were basing their bids on direct information.

With a view toward reassessing his approach to this kind of situation, Mr. Mason thought that it might be useful to prepare a whole schedule of bids. For each possible "true value" of the reserves, Mr. Mason felt that he should be able to establish an appropriate bid—given that value of the reserves. Thus, Mr. Mason felt that he ought to be able to complete a bid schedule similar to that given in Exhibit 3. He was wondering, however, what a reasonable schedule of bids might be like.

Exhibit 3
Gambit's bid schedule

If the true value of the reserves is:	Then Gambit's bid should be:
$ 1.7 million	$_____ million
2.7 million	_____ million
3.7 million	_____ million
4.7 million	_____ million
5.7 million	_____ million
6.7 million	_____ million
7.7 million	_____ million
8.7 million	_____ million
9.7 million	_____ million
10.7 million	_____ million
11.7 million	_____ million
12.7 million	_____ million
13.7 million	_____ million

Case 11–4A

American Grocery Products (A)

In late January 1970, Mr. John Roberts, Product Manager for American Grocery Products' new hot instant breakfast (code name Product B–14), was formulating a market strategy for introducing his new product. The product had been successfully designed, and limited consumption tests had been conducted to provide some data for predicting its market potential. The New Products Committee, which Mr. Roberts reported to, was then at the stage at which it had to decide whether to test-market or to actually launch the new product.

In 1970, American Grocery Products was one of the largest integrated manufacturers of packaged food products in the United States. The company marketed a wide and diversified line of food and allied products under many major brand names.

Product B–14

B–14 was conceived as a product fulfilling a specific need in the marketplace. In essence, B–14 was almost identical to the cold instant breakfast products that were promoted as meal replacements, but its important contribution was the fact that it was designed to be used with hot or warm water, thus giving a *hot* meal replacement. The product development had been based on the concept that, while many consumers accepted the idea of a beverage as a meal replacement, there were a substantial number who thought that cold milk was inconsistent with the idea of a hearty nutritious meal.

Preparation for a presentation at the February 28 meeting

On January 20, 1970, Mr. Roberts, after reviewing all relevant information, felt that the following courses of action were possible candidates for recommendation to top management. First, American Grocery Products (AGP) could launch the product nationwide in 1970. Second, AGP could conduct a test market in 1970 and delay the nationwide introduction until 1971. Finally, management could decide to drop the product altogether.

There were a number of considerations and problems that Mr. Roberts had to deal with in reaching a decision. B–14, because of its warmth, was likely to be a seasonal and somewhat regionally based product. Because of this likelihood of seasonality, all preparations must be made in the spring so that B–14 could be introduced in the fall at the beginning of the high-consumption season. It was felt that if the product were not introduced in the fall of 1970, then it would have to be delayed a full year before introduction.

The market potential

Roberts thought that the ultimate size of the hot instant breakfast (HIB) market would be about a third of the then existing instant breakfast market. The market research staff had spent a considerable amount of time running consumption tests and consumer panels on the product and had developed a model to project sales volume based on these results. The model gave a probabilistic forecast of sales potential, and the best available estimate in January 1970 is shown in Exhibit 1. American Grocery Products held the belief that the company was geared to high-volume production and had arbitrarily decided that any volume below 2 million packs would not be large enough to make HIB a viable ongoing business. In that event, the product would be phased out in three years.

The cooperative packer

If B–14 were introduced, it would be manufactured in a National Division plant in Indiana. The main problem in setting up production was that the plant was then used for the production of a cereal which was about to be phased out. On checking further with the Manufacturing Department, Roberts found that the changeover would not be completed until the fall of 1971. The setup cost and the capital outlay for the machinery to produce B–14 would be $1.6 million to be depreciated straight line over a period of ten years. After the plant began producing, the gross margin for each case

Exhibit 1
Probabilistic forecast of B–14 sales potential

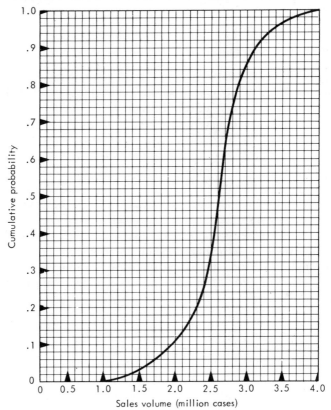

Sales volume (million cases)

would be $3. Because the product could only be introduced in the fall, an outside manufacturer had to be used if AGP wanted to launch the product in 1970. This outside manufacturer, known as a co-packer, was usually a company which specialized in supplying standard manufacturing machinery and facilities on a short-term interim basis. It would require an initial premium of $200,000 in addition to a higher cost per unit. The co-packer was capable of handling any volume in this situation, and if it were used, the gross margin would be $2.50 per case. The only alternative to using the co-packer would be to wait until the next fall before launching the product.

The test market

The test markets, if they were to be run, would be conducted in three major cities (Cleveland, Seattle, Boston). The main purpose of the results would be to establish a more accurate estimate of the market potential by looking at actual market performance in three different areas. Mr. Roberts felt that the most important piece of information would be the indication of final volumes, and he could visualize three fairly distinct test result categories: good, mixed, and poor. The cost of the test would be $400,000.

From AGP and the market research organization's past experience with this product, Mr. Roberts felt that the probability of obtaining different test results was dependent on the underlying market potential and would be different for different ranges of the true market volumes as shown in Exhibit 2.

Exhibit 2
Probability of observing different test results for different ranges of true market potential

1. *Market potential between 1 million and 2.25 million packs*

Good	0.3
Mixed	0.3
Poor	0.4
	1.0

2. *Market potential between 2.25 million and 2.75 million packs*

Good	0.6
Mixed	0.3
Poor	0.1
	1.0

3. *Market potential between 2.75 million and 4 million packs*

Good	0.8
Mixed	0.1
Poor	0.1
	1.0

The economics

The profitability of B–14 would depend on the sales volume achieved in the first year of its introduction. The New Products Committee was of the opinion that B–14 would most likely have a ten-year lifetime, with an annual sales volume for AGP equal to that achieved in the first year, regardless of when the product was launched.

AGP top management had arbitrarily decided that sales of more than 2 million packs per year must be maintained in order to keep the line. Otherwise, B–14 would be liquidated three years from the time of its introduction, with zero net salvage value (i.e., the salvage value of the machinery would probably just balance the cost of liquidation). Since B–14 was a new product introduced into a well-established cold instant breakfast market, a rather substantial advertising budget was envisioned for the first year. During the first six months of the introduction a $13.4 million advertising and promotion budget would be necessary. For the subsequent six months, a $2.5 million budget would be necessary if the product line were to be continued (i.e., sales rate at or exceeding 2 million cases per year) and $1.0 million would be necessary if it were to be discontinued. For the ongoing business in the years after the first, the annual advertising and promotion budget would be a function of sales volume, which is given in Exhibit 3. Although the business would be liquidated if sales were under 2 million cases, it was felt that some advertising and promotion expenditure was justified to try and recoup as much of the initial investment as possible. Furthermore, it was AGP company policy to use a discount rate of 20 percent for projects of this nature and the company tax rate was 50 percent.

Exhibit 3
Advertising and promotion expenditures for different sales volumes

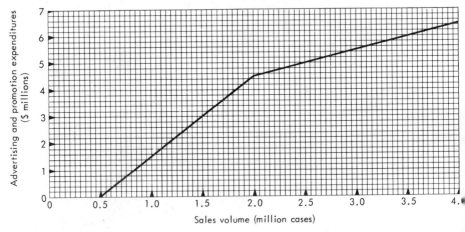

Note:
a. If sales volume is less than 2 million cases,

$$\text{A and P expenditures} = 3V - 1.5$$

b. If sales volume is greater than 2 million cases,

$$\text{A and P expenditures} = V + 2.5$$

where V = Sales volume in millions of cases and A and P expenditures are expressed in millions of dollars.

Case 11–4B

American Grocery Products (B)

At the February 28, 1970, meeting of the New Products Committee at which Mr. John Roberts made a preliminary presentation on his new hot instant breakfast (HIB), one of the crucial issues that cast some doubt on his analysis was the question of competitive reaction. A detailed study of the related cold instant breakfast (CIB) market revealed that it was dominated by one major competitor, the Pilgrim Foods Company. Looking into the history of the product showed that the cold instant breakfast market was originally established by Pilgrim in 1964. Although the success of CIB had attracted a number of attempted assaults on its position, in 1970 Pilgrim was still the dominant producer and maintained a 60 percent share of the market.

The members of the New Products Committee felt that because the HIB and the CIB markets were closely related, Pilgrim could very easily be attracted to introduce an HIB of its own. Since the formulations for CIB and HIB were so similar, no new technology would be involved and Pilgrim could possibly introduce an HIB with less than a year's lead time.

At the meeting, members of the New Products Committee felt that the likelihood of Pilgrim's reacting would depend on a number of factors, ranging from how lucrative Pilgrim thought the HIB business would be to how much CIB volume it was losing to the new product. One theory maintained that Pilgrim would be most unlikely to introduce an HIB. The rationale behind this theory was that Pilgrim might believe that HIB would not have a profitable enough market to justify the start-up cost of an introduction. Furthermore, should American Grocery Products (AGP) successfully build an HIB market, its franchise might be completely drawn from nonusers of CIB and would not adversely affect Pilgrim's CIB market. Finally, unless HIB sales cut deeply into Pilgrim's CIB franchise, the introduction of a Pilgrim HIB would only cannibalize Pilgrim's own CIB sales. To support this view, advocates cited a widely held belief that Pilgrim, being a milk-oriented company, might be averse to adding a product made with water, which would tend to downgrade its whole instant breakfast line.

Another theory was that Pilgrim would immediately introduce an HIB if it found the market lucrative. This would be desirable because by so doing Pilgrim would not only develop a new market, but would protect its franchise from AGP, although in the short run this action might cut into its CIB sales. Also, Pilgrim might fear that once AGP established an HIB market, it would only be a matter of time before it attempted a direct attack on CIB. These alternative viewpoints seemed to argue for and against Pilgrim's introduction of an HIB and, depending on which view one subscribed to, different assumptions could be made about the likelihood of a competitive response.

The competitive reaction and market share

Armed with these ideas from the New Products Committee meeting, Mr. Roberts decided to go back and reexamine his original analysis. After some thought he felt that despite the theory one subscribed to, if Pilgram did want to enter the market, it would be of paramount importance of AGP to be there first. The preemptive effect of being the first in the market would have a drastic impact on the ultimate market positions. Getting down to the question of how likely it would be for Pilgrim to introduce an HIB, Mr. Roberts felt that it was difficult to come up with an assessment because of the complexity of the factors involved. After long discussion, however, with other product managers at AGP who had competed with Pilgrim Foods on other occasions and with other product lines, he concluded that if AGP marketed the product in 1970, there would be no chance that Pilgrim would follow with a similar product. However, the test market alternative raised some interesting questions. It was felt that Pilgrim would find out about an AGP test market as soon as it was begun and could read the actual results along with AGP by conducting consumer surveys of its own in AGP's test areas. Pilgrim would then base its own strategies on essentially the same market information as AGP. Because of this fact, Mr. Roberts felt that Pilgrim's reaction would actually depend on the results of the market test. The higher the predicted market potential, the more likely it would be for Pilgrim to introduce an HIB. Mr. Roberts assessed the probability to be .5 after a good test result, .2 after a mixed result, and 0 after a poor result.

Turning next to the question of market share, Mr. Roberts concluded, after looking at some past cases of new product introductions, that with only two competitors and the appropriate advertising and promotion backing, AGP should not achieve less than 35 percent of the newly created HIB market. He felt that if AGP and Pilgrim launched the product in the same year, the odds were slightly in Pilgrim's favor and that the market share for AGP would be 45 percent with .6 probability, and 55 percent and 35 percent, both with .2 probability.

Having spent a considerable amount of time gathering this additional information to encompass competitive reaction, Mr. Roberts felt that he was ready to do his analysis again. However, he was afraid that this new competitive element might have an adverse affect on the economics of his product and that not only would his basic marketing strategy have to be changed but that the original set of very favorable profit figures that he obtained for his product might no longer be applicable.

_____ PART VI

Allocating scarce resources

Chapter 12

An introduction to
linear programming

Linear programming is one of the best developed and most widely applied disciplines of management science. It is concerned with the optimum allocation of limited resources among competing activities, under the constraints imposed by the problem being analyzed. Those constraints can be of a financial, technological, marketing, organizational, or any other nature. In broad terms, linear programming can be defined as a mathematical representation aimed at programming or planning the best possible allocation of scarce resources, where the mathematical model used is characterized exclusively by linear relationships.

Although the roots of linear programming could be traced back to the origins in the first optimization problems, it was not until 1947 that the general linear programming problem was formulated and solved by George B. Dantzig, as part of the effort of project SCOOP (Scientific Computation of Optimum Programs), a research group of the Air Force. At that time Dantzig developed the *simplex* method for solving the general linear programming problem. The extraordinary computational efficiency of the simplex method, together with the availability of digital computers, have made possible the application of linear programming to an enormous class of business, industrial, governmental, and military problems.

The purpose of this chapter is to give an intuitive overview of many of the important properties of linear programming. In the first section we present four examples, to give an idea of the types of problems that can be addressed by linear programming and some insight into how they can be formulated. We then consider one of these examples in detail, to illustrate the most important properties of linear programming models for understanding applications. Our approach is to analyze a problem involving only two decision variables so that our observations will have simple graphical interpretations. There is no attempt in this chapter to develop the underlying algebraic framework of linear programming, and the simplex method will not be discussed as such. However, a geometrical overview of the basics of linear programming, including concepts of shadow prices and sensitivity analyses, is presented. Next, the standard output of commercial linear programming computer systems is discussed by presenting the output for the examples already analyzed via the geometry. The stages involved in structuring, solving, and analyzing a linear programming model are presented in the final section.

FORMULATING LINEAR PROGRAMMING PROBLEMS

In order to provide a preliminary feeling about the types of problems to which linear programming can be applied and to illustrate the kind of rationale that should be used in formulating linear programming models, this section presents four highly simplified examples and describes their corresponding linear programming formulations.

Example 1: Insulation production

Suppose that a plant manager has one machine which can be used to produce two types of insulation material, referred to as type B and type R. Because of the difference in the densities of the two materials, 16⅔ carloads of type B can be produced per day, but only 8⅓ carloads of type R can be produced per day. The production process is such that any combination of these two levels can be produced as long as the total does not exceed an equivalent of 16⅔ carloads of type B per day. Further, although the demand for type R is unlimited, the demand for type B is limited to eight carloads per day. Finally, production is further restricted, since only ten boxcars can be made available for shipping each day. If the contribution is $300 per carload for type B and $400 per carload for type R, what should the manager's production schedule be in order to maximize total contribution?

In order to formulate this problem as a linear program, we first define the *decision variables*. The decision variables refer to the activities under the control of the decision maker whose levels must be set in order to solve the problem under consideration. For this example we are interested in knowing the number of carloads of each type of insulation to produce per day. We therefore define these variables as:

X_B = Number of carloads of type B produced per day
X_R = Number of carloads of type R produced per day

Next, the *objective function* must be specified. The objective function measures the performance, according to some criterion, for all possible settings of the levels of the decision variables. Thus the "best" settings for the decision variables can be made according to this criterion. In this example we want to maximize total contribution to overhead and profit, given by:

$$\text{Contribution} = 300X_B + 400X_R .$$

We can now develop the *constraints*. The constraints are limits placed on various combinations of the values of the decision variables. Since the plant can produce 16.67 carloads per day of insulation type B but only one half as much per day of insulation type R, the constraint imposed by limited machine capacity in units of carloads of insulation type B is:

$$X_B + 2X_R \leq 16.67 .$$

Since only 10 boxcars are made available each day and the decision variables are defined in terms of carloads per day, we have:

$$X_B + X_R \leq 10 .$$

Finally, the demand for insulation type B limits the amount that can be produced to:

$$X_B \leq 8 .$$

Since producing a negative number of carloads does not make any sense, we have nonnegativity constraints on the decision variables:

$$X_B \geq 0 , X_R \geq 0 .$$

Hence, the following linear program summarizes the problem above:

$$\text{Maximize } 300X_B + 400X_R,$$

subject to:

$$
\begin{aligned}
X_B + 2X_R &\leq 16.67 , \\
X_B + X_R &\leq 10 , \\
X_B &\leq 8 , \\
X_B \geq 0, X_R &\geq 0 .
\end{aligned}
$$

In the next section, we will return to this example to show how it can be solved and extensively analyze its properties.

Example 2: Aluminum alloy production

An aluminum producer makes a special alloy which is guaranteed to contain 90 percent or more aluminum, between 5 percent and 8 percent copper, and the remainder other metals. The demand for this alloy is very uncertain, so no supply is kept on hand. An order has been received for 1,000 pounds at 45 cents per pound. The alloy must be produced from two batches of scrap, pure copper, and pure aluminum. The analysis of the two batches of scrap shows that they contain the following:

	Al	Cu	Other
Scrap 1	95%	3%	2%
Scrap 2	85%	1%	14%

The costs of the various raw materials are:

	$/lb.
Scrap 1	0.15
Scrap 2	0.05
Al	0.50
Cu	0.60

In addition, it costs five cents a pound to melt down a pound of metal. There is no shortage of raw materials, as the producer has more than 1,000 pounds of each type of metal on hand. How would the producer charge his furnace so that he will maximize his contribution?

The first step in formulating a linear program is to define the decision variables of the problem. In the present example, these variables are simple to identify and correspond to the number of pounds of scrap 1, scrap 2, aluminum, and copper to be used in the production of the alloy. Specifically, we denote the decision variables as follows:

x_1 = Pounds of scrap 1
x_2 = Pounds of scrap 2
x_3 = Pounds of aluminum
x_4 = Pounds of copper

The next step to be carried out in the formulation of the problem is to determine the objective function. In this case, we want to maximize the total contribution resulting from the production of 1,000 pounds of the special alloy. Since we are producing exactly 1000 pounds of the alloy, the total revenue will be the selling price per pound times 1,000 pounds. That is:

$$\text{Total revenue} = 0.45 \times 1000 = 450 .$$

To determine the total cost incurred in the production of the alloy, we should add the melting cost of 5 cents a pound to the corresponding cost of each metal used. Thus, the relevant unit cost, in dollars per pound, is:

Scrap 1: $0.15 + 0.05 = 0.20$
Scrap 2: $0.05 + 0.05 = 0.10$
Al: $0.50 + 0.05 = 0.55$
Cu: $0.60 + 0.05 = 0.65$

Therefore, the total cost becomes:

$$\text{Total cost} = 0.20x_1 + 0.10x_2 + 0.55x_3 + 0.65x_4 \,,$$

and the total contribution we want to maximize is determined by the expression:

$$\text{Total contribution} = \text{Total revenue} - \text{total cost}.$$

Thus,

$$\text{Total contribution} = 450 - 0.20x_1 - 0.10x_2 - 0.55x_3 - 0.65x_4 \,.$$

It is worthwhile noticing in this example that since the amount of special alloy to be produced was fixed in advance, equal to 1,000 pounds, the maximization of the total contribution becomes completely equivalent to the minimization of the total cost.

We should now define the constraints on the problem. First, since the producer does not want to keep any supply of the alloy on hand, we should make the total amount to be produced exactly equal to 1,000 pounds:

$$x_1 + x_2 + x_3 + x_4 = 1,000 \,.$$

Next, the alloy should contain at least 90 percent aluminum. This restriction can be expressed as follows:

$$0.95x_1 + 0.85x_2 + x_3 \geqq 900 \,.$$

The left-hand side of this constraint gives the total amount of aluminum in the alloy derived from the two types of scrap and the pure aluminum. This amount must be at least 900 pounds, since 90 percent of the 1,000 pounds of alloy must be aluminum.

Similarly, the restrictions regarding copper content in the alloy can be represented by the following inequalities:

$$0.03x_1 + 0.01x_2 + x_4 \geqq 50 \,,$$
$$0.03x_1 + 0.01x_2 + x_4 \leqq 80 \,.$$

The first of these constraints requires that the copper content in the alloy be at least 5 percent, while the second indicates that the copper content can be no more than 8 percent.

Finally, we have the obvious nonnegativity constraints:

$$x_1 \geqq 0, x_2 \geqq 0, x_3 \geqq 0, x_4 \geqq 0 \,.$$

If we choose to minimize the total cost, the resulting linear programming problem can be summarized as follows:

$$\text{Minimize } 0.20x_1 + 0.10x_2 + 0.55x_3 + 0.65x_4 \,,$$

subject to:

$$x_1 + \quad x_2 + \quad x_3 + \quad x_4 = 1,000,$$
$$0.95x_1 + 0.85x_2 + \quad x_3 \quad\quad \geqq \quad 900,$$
$$0.03x_1 + 0.01x_2 \quad\quad + \quad x_4 \geqq \quad 50,$$
$$0.03x_1 + 0.01x_2 \quad\quad + \quad x_4 \leqq \quad 80,$$
$$x_1 \geqq 0, \quad x_2 \geqq 0, x_3 \geqq 0, x_4 \geqq 0.$$

Example 3: Trimming the ship

A ship has three cargo holds: forward, aft, and center. The capacity limits are:

	Weight (tons)	Volume (cubic feet)
Forward	2,000	100,000
Center	3,000	135,000
Aft	1,000	30,000

The following cargoes are offered; the shipowners may accept all or any part of each commodity:

Commodity	Amount (tons)	Volume per ton (cubic feet)	Contribution per ton ($)
A..............	6,000	60	6
B..............	4,000	50	8
C..............	2,000	25	5

In order to preserve the trim of the ship, the ratio of the weight in each hold to the capacity of that hold in tons must be the same for all holds. How should the cargo be distributed so as to maximize contribution?

To determine the decision variables of this problem, it is important to realize that what we need to know is the amount of each commodity to allocate to each of the three cargo holds. Thus, let the decision variables be:

x_{AF} = Tons of commodity A located in forward hold
x_{AC} = Tons of commodity A located in center hold
x_{AA} = Tons of commodity A located in aft hold

x_{BF} = Tons of commodity B located in forward hold
x_{BC} = Tons of commodity B located in center hold
x_{BA} = Tons of commodity B located in aft hold

x_{CF} = Tons of commodity C located in forward hold
x_{CC} = Tons of commodity C located in center hold
x_{CA} = Tons of commodity C located in aft hold

The objective function, which is to maximize the total contribution, is easily determined. Since $x_{AF} + x_{AC} + x_{AA}$ represents the total tons of commodity A being shipped, and $6 is the contribution per ton on that commodity, $6(x_{AF} + x_{AC} + x_{AA})$ is the total contribution from commodity A.

The total contributions from commodities B and C are determined in a similar manner, and the objective function is given by:

$$\text{Contribution} = 6(x_{AF} + x_{AC} + x_{AA}) + 8(x_{BF} + x_{BC} + x_{BA})$$
$$+ 5(x_{CF} + x_{CC} + x_{CA})$$

We now consider each of the restrictions of the problem in turn. The first set of constraints has to do with the total capacity, in tons, existing in each of the cargo holds. Since $x_{AF} + x_{BF} + x_{CF}$ is the amount located in the forward hold, the 2,000-ton limit on the forward hold is expressed by:

$$x_{AF} + x_{BF} + x_{CF} \leqq 2,000 \ .$$

Similarly, for the center hold we have:

$$x_{AC} + x_{BC} + x_{CC} \leqq 3,000 \ ,$$

and for the aft hold:

$$x_{AA} + x_{BA} + x_{CA} \leqq 1,000.$$

In order to express the cubic feet capacity limit we have to convert tons into cubic feet, by multiplying the tons shipped of each commodity by the corresponding cubic feet per ton. Thus we obtain as cubic feet capacity constraints for forward, center, and aft holds, respectively, the following:

$$60x_{AF} + 50x_{BF} + 25x_{CF} \leqq 100,000 \ ,$$
$$60x_{AC} + 50x_{BC} + 25x_{CC} \leqq 135,000 \ ,$$
$$60x_{AA} + 50x_{BA} + 25x_{CA} \leqq 30,000 \ .$$

A third set of restrictions has to do with the maximum availability of each commodity. Only 6,000 tons of commodity A are available, so the total amount shipped cannot exceed this supply. Thus:

$$x_{AF} + x_{AC} + x_{AA} \leqq 6,000 \ .$$

Similarly, a maximum of 4,000 tons is available of commodity B:

$$x_{BF} + x_{BC} + x_{BA} \leqq 4,000 \ ,$$

and, finally, only 2,000 tons are available of commodity C:

$$x_{CF} + x_{CC} + x_{CA} \leqq 2,000 \ .$$

The fourth set of constraints refers to the need for keeping the weight of each hold proportional to its capacity in tons. Thus the ratio of the weight shipped in any one hold to its capacity must equal the corresponding ratios for the other holds. That is to say;

$$\frac{x_{AF} + x_{BF} + x_{CF}}{2,000} = \frac{x_{AC} + x_{BC} + x_{CC}}{3,000} = \frac{x_{AA} + x_{BA} + x_{CA}}{1,500} \ .$$

The numerators of these fractions represent the total weight, in tons, allocated in the forward, center, and aft holds, respectively. The denominator gives the corresponding capacity, in tons, of these cargo holds. This last expression can be incorporated in the linear programming model by equating these ratios for any two holds, for example, between the forward and center and the center and aft;

$$\frac{x_{AF} + x_{BF} + x_{CF}}{2,000} - \frac{x_{AC} + x_{BC} + x_{CC}}{3,000} = 0 \ .$$

$$\frac{x_{AC} + x_{BC} + x_{CC}}{3,000} - \frac{x_{AA} + x_{BA} + x_{CA}}{1,500} = 0 \ .$$

Finally, we have the obvious nonnegativity constraints on all the variables involved:

$$
\begin{array}{lll}
x_{AF} \geqq 0, & x_{AC} \geqq 0, & x_{AA} \geqq 0 \ , \\
x_{BF} \geqq 0, & x_{BC} \geqq 0, & x_{BA} \geqq 0 \ , \\
x_{CF} \geqq 0, & x_{CC} \geqq 0, & x_{CA} \geqq 0 \ .
\end{array}
$$

Example 4: Electronics manufacturing

An electronics defense company manufactures three lines of products for sale to the government: transistors, micromodules, and circuit assemblies. It has four process areas: transistor production, circuit printing and assembly, transistor and module quality control, and circuit assembly test and packing.

Production of one transistor requires 0.1 standard hours of transistor production area capacity, 0.5 standard hours of transistor quality control area capacity, and 70 cents in direct costs.

Production of one micromodule requires 0.4 standard hours of the circuit printing and assembly area capacity, 0.5 standard hours of the quality control area capacity, three transistors, and 50 cents in direct costs.

Production of one circuit assembly requires 0.1 standard hours of the capacity of the circuit printing area, 0.5 standard hours of the test and packing area, one transistor, three micromodules, and $2 in direct costs.

Any of the three products may be sold in unlimited quantities at prices of $2, $8 and $25 each, respectively. If there are 200 hours of production time open in each of the four process areas in the coming month, what products and how much should be manufactured to yield the most contribution?

As with the previous examples, the first step in formulating a linear programming model is to select the decision variables to appropriately characterize the problem under consideration. In this example, however, the best choice of decision variables is certainly not obvious. Since transistors are used in micromodules which are in turn used in circuit assemblies, we need to keep track of production and sales separately. This suggests the following two sets of decision variables:

x_1 = Total number of transistors produced
x_2 = Total number of micromodules produced
x_3 = Total number of circuit assemblies produced

and,

y_1 = Total number of transistors sold as transistors
y_2 = Total number of micromodules sold as micromodules
y_3 = Total number of circuit assemblies sold as circuit assemblies

The objective function is now easily determined in terms of these variables by using the information provided in the statement of the problem with respect to the selling prices and the direct costs of each of the units produced. The total contribution is given by:

$$\text{Contribution} = 2.0y_1 + 8.0y_2 + 25y_3 - 0.7x_1 - 0.5x_2 - 2.0x_3$$

In order to be able to determine contribution in this way we need to know the number of transistors, micromodules, and circuit assemblies sold as such rather than consumed in the production of more complex components. Since each micromodule needs three transistors, and each circuit assembly needs one transistor, we have the total number of transistors sold as transistors given by:

$$y_1 = x_1 - 3x_2 - x_3 .$$

Similarly, for the total number of micromodules sold as micromodules, we have:

$$y_2 = x_2 - 3x_3 .$$

Finally, since all the circuit assemblies are sold as such, we have:

$$y_3 = x_3 .$$

The remaining constraints on production result from the 200-hour limit on production time available in each of the four process areas. Since the transistors are the only items requiring processing time in the transistor production area, and they consume 0.1 standard hours of production per transistor, we have:

$$0.1x_1 \leq 200 \text{ (transistor)}$$

Similarly, for the other three areas, we have:

$$0.4x_2 + 0.1x_3 \leq 200 \quad \text{(circuit printing)}$$
$$0.5x_1 + 0.5x_2 \qquad\quad \leq 200 \quad \text{(quality control)}$$
$$0.5x_3 \leq 200 \quad \text{(test and packing)}$$

Finally, we have the usual nonnegative conditions:

$$y_1 \geq 0, \quad y_2 \geq 0, \quad y_3 \geq 0, \quad x_1 \geq 0, \quad x_2 \geq 0, \quad x_3 \geq 0 .$$

We can summarize the formulations as follows:

Maximize $2y_1 + 8y_2 + 25y_3 - 0.7x_1 - 0.5x_2 - 2x_3$,

subject to:

$$
\begin{aligned}
y_1 &&&& - && x_1 + && 3x_2 - && x_3 &= && 0 \; , \\
&& y_2 &&&& - && x_2 + && 3x_3 &= && 0 \; , \\
&&&& y_3 &&&& - && x_3 &= && 0 \; , \\
&&&&&& 0.1x_1 &&&&&& \leq && 200 \; , \\
&&&&&&&& 0.4x_2 + 0.1x_3 && \leq && 200 \; , \\
&&&&&& 0.5x_1 + 0.5x_2 &&&&&& \leq && 200 \; , \\
&&&&&&&&&& 0.5x_3 \leq && 200 \; ,
\end{aligned}
$$

$$y_1 \geqq 0, \, y_2 \geqq 0, \, y_3 \geqq 0, \, x_1 \geqq 0, \, x_2 \geqq 0, \, x_3 \geqq 0 \; .$$

The first three constraints essentially define the y variables in terms of the x. It is not difficult to see that these constraints can also be solved to give the x variables in terms of the y. The implication of this is that the problem can also be formulated using only the y or only the x variables. In general, there are a number of equivalent formulations of any linear programming problem, and no one formulation is necessarily best.

A GEOMETRICAL OVERVIEW

Although we are not going to discuss actual computational procedures for solving linear programs, we can gain some insight into the properties of linear programs by looking at the geometry of a simple example. Since we want to be able to draw simple graphs depicting various possible situations, we will analyze the first example presented in the preceding section. Recall that the example included the production of two types of insulation subject to constraints on machine capacity, boxcar availability, and demand for type B insulation. The formulation developed in the preceding section is repeated here:

$$\text{Maximize } 300X_B + 400X_R \; ,$$

subject to:

$$
\begin{aligned}
X_B + 2X_R &\leq 16.67 \; , \\
X_B + X_R &\leq 10 \; , \\
X_B &\leq 8 \; , \\
X_B \geqq 0, \, X_R &\geqq 0 \; .
\end{aligned}
$$

Graphical representation of the decision space

All the values of X_B and X_R satisfying the constraints of the above linear programming problem can be geometrically represented by the cross-hatched area in Figure 12–1. Notice that each line in this figure is repre-

FIGURE 12–1
Graphical representation of feasible production possibilities

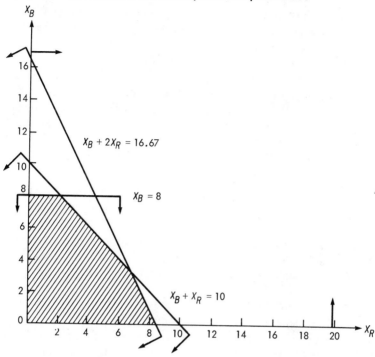

sented by a constraint expressed as an equality. To construct these lines, we need to determine values of X_B and X_R that satisfy the equality. For the first constraint, the points $X_B = 16.67$, $X_R = 0$ and $X_B = 0$, $X_R = 8.33$ satisfy the constraint with equality. These points are plotted in Figure 12–1 and connected by a straight line. The arrows associated with each line show the direction indicated by the inequality sign in each constraint. The set of values of X_B and X_R simultaneously satisfying all the constraints (indicated by the cross-hatched area) is the *feasible region* of production possibilities. Among these feasible production alternatives, we would like to find that one that maximizes the resulting contribution.

Finding the optimal solution

The optimal solution may be found by starting at some feasible solution (that is, a point within the cross-hatched area), say $X_B = 0$, $X_R = 0$, and looking for an improvement. Since producing R is worth \$400/carload while producing B is only worth \$300/carload, we might as a first step increase X_R as much as possible. Then $X_B = 0$, $X_R = 8\frac{1}{3}$, and the contribution = 3,333. Now we cannot increase X_B without decreasing X_R. If we increase X_B one unit, the return is \$300/carload; however X_R must be reduced one-half carload, since machine capacity is limited, in order to accommodate the increase in X_B; and this causes a loss of \$400/carload. The net effect on contribution is $300 - \frac{1}{2} \times 400 = 100$; hence we should increase X_B as much as possible while decreasing X_R appropriately. Then $X_B = 3\frac{1}{3}, X_R = 6\frac{2}{3}$, and the contribution = \$3,667. If we attempt to increase X_B further, we see that another carload of X_B must be balanced by a decrease in X_R of one carload, since boxcar availability is limited. The net effect is $1 \times 300 - 1 \times 400 = -100$, which is a decrease in contribution of \$100. Therefore, we do not want to increase X_B any further.

The values of the decision variables at the optimal solution can be determined graphically or by solving

$$X_B + 2X_R = 16.67 ,$$
$$X_B + X_R = 10$$

for the values of X_B and X_R, since the optimal solution is at the intersection of the binding constraints (i.e., the constraints that hold with equality). By subtracting the second equation from the first, we find $X_R = 6.67$; hence $X_R = 3.33$ and $X_B = 3.33$.

Note that any point in the interior of the feasible region cannot be the optimal solution, since more contribution would be made by increasing both X_B and X_R simultaneously. This process of starting at a feasible solution, finding and improving direction, and moving as far as possible in that direction is the basis of the simplex method, the computational procedure for solving linear programs.

An alternative way to graphically determine an optimal solution is to construct lines of constant contribution and observe the direction of increasing contribution. For example, all combinations of X_B and X_R that give a contribution of 1,200 fall on the straight line defined by

$$300X_B + 400X_R = 1,200 ,$$

while all combinations of X_B and X_R that give a contribution of 1,800 are given by

$$300X_B + 400X_R = 1,800 .$$

These two lines are plotted in Figure 12–2. Note that the lines of constant contribution are parallel to one another and increasing in a "northeasterly" direction. Maximizing contribution then amounts to moving the line of constant contribution as far as possible in this direction while still maintaining feasibility. The result is in the point labeled *optimal solution*. The line through this point is the optimal contribution line. This approach indicates that a linear program always has an optimal solution at a corner point, or *vertex*.

Figure 12–2
Finding an optimal solution

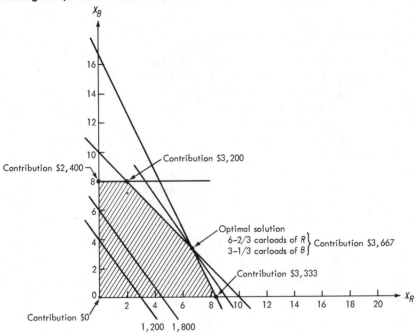

Integer solutions

In linear programming the decision space is continuous in the sense that fractional answers are always allowed. This is contrasted with discrete or integer programming, where integer answers are required for some or all variables. In this example if all ten carloads must be shipped each day, and mixed carloads are not permitted, then we must seek an integer solution. Our initial reaction is to round off the continuous solution yielding $X_R = 7$, $X_B = 3$. However, this solution is infeasible, since the production capacity constraint would be exceeded. Hence, rounding off is not always possible. Rounding down yields a feasible solution, $X_R = 6$, $X_B = 3$, and contribution $= 3,300$, but it is easy to see that $X_R = 6$, $X_B = 4$, and contribution $= 3,600$ is also a feasible solution, and it is clearly preferable because it has a higher contribution. Basically the integer programming problem is inherently difficult to solve and falls in the domain of what is called combinatorial analysis rather than simple linear programming. However, often what seem to be integer variables can be interpreted as rates, and then the integer difficulty disappears. In this example, if it is not necessary to ship all ten carloads each day, then the fractional carloads not completed by the end of the day are merely completed first the following day. Thus the rate of output will still be ten carloads per day. Finally, when the numbers involved are large, rounding to a feasible solution usually results in a good approximation.

Shadow prices on the constraints

Associated with any optimal solution are *shadow prices* (also referred to as dual variables, marginal values, or pi values) for the constraints. The shadow price on a particular constraint represents the change in the value of the objective function per unit increase in the right-hand-side value of the constraint.

For example, suppose that machine capacity were increased from 16.67 to 17.33, measured in units of carloads of insulation type B. What will be the improvement to the value of the objective function from such an increase? Since the constraints on machine capacity and available boxcars will remain binding with this increase, to determine the new values of the decision variables we solve

$$X_B + 2X_R = 17.33 ,$$
$$X_B + X_R = 10 ,$$

and find that $X_R = 7.33$ and $X_B = 2.67$. The new value of the objective function is then

$$300X_B + 400X_R = 300(2.67) + 400(7.33) = 3{,}733 ,$$

and the improvement in the value of the objective per unit increase in machine capacity is:

$$\frac{\text{Improvement in objective}}{\text{Increase in machine capacity}} = \frac{3{,}733 - 3{,}667}{17.33 - 16.67} = 100 .$$

The shadow price associated with machine capacity is then \$100 per unit increase of machine capacity, measured in carloads of insulation type B. If we had measured the machine capacity constraint in terms of carloads of insulation type R, the shadow price on machine capacity would have been \$200 per unit increase in machine capacity, measured in carloads of insulation type R. This is reasonable, since it takes twice as much machine capacity to produce a carload of insulation type R.

We could do a similar calculation to find the shadow price for the constraint on available boxcars by increasing the available boxcars from 10 to 11 and resolving. If this were done, we would find that:

$$\frac{\text{Improvement in objective}}{\text{Increase in boxcars available}} = \frac{3{,}867 - 3{,}667}{11 - 10} = 200 .$$

The shadow price on the third constraint must be zero, since there is excess demand for insulation type B. Since there is excess demand now, additional demand will be of no use, and hence its marginal value is zero. In general, the shadow prices remain unchanged only so long as the constraints that are binding at the optimal solution remain unchanged by the change in a particular right-hand-side value.

Besides the constraints explicitly stated in the formulation, there are also nonnegativity constraints on the variables. These constraints also have shadow prices associated with them; however, they are usually referred to by the special name of *reduced cost*. In this example, increasing the right-hand-side of $X_B \geqq 0$ from 0 to 1 causes no change in the optimal solution. Hence, the shadow prices, or reduced cost, associated with the nonnegativity constraint on X_B must be zero. A similar argument holds for X_R. However, had the optimal solution been $X_B = 8$ and $X_R = 0$, for example, producing any amount of type R would be nonoptimal. The reduced cost associated with the nonnegativity constraint on X_R would then indicate the amount by which the optimal value of the objective function would be changed (reduced in a maximization problem) for each unit of X_R produced. This idea will be developed further in the section on reduced costs and pricing out.

Ranges on objective coefficients

A natural question to ask about an optimal solution is how sensitive are the values of the decision variables to small changes in the problem data. In Figure 12–3, the optimal solution of this example is given. Changing

Figure 12–3
Ranges on objective coefficients

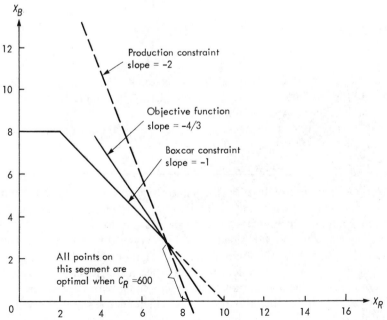

any coefficient in the objective function amounts to changing the slope of the objective function. It is clear from the figure that the optimal solution does not change so long as the slope of the objective function lies between the slope of the production capacity constraint and that of the constraint on boxcars. The slope of the production capacity constraint is -2, since for each one-unit increase in X_R a corresponding two-unit decrease in X_B is required to satisfy this constraint with equality. Similarly, the slope of the boxcar availability constraint must be -1. The slope of the objective function is $-400/300$, since for each one-unit increase in X_R a corresponding $400/300$ unit decrease in X_B is required to keep the contribution constant.

Now suppose that we consider making changes in the coefficient of X_B from 300 to, say, C_B, with all other problem data remaining unchanged. Then for the optimal solution to remain unchanged, the slopes must satisfy

$$-2 \leqq -\frac{400}{C_B} \leqq -1 .$$

or, equivalently,

$$200 \leqq C_B \leqq 400 .$$

If we consider varying the coefficient of X_R from 400 to, say, C_R, with all other data remaining unchanged, then the slopes must satisfy

$$-2 \leqq -\frac{C_R}{300} \leqq -1 ,$$

or, equivalently,

$$300 \leqq C_R \leqq 600 .$$

Since these ranges on the objective coefficients are relatively easy to compute for any linear program, they are always available from standard commercial linear programming systems.

It is interesting to note what happens at the boundary of one of these ranges. Suppose that the objective function is

$$C' = 300X_B + 600X_R .$$

Then the objective function has the same slope as one of the constraints, in this case the capacity constraint. For $C_R = 600$, all points on the line segment indicated in Figure 12–3 are optimal solutions.

If $C_R > 600$, then $X_R = 8.33$ and $X_B = 0$ become the new optimal solution. These changes in the optimal decisions that occur at the boundary of the ranges are also easy to determine, so they are generally reported by any commercial linear programming system along with the ranges.

The ranges on the objective function coefficients for which the solution remains unchanged can only be assumed to hold for changes in one objective coefficient, all other problem data remaining unchanged. Within these ranges, the values of the decision variables, as well as the slack and surplus in the various constraints, remain unchanged.

Ranges on the right-hand-side values

In determining the shadow prices on the constraints, small changes were made in the right-hand-side values and the problem resolved to determine the improvement in the objective function per unit of increase in a right-hand-side value. The changes made were small enough that the binding constraints at the optimal solution remained unchanged. How large can these changes be and the computation still be valid? Alternatively, over what range can a right-hand-side value vary without changing the values of the shadow prices?

To illustrate this, consider varying the right-hand-side value of the constraint on production capacity. The binding constraints at the optimal solution are the production capacity and boxcar availability. In Figure 12–4, if the production capacity constraint is relaxed by increasing its right-hand-side value, say b_1, the binding constraints at the optimal solution remain unchanged until $b_1 = 20$. At this point, the optimal solution is determined by the constraint on boxcars and the nonnegativity of

Figure 12–4
Ranges on right-hand-side values

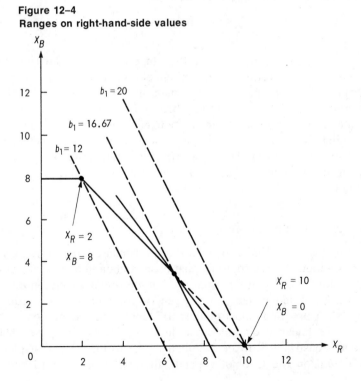

X_R; the optimal solution is then $X_B = 0$ and $X_R = 10$. If, on the other hand, the right-hand-side of the production capacity constraint is reduced to 12, then the binding constraints at the optimal solution are the capacity and demand constraints, and the optimal solution changes to $X_B = 8$ and $X_R = 2$. Hence, we have determined graphically that the range of b_1, the right-hand-side value of production capacity, is given by

$$12 \leqq b_1 \leqq 20 \, ,$$

where the current value of b_1 is 16.67. Further, we have also determined the change in the optimal solution that occurs at the boundaries of this range.

A similar analysis can be carried out on the constraint on the availability of boxcars. If this were done we would find that

$$8.33 \leqq b_2 \leqq 12.33$$

where the current value of b_2 is 10. The situation for the constraint on demand is slightly different. Since this constraint is not binding at the optimal solution, its right-hand-side value can be increased arbitrarily without changing the binding constraints at the optimal solution. However, if the upper bound on demand for type B insulation were reduced to 3.33, then this constraint and the limit on boxcar availability would determine the optimal solution. Hence we have

$$3.33 \leqq b_3 < + \infty \, ,$$

where the current value of b_3 is 8.

The right-hand-side ranges give the range on a particular right-hand-side value, all other problem data being held fixed, such that the binding constraints at the optimal solution remain unchanged. Since the binding constraints at the optimal solution remain unchanged, the shadow prices and reduced costs must also remain unchanged. Finally, in the process of determining the ranges, it is also easy to determine the change in the optimal solution that would occur if a particular range were exceeded, and this information is generally reported by any commercial system, along with the ranges.

Computational considerations

In some instances, linear programs are formulated that either have no feasible solution or have solutions that place no bound on the value of the objective function. In either situation, a finite optimal solution does not exist for the problem posed, and any general computational procedure for solving linear programs must be able to identify these conditions.

Infeasible linear programs arise in many ways. Suppose that an additional constraint is to be included in the formulation that places a lower bound on the level of capacity utilization in order to keep the machine operating efficiently. For example, suppose that the minimum production level for efficient capacity utilization is thought to be 20 carloads of type B insulation per day. Thus the following constraint,

$$X_B + 2X_R \geqq 20 \ ,$$

should be included in the formulation. However, this additional constraint raises the difficulty illustrated in Figure 12–5. There are no points that

Figure 12–5
Infeasible set of constraints

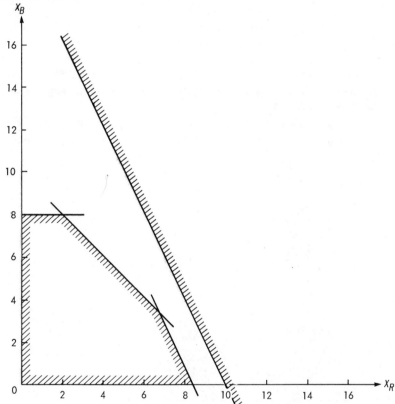

satisfy all the constraints simultaneously, and the problem is therefore *infeasible*. Computer routines for solving linear programming problems tell us when an error of this type has occurred. Infeasibility occurs, in general, whenever a set of constraints is so restrictive that no solution is possible. In large, complex formulations, it is often possible to pose an infeasible problem without being able to recognize this at the outset.

The other difficulty that can arise is that the optimal value of the objective function is unbounded. Suppose, in the original problem, that the constraints were incorrectly entered, so we are in fact trying to solve the following problem:

$$\text{Maximize } 300X_B + 400X_R \text{ ,}$$

subject to:

$$X_B + 2X_R \geqq 16.67 \text{ ,}$$
$$X_B + X_R \geqq 10 \text{ ,}$$
$$X_B \geqq 8 \text{ ,}$$
$$X_B \geqq 0, X_R \geqq 0 \text{ .}$$

This situation is shown in Figure 12–6. Clearly the maximum of the objective function is now unbounded. Linear programming solution techniques also indicate when this kind of error has been made. In practice, an unbounded solution is usually an indication that the problem has been poorly formulated, since no real situation produces an unlimited value of the objective function.

All of the standard commercially available linear programming computer systems indicate when infeasibility or unboundedness occurs. In

Figure 12–6
Unbounded linear program

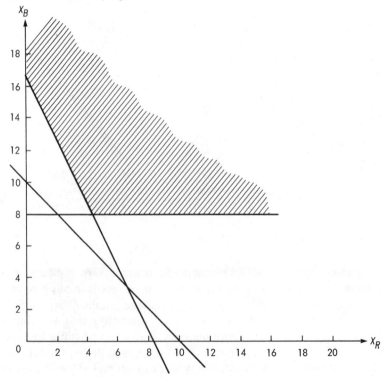

fact, all of these systems stop their calculations when one of the following three conditions occur:

1. A finite optimal solution has been determined.
2. An unbounded solution has been determined.
3. The formulation has been shown to be infeasible.

In the latter two cases, the formulation of the model needs to be reviewed.

Reduced costs and pricing out

The shadow price on a constraint has been interpreted as the change in the optimal value of the objective function, per unit of increase in the right-hand-side value. We can also interpret the shadow price as the opportunity cost of diverting resources away from the optimal set of decisions. That is, the objective function will change by the negative of the shadow price for each unit of decrease in the right-hand-side value. This interpretation is particularly useful in evaluating alternative activities.

Suppose that a new activity, one not included in the original formulation, arises. Can we determine from the shadow prices whether it would be an improvement to divert resources away from the current optimal activities into the new activity? To make this idea concrete, suppose that a new type of insulation can be manufactured that is a direct competitor of type B. The new product, insulation type Q, has a contribution of $325 per carload, can be produced at a rate of $11^{1}/_{9}$ carloads per day, and requires one boxcar per day. However, since type Q competes directly with type B, the upper bound on demand of eight carloads per day limits the total production of types B and Q together. The formulation of the model including the new activity of producing carloads of type Q is as follows:

$$\text{Maximize } 300X_B + 400X_R + 325X_Q ,$$

subject to:

$$
\begin{aligned}
X_B + \quad 2X_R + 1.5X_Q &\leq 16.67 , \\
X_B + \quad X_R + \quad X_Q &\leq 10 , \\
X_B + \qquad\qquad X_Q &\leq 8 , \\
X_B \geq 0, \quad X_R \geq 0, \quad X_Q &\geq 0 .
\end{aligned}
$$

Without solving this linear program, we can determine whether or not it is advantageous to divert resources from the current optimal solution into the new activity. Suppose one carload of type Q were produced; what would be the opportunity cost? The shadow prices determined for the problem without type Q are $100 per unit of machine capacity (measured in carloads of insulation type B), $200 per boxcar, and zero dollars per carload of type B demand. Type Q insulation uses 1.5 units of machine capacity (at a shadow price of $100), one boxcar (at $200), and one unit of demand (at $0). The opportunity cost of diverting resources from the current mix to produce one carload of type Q insulation is thus

$$100(1.5) + 200(1) + 0(1) = 350$$

However, the contribution from such production is only $325, hence the contribution to the company will be reduced by $325 - 350 = -25$ for each carload of type Q produced. The -25 is the reduced cost associated with the new activity. Since this value is negative, the opportunity cost of diverting resources from the optimal program exceeds the contribution. Hence, the new activity should not be pursued. In fact, if we solved the expanded linear program, the reduced cost associated with the non-negativity constraint on X_Q would be -25. This is often called the cost of nonoptimality, since for each unit of X_Q produced, the contribution is reduced by $25.

If, on the other hand, the contribution associated with the new activity were 360, then $360 - 350 = 10$ implies that the new activity is attractive to pursue. Sensitivity analysis does not tell us how much of the new insulation to produce in the event that it looks promising. The formulation given above must be solved to determine the new optimal program.

It is interesting to note what happens when the contribution from producing the new insulation is 350. In this case, the reduced cost is *zero*. What is the implication? The decision maker should be indifferent between producing some of the new type of insulation and not producing some. In the situation where resources can be diverted from the current optimal program into the new activity and the reduced cost of the new activity is zero, then there exist alternative optimal solutions to the linear program.

100 percent rules

Introducing the new activity is in essence diverting resources valued at their respective shadow prices from more than one constraint at a time. Under what conditions are the shadow prices valid when simultaneous changes are made in the right-hand-side values? The ranges are known to be valid for changes in one right-hand-side value with all other data being held fixed, but, unfortunately, it is *not* true in general that simultaneous variations within these ranges leave the shadow prices unchanged. However, it is possible to provide a conservative estimate to be used when simultaneous changes are valid.

If we consider the right-hand-side ranges determined for the insulation production problem involving only X_B and X_R as decision variables, we know that:

$$12 \leq b_1 \leq 20 ,$$
$$8.33 \leq b_2 \leq 12.33 ,$$
$$3.33 \leq b_3 .$$

Now suppose that we only consider making changes in the right-hand-side values of the first two constraints. We can graph these simultaneous changes in two dimensions, as shown in Figure 12–7. The diamond-shaped figure represents all simultaneous changes of production capacity, b_1, and boxcar availability, b_2, that are combinations of the individual ranges on each. The binding constraints at the optimal solution, and therefore the shadow prices and reduced costs, remain unchanged for simultaneous variations of b_1 and b_2 that are combinations of their respective ranges. This is a conservative estimate; it does not say that the shadow prices will change for variations outside the diamond figure but only that they might change. For example, it seems reasonable that once b_1 has been decreased from 16.67 to 12, so that any further decrease would change the shadow prices, any decrease in b_2 below 10 is likely to cause a change in the shadow prices.

Figure 12–7
Simultaneous variations in right-hand-side values

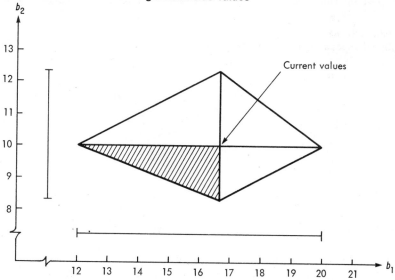

We can write an expression that summarizes making simultaneous changes away from the current solution that remain within the diamond figure. If the new right-hand-side values are to be b_1^* and b_2^*, respectively, and these values are both less than or equal to their respective current values (in the cross-hatched area of Figure 12–7), then

$$\frac{16.67 - b_1^*}{16.67 - 12} + \frac{10 - b_2^*}{10 - 8.33} \leqq 1 .$$

In essence, remaining within combinations of the ranges is equivalent to keeping the sum of the fractions formed by the ratio of the change to the maximum possible change in that direction less than or equal to one. Each fraction is the percent of the allowable range used and their sum must not exceed 100 percent; hence the 100 percent rule.

We should point out that if changes are made *only* in right-hand-side values of constraints that are not binding at the optimal solution, then the 100 percent rule does not apply. Such simultaneous changes are always possible until any one constraint becomes binding. However, if a right-hand-side value of any binding constraint is varied, the 100 percent rule must be applied to *all* right-hand-side values.

A similar 100 percent rule holds for simultaneous variations in the objective function coefficients. We have determined the ranges on the objective coefficients when varied individually:

$$200 \leq C_B \leq 400 ,$$
$$300 \leq C_R \leq 600 ,$$

where the current values of C_B and C_R are 300 and 400, respectively. The 100 percent rule for these coefficients is illustrated in Figure 12–8. If we

Figure 12–8
Simultaneous variations in objective coefficients

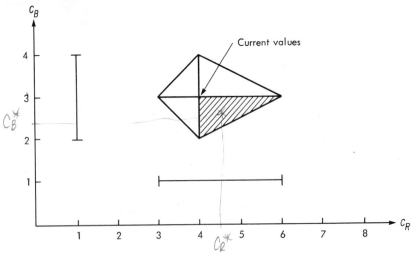

consider increasing C_R above the current value of 400 to C_R^* and decreasing C_B from its value of 300 to C_B^*, (in the cross-hatched area of Figure 12–8), the 100 percent rule states that:

$$\frac{C_R^* - 400}{600 - 400} + \frac{300 - C_B^*}{300 - 200} \leq 1 .$$

An example of simultaneous variations in the two coefficients that uses up to 100 percent of the ranges is $C_R^* = 500$ and $C_B^* = 250$. The slope of the objective function in this case would be $-C_R^*/C_B^* = -500/250 = -2$, and hence the objective function would be parallel to the production capacity constraint. Further increase in C_R^* or decrease in C_B^* would change the current optimal solution. However, to illustrate that the 100 percent rule is in fact conservative, consider increasing C_R^* and also increasing C_B^*. The 100 percent rule in this case states that:

$$\frac{C_R^* - 400}{600 - 400} + \frac{C_B^* - 300}{400 - 300} \leqq 1 \ .$$

If $C_R^* = 500$ and $C_B^* = 350$, the 100 percent rule is binding, but further changes in these coefficients are possible without changing the optimal solution, since the slopes of the production capacity constraint, objective function, and boxcar availability constraint are ordered as follows:

$$-2 < 500/350 < -1 \ .$$

Although the 100 percent rule is binding in this situation, further variations can be made without changing the optimal solution; hence, the 100 percent rule is conservative.

For the 100 percent rule on objective coefficients, it should be pointed out that if changes are made *only* in objective coefficients of decision variables with nonzero reduced costs, then the 100 percent rule does not apply. However, when changes are made in *any* objective function coefficient with zero reduced costs, then the 100 percent rule is applied to all coefficients being varied.

COMPUTER SOLUTION OF A LINEAR PROGRAM

The output of all commercially available computer systems for solving linear programs generally provides essentially the same information. In this section, we illustrate the various parts of the output for the example presented in the preceding one. Figure 12–9 gives the output for the example involving only insulation types R and B.

The output can generally be divided into three parts: Sections *1* and *2* give the solution, Sections *3* and *4* give shadow prices, and Sections *5* through *8* give sensitivity analysis.

The optimal value of the objective function is given as $3,667. Section *1* gives the optimal values of the decision variables that yield the given value of the objective function: $X_B = 3.33$ and $X_R = 6.67$. If any of the constraints are nonbinding, then the amount of slack or surplus in each constraint is given in Section *2*. The slack in demand for insulation type B is 4.67. Note that slack is *only* defined for "less-than-or-equal-to" constraints and measures the amount by which the left-hand side of such a constraint is less than the right-hand side. Surplus is *only* defined for "greater-than-or-equal-to" constraints and measures the amount by

Figure 12–9
Output for two-variable model

```
OPTION? OPT

DATA SET NAME? INSL1

TITLE: INSULATION PRODUCTION
PROCEED, DISPLAY, OR REJECT? D


OBJECTIVES:

                X-B         X-R

CONTRIB        300.0       400.0


CONSTRAINTS:

                X-B         X-R      RELATION  LIMITS

MACHINE        1.000       2.000       LE      16.67
BOXCARS        1.000       1.000       LE      10.00
DEMAND         1.000       .0000       LE      8.000

PROCEED OR REJECT? P

PARAMETRICS? N

MAXIMIZE OR MINIMIZE? MAX

OPTIMAL SOLUTION FOUND.
     CONTRIB      3666.70

OUTPUT OPTION? A

ALL ITEMS NOT LISTED IN SECTIONS 1 - 4 HAVE THE VALUE ZERO.

*1* DECISION VARIABLES
   1. X-B        3.33300
   2. X-R        6.66700

*2* SLACK(+) AND SURPLUS(-) IN CONSTRAINTS
   3. +DEMAND    4.66700

*3* SHADOW PRICES FOR CONSTRAINTS
   1. MACHINE    100.000
   2. BOXCARS    200.000

*4* REDUCED COSTS FOR DECISION VARIABLES

*5* RANGES ON COEFFICIENTS OF OBJECTIVE CONTRIB
      VARIABLE  LOWER BOUND  CURRENT VALUE  UPPER BOUND
   1. X-B        200.00        300.00        400.00
   2. X-R        300.00        400.00        600.00

*6* RANGES ON VALUES OF RIGHT-HAND-SIDE LIMITS
      CONSTRNT  LOWER BOUND  CURRENT VALUE  UPPER BOUND
   1. MACHINE    12.000        16.667        20.000
   2. BOXCARS    8.3335        10.000        12.334
   3. DEMAND     3.3330        8.0000        UNBOUNDED

*7* VARIABLE TRANSITIONS RESULTING FROM RANGING OBJECTIVE CONTRIB
      VARIABLE        LOWER BOUND              UPPER BOUND
                    VAR. IN    VAR. OUT     VAR. IN    VAR. OUT
   1. X-B           +BOXCARS    X-B         +MACHINE   +DEMAND
   2. X-R           +MACHINE   +DEMAND      +BOXCARS    X-B

*8* VARIABLE TRANSITIONS RESULTING FROM RANGING RHS LIMITS
      CONSTRNT        LOWER BOUND              UPPER BOUND
                    VAR. IN    VAR. OUT     VAR. IN    VAR. OUT
   1. MACHINE        +BOXCARS   +DEMAND      +MACHINE    X-B
   2. BOXCARS        +MACHINE    X-B         +BOXCARS   +DEMAND
   3. DEMAND         +BOXCARS   +DEMAND
```

which the left-hand side exceeds the right-hand side. For an equality constraint, neither slack nor surplus is defined.

The shadow price information is given in Sections *3* and *4*. These shadow prices give the change in the objective function per unit increase in the corresponding right-hand-side value. The shadow prices on the explicit constraints are given in Section *3*. The shadow price on production capacity is $100 per carload of type B machine capacity, while the shadow price on boxcar availability is $200 per boxcar. The shadow price on the demand constraint is zero, since there is slack in this constraint. That is, additional demand for insulation type B has zero value to the firm, since it currently has unfulfilled demand for this product. Section *4* provides the reduced costs or the shadow prices on the implicit nonnegativity constraints. Since the nonnegativity constraints on X_R and X_B are nonbinding at the optimal solution, these reduced costs are zero. In Figure 12–10 the example including insulation type Q is presented, and a nonzero reduced cost appears for insulation type Q.

In the first four sections of the computer output only the values that logically can be nonzero are printed. This leads to two interesting relationships. First, we know that if the shadow price on a constraint is nonzero, then the constraint must be binding (no slack or surplus) and if the constraint is nonbinding, then its corresponding shadow price must be zero. This is often referred to as *complementary slackness;* it implies that the names of all constraints are either included in Section *2* *or* Section *3* but *not* both. Second, a similar relationship exists between the names of the variables included in Sections *1* and *4*. If a decision variable has a nonzero value in Section *1*, then the reduced cost associated with the nonnegativity constraint on that variable must be zero and hence will not appear in Section *4*. Similarly, if a reduced cost is nonzero it will appear in Section *4* and the corresponding decision variable will be zero and hence will not appear in Section *1*.

The sensitivity results are given in Sections *5* through *8*. Sections *5* and *7*, which should be considered together, provide information on variations in the objective function coefficients. The range on a particular objective function coefficient gives the variation that is possible in that coefficient, all other problem data being held fixed such that the solution, the values of the decision variables and the slack and surplus in the constraints, remain unchanged. Section *5* gives the values for the range, for example $200 \leq C_B \leq 400$, while Section *7* gives the change in the solution that occurs if the boundaries of the range are exceeded. If C_B is less than 200, boxcar availability no longer is binding and decision variable X_R drops to zero. If C_B is greater than 400, the constraint on demand for type B becomes binding and the production capacity constraint becomes nonbinding.

Sections *6* and *8* should be considered together and provide information on variations in the right-hand-side values. The range on a particu-

Figure 12–10
Output for three-variable model

```
OPTION? OPT

DATA SET NAME? INSL2

TITLE: INSULATION PRODUCTION - 3 PRODUCTS
PROCEED, DISPLAY, OR REJECT? D


OBJECTIVES:

                X-B       X-R       X-Q

CONTRIB        300.0     400.0     325.0


CONSTRAINTS:

                X-B       X-R       X-Q      RELATION   LIMITS

MACHINE        1.000     2.000     1.500       LE       16.67
BOXCARS        1.000     1.000     1.000       LE       10.00
DEMAND         1.000      .0000    1.000       LE       8.000

PROCEED OR REJECT? P

PARAMETRICS? N

MAXIMIZE OR MINIMIZE? MAX

OPTIMAL SOLUTION FOUND.
    CONTRIB       3666.70

OUTPUT OPTION? A

ALL ITEMS NOT LISTED IN SECTIONS 1 - 4 HAVE THE VALUE ZERO.

*1* DECISION VARIABLES
   1. X-B        3.33300
   2. X-R        6.66700

*2* SLACK(+) AND SURPLUS(-) IN CONSTRAINTS
   3. +DEMAND    4.66700

*3* SHADOW PRICES FOR CONSTRAINTS
   1. MACHINE    100.000
   2. BOXCARS    200.000

*4* REDUCED COSTS FOR DECISION VARIABLES
   3. X-Q        -25.0000

*5* RANGES ON COEFFICIENTS OF OBJECTIVE CONTRIB
     VARIABLE   LOWER BOUND  CURRENT VALUE  UPPER BOUND
   1. X-B         250.00        300.00        400.00
   2. X-R         350.00        400.00        600.00
   3. X-Q        UNBOUNDED      325.00        350.00

*6* RANGES ON VALUES OF RIGHT-HAND-SIDE LIMITS
     CONSTRNT   LOWER BOUND  CURRENT VALUE  UPPER BOUND
   1. MACHINE     12.000        16.667        20.000
   2. BOXCARS     8.3335        10.000        12.334
   3. DEMAND      3.3330        8.0000       UNBOUNDED

*7* VARIABLE TRANSITIONS RESULTING FROM RANGING OBJECTIVE CONTRIB
     VARIABLE        LOWER BOUND            UPPER BOUND
                  VAR. IN   VAR. OUT     VAR. IN    VAR. OUT
   1. X-B          X-Q       X-B        +MACHINE    +DEMAND
   2. X-R          X-Q       X-B        +BOXCARS    X-B
   3. X-Q                                X-Q        X-B

*8* VARIABLE TRANSITIONS RESULTING FROM RANGING RHS LIMITS
     CONSTRNT        LOWER BOUND            UPPER BOUND
                  VAR. IN    VAR. OUT     VAR. IN    VAR. OUT
   1. MACHINE     +BOXCARS   +DEMAND     +MACHINE    X-B
   2. BOXCARS     +MACHINE   X-B         +BOXCARS    +DEMAND
   3. DEMAND      +BOXCARS   +DEMAND
```

lar right-hand-side value gives the variation that is possible in that value, all other problem data being held fixed, such that all the shadow prices and reduced costs remain unchanged. Section *6* gives the values for the range, for example, $12 \leqq b_1 \leqq 20$, while Section *7* gives the changes that occur when the boundary of the range is exceeded. If b_1 is less than 12, then the demand constraint becomes binding, and the boxcar availability constraint becomes nonbinding. If b_1 is greater than 20, then the production capacity constraint becomes nonbinding, and the decision variable X_R drops to zero.

All of the output given in Figure 12–9 should be compared to the results determined geometrically in the preceding section for the same example. As noted above, Figure 12–10 gives the computer output for the same example but includes the activity of producing insulation type Q. Note that the new activity is not promising at a contribution of $325, having a reduced cost of $-\$25$, as we determined graphically in the preceding section. The solution is therefore unchanged. Note, however, that the sensitivity results are somewhat different, since the new activity comes into play for some variations in the data.

SOLUTION STAGES OF A LINEAR PROGRAMMING PROBLEM

Although the practical applications of linear programming cover an increasingly broad range of problems, it is possible to distinguish five general stages that the solution of any linear programming problem should follow.

1. Formulating the model.
2. Gathering the data.
3. Obtaining the optimum solution.
4. Applying sensitivity analysis.
5. Testing and implementing the solution.

Obviously, these stages are not mutually exclusive but have common overlaps and strongly interact within one another. The main characteristics of each stage are discussed in general terms below.

Formulating the model

The first step to be taken in the application of linear programming to a practical situation is the development of the linear programming model. As we have seen, the basic aspects of the model formulation are:

Definition of the decision variables. On some occasions, a great amount of ingenuity is required to select those decision variables that are most adequate to describe the problem being examined. In some instances it is possible to decrease drastically the number of constraints or to transform an apparent nonlinear problem into a linear one by merely defining in a different way the decision variables to be used in the model formulation.

Selection of the objective function.   Once the decision variables are established, it is possible to determine the objective function to be minimized or maximized, provided that a measure of performance (or effectiveness) has been established and can be associated with the values that the decision variables can assume. This measure of performance provides a selection criterion used to evaluate the various courses of action that are available in the situation being investigated. The most common index of performance selected in business applications is some measure of dollar value; hence the objective function is usually the minimization of cost or the maximization of contribution. However, other objective functions could be more important in some instances. Examples of alternative objectives are:

Maximize total production, in units.

Minimize production time.

Maximize share of market for all or some products.

Maximize total sales, in dollars or units.

Minimize changes of production pattern.

Minimize the use of a particular scarce (or expensive) commodity.

Choosing an acceptable objective function could constitute a serious problem in some situations, especially when social and political problems are involved. In addition, there could be conflicting objectives, each one being important in its own right, that the decision maker wants to fulfill. In these situations it is usually helpful to define multiple objective functions and to solve the problem with respect to each one of them separately, observing the values that all the objective functions assume in each solution. If no one of these solutions appears to be acceptable, we could introduce as additional constraints the minimum desirable performance level of each of the objective functions we are willing to accept, and solve the problem again having as an objective the most relevant of those objective functions being considered. Sequential tests and sensitivity analysis could be quite valuable in obtaining satisfactory answers to this problem.

Description of the constraints.   Finally, all the constraints that characterize the problem under consideration should be described in terms of linear equations or inequalities. It is quite common that in the initial representation of the problem some vital constraints may be overlooked or some errors may be introduced into the model which will lead to unacceptable solutions to the problem under consideration. The linear programming solution, however, provides enough information to assist in the detection of these errors and their prompt correction. The problem then has to be reformulated and a new cycle has to be initiated.

Gathering the data

Having defined the model, it is necessary to collect all the data required for its solution. The data involve the objective function coefficients, the constraint coefficients, and the right-hand-side values of the linear program. This stage usually represents one of the most time-consuming and costly efforts required in the linear programming approach.

When dealing with large linear programs, often it is useful to write small computer programs to input automatically the required data and instructions. Those programs, called *matrix generators,* are designed to cover specific applications.

Obtaining the optimum solution

Because of the lengthy calculations required to obtain the optimum solution to a linear program, a digital computer is invariably used in processing any applied linear programming problem. In fact, almost all the computer manufacturers offer highly efficient linear programming codes which are available to the user without charge. These codes can presently handle general linear programming problems of up to 4,000 constraints and virtually an unlimited number of variables; they are equipped with sophisticated features which permit great flexibility in their operation and make them extraordinarily accurate and effective. Instructions to use these codes, which are provided by the manufacturers, vary only slightly among computer firms.

Computer programs are often written to translate the linear programming output, which is usually too technical in nature, into meaningful managerial reports ready to be used by middle and top managers. Most computer firms provide such general purpose *report writers*.

Applying sensitivity analysis

One of the most useful characteristics of the linear programming codes is their capability of performing sensitivity analyses on the optimum solutions obtained for the problem originally formulated. These postoptimum analyses are important for several reasons:

Data uncertainty. Much of the information that is used in formulating the linear program has a great degree of uncertainty. Future production capacities and product demand, product specifications and requirements, cost and revenue data, among other information, are usually evaluated through projections and average patterns which are far from being known with complete accuracy. Therefore, it is often important to determine how sensitive the optimum solution is to changes in these quantities, and how the optimum solution varies when actual experience deviates from the values used in the original model.

Dynamic considerations   Even if the data were known with complete certainty, we will still want to perform a sensitivity analysis on the optimum solution to find out how the recommended courses of action should be modified after some time, when changes most probably will take place in the original specification of the problem. In other words, instead of just getting a static solution to the problem, it is usually desirable to obtain at least some appreciation for a dynamic situation.

Formulation errors.   Finally, we want to inquire as to the effect on the optimum solution of errors we may have committed in the original formulation of the problem.

In general, the type of changes that are important to investigate are changes in the objective function coefficients, in the right-hand-side values, and in the constraint coefficients. Further, it is sometimes necessary to evaluate the impact on the objective function of introducing new variables or new constraints into the problem. Although it is often impossible to assess all of these changes simultaneously, the good linear programming codes provide several means of obtaining pertinent information about the impact of these changes with a minimum of extra computational work.

In addition to the information described in the preceding section, most codes allow for the use of multiple right-hand sides and multiple objective functions. This makes it possible to explore, in a very efficient manner, the changes observed in the optimum solution when the available resources or the costs are changed. Moreover, some codes permit parametric changes to be explored by specifying the resulting optimum solution when either right-hand-side values or objective function coefficients are continuously varied from one set of prescribed values to another.

Testing and implementing the solution

The solution should be fully tested to make sure the model clearly represents a real situation. We have already pointed out the importance of conducting sensitivity analyses as part of this testing effort. Should the solution be unacceptable, new refinements have to be incorporated into the model and new solutions obtained until the linear programming model is adequate.

When testing is complete, the model can be implemented. Implementation usually means the operation of the model with real data to arrive at a decision or set of decisions. We can distinguish two kinds of implementation—a single or one-time use, such as solving a plant location problem, and continual or repeated use of the model in production planning or blending. In the latter case routine operating systems should be established to provide input data to the linear programming model and to transform the output into routine operating instructions. Care must be taken to ensure that changes which take place in the real operating system are reflected in changes in the model.

EXERCISES

12.1. A machine shop has three types of equipment: lathes, drill presses, and milling machines. There are four products that can be made, each of which has a different contribution:

Product	Contribution per unit
1	$10.48
2	14.60
3	16.68
4	8.36

The availability of equipment depends on the number of machines available and men to run them. The resulting number of hours available of each is as follows:

Machine	Hours
Lathes.....................	1,000
Drill presses...............	4,000
Milling machines	2,500

To produce one unit of the first item requires: 1.5 hours of lathe time, 1 hour of drill press time, and 1.5 hours of mill time. For the second item, the hours are respectively 1, 5 and 3; for the third 2.4, 1, and 3.5, and for the fourth 1, 3.5 and 1.

Formulate the production decision problem as a linear programming problem.

12.2. J. Foster Smith was aggravated. The production manager of the Cooperative Dairy Company, to which his farm belonged, had just informed him that beginning next week the delivery of the 20,000 gallons per day of milk from his farm should be made to the 50,000-gallon Weirton Processing Facility, instead of to the Beaver Valley facility, of identical size, close to his farm.

It appeared that since the retirement of the previous production manager there had been nothing but change. In Smith's opinion, there was no real reason why the change was needed. Beaver Valley Processing Facility was only two miles from his farm, while Weirton was five. When Smith questioned the new production manager about the change he was told that the change was an attempt to save money, since Jones Dairy, which supplies 80,000 gallons of milk to the Cooperative, would be taking 50,000 gallons of its milk to Beaver, which was four miles from Jones Dairy, instead of carrying it to Weirton, eight miles distant. Since the Cooperative divided overall profits among the farmers in proportion to ownership, and costs were reported and reimbursed centrally, Smith reasoned that the change was probably reasonable but he wanted to think about it and satisfy himself completely that the change wouldn't lose money overall.

Formulate Smith's problem as a linear program.

12.3. A man in charge of a bond portfolio has $10 million to invest. The bonds available for investment are shown in Table A. His objective is to maximize after-tax earnings, subject to the following limitations:

1. Municipals must total no more than $3 million.

2. The average quality of the portfolio must not be worse than 1.4 on the bank's quality scale (see Table A).
3. The average years to maturity of the portfolio must not exceed five years.

Table A

Bond name	Bond type	*Quality scales*		Years to maturity	Yield to maturity	After-tax yield*
		(Moody's)	(Bank's)			
A	Municipal	Aa	2	9	4.5%	4.5%
B	Agency	Aa	2	15	5.4	2.7
C	Government	Aaa	1	4	5.0	2.5
D	Government	Aaa	1	3	4.4	2.2
E	Municipal	B	5	2	4.5	4.5

* Assume the tax on earnings to be 50 percent and that all bonds can be purchased at par.

Assume that all five bonds are available for investment, subject to the limitations given in the statement of the problem.

a. Formulate the optimum portfolio investment problem as a linear programming problem.

b. Indicate what changes are to be introduced in the formulation of this problem when in addition, it is possible to borrow up to $1 million at 5.5% before taxes.

12.4. Use the statement of Exercise 12.3 but assume that only bonds A and D are available for investment, subject to the same limitations given in the statement of the problem.

a. Formulate the optimal investment portfolio problem as a linear programming problem.

b. Construct a geometrical representation of the constraints defined in *a*.

c. From this geometrical representation, find the optimal values for the amounts to be invested in bonds A and D.

12.5. Outdoors, Inc., has as one of its product lines lawn furniture. They currently have three items in that line—a lawn chair, a standard bench, and a table. These products are produced in a two-step manufacturing process involving the tube bending department and the welding department. The time required by each item in each department is as follows:

	Product			
	Lawn chair	Bench	Table	Present capacity
Tube bending	1.2	1.7	1.2	1,000
Welding	.8	0	2.3	1,200

The contribution that Outdoors, Inc., receives from manufacture and sale of one unit of each product is $3 for a chair, $3 for a bench, and $5 for a table.

The company is trying to plan its production mix for the current selling season. They feel that they can sell any number they produce, but unfortunately production is further limited by available material because of a prolonged strike. The company currently has on hand 2,000 pounds of tubing. The three products require the following amounts of this tubing: 2 pounds per chair, 3 pounds per bench, and 4.5 pounds per table.

In order to determine the optimal product mix, the production manager has formulated the linear program shown in Figure A and obtained the results shown in Figure B.

Figure A
Formulation of Outdoors, Inc.

Objective:	Chair	Bench	Table		
Contribution:	$3	$3	$5		
Constraints:	Chair	Bench	Table	Relation	Limit
D-tube	1.2	1.7	1.2	$\leqq$	1,000
D-weld	.8	0	2.3	$\leqq$	1,200
TSuply	2.0	3.0	4.5	$\leqq$	2,000

Figure B

TITLE: OUTDOORS

OPTIMAL SOLUTION FOUND.
VALUE OF OBJECTIVE CONTRI   IS   2766.67

OUTPUT OPTION?   AA

1 DECISION VARIABLES
  1. CHAIR   7ØØ.ØØØ
  3. TABLE   133.333

2 SLACK (+) AND SURPLUS (−) IN CONSTRAINTS
  2. +D−WELD   333.333

3 SHADOW PRICES FOR CONSTRAINTS
  1. D−TUBE   1.16667
  3. TSUPLY   Ø.8ØØØØØ

4 REDUCED COSTS FOR DECISION VARIABLES
  2. BENCH   −1.38333

ALL ITEMS NOT LISTED HAVE THE VALUE ZERO.

5 RANGES ON COEFFICIENTS OF CONTRI

	VARIABLE	LOWER BOUND	CURRENT VALUE	UPPER BOUND
1.	CHAIR	2.2222	3.ØØØØ	5.ØØØØ
2.	BENCH	UNBOUNDED	3.ØØØØ	4.3833
3.	TABLE	3.ØØØØ	5.ØØØØ	6.75ØØ

6 RANGES ON COEFFICIENTS OF LIMIT

	CONSTRNT	LOWER BOUND	CURRENT VALUE	UPPER BOUND
1.	D−TUBE	533.33	1ØØØ.Ø	12ØØ.Ø
2.	D−WELD	866.67	12ØØ.Ø	UNBOUNDED
3.	TSUPLY	1666.7	2ØØØ.Ø	2555.6

REVISIONS? N

CONCLUDE OR RESTART?   C

a. What is the optimal production mix? What contribution can the firm anticipate by producing this mix?

b. What is the value of one unit more of tube-bending time? Of welding time? Of metal tubing?

c. A local distributor has offered to sell Outdoors, Inc., some additional metal tubing for 60 cents a pound. Should Outdoors buy it? If yes, how much would their contribution increase if they bought 500 pounds and used it in an optimal fashion?

d. If Outdoors, Inc., feels that it must produce at least 100 benches to round out its product line, what effect will that have on its contribution?

e. The R&D department has been redesigning the bench to make it more profitable. The new design will require 1.1 units of tube bending time, 2 hours of welding, and 2.0 pounds of metal tubing. If they can sell one unit of this bench with a unit contribution of $3, what effect will it have on overall contribution?

f. Marketing has suggested a new patio awning that would require 1.8 units of tube-bending time, 0.5 units of welding time, and 1.3 pounds of metal tubing. What contribution must this new product have to make it attractive to produce this season?

g. Outdoors, Inc., has a chance to sell some of its capacity in tube bending at a cost of $1.50 an hour. If it sells 200 hours at that price, how will this affect contribution?

h. If the contribution on chairs were to decrease to $2.50, what would be the optimal production mix, and what contribution would this production plan give?

Case 12–1A

Sherman Motor Company*

The Sherman Motor Company manufactured two specialized models of trucks in a single plant. Manufacturing operations were grouped into four departments: metal stamping; engine assembly; model 101 assembly; and model 102 assembly. Monthly production capacity in each department was limited as follows, assuming that each department devoted full time to the model in question:

| | Monthly capacity | |
Department	Model 101	Model 102
Metal stamping	2,500	3,500
Engine assembly	3,333	1,667
Model 101 assembly	2,250	—
Model 102 assembly	—	1,500

That is, the capacity of the metal stamping department was sufficient to produce stampings for either 2,500 model 101 trucks or 3,500 model 102 trucks per month if it devoted full time to either model. It could also produce stampings for both models, with a corresponding reduction in the potential output of each. Since each model 102 truck required five sevenths as much of the capacity of the department as one model 101 truck, for every seven model 102 trucks produced it would be necessary to subtract five from the capacity remaining for model 101. If, for example, 1,400 model 102 trucks were produced, there would be sufficient stamping capacity available for $2,500 - (5/7)(1,400) = 1,500$ model 101 trucks. Thus, the capacity restrictions in the four departments could be represented by the straight lines shown in Exhibit 1. Any production combination within the area bounded by the heavy portion of the lines was feasible from a capacity standpoint.

The prices to dealers of the two models, FOB the Sherman plant, were $2,100 for model 101 and $2,000 for model 102. Sherman followed the price leadership of one of the larger manufacturers in the industry.

As a result of a seller's market in 1953, Sherman was able to sell as many trucks as it could produce. The production schedules it had fol-

* Adapted from an example used by Robert Dorfman in "Mathematical or 'Linear' Programming: A Nonmathematical Approach," *American Economic Review,* December 1953.

Exhibit 1
Diagram showing production possibilities

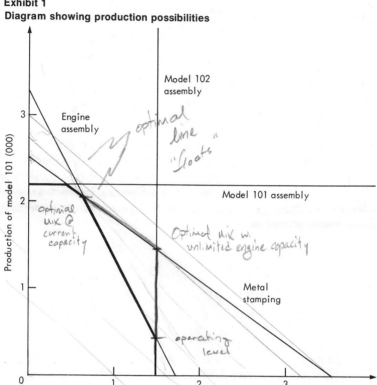

lowed during the first six months of the year resulted in a monthly output
of 333 model 101 trucks and 1,500 model 102 trucks. At this level of
production, both the model 102 assembly and the engine assembly departments were operating at capacity, but the metal stamping department
was operating at only 56.2 percent of capacity and the model 101 assembly

Exhibit 2
Standard costs of two truck models

		Model 101		*Model 102*
Direct materials		$1,200		$1,000
Direct labor				
Metal stamping	$ 40		$ 30	
Engine assembly	60		120	
Final assembly	100	200	75	225
Overhead*				
Metal stamping	$216		$169	
Engine assembly	130		251	
Final assembly	445	791	175	595
Total		$2,191		$1,820

* See Exhibit 3.

department was at only 14.8 percent. Standard costs at this level of production are given in Exhibit 2, and further details on overhead costs are given in Exhibit 3.

Exhibit 3
Overhead budget for 1953

Department	Total overhead per month*	Fixed overhead per month†	Variable overhead/unit Model 101	Variable overhead/unit Model 102
Metal stamping	$ 325,000	$135,000	$120	$100
Engine assembly	420,000	85,000	105	200
Model 101 assembly	148,000	90,000	175	—
Model 102 assembly	262,000	75,000	—	125
	$1,155,000	$385,000	$400	$425

  * Based on planned 1953 production rate of 333 model 101 trucks and 1,500 model 102 trucks per month.
  † Fixed overhead was distributed to models in proportion to degree of capacity utilization.

At a monthly planning session of the company's executives in July 1953, dissatisfaction was expressed with the company's profit performance as reported in the six-month income statement just prepared (see Exhibit 4). The sales manager pointed out that it was impossible to sell the model 101 truck to yield a profit and suggested that it be dropped from the line in order to improve overall profitability.

Exhibit 4
Income statement for six months ending June 30, 1953
(thousands of dollars)

Net sales	$21,950
Cost of goods sold	20,683
Gross Margin	$ 1,267
Selling, administrative, and general expense	1,051
Net income before taxes	$ 216
Taxes on income	115
Net income after taxes	$ 101

The controller objected to this suggestion. "The real trouble, Dick, is that we are trying to absorb the entire fixed overhead of the model 101 assembly department with only a small number of units production. Actually these units are making a contribution to overhead, even though it's not adequate to cover fixed costs, and we'd be worse off without them. In fact, it seems to me quite possible that we'd be better off by *increasing* production of model 101 trucks, cutting back if necessary on model 102 production."

The production manager pointed out that there was another way in which output of model 101 trucks could be stepped up, which would not require a cutback in model 102 production. This would be through purchase of engines from an outside supplier, thus relieving the present capacity problem in the engine assembly department. If this course of action were followed, Sherman would probably furnish the necessary materials but would reimburse the supplier for labor and overhead.

At this point the president entered the discussion. He asked the controller, the sales manager, and the production manager to get together to consider the two questions raised by their comments and to report their recommendations to him the next day. The two questions were: (1) Assuming no change in present capacity and demand, what would be the most profitable product mix? (2) What was the maximum labor and overhead charge that Sherman could afford to pay for engines if it purchased them from an outside supplier?

Case 12–1B

Sherman Motor Company Problems

1. *a.* Find the best product mix for Sherman Motors first when the capacities are those of the case and then with the engine capacity raised to 3,334 units of 101 engines. What is a unit of engine assembly capacity worth?
   b. The second unit of capacity added is worth the same as the first. Verify that if the capacity were increased to 4,333 the increased contribution is 1,000 times that in part *a*.
   c. How many units of 101 engine capacity can be added before there is a change in the value of an extra unit?
2. Sherman Motors is considering introducing a new economy truck, to be called Model 103. The total metal stamping capacity would be sufficient for 3,000 Model 103s per month, while the total engine assembly shop would be enough for 2,500 Model 103s. The 103s could be assembled in the 101 assembly department; each 103 would require only half as much time as a 101. Each Model 103 truck would give a contribution of $225.
   a. Formulate the production decision with the three trucks as a linear programming problem and then verify that no Model 103s should be produced.
   b. How much would it cost in terms of contribution if, for some other reasons, management insisted that at least one Model 103 be made?
   c. How high would the contribution on each 103 have to be before it became attractive to produce the new model?

3. The engine assembly line can be put on overtime. Suppose that
    efficiencies do not change and that 2,000 units of 101 overtime
    capacity are available. If direct labor costs increase by 50 percent
    on overtime and if the fixed overhead on the line on overtime is
    $40,000, the variable overhead remaining the same, would it pay
    to go on overtime?
4. The marketing manager, in arguing that maximizing short-run con-
    tribution was not necessarily to the long-run good of the company,
    wanted to produce as many Model 101s as possible. It was agreed
    to maximize the contribution for the month as long as the number
    101s produced was at least four times the number of 102s. What is
    the resulting product mix?

Case 12–2A

Red Brand Canners*

On Monday, September 13, 1965, Mr. Mitchell Gordon, Vice President of
Operations, asked the Controller, the Sales Manager, and the Production
Manager to meet with him to discuss the amount of tomato products to
pack that season. The tomato crop, which had been purchased at planting,
was beginning to arrive at the cannery, and packing operations would
have to be started by the following Monday. Red Brand Canners was a
medium-sized company which canned and distributed a variety of fruit
and vegetable products under private brands in the western states.

Mr. William Cooper, the Controller, and Mr. Charles Myers, the Sales
Manager, were the first to arrive in Mr. Gordon's office. Dan Tucker, the
Production Manager, came in a few minutes later and said that he had
picked up Produce Inspection's latest estimate of the quality of the incoming tomatoes. According to their report, about 20 percent of the crop was
Grade A quality and the remaining portion of the 3-million pound crop
was Grade B.

Gordon asked Myers about the demand for tomato products for the
coming year. Myers replied that they could sell all of the whole canned
tomatoes they could produce. The expected demand for tomato juice and
tomato paste, on the other hand, was limited. The Sales Manager then
passed around the latest demand forecast, which is shown in Exhibit 1.
He reminded the group that the selling prices had been set in light of the

---

* Reprinted from *Stanford Business Cases 1965* with the permission of the Publishers,
Stanford University Graduate School of Business, © 1965 by the Board of Trustees of the
Leland Stanford Junior University.

long-term marketing strategy of the company and that the potential sales had been forecast at these prices.

Exhibit 1
Demand forecasts

Product	Selling price per case	Demand forecast (cases)
24—2½ whole tomatoes	$4.00	800,000
24—2½ choice peach halves	5.40	10,000
24—2½ peach nectar	4.60	5,000
24—2½ tomato juice	4.50	50,000
24—2½ cooking apples	4.90	15,000
24—2½ tomato paste	3.80	80,000

Bill Cooper, after looking at Myers' estimates of demand, said that it looked like the company "should do quite well [on the tomato crop] this year." With the new accounting system that had been set up, he had been able to compute the contribution for each product, and according to his analysis the incremental profit on whole tomatoes was greater than the incremental profit on any other tomato product. In May, after Red Brand had signed contracts agreeing to purchase the grower's production at an average delivered price of 6 cents per pound, Cooper had computed the tomato products' contributions (see Exhibit 2).

Exhibit 2
Product item profitability

Product	24—2½ whole tomatoes	24—2½ choice peach halves	24—2½ peach nectar	24—2½ tomato juice	24—2½ cooking apples	24—2½ tomato paste
Selling price	$4.00	$5.40	$4.60	$4.50	$4.90	$3.80
Variable costs:						
Direct labor	1.18	1.40	1.27	1.32	0.70	0.54
Variable overhead	0.24	0.32	0.23	0.36	0.22	0.26
Variable selling........	0.40	0.30	0.40	0.85	0.28	0.38
Packaging material	0.70	0.56	0.60	0.65	0.70	0.77
Fruit*	1.08	1.80	1.70	1.20	0.90	1.50
Total variable costs	3.60	4.38	4.20	4.38	2.80	3.45
Contribution	0.40	1.02	0.40	0.12	1.10	0.35
Less allocated overhead ..	0.28	0.70	0.52	0.21	0.75	0.23
Net profit	0.12	0.32	(0.12)	(0.09)	0.35	0.12

* Product usage is as given below:

Product	Pounds per case
Whole tomatoes	18
Peach halves	18
Peach nectar	17
Tomato juice	20
Cooking apples	27
Tomato paste	25

Dan Tucker brought to Cooper's attention that although there was ample production capacity, it was impossible to produce all whole tomatoes since too small a portion of the tomato crop was "A" quality. Red Brand used a numerical scale to record the quality of both raw produce and prepared products. This scale ran from zero to ten, the higher number representing better quality. According to this scale, "A" tomatoes averaged nine points per pound and "B" tomatoes averaged five points per pound. Tucker noted that the minimum average input quality was eight points per pound for canned whole tomatoes and six points per pound for juice. Paste could be made entirely from "B"-grade tomatoes. This meant that whole tomato production was limited to 800,000 pounds.

Gordon stated that this was not a real limitation. He had been recently solicited to purchase 80,000 pounds of Grade A tomatoes at 8½ cents per pound and at that time had turned down the offer. He felt, however, that the tomatoes were still available.

Myers, who had been doing some calculations, said that although he agreed that the company "should do quite well this year," it would not be by canning whole tomatoes. It seemed to him that the tomato cost should be allocated on the basis of quality and quantity rather than by quantity only, as Cooper had done. Therefore, he had recomputed the marginal profit on this basis (see Exhibit 3), and from his results had concluded that Red Brand should use 2,000,000 pounds of the "B" tomatoes for paste, and the remaining 400,000 pounds of "B" tomatoes and all of the "A" tomatoes for juice. If the demand expectations were realized, a contribution of $48,000 would be made on this year's tomato crop.

Exhibit 3
Marginal analysis of tomato products

Z = Cost per pound of Grade A tomatoes in cents.
Y = Cost per pound of Grade B tomatoes in cents.

$$(600,000 \text{ lb} \times Z) + (2,400,000 \text{ lb} \times Y) = (3,000,000 \text{ lb} \times 6) \quad (1)$$

$$\frac{Z}{9} = \frac{Y}{5} \quad (2)$$

Z = 9.32 cents per pound
Y = 5.18 cents per pound

Product	Canned whole tomatoes	Tomato juice	Tomato paste
Selling price	$4.00	$4.50	$3.80
Variable cost			
(excluding tomato cost)	2.52	3.18	1.95
	$1.48	$1.32	$1.85
Tomato cost	1.49	1.24	1.30
Marginal profit	($0.01)	$0.08	$0.55

Case 12–2B

Red Brand Canners (supplement)

Late in the afternoon of Monday, September 13, 1965, while Messrs. Gordon, Cooper, Myers, and Tucker were discussing the production plans for the 1965 tomato crop they had bought, Mr. Gordon left to attend a dinner meeting of the local alumni club of the Graduate School of Business Administration of Stanford University.

He didn't want to go. In fact, he wouldn't have gone if he could have found some way out. The speaker for the evening was young, the topic was technical, and the whole thing promised to be boring.

To his surprise, the evening turned out to be exciting. The problems the speaker described were really just like the problems he had spent the afternoon discussing, as soon as he transferred the setting. So as the speaker went on, Mr. Gordon's doodling took the pattern of the table reproduced in Exhibit 1. He did (since he knew that Red Brand could sell to its forecast) have a linear programming problem!

After the talk, he found out from the speaker where he could get the computations done at a relatively small cost, and he sent to Compro, a local data processing firm, the table of Exhibit 1. He received back the data in Exhibit 2.

When he showed the results to Mr. Cooper, it was pointed out to him (Gordon thought that Cooper's tone got somewhat strident) that every accountant knows that one should attribute to the product the cost thereof: one should therefore deduct from every contribution the cost of the tomatoes, thus reducing the contributions by 6 cents per pound. Mr. Gordon's comment was that it shouldn't make one bit of difference since you had to pay for the tomatoes anyway, but he got a surprise when he submitted the revised data for a computer run. He got back the output of Exhibit 3. He sat and pondered awhile. He knew that pretty soon he was going to have to face Cooper, and he hated to lose this kind of argument.

The question of that other 80,000 pounds was also going to come up. He now thought he should go out and buy it all. He had called last evening's speaker and was informed that he would still make money on those tomatoes even if he paid as much as 9 cents per pound. At least, the young man said, that's what the computer printout told him. So he sent data for the purchase option to the computer center. He included data assuming that the fruit on hand cost nothing; the results for this run are shown in Exhibit 4. (An alternative formulation for the purchase option is shown in Exhibit 5.)

Exhibit 1

	AC	BC	AJ	BJ	AP	BP		
Juice market	0	0	1	1	0	0	≤	1,000
Paste market	0	0	0	0	1	1	≤	2,000
Grade A in crop	1	0	1	0	1	0	≤	600
Grade B in crop	0	1	0	1	0	1	≤	2,400
Can quality	1	−3	0	0	0	0	≥	0
Juice quality	0	0	3	−1	0	0	≥	0
Contribution*	82.2	82.2	66	66	74	74		

Note:

    AC—the quantity (in thousand pounds) of Grade A tomatoes used in the production of whole canned tomatoes.

    BC—thousands of pounds of Grade B in whole canned tomatoes.

    AJ—Grade A in juice.

    BJ—Grade B in juice.

    AP—Grade A in paste.

    BP—Grade B in paste.

* The contributions are $82.20 per 1,000 pounds, etc., or 8.22 cents per pound, etc.

Exhibit 2

OBJECTIVES:

	A-CANNED	B-CANNED	A-JUICE	B-JUICE	A-PASTE	B-PASTE
CONTR	82.20	82.20	66.00	66.00	74.00	74.00

CONSTRAINTS:

	A-CANNED	B-CANNED	A-JUICE	B-JUICE	A-PASTE	B-PASTE	RELATION	RHS-001
CE-MKT	.0000	.0000	1.000	1.000	.0000	.0000	LE	1000.
ST-MKT	.0000	.0000	.0000	.0000	1.000	1.000	LE	2000.
A-SUPPLY	1.000	.0000	1.000	.0000	1.000	.0000	LE	600.0
B-SUPPLY	.0000	1.000	.0000	1.000	.0000	1.000	LE	2400.
CAN-QUAL	1.000	−3.000	.0000	.0000	.0000	.0000	GE	.0000
CE-QUAL	.0000	.0000	3.000	−1.000	.0000	.0000	GE	.0000

Exhibit 2 (*continued*)

MAXIMIZE OR MINIMIZE? MAX

OPTIMAL SOLUTION FOUND.
    CONTR   225340.

OUTPUT OPTION? E

1 DECISION VARIABLES
  1. A-CANNED 525.000
  2. .B-CANNED 175.000
  3. A-JUICE   75.0000
  4. B-JUICE 225.000
  6. B-PASTE 2000.00

2 SLACK(+) AND SURPLUS(-) IN CONSTRAINTS
  1. +JCE-MKT 700.000

3 SHADOW PRICES FOR CONSTRAINTS
  2. PST-MKT   16.1000
  3. A-SUPPLY 90.3000
  4. B-SUPPLY 57.9000
  5. CAN-QUAL -8.10000
  6. JCE-QUAL -8.10000

4 REDUCED COSTS FOR DECISION VARIABLES
  5. A-PASTE   -32.4000

5 RANGES ON COEFFICIENTS OF OBJECTIVE CONTR

	VARIABLE	LOWER BOUND	CURRENT VALUE	UPPER BOUND
1.	A-CANNED	60.600	82.200	236.60
2.	B-CANNED	60.600	82.200	545.40
3.	A-JUICE	-88.400	66.000	87.600
4.	B-JUICE	14.533	66.000	80.311
5.	A-PASTE	UNBOUNDED	74.000	106.40
6.	B-PASTE	57.900	74.000	UNBOUNDED

6 RANGES ON VALUES OF RIGHT-HAND-SIDE RHS-001

	CONSTRNT	LOWER BOUND	CURRENT VALUE	UPPER BOUND
1.	JCE-MKT	300.00	1000.0	UNBOUNDED
2.	PST-MKT	1533.3	2000.0	2200.0
3.	A-SUPPLY	133.33	600.00	1200.0
4.	B-SUPPLY	2200.0	2400.0	2866.7
5.	CAN-QUAL	-600.00	.00000	466.67
6.	JCE-QUAL	-200.00	.00000	1400.0

OUTPUT OPTION? N

Exhibit 3

OBJECTIVES:

	A-CANNED	B-CANNED	A-JUICE	B-JUICE	A-PASTE	B-PASTE
CONTR	22.20	22.20	6.000	6.000	14.00	14.00

CONSTRAINTS:

	A-CANNED	B-CANNED	A-JUICE	B-JUICE	A-PASTE	B-PASTE	RELATION	RHS-001
JCE-MKT	.0000	.0000	1.000	1.000	.0000	.0000	LE	1000.
PST-MKT	.0000	.0000	.0000	.0000	1.000	1.000	LE	2000.
A-SUPPLY	1.000	.0000	1.000	.0000	1.000	.0000	LE	600.0
B-SUPPLY	.0000	1.000	.0000	1.000	.0000	1.000	LE	2400.
CAN-QUAL	1.000	-3.000	.0000	.0000	.0000	.0000	GE	.0000
JCE-QUAL	.0000	.0000	3.000	-1.000	.0000	.0000	GE	.0000

Exhibit 3 (*continued*)

```
MAXIMIZE OR MINIMIZE? MAX

OPTIMAL SOLUTION FOUND.
       CONTR          45760.0

OUTPUT OPTION? E

*1* DECISION VARIABLES
   1. A-CANNED   600.000
   2. B-CANNED   200.000
   4. B-JUICE    .000000
   6. B-PASTE    2000.00

*2* SLACK(+) AND SURPLUS(-) IN CONSTRAINTS
   1. +JCE-MKT   1000.00
   4. +B-SUPPLY  200.000

*3* SHADOW PRICES FOR CONSTRAINTS
   2. PST-MKT    14.0000
   3. A-SUPPLY   29.6000
   5. CAN-QUAL   -7.40000
   6. JCE-QUAL   -6.00000

*4* REDUCED COSTS FOR DECISION VARIABLES
   3. A-JUICE    -5.60000
   5. A-PASTE    -29.6000

*5* RANGES ON COEFFICIENTS OF OBJECTIVE CONTR
        VARIABLE   LOWER BOUND   CURRENT VALUE   UPPER BOUND
   1. A-CANNED     16.600        22.200          UNBOUNDED
   2. B-CANNED     5.4000        22.200          UNBOUNDED
   3. A-JUICE      UNBOUNDED     6.0000          11.600
   4. B-JUICE      .00000        6.0000          7.8667
   5. A-PASTE      UNBOUNDED     14.000          43.600
   6. B-PASTE      .00000        14.000          UNBOUNDED

*6* RANGES ON VALUES OF RIGHT-HAND-SIDE RHS-001
        CONSTRNT   LOWER BOUND   CURRENT VALUE   UPPER BOUND
   1. JCE-MKT      .00000        1000.0          UNBOUNDED
   2. PST-MKT      .00000        2000.0          2200.0
   3. A-SUPPLY     .00000        600.00          1200.0
   4. B-SUPPLY     2200.0        2400.0          UNBOUNDED
   5. CAN-QUAL     -600.00       .00000          600.00
   6. JCE-QUAL     -200.00       .00000          .00000

OUTPUT OPTION? N
```

Exhibit 4

OBJECTIVES:

	A-CANNED	B-CANNED	A-JUICE	B-JUICE	A-PASTE	B-PASTE	P-CANNED	P-JUICE	P-PASTE
CONTR	82.20	82.20	66.00	66.00	74.00	74.00	-2.800	-19.00	-11.00

CONSTRAINTS:

	A-CANNED	B-CANNED	A-JUICE	B-JUICE	A-PASTE	B-PASTE	P-CANNED	P-JUICE	P-PASTE	RELATION	RHS-001
JCE-MKT	.0000	.0000	1.000	1.000	.0000	.0000	.0000	1.000	.0000	LE	1000.
PST-MKT	.0000	.0000	.0000	.0000	1.000	1.000	.0000	.0000	1.000	LE	2000.
A-SUPPLY	1.000	.0000	1.000	.0000	1.000	.0000	.0000	.0000	.0000	LE	600.0
B-SUPPLY	.0000	1.000	.0000	1.000	.0000	1.000	.0000	.0000	.0000	LE	2400.
CAN-QUAL	1.000	-3.000	.0000	.0000	.0000	.0000	1.000	.0000	.0000	GE	.0000
JCE-QUAL	.0000	-3.000	3.000	-1.000	.0000	.0000	.0000	3.000	.0000	GE	.0000
P-SUPPLY	.0000	.0000	.0000	.0000	.0000	.0000	1.000	1.000	1.000	LE	80.00

Exhibit 4 (continued)

MAXIMIZE OR MINIMIZE? MAX

OPTIMAL SOLUTION FOUND.
      CONTR   225764.

OUTPUT OPTION? E

ALL ITEMS NOT LISTED IN SECTIONS 1 - 4 HAVE THE VALUE ZERO.

1 DECISION VARIABLES
   1. A-CANNED   600.000
   2. B-CANNED   205.000
   4. B-JUICE   195.000
   6. B-PASTE   2000.00
   7. P-CANNED   15.0000
   8. P-JUICE   65.0000

2 SLACK(+) AND SURPLUS(-) IN CONSTRAINTS
   1. +JCE-MKT   740.000

3 SHADOW PRICES FOR CONSTRAINTS
   2. PST-MKT   16.1000
   3. A-SUPPLY   90.3000
   4. B-SUPPLY   57.9000
   5. CAN-QUAL   -8.10000
   6. JCE-QUAL   -8.10000
   7. P-SUPPLY   5.30000

4 REDUCED COSTS FOR DECISION VARIABLES
   3. A-JUICE   .238419E-06
   5. A-PASTE   -32.4000
   9. P-PASTE   -32.4000

5 RANGES ON COEFFICIENTS OF OBJECTIVE CONTR
        VARIABLE   LOWER BOUND   CURRENT VALUE   UPPER BOUND
   1. A-CANNED   82.200   82.200   UNBOUNDED
   2. B-CANNED   68.067   82.200   545.40
   3. A-JUICE   UNBOUNDED   66.000   66.000
   4. B-JUICE   14.533   66.000   80.133
   5. A-PASTE   UNBOUNDED   74.000   106.40
   6. B-PASTE   57.900   74.000   UNBOUNDED
   7. P-CANNED   -7.5111   -2.8000   -2.8000
   8. P-JUICE   -19.000   -19.000   2.6000
   9. P-PASTE   UNBOUNDED   -11.000   21.400

6 RANGES ON VALUES OF RIGHT-HAND-SIDE RHS-001
        CONSTRNT   LOWER BOUND   CURRENT VALUE   UPPER BOUND
   1. JCE-MKT   260.00   1000.0   UNBOUNDED
   2. PST-MKT   1960.0   2000.0   2173.3
   3. A-SUPPLY   480.00   600.00   1120.0
   4. B-SUPPLY   2226.7   2400.0   2440.0
   5. CAN-QUAL   -520.00   .00000   120.00
   6. JCE-QUAL   -173.33   .00000   40.000
   7. P-SUPPLY   66.667   80.000   600.00

OUTPUT OPTION? N

Exhibit 5

OBJECTIVES:

	A-CANNED	B-CANNED	A-JUICE	B-JUICE	A-PASTE	B-PASTE	PURCHASE
CONTR	82.20	82.20	66.00	66.00	74.00	74.00	-85.00

CONSTRAINTS:

	A-CANNED	B-CANNED	A-JUICE	B-JUICE	A-PASTE	B-PASTE	PURCHASE	RELATION	RHS-001
JCE-MKT	.0000	.0000	1.000	1.000	.0000	.0000	.0000	LE	1000.
PST-MKT	.0000	.0000	.0000	.0000	1.000	1.000	.0000	LE	2000.
A-SUPPLY	1.000	.0000	1.000	.0000	1.000	.0000	-1.000	LE	600.0
B-SUPPLY	.0000	1.000	.0000	1.000	.0000	1.000	.0000	LE	2400.
CAN-QUAL	1.000	-3.000	.0000	.0000	.0000	.0000	.0000	GE	.0000
JCE-QUAL	.0000	.0000	3.000	-1.000	.0000	.0000	.0000	GE	.0000
P-SUPPLY	.0000	.0000	.0000	.0000	.0000	.0000	1.000	LE	80.00

Exhibit 5 (*continued*)

```
MAXIMIZE OR MINIMIZE? MAX

OPTIMAL SOLUTION FOUND.
      CONTR         225764.

OUTPUT OPTION? E

ALL ITEMS NOT LISTED IN SECTIONS 1 - 4 HAVE THE VALUE ZERO

*1* DECISION VARIABLES
   1. A-CANNED   615.000
   2. B-CANNED   205.000
   3. A-JUICE    65.0000
   4. B-JUICE    195.000
   6. B-PASTE    2000.00
   7. PURCHASE   80.0000

*2* SLACK(+) AND SURPLUS(-) IN CONSTRAINTS
   1. +JCE-MKT   740.000

*3* SHADOW PRICES FOR CONSTRAINTS
   2. PST-MKT    16.1000
   3. A-SUPPLY   90.3000
   4. B-SUPPLY   57.9000
   5. CAN-QUAL  -8.10000
   6. JCE-QUAL  -8.10000
   7. P-SUPPLY   .5.30000

*4* REDUCED COSTS FOR DECISION VARIABLES
   5. A-PASTE    -32.4000

*5* RANGES ON COEFFICIENTS OF OBJECTIVE CONTR
         VARIABLE   LOWER BOUND   CURRENT VALUE   UPPER BOUND
   1. A-CANNED     77.489         82.200          236.60
   2. B-CANNED     68.067         82.200          545.40
   3. A-JUICE     -88.400         66.000          87.600
   4. B-JUICE      14.533         66.000          80.133
   5. A-PASTE     UNBOUNDED       74.000          106.40
   6. B-PASTE      57.900         74.000          UNBOUNDED
   7. PURCHASE    -90.300        -85.000          UNBOUNDED

*6* RANGES ON VALUES OF RIGHT-HAND-SIDE RHS-001
         CONSTRNT   LOWER BOUND   CURRENT VALUE   UPPER BOUND
   1. JCE-MKT       260.00        1000.0          UNBOUNDED
   2. PST-MKT       1506.7        2000.0          2173.3
   3. A-SUPPLY      53.333        600.00          1120.0
   4. B-SUPPLY      2226.7        2400.0          2893.3
   5. CAN-QUAL     -520.00        .00000          546.67
   6. JCE-QUAL     -173.33        .00000          1480.0
   7. P-SUPPLY      .00000        80.000          600.00

OUTPUT OPTION? N

                  OPTION?
```

Case 12–3A

Mitchell Enterprises (A)*

Mr. Gordon Mitchell, President of Mitchell Enterprises, had called a special meeting of the company's Investment Review Committee in early December 1975. Members of that committee were Mr. Charles Gilbert, the Treasurer; Ms. Roberta Phillips, the Controller; and Mr. Paul Chesler, Special Assistant to Mr. Mitchell. The committee had spent its last meeting reviewing different methods for evaluating investment projects.

At that time, Mr. Gilbert had felt that it would be appropriate to use some method which took into account the value of funds over the entire project life, and Ms. Phillips had suggested the use of discounting to accomplish this. Unfortunately, the members of the committee could not agree on a hurdle rate which reflected the company's current financial position. Indeed, they had found it hard to accept any rate which would stay constant over the life of projects that might be considered. They had considered using a 10 percent hurdle rate for after-tax cash flows, typical of practice in their industry, but had not felt comfortable about that figure. Mr. Chesler had suggested that by use of linear programming they could determine a portfolio of projects and decide on the amount to be invested in each. In addition, he knew that a linear programming solution would help determine what hurdle rate or rates would be appropriate for the company. Overall, there had been much argument and little progress because they had been discussing the methods in abstract terms, and finally Mr. Mitchell suggested that Mr. Chesler prepare a list of projects which were typical of the projects they had evaluated that year. This list was to be circulated and used to focus the discussion at the next meeting. Subsequently, Mr. Chesler had circulated the attached memoranda.

---

* This case has been adapted from Gordon Enterprises (A).

MEMORANDUM

December 5, 1977

To: Investment Review Committee
From: Mr. Paul Chesler
Subject: Hypothetical investment projects

As you know, Mr. Mitchell has asked me to prepare a list of typical investment projects for us to consider at our next meeting. The accompanying table describes five projects which might compete for our investment dollar. The table shows the cash flow that will result from investing one dollar. Project A is a two-year investment available at the beginning of 1976 which pays 30 cents per dollar invested at the end of the first year and returns an additional dollar per dollar invested at the end of the second. At most, $500,000 can be invested in Project A. Project B is identical to Project A, except that it is available a year later. Project C is a one-year investment available only at the beginning of 1976 which pays $1.10 per dollar invested at the end of that year. Project D is a three-year investment available at the beginning of 1976 which pays $1.75 per dollar invested at the beginning of 1979. Project E will become available at the beginning of 1978 and will, after a year, pay $1.40 per dollar invested. Project E is limited to a maximum investment of $750,000. Of course, the cash we receive from any of these projects may be reinvested in others which are available at the time. In addition, we could obtain 6 percent via short-term bank accounts for any money not invested in a given year.

Cash flow per dollar invested

| | *Project* | | | | |
	A	B	C	D	E
1976	−1.00	0	−1.00	−1.00	0
1977	+0.30	−1.00	+1.10	0	0
1978	+1.00	+0.30	0	0	−1.00
1979	0	+1.00	0	+1.75	+1.40
Limit	$500,000	$500,000	None	None	$750,000

For the purpose of discussion I am assuming that we want to put $1 million of our money into some mix of these projects at the beginning of 1976 but no more thereafter, although we will reinvest throw-offs. All cash received on January 1, 1979, will be withdrawn.

The following table gives the results of discounting these projects as we had considered in our last meeting:

Project	Net present value at 10 percent*	Internal rate of return
A or B	$0.099	16.1%
C	0.000	10
D	0.314	20.5
E	0.273	40

* A hypothetical hurdle rate similar to ones we have seen used in the past. NPVs are calculated to the beginning of the year in which the outflow occurs.

In addition, I have formulated this investment portfolio problem as a linear program. The formulation and the results of the computer run will be forthcoming.

Case 12–3B

Mitchell Enterprises (B)

MEMORANDUM

December 8, 1975

To: Investment Review Committee
From: Mr. Paul Chesler
Subject: Linear programming formulation and results

As I remarked in my memorandum of last Friday, it is possible to formulate the portfolio problem proposed by Mr. Mitchell as a linear program. This formulation is shown in Exhibit 1. Notice that since there are no noncash expenses, posttax cash flow is strictly proportional to pre-tax flow. For this reason we can justify using pretax accumulated cash as the quantity to be maximized; this is equivalent to maximizing after-tax cash. The results of this weekend's computer run are shown in Exhibit 2.

Exhibit 1
Linear programming formulation

	Variables					Bank 76	Bank 77	Bank 78		Cash outlay ($000s)
	A	B	C	D	E					
Constraints										
1/1/76 investment	1.00	0	1.00	1.00	0	1.00	0	0	=	1,000
1/1/77 investment	−0.30	1.00	−1.10	0	0	−1.06	1.00	0	=	0
1/1/78 investment	−1.00	−0.30	0	0	1.00	0	−1.06	1.00	=	0
Limit on cash invested in A..........	1	0	0	0	0	0	0	0	≦	500
Limit on cash invested in B..........	0	1	0	0	0	0	0	0	≦	500
Limit on cash invested in E..........	0	0	0	0	1	0	0	0	≦	750
Objective function Payout at horizon (1/1/79)	0	1.00	0	1.75	1.40	0	0	1.06		

Exhibit 2
Results of LP computer run

```
MAXIMIZE OR MINIMIZE? MAX

OPTIMAL SOLUTION FOUND.
      PAYOUT          1797.60

OUTPUT OPTION? E

ALL ITEMS NOT LISTED IN SECTIONS 1 - 4 HAVE THE VALUE ZERO.

*1* DECISION VARIABLES
   1. A          500.000
   4. D          500.000
   5. E          659.000
   7. BANK-77    150.000

*2* SLACK(+) AND SURPLUS(-) IN CONSTRAINTS
   5. +B-LIMIT   500.000
   6. +E-LIMIT   91.0000

*3* SHADOW PRICES FOR CONSTRAINTS
   1. INV-76     1.75000
   2. INV-77     1.48400
   3. INV-78     1.40000
   4. A-LIMIT    .952000E-01

*4* REDUCED COSTS FOR DECISION VARIABLES
   2. B          -.640000E-01
   3. C          -.117600
   6. BANK-76    -.176960
   8. BANK-78    -.340000
```

Exhibit 2 (continued)

```
*5* RANGES ON COEFFICIENTS OF OBJECTIVE PAYOUT
        VARIABLE    LOWER BOUND   CURRENT VALUE   UPPER BOUND
    1.  A           -.95200E-01   .00000          UNBOUNDED
    2.  B           UNBOUNDED     1.0000          1.0640
    3.  C           UNBOUNDED     .00000          .11760
    4.  D           1.6324        1.7500          1.8452
    5.  E           1.3278        1.4000          1.5009
    6.  BANK-76     UNBOUNDED     .00000          .17696
    7.  BANK-77     -.64000E-01   .00000          .10691
    8.  BANK-78     UNBOUNDED     1.0600          1.4000

*6* RANGES ON VALUES OF RIGHT-HAND-SIDE RHS
        CONSTRNT    LOWER BOUND   CURRENT VALUE   UPPER BOUND
    1.  INV-76      500.00        1000.0          UNBOUNDED
    2.  INV-77      -150.00       .00000          85.849
    3.  INV-78      -659.00       .00000          91.000
    4.  A-LIMIT     .00000        500.00          569.04
    5.  B-LIMIT     .00000        500.00          UNBOUNDED
    6.  E-LIMIT     659.00        750.00          UNBOUNDED
```

Case 12–4

Rubicon Rubber Company

On Friday, February 13, 1970, Mr. George Nelson, Manager of the Tire
Division of Rubicon Rubber Company, was boarding a plane enroute to a
New York meeting with representatives of Eastern Auto Stores to
negotiate a final contract for the delivery of automobile snow tires. A
preliminary version of the contract called for the delivery of 15,000
medium-grade nylon-cord tires and 11,000 high-grade fiberglass-cord tires
over the three-month summer delivery period. Prices had tentatively been
set at $7 for the nylon tires and at $9 for the fiberglass.

Mr. Nelson had approximately two hours of time during the flight in
which to review his notes and to examine the analysis prepared for him by
Jim Leader, a new member of the staff and a recent MBA. Mr. Nelson felt
that there were a number of things which he had to resolve before he felt
secure in finalizing the contract, so he was anxious to get to work quickly
to avoid the possibility of a conversation with the fellow in the next seat.

Background

Rubicon Rubber Company was a small company located in Indepen-
dence, Ohio. It manufactured a variety of rubber products, including tires
for forklift trucks and small tractors. Founded in 1950, the company had
grown rapidly in its early years and more slowly recently. Sales last year
were $3 million. Future growth for the company appeared to be closely
linked to the development and sale of specialty tractors and forklift trucks
by the manufacturers of this equipment in western Ohio. Although most of
Rubicon sales were tires for the small tractor industry and rubber specialty products, Rubicon had for the past two years taken contracts to
manufacture small runs of regular automobile snow tires for Eastern Auto
Stores, one of the larger distributors of auto replacement tires. These
small contracts supplemented the larger ones placed with the major tire
manufacturers elsewhere in Ohio. Those produced under the contracts
bore the Eastern trademark and were to Eastern's specifications.

Rubicon had found it advantageous to take these short-leadtime contracts to utilize surplus capacity. (Expansion of plant and facilities in 1967
had left Rubicon with excess capacity that was expected to be fully
utilized in time.) Normal production planning allowed tire machine utilization to be determined relatively accurately eight months in advance.

The contract with Eastern called for a staged delivery schedule of the two types of snow tires over the three summer months, as indicated in Exhibit 1. The major problem in planning the production of these tires was the availability of sufficient tire machine capacity to ensure that the

Exhibit 1
Delivery schedule

Date	Nylon	Fiberglass
June 31	4,000	1,000
July 31	8,000	5,000
August 31	3,000	5,000
Total.........	15,000	11,000

contract could be satisfied. Only two types of machines, the Wheeling and Regal machines, could be used in molding tires of the sort covered by the contract. Virtually no time would be available on either type of machine until the first of June. After that time unused capacity would be available spasmodically between other contracts. A table of anticipated machine availability, prepared by Joe Tabler, the Production Supervisor, is shown in Exhibit 2.

Exhibit 2
Molding machine production hours available

	Wheeling machine	Regal machine
June	700	1,500
July	300	400
August	1,000	300

The two types of molding machines were similar except for their speeds. That the Wheeling machine was somewhat faster for both types of tires than the older Regal machine is shown by the production figures of Exhibit 3. This had tended to complicate production planning in previous years.

There was also a difference in productivity between nylon and fiberglass. This was due primarily to mold fastenings. The molds for the

Exhibit 3
Production capacity in hours/tire by type of machine for each type of tire

	Nylon	Fiberglass
Wheeling machine	0.15	0.12
Regal machine	0.16	0.14

nylon tires were somewhat more difficult to work with than those used for fiberglass tires. Since Eastern provided the molds, there was no easily made modification to basic equipment that was feasible in the short run. A machine shop modification could be made to improve efficiency, but it had never seemed practical in view of the short duration of the contract.

Costs (shown in Exhibit 4) had been prepared by the accounting department for use in production planning. The difference in costs between the two machines, shown in Exhibit 4, was due primarily to a difference in

Exhibit 4
Production planning costs by machine type

Wheeling machine
    Initial Cost: $50,000
    Depreciation method: Straight line
    Life: Five years

Machine amortization	$ 4.17/hr
Operating labor	3.75/hr
Supervision	0.25/hr
Overhead	2.00/hr
Total	$10.07/hr

Regal machine
    Initial cost: $45,000
    Depreciation method: Straight line
    Life: Five years

Machine amortization	$ 3.75/hr
Operating labor	3.75/hr
Supervision	0.25/hr
Overhead	2.00/hr
Total	$ 9.75/hr

the initial equipment purchase price. Material costs for the nylon tire were estimated to be $3.10, and for the fiberglass tire, $3.90. Finishing, packaging, and shipping were not expected to exceed 23 cents per tire. Costs were based on actual costs in the previous year, adjusted for price increases.

Warehouse space was not expected to be available within the company, since inventory would be at a seasonal high and the company would be receiving materials for fall production of new tractor tires. However, tires could be stored at a local warehouse at a cost of approximately ten cents per tire per month. There was a storage area adjacent to the production shop where up to one month's production could be kept until delivered to the warehouse or to Eastern. Monthly storage costs at the warehouse were assessed on the tires as they were placed in storage, and space had to be reserved ahead of time. Shipping was scheduled three days prior to the end of the month for delivery on the last day of the month.

The decision problem

As Mr. Nelson sat down he pulled the Eastern Auto file from his briefcase and thought back over the short meeting with Jim Leader that he had managed to squeeze in before rushing to the airport. He had assigned the job of planning the production schedule to Jim even though Jim was new with the company, because Jim was bright and appeared to be an independent thinker. Since time was short, Mr. Nelson remembered the misgivings he had experienced when he found that Jim had formulated the problem as a linear program. Now he was forced to think back to his own exposure to this subject in his attempt to understand what Jim had done. At the same time he remembered that he had often thought the problem "looked like" a programming problem but that there had never seemed to be time to work out the details. Jim had attached a short memo to the computer output, which Mr. Nelson planned to study (see Exhibit 5).

Mr. Nelson also thought back to his meeting with Tabler. Tabler had mentioned when he produced his equipment schedule that an additional Wheeling machine was due to arrive at the end of August. For a $200 fee it could be expedited to arrive a month earlier. Tabler had estimated that early arrival would make available 172 additional hours of Wheeling machine time in August.

Normally vacations were scheduled during the three summer months, with approximately one third of the staff gone during each month. Mr. Nelson felt that he would be able to put together the required manpower, though this would almost inevitably involve delaying some vacations until Christmas and hiring a few temporary employees. Providing supervisory staff would present similar problems.

About one half of overhead costs was equipment depreciation, and the other half was due to office expense. Overhead was allocated on the basis of direct labor and amounted to 50 percent of labor and supervision. The company had not computerized its clerical operations, so the presence of the Eastern contract would call for considerable office work.

As he prepared to go over the material, Mr. Nelson ticked off in his mind a few of the things that he would like to have at the conclusion of his analysis, whether or not he found Jim's LP approach satisfactory.

1. A summary of costs and revenues that he could show his boss, John Toms, President of Rubicon, when he returned from the meeting with Eastern.
2. Material for drafting a memo to Joe Tabler, telling him which machines to schedule for what, and when and whether to expedite the new machine.
3. A schedule of warehouse needs so that he could reserve space at the Bekson Warehousing Company.

4. A tentative schedule for the maintenance department indicating when the yearly maintenance check on the various machines could be performed.

One final worry that Mr. Nelson hoped to resolve before going into the meeting involved what his strategy should be if Eastern asked for more fiberglass tires. The Eastern representative to whom he had talked on the telephone the previous day had suggested that Eastern just might want more since sales had been very good the previous year. As Mr. Nelson turned to the task of analysis he noted the weather outside and thought to himself that if there were time due to delays in landing at the Kennedy Airport he would like to explain to himself what was going on with those dual variables, but the other matters seemed more important at the moment.

Exhibit 5

MEMORANDUM

To: George Nelson
From: Jim Leader
Subject: Scheduling for Eastern Auto tire contract

I have formulated the equipment and scheduling problem for this contract as a linear programming problem. I could see that there was not time to do what you wanted without taking this approach, and I also believe the answers to be better than I could do by hand.

The problem is one of minimizing the cost of producing and storing tires. (See the L.P. tableau of Attachment 1.)

From the tableau you can see that there are two kinds of choice variables:

1. The number of each type of tire to be scheduled on the Wheeling machine and on the Regal machine in each month. I have designated these as follows:

    W_n = No. of nylon tires to be produced on the Wheeling machine
    W_g = No. of fiberglass tires to be produced on the Wheeling machine
    R_n = No. of nylon tires to be produced on the Regal machine
    R_g = No. of fiberglass tires to be produced on the Regal machine

2. The number of each type of tire to be placed in inventory each month. For the inventory variables:

    I_n = No. of nylon tires to be carried into inventory at the end of each month
    I_g = No. of fiberglass tires to be carried into inventory at the end of each month

Note that I have used the subscripts n = nylon and g = fiberglass. I have also used superscripts above the numbers to indicate the month, since most of the variables are defined in all three time periods; 1 = June, 2 = July, and 3 = August.

Thus, the variable W_g^3 stands for the number of fiberglass tires to be produced in August on the Wheeling machine. (Please note that these superscripts are a

Exhibit 5 (continued)

symbolic way of distinguishing between the months; W_g^3 does *not* mean raise W_g to the third power.)

The constraints are of two types:

1. The constraints on the available machine time in each month.
2. The demand or delivery constraints in each month.

To determine the machine availability constraint in each month I took the number of nylon tires made on Wheeling equipment times the hours per nylon tire plus the number of fiberglass tires made on Wheeling equipment times the hours per fiberglass tire. This gives the total number of Wheeling machine hours for the month, which must be less than the Wheeling hours available in that month. For July:

$$0.15\ W_n^2 + 0.12\ W_g^2 \le 300 = \text{The availability of Wheeling hours in July}$$

The demand constraints stipulate that the tires produced in a month plus the tires in inventory from the last month less the amount returned to inventory at the end of the month must equal the amount demanded in the month. Thus, for July the nylon tire equation is:

$$W_n^2 + R_n^2 + I_n^1 - I_n^2 = 8{,}000 = \text{The demand for nylon tires in July}$$

The program seeks to minimize the total cost* of operating the tire machines and storing inventory over the entire three-month period. The computer output for the problem is shown in Attachment 2. For your convenience, I have also indicated the principal results from the computer output on the tableau itself.

Exhibit 5 (continued)
Attachment 1: The Linear Programming Tableau*

Columns are grouped by month: June variables $W_n^1, R_n^1, W_g^1, R_g^1, I_n^1, I_g^1$; July variables $W_n^2, R_n^2, W_g^2, R_g^2, I_n^2, I_g^2$; August variables $W_n^3, R_n^3, W_g^3, R_g^3$.

	W_n^1	R_n^1	W_g^1	R_g^1	I_n^1	I_g^1	W_n^2	R_n^2	W_g^2	R_g^2	I_n^2	I_g^2	W_n^3	R_n^3	W_g^3	R_g^3	Right-hand side	Shadow prices
June Wheeling	0.15		0.12														≤ 700	−0.333
Regal		0.16		0.14													≤ 1,500	0
Nylon	1	1			−1												= 4,000	0.8
Glass			1	1		−1											= 1,000	0.64
July Wheeling							0.15		0.12								≤ 300	−1.166
Regal								0.16		0.14							≤ 400	−0.625
Nylon					1		1	1			−1						= 8,000	0.9
Glass						1			1	1		−1					= 5,000	0.74
August Wheeling													0.15		0.12		≤ 1,000	−0.333
Regal														0.16		0.14	≤ 300	0
Nylon											1		1	1			= 3,000	0.8
Glass												1			1	1	= 5,000	0.64
Objective	0.75	0.80	0.60	0.70	0.10	0.10	0.75	0.80	0.60	0.70	0.10	0.10	0.75	0.80	0.60	0.70	Optimum value of	
Optimal solution	1,866.6	7,633.3	3,500.0		5,499.9	2,500.0	2,500.9		2,499.9				2,666.6	333.3	5,000.0		$19,173.33	

* The costs of operating the tire machines is taken to be the sum of operating cost and supervision plus half of the overhead charge. All blanks are zeros.

Exhibit 5 *(concluded)*
Attachment 2

MAXIMIZE OR MINIMIZE? MIN

OPTIMAL SOLUTION FOUND.
    OBJ   19173.3

OUTPUT OPTION? E

ALL ITEMS NOT LISTED IN SECTIONS 1 - 4 HAVE THE VALUE ZERO.

```
*1* DECISION VARIABLES
    1. W-1-N    1866.67
    2. R-1-N    7633.33
    3. W-1-G    3500.00
    5. I-1-N    5500.00
    6. I-1-G    2500.00
    8. R-2-N    2500.00
    9. W-2-G    2500.00
   13. W-3-N    2666.67
   14. R-3-N    333.333
   15. W-3-G    5000.00
```

```
*2* SLACK(+) AND SURPLUS(-) IN CONSTRAINTS
    2. +REGAL-1   278.667
   10. +REGAL-3   246.667
```

```
*3* SHADOW PRICES FOR CONSTRAINTS
    1. WHEEL-1   -.333333
    3. NYLON-1    .800000
    4. GLASS-1    .640000
    5. WHEEL-2   -1.16667
    6. REGAL-2   -.625000
    7. NYLON-2    .900000
    8. GLASS-2    .740000
    9. WHEEL-3   -.333333
   11. NYLON-3    .800000
   12. GLASS-3    .640000
```

```
*4* REDUCED COSTS FOR DECISION VARIABLES
    4. R-1-G    .600000E-01
    7. W-2-N    .250000E-01
   10. R-2-G    .475000E-01
   11. I-2-N    .200000
   12. I-2-G    .200000
   16. R-3-G    .600000E-01
```

```
*5* RANGES ON COEFFICIENTS OF OBJECTIVE OBJ
       VARIABLE  LOWER BOUND   CURRENT VALUE   UPPER BOUND
    1. W-1-N       .69063         .75000         .77500
    2. R-1-N       .75000         .80000         .87500
    3. W-1-G       .58000         .60000         .64750
    4. R-1-G       .64000         .70000        UNBOUNDED
    5. I-1-N       .45714E-01     .10000         .12500
    6. I-1-G       .80000E-01     .10000         .14750
    7. W-2-N       .72500         .75000        UNBOUNDED
    8. R-2-N      UNBOUNDED       .80000         .85429
    9. W-2-G      UNBOUNDED       .60000         .62000
   10. R-2-G       .65250         .70000        UNBOUNDED
   11. I-2-N      -.10000         .10000        UNBOUNDED
   12. I-2-G      -.10000         .10000        UNBOUNDED
   13. W-3-N       .67500         .75000         .80000
   14. R-3-N       .75000         .80000         .87500
   15. W-3-G     -.56923E+07      .60000         .66000
   16. R-3-G       .64000         .70000        UNBOUNDED
```

```
*6* RANGES ON VALUES OF RIGHT-HAND-SIDE RHS
       CONSTRNT   LOWER BOUND   CURRENT VALUE   UPPER BOUND
    1. WHEEL-1      438.75        700.00         1845.0
    2. REGAL-1      1221.3        1500.0        UNBOUNDED
    3. NYLON-1     -3633.3        4000.0         5741.7
    4. GLASS-1     -2500.0        1000.0         3177.1
    5. WHEEL-2      38.750        300.00         600.00
    6. REGAL-2      121.33        400.00         1280.0
    7. NYLON-2      2500.0        8000.0         9741.7
    8. GLASS-2      2500.0        5000.0         7177.1
    9. WHEEL-3      768.75        1000.0         1050.0
   10. REGAL-3      53.333        300.00        UNBOUNDED
   11. NYLON-3      2666.7        3000.0         4541.7
   12. GLASS-3      4583.3        5000.0         6927.1
```

Case 12–5A

Okanagan Lumber Company (A)*

In October 1968 the president of the Okanagan Lumber Company of Prince George, British Columbia, had asked a management consulting firm to consider possible uses of operations research techniques in the company. After a study of Okanagan's operations, the consultants had recommended that one of the most promising areas for the application of operations research was in improving the rules used for allocating logs among the company's five sawmills and its one plywood mill; the allocation decision was a difficult one because of the large number of possible alternatives and also because of the complex interdependences among the alternatives. On the basis of the recommendation, the president of Okanagan had appointed an operations research (OR) group and had assigned it the task of developing a log allocation model for the plywood mill and the sawmills.

The log test

The first part of the project was an extensive log test which was intended to establish a new scheme for classifying logs and for determining the value of the products obtained from the different log classes in the sawmills and the plywood mill. More specifically, the objectives of the test were to determine the factors which affected the recovery of lumber and veneer from timber, to classify the logs into homogeneous classes (as measured by the quality and quantity of their end products), and to measure the average yield for each log type in each possible use.

The OR group assumed that the geographic area from which a log came would not affect the yield (other characteristics being equal) and that the five sawmills would achieve very nearly the same recovery of lumber from the same timber. The group found that it was important, however, to classify logs according to species and diameter. In addition, there were certain secondary characteristics (such as the presence of more than a minimum amount of sway along the long axis of the trunk) which might make a log unacceptable for the plywood mill (and hence useful as a sawlog only). Logs which met the current standards for the plywood mill were called "peelers," while the other logs were called "sawlogs." The accompanying table shows the log classifications; the designations peeler

---

* Revised with permission from "Haida Lumber Company (A)," *Stanford Business Cases 1971,* Published by Stanford University Graduate School of Business, © 1971 by the Board of Trustees of the Leland Stanford Junior University.

and sawlog refer to the uses which would have been chosen for the logs *before* the study was undertaken.

Species	Name	Diameter range (inches)
1.......	Peeler	12 to 20
1.......	Peeler	Over 20
1.......	Sawlog	Under 16
1.......	Sawlog	16 to 24
1.......	Sawlog	Over 24
2.......	Peeler	12 to 20
2.......	Peeler	Over 20
2.......	Sawlog	12 to 20
2.......	Sawlog	Over 20
3.......	—	12 to 17
3.......	—	Over 17
4.......	—	All

One of the major purposes of the OR study was to reconsider the previous choices of peelers and sawlogs. Accordingly, a sample from each of the log classes from species 1, 2, and 3 was sent to the sawmills, where yield was carefully measured, and another sample from each class was sent to the plywood mill, where the yield of veneer was measured. The fourth species was considered suitable for the sawmills only. The Appendix gives a summary of the lumber and veneer yields for each of the log classes. The lumber yields could be converted to revenue (and then to contribution) figures quite easily, but the sales revenue from timber going into the plywood mill could not be calculated easily because the value of the veneer was a function of the plywood product mix, and obtaining the best yield therefore involved determining the best product mix. The problem of determining the best log and product mix in plywood and lumber was one which could be tackled with linear programming. Accordingly, the OR group next proceeded to develop a model of the plywood mill for use in a linear program.

Log allocation for the Quesnel region

Nearby forests supplied logs to the five sawmills and the Quesnel plywood mill. The mill managers and the regional managers met before the logging season started to determine a cutting schedule by species and to decide what quantities of each species would be shipped to each mill. Exhibit 1 gives the forecasts of log availability for the 1969 season.

The logging season started in April, and at that time the logging crews needed to know what portion of the estimated supply of each species should go to the plywood mill and what portion should go the sawmills. The logs sent to the sawmills were cut into lengths of 32 feet; the sawmills would then divide the logs further into 16-foot lengths. The logs destined

Exhibit 1
Logs available during 1969 season

Log description	Availability (MBF)*
1 peeler 12 to 20 inches	5,544
1 peeler over 20 inches	4,972
1 sawlog under 16 inches	4,224
1 sawlog 16 to 24 inches	13,596
1 sawlog over 24 inches	29,348
2 peeler 12 to 20 inches	5,302
2 peeler over 20 inches	2,948
2 sawlog 12 to 20 inches	21,406
2 sawlog over 20 inches	7,612
3 sawlog 12 to 17 inches	7,524
3 sawlog over 17 inches	10,076
4 all	85,008

* The figures were arrived at by multiplying the expected percentage of all logs falling into each class by the total logs for the 1969 season. The expected percentages were found in the log test.

for the plywood mill would be cut into 34-foot lengths; later these lengths would be divided into 8-foot blocks for processing into veneer. In general, the straighter, larger-diameter logs with fewer defects were sent to the plywood mill. The Quesnel mill had the capacity to handle at most 18,500 MBF (thousand board feet)[1] of timber per year.

The logs which arrived at the sawmills were processed into lumber. The only capacity limitation at the sawmills was headrig saw capacity. The amount of that capacity required to cut a specified number of board feet of lumber was primarily a function of the size of the log being cut; saw speed was independent of the log's diameter, so that differences in time per board foot were primarily a result of differences in the volume per unit of length for logs of various diameters. The accompanying table gives the headrig saw time required for each of the log classes. (Determining the values in the table was one of the early tasks of the OR group.)

Species	Name	Diameter range (inches)	Minutes per board foot (BF)
1	Peeler	12 to 20	0.007
1	Peeler	Over 20	0.005
1	Sawlog	Under 16	0.010
1	Sawlog	16 to 24	0.006
1	Sawlog	Over 24	0.004
2	Peeler	12 to 20	0.007
2	Peeler	Over 20	0.005
3	—	12 to 17	0.008
3	—	Over 17	0.005
4	—	All	0.010

[1] The basic unit of volume used by the timber industry is a board foot (BF), which is defined as the volume of a one-foot by one-foot by one-inch piece of wood.

Four of the sawmills had one saw each; the fifth mill had three saws. Most of the sawmills operated two shifts per day, but one of the smaller mills operated only one shift. The sawmills (and also the Quesnel plywood mill) operated on a 51-week, five-day, eight-hour-per-shift schedule. The sawmills lost about 13 percent of their operating time for breakdowns and delays. The OR team assembled information on the net realization of revenue per MBF for each type of log converted to lumber in the sawmills; these figures are included in the Appendix.

Sawmill	Number of headrig saws	Number of shifts per day
Alexandria	1	1
Hulatt	1	2
Soda Creek	1	2
Wells	3	2
Woodpecker	1	2

The Quesnel plywood mill

The production process in the plywood mill was considerably more complicated than that of the sawmills. Exhibit 2 gives a schematic picture of the process. Incoming logs were stacked in tiers in the mill yard and taken as needed into the mill. In outline, the process in the mill was first to debark the logs and then to cut them into blocks. Next, the logs were steamed to soften the wood fibers. They were then ready for peeling, a process which removed a thin layer of veneer in a continuous strip from the log (in much the same manner as paper is unwound from a roll). The

Exhibit 2
Process flow in the plywood mill

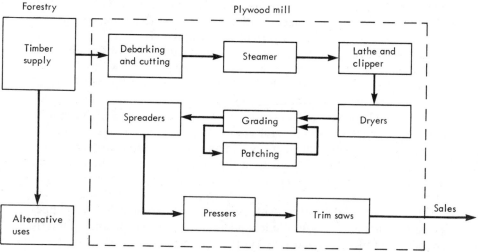

peeled veneer was then sent to the clipper, where it was cut manually into sheets of the size needed to form plywood panels. Next, the veneer was sorted into the heartwood and sapwood (which held different proportions of moisture) and was passed through a dryer. After that, the veneer was graded (and patched if necessary). Finally, layers of veneer were glued together into the various plywood products made by the mill; the panels were trimmed after gluing and were then ready for shipment.

In constructing the linear programming model of the plywood mill, the OR group had to consider the various operations of the mill in detail and, in particular, to determine the capacities of the parts of the mill. As outlined above, the first step in processing logs was to remove their bark (with a ring of scraper knives in the debarker) and then to cut them into eight-foot sections, called peeler blocks. The blocks were then loaded into a concrete vault, where they were steamed for 8 to 16 hours to soften the wood fibers for the peeling operation. There were four steaming vaults at Quesnel. These vaults provided ample capacity for any feasible production level even during the winter, when logs had to be steamed for long periods of time.

After steaming, the blocks were ready for the lathe and clipper operations. They were placed on a lathe and revolved against a knife which was bolted to a movable carriage. The lathe was a massive machine, sufficiently well bedded to withstand any shock or vibration that could have interfered with the smooth action of the block on the cutting knife. In order to maintain constant thickness of veneer as the diameter of the block decreased during cutting, a gear from the main drive automatically adjusted the position of the knife.

At first contact with the knife, the blocks did not produce full-length veneer; the uneven start was caused by unevenness in the shape of the block. It was necessary, therefore, to ''round up'' the block before a continuous layer of veneer could be obtained. In the interest of maximum recovery, certain usable pieces of the round-up veneer were salvaged for ultimate use in the interior layers of plywood panels.

At Quesnel the veneer was peeled to produce thicknesses of one-tenth inch and one-sixth inch. The veneer was peeled at these two thicknesses. It shrank a bit during drying, but the glue in the finished panels compensated for the shrinkage during drying.

The peeled veneer next went to a system of conveyors which carried it to the clipper, where an operator cut as much as possible of the veneer to 27-inch and 54-inch widths, using a manually activated drop-knife. Because of knots and other defects in the veneer, some of it had to be cut into narrower widths, called strips, which would be used in interior layers of panels.

The output of the lathe at Quesnel was constrained by the clipper. Since the clipper speed was independent of the veneer thickness (and the clipper's output depended only on the number of surface square feet it processed), greater volumes of thicker veneer could be produced. Exhibit 3 gives the output rates of the clipper for various log classifications. The lathe and clipper were operated two shifts a day, although an additional 32 hours a week was available on overtime. There were 12 workers in the lathe and clipper crew.

Exhibit 3
Lathe and clipper productivity

Log description	Net surface square feet ($^3/s$-inch basis) per hour	
	$^1/_{10}$ inch	$^1/_6$ inch
1 peeler 12 to 20 inches	10,500	17,500
1 peeler over 20 inches	8,850	14,800
1 sawlog under 16 inches ...	10,700	17,900
1 sawlog 16 to 24 inches	9,750	16,300
1 sawlog over 24 inches	8,200	13,700
2 peeler 12 to 20 inches	8,500	14,200
2 peeler over 20 inches	7,750	13,000
2 sawlog 12 to 20 inches....	8,060	13,500
2 sawlog over 20 inches	7,800	13,100
3 12 to 17 inches	8,950	15,400
3 over 17 inches	9,800	16,400

After peeling and clipping, the veneer was sorted into heartwood and sapwood. Sapwood is the outer layer of wood on a tree; it contains much more moisture than does the inner heartwood. Consequently, veneer made from sapwood required longer drying times in the mill than did veneer made from heartwood.

The sorted veneer was loaded into the dryer. Pieces of veneer were placed side by side in the loading section until the section was filled. The entire load was then pushed onto the dryer's conveyor belt. The veneer was carried through the dryer by a series of rollers which operated at whatever speed was appropriate for the particular type of veneer in the load. The maximum temperature of the dryer was 380 degrees fehrenheit, and the minimum time required to move a piece of veneer through the dryer was seven minutes. At that time setting, the dryer would process 652 surface square feet per minute. The time required to dry specific pieces of veneer to the desired moisture level varied, however, according to the thickness and species of the veneer and according to whether it was heartwood or sapwood. As the veneer came out of the dryer, it passed through a moisture detector; sheets which had not been dried sufficiently were sent through the dryer again. Exhibit 4 gives the required drying times (at normal operating temperatures) of different species for the thicknesses produced at Quesnel. The dryer was operated on three shifts and experienced about 11 percent downtime. A crew of six was required to feed the dryer and to stack the dried veneer.

Exhibit 4
Data on drying times

	Required dryer times (minutes)					
	Species 1		Species 2		Species 3	
Thickness (inches)	Heart	Sap	Heart	Sap	Heart	Sap
One-tenth	7.0	12.0	10.5	19.0	5.5	11.0
One-sixth	8.5	18.5	14.0	21.0	9.0	15.0

Proportion of heartwood to sapwood

Species	Heart/sap
1	45/55
2	12/88
3	55/45

The dried veneer was next routed to veneer graders, who had a thorough knowledge of veneer grades and gluing characteristics. The graders considered the size and number of defects in the veneer and the grain characteristics of the wood. They classified the veneer into grades B (the highest), C, and D; veneer grades below D were called noncertifiable (NC).

Part of the job of the graders was to identify pieces of veneer which should be patched. In the patching operation, knots, pitch pockets, and other defects were replaced with good veneer whose color and texture were similar to the color and texture of the surrounding wood. A machine cut a hole in the veneer to be repaired. Almost simultaneously the machine cut a patch of the same shape from other veneer and automatically fitted the patch into the hole. The entire operation took about three seconds.

After grading and patching, the veneer was ready to be used in assembling plywood panels. A panel consisted of either three or five layers of veneer which were glued together (with adjacent layers placed with their grains running at right angles to one another, as shown in Exhibit 5). Most types of veneer could be used in building one or more plywood products. In addition, a particular product could be made in several different ways. For example, ½ CD–5 meant a panel with five layers, a finished thickness of one-half inch, a grade C face (or front), and a grade D back. Such a panel could be produced with various species of veneer for the front and back. In addition, there was some choice as to the veneer for the middle layer (called the center) and the other two interior layers (called cores). Exhibit 6 shows the products which were currently being made at Quesnel and the choices of veneer which could be used in those products.

The assembly of veneer into plywood panels took place at a machine called a glue spreader. The machine had large rolls which transferred glue

Exhibit 5
Names of plywood panels

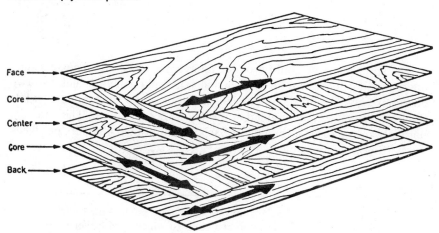

Face: The better side of a panel in any grade calling for a face and a back; also, either side of a panel where the grading rules draw no distinction between faces.
Back: The side reverse to the face of the panel.
Cores—crossbands: Inner plies running perpendicular to the panel face.
Centers: Inner plies running parallel to the panel face.

from storage troughs onto veneer pieces, coating both sides of the veneer at the same time. In addition, there were other rolls, called doctor rolls, which wiped the main rolls so that they would have only the desired amount of glue. The spreader operation required a crew of four. The crew placed a piece of pressboard on a platform in front of the glue spreader and then placed on the board the piece of veneer which would be the face of a panel or an assembled product. The next layer of veneer, called a core, was passed through the spreader to coat both of its sides with an even thickness of glue. The core was carefully laid on top of the face, with its grain running at right angles to that of the face. If the panel was to have five layers (or plies), the center (or middle layer) was next placed on top of the coreline, with its grain at right angles to that of the core. Another core was then glued and added to the pile, and then the back piece of veneer was added to complete the first panel and the front for the next panel was placed on the stack. For three-ply panels, the core of a panel was followed by the back completing that panel, and then the front for the next panel was placed on the stack. The process was repeated until a load was finished.

The amount of glue required for each core layer depended on the thickness of the core. Glue was prepared in batches which cost $20 each. The following table shows the amount of coreline footage (surface square feet of core material) which could be handled with one batch of glue:

Core thickness (inches)	Coreline footage (surface square feet) per batch
One-tenth	6,500
One-sixth	5,900

The spreader crew could produce an average of 3.9 corelines per minute, including allowance for delays. Thus, five-ply panels, which had two corelines each, could be assembled at a rate of 1.95 per minute, while three-ply panels could be glued at a rate of 3.9 per minute. The spreader normally operated on a three-shift basis; an additional 48 hours per week of overtime was available.

Exhibit 6
Panel lay-up alternatives

Each column gives one of the possible ways of making each of the four products listed. Thus, for each product, there was some choice as to which type of veneer to use for the layers of the product. For five-ply panels, it is assumed that both cores will be made of the same material.

Veneer specifications are given as follows:

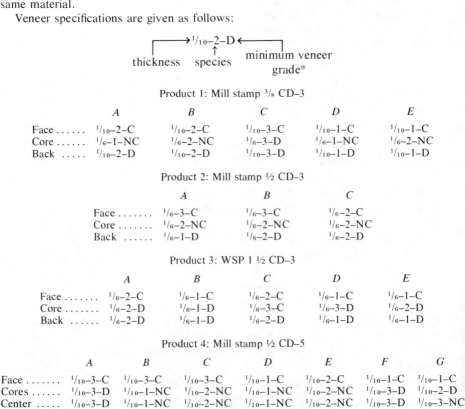

$$\xrightarrow{\hspace{2em}} {}^1/_{10}-2-D \xleftarrow{\hspace{2em}}$$
thickness   species   minimum veneer grade*

Product 1: Mill stamp $^3/_8$ CD–3

	A	B	C	D	E
Face	$^1/_{10}$–2–C	$^1/_{10}$–2–C	$^1/_{10}$–3–C	$^1/_{10}$–1–C	$^1/_{10}$–1–C
Core	$^1/_6$–1–NC	$^1/_6$–2–NC	$^1/_6$–3–D	$^1/_6$–1–NC	$^1/_6$–2–NC
Back	$^1/_{10}$–2–D	$^1/_{10}$–2–D	$^1/_{10}$–3–D	$^1/_{10}$–1–D	$^1/_{10}$–1–D

Product 2: Mill stamp ½ CD–3

	A	B	C
Face	$^1/_6$–3–C	$^1/_6$–3–C	$^1/_6$–2–C
Core	$^1/_6$–2–NC	$^1/_6$–2–NC	$^1/_6$–2–NC
Back	$^1/_6$–1–D	$^1/_6$–2–D	$^1/_6$–2–D

Product 3: WSP 1 ½ CD–3

	A	B	C	D	E
Face	$^1/_6$–2–C	$^1/_6$–1–C	$^1/_6$–2–C	$^1/_6$–1–C	$^1/_6$–1–C
Core	$^1/_6$–2–D	$^1/_6$–1–D	$^1/_6$–3–C	$^1/_6$–3–D	$^1/_6$–2–D
Back	$^1/_6$–2–D	$^1/_6$–1–D	$^1/_6$–2–D	$^1/_6$–1–D	$^1/_6$–1–D

Product 4: Mill stamp ½ CD–5

	A	B	C	D	E	F	G
Face	$^1/_{10}$–3–C	$^1/_{10}$–3–C	$^1/_{10}$–3–C	$^1/_{10}$–1–C	$^1/_{10}$–2–C	$^1/_{10}$–1–C	$^1/_{10}$–1–C
Cores	$^1/_{10}$–3–D	$^1/_{10}$–1–NC	$^1/_{10}$–2–NC	$^1/_{10}$–1–NC	$^1/_{10}$–2–NC	$^1/_{10}$–3–D	$^1/_{10}$–2–D
Center	$^1/_{10}$–3–D	$^1/_{10}$–1–NC	$^1/_{10}$–2–NC	$^1/_{10}$–1–NC	$^1/_{10}$–2–NC	$^1/_{10}$–3–D	$^1/_{10}$–3–NC
Back	$^1/_{10}$–3–D	$^1/_{10}$–3–D	$^1/_{10}$–3–D	$^1/_{10}$–1–D	$^1/_{10}$–2–D	$^1/_{10}$–1–D	$^1/_{10}$–1–D

* Higher grades of the same thickness from the same species can always be substituted.

Once the panels had been assembled they were pressed, an entire stack at a time, to complete the bond of the wood and the adhesive. The press had one stationary plate and one plate connected to hydraulic rams which were used to apply 175 to 200 pounds per square inch of pressure for 12 to 15 minutes per load. After pressing, the panels were trimmed to the standard 48-inch × 96-inch dimensions. They were then graded and marked for preparation for shipment. Since Quesnel had been producing only sheathing, or unsanded plywood, there was no sanding operation. Deliveries were made by boxcars.

Production planning at Quesnel

The Quesnel plant manager periodically received information from the corporate marketing group on the expected demand and price forecasts of the various products. During November, marketing gave the Quesnel manager the following forecasts for the 1969 season.

Product	Forecast net realization per thousand surface square feet (after discounts)	Sales limits set by marketing (in panels)	
		Minimum	Maximum
Mill stamp ⅜ CD–3	$51	—	250,000
Mill stamp ½ CD–3	66	5,000	50,000
WSP 1 ½ CD–3	69	800,000	2,000,000
Mill stamp ½ CD–5	71	—	250,000

Deciding on the best product mix was a difficult task. There was a seemingly infinite number of product mixes that could be produced to use the forecast log supply. The Quesnel manager wanted to choose the mix that would show the highest profits for the plant, but since plywood products were joint products (i.e., were produced simultaneously from the same process), costs could not be assigned easily to individual products and determining which products were most profitable was therefore difficult.

Scheduling production was another difficult part of the mill manager's job. He had some flexibility in determining the number of shifts which were scheduled, but Okanagan wanted to provide steady employment for its people, and so the main flexibility was in the amount of overtime used. Workers on the first shift received $2.50 per hour; those on the swing shift received an additional $0.075, while those on the owl shift received $0.15 above the base rate. Any overtime work was paid at 1½ times the first-shift rate. (There were no shift bonuses for overtime.) The pay scale did not vary significantly between operations.

Appendix: Results of the log tests

Realization for logs sent to the sawmills

The realizations per thousand board feet (MBF) for the various log classes are given below. The realizations are net of discounts, sales commissions, and log transportation to the mill.

Log description	*Net realization/MBF*
1 peeler 12 to 20 inches	$36.60
1 peeler over 20 inches	31.66
1 sawlog under 16 inches	39.15
1 sawlog 16 to 24 inches	28.78
1 sawlog over 24 inches	24.60
2 peeler 12 to 20 inches	30.90
2 peeler over 20 inches	23.20
2 sawlog 12 to 20 inches	29.50
2 sawlog over 20 inches	24.55
3 12 to 17 inches	35.44
3 over 17 inches	24.09
4 all	31.72

Recovery of veneer, by grade, for logs sent to the plywood mill

Log description	*Percent of veneer of each grade*				*Surface square feet (⅜-inch basis per BF)*
	B	*C*	*D*	*NC*	
1 peeler 12 to 20 inches	4	44	52	—	2.72
1 peeler over 20 inches	4	39	57	—	2.29
1 sawlog under 16 inches	1	30	66	3	2.77
1 sawlog 16 to 24 inches	3	25	68	4	2.53
1 sawlog over 24 inches	3	15	76	6	2.12
2 peeler 12 to 20 inches	—	52	48	—	2.20
2 peeler over 20 inches	—	36	64	—	2.01
2 sawlog 12 to 20 inches	—	23	72	5	2.09
2 sawlog over 20 inches	—	39	56	5	2.03
3 12 to 17 inches	—	60	4	36	2.32
3 over 17 inches	—	50	3	47	2.54

Notes:
1. Species 4 is not suitable for peeling.
2. Grade recoveries are after estimated waste.
3. Net yields include upgraded veneer obtained by patching.
4. Volume of veneer is usually expressed in terms of surface square feet on a ⅜-inch basis—i.e., the unit of measure is defined as a piece which is one foot by one foot by three-eighths inch. The first four columns for each log type give the *percentage* yields of each grade. The last column gives the *volume* yield of veneer for each board foot (BF) of log of that particular type.

Case 12–5B

Okanagan Lumber Company (B)*

This case describes the formulation as a linear program of the log allocation problem described in Okanagan Lumber Company (A). It also includes computer output for the LP problem.

The 12 classes of logs are coded as follows:

Code number	Species	Name	Diameter range (inches)
1	1	Peeler	12 to 20
2	1	Peeler	Over 20
3	1	Sawlog	Under 16
4	1	Sawlog	16 to 24
5	1	Sawlog	Over 24
6	2	Peeler	12 to 20
7	2	Peeler	Over 20
8	2	Sawlog	12 to 20
9	2	Sawlog	Over 20
10	3	—	12 to 17
11	3	—	Over 17
12	4	—	All

Decision variables and objective function

The objective function is revenue minus glue costs minus overtime labor costs. (Charges for regular labor are assumed to be fixed and so are not included. Similarly, timber costs are not included.) The objective function is given in units of tens of thousands of dollars.

The decision variables are:

1. How many tens of thousands of board feet (10MBF) of each of the 12 log types to send to the sawmills (variables 1 through 12).
2. How many 10MBF of each of the first 11 log types to send to the plywood mill to be made into one-tenth-inch veneer (variables 13 through 23). (Type 12 logs are never sent to the plywood mill.)
3. How many 10MBF of each of the first 11 log types to send to the plywood mill to be made into one-sixth-inch veneer (variables 31 through 41).
4. It is possible to use better quality veneer than is actually required in a

---

* Revised with permission from "Haida Lumber Company (B)," *Stanford Business Cases 1971*, Published by Stanford University Graduate School of Business, © 1971 by the Board of Trustees of the Leland Stanford Junior University.

particular product. Species 1 gives B, C, and D quality. Variables 24 and 42 allow downgrading the B to C for one-tenth inch and one-sixth inch, respectively. Similarly, variables 25 and 43 allow downgrading species 1 from C to D. Variables 26 and 44 allow downgrading species 1 from D to noncertifiable (or NC). Species 2 produces only grades C and D. Variables 27 and 45 allow downgrading species 2 from C to D, while variables 28 and 46 allow downgrading it from D to NC. Similarly, variables 29 and 47 allow downgrading species 3 from C to D, while variables 30 and 48 allow downgrading it from D to NC.

5. How many tens of thousands of minutes of lathe and clipper overtime to use (variable 49).

6. How many tens of thousands of panels to make of each of the products listed in Exhibit 6 of Okanagan Lumber (A) (variables 50 through 69).

7. How many tens of thousands of minutes of spreader overtime to use (variable 70).

The decision variables, their units and their coefficients in the objective function are listed in Table 1. Sample calculations of coefficients for the objective function are given in Exhibit 1.

Table 1
Decision variables

Number	Description	Dimensions	Coefficient of objective function
1	Logs to sawmill—1	10MBF	0.03660
2	Logs to sawmill—2	10MBF	0.03166
3	Logs to sawmill—3	10MBF	0.03915
4	Logs to sawmill—4	10MBF	0.02878
5	Logs to sawmill—5	10MBF	0.02460
6	Logs to sawmill—6	10MBF	0.03090
7	Logs to sawmill—7	10MBF	0.02320
8	Logs to sawmill—8	10MBF	0.02950
9	Logs to sawmill—9	10MBF	0.02455
10	Logs to sawmill—10	10MBF	0.03544
11	Logs to sawmill—11	10MBF	0.02409
12	Logs to sawmill—12	10MBF	0.03172
13	Logs to $^1/_{10}$-in. veneer—1	10MBF	0
14	Logs to $^1/_{10}$-in. veneer—2	10MBF	0
15	Logs to $^1/_{10}$-in. veneer—3	10MBF	0
16	Logs to $^1/_{10}$-in. veneer—4	10MBF	0
17	Logs to $^1/_{10}$-in. veneer—5	10MBF	0
18	Logs to $^1/_{10}$-in. veneer—6	10MBF	0
19	Logs to $^1/_{10}$-in. veneer—7	10MBF	0
20	Logs to $^1/_{10}$-in. veneer—8	10MBF	0
21	Logs to $^1/_{10}$-in. veneer—9	10MBF	0
22	Logs to $^1/_{10}$-in. veneer—10	10MBF	0
23	Logs to $^1/_{10}$-in. veneer—11	10MBF	0
24	$^1/_{10}$ in. downgraded B to C—species 1	10MSF*	0

Table 1 (continued)

Number	Description	Dimensions	Coefficient of objective function
25	$^{1}/_{10}$ in. downgraded C to D—species 1	10MSF*	0
26	$^{1}/_{10}$ in. downgraded D to NC—species 1	10MSF*	0
27	$^{1}/_{10}$ in. downgraded C to D—species 2	10MSF*	0
28	$^{1}/_{10}$ in. downgraded D to NC—species 2	10MSF*	0
29	$^{1}/_{10}$ in. downgraded C to D—species 3	10MSF*	0
30	$^{1}/_{10}$ in. downgraded D to NC—species 3	10MSF*	0
31	Logs to $^{1}/_{6}$-in. veneer—1	10MBF	0
32	Logs to $^{1}/_{6}$-in. veneer—2	10MBF	0
33	Logs to $^{1}/_{6}$-in. veneer—3	10MBF	0
34	Logs to $^{1}/_{6}$-in. veneer—4	10MBF	0
35	Logs to $^{1}/_{6}$-in. veneer—5	10MBF	0
36	Logs to $^{1}/_{6}$-in. veneer—6	10MBF	0
37	Logs to $^{1}/_{6}$-in. veneer—7	10MBF	0
38	Logs to $^{1}/_{6}$-in. veneer—8	10MBF	0
39	Logs to $^{1}/_{6}$-in. veneer—9	10MBF	0
40	Logs to $^{1}/_{6}$-in. veneer—10	10MBF	0
41	Logs to $^{1}/_{6}$-in. veneer—11	10MBF	0
42	$^{1}/_{6}$-in. downgraded B to C—species 1	10MSF	0
43	$^{1}/_{6}$-in. downgraded C to D—species 1	10MSF	0
44	$^{1}/_{6}$-in. downgraded D to NC—species 1	10MSF	0
45	$^{1}/_{6}$-in. downgraded C to D—species 2	10MSF	0
46	$^{1}/_{6}$-in. downgraded D to NC—species 2	10MSF	0
47	$^{1}/_{6}$-in. downgraded C to D—species 3	10MSF	0
48	$^{1}/_{6}$-in. downgraded D to NC—species 3	10MSF	0
49	Lathe overtime	10,000 minutes	-0.750
50	Panels—product 1, alternative A	10,000 panels	1.5235
51	Panels—product 1, alternative B	10,000 panels	1.5235
52	Panels—product 1, alternative C	10,000 panels	1.5235
53	Panels—product 1, alternative D	10,000 panels	1.5235
54	Panels—product 1, alternative E	10,000 panels	1.5235
55	Panels—product 2, alternative A	10,000 panels	2.0035
56	Panels—product 2, alternative B	10,000 panels	2.0035
57	Panels—product 2, alternative C	10,000 panels	2.0035
58	Panels—product 3, alternative A	10,000 panels	2.0995
59	Panels—product 3, alternative B	10,000 panels	2.0995
60	Panels—product 3, alternative C	10,000 panels	2.0995
61	Panels—product 3, alternative D	10,000 panels	2.0995
62	Panels—product 3, alternative E	10,000 panels	2.0995
63	Panels—product 4, alternative A	10,000 panels	2.0751
64	Panels—product 4, alternative B	10,000 panels	2.0751
65	Panels—product 4, alternative C	10,000 panels	2.0751
66	Panels—product 4, alternative D	10,000 panels	2.0751
67	Panels—product 4, alternative E	10,000 panels	2.0751
68	Panels—product 4, alternative F	10,000 panels	2.0751
69	Panels—product 4, alternative G	10,000 panels	2.0751
70	Spreader overtime	10,000 minutes	-0.25

* MSF = thousand surface square feet.

Exhibit 1
Sample calculations of coefficients of the objective function

1. *For type 4 logs to the sawmill.* The Appendix of the (A) case gives $28.78/MBF for species 1 sawlogs with 16–24-inch diameters. That gives $278.8 per 10,000 BF, or 0.02878 tens of thousands of dollars per 10,000 BF.

2. The various types of veneer do not generate revenue until they are parts of panels. Hence, the end products (the panels) have positive coefficients in the objective function, but the variables for veneer have zero coefficients.

3. *For lathe and clipper overtime.* Twelve workers at 1½ times the regular rate of $2.50 per hour gives $45 per hour, or $7.50 for ten minutes. That gives $7,500 (or 0.75 in tens of thousands of dollars) for 10,000 minutes.

4. Similarly, the spreader overtime requires four workers and gives 0.25 in tens of thousands of dollars for 10,000 minutes.

5. *For product 4, alternative A.* The (A) case gives a net realization of $71 per 1,000 surface square feet. Since each panel is 4 feet × 8 feet (or 32 square feet), this amount is

$$\frac{71}{1,000} \times 32 = \$2.272$$

per panel. We must then subtract glue costs. This product uses two one-tenth-inch cores for a total of 64 square feet of one-tenth-inch core. The (A) case states that $20 (one batch) of glue will take care of 6,500 square feet of one-tenth-inch cores. Thus, one panel will use $20/6,500 per square foot, or

$$\frac{\$20}{6,500} \times 64 = \$0.196923$$

of glue. The panel nets $2.272 minus $0.1969, or $2.075; 10,000 panels give 2.075 tens of thousands of dollars.

Constraint names and right-hand-sides

1. *Log availability constraints* (1 through 12) For each log type, Exhibit 1 of the (A) case gives the number of MBF which will be available. (The constraints are stated in terms of 10MBF.) For each log type, the use of logs cannot exceed the supply. For log types 1 through 11, the constraints therefore require that use in the sawmill plus use in one-tenth-inch veneer plus use in one-sixth-inch veneer not exceed the available supply. For log type 12 the logs sent to the sawmill cannot exceed the supply.

2. *Plywood mill capacity constraint* (13). Total logs processed at the plywood mill (whether for one-tenth-inch veneer or for one-sixth-inch veneer) cannot exceed 18,500 MBF (or 1,850 in tens of MBF).

3. *Veneer supply constraints* (14 through 33). For each log type, the information from the log test in the Appendix of the (A) case can be used to determine how much veneer will be produced (for either thickness) for each 10MBF sent to the plywood mill to produce veneer. For each

log type and thickness there is a constraint requiring that the veneer used not exceed the veneer supply. The veneer may be used in the various products given in the (A) case, and if appropriate, it may be downgraded. Exhibit 2 of this case gives sample calculations of veneer supply constraints. The supply constraints are stated in the form USE − SUPPLY $\leqq$ 0.

Exhibit 2
Plywood mill capacity and veneer supply constraints

1. Plywood capacity is 18,500 MBF per year. Total logs processed at the plywood mill equals the sum of variables 13–23 and 31–41.
2. *Veneer supply constraints for one-tenth-inch veneer.*
Example 1: Grade B veneer from species 1 (constraint 14). The Appendix of the (A) case says that one BF of this type of log gives 2.72 surface square feet of three-eighths-inch basis veneer in all; in other words, the total volume of veneer per BF is 2.72 times three-eighths-inch. We assume that the total volume yield is fixed, so that we would get different amounts (in surface square feet) for different thicknesses. For three-sixteenths-inch we would get twice as many (or 5.44) surface square feet, for example. For one-tenth-inch veneer we get

$$\frac{^3/_8}{^1/_{10}}$$

as much total veneer, or

$$^3/_8 \times {}^{10}/_1 \times 2.72 = 10.2$$

surface square feet. According to the Appendix of the (A) case, 4 percent of this amount (or 0.408 surface square feet) is grade B. In a similar way we can find that one board foot of type 2 log provides 0.343 square feet; the corresponding figures for log types 3, 4, and 5 are 0.104, 0.285, and 0.239, respectively. The yield of surface square feet per board foot is the same number as the yield of 10MSF per 10MBF, so these numbers are the appropriate ones for the constraint.

No products require grade B veneer, so that any such veneer which is used would first be downgraded. Thus, constraint 14 states that the total use (which is variable 24) cannot exceed the total supply.

Variable 24 − 0.408 × (variable 13) − 0.343 × (variable 14) − 0.104 × (variable 15)
− 0.285 × (variable 16) − 0.239 × (variable 17) $\leqq$ 0

Example 2: One-tenth-inch veneer of grade C from species 1. The initial availability of such veneer can be found (by calculations analogous to those above) as

4.488 × (variable 13) + 3.349 × (variable 14) + 3.116 × (variable 15)
+ 2.372 × (variable 16) + 1.193 × (variable 17)

To this amount we must add the veneer downgraded from B to C (variable 24). The veneer can be used for

Exhibit 2 *(continued)*

---

a. Downgrading to D (variable 25).

b. Product 1 alternatives D or E (variables 53 and 54), with 32 square feet required per panel (or 32 10MSF per 10,000 panels).

c. Product 4, alternatives D, F, or G, with 32 square feet per panel (variables 66, 68, and 69).

Thus, the total use is

Variable 25 + 32 × (variable 53) + 32 × (variable 54)
$$+ 32 \times (\text{variable } 66) + 32 \times (\text{variable } 68) + 32 \times (\text{variable } 69)$$

3. *Veneer supply constraints for one-sixth-inch veneer*. These constraints are analogous to the one-sixth-inch veneer constraints discussed above.

4. *Sawmill capacity constraint* (34). The (A) case gives the times required to cut the various log types at the sawmills. As shown in Exhibit 3 of this case, that information can be used to derive coefficients for a constraint requiring that sawmill use not exceed the combined capacity of the five mills.

5. *Lathe and clipper capacity constraints* (35 and 36). Constraint 35 requires that regular lathe and clipper use (which is total use minus the overtime used) cannot exceed regular lathe and clipper time available. Exhibit 4 explains how the coefficients can be calculated for that constraint. Constraint 36 places a limit on the overtime available for the lathe and clipper; the maximum is 32 hours per week for 51 weeks of the year (or 1,632 hours, which is also 97,920 minutes).

6. *Dryer capacity constraint* (37). Constraint 37 requires that regular dryer capacity, net of downtime, not exceed availability. The values for usage and availability are explained in Exhibit 5.

Exhibit 3
Sawmill capacity constraint

The (A) case gives time requirements in minutes/BF (or equivalently, 10,000 minutes per 10MBF). Thus, usage is 0.007 * (variable 1) + · · · + 0.010 * (variable 12).

The five sawmills have a total of 13 saw shifts per day. At eight hours per shift and 255 days per year, there are

$$13 \times 8 \times 255 \times 60 = 1,591,200 \text{ minutes} .$$

Eliminating 13 percent for downtime leaves 1,384,344 (or 138.4 in 10,000-minute units). The constraint states that use must not exceed availability.

Exhibit 4
Lathe and clipper capacity

1. To calculate the use of lathe and clipper capacity, consider, for example, one-tenth-inch veneer from logs of type 1. The (A) case says that the lathe and clipper can handle 10,500 surface square feet (three-eighths-inch basis) per hour and also that the total veneer yield for this type of log is 2.72 such square feet. Thus, for every BF the requirement is

$$\frac{2.72 \text{ sq ft}}{\text{BF}} \times \frac{1 \text{ hr}}{10,500 \text{ sq ft}} \times \frac{60 \text{ min}}{\text{hr}}$$

or 0.0155428 minutes per BF (or 0.0155428 in ten thousands of minutes per 10MBF).

The other usages are calculated similarly.

2. Regular time is available 16 hours per day, five days a week, 51 weeks a year, or 4,080 hours (equals 244,800 minutes, or 24.48 ten thousands of minutes).

3. Constraint 35 states that regular use (which is total use minus overtime) must not exceed the available regular time.

4. Overtime is available 32 hours per week, or 1,632 hours per year (or 97,920 minutes per year). Constraint 36 states that overtime use may not exceed the time available.

Exhibit 5
Dryer capacity

1. Total availability is 24 hours per day, 255 days per year. This amount is 367,200 minutes per year. Subtracting 11 percent for downtime leaves 326,808 minutes.

2. The (A) case states that the dryer handles 652 square feet per minute when it is set at seven minutes. Set at one minute, it should handle 7×652 square feet, or 4,564 square feet, per minute; set at two minutes, it should handle half that amount per minute, etc.

3. As an example, consider species 1, one-tenth-inch veneer. That species gives 45 percent heartwood (which requires a setting of 7 minutes) and 55 percent sapwood (which requires a setting of 12 minutes). The heartwood can be processed at 652 square feet/minute; the sapwood at 4,564/12, or 380.3 square feet/minute. Because 1,000 square feet will contain 450 square feet of heartwood and 550 square feet of sapwood, the total time to dry 1,000 square feet of species 1, one-tenth-inch veneer is the sum of

$$\frac{450 \text{ sq ft}}{652 \text{ sq ft/min}} = 0.6902 \text{ min}$$

and

$$\frac{550 \text{ sq ft}}{380.3 \text{ sq ft/min}} = 1.4461 \text{ min}$$

or 2.136 minutes in all.

Exhibit 5 *(continued)*

4. To determine how much time it takes to process some number of MBF of one of the species 1 log classes which has been sent to be made into one-tenth-inch veneer, for example, we must consider the yield in square feet of veneer for that class. The yield numbers were discussed in Exhibit 2. For example, for type 1 logs the yield of one-tenth-inch veneer is 10.2 MSF/MBF. Thus, drying 1,000 BF requires

$$\frac{2.136 \text{ min}}{\text{MSF}} \times \frac{10.2 \text{ MSF}}{\text{MBF}} = 21.7872 \text{ min/MBF}$$

which is 217.872 min/10MBF, or 0.0217872 in ten thousands of minutes per 10MBF.

The other figures are found in a similar way.

Exhibit 6
Spreader capacity

1. The spreader can handle 3.9 corelines per minute. Thus, products 1, 2, and 3 (with one coreline each) require 1/3.9, or 0.2564, minute/panel (and the same number of tens of thousands of minutes per 10,000 panels). Product 4 has two corelines and so requires twice as much time.

2. Regular time available is 24 hours per day, 255 days per year, or 367,200 minutes in all.

3. Constraint 38 requires that the use of regular spreader time (which is total use minus overtime) must not exceed available time.

4. Spreader overtime is available up to 48 hours per week, or 146,880 minutes per year. Constraint 39 states that the use of overtime may not exceed the time available.

7. *Spreader capacity constraints* (38 and 39). Constraint 38 requires that use of regular spreader time (total time minus overtime) not exceed availability. Exhibit 6 explains the coefficients for that constraint. Constraint 39 requires that spreader overtime not exceed 48 hours per week (or 146,880 minutes per year).

8. *Sales restrictions* (40 through 45). Constraint 40 gives the maximum for product 1 (the total for all of the different realizations which might be made of that product) in tens of thousands of panels. Constraints 41 and 42 give the minimum and maximum for product 2 (in all its forms). Constraints 43 and 44 give the limits for product 3, while constraint 45 gives the maximum for product 4.

Table 2 lists the constraints and gives their right-hand-side values. *Important note:* Because of the way the units have been chosen in this problem, the shadow prices for these constraints will turn out to have the natural units of dollars per board foot, dollars per minute, etc.

Table 2
Constraint names and right-hand sides

Number	Description	Dimensions	Right-hand side
1	Log availability—1	10MBF	554.4
2	Log availability—2	10MBF	497.2
3	Log availability—3	10MBF	422.4
4	Log availability—4	10MBF	1,359.6
5	Log availability—5	10MBF	2,934.8
6	Log availability—6	10MBF	530.2
7	Log availability—7	10MBF	294.8
8	Log availability—8	10MBF	2,140.6
9	Log availability—9	10MBF	761.2
10	Log availability—10	10MBF	752.4
11	Log availability—11	10MBF	1,007.6
12	Log availability—12	10MBF	8,500.8
13	Plywood mill—overall capacity	10MBF	1,850.0
14	Veneer supply $1/_{10}$-in. B—1	10MSF	0
15	Veneer supply $1/_{10}$-in. C—1	10MSF	0
16	Veneer supply $1/_{10}$-in. D—1	10MSF	0
17	Veneer supply $1/_{10}$-in. NC—1	10MSF	0
18	Veneer supply $1/_{10}$-in. C—2	10MSF	0
19	Veneer supply $1/_{10}$-in. D—2	10MSF	0
20	Veneer supply $1/_{10}$-in. NC—2	10MSF	0
21	Veneer supply $1/_{10}$-in. C—3	10MSF	0
22	Veneer supply $1/_{10}$-in. D—3	10MSF	0
23	Veneer supply $1/_{10}$-in. NC—3	10MSF	0
24	Veneer supply $1/_{6}$-in. B—1	10MSF	0
25	Veneer supply $1/_{6}$-in. C—1	10MSF	0
26	Veneer supply $1/_{6}$-in. D—1	10MSF	0
27	Veneer supply $1/_{6}$-in. NC—1	10MSF	0
28	Veneer supply $1/_{6}$-in. C—2	10MSF	0
29	Veneer supply $1/_{6}$-in. D—2	10MSF	0
30	Veneer supply $1/_{6}$-in. NC—2	10MSF	0
31	Veneer supply $1/_{6}$-in. C—3	10MSF	0
32	Veneer supply $1/_{6}$-in. D—3	10MSF	0
33	Veneer supply $1/_{6}$-in. NC—3	10MSF	0
34	Headrig saw capacity	10,000 minutes	138.4
35	Regular lathe and clipper time	10,000 minutes	24.48
36	Overtime lathe and clipper	10,000 minutes	9.792
37	Dryer capacity	10,000 minutes	32.68
38	Regular spreader time	10,000 minutes	36.72
39	Overtime spreader	10,000 minutes	14.688
40	Sales max—product 1	10,000 panels	25
41	Sales min—product 2	10,000 panels	0.5
42	Sales max—product 2	10,000 panels	5
43	Sales min—product 3	10,000 panels	80
44	Sales max—product 3	10,000 panels	200
45	Sales max—product 4	10,000 panels	25

The tableau for the linear programming formulation of the log allocation problem follows the computer output.

Computer output

```
TITLE: OKANAGAN LUMBER COMPANY
PROCEED, DISPLAY, OR REJECT? P

MAXIMIZE OR MINIMIZE? MAX

OPTIMAL SOLUTION FOUND.
     CONTRIB        763.283

OUTPUT OPTION? E

ALL ITEMS NOT LISTED IN SECTIONS 1 - 4 HAVE THE VALUE ZERO.

*1* DECISION VARIABLES
   1.  L1-SAW      167.747
   2.  L2-SAW      497.200
   3.  L3-SAW      216.020
   4.  L4-SAW      149.088
   5.  L5-SAW      2934.30
   6.  L6-SAW      530.200
   7.  L7-SAW      291.262
   8.  L8-SAW      2140.60
   9.  L9-SAW      761.200
  10.  L10-SAW     747.291
  11.  L11-SAW     1007.60
  12.  L12-SAW     8500.80
  13.  L1-V10      66.0129
  22.  L10-V10     .000000
  24.  DG10-BC1    26.9333
  26.  DG10-DN1    26.9333
  27.  DG10-CD2    .000000
  31.  L1-V6       320.640
  33.  L3-V6       206.380
  34.  L4-V6       1210.51
  37.  L7-V6       3.53786
  40.  L10-V6      5.10856
  42.  DG6-BC1     298.080
  45.  DG6-CD2     5.76000
  46.  DG6-DN2     16.0000
  53.  PAN1-D      9.81942
  55.  PAN2-A      .500000
  59.  PAN3-B      102.157
  61.  PAN3-D      .333333E-01
  63.  PAN4-A      .000000
  64.  PAN4-B      .000000
  65.  PAN4-C      .000000
  66.  PAN4-D      .280555
  69.  PAN4-G      .000000
```

Computer output *(continued)*

```
*2* SLACK(+) AND SURPLUS(-) IN CONSTRAINTS
 13. +CP-PLY    37.8086
 33. +V6-NC-3    9.60000
 35. +CP-LC-RG   7.19531
 36. +CP-LC-OT   9.79200
 38. +CP-SP-RG   7.77388
 39. +CP-SP-OT  14.6880
 40. +PAN1-MAX  15.1806
 42. +PAN2-MAX   4.50000
 43. -PAN3-MIN  22.1903
 44. +PAN3-MAX  97.8097
 45. +PAN4-MAX  24.7194
```

```
*3* SHADOW PRICES FOR CONSTRAINTS
  1. SUP-L1    .226370E-01
  2. SUP-L2    .216864E-01
  3. SUP-L3    .192028E-01
  4. SUP-L4    .168117E-01
  5. SUP-L5    .166211E-01
  6. SUP-L6    .169370E-01
  7. SUP-L7    .132264E-01
  8. SUP-L8    .155370E-01
  9. SUP-L9    .145764E-01
 10. SUP-L10   .194823E-01
 11. SUP-L11   .141164E-01
 12. SUP-L12   .117728E-01
 14. V10-B-1   .192688E-01
 15. V10-C-1   .192688E-01
 16. V10-D-1   .113945E-01
 17. V10-NC-1  .113945E-01
 18. V10-C-2   .159548E-01
 19. V10-D-2   .159548E-01
 20. V10-NC-2  .113945E-01
 21. V10-C-3   .192688E-01
 22. V10-D-3   .113945E-01
 23. V10-NC-3  .227406E-02
 24. V6-B-1    .238288E-01
 25. V6-C-1    .238288E-01
 26. V6-D-1    .208903E-01
 27. V6-NC-1   .169461E-01
 28. V6-C-2    .297118E-01
 29. V6-D-2    .297118E-01
 30. V6-NC-2   .297118E-01
 31. V6-C-3    .307381E-01
 32. V6-D-3    .208903E-01
 34. CP-SAW   1.99472
 37. CP-DRYER  6.06423
 41. PAN2-MIN -.599386
```

Computer output *(continued)*

```
*4* REDUCED COSTS FOR DECISION VARIABLES
  14. L2-V10      -.600752E-02
  15. L3-V10      -.100549E-01
  16. L4-V10      -.106979E-01
  17. L5-V10      -.177584E-01
  18. L6-V10      -.823975E-01
  19. L7-V10      -.730385E-01
  20. L8-V10      -.795176E-01
  21. L9-V10      -.767227E-01
  23. L11-V10     -.984549E-02
  25. DG10-CD1    -.787424E-02
  28. DG10-DN2    -.456023E-02
  29. DG10-CD3    -.787424E-02
  30. DG10-DN3    -.912046E-02
  32. L2-V6       -.338382E-02
  35. L5-V6       -.431199E-02
  36. L6-V6       -.245805E-02
  38. L8-V6       -.178229E-02
  39. L9-V6       -.107648E-01
  41. L11-V6      -.115415E-01
  43. DG6-CD1     -.293845E-02
  44. DG6-DN1     -.394423E-02
  47. DG6-CD3     -.984782E-02
  48. DG6-DN3     -.208903E-01
  49. LATHE-OT    -.750000
  50. PAN1-A      -.398793E-01
  51. PAN1-B      -.448381
  52. PAN1-C      -.126215
  54. PAN1-E      -.408502
  56. PAN2-B      -.282287
  57. PAN2-C      -.249443
  58. PAN3-A      -.752829
  60. PAN3-C      -.785673
  62. PAN3-E      -.282286
  67. PAN4-E      -.398793E-01
  68. PAN4-F       .000000
  70. SPRDR-OT    -.250000
```

```
*5* RANGES ON COEFFICIENTS OF OBJECTIVE CONTRIB
        VARIABLE   LOWER BOUND   CURRENT VALUE   UPPER BOUND
   1. L1-SAW      .36600E-01     .36600E-01      .41737E-01
   2. L2-SAW      .28276E-01     .31660E-01      .31660E-01
   3. L3-SAW      .34429E-01     .39150E-01      .39150E-01
   4. L4-SAW      .28780E-01     .28780E-01      .31687E-01
   5. L5-SAW      .24600E-01     .24600E-01      .52586E+06
   6. L6-SAW      .28442E-01     .30900E-01      UNBOUNDED
   7. L7-SAW      .99736E-02     .23200E-01      .24914E-01
   8. L8-SAW      .27718E-01     .29500E-01      UNBOUNDED
   9. L9-SAW      .13785E-01     .24550E-01      UNBOUNDED
  10. L10-SAW     .28318E-01     .35440E-01      .39343E-01
  11. L11-SAW     .14245E-01     .24090E-01      .12209E+07
  12. L12-SAW     .19947E-01     .31720E-01      .31720E-01
  13. L1-V10     -.50911E-02     .00000          .00000
```

Computer output *(continued)*

```
14.  L2-V10     UNBOUNDED       .00000      .60075E-02
15.  L3-V10     UNBOUNDED       .00000      .10055E-01
16.  L4-V10     UNBOUNDED       .00000      .10698E-01
17.  L5-V10     UNBOUNDED       .00000      .17758E-01
18.  L6-V10     UNBOUNDED       .00000      .82398E-01
19.  L7-V10     UNBOUNDED       .00000      .73039E-01
20.  L8-V10     UNBOUNDED       .00000      .79518E-01
21.  L9-V10     UNBOUNDED       .00000      .76723E-01
22.  L10-V10    -.39032E-02     .00000      .71224E-02
23.  L11-V10    UNBOUNDED       .00000      .98455E-02
24.  DG10-BC1   -.12478E-01     .00000      .33977E-01
25.  DG10-CD1   UNBOUNDED       .00000      .78742E-02
26.  DG10-DN1   .00000          .00000      .29038E-02
27.  DG10-CD2   -.12462E-02     .00000      .19207E-01
28.  DG10-DN2   UNBOUNDED       .00000      .45602E-02
29.  DG10-CD3   UNBOUNDED       .00000      .78742E-02
30.  DG10-DN3   UNBOUNDED       .00000      .91205E-02
31.  L1-V6      .00000          .00000      .32367E-02
32.  L2-V6      UNBOUNDED       .00000      .33838E-02
33.  L3-V6      .00000          .00000      .47210E-02
34.  L4-V6      -.29071E-02     .00000      .00000
35.  L5-V6      UNBOUNDED       .00000      .43120E-02
36.  L6-V6      UNBOUNDED       .00000      .24580E-02
37.  L7-V6      -.17141E-02     .00000      .00000
38.  L8-V6      UNBOUNDED       .00000      .17823E-02
39.  L9-V6      UNBOUNDED       .00000      .10765E-01
40.  L10-V6     -.12650E-01     .00000      .30843E-01
41.  L11-V6     UNBOUNDED       .00000      .11541E-01
42.  DG6-BC1    -.25232E-01     .00000      .00000
43.  DG6-CD1    UNBOUNDED       .00000      .29385E-02
44.  DG6-DN1    UNBOUNDED       .00000      .39442E-02
45.  DG6-CD2    -.29155E-02     .00000      .00000
46.  DG6-DN2    .00000          .00000      .12766E-01
47.  DG6-CD3    UNBOUNDED       .00000      .98478E-02
48.  DG6-DN3    UNBOUNDED       .00000      .20890E-01
49.  LATHE-OT   UNBOUNDED       -.75000     .00000
50.  PAN1-A     UNBOUNDED       1.5235      1.5634
51.  PAN1-B     UNBOUNDED       1.5235      1.9719
52.  PAN1-C     UNBOUNDED       1.5235      1.6497
53.  PAN1-D     1.5235          1.5235      1.6471
54.  PAN1-E     UNBOUNDED       1.5235      1.9320
55.  PAN2-A     2.0035          2.0035      2.6029
56.  PAN2-B     UNBOUNDED       2.0035      2.2858
57.  PAN2-C     UNBOUNDED       2.0035      2.2529
58.  PAN3-A     UNBOUNDED       2.0995      2.8523
59.  PAN3-B     2.0995          2.0995      2.1972
60.  PAN3-C     UNBOUNDED       2.0995      2.8852
61.  PAN3-D     1.9733          2.0995      2.3949
62.  PAN3-E     UNBOUNDED       2.0995      2.3818
63.  PAN4-A     2.0751          2.0751      2.1520
64.  PAN4-B     2.0569          2.0751      2.0751
65.  PAN4-C     2.0352          2.0751      2.5129
66.  PAN4-D     2.0751          2.0751      2.0933
67.  PAN4-E     UNBOUNDED       2.0751      2.1150
68.  PAN4-F     UNBOUNDED       2.0751      2.0751
69.  PAN4-G     2.0352          2.0751      2.6953
70.  SPRDR-OT   UNBOUNDED       -.25000     .00000
```

Computer output *(concluded)*

```
*6* RANGES ON VALUES OF RIGHT-HAND-SIDE RHS
     CONSTRNT  LOWER BOUND  CURRENT VALUE  UPPER BOUND
 1.  SUP-L1       477.84        554.40        657.91
 2.  SUP-L2       390.02        497.20        642.12
 3.  SUP-L3       368.81        422.40        531.43
 4.  SUP-L4      1303.7         1359.6        1480.4
 5.  SUP-L5      2800.3         2934.3        3115.4
 6.  SUP-L6       453.64        530.20        633.71
 7.  SUP-L7       187.62        294.80        439.72
 8.  SUP-L8      2064.0         2140.6        2244.1
 9.  SUP-L9       654.02        761.20        906.12
10.  SUP-L10      685.41        752.40        842.97
11.  SUP-L11      900.42       1007.6         1152.5
12.  SUP-L12     8447.2         8500.8        8573.3
13.  CP-PLY      1812.2         1850.0        UNBOUNDED
14.  V10-B-1      -30.230        .00000        24.285
15.  V10-C-1     -866.58         .00000        24.285
16.  V10-D-1      -26.218        .00000      1881.6
17.  V10-NC-1     -26.218        .00000      1881.6
18.  V10-C-2       .00000        .00000        .00000
19.  V10-D-2       .00000        .00000        .00000
20.  V10-NC-2      .00000        .00000        .00000
21.  V10-C-3       .00000        .00000        .00000
22.  V10-D-3       .00000        .00000        .00000
23.  V10-NC-3      .00000        .00000        .00000
24.  V6-B-1      -290.66         .00000       295.16
25.  V6-C-1      -290.66         .00000       295.16
26.  V6-D-1      -590.32         .00000       581.33
27.  V6-NC-1     -329.29         .00000       509.07
28.  V6-C-2        -9.0000       .00000        16.000
29.  V6-D-2     -1317.2          .00000        16.000
30.  V6-NC-2    -1317.2          .00000        16.000
31.  V6-C-3      -358.16         .00000        16.000
32.  V6-D-3        -1.0667       .00000       581.33
33.  V6-NC-3       -9.6000       .00000       UNBOUNDED
34.  CP-SAW       137.71        138.43        138.97
35.  CP-LC-RG      17.285        24.480       UNBOUNDED
36.  CP-LC-OT       .00000        9.7920      UNBOUNDED
37.  CP-DRYER      30.601        32.680        33.266
38.  CP-SP-RG      28.946        36.720       UNBOUNDED
39.  CP-SP-OT       .00000       14.688       UNBOUNDED
40.  PAN1-MAX       9.8194       25.000       UNBOUNDED
41.  PAN2-MIN       .65565E-06    .50000        5.0000
42.  PAN2-MAX       .50000        5.0000       UNBOUNDED
43.  PAN3-MIN     UNBOUNDED      80.000       102.19
44.  PAN3-MAX     102.19        200.00        UNBOUNDED
45.  PAN4-MAX       .28056       25.000       UNBOUNDED
```

Case 12–6

Mutual Life Insurance Company*

The Mutual Life Insurance Company (MLIC) offered various types of life insurance, annuities, and group health and accident insurance. Life insurance was sold through full-time agents of the company. In 1962, the 1,679 full-time MLIC agents sold $812 million of new insurance, bringing the total life insurance in force to $8.24 billion. Although 1962 sales represented a 2.5 percent increase over sales of the previous year, the company's total life insurance in force slipped in the national ranking from fifth to seventh. This was of particular concern to management since one of the primary objectives of the company was to maintain its position relative to the industry. Heavy emphasis was placed on this objective because profits were closely regulated by the government.

The Economic Research Section of Mutual Life was continually seeking new techniques for long-range planning. The most recent products of this effort were projections to 1970 of general economic conditions, and of conditions within the insurance industry. Dr. Robert Bates, Director of Economic Research, felt that the next step should be the development of a model of company operations for use in predicting the internal requirements for various levels of sales growth. Dr. Bates assigned a team of one economist and two actuaries to study the problem of developing a long-range planning model.

The study was begun by selecting three alternative sales goals for the year 1970:

> Goal 1: *$860 million*. This represented 1.0 percent of the industry sales forecast for 1970—a level to which Mutual Life's market share would fall if recent trends continued.
>
> Goal 2: *$1,145 million*. This was based on Mutual's current share of industry sales—1.46 percent.
>
> Goal 3: *$1,465 million*. At 1.88 percent of industry sales, this equaled Mutual's highest market share in the past decade.

The problem was stated as one of determining the agency personnel requirements, premium income, commissions, other expenses, and policy terminations associated with each of the alternative sales goals. The critical element was identified as agency personnel requirements, since

---

* From K. R. Davis and F. E. Webster, Jr., *Sales Force Management–Text and Cases,* published in 1968 by The Ronald Press, New York. Not to be reproduced or quoted without the written permission of the authors and publisher. Used with permission.

this was the variable most likely to affect sales of new life insurance. It was felt that sales would be a function of both the size and quality of the agency field force. Sales would in turn affect premium income and insurance in force. And all of these would affect commissions, other expenses, and policy terminations.

Because the development of a mathematical model would require a high level of sophistication in operations research and computer techniques, Dr. Bates requested authorization to employ the services of a management consulting firm. Although Mutual's top management did not share Bates' enthusiasm for mathematical models as planning tools, they granted him a free hand in determining how the budget of the Economic Research Section was to be spent.

In a memo to Bates, the Vice President of Finance reminded him that the research expenditures of mutual life insurance companies were limited by government regulation, and that the present budget allocation to the Economic Research Section was the maximum allowable.

Dr. Bates knew that the budget constraint would limit the effectiveness of outside consultants, but he felt that there was not sufficient experience with model-building within his section to successfully complete the project. Consequently, he retained the services of a well-known management consulting firm—Coolidge Associates.

Allen Faber, a senior consultant on the Coolidge Associates staff with extensive experience in mathematical programming, was given the MLIC assignment. Mr. Faber and Dr. Bates agreed that the MLIC research team that had begun the project should continue their work with the assistance of the consultant. In this way, when the consultant's job was completed, there would remain within the company a group capable of using and improving the planning model.

As Faber went over the work that had been done by the team up to that time, it became apparent that the members of the team did not feel that his presence was necessary. One bright, young actuary, in particular, thought that he knew more about the insurance company and its problems than an outside consultant could possibly know.

Faber's initial reaction to the work that had been done was that the basic objectives of the modeling procedure were well conceived. He was concerned, however, with a weakness in the team's approach to actual construction of the model. The sales goals were expressed only in terms of the 1970 sales level. Thus, an attempt to minimize the costs of providing the agency personnel necessary to meet a given goal might result in a hiring pattern as shown in the accompanying curve. Faber pointed out that, while this approach might result in a minimum cost program for reaching the 1970 sales goal, it might also result in excessive costs in later years. As the curve shows, the company might find itself in 1970 with the majority of the agency force made up of employees who were recently

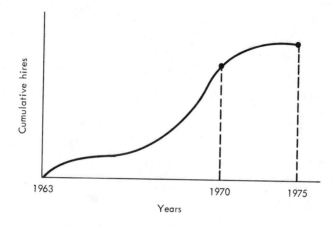

hired. The relatively low productivity of these new employees would necessitate an increase in the hiring rate if the desired rate of growth were to be maintained beyond 1970. To overcome this problem of suboptimization, Faber suggested that sales goals be specified for each of the years 1970–75 in order to ensure some continuity in sales growth.

The research team agreed with this observation, but relations between the actuary and the consultant did not improve. Finally, the actuary was taken off the team by Dr. Bates and the project began to move forward.

Faber decided that the problem of agency personnel requirements could be set up in a linear programming (LP) format. Using LP, it would be possible to determine, for each set of sales goals, the number of new agents to be hired in each of the years 1963–75, with the objective of minimizing total hiring and training costs. The problem could then be expressed as one of determining the minimum number of new agents hired over the 13-year period, within the constraint of meeting the sales goal in each year.

The consultants requested permission to speak with operating personnel to obtain their judgments concerning the range over which the hiring and training costs per employee remained relatively stable. At the same time, the consultants hoped to uncover other areas of information relevant to the model. Due to budget limitations, their request was denied. As a consequence, they were forced to rely upon accounting records and upon the judgments of the members of the research section. Based on their investigation, the consultants decided that hiring and training costs could be assumed to vary linearly.

To realize Mutual's objective of being a growth company, MLIC management established the policy that the number of agents hired in a given year should be at least as large as the number hired in the previous year. But because Mutual did not want to grow so fast as to become unmanageable, it decided that the number of agents hired in a given year, should not exceed 150 percent of the number hired in the previous year. These sets of constraints were expressed mathematically as:

$$H_i \geqq H_{i-1} \quad \text{or} \quad H_{i-1} - H_i \leqq 0 ,$$
$$H_i \leqq 1.5H_{i-1} \quad \text{or} \quad H_i - 1.5H_{i-1} \leqq 0 ,$$

where H_i represents the number of new agents hired in year i.

The next step in setting up the linear program was to establish a relationship between the number of new agents hired in each year and the volume of sales that these agents could be expected to produce in the years 1970 through 1975. The consultants asked the research section to provide them with two sets of historical data:

1. The agent survival rates as a function of length of service, i.e., the average percentage of the agents hired in a year who remained with the company at the end of the year; the average percentage of agents entering their second year who remained with the company at the end of the second year; etc.
2. The agent productivity rates, in dollars of sales per agent, for survivors and terminators in each length of service category.

Using these data, the consultants constructed the table given in Exhibit 1. The productivity coefficients were then used in the sales volume constraints as follows:

$$104.50H_i + 157.50H_{i-1} + 113.20H_{i-2} + 95.60H_{i-3}$$
$$+ 76.95H_{i-4} + \ldots = G_i ,$$

where H_i again equals the number of agents hired in year i, and G_i equals the sales goal for year i.

The basic assumption underlying the above analysis of agent productivity was that all agents to be hired in a given year would be of a caliber equal to that of MLIC agents hired in the past. The consultants felt that, as the need for new agents increased each year, some portion of the new agents would be of a lower caliber. In addition, they realized that an increasing number of new agents would infringe on the territories of established MLIC agents. The restriction of no more than a 50 percent increase in new hires from one year to the next would limit infringement to some extent. However, it was felt that further allowance should be made for diminishing agent productivity.

Allen Faber reasoned that total dollar sales volume would increase at a somewhat lower rate than the number of agents hired. This relationship reflected the fact that the best agents would be hired first and that productivity per agent therefore tended to decrease as the number of agents hired increased. This line of reasoning could be expressed by the solid line in the accompanying graph. To fit the requirements of the LP model, this relationship could be quite accurately approximated by two linear segments as indicated by the broken lines above.

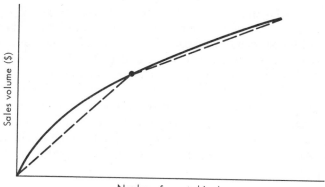

Number of agents hired

It was therefore possible to think of agents hired in a given year as being of two classes. One class would be assumed to follow the same patterns of survival and productivity as agents hired in the past. However, it was assumed that there would be no more than 100 of these "first class" agents available for hire in a given year. The survival and productivity characteristics of the remaining, "second class" agents would be somewhat lower.

In order to introduce this new set of conditions into the model, it was necessary to establish two variables for each of the 13 years: the number of first-class agents hired in a given year, F_i, and the number of second-class agents hired in a given year, S_i. The total number of agents to be hired each year would be the sum of the two variables:

$$H_i = F_i + S_i ,$$

with the additional set of conditions that

$$F_i \leqq 100 .$$

The productivity coefficients for first-class agents were those calculated in Exhibit 1. The higher proportion of failures among the second-class agents was taken into account by adjusting the survival rates for these agents in their first two calendar years of service. It had been found that most of the unsuccessful agents would terminate during the first two years, leaving as survivors those who conformed to the historical standards of MLIC. The effect of the lower survival rates on the productivity coefficients for second-class agents is shown in Exhibit 2.

A summary of the 45 constraints thus established is given in Exhibit 3. The objective function was:

$$\text{Minimize} \sum_{i=63}^{75} F_i + S_i .$$

In determining the sales goals for use as inputs to the model, the three originally determined goals for 1970 were combined with several assumed growth patterns for the years 1970–75. The 12 resulting goals (Exhibit 4) were then tested in the personnel planning model to determine the optimal hiring strategies associated with each. The results of the computations are shown in Exhibit 5. These were presented to Dr. Bates with a memo explaining the restrictions and the difficulties of obtaining feasible solutions (Exhibit 6).

Dr. Bates felt that before any further work was done in expanding the planning model, these initial results should be shown to management since the ultimate success of the proposed long-range planning model would depend upon management's willingness to accept a model of this sort as a planning tool.

Exhibit 1
Average survival and production rates for "first class" MLIC agents

| Calendar year of service | Percent of entrants surviving the year | Percent of agents hired at beginning of first year | | Average production ($000) | | Productivity coefficient ($000) |
		Surviving	Terminating	Survivors	Terminators	
First	74	74	26	$126	$ 42	$104.50
Second	55	41	33	336	61	157.50
Third	71	29	12	366	62	113.20
Fourth*	77	22	7	404	84	95.60
Fifth	79	18	4	417	75	76.95
Sixth or more	91	16	2	474	116	†

* Sample calculations—fourth year of service:

Percent of entrants surviving the year
　From historical data, of those agents entering their fourth year of service, 77 percent will remain with the company at the end of the year.

Percent of agents hired at beginning of first year
　Surviving:　　22 percent ($= 0.74 \times 0.55 \times 0.71 \times 0.77 \times 100$ percent) of all agents hired remain with the company for at least four years.
　Terminating:　7 percent ($= 29$ percent $- 22$ percent) of all agents hired leave the company during their fourth year of service.

Average production ($000)
　Survivors:　　From historical data, the average dollar sales during the fourth year of service of agents remaining with the company at the end of the fourth year is $404,000.
　Terminators:　The average fourth-year sales of agents terminating in that year is $84,000.

Productivity coefficient
　The agents hired in a given year can be expected to produce $95,600 in annual sales per agent four years later ($404 \times 0.22 + \$84 \times 0.07 = \$95.60$) (slight errors due to rounding).

† Productivity coefficients for six years or more of service continue to decline, due to the 91 percent survival rate.

Exhibit 2
Average survival and production rates for "second class" MLIC agents

Calendar year of service	Percent of entrants surviving the year	Percent of agents hired at beginning of first year		Average production ($000)		Productivity coefficient ($000)
		Sur- viving	Termi- nating	Sur- vivors	Termi- nators	
First	68	68	32	$126	$ 42	$ 99.12
Second	50	34	34	336	61	134.98
Third	71	24	10	366	62	94.35
Fourth	77	18	6	404	84	79.76
Fifth	79	14	4	417	75	61.38
Sixth or more	91	13	1	474	116	†

†Productivity coefficients for six years or more of service continue to decline, due to the 91 percent survival rate.

Exhibit 3
The LP model

Constraints:

1 . . . . $F_{63} + S_{63} \geqq 430$

2–13 . . . . $F_{i-1} + S_{i-1} - F_i - S_i \leqq 0;$ $\qquad i = 64, 65, \ldots, 75$

14 . . . . $F_{63} + S_{63} \leqq 645$

15–26 . . . . $-1.5F_{i-1} - 1.5S_{i-1} + F_i + S_i \leqq 0;$ $\qquad i = 64, 65, \ldots, 75$

27–39 . . . . $F_i \leqq 100;$ $\qquad i = 63, 64, 65, \ldots, 75$

40–45 . . . . $104.50F_i + 99.12S_i + 157.50F_{i-1} + 134.98S_{i-1} + 113.20F_{i-2}$
$\qquad\qquad + 94.35S_{i-2} + 95.60F_{i-3} + 79.76S_{i-3} + \ldots = G_i;$
$\qquad i =$ $\qquad\qquad 70, 71, 72, 73, 74, 75$

Observe function:

$$\text{Minimize } \sum_{i=63}^{75} F_i + S_i$$

Exhibit 4
Sales goals, 1970–1975 (millions of dollars)

Goal	1970	1971	1972	1973	1974	1975
A–1	351	416	482	548	615	682
B–2	636	712	793	874	958	1,042
C–3	956	1,057	1,155	1,255	1,357	1,463
D–1	351	379	406	430	452	472
E–1	351	382	411	438	463	486
F–2	636	704	772	840	907	975
G–2	636	715	796	877	960	1,043
H–2	636	727	820	916	1,014	1,114
I–3	956	1,037	1,119	1,200	1,282	1,364
J–3	956	1,051	1,149	1,248	1,349	1,452
K–3	956	1,066	1,180	1,297	1,418	1,542
L–3	956	1,088	1,227	1,372	1,524	1,685

The above figures for the 12 alternative sales goals are *exclusive* of business produced by non-full-time agent groups (brokers, agents of other companies, etc.). We have also subtracted the business expected to be produced in the 1970–75 period by full-time agents now with the company.

Exhibit 5
Agent hiring strategy for various sales goals

Year	A	B	C	D	E	F	G	H	I	J	K	L
									Sales goal			
1963	430	430	500	430	430	430	430	430		571	430	430
1964	430	430	751	430	430	430	430	430		857	546	438
1965	430	480	1,127	474	430	626	456	430		1,285	819	657
1966	430	720	1,184	532	457	792	684	569		1,285	1,228	985
1967	430	1,080	1,775	556	523	1,189	1,026	854		1,710	1,843	1,477
1968	430	1,258	1,775	556	587	1,189	1,283	1,281		1,710	1,860	2,048
1969	598	1,258	1,775	556	587	1,189	1,283	1,381	No	1,710	1,860	2,048
1970	813	1,258	1,775	556	587	1,189	1,283	1,381	feasible	1,710	1,860	2,048
1971	813	1,258	1,775	556*	587*	1,189	1,283	1,381	solution	1,710	1,860	2,048
1972	939	1,353	1,784	556	587	1,209	1,359	1,492		1,786	1,946	2,239
1973	976	1,379	1,901	556	587	1,269	1,388	1,544		1,864	2,049	2,309
1974	1,081	1,508	1,979	556	600	1,310	1,500	1,662		1,980	2,189	2,546
1975	1,113	1,558	2,140	577	611	1,402	1,556	1,756		2,098	2,328	2,723
Total hired in 13 years	8,913	13,970	20,141	6,901	7,003	13,413	13,961	14,591		20,276	20,818	21,996

* These sales goals could only be met by reducing the sales efficiency for agents hired in 1971 by a small amount.

Exhibit 6

October 4, 1963

Dr. Robert Bates, Director
Economic Research Section
Mutual Life Insurance Company
Springfield, Missouri

Dear Dr. Bates:

Enclosed are the results of our computation of the personnel planning model.

In setting up the problem in a linear programming format, we used essentially four sets of restrictions, i.e.:

1. All sales goals for new full-time agents for 1970 to 1975 have to be met exactly.
2. The number of new agents hired in one year must be at least as large as the number hired in the previous year.
3. The number of new agents hired in one year shall not exceed 150 percent of the number of agents hired the previous year.
4. The first 100 agents hired each year will have somewhat higher survival and productivity rates than the other agents hired in the same year.

The problem as stated involved a matrix of 46 equations and 65 variables, and, of course, 12 sets of requirements. As such, the problem exceeded the capacity of our 1401 program, which is limited to 40 equations. We therefore used the 7090 computer, and total computation time amounted to 0.13 hour. In addition to this we used an IBM 1401 computer for data preparation and the printing of results.

The answers obtained appear to be very interesting. One sales goal, case I, could not be met at all within the leeway allowed by the agent hiring policy restrictions. This case increased sales rapidly to $956 million in 1970, and then increased sales at a much lower rate beyond 1970. In order to meet this 1970 goal, a large number of new agents need to be hired in the late 1960s. The policy as stated necessitates that each year thereafter at least as many new agents need to be hired. This apparently is not feasible without either reducing the productivity of new agents or relaxing this 100 percent restriction.

Similarly, cases D and E were only barely feasible, because the computation shows that in order to meet these goals, only 93 and 54 agents, respectively, with an expected higher survival rate should be hired in 1971 instead of the normal complement of 100 in this class.

The computation also shows that for some of the projected sales goals, and especially for cases B, C, J, K, and L, the 150 percent maximum hiring rule is limiting in one year and the 100 percent minimum becomes restrictive 1, 2, or 3 years later.

Finally, the results from the computations indicate that for most sales goals, the annual hiring rates can only be varied over a narrow range while still yielding feasible solutions.

I am sincerely looking forward to discussing these results with you further.

Yours very truly,

Allen J. Faber

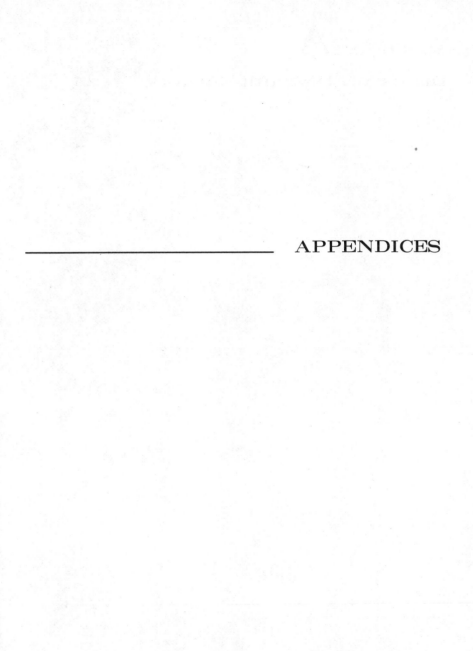

APPENDICES

Appendix A
Tables of Discount Factors

Table A-1
Single payment discount factors

Number of years	1%	2%	3%	4%	5%	6%	7%	8%	9%	10%
1	.990	.980	.971	.962	.952	.943	.935	.926	.917	.909
2	.980	.961	.943	.925	.907	.890	.873	.857	.842	.826
3	.971	.942	.915	.889	.864	.840	.816	.794	.772	.751
4	.961	.924	.888	.855	.823	.792	.763	.735	.708	.683
5	.951	.906	.863	.822	.784	.747	.713	.681	.650	.621
6	.942	.888	.837	.790	.746	.705	.666	.630	.596	.564
7	.933	.871	.813	.760	.711	.665	.623	.583	.547	.513
8	.923	.853	.789	.731	.677	.627	.582	:540	.502	.467
9	.914	.837	.766	.703	.645	.592	.544	.500	.460	.424
10	.905	.820	.744	.676	.614	.558	.508	.463	.422	.386
11	.896	.804	.722	.650	.585	.527	.475	.429	.388	.350
12	.887	.788	.701	.625	.557	.497	.444	.397	.356	.319
13	.879	.773	.681	.601	.530	.469	.415	.368	.326	.290
14	.870	.758	.661	.577	.505	.442	.388	.340	.299	.263
15	.861	.743	.642	.555	.481	.417	.362	.315	.275	.239
16	.853	.728	.623	.534	.458	.394	.339	.292	.252	.218
17	.844	.714	.605	.513	.436	.371	.317	.270	.231	.198
18	.836	.700	.587	.494	.416	.350	.296	.250	.212	.180
19	.828	.686	.570	.475	.396	.331	.277	.232	.194	.164
20	.820	.673	.554	.456	.377	.312	.258	.215	.178	.149
21	.811	.660	.538	.439	.359	.294	.242	.199	.164	.135
22	.803	.647	.522	.422	.342	.278	.226	.184	.150	.123
23	.795	.634	.507	.406	.326	.262	.211	.170	.138	.112
24	.788	.622	.492	.390	.310	.247	.197	.158	.126	.102
25	.780	.610	.478	.375	.295	.233	.184	.146	.116	.092
26	.772	.598	.464	.361	.281	.220	.172	.135	.106	.084
27	.764	.586	.450	.347	.268	.207	.161	.125	.098	.076
28	.757	.574	.437	.333	.255	.196	.150	.116	.090	.069
29	.749	.563	.424	.321	.243	.185	.141	.107	.082	.063
30	.742	.552	.412	.308	.231	.174	.131	.099	.075	.057
31	.735	.541	.400	.296	.220	.164	.123	.092	.069	.052
32	.727	.531	.388	.285	.210	.155	.115	.085	.063	.047
33	.720	.520	.377	.274	.200	.146	.107	.079	.058	.043
34	.713	.510	.366	.264	.190	.138	.100	.073	.053	.039
35	.706	.500	.355	.253	.181	.130	.094	.068	.049	.036
36	.699	.490	.345	.244	.173	.123	.088	.063	.045	.032
37	.692	.481	.335	.234	.164	.116	.082	.058	.041	.029
38	.685	.471	.325	.225	.157	.109	.076	.054	.038	.027
39	.678	.462	.316	.217	.149	.103	.071	.050	.035	.024
40	.672	.453	.307	.208	.142	.097	.067	.046	.032	.022
41	.665	.444	.298	.200	.135	.092	.062	.043	.029	.020
42	.658	.435	.289	.193	.129	.087	.058	.039	.027	.018
43	.652	.427	.281	.185	.123	.082	.055	.037	.025	.017
44	.645	.418	.272	.178	.117	.077	.051	.034	.023	.015
45	.639	.410	.264	.171	.111	.073	.048	.031	.021	.014
46	.633	.402	.257	.165	.106	.069	.044	.029	.019	.012
47	.626	.394	.249	.158	.101	.065	.042	.027	.017	.011
48	.620	.387	.242	.152	.096	.061	.039	.025	.016	.010
49	.614	.379	.235	.146	.092	.058	.036	.023	.015	.009
50	.608	.372	.228	.141	.087	.054	.034	.021	.013	.009

Table A–1 *(continued)*

Number of years	11%	12%	13%	14%	15%	16%	17%	18%	19%	20%
1	.901	.893	.885	.877	.870	.862	.855	.847	.840	.833
2	.812	.797	.783	.769	.756	.743	.731	.718	.706	.694
3	.731	.712	.693	.675	.658	.641	.624	.609	.593	.579
4	.659	.636	.613	.592	.572	.552	.534	.516	.499	.482
5	.593	.567	.543	.519	.497	.476	.456	.437	.419	.402
6	.535	.507	.480	.456	.432	.410	.390	.370	.352	.335
7	.482	.452	.425	.400	.376	.354	.333	.314	.296	.279
8	.434	.404	.376	.351	.327	.305	.285	.266	.249	.233
9	.391	.361	.333	.308	.284	.263	.243	.225	.209	.194
10	.352	.322	.295	.270	.247	.227	.208	.191	.176	.162
11	.317	.287	.261	.237	.215	.195	.178	.162	.148	.135
12	.286	.257	.231	.208	.187	.168	.152	.137	.124	.112
13	.258	.229	.204	.182	.163	.145	.130	.116	.104	.093
14	.232	.205	.181	.160	.141	.125	.111	.099	.088	.078
15	.209	.183	.160	.140	.123	.108	.095	.084	.074	.065
16	.188	.163	.141	.123	.107	.093	.081	.071	.062	.054
17	.170	.146	.125	.108	.093	.080	.069	.060	.052	.045
18	.153	.130	.111	.095	.081	.069	.059	.051	.044	.038
19	.138	.116	.098	.083	.070	.060	.051	.043	.037	.031
20	.124	.104	.087	.073	.061	.051	.043	.037	.031	.026
21	.112	.093	.077	.064	.053	.044	.037	.031	.026	.022
22	.101	.083	.068	.056	.046	.038	.032	.026	.022	.018
23	.091	.074	.060	.049	.040	.033	.027	.022	.018	.015
24	.082	.066	.053	.043	.035	.028	.023	.019	.015	.013
25	.074	.059	.047	.038	.030	.024	.020	.016	.013	.010
26	.066	.053	.042	.033	.026	.021	.017	.014	.011	.009
27	.060	.047	.037	.029	.023	.018	.014	.011	.009	.007
28	.054	.042	.033	.026	.020	.016	.012	.010	.008	.006
29	.048	.037	.029	.022	.017	.014	.011	.008	.006	.005
30	.044	.033	.026	.020	.015	.012	.009	.007	.005	.004
31	.039	.030	.023	.017	.013	.010	.008	.006	.005	.004
32	.035	.027	.020	.015	.011	.009	.007	.005	.004	.003
33	.032	.024	.018	.013	.010	.007	.006	.004	.003	.002
34	.029	.021	.016	.012	.009	.006	.005	.004	.003	.002
35	.026	.019	.014	.010	.008	.006	.004	.003	.002	.002
36	.023	.017	.012	.009	.007	.005	.004	.003	.002	.001
37	.021	.015	.011	.008	.006	.004	.003	.002	.002	.001
38	.019	.013	.010	.007	.005	.004	.003	.002	.001	.001
39	.017	.012	.009	.006	.004	.003	.002	.002	.001	.001
40	.015	.011	.008	.005	.004	.003	.002	.001	.001	.001
41	.014	.010	.007	.005	.003	.002	.002	.001	.001	.001
42	.012	.009	.006	.004	.003	.002	.001	.001	.001	.000
43	.011	.008	.005	.004	.002	.002	.001	.001	.001	.000
44	.010	.007	.005	.003	.002	.001	.001	.001	.000	.000
45	.009	.006	.004	.003	.002	.001	.001	.001	.000	.000
46	.008	.005	.004	.002	.002	.001	.001	.000	.000	.000
47	.007	.005	.003	.002	.001	.001	.001	.000	.000	.000
48	.007	.004	.003	.002	.001	.001	.001	.000	.000	.000
49	.006	.004	.003	.002	.001	.001	.000	.000	.000	.000
50	.005	.003	.002	.001	.001	.001	.000	.000	.000	.000

Table A-1 (continued)

Number of years	21%	22%	23%	24%	25%	26%	27%	28%	29%	30%
1	.826	.820	.813	.806	.800	.794	.787	.781	.775	.769
2	.683	.672	.661	.650	.640	.630	.620	.610	.601	.592
3	.564	.551	.537	.524	.512	.500	.488	.477	.466	.455
4	.467	.451	.437	.423	.410	.397	.384	.373	.361	.350
5	.386	.370	.355	.341	.328	.315	.303	.291	.280	.269
6	.319	.303	.289	.275	.262	.250	.238	.227	.217	.207
7	.263	.249	.235	.222	.210	.198	.188	.178	.168	.159
8	.218	.204	.191	.179	.168	.157	.148	.139	.130	.123
9	.180	.167	.155	.144	.134	.125	.116	.108	.101	.094
10	.149	.137	.126	.116	.107	.099	.092	.085	.078	.073
11	.123	.112	.103	.094	.086	.079	.072	.066	.061	.056
12	.102	.092	.083	.076	.069	.062	.057	.052	.047	.043
13	.084	.075	.068	.061	.055	.050	.045	.040	.037	.033
14	.069	.062	.055	.049	.044	.039	.035	.032	.028	.025
15	.057	.051	.045	.040	.035	.031	.028	.025	.022	.020
16	.047	.042	.036	.032	.028	.025	.022	.019	.017	.015
17	.039	.034	.030	.026	.023	.020	.017	.015	.013	.012
18	.032	.028	.024	.021	.018	.016	.014	.012	.010	.009
19	.027	.023	.020	.017	.014	.012	.011	.009	.008	.007
20	.022	.019	.016	.014	.012	.010	.008	.007	.006	.005
21	.018	.015	.013	.011	.009	.008	.007	.006	.005	.004
22	.015	.013	.011	.009	.007	.006	.005	.004	.004	.003
23	.012	.010	.009	.007	.006	.005	.004	.003	.003	.002
24	.010	.008	.007	.006	.005	.004	.003	.003	.002	.002
25	.009	.007	.006	.005	.004	.003	.003	.002	.002	.001
26	.007	.006	.005	.004	.003	.002	.002	.002	.001	.001
27	.006	.005	.004	.003	.002	.002	.002	.001	.001	.001
28	.005	.004	.003	.002	.002	.002	.001	.001	.001	.001
29	.004	.003	.002	.002	.002	.001	.001	.001	.001	.000
30	.003	.003	.002	.002	.001	.001	.001	.001	.000	.000
31	.003	.002	.002	.001	.001	.001	.001	.000	.000	.000
32	.002	.002	.001	.001	.001	.001	.000	.000	.000	.000
33	.002	.001	.001	.001	.001	.000	.000	.000	.000	.000
34	.002	.001	.001	.001	.001	.000	.000	.000	.000	.000
35	.001	.001	.001	.001	.000	.000	.000	.000	.000	.000
36	.001	.001	.001	.000	.000	.000	.000	.000	.000	.000
37	.001	.001	.000	.000	.000	.000	.000	.000	.000	.000
38	.001	.001	.000	.000	.000	.000	.000	.000	.000	.000
39	.001	.000	.000	.000	.000	.000	.000	.000	.000	.000
40	.000	.000	.000	.000	.000	.000	.000	.000	.000	.000
41	.000	.000	.000	.000	.000	.000	.000	.000	.000	.000
42	.000	.000	.000	.000	.000	.000	.000	.000	.000	.000
43	.000	.000	.000	.000	.000	.000	.000	.000	.000	.000
44	.000	.000	.000	.000	.000	.000	.000	.000	.000	.000
45	.000	.000	.000	.000	.000	.000	.000	.000	.000	.000
46	.000	.000	.000	.000	.000	.000	.000	.000	.000	.000
47	.000	.000	.000	.000	.000	.000	.000	.000	.000	.000
48	.000	.000	.000	.000	.000	.000	.000	.000	.000	.000
49	.000	.000	.000	.000	.000	.000	.000	.000	.000	.000
50	.000	.000	.000	.000	.000	.000	.000	.000	.000	.000

Table A–1 (continued)

Number of years	35%	40%	45%	50%	55%	60%	70%	80%	90%	100%
1	.741	.714	.690	.667	.645	.625	.588	.556	.526	.500
2	.549	.510	.476	.444	.416	.391	.346	.309	.277	.250
3	.406	.364	.328	.296	.269	.244	.204	.171	.146	.125
4	.301	.260	.226	.198	.173	.153	.120	.095	.077	.062
5	.223	.186	.156	.132	.112	.095	.070	.053	.040	.031
6	.165	.133	.108	.088	.072	.060	.041	.029	.021	.016
7	.122	.095	.074	.059	.047	.037	.024	.016	.011	.008
8	.091	.068	.051	.039	.030	.023	.014	.009	.006	.004
9	.067	.048	.035	.026	.019	.015	.008	.005	.003	.002
10	.050	.035	.024	.017	.012	.009	.005	.003	.002	.001
11	.037	.025	.017	.012	.008	.006	.003	.002	.001	.000
12	.027	.018	.012	.008	.005	.004	.002	.001	.000	.000
13	.020	.013	.008	.005	.003	.002	.001	.000	.000	.000
14	.015	.009	.006	.003	.002	.001	.001	.000	.000	.000
15	.011	.006	.004	.002	.001	.001	.000	.000	.000	.000
16	.008	.005	.003	.002	.001	.001	.000	.000	.000	.000
17	.006	.003	.002	.001	.001	.000	.000	.000	.000	.000
18	.005	.002	.001	.001	.000	.000	.000	.000	.000	.000
19	.003	.002	.001	.000	.000	.000	.000	.000	.000	.000
20	.002	.001	.001	.000	.000	.000	.000	.000	.000	.000
21	.002	.001	.000	.000	.000	.000	.000	.000	.000	.000
22	.001	.001	.000	.000	.000	.000	.000	.000	.000	.000
23	.001	.000	.000	.000	.000	.000	.000	.000	.000	.000
24	.001	.000	.000	.000	.000	.000	.000	.000	.000	.000
25	.001	.000	.000	.000	.000	.000	.000	.000	.000	.000
26	.000	.000	.000	.000	.000	.000	.000	.000	.000	.000
27	.000	.000	.000	.000	.000	.000	.000	.000	.000	.000
28	.000	.000	.000	.000	.000	.000	.000	.000	.000	.000
29	.000	.000	.000	.000	.000	.000	.000	.000	.000	.000
30	.000	.000	.000	.000	.000	.000	.000	.000	.000	.000
31	.000	.000	.000	.000	.000	.000	.000	.000	.000	.000
32	.000	.000	.000	.000	.000	.000	.000	.000	.000	.000
33	.000	.000	.000	.000	.000	.000	.000	.000	.000	.000
34	.000	.000	.000	.000	.000	.000	.000	.000	.000	.000
35	.000	.000	.000	.000	.000	.000	.000	.000	.000	.000
36	.000	.000	.000	.000	.000	.000	.000	.000	.000	.000
37	.000	.000	.000	.000	.000	.000	.000	.000	.000	.000
38	.000	.000	.000	.000	.000	.000	.000	.000	.000	.000
39	.000	.000	.000	.000	.000	.000	.000	.000	.000	.000
40	.000	.000	.000	.000	.000	.000	.000	.000	.000	.000
41	.000	.000	.000	.000	.000	.000	.000	.000	.000	.000
42	.000	.000	.000	.000	.000	.000	.000	.000	.000	.000
43	.000	.000	.000	.000	.000	.000	.000	.000	.000	.000
44	.000	.000	.000	.000	.000	.000	.000	.000	.000	.000
45	.000	.000	.000	.000	.000	.000	.000	.000	.000	.000
46	.000	.000	.000	.000	.000	.000	.000	.000	.000	.000
47	.000	.000	.000	.000	.000	.000	.000	.000	.000	.000
48	.000	.000	.000	.000	.000	.000	.000	.000	.000	.000
49	.000	.000	.000	.000	.000	.000	.000	.000	.000	.000
50	.000	.000	.000	.000	.000	.000	.000	.000	.000	.000

Table A–2
Year-end accumulations of periodic payments

Interest rate	1 year	½ year	¼ year	1 month	1 week	1 day	0
				Period			
.01	1.000	1.002	1.004	1.005	1.005	1.005	1.005
.02	1.000	1.005	1.007	1.009	1.010	1.010	1.010
.03	1.000	1.007	1.011	1.014	1.015	1.015	1.015
.04	1.000	1.010	1.015	1.018	1.019	1.020	1.020
.05	1.000	1.012	1.019	1.023	1.024	1.025	1.025
.06	1.000	1.015	1.022	1.027	1.029	1.030	1.030
.07	1.000	1.017	1.026	1.032	1.034	1.035	1.035
.08	1.000	1.020	1.030	1.036	1.039	1.039	1.039
.09	1.000	1.022	1.033	1.041	1.043	1.044	1.044
.10	1.000	1.024	1.037	1.045	1.048	1.049	1.049
.11	1.000	1.027	1.040	1.049	1.053	1.054	1.054
.12	1.000	1.029	1.044	1.054	1.058	1.059	1.059
.13	1.000	1.032	1.048	1.058	1.062	1.063	1.064
.14	1.000	1.034	1.051	1.063	1.067	1.068	1.068
.15	1.000	1.036	1.055	1.067	1.072	1.073	1.073
.16	1.000	1.039	1.058	1.071	1.076	1.078	1.078
.17	1.000	1.041	1.062	1.076	1.081	1.083	1.083
.18	1.000	1.043	1.065	1.080	1.086	1.087	1.088
.19	1.000	1.045	1.069	1.084	1.090	1.092	1.092
.20	1.000	1.048	1.072	1.089	1.095	1.097	1.097
.21	1.000	1.050	1.076	1.093	1.100	1.101	1.102
.22	1.000	1.052	1.079	1.097	1.104	1.106	1.106
.23	1.000	1.055	1.083	1.101	1.109	1.111	1.111
.24	1.000	1.057	1.086	1.106	1.113	1.115	1.116
.25	1.000	1.059	1.089	1.110	1.118	1.120	1.120
.26	1.000	1.061	1.093	1.114	1.122	1.125	1.125
.27	1.000	1.063	1.096	1.118	1.127	1.129	1.130
.28	1.000	1.066	1.100	1.123	1.132	1.134	1.134
.29	1.000	1.068	1.103	1.127	1.136	1.138	1.139
.30	1.000	1.070	1.106	1.131	1.141	1.143	1.143
.35	1.000	1.081	1.123	1.152	1.163	1.166	1.166
.40	1.000	1.092	1.140	1.172	1.185	1.188	1.189
.45	1.000	1.102	1.156	1.192	1.207	1.210	1.211
.50	1.000	1.112	1.172	1.212	1.228	1.232	1.233
.55	1.000	1.122	1.187	1.232	1.250	1.254	1.255
.60	1.000	1.132	1.203	1.252	1.271	1.276	1.277
.70	1.000	1.152	1.234	1.290	1.312	1.318	1.319
.80	1.000	1.171	1.263	1.328	1.353	1.360	1.361
.90	1.000	1.189	1.293	1.365	1.394	1.401	1.402
1.00	1.000	1.207	1.321	1.401	1.433	1.441	1.443

Appendix B

Random Number Table

	00–04	05–09	10–14	15–19	20–24	25–29	30–34	35–39	40–44	45–49
00	64249	63664	39652	40646	97306	31741	07294	84149	46797	82487
01	26538	44249	04050	48174	65570	44072	40192	51153	11397	58212
02	05845	00512	78630	55328	18116	69296	91705	86224	29503	57071
03	74897	68373	67359	51014	33510	83048	17056	72506	82949	54600
04	20872	54570	35017	88132	25730	22626	86723	91691	13191	77212
05	31432	96156	89177	75541	81355	24480	77243	76690	42507	84362
06	66890	61505	01240	00660	05873	13568	76082	79172	57913	93448
07	48194	57790	79970	33106	86904	48119	52503	24130	72824	21627
08	11303	87118	81471	52936	08555	28420	49416	44448	04269	27029
09	54374	57325	16947	45356	78371	10563	97191	53798	12693	27928
10	64852	34421	61046	90849	13966	39810	42699	21753	76192	10508
11	16309	20384	09491	91588	97720	89846	30376	76970	23063	35894
12	42587	37065	24526	72602	57589	98131	37292	05967	26002	51945
13	40177	98590	97161	41682	84533	67588	62036	49967	01990	72308
14	82309	76128	93965	26743	24141	04838	40254	26065	07938	76236
15	79788	68243	59732	04257	27084	14743	17520	95401	55811	76099
16	40538	79000	89559	25026	42274	23489	34502	75508	06059	86682
17	64016	73598	18609	73150	62463	33102	45205	87440	96767	67042
18	49767	12691	17903	93871	99721	79109	09425	26904	07419	76013
19	76974	55108	29795	08404	82684	00497	51126	79935	57450	55671
20	23854	08480	85983	96025	50117	64610	99425	62291	86943	21541
21	68973	70551	25098	78033	98573	79848	31778	29555	61446	23037
22	36444	93600	65350	14971	25325	00427	52073	64280	18847	24768
23	03003	87800	07391	11594	21196	00781	32550	57158	58887	73041
24	17540	26188	36647	78386	04558	61463	57842	90382	77019	24210
25	38916	55809	47982	41968	69760	79422	80154	91486	19180	15100
26	64288	19843	69122	42502	48508	28820	59933	72998	99942	10515
27	86809	51564	38040	39418	49915	19000	58050	16899	79952	57849
28	99800	99566	14742	05028	30033	94889	53381	23656	75787	59223
29	92345	31890	95712	08279	91794	94068	49337	88674	35355	12267
30	90363	65162	32245	82279	79256	80834	06088	99462	56705	06118
31	64437	32242	48431	04835	39070	59702	31508	60935	22390	52246
32	91714	53662	28373	34333	55791	74758	51144	18827	10704	76803
33	20902	17646	31391	31459	33315	03444	55743	74701	58851	27427
34	12217	86007	70371	52281	14510	76094	96579	54853	78339	20839
35	45177	02863	42307	53571	22532	74921	17735	42201	80540	54721
36	28325	90814	08804	52746	47913	54577	47525	77705	95330	21866
37	29019	28776	56116	54791	64604	08815	46049	71186	34650	14994
38	84979	81353	56219	67062	26146	82567	33122	14124	46240	92973
39	50371	26347	48513	63915	11158	25563	91915	18431	92978	11591
40	53422	06825	69711	67950	64716	18003	49581	45378	99878	61130
41	67453	35651	89316	41620	32048	70225	47597	33137	31443	51445
42	07294	85353	74819	23445	68237	07202	99515	62282	53809	26685
43	79544	00302	45338	16015	66613	88968	14595	63836	77716	79596
44	64144	85442	82060	46471	24162	39500	87351	36637	42833	71875
45	90919	11883	58318	00042	52402	28210	34075	33272	00840	73268
46	06670	57353	86275	92276	77591	46924	60839	55437	03183	13191
47	36634	93976	52062	83678	41256	60948	18685	48992	19462	96062
48	75101	72891	85745	67106	26010	62107	60885	37503	55461	71213
49	05112	71222	72654	51583	05228	62056	57390	42746	39272	96659

50-54	55-59	60-64	65-69	70-74	75-79	80-84	85-89	90-94	95-99	
59391	58030	52098	82718	87024	82848	04190	96574	90464	29065	00
99567	76364	77204	04615	27062	96621	43918	01896	83991	51141	01
10363	97518	51400	25670	98342	61891	27101	37855	06235	33316	02
86859	19558	64432	16706	99612	59798	32803	67708	15297	28612	03
11258	24591	36863	55368	31721	94335	34936	02566	80972	08188	04
95068	88628	35911	14530	33020	80428	39936	31855	34334	64865	05
54463	47237	73800	91017	36239	71824	83671	39892	60518	37092	06
16874	62677	57412	13215	31389	62233	80827	73917	82802	84420	07
92494	63157	76593	91316	03505	72389	96363	52887	01087	66091	08
15669	56689	35682	40844	53256	81872	35213	09840	34471	74441	09
99116	75486	84989	23476	52967	67104	39495	39100	17217	74073	10
15696	10703	65178	90637	63110	17622	53988	71087	84148	11670	11
97720	15369	51269	69620	03388	13699	33423	67453	43269	56720	12
11666	13841	71681	98000	35979	39719	81899	07449	47985	46967	13
71628	73130	78783	75691	41632	09847	61547	18707	85489	69944	14
40501	51089	99943	91843	41995	88931	73631	69361	05375	15417	15
22518	55576	98215	82068	10798	86211	36584	67466	69373	40054	16
75112	30485	62173	02132	14878	92879	22281	16783	86352	00077	17
80327	02671	98191	84342	90813	49268	95441	15496	20168	09271	18
60251	45548	02146	05597	48228	81366	34598	72956	66762	17002	19
57430	82270	10421	05540	43648	75888	66049	21511	47676	33444	20
73528	39559	34434	88596	54086	71693	43132	14414	79949	85193	21
25991	65959	70769	64721	86413	33475	42740	06175	82758	66248	22
78388	16638	09134	59880	63806	48472	39318	35434	24057	74739	23
12477	09965	96657	57994	59439	76330	24596	77515	09577	91871	24
83266	32883	42451	15579	38155	29793	40914	65990	16255	17777	25
76970	80876	10237	39515	79152	74798	39357	09054	73579	92359	26
37074	65198	44785	68624	98336	84481	97610	78735	46703	98265	27
83712	06514	30101	78295	54656	85417	43189	60048	72781	72606	28
20287	56862	69727	94443	64936	08366	27227	05158	50326	59566	29
74261	32592	86538	27041	65172	85532	07571	80609	39285	65340	30
64081	49863	08478	96001	18888	14810	70545	89755	59064	07210	31
05617	75818	47750	67814	29575	10526	66192	44464	27058	40467	32
26793	74951	95466	74307	13330	42664	85515	20632	05497	33625	33
65988	72850	48737	54719	52056	01596	03845	35067	03134	70322	34
27366	42271	44300	73399	21105	03280	73457	43093	05192	48657	35
56760	10909	98147	34736	33863	95256	12731	66598	50771	83665	36
72880	43338	93643	58904	59543	23943	11231	83268	65938	81581	37
77888	38100	03062	58103	47961	83841	25878	23746	55903	44115	38
28440	07819	21580	51459	47971	29882	13990	29226	23608	15873	39
63525	94441	77033	12147	51054	49955	58312	76923	96071	05813	40
47606	93410	16359	89033	89696	47231	64498	31776	05383	39902	41
52669	45030	96279	14709	52372	87832	02735	50803	72744	88208	42
16738	60159	07425	62369	07515	82721	37875	71153	21315	00132	43
59348	11695	45751	15865	74739	05572	32688	20271	65128	14551	44
12900	71775	29845	60774	94924	21810	38636	33717	67598	82521	45
75086	23537	49939	33595	13484	97588	28617	17979	70749	35234	46
99495	51434	29181	09993	38190	42553	68922	52125	91077	40197	47
26075	31671	45386	36583	93459	48599	52022	41330	60651	91321	48
13636	93596	23377	51133	95126	61496	42474	45141	46660	42338	49